W9-CHP-187

VIOLENT OFFENDERS

The LAW AND PUBLIC POLICY: PSYCHOLOGY AND THE SOCIAL SCIENCES series includes books in three domains:

Legal Studies—writings by legal scholars about issues of relevance to psychology and the other social sciences, or that employ social science information to advance the legal analysis;

Social Science Studies—writings by scientists from psychology and the other social sciences about issues of relevance to law and public policy; and

Forensic Studies—writings by psychologists and other mental health scientists and professionals about issues relevant to forensic mental health science and practice.

The series is guided by its editor, Bruce D. Sales, PhD, JD, ScD(*hc*), University of Arizona; and coeditors, Bruce J. Winick, JD, University of Miami; Norman J. Finkel, PhD, Georgetown University; and Valerie P. Hans, PhD, University of Delaware.

* * *

Violent Offenders

APPRAISING AND MANAGING RISK

SECOND EDITION

Vernon L. Quinsey

Grant T. Harris

Marnie E. Rice

Catherine A. Cormier

AMERICAN PSYCHOLOGICAL ASSOCIATION • WASHINGTON DC

Copyright © 2006 by the American Psychological Association. All rights reserved. Except as permitted under the United States Copyright Act of 1976, no part of this publication may be reproduced or distributed in any form or by any means, including, but not limited to, the process of scanning and digitization, or stored in a database or retrieval system, without the prior written permission of the publisher.

Second Printing, November 2006

Published by
American Psychological Association
750 First Street, NE
Washington, DC 20002
www.apa.org

To order
APA Order Department
P.O. Box 92984
Washington, DC 20090-2984
Tel: (800) 374-2721; Direct: (202) 336-5510
Fax: (202) 336-5502; TDD/TTY: (202) 336-6123
Online: www.apa.org/books/
E-mail: order@apa.org

In the U.K., Europe, Africa, and the Middle East, copies may be ordered from
American Psychological Association
3 Henrietta Street
Covent Garden, London
WC2E 8LU England

Typeset in Goudy by Stephen McDougal, Mechanicsville, MD

Printer: Edwards Brothers, Inc., Ann Arbor, MI
Cover Designer: Berg Design, Albany, NY
Technical/Production Editor: Tiffany Klaff

The opinions and statements published are the responsibility of the authors, and such opinions and statements do not necessarily represent the policies of the American Psychological Association.

Library of Congress Cataloging-in-Publication Data

Violent offenders : appraising and managing risk / Vernon L. Quinsey . . . [et al.]. — 2nd ed.
   p. cm. — (The law and public policy)
  Includes bibliographical references.
  ISBN 1-59147-343-8
  1. Mentally ill prisoners—United States. 2. Sex offenders—United States.
3. Violent offenders—United States. I. Quinsey, Vernon L. II. Series.

HV9304.V56 2006
616.85'82075—dc22   2005015453

British Library Cataloguing-in-Publication Data
A CIP record is available from the British Library.

Printed in the United States of America
Second Edition

We dedicate this book to our spouses, Jill, Emily, and Greg, whose love and support have facilitated an enduring close collaboration that has made possible the work described in this book, and to all the offenders who have substituted constructive and prosocial behaviors for antisocial ones.
—VLQ, GTH, and MER

I dedicate this work to my children, Denis and Elise, and my granddaughter, Madison, because everything I do, I do for you, and to all the victims of violence—that one day there will be no more.
—CAC

CONTENTS

ACKNOWLEDGMENTS

The research reported in this book was supported by operating funds from the Mental Health Centre, Penetanguishene; contracts from the Ministry of the Solicitor General and the Ontario Ministry of Health; and research grants from the Laidlaw Foundation, the Ontario Mental Health Foundation, the Ontario Ministry of Health, Physicians Services Incorporated of Ontario, and the Social Sciences and Humanities Research Council of Canada. Preparation of the book itself was partially supported by a contract from the Kingston Psychiatric Hospital.

Many people helped with the research reported herein. Although most of these people are acknowledged in the original publications, we express our gratitude to all who are or have been directly involved in our research program: Rudy Ambtman, Kirsten Barr, Valerie Bell, Sid Bergersen, Angela Book, Barry Boyd, Peggy Buck, Joe Camilleri, Wayne Carrigan, Terry Chaplin, Garth Coleman, Mireille Cyr, Sonja Dey, Christopher Earls, Andrew Harris, Manuel Helzel, Zoe Hilton, Jim Horley, Randerson Houghton, Martin Lalumière, Carol Lang, Nancy Link, Anne Maguire, Joelle Mamuza, Carolyn Ostrowski, Denise Preston, Manfred Pruesse, Marlene Pruesse, Kelly Reid, Michael Seto, Tracey Skilling, Lana Stermac, Douglas Upfold, George Varney, Bill Walker, Anita Warneford, and Bill Whitman.

We are grateful to Howard Danson, Wayne Barnett, Russel Fleming, Malcolm MacCulloch, and Deborah Sattler for their encouragement and administrative support. Thanks are due to Brenda Durdle, Emily Harris, Zoe Hilton, Martin Lalumière, John Monahan, and Tracey Skilling for constructive comments on drafts of this book.

VIOLENT OFFENDERS

INTRODUCTION

Typically, problems in offender management surface when offenders are considered for release from an institution in which they were initially placed because of some violent behavior. It is difficult to strike the proper balance between offenders' civil liberties and community safety: that is, to decide who should be released and when. In the recent past, such decisions had to be made with little help from the literature on the prediction of violence. Historically, this literature has asserted that although certain historical variables statistically predict future violence, a large proportion of offenders, perhaps the majority, who are assessed as dangerous (by whatever method) in fact turn out to have been inaccurately judged to be dangerous (false positives). Regardless of the scientific indefensibility of these predictions, they are ubiquitous, making it difficult to meet the very real political need for decision makers to appear to have done a proper and careful "scientific" assessment in case the offender commits a further violent act that becomes public knowledge.

Persons who are responsible for the community management of offenders with histories of serious aggressive behaviors, sex offenses, or fire setting often greet their task with a mixture of worry and despair. And no wonder: Much of the scientific literature argues that neither treatment nor supervision has demonstrable effects on recidivism; thus, it is often unclear to practitioners what should be done with or for the offender. We have written extensively on interventions for mentally disordered offenders (G. T. Harris, Rice, Quinsey, & Durdle, 1995; Quinsey, 1981; Rice & Harris, 1997b; Rice, Harris, Cormier, et al., 2004; Rice, Harris, & Quinsey, 1996; Rice, Harris, Quinsey, & Cyr, 1990), so in this book we will cover treatment issues primarily as they relate to risk assessment.

The community commonly serves as the final common path for patients discharged from psychiatric facilities, developmentally disabled persons discharged from institutions, and inmates released from correctional institutions. Within the psychiatric hospital system, the "revolving door" syndrome of frequent short hospital admissions is well known. Regarding the system for intellectually disabled persons, policies of normalization and deinstitutionalization have resulted in large numbers of these individuals living in the community with varying amounts of support. Similarly, because of probation and parole orders, large numbers of convicted offenders live in the community under supervision.

It is striking that the issues involved in managing or reducing the risk of violence posed by offenders in these three traditionally separate human service sectors are almost identical. These similarities are ironic, given the great attention paid to making the initial disposition to a particular human service system and the difficulties in dealing with persons who do not fit neatly within any one of the three, such as dually diagnosed persons or mentally disordered offenders. This concern with initial placement, as reflected in such legal dispositions as "not guilty by reason of insanity," is based not so much on the behaviors that initially led to institutionalization or the kind of programs delivered within a sector, but rather on the perceived appropriateness of the confine and medicate, confine and train, or confine and punish paradigms traditionally characterizing the three human service sectors.

This is not, of course, to assert that the same proportions of offenders in each sector pose a risk for violence or that the type of violent behavior of concern is necessarily of the same kind or severity. Although one associates a propensity for violence primarily with the criminal justice system, the proportion of persons posing such a risk within any service sector is dependent on a variety of substantively uninteresting bureaucratic and legal arrangements within particular jurisdictions. This is summed up for mental health and corrections by Penrose's law, which asserts that the number of persons in the mental health and correctional systems is a constant (Penrose, 1939). Although in fact only a minority of offenders within any of the three service sectors pose a high risk of exhibiting serious violent behaviors, there are a sufficient number in each that the absolute number living in the community is large.

We argue in this volume that community risk management can be improved by combining what is already known from three areas of inquiry: the prediction of violence, the study of decision making and clinical judgment, and the literature on treatment outcomes and program evaluation. We will argue that although these literatures certainly can induce predictive, therapeutic, and supervisory nihilism among practitioners, more recent developments offer grounds for some optimism, particularly when an integrative approach is taken. Finally, we hope to show that the type of technological or engineering work that is necessary to improve practice provides information that can also inform scientific theory.

This book reports on a sustained program of research that began 35 years ago. Most of the authors' research reported herein has focused on the maximum-security Oak Ridge Division of the Mental Health Centre, Penetanguishene (Ontario, Canada). This institution is probably the most thoroughly studied maximum-security psychiatric facility in the world. Although most of this research has been reported in the form of book chapters and journal articles, from which we occasionally borrow, these are too scattered to permit integration, and their cumulative effect is therefore minimized. Because of the duration and size of this concentrated research effort, we believe that a unique opportunity exists to draw some firm conclusions about the prediction of violent behavior, conclusions that, although originating primarily from a single institution and forensic system for dealing with mentally disordered offenders, apply to policy and clinical issues arising in the management of violent offenders in a wide variety of contexts.

Our primary concern in this book is with the criminal violence of both mentally disordered offenders and criminal inmates, not with politically inspired terrorism, civil war, or war between states. In addition, although it is clear that violence of a variety of kinds can arise out of the social disintegration and large-scale drug trafficking found in some large urban areas, this book does not address such social issues. This book concerns persons whose histories of criminal violence raise serious societal concerns about whether they will commit further violent acts. As illustrated by the case of Robert Phillip, presented in Exhibits A and B, these concerns are very real. Because the overwhelming majority of these persons are men, they are the focus of this book (and are reflected in the single-sex pronouns throughout). We also do not discuss institutional violence or violence in the everyday lives of young people herein, because we have dealt with these topics elsewhere (Rice, Harris, Varney, & Quinsey, 1989, and Hilton, Harris, & Rice, 2000, respectively).

There has been substantial change in the field of risk assessment in the 7 years since the first edition of this book appeared. Most important, the empirical literature on the prediction of recidivism is now much larger and richer than it was. Much of this new literature consists of follow-up studies of various offender and psychiatric populations in which already developed predictive instruments were compared or new actuarial instruments were devised. A small but growing literature has investigated the use of dynamic predictors in the management of risk among supervised offenders. Accompanying these empirical studies is a large body of commentary: review papers that debunk or celebrate the empirical findings, criticize or praise the technology of prediction, relate the empirical to the legal literatures, revisit the clinical versus actuarial debate (giving rise to a sense of déjà vu all over again), and so forth (cf. Dvoskin & Heilbrun, 2001; Maden, 2003; Szmukler, 2003). The commentaries reveal anything but an emerging consensus about the status of the technology of prediction or even the advisability of its use.

The following story helps explain why we do this work—to understand such persons and to prevent the harm they cause. The name and dates have been changed, but otherwise the story is true.

Robert Phillip was born in Ottawa to a mother who already had 10 children. Almost all members of the family were eventually institutionalized for low intelligence or criminal activity. Within a year of his birth, Phillip was placed in foster care. He experienced a series of foster homes, the longest lasting a year, until he was 9, when he was placed in an orphanage. Unmanageable in the orphanage, he went back into foster care, but he was a continual runaway and was frequently in trouble with the police for an escalating series of juvenile crimes, including sexual assaults against younger children.

When he was 11, Phillip was sent to an institution for intellectually disabled persons near Ottawa (although he was actually quite bright). There he was one of the most difficult inmates the institution had ever had. He was violent, he ran away, and he brutally sexually assaulted other residents, especially those who were younger and more vulnerable. At the age of 16, he was sent to Oak Ridge, a maximum-security psychiatric facility. There he was involved in coercive sexual activity with other patients. At the age of 20, however, he was transferred to the neighboring minimum-security facility.

Almost immediately, he escaped. He stole a knife, a gun, and ammunition from a nearby cottage. He made his way to Toronto (150 km away), and there he raped a teenage boy at gunpoint and then sexually assaulted a young girl. The girl's mother arrived on the scene while Phillip was assaulting her daughter. She grabbed the gun, aimed at Phillip, and pulled the trigger. Because Phillip had loaded the gun with the wrong ammunition, it did not fire. The police apprehended Phillip, but he was not charged with a criminal offense. He was returned to Oak Ridge, where his institutional file bore a red caution flag for many years: "This man should not be considered for release from Oak Ridge without due and careful consideration of the events of September 13, 1963." The Actuarial Risk Appraisal Report excerpted in Exhibit B treats the events of that day as the index offense and is based on Phillip's life up to that point.

After many more years in Oak Ridge, during which Phillip participated in behavioral treatment for sexual deviance and an intensive therapeutic community program, he was transferred in 1980 to a medium-security psychiatric institution several hundred kilometers away. There he was reported to be difficult to manage and a poor treatment candidate. He sexually assaulted a young mentally handicapped patient, but he was not criminally charged. Instead, he was returned to Oak Ridge, where he minimally involved himself in treatment and was frequently noted to be engaged in sexual misconduct.

In 1983, the medical director for the institution of which Oak Ridge was a part decided to transfer patients who were personality disordered and not psychotic to regular psychiatric institutions. When apprised of the risk Phillip posed (our actuarial tool did not yet exist), the medical director replied that although a violent offense was very likely, Phillip would then go where he belonged—to the correctional system. An expurgated version of his file accompanied him, and in 1983 Phillip was transferred to another minimum-security psychiatric hospital hundreds of kilometers away (and almost a thousand kilometers from the place he had gone in 1980).

Phillip quickly escaped and forcibly sexually assaulted a young boy and a teenage girl at knifepoint. He was criminally charged with assault, but not sexual assault, because it was thought that testifying would be too traumatic for the victims. He was sentenced to 22 months. During this sentence, Phillip participated in a treatment for sex offenders but was also transferred to a maximum-security institution because of problem behavior. He was released on parole. Two weeks after release, he was living in a halfway house in Ottawa, from which he escaped. Using force, threats of death, and a guard dog he had stolen from the halfway house, he raped a 10-year-old boy. The boy, son of a foreign diplomat who did not want him to testify, left the country. The prosecution agreed to a plea bargain and a sentence of 5 years. During this incarceration, Phillip participated in yet another specialized treatment program for sex offenders.

In 1988, Phillip was released to Toronto. He volunteered as a Little League coach and visited schools lecturing children about avoiding crime. During a mix-up at two parole offices (each of two officers thought he was supervised by the other), he abducted an 11-year-old boy at knifepoint from a shopping mall parking lot. Phillip kept the boy for 2 days in his apartment, where he repeatedly sexually assaulted the child. He stabbed the boy to death and left the body in a vacant lot. Convicted of murder, Phillip was himself stabbed to death during the ensuing incarceration. No charges have ever been laid in connection with his death.

In this second edition, we update our review of the empirical literature, focusing on the actuarial instruments that we developed and described in the first edition of this book and the measures of dynamic risk that we have continued to develop. We also review some of the commentaries on risk appraisal, raising our list of 15 common arguments against actuarial risk appraisal to 20. We have clarified our descriptions of how to score certain items of the Violence Risk Appraisal Guide (VRAG) and Sex Offender Risk Appraisal Guide (SORAG) based on an extensive number of inquiries from professionals who have used these instruments in the field. Lastly, we have provided a more detailed description of the development of the SORAG.

The book is organized in four major parts and a series of appendixes. The first part deals with the historical and methodological context of risk appraisal and is designed to give the reader the background necessary to understand the necessity for and the mechanics of developing actuarial risk appraisal instruments. The second part reviews follow-up and etiological research on three populations of offenders: mentally disordered offenders, sex offenders, and fire setters, providing the substantive knowledge required for understanding the third section, which deals with the development of violence prediction instruments, their level of accuracy, and some common misconceptions about their use and interpretation. The fourth part describes methods of altering the risk of violence and ends with a brief discussion of what we consider to be the principal broad conclusions that can be drawn from this work and their implications for future research. The appendixes are practically oriented, providing a detailed description of how the VRAG and SORAG are scored and interpreted and how narrative case histories can be compiled that are optimal for use in risk appraisal reports. We hope that our book provides up-to-date substantive and technical knowledge necessary to conduct and interpret individual risk appraisals and to understand the literature on violence prediction.

Robert Phillip's Actuarial Risk Appraisal Report

The following is excerpted from the Actuarial Risk Appraisal Report based on the events of September 13, 1963:
Name: Robert Phillip
Date of birth: July 11, 1943
Index offense: Sexual assault with a weapon
Date of offense: September 13, 1963

CHILDHOOD HISTORY

Factors indicating *low risk* of violent recidivism are that Mr. Phillip had not been suspended or expelled from school. Factors indicating *high risk* of violent recidivism are that Mr. Phillip did not live with both of his biological parents to the age of 16, was arrested under the age of 16, and had a history of childhood behavior problems and aggression, low educational achievement, and poor elementary school adjustment.

ADULT ADJUSTMENT

Factors indicating *low risk* are that Mr. Phillip was not living alone at the time of the index offense and had not been admitted to corrections. Factors indicating *high risk* are that Mr. Phillip had previously escaped from custody, did not have a period of employment while living in the community, had not been involved in a marital relationship, had failed on a prior conditional release, and had a history of violent sexual and nonviolent offenses. Mr. Phillip's history of alcohol problems (which includes parental alcohol abuse) was such that it did not factor either positively (high risk) or negatively (low risk) as a predictor of violent recidivism.

OFFENSE CHARACTERISTICS

Factors indicating *high risk* are that Mr. Phillip was young (20) at the time of the index offense, the offense was sexually motivated, and the victim was a young male who was a stranger.

ASSESSMENT RESULTS

A factor indicating *low risk* is that Mr. Phillip's IQ is at least average. Factors indicating *high risk* are that Mr. Phillip met the criteria for a *DSM–III* psychiatric diagnosis of personality disorder but not schizophrenia, he was recorded as having attitudes supportive of crime and unfavorable toward convention, his score on the Revised Psychopathy Checklist was 38, and he exhibited deviant preferences in a phallometric assessment.

APPRAISAL

On the basis of his score on a risk appraisal instrument constructed from the variables previously noted, Mr. Phillip's category for risk of violent recidivism is the highest of nine categories. Among offenders in the studies described earlier, fewer than 3% obtained higher scores, and all, or 100%, in that category reoffended violently within an average of 7 years after release.

I

HISTORICAL AND METHODOLOGICAL CONTEXT

1

HISTORICAL PERSPECTIVE

The treatment and management of violent offenders have a very long history. Some knowledge of this history may help society avoid attempts to reinvent the wheel. As we demonstrate in this book, there is a curious repetitiveness in the manner with which society conceptualizes and deals with the problem of criminal violence. A sense of déjà vu arises from a consideration of the history of the management of offenders.

In our view, the repetitive nature of policy shifts is at least partly a result of the lack of sustained empirical work on the problem of reducing offender risk. The assessment and management of offenders have primarily been driven by ideology and fashion. Offender assessment has been (and to a large degree still is) an essentially lay activity, in the sense that it usually involves commonsense predictors combined in an intuitive and informal manner. Treatment has been, and often still is, driven by theoretically feeble fads and fashions. Treatment to reduce risk has been, and often continues to be, delivered with low fidelity of implementation and in the absence of any scientifically sound knowledge of what has been effective. Until fundamental changes in training and practice are made, this aimlessness and ineffectiveness will undoubtedly continue.

When thinking about what has been learned from history, however, one must remain aware of the ubiquity of hindsight bias. *Hindsight bias* is the erroneous belief, once an outcome is known, that it was in fact predictable all along (Hawkins & Hastie, 1990). Hindsight bias is akin to a perceptual illusion. This phenomenon can lead to a serious underestimation of the amount of scientific and conceptual change that has actually occurred. The hindsight bias is nicely illustrated in a statement by Kettering, quoted in Allyon and Azrin (1968) in their discussion of implementing behavioral procedures in a psychiatric hospital: "First they tell you you're wrong, and they can prove it. Then they tell you you're right, but it's not important. Then they tell you it's important, but they've known it for years" (p. 1). Perhaps the most general conclusion that can be drawn from the hindsight bias literature is that people are not now as smart as they think and that people used to be smarter than we now think they were.

This chapter outlines the historical and legal context of our research program on the prediction of violence. We begin with a brief outline of the history of North American (i.e., Canadian and U.S.) institutions and then become more specific, covering the insanity defense and mental health policy in Ontario, Canada; we conclude with a discussion of the forensic system in Ontario. As will be apparent to readers with experience in the criminal justice system, the system within which this research was conducted is similar to forensic and correctional systems in the United States and the United Kingdom, and the problems with which these systems deal have remained similar at least throughout the past century (cf. Quinsey, 1999). The similarity of different institutions for offenders and forensic psychiatric patients is so striking that it has inspired *Quinsey's conjecture*: The universe is homogeneous with respect to forensic institutions.

NORTH AMERICAN INSTITUTIONS

Unless otherwise noted, two books by historian David J. Rothman, *The Discovery of the Asylum: Social Order and Disorder in the New Republic* (1971) and *Conscience and Convenience: The Asylum and Its Alternatives in Progressive America* (1980), form the basis of the historical discussion that follows. A broad survey of the history of asylums in North America and the United Kingdom was provided by Dwyer (1988). As we have described elsewhere (Rice & Harris, 1997b), the management of offenders has oscillated between two seductive ideas: (a) punishment and harsh treatment induce people not to commit crimes, and (b) something about an institutional milieu can repair the defects that cause people to commit crimes and thereby induce them to stop.

The prison, the reformatory, the workhouse or poor house, and the insane asylum all began in North America for the same reasons and at about the same time. Centralized workhouses and prisons were originally established following European models in the late 1700s as a state response to public disorder (Takagi, 1975). In the 1820s and 1830s, institutions were established to rehabilitate criminals, delinquents, the poor, and the insane. This rehabilitation was posited to occur by returning these deviants to life as it was supposed to have been in earlier, colonial times: simple, hierarchical, orderly, well disciplined, and work oriented. The institutions would both rehabilitate individuals and set an example for the rest of the population. This was necessary, it was believed, because societal permissiveness, poverty, and the availability of alcohol were what had caused these problems in the first place.

There was strident debate in the pre–Civil War period concerning the relative rehabilitative merits of the Pennsylvania penitentiary system (involving total isolation of the inmate in a cell) and the Auburn or congregate system, in which inmates were allowed to work together during the day. Both systems involved total silence: It was believed that silence, labor, and obedience would produce rehabilitation. Unfortunately, a variety of abuses (including bribery of guards, very harsh punishment, and exploitation of convict labor through contracting) crept into the penitentiaries, and hopes of reform rapidly vanished.

As in the case of the new penitentiaries, "moral" or psychological treatment of insanity in specially designed asylums was at first touted as extremely successful. The statistics turned out, however, to be much too optimistic. At first, staffing ratios in mental hospitals were relatively good, patients with good prognoses were admitted, and classification schemes for the management of patients were administered with care. However, all of these institutions soon silted up with chronic patients, and they became human warehouses. Soon, even the pretense of treatment was dropped.

The emphasis was then placed on custodial "care" as opposed to reform or rehabilitation in all of these types of institution. Orderliness, hierarchical authority, and discipline were transformed into neglect and harsh punishment as a result of crowding and lack of attention to individuals' specific problems and deficits. None of these types of institutions fulfilled either the rehabilitative or the social reform goals of their original advocates. Despite repeated and detailed exposés of their abuses and failures, however, they flourished for the next 170 years.

Similar discrepancies between rhetoric and practice are illustrated by the ways in which North American society has tackled the problem of juvenile crime. At their outset, juvenile institutions were forward looking, optimistic, and program oriented. The Ontario Reformatory at Penetanguishene was established in the 1860s on the site of the present maximum-security Oak Ridge Division of the Mental Health Centre that is the subject of our research program. It is an excellent example of the optimistic and humane approach to juvenile offenders at that time (Quinsey, 1982; Shoom, 1972). The approach involved incentive systems to manage behavior that are as sensible and persuasive now as they were when the institution's administrator described the program toward the end of the 19th century (Christie, 1882), when its primitive incentive system was embedded in a humanistic philosophy but bedeviled by a discrepancy between the philosophy and what was possible in practice:

> The boys should have no little share in their own self-improvement, and in order that they may be stimulated to cooperate heartily in the work, an incentive in the shape of a system of fixed rewards becomes a necessity. To that end such means as are at present available should be at once taken to ensure the establishment and perpetuation of a system of grading, whereby the boys would, from the beginning, feel that their early restoration to liberty altogether depended on the manner in which they conducted themselves and the progress made by them. (p. 90)
>
>   * * *
>
> But on entering the building, there may be seen the effects of introducing the modern and humane system which looks upon a boy as needing moral training and influence more than rigorous discipline; interesting and useful work, with proper recreation, more than hard tasks; home comforts and surroundings more than the solitary cell; healthy food more than prison diet; a respectable dress rather than prison uniform. (p. 80)
>
>   * * *
>
> When one is dealing with the moral, mental, and physical progress of over 260 boys, varying in race, creed, colour, character, and early training, there is a great temptation, when framing an annual report, to dilate on the many idiosyncrasies of mind and body represented by the group; or to attempt an analysis of the characteristics developed in each class, and to enlarge on the peculiarly careful handling required for the present and prospective good of each boy.
>
> But one might as well attempt to catch and hold a sunbeam, as to strive to depict the ever varying shades of character indicated in the foregoing paragraphs. For, no matter how familiar one may be with them, their transmission through the medium of a written report to the minds, no matter how receptive, of others, would be a feeble endeavour. (p. 89)

The Ontario Reformatory at Penetanguishene continued to operate until about 1900, when it became a victim of the "progressive" deinstitutionalization movement of that time (A. Jones, 1978). Unfortunately, but predictably, the humanistic philosophy of treatment did not provide a reliable way for managers to keep order and ensure that the boys went along with the plan. In practice, the system increasingly relied on brutal punishment, and abuse of the boys (as well as of the guiding philosophy) was not uncommon (Nielson, 2000).

In the first 40 years of this century, reformers rediscovered the evils of institutions. In this "progressive" era, reformers believed that deviants differed from each other in ways that could be identified using the case study method. This method involved recording the facts of each individual case.

The observed differences would then lead to different treatments and disposition decisions. Treatment was believed to be more effective with younger than older individuals. Broad discretionary powers were considered necessary to implement interventions such as parole, probation, and open-ended sentences in a flexible system. In the correctional system, reformers sought to treat the criminal, not to punish the crime. To this end, they used the case study method (it was basically the same in psychiatry, psychology, and social work) to choose the best disposition for the person. Lengthy or indeterminate sentences were used so that suitable inmates could earn parole.

Despite the zeal with which the reformers advocated their reforms, their ideas did not constitute anything remotely resembling a complete theory of crime, poverty, mental disorder, or social deviance. In practice, the reforms were never truly implemented with integrity. Nevertheless, the system was retained, even though it became apparent almost immediately that, in general, there was no supervision of offenders on parole, parole decisions were based on idiosyncratic subjective criteria applied in the most perfunctory manner, and the popular media blamed the parole system for each new crime wave.

Wardens supported the parole system because it gave them some control over who would be released (prison authorities participated in parole decisions) and because diminution of parole possibilities could lead to inmate mutiny. Prosecutors favored parole because a released inmate could be returned to prison without trial on reoffense. In any event, it was doubtful that parole actually decreased the amount of time inmates spent imprisoned, because judges simply raised the maximum time to be served for the offense, effectively increasing the amount of time offenders were involved in the criminal justice system. Plea bargaining was facilitated by threatening defective delinquent, psychopathy, or habitual offender dispositions, or simply the specter of long maximum sentences.

Progressive reformers invented juvenile court systems so that alternatives could be broadened beyond merely incarcerating or ignoring youthful offenders. The central ideas were the separation of adult and juvenile offenders, individualization, broadened discretion, informal proceedings, and the use of probation. Procedural legal safeguards were considered unnecessary, because the goal was to help the child. Psychiatric court clinics were established in some urban centers.

The juvenile court system also did not live up to expectations. It probably did not reduce the amount of incarceration (offenders who previously would have been ignored were given probation), trained probation officers (or any officers at all, outside urban areas) could not be obtained, and court clinics simply offered diagnoses after perfunctory examinations (in any case, these were often ignored). Other than common sense, there was no treatment technology to which to appeal. It was difficult to distinguish discretion from arbitrariness. Reformatories or training schools tended to become like prisons and to introduce the regimentation and brutality that the progressive reformers most wanted to avoid.

Criminal justice and mental health administrators embraced these progressive reforms to the adult and juvenile systems because they enhanced the ability of these systems to function bureaucratically. Reformers did not understand the real nature of their alliance with the administrative system or that "reforms" could be implemented and defended without accomplishing the reformers' objectives. Nor did they realize that their goals, the goals of administrators, and the goals of the clients in this system could be incompatible.

Thus, the reformers of the 1920s and 1930s believed that

> . . . failure . . . reflected faulty implementation, not underlying problems with theory or politics; incompetent administrators and stingy legislators, not basic flaws within the design, undercut the strengths of the innovations. Hence, reformers responded to disappointment in one-note fashion: they urged better training for probation and parole officers; better programs for prisons and training schools; more staff for juvenile courts and more attendants for mental hospitals. Do more of the same so that the promise of these innovations would be realized. (Rothman, 1980, p. 9)

The fundamental problem of the progressive reformers was that their enthusiasm blinded them to their lack of an effective treatment technology for the accomplishment of their objectives. The case method, as either an empirical or clinical means to understand the phenomena of interest, resulted in a mere collection of facts. The reforms did not end institutional abuses or even ameliorate them; instead, the reforms sometimes had the effect of increasing the coercive power of the state (Rothman, 1980).

The degree of discrepancy between progressive rhetoric and reality has created a burden of justifiable mistrust and skepticism. Public officials and the general public often distrust the assertions of "professionals" regarding the source and remediation of human problems. This distrust is justified by the failure of the "experts" to adhere to sensible epistemological standards as a basis for their assertions. In our view, this distrust continues to this day and is, to a large extent, as justified as it ever was.

The lack of effective treatments for mental illness led to the credulous endorsement of radical physical interventions for asylum inmates in the mid-20th century. Valenstein (1986) documented this phenomenon in his book *Great and Desperate Cures: The Rise and Decline of Psychosurgery and Other Radical Treatments for Mental Illness*. It begins with a quote written by English preacher and author John Bunyan in 1668:

> Physicians get neither name nor fame by pricking of weals, or picking out thistles, or by laying plasters to the scratch of a pin: . . . [anyone] can do this. But if they would have a name and fame, if they will have it quickly,

they must . . . do some great and desperate cures. Let them fetch one to life that was dead: let them recover one to his wits that was mad; let them make one that was born blind to see; or let them give ripe wits to a fool; these are notable cures, and he that can do thus, if he doth thus first, he shall have the name and fame he desires; he may lay abed till noon. (p. vi)

Valenstein's book is a cautionary tale of a technology wrongly conceived, hastily implemented, received with great enthusiasm, and widely applied, causing great and irreparable harm to tens of thousands of helpless people.

In the 1930s and 1940s, psychiatrists and neurologists disagreed over the nature of mental illness and the appropriateness of various treatments. Neurologists favored somatic treatments, often using the model of general paresis, for which a physical cure had been found. In contrast, psychiatrists favored the psychodynamic model that had been developed by Freud. Both hoped to retain control of the treatment of mental illness by physicians so as to exclude nonmedical professionals. Insane asylums, which had become huge warehouses for the hopelessly mentally ill population, were severely underfunded, and therapy was notable primarily by its absence. There were, however, a number of radical physical therapies in use at the time, including various forms of shock therapy and continuous baths.

Egas Moniz, an influential Portuguese neurologist who had done important work in cerebral arteriography, learned about an operation that had been performed on the frontal lobes of two chimpanzees in 1935 that left one of them more placid. The thought occurred to him that such an operation might be useful for humans with mental illness. He theorized that the frontal lobes were the site of "psychic activity," that thoughts were in the fiber connections, and that mental disorder was a result of "fixed" interfering thoughts. The solution, therefore, was to destroy the stabilized pathways in the frontal lobes. Moniz did not appear concerned about possible dysfunction that might be caused by frontal lobe damage, because he had seen a report on a patient with severe frontal lobe damage who could adequately perform well-rehearsed tasks, although it was also reported that this patient had become irritable and childish and could not learn new material readily. Moniz focused on the faculties that this patient had retained and disregarded the considerable evidence available at the time that the frontal lobes were important for normal functioning.

Moniz immediately began to operate on a small series of patients using a variety of techniques to sever fiber tracts in the frontal lobes. His evaluation of impact was based on a casual conversation with the patient held shortly after the operation. A number of patients were pronounced "cured" of their symptoms (primarily those of agitated depression). Moniz made no statement regarding the level of their functioning or whether they were released from hospital.

Moniz rushed into print. Within three months, operations had occurred in five countries. A flamboyant and brilliant American neurologist, Walter Freeman, read about the technique and soon published an article that described a small number of patients operated on because of agitation and depression. His report attracted an enormous amount of popular publicity. Freeman performed a larger series of operations and published the results in a book. Its cover depicted a trepanned skull with escaping black butterflies. Freeman argued that the operation severed the thinking from the feeling brain, that it removed the "sting" of psychosis and made patients less worried. However, Freeman also believed that the operation was a last resort. Between 1948 and 1952, tens of thousands of psychosurgical operations were performed. In 1949, Moniz won the Nobel Prize for his work.[1] In the 1940s, "promising new somatic therapies" were being advanced to solve the disgraceful conditions of public mental hospitals. More and more, lobotomies were suggested for violent schizophrenic individuals and other hopeless patients for whom nothing else worked. Subsequently, lobotomies were advocated for persons with better prognoses earlier in their illness—"before it was too late."

Although psychoanalysts were opposed to psychosurgery, they had no practical alternative treatment for psychosis. Psychiatrists objected (at first privately) to the procedure on the grounds that it produced partial euthanasia or substituted an organic syndrome for a pre-existing psychosis. They noted that many patients became worse. By and large, however, only a few isolated individuals complained. The frequency of lobotomies gradually declined, partly because of their ineffectiveness but mostly because of the introduction of antipsychotic medications that greatly helped alleviate the positive symptoms of schizophrenia. Although infrequent, however, lobotomies continued to be performed on assaultive patients with chronic schizophrenia into the early 1970s.

The more recent status of public mental hospitals was well summarized by Talbott (1978) in his book *The Death of the Asylum*. Talbott outlined the competing legal, professional, and advocacy interests that, together with the civil service bureaucracy and budgetary and political constraints, paralyzed the implementation of therapeutic programs. That is, because of the absence of a systemic commitment to an empirical (i.e., scientific) approach to these problems, ideology, self-interest, and professional rivalry ruled the day by default.

The development of mental health services in our own jurisdiction (the province of Ontario, Canada) was well described by Simmons (1990) in his book *Unbalanced: Mental Health Policy in Ontario, 1930–1989*. In 1987, the auditor general of Ontario noted that work in Ontario's mental hospitals (with their 90% occupancy rate) was stressful, the facilities were inadequate,

---

[1] Ironically, Moniz was shot and paralyzed by a patient on whom he had earlier operated.

and 25% of the patients could be housed in the community if there were suitable facilities for them. However, the investment in community facilities never materialized, largely because of the influence of psychiatrists who wanted to hold on to hospital treatment for the mentally ill population to preserve their own status as medical specialists. Despite evidence showing that psychiatric units in general hospitals were the most expensive way to provide service and that the wrong clientele was being served, general hospital psychiatric units flourished at the direct expense of the development of community treatment. Simmons argued that by the end of the 1980s, the tripod of psychiatric services was woefully unbalanced, with psychiatric hospitals and psychiatric wings of general hospitals predominating over a weak community treatment system. Although this problem had been known to the Ministry of Health for more than 50 years,

> Not once in the half-century under consideration did the government attempt to formulate and then implement a coherent long-term plan for mental health services in Ontario. For more than half a century, incremental politics has been the order of the day in mental health policymaking. (Simmons, 1990, p. xiii)

It should be noted that although these difficulties resulting from inability to plan and implement coherent mental health policy characterize other jurisdictions in North America (Talbott, 1978), large-scale planning has been successful in other contexts (e.g., policies dealing with the intellectually handicapped in Ontario in the 1970s). It is fair to claim that the ministry responsible for persons with intellectual disabilities successfully transferred the bulk of services for its clientele from institutions to local community agencies. The hallmark of this shift was the provision of genuine support for such community agencies so that community-based services were in place when the change occurred. Such foresight has not characterized "deinstitutionalization" for mental patients throughout North America over the past two decades.

The lack of planning, itself the result of a number of bureaucratic and political processes, has resulted in inadequate community mental health services in a disorganized system. The relative lack of aftercare and community resources has been reflected in the institutional focus of forensic services in Ontario and been implicated in the criminalization of chronic mental patients. In most jurisdictions, efforts toward "deinstitutionalization" are severely hampered by the twin plagues of underfunding and squabbling (always carried out in an empirical vacuum about what has actually been demonstrated to be effective) over the allocation of those scarce resources. For example, in our own jurisdiction, psychiatric hospital beds are currently being decreased, whereas the publicly funded billing rates for psychiatrists have been increased, practically ensuring even less access to even scarcer community-based resources provided by any other clinicians. Most of these private practice psychiatrists are located in urban areas, treat only the least severely mentally ill patients, and accept few forensic patients. Yet abundant empirical evidence suggests that patient outcomes could be much better if services were structured much differently and if social policy in this area were driven by empirical evidence. In reality, policy is more influenced by short-term political agendas and by professional self-interest.

ADJUDICATION OF INSANITY ACQUITTEES

If the assessment and management of offenders in general has been marked by unscientific and unsystematic approaches, the entire topic of insanity has been even more subject to ideology and fads. Since the 19th century, the "criminally insane" have been a controversial group of offenders. They are of great interest because they are a focus of both public fear and civil rights litigation and because issues involving them are at the intersection of criminal justice and mental health policies. Before discussing insanity acquittees in more detail, some legal history may be helpful. For this purpose we draw heavily on *Crime and Insanity in England: Volume 1. The Historical Perspective* by N. Walker (1968).

The earliest statement of legal principle concerning mentally ill offenders is a response to a query from a Roman governor written by Marcus Aurelius about 179 CE and preserved in the Justinian Code (Spruit, 1998):

> The deified Marcus and Commodus issued a rescript to Scapula Terullus in these words: If you have clearly ascertained that Aelius Priscus is in such state of insanity that he is permanently out of his mind and so entirely incapable of reasoning, and no suspicion is left that he was simulating insanity when he killed his mother, you need not concern yourself with the question how he should be punished as his insanity itself is punishment enough. At the same time he should be kept in close custody, and, if you think it advisable, even kept in chains; this need not be done by way of punishment so much as for his own protection and the security of his neighbours. If however, as is very often the case, he has intermittent periods of relative sanity, you must carefully investigate the question whether he may not have committed the crime on one of these moments, and so have no claim to mercy on the ground of mental infirmity; and, if you should find that anything of this kind is the fact you must refer the case to us, so that we may consider, supposing he committed the act at a moment when he could be held to know what he was doing, whether he ought not to be visited with punishment corresponding to the enormity of his crime.
>
> But since we have learned from you by letter that his position and rank are such that he is in the hands of his friends, even confined to his own house indeed, your proper course will be, in our opinion, to summon the persons who had the charge of him at the time and ascertain how they came to be so remiss, and then pronounce upon the case of

each separately, according as you see anything to excuse or aggravate his negligence. The object of providing keepers for lunatics is to keep them not merely from doing harm to themselves, but from bringing destruction upon others; and if this last-mentioned mischief should come to pass, it may well be set down to the negligence of any who were too neglectful in performing of their duties. (p. 316)

The punishment that the said Priscus would escape would be to be sewn up in a bag with a dog and some snakes and thrown into the sea.

In England during the 13th century, Henry de Bracton united ecclesiastical and secular law into one legal system. He enunciated the common law principle that a crime consists of two parts: *actus rea* (wrongful act) and *mens rea* (criminal intent). This distinction remains central today. A variety of very different insanity tests have been proposed. On the liberal side, Lord Chief Justice of England Matthew Hale suggested in 1736 that a defendant whose understanding is less than that of a typical 14-year-old should be exonerated. On the restrictive side, Justice Tracy argued in a 1724 trial that defendants should be acquitted only if they were totally deprived of their understanding and memory and if their comprehension of their acts was comparable to that of infants, brutes, or wild beasts. This is known as the "wild beast test."

In 1843, a Scottish wood turner named Daniel M'Naghton shot Edward Drummond, private secretary to England's prime minister, Robert Peel, mistakenly believing that he was Peel. He explained that the Tories were persecuting him; had followed him to France, Scotland, and England; accused him of crimes of which he was innocent; and wished to murder him. The medical opinion was unanimous that M'Naghton suffered from psychotic delusions of reference; he was acquitted on account of insanity.

Public outcry over this acquittal was so great that the House of Lords asked the 15 judges of the Queen's Bench to clarify the question of the insanity defense. The Queen's Bench promulgated the M'Naghton rule:

> At the time of committing the act, the party accused was labouring under such a defect of reason, from disease of the mind, as not to know the nature and quality of the act he was doing or if he did know it, that he did not know that what he was doing was wrong. (Quen, 1981, p. 5)

The M'Naghton rule implied that M'Naghton should have been found guilty because he knew that what he was doing was against the law. Section 16 of the *Criminal Code of Canada* substitutes "appreciate" for "know" to broaden the defense to include emotional factors (see Exhibit 1.1).

As illustrated by the Shortis (see Exhibit 1.2) and M'Naghton cases (as well as the trial of John Hinckley, who was tried for the 1981 attempted assassination of U.S. President Ronald Reagan), the insanity defense attracts the most attention when it is used against a charge of homicide. As Rice and Harris (1990) and others have demonstrated, insanity acquittals are almost

EXHIBIT 1.1
An Examination of the Insanity Defense

As an illustration of the legal technicalities inherent in the insanity defense and verdict, we examine the Canadian jurisprudence. The emergent themes are, however, common to all North American jurisdictions (Shah, 1986).

Until 1991, under the old legislation (Section 542(2) of the *Criminal Code of Canada*), the Advisory Board of Review was to keep persons found not guilty by reason of insanity "in strict custody in the place and in the manner that the court, judge, or magistrate directs, until the pleasure of the lieutenant-governor of the province is known."

According to Section 547(5d), the Advisory Board of Review was to advise "whether . . . that person has recovered and, if so, whether in its opinion it is in the interest of the public and of that person for the lieutenant-governor to order that he be discharged absolutely or subject to such conditions as the lieutenant-governor may prescribe."

The warrant was thus fully indeterminate and remained in effect until the Advisory Board of Review decided that the person should be released. The decision was explicitly based on the person's recovery and implicitly based on an appraisal of dangerousness, raising questions about the accuracy of these appraisals that are addressed in this book.

The lieutenant-governor's system was often criticized, perhaps most trenchantly by the Law Reform Commission of Canada (1976), which argued that the lieutenant governor's warrant (L.G.W.) "has five distinguishing characteristics: (1) jurisdictional complexity, (2) emphasis on custody rather than therapy, (3) indeterminacy, (4) non-reviewability, and (5) problems of termination" (p. 36): "Our position [is] that dispositions should be made openly, according to known criteria, be reviewable and of determinate length. The present L.G.W. offends on all counts" (p. 38).

These and related criticisms did not result in fundamental change until the Canadian Supreme Court decided in *Regina v. Swain* (1991) that the automatic detention of persons found not guilty by reason of insanity was contrary to provisions of the Canadian Charter of Rights and Freedoms. This decision caused the federal parliament to pass amendments to the *Criminal Code of Canada* on this issue that had been planned for a long time. The revised Section 16 reads as follows:

> No person is criminally responsible for an act committed or an omission made while suffering from a mental disorder that rendered the person incapable of appreciating the nature and quality of the act or omission or of knowing that it was wrong.

A *mental disorder* is explicitly defined as a "disease of the mind." Section 16 further states that the accused is presumed not to suffer from a mental disorder until proved otherwise on the balance of probabilities and that the burden of proof rests on the party that raises the issue.

Under the current legislation, the court or Ontario Review Board is to make the least-onerous and least-restrictive disposition of persons found not criminally responsible on account of mental disorder (NCRMD), taking into consideration their mental condition, their reintegration into society and their other needs, and the need to protect the public from dangerous persons. The court or Ontario Review Board is to discharge NCRMD offenders absolutely, if they do not present a significant threat to the safety of the public, and otherwise is to discharge them subject to conditions or detain them in custody in a hospital.

The new legislation contains as yet unenacted sections that provide for determinate "sentences" for mentally disordered offenders that are related to the severity of their offense (either 2 or 10 years depending on the maximum sentence that convicted persons are eligible to receive) with the exception of those offenders whose index offense involves homicide or treason and those who are determined to be "dangerous mentally disordered offenders."

The *Criminal Code of Canada* specifies the criteria by which the Ontario Review Board or court is to make decisions about mentally disordered offenders. There was less specification of the criteria to be used in the old legislation than there is in the new. In the old legislation, the Advisory Board of Review was to decide whether it was in the best interest of the public and the mentally disordered offender for him to be released absolutely or under conditions; in the new legislation, the discretion of the Ontario Review Board is limited by an injunction to use the least-restrictive and least-onerous disposition while protecting the public. For helpful discussions of Canadian legislation from a legal perspective, see R. M. Gordon and Verdun-Jones (1986) and O'Marra (1993).

---

always for very serious violent offenses.[2] Successful insanity defenses, however, are rare. Thus, in Canada, the number of persons convicted is about 10 times the number found unfit or not guilty by reason of insanity; half of the insanity acquittals and unfits are homicide cases (see also Wright, 1991). As we will describe in chapter 4, the situation is similar across U.S. jurisdictions, although many different legal tests of insanity are used. Evidence from both the United States (Packer, 1985) and Canada (Rice, Harris, Cormier, et al., 2004) suggests that the elimination of mandatory institutionalization of insanity acquittees increases the number of insanity verdicts for minor offenses.

The insanity defense embodies philosophical assumptions about the causes of behavior.[3] From a legal viewpoint, the issue is a moral one: Only persons who have free will and who have criminal intent should be punished. Thus, people who are insane should be exempt from the penal system (N. Walker, 1968). In this context, the concepts "disease of the mind" and "mental disorder" are neither clinical nor scientific but rather legal entities, and clinicians and scientists can advise the courts with regard to their assessments but cannot address the ultimate issue. Courts and juries can and do disregard expert advice. It should also be noted that expert opinion on such legal abstractions as "disease of the mind" and whether a person appreciated the nature and quality of a past act is often divided. It is hard enough to get adequate agreement on actual psychiatric diagnoses. From a utilitarian perspective, such a moralistic approach results in avoidable harm: Criminal intent aside, people who are insane may repeat their offenses (N. Walker, 1968).

As N. Walker (1968) has noted, the history of the insanity defense in countries influenced by English common law has been a series of compro-

---

[2]Homicide, however, is among the rarest of crimes: In Canada, the homicide rate was 2.47 homicides per 100,000 persons in 1990. This rate, which has not changed in more than 10 years, is about a quarter of the U.S. rate (Wright, 1991). To put it in perspective, the rate of deaths from motor vehicle accidents in Canada in 1973 was 12 times higher than the homicide rate, the suicide rate was 3 times higher than the homicide rate, and the rate of deaths from accidental falls was 3 times higher than the homicide rate (Statistics Canada, 1975). The homicide rate has fallen to 1.73 in 2003 (Statistics Canada, www40.statcan.ca).

[3]Given the centrality of free will to legal understandings of human conduct, it often is difficult to see how scientific findings can be applied to legal decision making. That is, "free will" probably has no sensible (and certainly no agreed-on) scientific meaning. Walker's distinction between utilitarian and moralistic approaches is the same made in contemporary philosophy between consequential and deontological moral philosophies (Morton, 2003).

EXHIBIT 1.2
The Shortis Case

The controversial issues involved in the insanity defense are well illustrated in an interesting book entitled *The Case of Valentine Shortis: A True Story of Crime and Politics in Canada* (Friedman, 1986). In 1895, Valentine Shortis was tried for murder in Valleyfield, Quebec. Shortis was the only child of exceptionally wealthy parents; his father exported cattle from southern Ireland. He came to Canada at the age of 18, in 1893, to "finally learn to stand on his own two feet." Shortis was a reluctant immigrant, weeping bitterly on the boat to Canada.

At first, he tried to set up a bicycle business using money supplied by his parents, but he accomplished nothing. He drifted from scheme to scheme, spending most of his time collecting catalogues of bicycles and guns. His mother finally came over from Ireland and arranged for him to have a job at the Globe Woollen Mills in Montreal. He was then hired for a 2-month period, after which he was cut off the payroll but was allowed to stay without pay. Shortly thereafter, he was told he was not wanted even as a volunteer.

On a Friday evening, employees at the company were placing $12,000 in pay envelopes. Shortis visited the company office, grabbed a revolver that was kept in a drawer, and shot three men, two of whom died. It was clear that he was interested in robbing the office. Shortly after being outwitted by the surviving employees, who locked themselves in the company vault, Shortis was arrested. Given the circumstances, the only possible defense against the death penalty was a plea of insanity.

A modified M'Naghton rule was used in Canada to determine whether an offender was not guilty by reason of insanity. Unfortunately, however, a transcription error had been made in the 1892 *Criminal Code of Canada* and not noticed and corrected until 1931. The mistake consisted in substituting *and* for *or,* so that the accused had to prove that he did not know the nature and quality of the act *and* that he did not know that it was wrong.

Based partly on evidence of Shortis's history of impulsive and erratic behavior gathered by a private detective sent to Ireland by the defense, C. K. Clarke, superintendent of Kingston's Rockwood asylum, and three other psychiatrists argued that Shortis was a moral imbecile or morally insane and thus not influenced by legal deterrents, having been overcome by an irresistible impulse. Years later, after Kraepelin's work (Neale & Oltmanns, 1980) had become known, Clarke wrote that Shortis was "a high grade mental defective with paranoid dementia praecox," although the term *moral imbecile* is closer to what is now called *psychopathy*.

This insanity defense was not popular in the local community. The *Montreal Herald,* for example, declared that the "gallows is a safer place than any asylum for a man whose sanity is first suspected after he has slaughtered two inoffensive fellow beings." Despite the evidence of insanity presented by the four defense psychiatrists, Shortis was sentenced to hang.

The case precipitated a constitutional crisis in which the privy council of Prime Minister Bowell was pitted against the Governor General, who tried to prevent the hanging. Part of the controversy was related to ethnic and religious tensions within Canada. Louis Riel, a French-speaking Catholic Métis who had led a rebellion against the government, had been in a similar situation and had been hanged; Shortis was an English-speaking Protestant. Eventually, the cabinet commuted the sentence to life imprisonment. Shortis barely escaped being lynched because a train carrying a party of outraged citizens was delayed by a blizzard. He spent the next 42 years in continuous confinement. He spent time in the Laval and Kingston penitentiaries, the Guelph Reformatory, and the Oak Ridge maximum-security psychiatric facility before his release.

mises between the utilitarian and the moralistic approaches to the problem of disposition. Sometimes the issue has been decided according to abstract legal principle and sometimes according to whether a penal or a mental hospital disposition was deemed more suitable. It is of interest that broad historical trends in disposition have been independent of landmark legal cases. The gap between courtroom rhetoric and practice has been wide in all jurisdictions. For example, it is not uncommon for offenders to be found guilty after strenuous debate and later to be transferred to a secure mental hospital from prison because of mental illness, completely circumventing the disposition made at trial.

Steadman et al. (1993) evaluated American attempts to reform the insanity defense during the 1980s. Reform efforts have been designed to enhance the public's perception of community safety by reducing the number of insanity acquittals or preventing the early release of insanity acquittees from hospitals. Steadman et al. studied two types of "front-end," or adjudication, reforms, altering the test used and changing the burden of proof, and a variety of "back-end," or dispositional, reforms that related to release decisions. In California, a more conservative reformulation of the insanity test had no effect on the number of insanity pleas or their success rate, on the characteristics of those found acquitted on account of insanity, or on the confinement pattern of insanity acquittees. There was a steady decrease, however, in the number of pleas throughout the study period; this decrease was initiated not by the change in the test, but rather by a dispositional reform that set the commitment time for insanity acquittees equal to the maximum sentence they would have received had they been convicted.

Georgia and New York shifted the burden of proof from the state to the defendant and changed the evidentiary requirement from reasonable doubt to a preponderance of the evidence. In both states, the number of insanity pleas declined. The success rate of the pleas remained constant in Georgia and increased in New York. In both states, individuals who were not diagnosed with a major mental illness were less likely to use an insanity defense. Reforms that abolished the insanity defense or introduced "guilty but mentally ill" statutes were relatively ineffective in achieving their aims. Some offenders are so obviously and seriously mentally ill that some legal mechanism is invariably found to divert them to a psychiatric institution.

Overall, Steadman et al. (1993) found that although the insanity defense may be philosophically important, it was raised at trial only 0.9 times in every 100 felony cases and led to an acquittal only 23% of the time. Moreover, attempts at reform often produced subtle and unintended consequences, leading Steadman et al. to conclude that reforms of the insanity defense should be informed by a "systemic perspective and solid empirical data, not the usual anecdote, hysteria, and hyperbole" (p. 152).

Thus, despite all of the arguments concerning the most appropriate wording of the insanity defense rule, it remains unclear whether it makes much difference. As is discussed in more detail later, offenders found not guilty by reason of insanity are easily discriminable from those who are evaluated by psychiatrists to determine whether an insanity defense is applicable but who are later convicted. Offenders acquitted by reason of insanity have more serious index offenses than a randomly selected group of subsequently convicted insanity evaluatees and are more likely to have a diagnosis of psychosis than subsequently convicted insanity evaluatees who are matched on index offense (G. T. Harris & Rice, 1990). This suggests an alternate rendering of the M'Naghton rule: No person shall be convicted after having committed homicide or attempted homicide if found to be psychotic shortly afterwards.

It is also unlikely that the actual task of appraising dangerousness varies greatly with legislative details. Clinicians and decision makers must relate the legislative language to the empirical literature on the prediction of recidivism if they are to effectively balance the rights of the offender with the protection of the public.

PREVENTIVE DETENTION

The issues of indeterminate confinement, provision of effective treatment, and assessment of dangerousness involved in the preventive detention of offenders are very similar to those involved in the hospitalization of the "criminally insane." Preventive detention of individuals presumed to be dangerous began in the mid-19th century (Petrunik, 1982). In North America, it was designed to incapacitate dangerous individuals until treatment rendered them fit for safe release. Preventive detention has recently been revived. By the 1980s, habitual criminal status had been widely repealed or fallen into disuse, but in the 1990s many U.S. jurisdictions have revived or passed new preventive detention legislation, the most famous of which is the "sexual predator law" of the state of Washington (for details on this legal history, see Lieb, Quinsey, & Berliner, 1998). In Canada, the 1948 Dangerous Sex Offender legislation provided for the determination of the dangerousness of sex offenders through the expert testimony of psychiatrists in court (Greenland, 1984). In 1977 this legislation was renamed Dangerous Offender legislation and was broadened to include all dangerous offenders, whether sexual or not. Although both versions rarely have been used, the number of offenders incarcerated as Dangerous Offenders has been increasing over the past 25 years (Solicitor General Canada, 2001).

Under current Canadian legislation, to be designated as a dangerous offender, a person must first be convicted of a personal injury offense. A *personal injury offense* is an indictable offense for which one is liable for imprisonment for 10 or more years involving actual or attempted interpersonal violence or conduct endangering the life or safety of another person or inflicting or being likely to inflict severe psychological damage on another, or the commission or attempted commission of sexual assault, sexual assault with a weapon, threat or the infliction of bodily harm, or aggravated sexual assault. A person is judged to be such a threat to the life, safety, or physical or mental well-being of others

- if there is a pattern of repetitive behavior that shows a failure of self-restraint or a pattern of persistent aggressive behavior that shows indifference to reasonably foreseeable consequences to others;
- if any behavior associated with the index offense is so brutal as to compel the conclusion that the offender's future behavior is unlikely to be inhibited by normal standards of behavior restraint; or
- if the offender's conduct has shown a failure to control sexual impulses and a likelihood of causing injury, pain, or other evil to others.

Because both the Dangerous Offender and Dangerous Sexual Offender legislation was designed (as is the case in most North American jurisdictions) to provide community protection and offender treatment, it "carried implicit assumptions about the ability of professionals to act equitably, to provide treatment for offenders, and to predict their behavior" (Wormith & Ruhl, 1986, p. 401). Wormith and Ruhl's study of offenders held under the Dangerous Sex Offender legislation indicated that these assumptions were not justified. There were gross geographic disparities in the frequency of application; economic bias, in that poor offenders were more likely to be designated as Dangerous Sex Offenders; inaccurate application, in that a sizeable proportion of these offenders had no history of violent offending; and, finally, very limited availability of treatment to these offenders while they were incarcerated. Referring to the very similar Canadian Habitual Offender legislation, Mewett (1961) stated, "It is impossible to deny that our present system is a half-hearted attempt, weak in its inception and savage in its execution" (p. 58).

MENTALLY DISORDERED OFFENDERS IN ONTARIO

If Quinsey's conjecture holds true for institutions, it is just as valid for entire systems. Thus, the jurisdiction of Ontario serves as a typical example of the difficulties inherent in the traditional informal and unscientific approaches to the problems of assessing and managing violent mentally disordered offenders. Although the system for mentally disordered offenders in Ontario changed very slowly over the first part of the 20th century (Downey, 1915; Lynch, 1937; McKnight, Mohr, & Swadron, 1962; Rice, 1985; N. C. Wallace, 1925), change came more quickly after the opening of the first medium-security units in the province (Rice, 1986). Throughout the 20th century, however, there were remarkable strands of continuity. The approach to the management of mentally disordered offenders remained institution focused, with new mentally disordered offenders usually beginning their institutional careers in the most secure institution of the Ontario psychiatric hospital system. Since 1933, the most secure psychiatric institution in Ontario has been the Oak Ridge Division of the Mental Health Centre, Penetanguishene.

A further thread of continuity is the difficulty in determining when, if ever, a particular mentally disordered offender should be released to an area of lower security or to the community. Such a decision traditionally has been seen as contingent on the offender's recovery from his mental illness. Unfortunately, the relationship between an offender's mental disorder and his dangerousness is often nebulous (Monahan, 1981; Quinsey, 1977b). In fact, as we discuss in more detail in chapter 5 (see the section entitled "A Comparison of Criminal Recidivism Among Schizophrenic and Nonschizophrenic Offenders"), offenders diagnosed with major mental disorders are typically less dangerous to the community than other serious offenders (Rice & Harris, 1992). For example, some mentally disordered offenders may remain quite psychotic yet not present much risk, and others suffer from disorders for which no specific treatment is available (e.g., intellectual handicap) or that are at least in part defined by their histories (e.g., antisocial personality disorder). Because no specific treatments are available for mental retardation and antisocial personality disorder, these persons cannot be said to recover. We maintain that release policies for such individuals should be based on level of risk rather than recovery from mental disorder.

Historically, the response to these ambiguities has been to err on the side of caution by institutionalizing mentally disordered offenders for very long periods under custodial conditions. However, since the Lieutenant Governor's Advisory Board of Review was established in Ontario in 1967, length of hospital stay in maximum security has generally decreased. This has occurred in the context of an increasingly adversarial atmosphere in review board hearings, an increasing emphasis on the right of mentally disordered offenders to the least restrictive disposition, and growing public dissatisfaction with the release of dangerous offenders. The confluence of these developments has led to ever-growing pressure on mental health professionals to predict the occurrence of future violent behavior more accurately.

It is clear, however, that any system of prediction, supervision, or management of dangerous offenders is part of a much larger legal and bureaucratic enterprise with a long history. It is unlikely that any marked improvement in prediction or management can be obtained without attempting to change a variety of institutional and systemic practices. The problems of prediction and management cannot be ameliorated without a scientifically adequate approach to the accumulation of knowledge, an accurate method of appraising risk, and an effective technology of supervision and treatment.

OAK RIDGE

Finally, in this journey from the general to the specific, it remains for us to describe these issues as they apply in Oak Ridge, our own home institution, in which most of the research reported in this book was conducted. Oak Ridge is a psychiatric facility for men operated by the Ontario Ministry of Health. Administratively, it is a division of the Mental Health Centre of Penetanguishene, Ontario. Half of Oak Ridge was opened in 1933, and the other half was built in 1956. The physical structure consisted of eight 36-bed wards (now seven 20-bed wards). The original structure was that of a not very elegant prison; offices for professional staff were not added until the 1970s. Each patient has an individual cell (a "room"). A visiting area was added in the 1980s, and an indoor pool was constructed in the 1990s. At the same time, most wards were renovated.

Oak Ridge was originally built and operated as a maximum-security custodial psychiatric facility for housing the "criminally insane" for very long periods. Until the 1980s, Oak Ridge operated at close to capacity (about 300 patients). Since the mid-1960s, the general trend has been for the number of professional staff to increase; since the mid-1980s, the trend has been for the patient population to decrease, although most recently the number of beds has begun to climb, from a low of 120 in 1990 to 140 in 1997. More about the history of Oak Ridge can be found in other sources (Nielson, 2000; Rice & Harris, 1993; Weisman, 1995).

Oak Ridge has received various types of referral: offenders remanded by the courts for a 30- to 60-day psychiatric assessment of their fitness to stand trial or the applicability of an insanity defense; patients detained after having been found not guilty by reason of insanity (presently termed *not criminally responsible on account of mental disorder*) or unfit for trial; mentally ill offenders from jails, provincial reformatories, or federal prisons; and patients who have been involuntarily certified (civilly committed) under the Ontario Mental Health Act and who are too difficult to manage in the less-secure settings of other Ontario psychiatric hospitals or (much more rarely) too difficult to manage in facilities for the intellectually handicapped. More recently, Oak Ridge housed a small number of offenders following expiration of their sentences by virtue of civil commitment, a use similar in some respects to the sexual predator laws in several American states. The characteristics of the patient population have changed with time. Descriptive data on the characteristics of the admission, discharge, and cross-sectional characteristics of Oak Ridge patients are presented in Appendix O. The demographic data reveal that the admission population strongly resembles that of a prison, whereas the cross-sectional population tends to be much more severely mentally disordered.

Through much of its history, Oak Ridge had two kinds of programs (Rice & Harris, 1992). One was designed to treat patients who frequently exhibited problem behaviors within a hospital setting and who were deemed unsuitable for verbal therapies. Ward programs were based on security and behavior modification principles (Quinsey, 1981; Quinsey & Sarbit, 1975). Patients earned privileges for exhibiting carefully specified desirable behaviors and lost privileges for undesirable behaviors. The programs and ward structures were designed so that as patients developed more stable and acceptable patterns of behavior, they were moved from the more secure, minimum-privilege upper wards to the less secure, maximum-privilege lower wards. Transfer to the next level in the progression occurred only when the patients had met well-defined criteria for changes in status laid down by the ward staff. The upper-ward programs were primarily aimed at reducing the incidence of assaultive behavior, teaching basic hygiene skills and simple work habits, and improving the patients' mood and cooperation. In the lower wards, rewards were less immediate and direct. During the day, most patients on the lower wards worked in off-ward shop areas. (A follow-up study of patients from this program is discussed in chap. 5.)

The other class of programs emphasized verbal, insight-oriented, emotionally evocative therapy in several forms. In its most coherent form, the Social Therapy Unit occupied four wards and used the traditional division of upper (more secure) and lower (less secure) wards. The program was designed to treat personality-disordered and psychotic patients in roughly equal proportions. Patients were usually young and average or above in intelligence. The basic idea behind the milieu therapy approach was that mental illness is a form of disturbed communication that can best be resolved through interactions of patients with each other. Because many of the patients habitually exploited and manipulated others, both the duration and intensity of social interactions were deliberately enhanced so that these exploitative behaviors became obvious to both the patient himself and others and so the long-term consequences of these antisocial styles of interaction could not be escaped. (An evaluation of the Social Therapy Unit program is discussed more fully in chap. 5.)

Successively over the years between 1971 and 1988, each of the first three present authors worked as the behavioral psychologist for the behavioral program. In that role, we each felt a keen desire to bring some science to the task faced by the rest of the Oak Ridge staff. We tried to initiate and maintain high-quality behavioral treatment. We tried to help systematize decision making, especially as it applied to release. We ran social skills training groups for patients aimed at remediation of the skill deficits that had, in theory at least, led to their violent offenses. We examined assaultive patients and their violent acts, leading to efforts to teach ward staff members the skills necessary to prevent such incidents (Rice, Harris, Varney, & Quinsey, 1989). We each became embroiled in ward politics, worked to change the role of psychology away from psychometric testing, and did research on violence and crime.

Ultimately, each of us left our direct clinical duties in the behavioral program behind to become a full-time researcher. In recent years, Oak Ridge has lost its unique treatment focus, and the wards can be characterized as a nonspecific milieu—custodial care with a security-oriented level system, plus drug treatment and educational, recreational, and vocational opportunities for some patients. Since 1988, our research efforts on the prediction and control of violence have intensified. Throughout, however, our aim was to produce knowledge that would help with those concerns that had originally consumed our attention as practitioners on the behavioral program: What treatments are indicated by the scientific evidence? Which offenders can safely be released? What methods most accurately appraise the risk of offenders to be released? How can scientific methods be made paramount in decisions about what to do?

CONCLUSION

In the criminal justice system, sentencing is thought to serve several quite different purposes: general deterrence (deterring others who might be tempted to commit a similar offense by example), specific deterrence (deterring the person sentenced from committing a similar offense), incapacitation (prevention of criminal activity by curtailing opportunity), rehabilitation, endorsement of community values, and discouragement of vigilante justice by the relatives and friends of victims. The extent to which sentencing practices actually accomplish these goals is a subject of continuing controversy among criminologists.

Offenders who cannot assist in their own defense or who are considered not to have criminal intent are given special (psychiatric hospital) dispositions. These dispositions are generally meant to incapacitate offenders until they are unlikely to commit further offenses because of treatment-induced improvement in their mental condition, spontaneous recovery, or age-related infirmity.

Many of the purposes of sentencing or special dispositions depend on knowing the likelihood that a particular offender will commit a new serious offense. If an offender is very unlikely to commit a new serious offense, it is pointless to incapacitate him, to attempt to reduce his risk through rehabilitation or treatment, or to worry about special deterrence.

Risk management was extremely conservative in the first half of the 20th century, particularly within the forensic mental health system. The rationale for incapacitating, and often indeterminate, dispositions has usually included the promise of treatment or rehabilitation in addition to the protection of the public. However, the gap between the promise of rehabilitation and the results of such attempts (when they have actually been made) has usually been very wide. More recently, the pendulum has swung between an emphasis on the civil rights of inmates and forensic patients and increasing sentences for specific categories of crime. The recent passage of U.S. sexual predator laws, which combine an indeterminate sentence with treatment designed to lower the likelihood of reoffending, illustrates that the North American pendulum is currently once again on the conservative side.

The historical review presented in this chapter shows that policy and dispositional decisions concerning serious offenders, as well as their treatment, have been driven primarily by historical inertia and ideology. The pendulum-like policy swings demonstrate the need for a more scientifically informed approach to risk management. One important aspect of this approach involves measuring the risk that offenders actually present to the community.

2

PREVIOUS RESEARCH ON PREDICTION

Society has an interest in knowing which adjudicated offenders are likely to commit further offenses. Sentencing, parole, probation, admission, and discharge from hospital and adjustments in the conditions of supervised community release necessitate implicit and usually explicit judgments about the likelihood of future antisocial behavior. Even so-called "truth in sentencing" or "just deserts" approaches to determine sentencing make sentence length partly contingent on factors presumably related to public safety. A major assumption underlying all social policy in this area is that certain characteristics pertaining to an individual are actually related to future criminal conduct. In other words, if all the variance in criminal conduct were attributed to measurement error and the environment, and none of the variance were accounted for by individual characteristics, the occurrence of crime could never be affected by decisions about the institutionalization of individual offenders. In fact, however, there is a long history of research aimed at discovering the predictors of recidivism—individual characteristics that are related to future antisocial conduct among individuals already identified as having committed offenses.

In this chapter, we review the empirical research on this topic reported before our own attempts to study the prediction of violence (i.e., up to the mid-1980s). More recent findings are reviewed in chapter 5. Before summarizing the earlier work, some initial observations must be made. First, the work is fragmented. Some investigators have studied the predictors of recidivism among adult felons released from prison, whereas others have studied antisocial conduct among insanity acquittees discharged from hospitals. Some have studied juvenile offenders, whereas others have examined recidivism among adults. Almost all studies were conducted in North America and Europe. If the predictors of recidivism were dependent on such variations in population characteristics, sensible statements about the predictors of recidivism would be impossible. Fortunately, however, the same personal characteristics are related to recidivism regardless of the population of offenders examined.

Second, recidivism can be defined in a number of ways. Thus, many studies of prisoners include technical parole violations in the definition of recidivism—behaviors that would be neither criminal nor antisocial if the individual were not a parolee. Similarly, many studies of discharged forensic patients include rehospitalization for noncriminal actions in the definition of recidivism. More important, most criminal behavior is minor. That is, the vast majority of crimes (e.g., theft, drug possession, public intoxication, prostitution, fraud) have no direct impact on the personal safety of the public in general. This means that legal jurisdictions vary considerably in whether they consider such behaviors to constitute crimes in the first place and, even when they are considered to be criminal offenses, in how much effort officials expend in apprehending their perpetrators. Again, to the extent that recidivism includes such behaviors, geographic variability would preclude any hope that sensible statements could be made about the predictors of recidivism. In the remainder of this chapter and this book, we confine ourselves (with a few exceptions that are clearly noted) to the discussion and prediction of violent recidivism or, at least, recidivism defined by the commission of serious antisocial conduct, such as homicide, sexual assault, arson, and armed robbery.

A related matter concerns the way in which most of the research was conducted. Almost all the research involves follow-up studies in which a group of individuals released from institutions was examined to determine which personal characteristics that were measured (or could have been measured) at the time of release are statistically related to subsequent violent or antisocial behavior. The measures of recidivism have almost always come directly from official records (e.g., police records, data on hospital admissions). These kinds of studies have several strengths. Policymakers are very concerned about institutionalized or, at least, apprehended offenders. There is, of course, societal and theoretical interest in the predictors of crime among persons who have never before been apprehended (i.e., in the antecedents of entry into a criminal career), but the focus of the present book is on the relative persistence of offending among identified offenders.

Follow-up studies also have weaknesses. Little is known, for example, about the possible predictors of recidivism among those rare persons who are never released, such as assassins of heads of state or mass murderers. Police records and other official data are probably conservative in that they are unlikely to record an innocent person as having recidivated. However, police records undoubtedly underestimate the actual prevalence of crime. Some victims do not report crimes, some perpetrators escape apprehension, and some guilty people go free. It is likely that these sources of "error" in detecting recidivism are related to some actual predictors of recidivism. As an example, it is very likely that released offenders with the fewest emotional ties to other people in their communities are erroneously recorded as not having recidivated when, in fact, they are committing crimes under aliases in other jurisdictions. Such "biases" in the measurement of outcome obscure true predictors of recidivism, although recidivists are more likely to be identified in follow-up studies to the extent that they commit more serious offenses with greater frequency over longer time periods. Thus, the weight given to reported findings should (and does in our review in this chapter) reflect the methodological rigor of the empirical work and the frequency with which the findings are replicated in different populations.

The most commonly predicted data are police reports of charges or convictions. Follow-up studies actually measure violent behaviors for which members of the sample are first caught, then charged, and (in the case of conviction data) then convicted. In addition, plea bargaining often changes the label attached to the offense into one connoting nonviolent crime. Thus, the dependent measure might not be so much one of violence as the offender's luck, police efficiency, social judgments of the offense, plea bargaining, and the outcome of an adversarial legal process.

Moreover, different researchers have used different definitions of violence. Criminal offenses such as robbery and carrying a weapon are sometimes and sometimes not considered to be violent. The broadness of the definition could have a large effect on how well variables can discriminate between violent and nonviolent released persons and does necessarily affect the inevitable tradeoff between false positives and false negatives.

Finally, a global definition of violent recidivism is actually a composite of theoretically unrelated behaviors ranging from sexual murder to armed robbery. Increasing the breadth of the definition of violence increases the number and proportion of recidivists classified as violent but might do so at the cost of forcing unrelated behaviors into the same behavioral class.

EMPIRICAL PREDICTION OF RECIDIVISM

As mentioned already, with very few exceptions, the personal characteristics empirically related to violent recidivism do not vary as a function of the type of population studied. Thus, the predictors of violent recidivism are essentially the same in the populations of prisons, secure psychiatric facilities, and ordinary mental hospitals (Bonta, Law, & Hanson, 1998).

Secure Hospitals

Before 1960, there was little follow-up information on persons released from special or secure hospitals. The small amount of research available on the prediction of violence (usually and inelegantly called the *prediction of dangerousness*) primarily addressed the issue of the overall dangerousness of mentally ill persons. Such persons had been found in several studies to have been charged less frequently than members of the general public. The issue of dangerousness rarely arose because of the extremely conservative way in which mentally disordered offenders were managed: They were kept for very long periods in maximum-security psychiatric institutions and then usually transferred to regular mental hospitals before reaching the community.

In the 1960s, however, there was growing concern with procedural safeguards and the civil liberties of mentally disordered offenders. Generally, it was held in the mental health community that psychiatric expertise was relevant and reasonably accurate in determining when someone had achieved maximum benefit from hospitalization and in identifying persons who were dangerous to the public. The idea of laypersons (defined as nonpsychiatrists) being involved in these decisions was thought to be lamentable but required by public concerns. In particular, the involvement of lawyers was strongly resisted.

In the 1960s and early 1970s, the secure hospitals were very insular in their outlook and were dominated by psychiatry. No one seemed to have heard of Meehl's (1954) devastating critique of clinical judgment. Few professionals considered base rates to be a problem in the prediction of violence as they were in the prediction of suicide, and few professionals attended to the correctional follow-up studies that indicated inaccurate prediction of violence and low base rates of violent offending.

The momentum of change picked up markedly in 1974, when Steadman and Cocozza published their book on the Baxstrom cohort. This was a sociologically oriented follow-up study of individuals released from a maximum-security hospital as a result of the *Baxstrom* decision. In 1966, the U.S. Supreme Court, in *Baxstrom v. Herold*, held that Johnny K. Baxstrom had been denied equal protection by being confined in Dannemora (a maximum-security correctional psychiatric hospital) beyond the expiration of his sentence (U.S. Supreme Court, 1966). Baxstrom was held in Dannemora because of mental illness but was not given the legal safeguards for contested civil commitments. It should be noted that Dr. Herold of Dannemora had tried to have Baxstrom transferred to a civil facility, but none would accept him. Because of this successful appeal (handled essentially alone by Baxstrom), 967 offenders were released to hospitals throughout New York state. None of them had been found not guilty by reason of insanity. Havoc was expected, but none occurred. These offenders had very low rates of reoffending. Within a year of transfer, 176 patients had been discharged to the community, and seven had returned to security hospitals. Over a 4.5-year period, more than half of the patients were discharged to the community, and fewer than 3% returned to security hospitals. Of a subsample of 199 patients, half were in a mental hospital, 34% were in the community, 14% were dead, and 2.5% were in secure hospitals or prisons at the end of the follow-up period. Of 98 released, 44 were rehospitalized or rearrested (or both).

The Baxstrom natural experiment was important because it demonstrated a very low base rate of postrelease violent behavior (only two men were reconvicted for a violent crime) in an uncensored cohort of maximum-security releasees. It indirectly questioned the accuracy of clinical judgment (these people had previously not been released mostly because clinicians had thought they were too dangerous). Most important, it was very widely publicized.

In 1979, Thornberry and Jacoby published a very similar and much more detailed study of the Dixon cohort released from the wretched Farview Institution in Farview, Pennsylvania. There were 586 patients released; they averaged 47 years of age and had been in Farview an average of 14 years. The 3-year recidivism rate was 23.7%. Fourteen percent were rearrested or returned for a violent offense. Ironically, the Dixon patients had been seen as ineligible for community release by both Farview and the civil hospitals to which they were transferred: "While at Farview they were too young and dangerous, but once transferred to a civil hospital they were too old and frail" (p. 123). Despite this conclusion, this recidivism rate is not that low; with a longer follow-up, a different conclusion might have been drawn (see Hodgins & Janson, 2002).

During the 1970s, a number of studies were conducted on the dangerousness of Ontario security hospital patients. These studies were similar in intent and outcome to those reported earlier in this chapter. Quinsey, Pruesse, and Fernley (1975a) followed 56 forensic patients who had been found not guilty by reason of insanity or unfit for trial and were later released from Oak Ridge. Most were initially transferred to regular psychiatric hospitals. They averaged 42 years of age at release and had been in Oak Ridge for an average of 8 years. Over an average follow-up period of 30.5 months, 5 (9%) of these patients were readmitted to Oak Ridge or reconvicted. Only two patients were convicted for (rather minor) violent offenses. Twenty-seven were interviewed and administered the Environmental Deprivation Scale (Jenkins et al., 1972) and the Brief Psychiatric Rating Scale (Overall & Gorham, 1962). Fourteen were living in the community and 13 in institutions. In general, these patients had experienced few problems in hospital, were relatively asymptomatic, had good work records, but had very limited community social support (partly because they had killed family members). The hospitalized patients complained chiefly of boredom; few were involved in therapeutic programs or had hobbies or interests other than television. These patients resembled the type of offenders described by Megargee, Cook, and

Mendelsohn (1967) who were unassertive and had no past criminal history, but who had nevertheless committed acts of extreme violence.

Quinsey, Warneford, Pruesse, and Link (1975) followed up on 91 civilly committed patients discharged directly to the community against psychiatric advice by a newly established Board of Review. One might have expected these patients to be relatively dangerous, because hospital clinicians were reluctant to transfer them to a less secure facility or release them to the community. The average patient was 32 years old on discharge and had been in Oak Ridge an average of 2 years. In a 1- to 4-year follow-up period, 39% of the patients were readmitted to Oak Ridge or convicted for additional offenses (23% within the first year); 17% committed a violent offense against persons. Personality-disordered patients were more likely to commit a crime than psychotic patients. The only significant predictor of postrelease violence was previous violence.

In a subsequent study, Quinsey, Pruesse, and Fernley (1975b) followed 20 insanity acquittees (held on Warrants of the Lieutenant Governor, or WLGs), 20 discharged involuntary patients, and 20 civilly committed patients discharged by the Regional Board of Review for involuntary (civilly committed) patients. Thirty percent were rearrested over the 39-month follow-up, 20% of these for committing a violent offense. The civilly committed patients, whether released by the Regional Board of Review or by the hospital, had higher recidivism rates than the WLG patients. A scale was constructed, very similar to N. Walker and McCabe's (1973) in England and Steadman and Cocozza's (1974) in the United States, by using the Burgess (1925) method in which one point was assigned for each of the variables that discriminated between successes and failures: diagnosis of personality disorder, being under 31 at discharge, having spent less than 5 years in psychiatric hospitals, having an admission offense not against persons, and not having lived until age 16 with both parents. This scale classified the releasees with 78% accuracy.

Pruesse and Quinsey (1977) followed 206 patients for a 37- to 49-month period. These patients were all released from maximum security during 1972 (89% were civilly committed). Members of this sample had spent less time in psychiatric hospitals and had less often been committed for a violent offense than the members of the Quinsey, Pruesse, and Fernley (1975b) sample; 46% of the sample were reconvicted or returned to Oak Ridge, and 17% committed a new violent offense. Accuracy in predicting failure dropped from 78% in the original sample to 65%, not because of shrinkage, which would have resulted from the use of multiple regression (a statistical method to identify the shortest and most accurate combination of predictors), but because of this sample's different characteristics.

The only study that supported psychiatric expertise in the prediction of violent reoffending was conducted at Bridgewater Institution in Massachusetts. Bridgewater was the subject of Wiseman's (1967) controversial film

Titicut Follies that illustrated the abysmal side of total institutions (Appelbaum, 1989; McGarry, 1970). Kozol, Boucher, and Garofalo (1972) purported to show that offenders released against medical advice did worse than offenders released by the hospital. This study was seriously confounded, however, by unequal follow-up times. In addition, the criteria for the decisions were very poorly specified.

The most authoritative review of the use of psychological tests in the prediction of violence was conducted by Megargee (1970), who concluded that no single test had been shown to be valuable in the prediction of violence. By the late 1970s, most mental health professionals, including many psychiatrists, capitulated to the sociologists and were ready to endorse the proposition "Of course, you can't predict dangerousness." This new popular wisdom meant primarily that new legal safeguards and greater legal scrutiny accompanied the variety of decisions that involved assessments of dangerousness in the mental health system (commitment, transfer to less secure settings, and release). Ironically, these decisions became more closely related to clinicians' assessments of dangerousness, rather than less.

Predictors of Recidivism

The prediction of both general and violent criminal recidivism of persons released from correctional institutions has received extensive study (for early reviews, see Gabor, 1986; Monahan, 1981; Quinsey, 1984; Waller, 1974). Enough work has been completed to establish a general consensus within the correctional research community about the classes of variables that are valid predictors of recidivism and the degree to which they are related to the criterion behaviors of interest. Most of this research has examined the predictors of general, rather than exclusively violent, recidivism.

In addition to the studies already mentioned, there are a large number of Canadian follow-up studies of released inmates and forensic patients.[1] These studies all agree that youthfulness and number of previous convictions (for crime in general or violence in particular) are positively related to the probability of general criminal recidivism. Other predictors, including age at first

---

[1]Andrews and Friesen (1987); Andrews, Kiessling, Robinson, and Mickus (1986); Bonta and Motiuk (1985, 1987, 1990); Carlson (1973); Gendreau, Grant, and Leipciger (1979); Gendreau, Madden, and Leipciger (1979, 1980); Hart, Kropp, and Hare (1988); Hodgins (1983); Mandelzys (1979); Motiuk, Bonta, and Andrews (1986); Motiuk and Porporino (1989); Waller (1974); Wormith (1984); and Zarb (1978). American and British studies include Adams (1983); Ashford and LeCroy (1988); R. R. Barton and Turnbull (1979); A. J. Beck and Shipley (1987); Bieber, Pasewark, Bosten, and Steadman (1988); Bogenberger, Pasewark, Gudeman, and Bieber (1987); Bowden (1981); R. C. Brown, D'Agostino, and Craddick (1978); Gathercole, Craft, McDougall, Barnes, and Peck (1968); Gibbens, Pond, and Stafford-Clark (1959); M. R. Gottfredson, Mitchell-Herzfeld, and Flanagan (1982); Gulevich and Bourne (1970); Hedlund, Sletten, Altman, and Evenson (1973); A. B. Heilbrun, Heilbrun, and Heilbrun (1978); Hoffman and Beck (1985); Holland, Holt, and Brewer (1978); Klassen and O'Connor (1988); Monahan and Steadman (1983); Morrow and Peterson (1966); Rhodes (1986); Steadman and Keveles (1972); Taylor (1985); Tong and MacKay (1959); and N. Walker and McCabe (1973).

arrest, criminal versatility (variety of offending), alcohol abuse, and low educational attainment, are usually found to be positively but more weakly related to recidivism rates. Although findings on the relation of institutional behavior to postrelease recidivism are conflicting, escape and escape attempts have always been found (when examined) to be related to higher recidivism rates.

Perhaps the largest scale follow-up studies of the prediction of violence among released offenders have been conducted by the California Youth Authority (Molof, 1965; Wenk, Robison, & Smith, 1972). These studies of youthful offenders indicated that attempts to predict which offenders would commit violent crimes on release resulted in unacceptably high numbers of persons misclassified as dangerous. With very low frequencies of postrelease violence, maximal proportion of correct judgments is attained by predicting that no one will be violent.

N. Walker, Hammond, and Steer (1967) followed for an 11-year period the criminal records of 4,301 persons who had been convicted of any offense in 1947 in Scotland. These investigators also obtained the previous criminal records of 4,239 Londoners convicted of an indictable offense during part of 1957, as well as their records for a subsequent 5-year period. Offenses of "personal violence" included murder, threatening, use of firearms, robbery, and assaults, but they did not include cruelty to children, causing death by dangerous driving, or sexual offenses involving violence. Of the Scots, 264 men (6%) committed a violent offense in 1947 or later, and of the Londoners, 500 (12%) had committed a violent offense. In both samples, the probability with which a person would be reconvicted of a violent offense increased slightly with each nonviolent offense; however, the probability of a further violent offense rose much more sharply with each violent offense. In the Scottish sample, for example, 14% of the 264 men who had been convicted of a violent offense were reconvicted of another, whereas 40% of the 45 men with two previous convictions for violence were reconvicted for a violent offense, and 55% of the 11 men with four or more previous convictions for violence were reconvicted for a violent offense. These data indicate that a very small number of men have frequent previous convictions for violent offenses and that such a history is a predictor of violent recidivism.

Although more often studied in psychiatric populations, diagnosis has been examined in both released prisoners and forensic patients (Bonta, Law, & Hanson, 1998; Phillips et al., 2005). With very few exceptions, antisocial personality disorder (or personality disorder of any type or psychopathy) has been consistently found to predict criminal and violent recidivism. A few studies have reported that mental retardation is related to recidivism (Farrington, 2000).

Nuffield (1982) followed 2,475 men released from Canadian penitentiaries over a 3-year period. Violent recidivism was counted as any charge for homicide, assault, violent sexual offense, armed robbery, and robbery. The base rate of charges for violent crimes was 12.6% (nearly half of these involved armed or unarmed robbery). The Burgess (1925) method of prediction divided the validation half of the sample into four risk categories with success rates (i.e., no violent offenses) of 69%, 82%, 87%, and 93%, respectively. Unfortunately, the accuracy of this predictive method, although higher than that previously obtained with multiple regression or predictive attribute methods, did not seem high enough to be useful in the real world. It was clear from these data, however, that inmates who are almost certain not to recidivate violently could be reliably identified. The following variables were weighted in the Burgess system of predicting future violence: young age at first conviction; previous convictions for a violent crime; previous convictions for nonsexual assault; previous history of escape; five or more previous imprisonments; current offense a violent crime, sexual crime, or illegal possession of a firearm; and young age at release. This research was successful, however, in developing an actuarial instrument, the General Statistical Information About Recidivism (SIR) Scale, to predict general criminal recidivism. Accurate prediction of general recidivism was replicated in a study of Canadian federal inmates using the SIR Scale more than 10 years later (Bonta, Harman, Hann, & Cormier, 1996). Similar stability in the accuracy of predicting general recidivism has been demonstrated in the United States for the Salient Factor Score over a 17-year period (Hoffman, 1994).

CRITIQUE

Monahan (1981) suggested several issues for clinicians to consider in evaluating dangerousness:

- contexts and precipitating events for previous violence,
- demographic characteristics,
- history of violence,
- base rate of violence among similar persons,
- current stresses,
- cognitive and affective predispositions to violence,
- similarity of future environment to past environments that occasioned violence,
- availability of victims, and
- means of committing violence.

Until recently, very little research has been conducted to determine the relative importance of these potential factors or how they should be evaluated, quantified, or combined to yield predictions.

How are we to account for the small amount of progress made by this follow-up literature through the early 1980s? Was it because the problems in the prediction of violence were intractable, or were there remediable methodological difficulties that, if addressed, would lead to better predictive methods? So far, we have mentioned several limitations in the follow-up literature: the reliance on historical or static predictor variables, the base rate problem, and the failure to identify antecedents of recidivism. Before discussing a variety of attempts to circumvent these and other problems in the more recent literature, a more complete discussion of methodological issues in the prediction of violence is required.

Inadequate Predictors

Researchers typically have relied on predictors of convenience, those that are usually available in institutional files. This choice of predictors often leaves the researcher at the mercy of the accuracy and completeness of the institutional files. File data may have been entered by the most junior clerk in the organization or by a variety of persons who did not coordinate their data gathering. In many cases, file data are based directly on the self-report of the offender, with no attempts at corroboration. The quality of the predictors, therefore, varies markedly over studies and is often very poor. This problem is frequently exacerbated by investigators not performing interrater reliability checks on the coding and entry of file data.

More generally, predictors of convenience rarely are those that one would choose on theoretical grounds. For example, one might wish to use a theoretically interesting typology of homicide offenders as a predictor variable, and Darwinian theory suggests that naturally occurring types of homicide offenders might be identifiable by an examination of offender motives related to their inclusive and personal fitness concerns (Daly & Wilson, 1988). Thus, homicide might be motivated by sexual jealousy, paternity uncertainty, status competition between men, and so on. Unfortunately, useful data on motives are rarely available in routinely collected information.

Predicting recidivism is much like predicting the winner in a horse race: Atheoretical actuarial schemes attempt to predict who wins by deriving the odds from a consideration of a horse's previous history. Although such handicapping is a sensible way to make these decisions, a more satisfying scientific approach would attempt to predict winners directly from a theory of horse race performance relating the characteristics of the horses (e.g., lung capacity, training method) to outcome. Such an approach is better suited to improve understanding than an atheoretical actuarial approach (Quinsey, 1995), and there is no reason why theoretically relevant predictors could not be used in an actuarial model.

A further problem involves the historical nature of these predictors. Both the secure hospital and correctional empirical literatures deal almost exclusively with static predictors—that is, predictors that are fixed and unchanging, such as age on admission, number of prior offenses, length of institutionalization, and so on. As we demonstrate in chapter 8 (see the section entitled "Violence Risk Appraisal Guide; VRAG"), static predictors are useful in determining the long-term risk of recidivism for individual offenders and in identifying those who require intervention and supervision. However, there has been very little work on dynamic predictors, or those variables that change or can be made to change, until recently. Of 28 follow-up studies of released mentally disordered offenders (Quinsey, 1988), 25 involved the use of only static predictors, and only 3 (of which 2 were essentially pilot investigations) attempted to predict recidivism from measures of therapeutic change. The proximal causes of new offenses are among the theoretically relevant variables about which little is known. As Mandelzys (1979) pointed out, it was unclear from this earlier literature how much criminal recidivism is the result of unresolved problems with a released offender that could have been addressed during a period of custody and what proportion of new offenses are due to new environmental or offender problems.

Thus, most of the follow-up literature provides very little information to help in choosing appropriate programs for offenders or in making decisions on the basis of offender change. The paucity of well-designed intervention evaluation studies further contributes to this problem. Research on the determinants of recidivism should be linked to questions of how to reduce or prevent it in the community.

One obvious factor that should be considered is the effectiveness of supervision under early release. Unfortunately, the early literature on the effectiveness of parole and mandatory supervision contains few studies and is methodologically weak (Nietzel & Himelein, 1987). In summarizing the best-executed research on the efficacy of some versus no supervision, M. R. Gottfredson et al. (1982) concluded that supervision had only small effects on recidivism. The limited effectiveness of supervision in the early literature is related to inadequate knowledge of the specific antecedents of recidivism. In this context, *antecedents* means dynamic (changing) conditions of the offender or identifiable environmental events that cause recidivism. Static personal characteristics of offenders may be useful in this context as variables that define the risk group to which an offender belongs and as potential moderator variables—that is, variables that determine the manner in which antecedents affect behavior.

Issues and Problems With Dynamic Predictors

Predictors that change with time or that can be made to change are potentially of great practical importance in the management of offenders. Dynamic predictors provide targets for supervision and cues as to when supervision may be relaxed or needs to be intensified. Exposure to particular treatments and offenders' behavior during treatment are also dynamic predictors; the degree of the predictive accuracy of treatment-related variables speaks to treatment efficacy.

The issues involved in dynamic prediction, however, are more complex than those involved in predictions made from static variables, in part because dynamic predictors are of several types. Some (like the antecedents of recidivism described earlier in this chapter) vary continuously in real time; these may be more or less continuously fluctuating changes in the state of the offender (e.g., whether or not the offender is currently under the influence of alcohol or other substances) or more or less rapidly changing environmental events (e.g., a recent death in the offender's family or other change in the family support system). Other dynamic predictors may be continually changing but predictably so, such as age, or they may change with time in a foreseeable but not completely predictable manner, such as a gradual loss of treatment gains. Still others, such as the provision of a discrete treatment at a given point in time, change once and then become static. The methodological and logistical problems occasioned by these various different kinds of dynamic predictors are often different. For example, a limitation in the use of dynamic predictors that potentially change continuously and unpredictably relates to the time interval of prediction. Whenever the desired prediction interval is long (i.e., if one is interested in the likelihood of a person recidivating over a period longer than 6 months or so), the prediction cannot involve these continuously changing variables, because the prediction must be made at the beginning of the period. Furthermore, the frequency with which observations are made is of critical importance. If the observations are made monthly, for example, antecedents that vary more quickly are difficult to link to recidivism.

Unfortunately, even the recent correctional psychological literature does not distinguish among the various kinds of dynamic predictors, leading to the mixing of dynamic and static items within predictive instruments. Results obtained with such heterogeneous scales can be difficult to interpret, such as those involving test–retest reliability coefficients. It has nevertheless been the practice to use heterogeneous scales in the prediction of recidivism. Moreover, it is sometimes not a simple matter to know whether a given variable should be classified as dynamic or static. For example, it is not uncommon for personality variables to be classified as dynamic, presumably on the grounds that they can change or be made to change. Unfortunately, however, personality variables have been found to be very stable. Personality traits are defined as enduring behavioral dispositions, and as such they are not attractive as candidate dynamic variables. The stability coefficients for the NEO Personality Inventory—Revised (Costa & McCrae, 1992) Big Five personality factors, for example, are extremely high over years among adults. Similarly, a diagnosis such as Antisocial Personality in the *Diagnostic and Statistical Manual of Mental Disorders* (4th ed.; *DSM–IV*; American Psychiatric Association, 1994) is made on the basis of a person's lifetime history. The other major measure of antisociality, the Psychopathy Checklist—Revised (PCL–R; Hare, 1991), contains many purely historical items, and those that are not historical are scored in a manner informed by the person's entire history.

The methodological difficulties in identifying dynamic predictors and assessing their accuracy tend to be underestimated. That a variable can conceivably change or be made to change does not guarantee that it is dynamic in any useful sense. First, the candidate dynamic variable may be entirely accounted for by static variables. To the extent that a candidate dynamic variable can be predicted by static ones, it is not dynamic. The surest way to overcome this problem is to use change scores for each participant, although static predictors can also be covaried.[2] Difference scores, by nature, are less reliable than the scores they are calculated from to the extent that these scores are correlated with each other. This decrease in reliability must often be compensated for by increasing the number of participants in the study. Also, predictors that change may lose their predictive ability with remeasurement. For example, pretreatment, but not posttreatment, phallometric deviance indexes predict sexual recidivism; in addition, among a large number of psychological tests administered before and after sex offender treatment, pretreatment measures were more highly correlated with violent and sexual recidivism than posttreatment measures (Quinsey, Khanna, & Malcolm, 1998).

The accuracy of prediction from static variables and that of prediction using dynamic variables are usually impossible to compare unless one uses dynamic predictors as measured at a particular point in time. The issue in such a comparison, however, is the degree to which dynamic prediction adds to predictive accuracy determined by static variables. Finally, the ultimate accuracy of dynamic prediction is constrained in other ways. To the extent that static predictors are accurate in forecasting the likelihood of recidivism over a particular temporal interval, the accuracy of dynamic prediction declines, and any treatment effects must be smaller. This is a very real limitation with current treatment technologies. We will return to dynamic prediction in chapter 10, where we present some empirical information and suggest how dynamic prediction might best be used.

Inadequate Samples

Samples of offenders, like predictors, are usually chosen by convenience. Often the individuals in the sample have little in common except their being housed at one time or another in the same institution. The heterogeneity of the samples in conjunction with the homogeneity of the predictors often means that small groups of persons for whom more accurate prediction might be possible from appropriate predictors are not identified. As Grove and Meehl (1996) pointed out, whether prediction is more accurate when based on a

---

[2]Cox regression analysis with time-dependent covariates offers another approach to this problem.

large and heterogeneous sample than when based on a smaller sample (the members of which closely resemble the individual for whom the prediction is to be made) is an empirical question.

Samples of released offenders are also often severely biased; this form of bias is called *sample censoring*. In cases where there are indeterminate sentences, only those who are judged as fit for release can be followed up. The adoption of a prediction scheme on the basis of such severely censored samples might lead to a more conservative release strategy than that already used, that of deciding who not to release among those formerly thought to be releasable. To the extent that releasees are different from retained offenders, one learns nothing about the dangerousness of the retained offenders. One's interpretation of the accuracy of release decisions is determined by one's estimate of the likely dangerousness of the retained population. To the extent that sentences are long and discretion is involved in parole decisions, similar censoring occurs in correctional samples.

Low Base Rates

The *base rate* is the proportion of a population that exhibits the phenomenon of interest—in this case, violent recidivism. Because offense prevalence in almost all populations is inversely related to offense severity, most studies of violent recidivism, even those with large samples, often actually examine the predictors of robbery and relatively minor assaults.

A low base rate of violent recidivism affects the apparent accuracy of predictions. For example, if only 50 in a population of 1,000 (5%) were actually later violent, the prediction that none would be violent is 95% accurate. It would require a very efficient prediction (or a large imbalance in the relative cost of liberal and conservative type errors) to make it worthwhile ever to predict that an offender will reoffend violently. It is often very difficult to know the base rate of truly dangerous individuals in a true cross section of an institutionalized population. It does seem that for the durations of follow-up usually examined in the studies reviewed in this chapter, the base rates were generally under 20%. Obviously, with more opportunity, base rates can be expected to increase. Moreover, because an institution cannot release a random sample of its population to obtain a precise unbiased estimate of the base rate, base rates often can only be estimated.

What opinions do institutional staff have about the base rates of truly violent persons? Sixteen Oak Ridge staff were asked, "If 100 men were randomly chosen from this maximum-security mental hospital and released, how many would commit an offense causing bodily harm to another person within 1 year?" In random order, they were also asked about men from a regional mental hospital, a provincial correctional institution, and various Canadian streets at noontime. Respondents were divided into medically trained (the present and former medical directors, two psychiatrists, the director of nursing, and three nursing supervisors) and nonmedically trained (psychologists, social workers, and hospital administrators) professionals. All respondents made base rate estimates for the street that were much too high, and medically trained respondents estimated much higher base rates than nonmedically trained staff (Quinsey, 1981). These differences of opinion regarding base rates should lead to differences of opinion about the dangerousness of individuals.

From a research perspective, low outcome base rates make it difficult to observe empirical relationships between predictors and that outcome. Thus, base rates closest to .50 offer optimal opportunities to discover efficient predictors of violent recidivism. Researchers have several reasons to be optimistic on this score. First, Monahan (1978) suggested that base rates of violence might be higher in emergency commitment decisions and in bail decisions. He argued that higher base rates (and greater accuracy) should be obtained because the context of prediction and the behavior to be predicted would be close both temporally and situationally.

Second, higher base rates inevitably occur in institutions with relatively stable selection ratios (probably a very common situation) and even slightly-better-than-chance accuracy of release decisions. This was demonstrated by Quinsey (1980), who used the selection ratio typically used in a maximum-security psychiatric hospital (60% of patients in treatment retained each year) and a 10% base rate of truly seriously violent patients (estimated from earlier studies using fairly short follow-ups) to explore the effects of varying degrees of predictive accuracy on the outcome of release decisions. In the first year (with a particular cohort), there is unlikely to be any value in making predictions. However, as long as predictions are even slightly better than random, systematic changes occur in that cohort. With no change in either the base rate or selection ratio, the institution rapidly accumulates more and more truly dangerous persons (see also Quinsey & Maguire, 1986).

A third reason for optimism is that most of the studies reviewed in this chapter used mean follow-up periods of less than 4 years. In more recent studies of released offenders that used longer follow-ups, base rates were higher. In some studies with follow-up durations as long as 10 years, base rates approached 50% (G. T. Harris, Rice, & Cormier, 1991b; Rice, Harris, & Cormier, 1992; Rice, Harris, Lang, & Bell, 1990). In fact, long follow-up periods used with high-risk offenders such as sex offenders have yielded base rates of violent recidivism well over 50% (Rice & Harris, 1997a).

Measures of Predictive Accuracy

Many problems presented by low base rates, both for decision makers and researchers, are obviated by an index of predictive efficiency that is independent of the base rate and selection ratio. Such a measure of accuracy means that questions of the utility of predictions can be logically and practically separated from the strict accuracy of predictions. Such an index is the relative operating characteristic (ROC), first derived in communications engineering and psychophysics (see Rice & Harris, 1995b; chap. 3 of this volume). We address issues of measurement and the evaluation of predictive accuracy in chapter 3, but for now we note that the actuarial tool developed by Nuffield (1982) for the prediction of violent recidivism possessed moderate predictive accuracy, even though it had earlier been rejected because of its very low base rate. ROC analysis showed that Nuffield's instrument could be useful if applied in a population with a higher base rate (as would occur in a longer follow-up; Nuffield's was less than 3 years). ROCs, of course, cannot compensate for data that have not been collected. ROCs cannot be usefully computed when only a single dichotomous prediction is tested. In addition, ROCs cannot compensate for methodological weaknesses inherent in the use of inadequate predictor and criterion variables, unreliable measurement, or inappropriate samples.

CONCLUSION

The limitations in the accuracy of appraisals of dangerousness found by the research up through the early 1980s do not appear to have been imposed by nature. Contrary to the impression given by much of the prediction literature, the base rate of violence is sometimes high enough to make predictions well worthwhile. First, it is certain that the base rate of violent behavior has often been underestimated by recidivism research because investigators have used "rap sheet" information instead of police descriptions of the behaviors involved, follow-up periods that are too short (because serious violent crimes are often low-frequency phenomena), and unlikely populations of offenders (e.g., older persons). Offenders likely to exhibit high base rates of violent behaviors include those with lengthy histories of violent crime, psychopathic individuals, and persons repeatedly passed over for release when held under fully indeterminate conditions. In addition to base rate problems, a number of serious measurement and other methodological difficulties in this research could be remedied with a concomitant increase in predictive accuracy. These difficulties include restriction of range in predictor or outcome variables, confusion about the definition and potential role of dynamic predictors, sample censoring, poor reliability of predictor and criterion variables, and inadequate measures of predictive accuracy.

3

METHODS AND MEASUREMENT

Each field of knowledge has specialized terms and unique concepts readers must understand if they are to make use of the research and other information from that field. Often understanding is made difficult by the use of everyday words for specialized, noneveryday meanings; for example, such common terms as *reinforcement*, *punishment*, *extinction*, and *superstition* are part of the lexicon of behavior analysts. However, special, newly created terms often seem to be jargon (examples from behavior analysis include *autoshaping*, *negative reinforcement*, and *consequation*). To reduce the likelihood of both difficulties, in this chapter we explain the meanings of some special terms used in following chapters that deal with actuarial prediction. Then we explain some difficulties inherent in evaluating the accuracy of any prediction and present a solution to these difficulties and methods for incorporating other considerations in prediction decisions.

WHAT WE DO NOT DEFINE

Although our goal is to explain actuarial prediction in as nontechnical a manner as possible, some use of technical terms is unavoidable. The reader may already (and, by the end of the book, will certainly) have encountered some terms used throughout scientific psychology, such as *probability, empirical, norm, population, sample, estimate, measurement error, continuous, categorical, dichotomous, variable, independent* (or *predictor*) *variable, dependent* (or *criterion* or *outcome*) *variable, mean, variability, variance, standard deviation, standard error, interaction, correlation, univariate, regression, multiple regression, covariance, least squares, maximum likelihood,* and *statistical significance*. Readers wanting definitions of these terms so that they can closely follow the methodological details in the following chapters may consult an introductory psychology textbook or other source (e.g., Christiansen, 1988; Kanji, 1993; Vogt, 1993).

SOME TERMS DEFINED

Although they are common, we define some terms as they apply especially to the prediction of which offenders will commit new offenses if given the opportunity to do so.

Reliability and Validity

Reliability refers to the consistency or stability of a measure from one use to the next. In the prediction of recidivism, reliability is assessed by comparing the scores the same individuals receive when independently evaluated by two or more assessors (e.g., clinicians or research assistants). As noted earlier, reliability is a necessary but not sufficient condition of accuracy. Reliability places an upper bound on accuracy—an inaccurate assessment can be reliable, but an unreliable assessment cannot be accurate.

Validity refers to accuracy of measurement—the degree to which an assessment measures what it is supposed to. In practice, validity is more difficult to evaluate than reliability. The validity that matters most in predicting recidivism is predictive validity (or criterion-related validity). Simply put, *predictive validity* refers to the degree to which actual outcomes match predicted outcomes. As much of the rest of this chapter explains, the ways to evaluate this matching are not quite so simple, but accurate predictions are said to be valid. As we document later in this volume, a persuasive amount of research demonstrates that actuarial prediction systems are more valid than clinical judgment, especially in the prediction of violence, in part because actuarial systems are more reliable.

Incremental validity refers to the amount that validity is improved with the addition of new information. For example, the number of prior charges for criminal offenses and the number of previous admissions to penitentiary both exhibit validity in the prediction of criminal recidivism. However, number of previous admissions to penitentiary provides little incremental validity after the number of prior charges is considered. The idea of incremental validity helps explain why it is possible to make accurate predictions without the use of every predictor variable known to be valid.

Recidivism and Opportunity

The *Oxford Dictionary of Current English* defines *recidivism* as "habitual relapse into crime" (Fowler & Fowler, 1970, p. 686). Some writers use the term to mean repetition of the same crime. Throughout this book, we focus on violent recidivism and mean any violent offense that occurs after release, regardless of the offense or offenses that originally brought the individual into the cohort. In most cases, the original or index offense was also violent.

Related to recidivism is opportunity. There is little point in evaluating the recidivism of offenders who have not had the opportunity to commit new crimes because they are still incarcerated. Studies of recidivism incorporate some criterion to say which individuals have had an opportunity to recidivate. Release to the community from prison is a clear instance of opportunity, but what about release to a halfway house? What about transfer from a maximum-security psychiatric facility to an open psychiatric ward? The point is that to study recidivism, a somewhat arbitrary decision about when individuals have opportunity must be made. Also, when the speed of violent recidivism is studied, time spent in subsequent incarcerations for nonviolent offenses must not be counted as opportunity. Finally, opportunity is more crucial for those who have not (apparently) recidivated. Thus, some investigators check death records to ensure that released offenders are not recorded as having been successful (i.e., as not having recidivated) when they actually had no opportunity (because they were dead). For those who have committed a subsequent violent offense, it does not matter much whether they have met the operational definition for having had the opportunity to do so. Thus, we include among violent recidivists those who commit a violent offense while still in prison or maximum-security hospital and record their time at risk as 0.

THINKING ABOUT EFFECT SIZES

Effect size is the degree to which a phenomenon is present in a population. This concept is in contrast to tests of the null hypothesis (i.e., most standard inferential statistics), which merely make a probabilistic statement about whether a phenomenon is present. That is, inferential hypothesis testing gives the probability that a phenomenon exists, whereas effect size statistics tell the size of that phenomenon. Several measures have been proposed for indexing effect sizes, and each has advantages. Effect size is illustrated in Figure 3.1. The figure shows two distributions, one for offenders who were actually violent after release and one for an equal number of offenders who

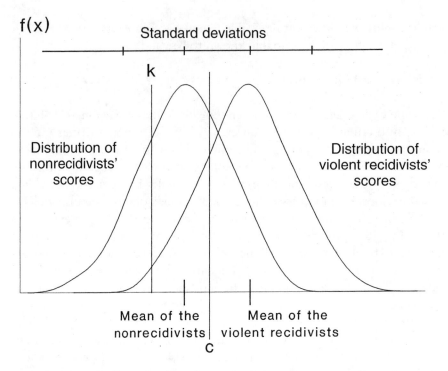

Figure 3.1. Hypothetical prediction tool scores for a base rate of 50%.

were not violent. Each distribution plots number of offenders (actually a probability density function) on the vertical axis as a function of the score they received on a test to predict violent recidivism. The actually violent offenders scored, on average, higher on the test than the nonviolent offenders, but there is some overlap between the groups—some nonviolent offenders scored higher (worse) than some violent offenders. In addition, the standard deviation of the two distributions is shown; for simplicity, we assume that the distributions have the same standard deviation. Now one of the most useful measures of effect size can be derived: the number of standard deviations between the two means. In the case of our illustration in Figure 3.1, the two means are exactly one standard deviation apart, so that this measure of effect size, usually called *d* (first derived by Cohen; see Cohen, 1969), is equal to 1.0.

Figure 3.1 also illustrates other important concepts in the prediction of violence. First, the two distributions are the same size, indicating that the number of violent recidivists was equal to the number of nonviolent ones; the proportion of violent offenders was half the total. In other words, the base rate of violent recidivism was 50%. Furthermore, before the actual outcome was known, a prediction was made by adopting a cutoff score indicated by the vertical line labeled *c*—every offender with a test score above *c* was predicted to recidivate, and every offender at *c* or below was predicted to be safe to release. The proportion of offenders predicted to be violent by c is called the *selection ratio*. Once outcome is known, all the offenders could then be separated into four groups: the violent recidivists who were correctly predicted (appropriately called *hits*, or *true positives*), the violent recidivists who were not predicted (*misses*, or *false negatives*), the nonviolent offenders predicted correctly (*true negatives*), and the nonviolent offenders incorrectly predicted to recidivate (*false alarms*, or *false positives*). In addition, the proportion of violent recidivists correctly predicted is called the *hit rate* (*hit rate* is a synonym for *sensitivity*), and the proportion of nonviolent offenders incorrectly predicted to be violent is called the *false alarm rate* (*specificity* is defined as the false alarm rate subtracted from 1). Finally, the adoption of c defines two sets of correct predictions (hits and true negatives) and two sets of errors (misses and false alarms). The proportion of correct predictions is the sum of the correct sets divided by the total and can be expressed as a percentage (*percent correct*).

Next, if one decided that the number of misses in the situation illustrated in Figure 3.1 was too large—that too many violent people were being released—what could be done? Obviously, using a much better test, one with a larger effect size, would be ideal. If $d = 2.0$ instead of 1.0, it is clear that errors of both kinds could be greatly reduced. Suppose, however, that the present test is optimal (i.e., the best available). What could be done then? The only solution is to adopt a different value for c, a lower value (indicated in the figure by k) that results in fewer misses. When a new cutoff score is adopted, almost everything else changes—misses are lower and the hit rate is higher, but the false alarm rate is higher too (and the number of true negatives lower). The percent correct also changes. In fact, the only thing that does not change when k is adopted rather than c is the effect size, d. What would have happened if we had decided that it was the false alarm rate that was too high when c was the cutoff? What would be the result if an even higher value for c had been adopted? The result would have been a reduction in false alarms but a countervailing increase in misses and another change in the percentage of correct predictions; d would still be unchanged.

Moving the cutoff around in this way illustrates a number of important things about prediction. First, with a given test (i.e., with a given d), there is an absolutely inevitable tradeoff between misses and false alarms: One cannot be reduced without an increase in the other. This unavoidable dilemma is often called the *sensitivity–specificity tradeoff* to imply that improving a test's hit rate always comes at the expense of a higher false alarm rate. Second, with a given test, there is no definitive way to set a value for c. The cutoff could be set to maximize percent correct, but that is unlikely to be satisfactory for several reasons, one of which pertains to the relative importance of the two types of errors. That is, the value (actually, the cost) one attaches to the two types of errors depends on one's point of view. The families of homicide victims and survivors of sexual assault, if asked about the importance of misses compared with false alarms in predicting violent recidivism, would respond differently from prisoners applying for parole. Without doubt, the latter group would accept more misses to minimize false alarms than would the former, who are likely to demand that the number of misses (i.e., actually violent men who are erroneously released) approach 0.

Decision makers are unlikely to satisfy both groups completely, even though they would probably adopt a cutoff between that desired by each. Furthermore, decisions about the relative importance of the two types of error are value judgments and cannot be derived from knowing the accuracy (i.e., effect size) of a test. The arena for resolving questions about value judgments is politics (rather than science[1]), where it seems that implicit decisions about c result in swings of the social policy pendulum. The illustration does point out, however, that if costs were settled and the test's d known (plus the base rate, as pointed out later in this chapter), the single optimum value for c can be determined precisely.

As mentioned earlier, the ideal way to reduce both types of error is to increase d by developing a new, more accurate test—one with a larger effect size. Over a given length of opportunity, use of a more accurate test should result in a lower base rate of violent recidivism than a less accurate test. Many other things might also affect the base rate of recidivism—changing the average length of opportunity, applying the test in a new higher- (or lower-) risk population, changing the operational definition of violent recidivism, applying the test in a different jurisdiction where the authorities have higher arrest and conviction rates, and so on. In fact, studies of recidivism commonly report quite different base rates. Figure 3.2 illustrates some of the problems presented for the prediction of violent recidivism by a base rate different from that shown in Figure 3.1.

In Figure 3.2, the size of the distribution of violent recidivists is much smaller than that of the distribution for nonrecidivists. In fact, the violent offenders are outnumbered 3 to 1; the base rate of violent recidivism is .25. We illustrate the same effect size (test accuracy) as shown in Figure 3.1, $d =$ 1.0, and again for simplicity we assume that the standard deviations of the two groups are equal. This assumption of equal variation turns out to be quite reasonable, and a lower base rate about .25 is more typical of published follow-up studies of violent recidivism than is a base rate near 50%. The following happens when the same value for c (from Figure 3.1) is adopted: The numbers of hits, misses, false alarms, and true negatives; the hit and false alarm rates; and the percent correct are all different (compared with those associated with c in Figure 3.1). Again, the only constant is the effect size,

---

[1]"How wrong is this crime?" is purely a question of values and cannot be answered scientifically. However, "How wrong does this crime seem?" or "How much would people punish the perpetrator of this crime?" can be addressed scientifically (and have been; Wolfgang, Figlio, Tracy, & Singer, 1985; see also Hilton, Harris, & Rice, 2003a)—by asking people's opinions in a survey.

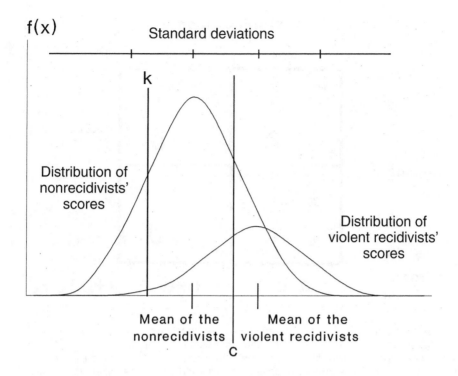

Figure 3.2. Hypothetical prediction tool scores for a base rate of 25%.

d—the true accuracy of the test. This example illustrates the impossibility of comparing the accuracy of two tests using percent correct, sensitivity, or specificity when the tests have been evaluated in research using different base rates. Because researchers have little control over the base rate (in contrast to the selection ratio), this problem is not easy to solve. In the next section we describe the solution.

MEASURING PREDICTIVE ACCURACY

Considering Figures 3.1 and 3.2, the accuracy (effect size) of a test may be captured in many ways. Many methods involve computations on the basis of a single cutoff value for *c* and therefore use the four key values (hits, misses, false alarms, and true negatives) in various ways. The computation of some of these statistics is given in Figure 3.3. As we have shown in detail elsewhere (Rice & Harris, 1995b) and in our analysis of Figures 3.1 and 3.2, none of these indexes of accuracy is adequate. Although they are affected by the test's accuracy (i.e., *d*), they are doomed by their dependence on the selection ratio (i.e., *c*), the base rate, or both.

Some measures of effect size are acceptable for many purposes but are not appropriate here; the most well known of these is the correlation coeffi-

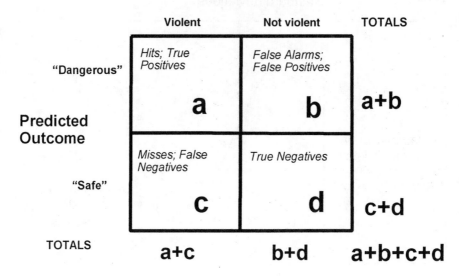

Actual Outcome

	Violent	Not violent	TOTALS
"Dangerous"	Hits; True Positives **a**	False Alarms; False Positives **b**	**a+b**
"Safe"	Misses; False Negatives **c**	True Negatives **d**	**c+d**
TOTALS	**a+c**	**b+d**	**a+b+c+d**

Predicted Outcome (row label)

Figure 3.3. Contingency table. The equations are as follows: correlation $(\varphi) = (bc - ad)/((a + b)(c + d)(a + c)(b + d))^{1/2}$; relative improvement over chance $= (a(a + b + c + d) - (a + b)(a + c))/((a + b)(b + d))$; odds ratio $= ad/bc$; $\chi^2 = ((a + b + c + d)(ad - bc)^2)/((a + b)(a + c)(c + d)(b + d))$; base rate $= (a + c)/(a + b + c + d)$; selection ratio $= (a + b)/(a + b + c + d)$; hit rate $= a/(a + c) =$ sensitivity; false alarm rate $= b/(b + d) = 1 -$ specificity; proportion correct $= (a + d)/(a + b + c + d)$; positive predictive power $= a/(a + b)$; negative predictive power $= d/(c + d)$.

cient. It is beyond our present scope to explain, but suffice it to say that the base rate places a limit on the correlation coefficient so that the correlation also depends on the base rate. There are correction formulas for this problem, and some other statisticians suggest a solution in which the table illustrated in Figure 3.3 is artificially rewritten so that the base rate is exactly 50% (the binomial effect size display; Rosenthal, 1991), but neither of these is ideal. Instead, we and others (e.g., Swets, 1992) have suggested a different solution: the relative operating characteristic (ROC).

Relative Operating Characteristic

At a given value of d (effect size), sensitivity (hit rate) and specificity (1 – false alarm rate) vary as a function of the base rate and the selection ratio, but it has been shown in decision making generally and in the prediction of violence in particular that the tradeoff between the two varies much less. Figure 3.4 illustrates the tradeoff between hits and false alarms for the data in Figure 3.1; the tradeoff for the data in Figure 3.2 is also illustrated. It is hard to discern the two tradeoffs because they lie exactly on top of each other; only the individual data points are different. The data points for the

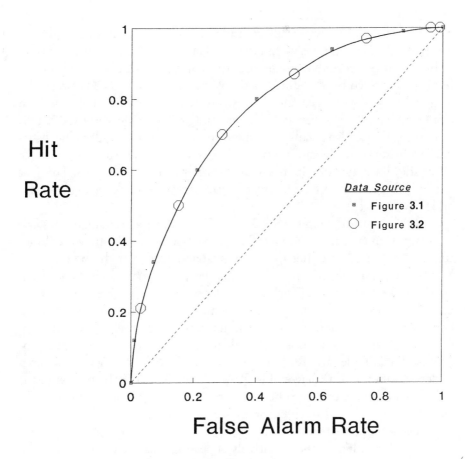

Figure 3.4. Relative operating characteristic (ROC).

respective figures come from calculating the hit rate and false alarm rate at each of several possible values of c and then plotting the hit rate as a function of the false alarm rate. This tradeoff is called the *relative operating characteristic* (ROC) and was first developed in communications technology and in signal detection theory in psychophysics. Recently, it has been applied to the prediction of violent recidivism (Mossman, 1994), and we have shown that the tradeoff, for a given test, remains invariant over large variations in selection ratio and base rate (Rice & Harris, 1995b).

Consider the ROC shown in Figure 3.4. A perfectly accurate test (i.e., one with a huge value for d so that the two distributions in Figure 3.1 had no overlap) would yield a peculiar ROC—the hit rate of 1.0 would be plotted for the false alarm rate equal to 0 and for every other possible false alarm rate. That is, the "curve" (for a perfect test) travels up the vertical axis and then along the top of the box until it reaches the top right-hand corner. It is obvious, we hope, that a completely useless test would yield an ROC described by the dotted diagonal line—the hit rate never exceeds the false alarm rate; the test would have an effect size of 0. The test we illustrate ($d = 1$) yields an ROC that lies between perfection and worthlessness. It is valuable to have a single score that summarizes this curve. Classically, the effect size has been captured by d', defined as the perpendicular distance between the diagonal (no information) and the test's ROC at the point where the false alarm rate equals .5 (essentially the amount of "bend" in the ROC). It is interesting that d' also equals the distance between the two underlying distributions in standard deviation units. That is, $d' = d$ (our earlier measure of effect size) if the two distributions have equal standard deviations. This fact explains why a test's ROC is invariant with respect to alterations in base rate and selection ratio.

ROCs for the data in Figures 3.1 and 3.2, as illustrated in Figure 3.4, are perfectly symmetrical. Sometimes ROCs are asymmetrical—they are sometimes more bulged at either the top right-hand corner or the bottom left-hand corner. This occurs when the two underlying distributions do not have equal standard deviations. (Technically, "lopsided" ROCs can also result from underlying distributions that are not normal, but it turns out that they are very robust to deviations from this assumption.) Nevertheless, because lopsided ROCs are possible, it is preferable to measure accuracy using the proportional area under the ROC rather than d'. Thus, the proportional area under the (useless test) diagonal is .50, and the area under the perfect test is 1.0. The area under our hypothetical test ($d = d' = 1.0$) is approximately .75 (i.e., our hypothetical test's accuracy seems to lie about halfway between worthlessness and perfection).

Another valuable and intuitively appealing measure of effect size, the *common language effect size* (CLES), can be derived once d is known (McGraw & Wong, 1992). In our example, the CLES is defined as the probability that a randomly selected violent recidivist has a higher score on the test than a randomly selected nonrecidivist. That is, the CLES is the probability that, if a recidivist and nonrecidivist were chosen at random, the recidivist has the higher test score. As we demonstrated elsewhere (Rice & Harris, 1995b), the CLES and the ROC area are conceptually and mathematically equivalent, making the interpretation of the ROC area intuitively straightforward. Thus, CLES values also do not depend on selection ratio or base rate.

The point is that ROCs permit an estimate of d, the true accuracy. They yield an index of effect size, the area under the ROC, that is unaffected by variations in selection ratio and base rate, in turn permitting direct comparisons of the accuracies of different tests used with different selection ratios and base rates. ROCs yield additional measures of effect size that lend themselves to easy interpretation. Finally, once the true size and shape of a test's ROC is known (and the relative costs of errors worked out), the absolute best selection ratio (cutoff score) can be calculated for any given base rate.

It is interesting to return to earlier investigations to re-examine the conclusion that violent recidivism was too rare to have been predictable. Quinsey, Pruesse, and Fernley (1975b) examined the ability of a number of predictors to forecast outcome among patients released from Oak Ridge. The outcome of interest was avoiding any readmission or criminal conviction, and there were five predictors (a nonpersonality disorder diagnosis, age, history of psychiatric admissions, a violent index offense, and living with both parents to age 16). An ROC computed from the results gives an area of .86. An ROC area of .76 was achieved using only two attributes in an earlier study (Quinsey, Warneford, Pruesse, & Link, 1975). In the original article, however, it was concluded that violent recidivism was not predictable—only a single variable (history of violent crime) was significantly related to which offenders (16%) met the criterion for violent reoffense. In the original studies, ROCs were not used, but computing an ROC yields an area about .80. Thus, if the base rate had been higher (the average follow-up was about 2 years), more relationships would been significant, and a multi-item tool would have had a larger effect size.

Comments

We now confess that our illustrative test (with $d = 1.0$ and CLES = .75) is not a hypothetical test after all. The data used in this chapter to illustrate concepts about measurement and accuracy came from our own research and reflect the accuracy of our actuarial instrument for the prediction of violent recidivism. As we explain in more detail in chapter 8, the accuracy of our instrument, assessed using ROC statistics, was unaffected by many wide variations in base rate as well as other variations in the population considered. This is exactly what would be expected; indeed, such invariance is axiomatic, given that the test and event to be predicted do not change. Thus, in addition to all the illustrations just discussed, our research results strongly suggest that over the variations in population and base rate we have studied, the process or mechanism that produces the performance of our instrument in predicting violent recidivism is also invariant. We return to this suggestion in chapter 11.

Finally, the question remains: How large is an effect where $d = 1.0$? Is it significant statistically or clinically? Is it useful? How does this effect size compare with other well-established effects in psychology or science in general? The great thing about a common metric for effect sizes is that one could attempt to answer this last question. We note the following facts: First, the ROC area of .75 we have reported is certainly statistically significant (i.e., significantly different from .50). Second, it is certainly clinically significant, given the base rates of violent recidivism exhibited in recent studies in the literature, and given any decision about relative costs of errors that could be conceivably arrived at. Third, in examining many effects (including therapy) in psychology, Cohen (1969) proposed the following guidelines for effect sizes: $d = .20$ is a small effect; .50 is moderate; and .80 is a large effect. In medicine and psychiatry, effect sizes for treatment as large as this are rare (Lipsey & Wilson, 1993). Compared with other findings in psychology and medicine more generally, the accuracy ($d = 1.0$) of our actuarial instrument for the prediction of violent recidivism has to be considered large.

4

CLINICAL JUDGMENT

If we believe that it is possible for us to learn from experience, is it possible for us to learn that we can't?
—Einhorn and Hogarth, 1978, p. 395

The past quarter century of research has severely shaken confidence in the accuracy of clinical judgment, both in absolute terms and in comparison to actuarial methods. As we described in chapter 2, previous researchers have indirectly evaluated clinical assessments of dangerousness by following offenders who were released from secure psychiatric institutions by court order. Because these offenders were at least implicitly considered to be dangerous, their apparently very low rates of violent recidivism spoke to the conservative bias of clinical judgment.

HUMAN JUDGMENT

When people are asked to make judgments on the basis of probabilistic data (as when a clinician tries to predict which persons will commit violence, or when a sports fan tries to predict which teams will have winning seasons), a variety of task features can lead them to make systematic and gross errors. Laboratory studies of probability learning and other tasks involving the combination of probabilistic data to arrive at a prediction have convincingly demonstrated that people make predictions on the basis of the frequencies of various individual events and not on their actual probabilities:

Specifically, people do not take into account the opportunities an event has to occur, only how often it does occur (Estes, 1976). Thus, accuracy in judgment is possible only when the alternative events have equal opportunities to occur. Needless to say, this rarely occurs under natural circumstances. In addition, accuracy in judgment is possible only when the various events are equally attended to and equally remembered.

The influence of encoding frequencies rather than probabilities and the tendency to ignore negative outcome information is exacerbated by a number of other features present in applied decision-making situations. Kahneman and Tversky (1973) argued that because people use simplifying heuristics such as "availability" rather than probabilities (e.g., believing that being struck by lightning is very likely just after reading a newspaper story about it), they ignore the profound effects that differing base rates of occurrence have on probabilistic judgments (Slovic, Fischhoff, & Lichtenstein, 1982).

Problems of a different kind occur because different predictors may be correlated. People seem unable to adjust their predictions according to the interrelationships among predictive variables. In practical terms, this means that people often think they have more information (or are using more information) than they actually have, they are therefore willing to make more extreme judgments than warranted, and they have more confidence than justified (Einhorn & Hogarth, 1978; Kahneman & Tversky, 1973; Wiggins, 1973). Similarly, people tend to be unaware of regression effects—specifically, because of measurement error, the more extreme the value of a predictive variable, the less reliable a predictor it becomes, and the more the prediction should be moved toward the mean. Humans are, in fact, most confident when making extreme judgments: This ubiquitous phenomenon has been termed the *illusion of validity* (Einhorn & Hogarth, 1978, p. 395).

CLINICAL JUDGMENT

From the review of the literature on human judgment, one might expect clinicians' predictions to be suboptimal under certain conditions. An extensive literature amply confirms this suspicion (for a recent review, see Garb & Boyle, 2003). Goldberg (1968) summarized studies of psychologists' clinical judgments and concluded that the amount of clinical training and experience of the psychologist was unrelated to accuracy. More important, the amount of information available to the clinician was unrelated to accuracy but was highly related to the degree of confidence in the judgment. Experienced clinicians' judgments that are based on different data sources do not show high agreement (convergence); neither do clinicians show high levels of agreement with each other when judging the same data (Goldberg, 1968).

Goldberg (1970) showed that multiple linear regression models (statistical models of the relationship among available information and clinicians' actual decisions) that are based only on clinicians' previous judgments are more accurate on new cases than the clinicians themselves. When judgments are averaged over clinicians, however, the "composite judge" performs about as well as the regression model. Goldberg argued on the basis of experiments performed in situations where outcome data were available that when criterion or outcome data are unavailable, a model of the clinician's judgments is likely to increase judgmental accuracy over the clinician's own predictions.

Results of experimental training programs designed to improve clinicians' accuracy through outcome feedback have been very disappointing (Goldberg, 1968). Chapman and Chapman (1967) even demonstrated that clinicians learn insights that are the opposite of that indicated by feedback when these insights make intuitive sense or fit preconceived notions. In light of such data, it is not surprising that Wiggins (1973), in a lucid review of the earlier literature, recommended that clinicians would most profitably be used to gather clinical data, which could then be assimilated and evaluated by an actuarial model.

PREDICTION OF VIOLENCE

Quinsey and Ambtman (1979) controlled the amount and kind of clinical file information available to forensic psychiatrists who were asked to make predictions of future violent behavior and mock release decisions concerning mentally disordered offenders who had been admitted to Oak Ridge at some time in the past. This study examined three criteria for expertise (Einhorn, 1974): Experts should make different judgments than laypersons, should make more accurate judgments than laypersons (the amount of accuracy being limited by the amount of agreement shown in their judgments), and should use any specialized assessments or measurements in arriving at their judgments.

Nine high school teachers and four senior forensic psychiatrists rated the histories, index offense descriptions, and postoffense assessment data and progress reports of 9 child molesters, 10 property offenders, and 11 serious violent offenders against adults. The three types of patient data were rated separately and together on the likelihood of a property offense, the likelihood of an assaultive offense, and the seriousness of an assault should one occur, if these patients were to be released from a maximum-security mental hospital. Raters also judged whether the patients should be released.

Each patient was rated by each rater on two occasions. On the first, the three summaries were rated separately for half of the patients, whereas the combined information (the "total file") was rated for the remainder; on the second occasion, the remaining material for each patient was rated. The rating occasions were separated by a minimum of 5 weeks so that the raters would not remember which summaries went together; in addition, the researchers implied that the raters were to rate 60 different patients. Order effects were controlled by counterbalancing.

The average interrater reliabilities within rater occupational class were quite low; the highest was .68, for the teachers' prediction of the seriousness of an assaultive offense should one occur judged on the basis of the patients' offense data, and the lowest was −.10, for the psychiatrists' seriousness predictions judged on the basis of the patients' assessment data. The average ratings of the psychiatrists were very highly correlated with the average ratings of the teachers. Kappa coefficients of agreement on the release recommendations among pairs of raters were low for all information types.

The average rating of the total file was well predicted from the average ratings of its components for both groups of raters and all three variables (all correlations were above .78, with the exception of the psychiatrists' ratings of likelihood of an assaultive offense, .47). Index offense information made by far the greatest contribution to the ratings of the total file, whereas the assessment data made a very small contribution to either occupational group's ratings of the total file.

None of the criteria for expertise in the prediction of violence were met by the forensic psychiatrists. They did not agree among themselves, could not on average have made accurate judgments because validity coefficients cannot be higher than reliability coefficients, made on average judgments very similar to those of laypersons, weighted the three information types similarly to laypersons in arriving at a judgment of the total file, and gave little weight to the specialized assessment data that were available to them. Agreement did not improve with additional information (i.e., it was not higher when the total file was assessed), but judgments of the total file were more conservative than judgments that were based on its components. It appeared that raters were looking for signs that the patients were dangerous and were more likely to find them the more information they had.

Considering only the judgments made about the serious offenders against persons, it was of interest that both the psychiatrists and the teachers rated the total file and the offense descriptions much more conservatively than they did the history and assessment information. It is instructive to examine the characteristics of offenders who are regarded by clinicians as high risk if and only if the nature of their index offense is known. These serious offenders against persons often had relatively normal, noncriminal histories and exhibited good institutional adjustment. They resembled offenders described by Megargee, Cook, and Mendelsohn (1967) who scored high on the Over-controlled–Hostility (O-H) subscale of the Minnesota Multiphasic Personality Inventory (MMPI; Hathaway & McKinley, 1967).

Quinsey, Maguire, and Varney (1983) compared 14 Oak Ridge patients who had been charged with murder or attempted murder and who had a *T* score of 70 or above on the O-H subscale (Megargee et al., 1967) with 18 patients with similar charges and a *T* score of 52 or less, 15 patients who had not been charged with an offense against persons, and 20 volunteers from the local community. Five measures of assertion were taken on each participant:

1. The Fear of Negative Evaluation Scale (D. Watson & Friend, 1969) measures negative assertion as exemplified by the item "The disapproval of others would have little effect on me."
2. The Negative Assertion Questionnaire, designed by Quinsey et al. (1983) for this study, contained simply worded items, such as, "When someone treats me badly, I am hurt but keep quiet." All of its items were written to be applicable for patients living in a maximum-security institution.
3. In the role-play assertion measure, participants were rated on their degree of assertion in nine situations role-played with confederates.
4. Participants were asked to write a letter seeking to redress a hypothetical injustice they had suffered in a correspondence course; the letter was then rated on the degree of assertiveness shown in it.
5. The Provocative Situation Questionnaire, also designed by Quinsey et al. for this study, contained 29 descriptions of moderately to extremely provocative situations; participants rated how much anger they would feel, what they would say, and what they would do in each. An example of one situation is the following:

> You and your wife go to a dance and have a few drinks. Some guy keeps asking her to dance, and you sit by yourself drinking beer. After one of the sets she doesn't come back, and you go to find her. When you go out into the hall to look, you find her necking with the guy she's been dancing with. Your wife looks scared and goes into the washroom, but the guy says, "Don't worry honey, I'll take care of him." You walk up to him and he pushes you on the chest, hard.

In a multiple discriminant analysis, ratings of assertion in the role-plays best discriminated the high O-H participants from all others; the Provocative Situation Questionnaire was the next best discriminator. Moreover, each of these measures of assertion significantly differentiated the high O-H participants from each of the comparison groups. None of the other measures were significant.

The assertive deficits of the high O-H participants were very striking.[1] In the role-plays, the confederates behaved less assertively with high O-H participants than with other participants, because the former gave in to the requests almost immediately. For example, high O-H participants would watch a female stranger's luggage at her request while she made a phone call until they missed their own bus. In the Provocative Situation Questionnaire, high O-H participants typically indicated that they would neither be very angry nor say or do very much to the male stranger in the dance scenario.

High O-H individuals, therefore, are model patients who pose little problem for other patients or for clinical staff. They tend to have little in the way of a criminal history except for a single very serious index offense. Clinicians who are unaware of their index offense, therefore, would be likely to assess their dangerousness as being extremely low, but those aware of the seriousness of their index would conclude that they were highly dangerous. Because of the low frequency of their criminally violent acts, high O-H offenders bring the problem of low base rates and the heterogeneity of offender samples into sharp relief. They also provide a dramatic illustration of clinicians' tendency to rely heavily on offense history in the prediction of future offenses (just as do laypersons).

Huss, Odeh, and Zeiss (2004) recently reported a study similar to the one conducted by Quinsey and Ambtman (1979). Sixty-seven mental health professionals, including psychologists, psychiatrists, nurses, and social workers, were given admission evaluations and clinical notes for the first 24 hours after admission from actual patients. On the basis of their readings of the material, clinicians were asked to make a dichotomous prediction about dangerousness, rate the probability of a future assault, make a prediction about the severity of any future violence, and finally list the risk cues they used when making their violence predictions. The risk cues clinicians used in their judgments were found to be unrelated to the actual violence of the patients, and the interrater reliabilities of the clinicians' ratings were poor. It seems that even though there has been much more research on the individual predictors of violence in the near quarter-century since Monahan published his 1981 monograph, there is still no evidence of expertise in unaided clinical judgment.

Given this unreliability, methods should be used to increase the reliability of clinical judgments whenever they enter into appraisals of dangerousness. The most straightforward manner of doing this is to average over *independent* judges. The number of judges required to achieve a given level of reliability is given by the inverse form of the Spearman–Brown prophecy formula (Meehl, 1992). Given a known pairwise reliability coefficient, r, and

---

[1]Rice and Josefowitz (1983) found that men with assertive deficits who were given assertion training in Oak Ridge became less popular both with attendant staff and with other patients, an illustration of the importance of determining the ecological validity of particular skills.

the desired reliability, r^*, the required number of raters is given as $n = r^*(1-r)/r(1-r^*)$. The strong agreement between the average ratings of dangerousness made by the teachers and the psychiatrists in the Quinsey and Ambtman (1979) study provided indirect evidence that averaging is a powerful method of increasing reliability in appraisals of dangerousness. However, the validity of these averaged judgments is not assured by this procedure.

In another study (Rice, Harris, & Quinsey, 1996), we asked forensic clinicians to make recommendations about release for a large group of forensic patients and to specify what kinds of community supervision would be necessary to keep these patients safely in the community. We found that clinicians seemed most ready to release without supervision those patients who were actually the most likely to reoffend violently and to retain or recommend intensive supervision for the least dangerous patients. This anomaly occurred because the clinicians tended to concentrate on symptoms that were not accurate predictors of violence.

Of the variety of clinical prediction tasks, it would be expected that violence prediction would be among the most problematic because the base rate of violent behavior varies with the population concerned. Judges are known to be insensitive to differing base rates under a variety of conditions, such as when they are asked to assess the likelihood of some event given the base rate of the phenomenon to be predicted plus worthless diagnostic information. C. K. Cannon and Quinsey (1995) found that university students made the same prediction of violent recidivism for identical cases described as being sampled from populations with base rates of 30% and 70%.

One might expect forensic clinicians to do better in assessing the treatability of offenders and in selecting specific treatments for them than in assessing dangerousness. Although there is less information concerning this form of judgment than there is on the clinical prediction of future violence, the available data are even more discouraging. Quinsey and Maguire (1983) studied 200 consecutive court remands to the maximum-security Oak Ridge psychiatric facility. The treatability of each offender was independently rated by forensic clinicians from a variety of disciplines after each case conference preceding his return to the court. The clinicians showed poorer agreement on the rating of general treatability than they did on the dangerousness of these offenders. Interclinician agreement on ratings of the efficacy of discrete types of treatment was extremely low, with the exception of neuroleptic medication. Agreement did not improve when the most senior or the most optimistic pair of clinicians were compared.

Clinicians were extremely pessimistic about the prospects for treatment, especially for offenders diagnosed with personality disorder as opposed to psychosis. Ratings of treatability were well predicted from various sorts of data. Expected improvement with an optimal program of treatment was related to the clinicians' ratings of degree of personality disorder ($r = -.71$) and degree of psychosis ($r = .59$), as well as the number of previous correctional institutionalizations ($r = -.35$). On the basis of these results, it could be argued that clinicians simply note whether the offender is psychotic and whether he has committed many previous offenses in deciding whether he is treatable or not (see also Konecni & Ebbesen, 1984). Ironically, clinicians tend to recommend for treatment the patients who are at the lowest risk for likelihood of future violence.

In view of the research summarized so far, it does not appear that our conceptualization of how clinicians determine treatability and dangerousness is likely to be found in an organized body of clinical lore. Rather, it should be sought in how persons in general perceive the causes of behavior. Attribution theory deals with how laypersons perceive these causes (e.g., B. Harris & Harvey, 1981) and has successfully been applied to a variety of forensic and correctional issues (Henderson & Hewstone, 1984; Perlman, 1980; Saulnier & Perlman, 1981a, 1981b).

Assessments of dangerousness and treatability made by laypersons and clinicians were compared in a study using fictitious case histories (Quinsey & Cyr, 1986). Each of 24 laypersons and 24 clinicians (21 psychologists and 3 psychiatrists) was asked to evaluate 4 of 16 case histories. The histories culminated in a theft, an armed robbery, a murder, or an attempted suicide. Half of the participants read histories that were designed to produce an internal attribution of causality, and half read histories that would elicit an external attribution. In the internal condition, many prior instances of the same type of behavior as that involved in the offense and little immediate environmental provocation were described; opposite descriptions occurred in the external condition.

The laypersons and the clinicians had few differences of opinion. The internal condition was associated with higher ratings of stability, internality, and controllability of cause; as predicted, it was related to higher ratings of dangerousness. Offenders in the internal condition were seen as less likely to benefit from treatment than offenders in the external condition; this is an interesting result, because the offenders in the external condition were portrayed as essentially ordinary (i.e., noncriminal) individuals acting under the stress of unusual provocation. The result suggests that assessments of treatability are similar to moral judgments, thus explaining the negative correlation ($r = -.43$) that was obtained between perceived treatability and perceived dangerousness. Taken together, these findings support the view that, with respect to personality-disordered offenders, assessments of treatability and dangerousness are made on the basis of the same criteria by both laypersons and clinicians and that both groups confuse treatability with prognosis.

One might expect to discover strong evidence of specialized clinical expertise in the treatment of psychotic patients using psychotropic drugs. A study directly relevant to expertise in this area (G. T. Harris, 1989, and described in more detail in chap. 10) examined the association between neuroleptic drug prescriptions and the performance of 177 men in Oak Ridge ward programs over an 18-month period. Many patients improved with no adjustments in their prescriptions, but for those who did not, adjustments (totaling up to 20 or more) in drug type or dose were unrelated to improvements in their condition. After the initial improvement associated with admission and initial drug administration experienced by some patients, nothing the physicians did with patients' drugs and doses effected ameliorations in performance.

CLINICAL AND ACTUARIAL MODELS

Quinsey and Maguire (1986) attempted to circumvent the base rate and sample censoring problems (problems related to the fact that many patients are not released) of most previous prediction of violence studies in comparing actuarial and clinical decision methods. This study used two composite samples to develop a judgment and an actuarial model that could be compared with one another. The judgment sample of 360 men comprised four groups: 86 insanity acquittees, 47 involuntary patients, 199 remanded offenders, and 28 long-stay patients. The assessment of dangerousness for the judgment model was the average rating of two to five experienced forensic psychologists or psychiatrists for each patient except the long-stay patients, who were assigned maximal dangerousness ratings on the basis of their retention over a long period. Ratings were scored on a scale of 0 to 100.

The outcome sample of 85 men was specially constructed to represent the outcomes of interest in an 11-year follow-up: no offense, property offenses, minor offenses against persons, and serious offenses against persons. To be included in this sample, *successes* were defined as individuals who had long opportunities to reoffend but did not, and new offenses had to be unambiguously classifiable into one of the categories. Serious offenses against persons were those that resulted in sentences of over 5 years, except when the patient entered the mental health system instead of the correctional system. In these latter cases, very serious offenses, such as murder or attempted murder, which would have received long sentences, were required. The outcomes were scored as 0, 20, 60, and 100. (Other scoring schemes yielded similar results.)

Thirty-three predictor variables were organized into three classes: preoffense, offense, and postoffense. Using stepwise regression, two variables, seriousness of index offense and monthly institutional assaults, yielded a multiple correlation of .51 with dangerousness ratings. In the prediction of outcome, two variables, seriousness of index offense (scored by giving one point each for victim death, sexual element, multiple victims, offending on more than one occasion, bizarre elements, and no previous relationship to victim) and an economic or property offense yielded a multiple correlation of .38. In blockwise analyses, the three classes of variables contributed roughly equally to both the clinical judgment and actuarial models.

The judgment model derived from the judgment sample did not significantly predict the outcome of the outcome sample. Clinicians perceived the following characteristics to be related to dangerousness: a homicide offense, high institutional assault frequency, an involuntary admission, low IQ, and admission to the Activity Treatment Unit (a behaviorally oriented program). The outcome model weighted an economic or sexual offense (not homicide), a remand (not involuntary) admission status, a higher IQ, and admission to the Social Therapy Unit (a program for relatively highly functioning patients, particularly those diagnosed with psychopathy). The outcome model did not use institutional assaults. The clinical judgment model appeared to go awry in overemphasizing an index offense of murder and institutional assaults and in underemphasizing sexual offending as predictors. Clinicians saw low instead of high IQ as related to dangerousness. Consistent with these results, Quinsey (1979) found that index offense severity (particularly homicide) and a diagnosis of retardation were the best predictors of length of stay at Oak Ridge. Diagnosis was related to neither the clinical nor the actuarial model. Many of the findings of this study are subject to a variety of limitations and qualifications, especially the fact that the outcome sample was selected for having a long period of opportunity to reoffend (subsequent institutional violence was not examined).

The poor performance of the clinical judgment model, however, must not blind one to common sense. It defies imagination to assert that clinicians (or anyone else, for that matter) cannot validly forecast violent behavior for any patient. The 28 long-term patients who were assigned maximal dangerousness ratings in the judgment sample should contain a high proportion of truly dangerous individuals if there is any validity to clinical judgment at all (Quinsey, 1980). Of these individuals, 20 were released or transferred to a less-secure setting before the end of the follow-up period: of these, 6 were returned to Oak Ridge from other institutions for assault, sexual misbehaviors, or threats, and 6 others were convicted of new offenses. One offender (Robert Phillip, described in the Introduction to this volume) committed a serious sexual assault on a child using a weapon (and later committed a sexual child murder), one received life imprisonment for a series of aggressive sexual crimes against children, one received life for a sadistic rape, two were given life for attempted murder, and one was convicted of mischief and theft. Given the short follow-up period for this group (5 years maximum), their dangerousness is unambiguous. Therefore, for some individuals the issue of dangerousness is obvious. However, because there are so few of these individuals, they are masked in most prediction studies by the large majority for whom the issue of dangerousness is opaque to clinical judgment.

Lidz, Mulvey, and Gardner (1993) followed 714 patients seen in a psychiatric emergency room by a psychiatrist and another mental health professional. Half of these patients were assessed as having some potential for violence and the other half as not having that potential. The two groups of patients were matched on age, sex, race, and whether they were admitted to the hospital. Follow-up data included official records and data collected from the patients and collateral informants during a 6-month follow-up period. Fifty-three percent of the patients predicted to be violent did in fact exhibit some form of violence; so did 36% of those predicted to be nonviolent. These data indicate that clinical judgment can function above chance levels but say nothing about the expertise of clinicians or the relative efficacy of clinical judgment and actuarial prediction. However, Gardner, Lidz, Mulvey, and Shaw (1996) later found, as expected, that an actuarial model outperformed the clinicians in predicting violent crimes committed by mental patients.

Wormith and Goldstone (1984) provided a useful summary of the correctional literature on clinical and statistical prediction of general recidivism. This literature review and several previous studies led to a follow-up of 200 inmates released in the prairie region of mid-Western Canada designed to test a method of statistical synthesis in which clinical judgments are incorporated into an actuarial model. Sixty percent of these offenders were released on mandatory supervision. *Release outcome* was defined as any rearrest or parole violation leading to revocation or reincarceration within 1 year of release. Prediction variables included three legal–demographic variables—previous convictions, marital status, and age at release—and three subjective judgment variables—police recommendations, employment plans, and prognosis at release.

Sixty-six percent of the offenders reoffended within 1 year. The three legal–demographic variables significantly predicted outcome ($R = .52$) and correctly classified 80% of the 130 offenders in the construction sample. The correlations did not shrink on cross validation with 70 additional offenders. Similar results were obtained with the subjective judgment variables. Good interrater reliabilities were obtained on these variables in coding from files. The multiple correlation with outcome was .55 in the construction sample; 81% of the offenders in the construction sample and 79% of the offenders in the validation sample were correctly classified.

When variables from both sets were included, the multiple correlation rose to .63 and the classification accuracy in the construction sample to 85%. Upon cross-validation, the multiple correlation was .57, and 77% of the offenders were correctly classified. It appeared that although the subjective judgments could be reliably coded from the files and were as closely related to outcome as the legal–demographic variables, they did not greatly increase the predictive accuracy obtained by using the standard static predictors.

Whether clinical adjustment can ever improve the predictive accuracy of actuarial prediction schemes seems doubtful. Its success depends on how much variance in outcome remains after the actuarial instrument is used and how accurately decision makers can deal with this residual individuating information. Put baldly, the literature previously cited and more generally (e.g., Dawes, Faust, & Meehl, 1989) does not make one sanguine about the prospect that intuitive clinical judgment can increase the accuracy of actuarially devised instruments, even when the independent judgments of clinicians are averaged to increase their reliability (Ashton, 1986). As has been pointed out elsewhere (Wiggins, 1973), however, clinical judgments in the form of structured behavioral rating scales might be useful as input to actuarial prediction instruments. In fact, as we discuss in chapter 8, human judgments applied in a very structured way play a large role in the actuarial prediction of violence.

The question of the relation of actuarial instruments and clinical judgment can also be reversed—that is, can the provision of actuarial information remediate problems of clinical judgment such as base rate neglect, in which people frequently disregard the relative frequency of an outcome in a population when making predictions about whether it will occur in a particular case? Mamuza (2000) attempted to overcome base rate neglect in the prediction of offender recidivism in two studies. In Study 1, the attempt to overcome base rate neglect involved linking the base rate to a causal explanation of the offender's criminality. The causal explanation was expected to make the base rate more salient. Three hundred and sixty university students rated two offender histories, one of which was associated with a 30% base rate of recidivism and the other with a 70% base rate. The base rates were associated with either a causal (neurotransmitter or social learning "cause" of criminal behavior) or noncausal (release from a particular institution) explanation. Average predictions in the noncausal and two causal conditions were all above 70% in the 30% condition and were about 80% in the three 70% conditions. Base rate neglect was clearly not overcome by providing a causal rationale. In Study 2, base rate information was presented in the context of an actuarial risk assessment. One hundred and eighty students rated two case histories with or without base rate information presented as scores on actuarial risk prediction instruments. Mean predictions with no base rate, a 30% base rate, and a 70% base rate were 67%, 41%, and 68%, respectively, suggesting that base rates presented within the context of actuarial instruments can at least partially overcome base rate neglect.

Although it appears possible to reduce base rate neglect, the way in which clinicians interpret probabilistic information, such as that provided by an actuarial instrument, depends in a complex way on how exactly that information is communicated to them. In a thoughtful series of studies of forensic clinicians, K. L. Heilbrun, O'Neill, Strohman, Bowman, and Philipson (2000) found that although frequency scales (e.g., 20 out of 100) evoke lower likelihood judgments than probability statements (e.g., .20), they are paradoxically associated with higher perceptions of risk. Similar findings were reported by Slovic and Monahan (1995) and Slovic, Monahan, and MacGregor (2000). K. Heilbrun et al. found that the difference between frequency and probability formats obtained whether the likelihood assessments were made by the same person who judged the risk or whether they were made by someone else and communicated to the risk assessor. They interpreted this finding to mean that clinicians rely on an affect heuristic that is stimulated more readily by frequency scales than probability statements—that is, frequency scales engender more vivid and frightening images. It follows, therefore, that the feeling of risk induced by a case will be translated into a relative frequency (e.g., 10 out of 100) that is smaller than the probability (e.g., 20%) that would be derived from that same feeling about the case. Similarly, a particular frequency (e.g., 10 out of 100) will be linked to a higher risk category than a numerically equivalent probability (10% in this example).

In support of this idea, Monahan et al. (2002) found that psychologists who worked in forensic facilities made more conservative decisions when risk information was communicated in the form of frequencies than in the form of probabilities but that other clinical psychologists did not. The authors interpreted this finding to mean that forensic clinicians' experience with severe cases increased the salience of the affect heuristic.

The format in which risk is communicated would be expected to affect what probability threshold is used in deciding on the disposition of a case that is predicated on risk assessment. Monahan and Silver (2003) found that, on average, judges recommended civil commitment in hypothetical cases where the probability of a violent act was estimated to be 26%. Thirteen of the 26 judges were given the risk information in frequency format, and the remainder were given this information in probability format. As expected, the frequency format was associated with more conservative decisions, but the difference with this small sample was not significant. Fortunately, it appears that with practice, forensic clinicians can overcome the tendency to treat frequency and probability information differently. In a test of forensic clinicians who were accustomed to probability-based assessments for their own patients, Hilton, Harris, Rawson, and Beach (2005) reported appropriate risk-related decisions whether clinicians received frequency or probability summary information for hypothetical cases.

EVIDENCE-BASED CLINICAL PRACTICE IN FORENSIC FACILITIES

The traditional way to evaluate the quality of an organization's clinical service is accreditation, usually involving the comparison of the organization's documented information about clinical services against standards or benchmarks. This occurs because few organizations conduct empirically sound evaluations of their services based on client outcomes. Unfortunately, many accreditation standards are known to be invalid indicators of clinical effectiveness (e.g., professional qualifications of the staff) or are of unknown validity (G. T. Harris & Rice, 1997; Rice, Harris, Quinsey, & Cyr, 1990). As a partial remedy, we conducted evaluations of forensic mental health services using benchmarks for which there was an empirical basis (Rice, Harris, & Quinsey, 1996; Rice, Harris, Cormier, et al., 2004). These evaluations revealed ways that clinical service lagged behind best practices based on empirical evidence.

First, forensic clinicians were poorly informed about their patients' risk-relevant histories. Data about past criminal and violent behavior and addiction, for example, were not systematically recorded despite compelling evidence that valid decisions about risk could not be made without them (also reported by Elbogen, Tomkins, Pothuloori, & Scalora, 2003). Second, treatment services did not reflect the current evidence, especially in failing to implement high-integrity psychosocial therapies. Finally, many decisions about release and supervision were relatively insensitive to patients' actuarially assessed risk (see also Hilton & Simmons, 2001); decisions were inappropriately driven by the severity of patients' active psychotic symptoms, even though no evidence can be found that, in forensic populations, such symptoms constitute valid static or dynamic violence risk factors (also see chap. 10). These primary shortcomings meant suboptimal performance with respect to the protection of public safety and patients' rights—more than necessary, dangerous patients were released to the community and nondangerous patients were held in custody. It is clear that a crucial research question is, How can forensic mental health agencies ensure that clinical practice reflects current scientific information?

PROFESSIONAL TRAINING AND EXPERTISE

The literature in the foregoing section supports the view that, in the prediction of violent reoffending and in the determination of treatability, mental health professionals are (or, at least have been) functioning effectively as laypeople. The question naturally arises whether mental health professionals possess expertise in other domains of professional activity that rely on clinical judgment. In this context, an overview of the literature on psychological training and intervention effectiveness is relevant, not only because psychological interventions are frequently used to reduce recidivism, but also to illustrate that the conclusions drawn from the literature on clinical prediction apply equally to the provision of psychological treatments, with implications that are explored in chapter 10.

Over 2 decades ago, the American Psychological Association (1982) Task Force on the Evaluation of Education, Training, and Service in Psychology asserted that there was no evidence that professional training and experience was related to professional competence. Although no evidence of a relationship does not prove the absence of a relationship, it does place the burden of proof on those who assert that they have special competence or expertise on account of their training or credentials. In the literature review in this section, we show that with a number of instructive but highly circumscribed exceptions, the evidence is unfavorable. Dawes (1994) published an entire book on the relationship of training and effectiveness, reaching the same conclusions.

The most ambitious study on the training of clinical psychologists was begun shortly after World War II (Kelly & Fiske, 1951). Several hundred clinical psychology trainees were studied cross-sectionally and longitudinally at 40 sites. In addition to objective tests, four projective tests, two interviews, a series of situation tests, and ratings by university supervisors, site supervisors, and peers were used as predictors.

The results of this project showed that no single criterion of success in training or practice was identifiable. University and clinical site supervisors showed wide differences in their conceptions of success. Judges agreed better about academic progress than about the clinical or social skills of the trainees. In particular, ratings of clinical competence appeared to be as much a function of the rater's role as of the person being rated. Supervisors' ratings did not adequately differentiate the various tasks of the clinical psychologist. Scores from the Miller Analogies Test (The Psychological Corporation, 1994) and the Strong (1943) Vocational Interest Blank predicted the various criterion measures as well as or better than the rating data. Ratings based on the academic file plus the objective test profile were almost as accurate as ratings based on much more extensive information.

Academic performance and research competence were the best-predicted outcomes among clinical psychology trainees. The Miller Analogies Test was the best predictor of academic performance as measured by examinations in general psychology ($r = .58$) and clinical psychology ($r = .58$) and among the best for supervisors' ratings ($r = .47$). Research competence was best predicted by the faculty's review of credentials and objective test results, although the Miller Analogies Test and several tests of interests were also good predictors. Rated diagnostic competence was not well predicted by any measure and was not related to scores on a diagnostic prediction examination.

Among the tasks the investigators set themselves was the development of a measure of therapeutic competence. They were unsuccessful in this endeavor, concluding "that therapeutic competence is a complex of relatively unrelated skills or that some of these measures of the process are not related to skill in therapy" (Kelly & Fiske, 1951, p. 113). Therapeutic competence was not related to academic performance or to amount of experience. Test results indicated that a variety of kinds of individuals earn the reputation of being good therapists, a result to be expected given the investigators' finding of low consensus about what constitutes good therapy.

Kelly and Fiske (1951) discussed the lack of relationship between the results obtained and the confidence the assessment project staff had in the validity of particular methods of predicting aspects of trainee performance. Simple and inexpensive assessments generally outperformed more expensive and complex ones. Both of these findings have been replicated in many settings over the years. Tucker (1970), for example, could persuasively review the literature on interviews in 1970 and conclude that they should never be used to select personnel. Such recommendations have been futile, leading some psychologists to invoke the "fallacy of personal validation" (Forer, 1949, p. 118) to explain the continuance of such practices.

In a book on the evaluation of professional psychology, Sechrest and Chatel (1987) concluded as follows:

> A major problem for professional psychology is, of course, that we do not really know how to specify what psychologists ought to be able to do, ought in fact to do, and we know even less about how well they ought to be able to do anything. The problem is made worse by the insistence of many psychologists that practice is an art and that it cannot be prescribed or assessed . . . . There is no evidence that any specific educational or training program or experience is related to professional competence. (p. 5)

Training and Effectiveness

A 1995 issue of the *Journal of Consulting and Clinical Psychology* had a special section on training and therapy outcome. The conclusions reached were similar to those reached in earlier reviews:

> Given the enormous national investment of physical and human resources in graduate programs, it is quite remarkable that more compelling evidence is not available that demonstrates that graduate training directly relates to enhanced therapy outcomes. (Stein & Lambert, 1995, p. 194; see also Holloway & Neufeldt, 1995)

In addition, mental health professionals have not fared well in comparison to paraprofessionals (therapists without professional certification): "Current research evidence does not indicate that paraprofessionals are more effective, but neither does it reveal any substantial superiority for the professionally trained therapist" (Berman & Norton, 1985, p. 401). Durlak (1979) observed that

> paraprofessionals achieve clinical outcomes equal to or significantly better than those obtained by professionals. In terms of measurable outcome, professionals may not possess demonstrably superior clinical skills when compared with paraprofessionals. Moreover, professional mental health education, training, and experience do not appear to be necessary prerequisites for an effective helping person. The strongest support for

paraprofessionals has come from programs directed at the modification of college students' and adults' specific target problems and, to a lesser extent, from group and individual therapy programs for non-middle-class adults. Unfortunately, there is little information on the factors that account for paraprofessionals' effectiveness. (p. 80; see also Hattie, Sharpley, & Rogers, 1984)

Weisz, Weiss, Han, Granger, and Morton (1995) provided additional evidence regarding therapist training in a meta-analysis of psychotherapy effects with children and adolescents. They found that paraprofessionals (usually trained by professionals) produced larger effect sizes than students or professional therapists; students and fully trained professionals did not differ. However, Weisz et al. observed that their study was not definitive and that they did find that professionals achieved larger effects than paraprofessionals with overcontrolled (inhibition or anxiety) problems.

J. L. Binder (1993) observed that "there is a paucity of empirical information about the procedures and processes involved in psychotherapy training, and empirical evidence for the effectiveness of current practices is practically nonexistent" (p. 301). One of the difficulties in evaluating training programs is that most of the skills that clinical psychologists require to be effective therapists have not been identified. To develop practical skills, we must be able to specify them, relate their effectiveness to outcome, and measure their acquisition. Some of this work has been done. For example, studies of paraprofessional skill acquisition have demonstrated that specific instructional methods are necessary and sufficient for the acquisition and generalization of behavioral treatment methods (Ducharme & Feldman, 1992). For the most part, however, the methods used in professional training programs have gone unevaluated (e.g., Osipow & Reed, 1987); for example, the practice of sending students to any of a variety of clinical settings and hoping that they learn something useful seems suboptimal. In general, very little scientific information is available on the relationship between specific clinical skills and client outcomes, and credentialing has not addressed this issue.

> Various boards that grant credentials, such as the state licensing boards, the American Board of Professional Psychology (ABPP), and other nonstatutory boards, face the problem of evaluating professional competence to practice psychology. Unfortunately, such groups have yet to take advantage of the expertise in psychological measurement of those professionals they attempt to certify. The national licensing examination (Examination for Professional Practice in Psychology, or EPPP) is a knowledge-based paper-and-pencil test that measures psychological background rather than competence to practice psychology. Licensing boards may use oral examinations or essays to focus on practice, but these methods lack the standardization of the EPPP. The ABPP examination relies on work samples brought in by candidates, but it also lacks standardization; reliability and validity remain unchecked. Other boards have ex-

perimented with measurement methods but have so far failed to establish their reliability and validity for the evaluation of competence. In evaluating itself, psychology has not stood up to its own standards. (Howard, 1987, p. 56)

Meta-Analytic Investigations of Treatment Effectiveness

Lipsey and Wilson (1993) conducted the most extensive meta-analyses of the effectiveness of psychological interventions. These analyses show at least modest positive effect sizes for interventions of almost all types for almost all problems. The welcome news is that psychological treatments are generally helpful, as opposed to harmful or ineffective. This robust finding of positive treatment effects is not discredited or diminished by a lack of consensus about how the effect is produced (e.g., Parloff, 1986). The not-so-welcome implication for the effort expended in training therapists is that the type of treatment administered appears at this level of analysis to be irrelevant. These findings are compatible with the repeated finding that level of practitioner training and experience is unrelated to treatment effectiveness (Berman & Norton, 1985; J. L. Binder, 1993; Durlak, 1979; Hattie et al., 1984; Kelly & Fiske, 1951; Sechrest & Chatel, 1987).

Despite Lipsey and Wilson's (1993) meta-analyses, the universe is in fact not homogeneous with respect to treatment outcome. A more fine-grained analysis indicates that particular approaches to intervention yield much larger treatment effect sizes. In the area of child and adolescent psychotherapy, behavioral treatments have been shown to produce much larger treatment effect sizes than nonbehavioral treatment (Weisz et al., 1995; see also Giles, 1990). Similarly, behavioral and cognitive–behavioral treatments directed toward theoretically relevant problems of moderately high-risk offenders have been shown to reduce criminal recidivism more than alternative treatment approaches (Andrews, Zinger, et al., 1990; Lipsey, 1992).

The Andrews, Zinger, et al. (1990) meta-analysis indicates that some treatments either do not affect or may actually increase criminal recidivism. An example of such a treatment is provided by J. McCord (1978), who reported data from the Cambridge–Somerville Youth Study on 253 boys who received (when they were between the ages of 5 and 13 years) a combination of vocational counseling, medical or psychiatric attention, a sojourn in summer camps, and referrals to the Boy Scouts, YMCA, and other community programs. Another 253 boys matched for risk (age, delinquency-prone histories, family background, home environment) and randomly assigned to a control group did not receive any intervention. Both groups contained "average" and "difficult" children.

All participants were followed for about 30 years. Official offense records and personal contacts were used to provide outcome data. Ninety-five percent of participants still living were located. There was no significant difference in juvenile and adult official and unofficial records between the two groups and no difference between difficult and average participants. Nineteen percent of the treated participants committed a serious crime; the comparable value for the untreated participants was 17%. There was also no significant difference between the two groups in the number of serious crimes committed or the age when the first crime (serious or not serious) was committed. However, more treated participants committed more than one crime.

No difference was found in the number of men subsequently treated for alcoholism, but more treated participants reported problems with drinking. Treated participants tended to report more stress-related diseases and tended to die younger. More control group participants were professionals (43% vs. 29%). Although a majority of treated participants reported satisfaction with the program, no attempt was made to relate level of satisfaction and outcome. A substantial portion of treated participants reported having developed a strong attachment to their counselors. The researcher speculated that the deleterious outcome of treated participants might be because of a development of harmful dependency on counselors.

As for treatments that are associated with large treatment effect sizes, individual studies can be instructive in cases where there are too few exemplars of a particular treatment type for meta-analysis. To discover what can be accomplished, researchers must turn to exemplary outliers (see Paul, 1986). In what is probably the best and most definitive psychological intervention evaluation ever accomplished, Paul and Lentz (1977) demonstrated the superiority of a social learning intervention in the form of a sophisticated token economy over a milieu therapy approach and traditional treatment for individuals with chronic schizophrenia. So powerful was this intervention that there was no individual difference variable that could predict outcome because there was so little variance left to predict. To achieve this magnitude of effect, Paul and Lentz trained all of their treatment staff and their data coders according to rigorous criteria, the patients' routine was designed for its rehabilitative effect, senior clinicians functioned as models and coaches for their staff, and fidelity of implementation was monitored continuously over a 4-year period.

When one considers the success of Paul and Lentz's (1977) program, the rigor of its evaluation, and the fact that it was three times more cost effective than the traditional treatment, one is shocked to observe what little impact it has had on the field (see Bellack, 1986). Backer, Liberman, and Kuchnel (1986) studied the dissemination and adoption of innovative psychosocial interventions. After reviewing the literature, they concluded that the scientific literature on program effectiveness has little influence on clinicians because they read little of it and because the literature is written primarily for researchers as opposed to clinicians. Professional meetings and workshops similarly have limited effectiveness because they are primarily didactic and do not involve the active–directive training known to be more effective with adult learners. The effectiveness of all forms of dissemination of program information is limited by the compatibility of the programs or methods themselves with the office-based clinical practice engaged in by the majority of clinicians. The conservatism of clinical practice that results from these limitations is an indirect but powerful indictment of the viability of the scientist–practitioner model.

Backer et al. (1986) documented the characteristics of three successful program dissemination efforts. The common characteristics of these efforts were personal contact between developers and potential adopters, outside consultation on the adoption process, organizational support for the innovation and consistent advocacy by agency staff, adaptability of the innovation to new circumstances, credible evidence of the innovation's effectiveness (although this is obviously not a necessary condition), and "off-the-shelf" complete descriptions of how to conduct the treatment.

Other exemplary outliers come from the expressed emotion and behavior family management literature. Behavior family management uses a social learning approach; it is highly structured and directive and involves the use of goal setting, modeling, behavioral rehearsal, reinforcement, and homework assignments. Patients and their relatives learn about schizophrenia, treatment, problem solving, and communication. The general goals are to improve the emotional climate in the home and to reduce parental guilt and hostility toward the patient.

Hogarty et al. (1986) studied 103 patients meeting research diagnostic criteria (Spitzer, Endicott, & Robins, 1978) for schizophrenia or schizoaffective disorder residing in homes high in expressed emotion over a 2-year period. Patients were randomly assigned to one of four conditions: family treatment and medication; social skills training and medication; family treatment, social skills, and medication; and medication alone. The first-year relapse rates were 19% for family treatment, 20% for social skills, 0% for the combination, and 41% for medication alone.

A further example of very large treatment effects in comparison to alternate treatments and other control conditions is provided by behaviorally oriented and communication skills–oriented parent training, such as Patterson's parent management training model (Patterson & Fleischman, 1979) and, in interventions with adolescents, behavioral family system therapy, such as Alexander's functional family therapy model (Alexander & Parsons, 1973; Klein, Alexander, & Parsons, 1977). Not surprisingly, in view of its concrete specificity, Alexander's functional family therapy model can be effectively used by paraprofessionals (C. Barton, Alexander, Waldron, Turner, & Warburton, 1985). More effective interventions seem to be ones that use pragmatic, case-specific, broad-based but problem-focused strategies provided in multiple settings (D. A. Gordon & Arbuthnot, 1987; Henggeler, 1989; Kazdin, 1987; Michelson, 1987; Miller & Prinz, 1990; M. F. Shore & Massimo, 1979).

These examples of unusually effective treatments share common elements, the most important of which for our argument is that the treatment methods are sufficiently well specified that they can be taught to intelligent laypeople. As we demonstrate in chapter 8, the same is true of actuarial prediction methods. The general conclusion seems to be that clinical intuition, experience, and training, at least as traditionally conceived, are not helpful in either prediction or treatment delivery. Although discouraging, this conclusion is not nihilistic. Training, in the sense of knowing the empirical literature and relevant scientific and statistical techniques, can improve the selection of appropriate treatments, treatment program planning, and evaluation.

II

A NEW GENERATION OF FOLLOW-UP STUDIES

5

MENTALLY DISORDERED OFFENDERS

In Part II, we summarize follow-up studies published after 1990 of men admitted to Oak Ridge. In this chapter, we describe all our studies on mentally disordered offenders except for those about fire setters and sex offenders, which are described in subsequent chapters because we have conducted separate follow-ups and examined more specific outcomes for these groups.

The term *mentally disordered offender* encompasses a heterogeneous and poorly defined group. In its narrowest interpretation, the category is a legal one that includes insanity acquittees, people found guilty but mentally ill, people found unfit to stand trial, mentally disordered sex offenders, sexual predators, and prisoners transferred to mental health facilities. In a 1978 survey (Monahan & Steadman, 1983), 6.6% of all the offenders detained in the United States met this legalistic definition of mentally disordered offender. Of these, 8% were insanity acquittees, 32% were incompetent to stand trial, 6% were mentally disordered sex offenders, and the majority (54%) were convicted prisoners who had been transferred to mental health facilities.

More recently, persons designated as sexual predators have formed an increasing proportion of mentally disordered offenders in the United States. For example, statistics from Atascadero State Hospital (a maximum-security forensic psychiatric facility serving the state of California) in the third quarter of 2002 showed that about 35% of the 1,145 patients were sexually violent persons (M. Hunter, personal communication, October 24, 2002). In addition, broader definitions of the term include persons sent to forensic hospitals for assessments of competency or for treatment to restore competency. Even broader definitions might include persons assessed for competency within jails and persons referred to mental health courts. No matter how defined, however, the overwhelming majority of mentally disordered offenders are men (e.g., Menzies, Chunn, & Webster, 1992; Rice, Harris, Cormier, Lang, Coleman, & Smith Krans, 2004; Steadman & Halfon, 1971).

CHARACTERISTICS OF MENTALLY DISORDERED OFFENDERS

Most forensic researchers would estimate that the true number of mentally disordered offenders is many times higher than estimates using the categories described in the introduction to this chapter. Studies of the prevalence of mental disorder among incarcerated offenders reveal a surprisingly high prevalence. For example, Hodgins and Coté (1990) used the Diagnostic Interview Schedule (Robins, Helzer, Croughan, & Ratcliff, 1981) to establish diagnoses and found that only 5% of penitentiary inmates in one Canadian province did not have a mental disorder. Nearly one quarter met the criteria for a psychosis (schizophrenia, major depression, bipolar disorder, or organic brain syndrome) at some time in their lives, half of the remainder presented a problem with substance abuse or dependence, and nearly half the sample qualified for a diagnosis of antisocial personality disorder (APD). Although prevalence rates have been found to be somewhat lower in other jurisdictions and other correctional populations (e.g., Fazel & Danesh, 2002; Motiuk & Porporino, 1991; Steadman, Fabisiak, Dvoskin, & Holohean, 1987; Teplin, 1990a, 1990b; Wormith & Borzecki, 1985), it is clear that many prisoners meet the criteria for some form of mental disorder.

The insanity defense is raised in only about 1% of felony cases in the United States, and although success rates vary widely across jurisdictions, on average it is successful in only 26% of cases in which it is raised (Callahan, Steadman, McGreevy, & Robbins, 1991; Melton, Petrila, Poythress, & Slobogin, 1997). One might expect, then, that cases resulting in successful insanity acquittals would involve offenders who were clearly mentally disordered. Yet there is evidence of considerable overlap between those found guilty and those found insane in both diagnosis and psychiatric history.

Rice and Harris (1990) compared male insanity acquittees with a randomly selected sample of offenders who had been sent for pretrial psychiatric assessments and subsequently convicted and with a sample of convicted offenders matched for offense type and severity. Compared with the randomly selected convicted offenders, the insanity acquittees were much more likely to have committed murder or attempted murder (74% vs. 7%), were more likely to be diagnosed as psychotic (75% vs. 41%), and were less likely to be diagnosed as personality disordered (13% vs. 46%) than the other offenders. Compared with convicted offenders matched for offense severity, the insanity acquittees were even more likely to be diagnosed as psychotic (75% vs. 13%) and even less likely to be diagnosed as personality disordered (13% vs. 65%). Surprisingly, the insanity acquittees had, on average, fewer prior psychiatric admissions than the randomly selected control group.

How does a finding of guilty or not guilty by reason of insanity affect placement, length of stay, and treatment? The answer is, surprisingly little. Although most insanity acquittees are sent to hospitals (usually to secure hospitals), and most convicted persons are sent to prison, the differences between secure hospitals and prisons are often slight. Although the presumption is that insanity acquittees require treatment for their mental disorder, sometimes no effective treatments are available. In addition, when treatments are available, some patients refuse them. Moreover, even when effective treatments are known and patients are willing to participate, programs are sometimes not available. Conversely, treatment programs are often available inside prisons (see Cullen, 1993; Gunn, Robertson, & Dell, 1978). For both insanity acquittees and convicted offenders, length of stay is strongly related to the seriousness of the index offense and offense history (Green & Baglioni, 1998; G. T. Harris, Rice, & Cormier, 1991a; Steadman, Pasewark, Hawkins, Kiser, & Bieber, 1983). Indeed, some studies have shown that, especially for serious offenses, average lengths of stay do not differ between the two groups (Braff, Arvanties, & Steadman, 1983; G. T. Harris, Rice, & Cormier, 1991b; Pantle, Pasewark, & Steadman, 1980). One might wonder why a large investment is often made in determining which system the patient should be attached to, when the consequences differ so little.

Thus, there is considerable overlap between the "offender" populations of criminal justice systems and the "forensic" populations of ordinary psychiatric hospitals. After studying prison and mental hospital populations in several European countries, Penrose (1939) noted a strong negative correlation between them. As mentioned in the introduction to this volume, he proposed what has become known as Penrose's law: As the size of the prison population goes up, the size of the mental hospital population goes down proportionately, and vice versa, presumably because people move from one system to the other.

In North America, evidence for this hydraulic model has been mixed (e.g., Hiday, 1999; Smiley, 2001; Steadman, Monahan, Duffee, Hartstone, & Robbins, 1984; Teplin, 1991). It is clear, however, that the number of individuals having contact with both the mental health and criminal justice systems is increasing. Teplin (1984; Rice, Harris, & Quinsey, 1996) provided evidence for the "criminalization" of the mentally ill population; mentally ill persons were increasingly involved in the criminal justice system because of restrictions on involuntary civil commitment and the trend toward deinstitutionalization. She found that mentally disordered persons were more likely to be arrested, even when committing the same offense, than non–mentally disordered persons. In her study, police frequently tried unsuccessfully to have the mentally disordered offenders admitted to a psychiatric hospital.

However, there is evidence that the net for identifying those eligible for mental health services has been widened through the "psychiatrization" of criminal behavior (Cocozza, Melick, & Steadman, 1978; Monahan, Davis, Hartstone, & Steadman, 1983). That is, the scope of mental health intervention has expanded to include more forms of deviant behavior, and individuals who would previously have been dealt with exclusively by the criminal justice system are now referred to mental health professionals. Consistent with this view, Cocozza et al. (1978) found that the proportions of New York State Psychiatric Hospital patients with previous arrests rose over time and that arrest rates on release were much higher among those with previous arrests than among other patients. More recently, mental health courts have been created in an effort to prevent criminalization of the mentally ill population by providing mental health services without criminal sentencing (Slate, 2003; A. Watson, Hanrahan, Luchins, & Lurigio, 2001). Although there are few data as yet to show the success of such efforts, there is some reason to believe that they can reduce incarceration and increase the use of mental health services among mentally ill offenders (Boothroyd, Poythress, McGaha, & Petrila, 2003; Cosden, Ellens, Schnell, Yamini-Diouf, & Wolfe, 2003; Trupin & Richards, 2003). They may also reduce the use of forensic hospital beds (Fisher et al., 2002).

Whatever the reason, there is no doubt that many people shift back and forth between the mental health and criminal justice systems. Menzies and Webster (1987) followed up 571 accused individuals admitted to a brief assessment unit for a pretrial psychiatric assessment. Within two years, 349 individuals (61%) received a total of 663 terms of imprisonment, 281 (49%) received a total of 592 psychiatric admissions, and 141 patients (25%) spent time in both prison and hospital. The authors asserted that their data provide evidence for what Toch (1982) referred to as *bus therapy*, wherein mental health and correctional facilities fight to "off-load" difficult individuals on one another in such rapid cycles that the bus rides between facilities seem to be the only "therapy" provided.

The *mentally disordered offender* designation is often influenced by political as well as legal and clinical considerations. A good example is the category of *mentally disordered sex offenders*. Since the enactment of the first "sexual psychopath" statute in 1937, the enactment of similar statutes rose until the early 1970s and then waned until the present. Renewed public concern about serious reoffenses by released sex offenders has led to a recent trend toward reenactment of special laws to permit the indefinite detention and treatment of the most serious sex offenders (usually child molesters and rapists who qualify for the *sexual predator* label; see also Community Protection Act, 1990, for Washington State's law).

Unlike most other officially designated mentally disordered offenders, only a minority of mentally disordered sex offenders suffer from schizophrenia or other psychoses (Sturgeon & Taylor, 1980), and most sex offender treatment programs specifically exclude acutely psychotic offenders (e.g., Marques, Nelson, West, & Day, 1994; Pithers, Martin, & Cumming, 1989). The diagnosis most commonly responsible for designation as a mentally disordered sex offender under the sexual psychopath laws was one of the paraphilias (almost always pedophilia or sexual sadism) in the various editions of the *Diagnostic and Statistical Manual of Mental Disorders* (DSM; American Psychiatric Association, 1968, 1980, 1987). A diagnosis of antisocial personality disorder, although very common among sex offenders, was often not sufficient to qualify one as a mentally disordered sex offender (Monahan & Davis, 1983). Under the sexual predator laws, however, APD is recognized as sufficient evidence of disorder (e.g., Community Protection Act, 1990).

Thus, mentally disordered offenders overlap heavily with both offender and mentally disordered populations (Seto, Harris, & Rice, 2004). Mentally disordered offenders, like other offenders, have committed a wide range of offenses, ranging from fraud, shoplifting, or vagrancy to multiple murders. The disorders from which they suffer also cover a broad range, including undoubtedly all those listed on Axes I and II of the fourth edition of the *DSM* (*DSM–IV*; American Psychiatric Association, 1994), although not all would be sufficient in themselves to earn them the label *mentally disordered offender*. Some are adults, some juveniles; some are felons, some misdemeanants; some are institutionalized, some are maintained in the community; most are men, but some are women. They live in a wide variety of circumstances, including prisons, psychiatric hospitals, boarding houses, nursing homes, family homes, and cardboard boxes on city streets, and they come from every ethnic background. Little is known about effective interventions for mentally disordered offenders specifically, and almost nothing is known about how these other demographic and status variables moderate any treatment effects.

In this chapter, we summarize six follow-up studies published after 1990 of men admitted to Oak Ridge. All of the studies had several elements in common. The majority of the men in the studies were sent for an assessment prior to trial; most of them were subsequently found guilty and convicted. A minority of the men were found unfit to stand trial or not guilty by reason of insanity, and they were returned to Oak Ridge for treatment. An even smaller group of men were involuntary admissions who came to Oak Ridge because they were considered to be unmanageable in less secure facilities.

There is also a considerable amount of overlap among the participants of the six studies. Although the sum of the numbers of participants mentioned in each study described in this chapter totals approximately 2,700, the actual number of individuals whose data were included in at least one study is only 866. More detail about participant overlap can be found in the original reports of each of the studies. All of the studies used the same primary definition of outcome: *Violent recidivism* was defined as any new charge for a violent offense or (much more rarely, except in the first study reported) returned to Oak Ridge for an act that, in the judgment of the raters, would otherwise have resulted in a criminal charge for a violent offense.

Violent offenses ranged from common assault to multiple murders and included all sexual assaults. Armed robbery and pointing a firearm were included as violent offenses; robbery, possession of a weapon, and arson were not. In one of the studies, we reported results obtained using any criminal offense as an outcome measure.

For all studies, the variables used to predict recidivism were coded from institutional files by a team of research assistants. The institutional files were exceptionally complete and included information from a number of sources (e.g., psychosocial histories, information from other institutions, police reports, psychological test reports, medical reports, questionnaires from patients' families, performance in programs). Except in the first study described, the coding of diagnosis was done by research assistants by applying *DSM–III* (American Psychiatric Association, 1980) criteria to the information on the clinical record pertaining to the patient's behavior before the admission that resulted in his being in the study.

Recidivism data were obtained from the files of the coroner's office, the lieutenant governor's Review Board (now the Ontario Review Board, which maintains information about every insanity acquittee in the jurisdiction), the Royal Canadian Mounted Police (a national database sometimes including Interpol reports), the National Parole Service of Canada, and provincial correctional and parole systems. To prevent inadvertent contamination of the historical variables by raters' knowledge of recidivism, variables pertaining to childhood history, adult adjustment, offense, and assessment were all coded using only file information that was available at the time of the index offense. Then recidivism data were obtained and coded, in most cases by a separate team of raters. Follow-up times were calculated by determining the time at risk for each participant. Participants were deemed to be at risk to recidivate when they had regular unsupervised leaves of absence from a correctional or psychiatric facility, when they were released from a maximum- or medium-security hospital to an open facility, or when they were released to the street.

Reliability checks were done for each study to ensure the accuracy of coding for all of the study variables. Reliabilities obtained for all variables included in the prediction analyses were high; more details about reliability are given in each of the original reports.

A FOLLOW-UP OF A MAXIMUM-SECURITY TOKEN ECONOMY

A *token economy* is a behavioral program designed to alter the behavior of participants by offering points or tokens for desired behaviors. Most token economies also include response costs in the form of points or tokens lost for undesired behaviors. Token economies were first developed in the 1960s for chronic psychiatric patients (Allyon & Azrin, 1968), but they have since been applied to many other populations, including prisons (Milan, 1987) and, as described in this section, forensic hospitals.

Token economy programs, or any treatment programs for that matter, ideally are designed to shape the behavior of participants in such a way that they demonstrate more prosocial, and less antisocial, behavior both within the institution and later in the community. Good performance and improvement in the program likewise should be related to early release from the institution and to positive outcome after release. Unfortunately, with few exceptions (e.g., Liberman, Mueser, & Wallace, 1986; Paul & Lentz, 1977), there has been little empirical evidence that these goals have been met for any institutional treatment program and even less evidence that any of these ideals have been met in token economy programs in maximum-security settings. However, encouraging results have been reported in one forensic hospital (N. C. Beck, Menditto, Baldwin, Angelone, & Maddox, 1991; Menditto, 2002; Menditto et al., 1996).

In the study reported in this section (Rice, Quinsey, & Houghton, 1990), variables reflecting performance in a maximum-security token economy program, as well as demographic, historical, and diagnostic variables, were used to predict subsequent recidivism. It was predicted that good performance in the program would be related to shorter stay and lower recidivism on release. The study focused on 113 men admitted to the admission ward of the maximum-security Oak Ridge Activity Treatment Unit between March 1975 and April 1976. These men were all those admitted for treatment except for 17 patients who remained on the unit for less than 7 weeks.

On arrival to the unit, each patient was assessed informally by the ward staff and assigned to confined or semiconfined status on the basis of whether his initial behavior toward staff members was cooperative and whether the staff member assessed that patient to be too dangerous to let out on the corridor. Patients could earn points on daily assessments of their ward work, mood, and cooperation; room care and self-care; and weekly attendance at ward meetings. The points were accumulated weekly and determined the patient's privilege category for the next week. Privilege categories determined how much time a patient was allowed to spend out of his room, his yard privileges, his attendance at the off-ward dining room and paid work areas, and his access to material reinforcers such as cigarettes, candies, lighters, and books. Patients were fined according to a fixed schedule for various misbehaviors. If the fines were large enough, they resulted in an immediate drop in privilege category and were also subtracted from the total accumulated toward the next week's privilege category. Certain serious misbehaviors (e.g., assaults) resulted in the loss of all points plus lengthy seclusion. Records were also kept of the number of assaults by each patient during his 12 weeks in the program. *Assaults* were defined as incidents of patient-initiated forceful physical contact or attempted physical contact against one or more persons.

During the follow-up period, which averaged 6.6 years, 22 of the 92 patients committed a violent offense subsequent to their release from Oak Ridge or were returned to Oak Ridge because of a violent offense against persons, yielding a 24% violent failure rate. Twelve patients incurred subsequent charges for violent offenses, and 13 committed acts of violence in other hospitals for which they were not charged. The majority of the violent acts were assaults or sexual assaults; there were one charge of robbery with violence and one charge of murder.

A discriminant analysis using the best combination of 5 of the 16 predictor variables used in this study yielded a multiple correlation for violent recidivism of .44. The variables included were total months in institutions, lack of previous employment, referral from other than a psychiatric hospital, lack of psychosis, and seclusions for misbehavior in weeks 7 to 12. A noteworthy (if disappointing) finding of this study was the general lack of a relationship between the program variables and outcome. Only the number of seclusions for misbehavior was related to violent recidivism. The data from a study at our institution described in chapter 4 (Quinsey & Maguire, 1986) suggested that clinicians, when making release decisions about patients, consider patients who do poorly in treatment programs to be poor risks. However, the data from this study suggested that program variables of the sort used in this study were so weakly related to later outcome that they should not be given much weight in making release decisions. The next follow-up study involved a program much different from this behavioral one.

A COMPARATIVE FOLLOW-UP OF A MAXIMUM-SECURITY THERAPEUTIC COMMUNITY

The therapeutic community approach evolved in psychiatric settings in England during the late 1940s, notably under the leadership of Maxwell Jones. Citizens of therapeutic communities care materially and emotionally for one another, follow the rules of the community, submit to the authority of the group, and suffer sanctions imposed by the group (M. Jones, 1956, 1968). Honesty, sincerity, and empathy for others are highly valued. Reports of the efficacy of therapeutic communities, however, have been more testimonial than scientific (Fairweather, Saunders, Maynard, Cressler, & Black, 1969; A. Jones, 1978; M. Jones, 1968; Maller, 1971). Unfortunately, the few controlled studies evaluating the ability of therapeutic communities to increase postdischarge socialization or work skills, or to prevent rehospitalization, showed modest effects, at best, compared with more traditional hospital programs (Paul & Lentz, 1977). Yet therapeutic communities continue to be recommended for persons with alcohol and drug addictions, for mentally disordered offenders, and for criminal offenders (Deitch, Carleton, Koutsenok, & Marsolais, 2002; DeLeon, 1985; Dolan, 1998; D. S. Lipton, 1998; Rawlings, 1999; W. H. Reid, 1989; Toch, 1980).

Offenders classifiable as being psychopathic occupy many beds in correctional and forensic mental health facilities. Wong (1984) found that as many as 30% of Canadian federal prisoners could be categorized as psychopaths; the percentage increased with institutional security level. The treatability of psychopathic individuals has long concerned criminologists and mental health experts. Early reports indicated positive effects of psychotherapy (Corsini, 1958; H. Lipton, 1950; Rodgers, 1947; Rosow, 1955; Schmideberg, 1949; Showstack, 1956; Thorne, 1959), but most more recent reports have concluded that current treatments for psychopathic adults are ineffective (e.g., Cleckley, 1982; Hare, 1970, 2003; G. T. Harris & Rice, 2005; W. M. McCord, 1982; Woody, McLellan, Rubersky, & O'Brien, 1985; but see also Salekin, 2002; Skeem, Monahan, & Mulvey, 2002, for contrary views).

Acknowledging negative evidence available at the time, Hare (1970) suggested that a therapeutic community that reshaped the social milieu might change some of the basic personality characteristics and interpersonal behavior of psychopathic individuals. Although not substantiated by comparative outcome data, several reports of therapeutic community programs for psychopathic individuals have been positive (Barker & Mason, 1968; Copas, O'Brien, Roberts, & Whiteley, 1984; Dolan, 1998; W. M. McCord, 1982; Whiteley, 1970).

One of the major problems in evaluating the effectiveness of various treatments on the recidivism of psychopathic individuals relates to the circularity in the definition of *psychopathy* (and the closely related term *antisocial personality disorder*; APD) in that criminal behavior has been identified both as a defining property and as a result of the disorders (Gunn, 1977). It is axiomatic that future behavior is best predicted by past behavior, and thus it is not surprising that those diagnosed as psychopathic have been reported to have worse outcomes than other offenders with less serious criminal histories. Although the Hare Psychopathy Checklist—Revised (PCL–R; Hare, 1991, 2003) contains some items obviously related to criminal history, it primarily comprises items conceptually quite distinct from criminal behavior. The PCL–R correlates highly with such clinical–behavioral measures as Cleckley's (1982) criteria for psychopathy and the *DSM–III*, *DSM–III–R*, and *DSM–IV* diagnosis of APD (Hare, 1983, 1985; Hare, Hart, & Harpur, 1991). When *DSM–IV* items are each scored individually and summed, as are the items on the PCL–R scale, the correlation between the PCL–R and APD scores (as opposed to binary diagnosis) are in the .90s, indicating that the PCL–R and APD measure the same underlying construct but that the dichotomous manner in which the APD diagnosis is arrived at wastes information (Skilling, Harris, Rice, & Quinsey, 2002).

In the study reported in this section (Rice, Harris, & Cormier, 1992), we evaluated an intensive therapeutic community for mentally disordered offenders that was thought to be especially suitable for psychopaths. The program operated for more than a decade in the Social Therapy Unit of Oak Ridge and drew worldwide attention for its novel approach to treatment (Barker, 1980; Barker & Buck, 1977; Barker & Mason, 1968; Barker, Mason, & Wilson, 1969; Barker & McLaughlin, 1977). Treated offenders were compared with untreated offenders matched with the treated offenders on variables consistently reported in the literature to be related to recidivism (age, criminal history, and index offense). The offenders in the study were a particularly serious group of offenders in that almost all had a history of violent criminality. The PCL–R was used to identify psychopathic and nonpsychopathic individuals to examine the interrelationships among treatment, psychopathy, and recidivism. In almost all cases, the comparison offenders were convicted of some offense or offenses and served prison sentences. The outcome measures were criminal recidivism and violent recidivism, and the average follow-up period exceeded 10 years.

The therapeutic community program has been described at length elsewhere (Barker & Buck, 1977; Barker & Mason, 1968; Barker et al., 1969; Barker & McLaughlin, 1977; Maier, 1976; Quinsey, 1981; Weisman, 1995). Briefly, the program was peer operated and involved intensive group therapy for up to 80 hours weekly. The goal was to create an environment where patients could develop empathy and responsibility for their peers. Patients participated in fixed and long-term daily sessions with one or two other patients and sat on committees that monitored and structured all aspects of their lives. Patients who performed well in the program and who showed organizational talent were appointed to program leadership roles and led therapy groups and security and administrative committees. Patients participated in decisions about release and transfer.

Other features of the program may have been important. Patients had very little contact with professional staff. Very little effort was expended in organized recreational programs. Very few patients participated in academic upgrading or vocational training. Some patients worked in contract workshops, in the kitchen, or on cleaning gangs. However, such work was regarded as a temporary "rest" from therapy, and patients who worked shared the wages they earned with the patients involved in intensive therapy. No programs were specifically aimed at altering procriminal attitudes and beliefs, teaching social skills or social problem solving, or training in life skills. A minority of the patients were diagnosed as psychotic and were prescribed neuroleptic drugs, but efforts were made to keep doses as low as possible. One reason for including psychotic patients in the program was to give psycho-pathic individuals an opportunity to care for such individuals. Tight internal and external security was maintained by patients in cooperation with psychi-atric attendants. Patients had very little opportunity for diversion; tight lim-its were imposed on viewing television, reading material, and even on social interactions among patients.

Entry to and participation in the therapeutic community was not vol-untary, and stated willingness to participate was not a selection criterion. For example, an individual found not guilty by reason of insanity or convicted of a violent crime and then civilly committed could be assigned to the program even if he did not wish to be. Once in the program, patients who refused to engage in detailed discussion of their offenses, backgrounds, and feelings were sent to a subprogram where they discussed their motivation, attitudes, and participation until they complied with program requirements. Although pa-tients could leave the therapeutic community by convincing staff or an inde-pendent review board that they had made clinical progress, they could not get out simply by misbehaving. Noncompliance and disruption were regarded as symptoms to be changed, and this form of attrition was not permitted.

Several aspects of the program might be seen to violate patients' rights by today's standards, but in the 1970s the program was very favorably re-viewed on both ethical and clinical grounds. For example, one blue-ribbon panel of experts who reviewed the program commented glowingly,

> This is an exciting program which has the hallmark of being right as . . .
> the final model of the DNA molecule looked right to Watson & Crick.
> Here the impossible is apparently happening—psychopaths are being
> treated with success. . . . Results of the program [include] a very low
> recidivism rate. (Butler, Long, & Rowsell, 1977, pp. 3, 28)

The Government of Canada (1977) stated, "[The program designer has] de-veloped the techniques that are the most fruitful of any in the universe at the present time" (p. 45).

Our evaluation of the program was entirely retrospective; we had no control over any aspect of the program. The treated offenders in this study were 176 patients who spent at least 2 years in the therapeutic community program during the period of its most active operation (January 1968 to Feb-ruary 1978). *Being at risk to reoffend* was defined as being released to the street or being held in an open psychiatric institution. Three offenders reoffended after leaving the maximum-security program but while still in another secure hospital; they reoffended although technically not yet at risk to do so.

For most treated offenders, a matched comparison offender was selected from among the many forensic assessment cases (>100 individuals) admitted each year. Because of the strictness of the matching criteria, 30 treated of-fenders could not be matched. Preliminary analyses showed no differences between matched and unmatched patients. For the matched pairs, the matching was performed according to several criteria: The treated and comparison offenders had to be

- the same age within 1 year at the time of the index offense,
- charged with the same index offense,
- equivalent in criminal history for each of property and violent offenses according to a system developed by Akman and Normandeau (1967), and
- charged with their index offenses no more than 2 years apart.

In addition, comparison offenders could not have returned to the study institution for any treatment. Almost all (84%) of the 146 comparison offenders spent some time (M = 50.7 months, SD = 46.4 months) in a correctional institution.

The mean duration of follow-up was 10.5 years (SD = 4.94 years), and there were no differences in mean follow-up time for treated versus untreated or for psychopathic versus nonpsychopathic offenders. Of the 176 offenders treated, 169 were at risk to reoffend for some time (or failed anyway) during the follow-up period ending in April 1, 1988; of the 146 untreated matches, 136 were at risk to reoffend.

The results did not match the glowing judgments made by observers. Overall, there was very little evidence of a treatment effect. The rates of violent reoffense were 39% and 46% for treated and untreated offenders, respectively, and 40% for both matched treated and untreated offenders. Because the therapeutic community had been regarded as an especially promising treatment for psychopathic individuals, treatment and outcome were compared for psychopathic and nonpsychopathic individuals separately. To make this comparison, we had to decide on a cutoff score on the PCL–R to categorize offenders as psychopaths. PCL–R scores were based solely on file information, rather than on a combination of file and interview information. Wong (1984) reported that the correlation between the file-only versus the file-plus-interview methods of gathering data for the PCL–R was very high (r = .93). Wong also proposed that a cutoff of 25 would be more appropriate than the traditional cutoff of 30 when using the file method only, and we found in other analyses that a cutoff of 25 would identify a nearly pure sample of psychopathic individuals (Harris, Rice, & Quinsey, 1994). In view of Wong's findings, we adopted a cutoff of 25 out of 40. More recently, Hare (2003) presented data suggesting that file-based PCL–R ratings are, on average, about 4 points lower than scores obtained from the file-plus-interview method.

For the 46 treated matched psychopathic offenders (with opportunity to reoffend) and their comparison offenders, the rates of violent recidivism were 78% and 55%, respectively, suggesting that, especially for violent reoffense, the therapeutic community treatment was associated with poorer outcomes for psychopathic offenders. However, most treated psychopathic

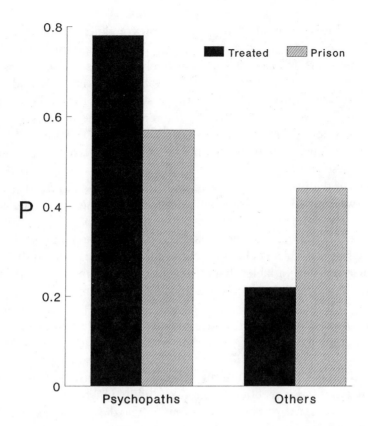

Figure 5.1. Violent recidivism by treatment and psychopathy. *P* = probability of violent recidivism.

offenders were matched to comparison offenders who did not meet the criterion for psychopathy. We examined the effects of treatment on outcome for psychopathic and nonpsychopathic offenders separately. All treated (not just those who had been matched) and untreated offenders who had an opportunity to reoffend were included in this analysis. As can be seen in Figure 5.1, there was an interaction of treatment with psychopathy on violent recidivism such that treatment was associated with lower recidivism for nonpsychopathic offenders but higher recidivism for psychopathic offenders. A log-linear analysis yielded a significant interaction effect.

To evaluate the importance of this interaction, a multiple discriminant analysis was performed in which the predictor variables were psychopathy (or not), treatment (or not), and the interaction of these two; the dependent variable was violent reoffense (or not). The analysis showed that treatment made no significant contribution to the discriminant function, but the other two variables (psychopathy and the interaction of psychopathy and treatment) yielded a statistically significant solution (regression $R = .35$).

Because retrospectively coded *DSM–III* diagnosis was one of the few variables on which the treated and untreated groups differed at the outset, this relationship was examined further. The rates of violent reoffense among matched treated and untreated psychotic (schizophrenia or affective disorder) offenders were 15% and 25%, respectively, whereas among nonpsychopathic, nonpsychotic offenders, the comparable rates were 26% and 40%. Although neither comparison was statistically significant, they indicated that the main results were not because of differences in the diagnoses of the nonpsychopathic groups.

The final analyses concerned the variables specific to the treatment program. These variables pertained at least in a general way to the patient's adjustment to the institution, his success in the program, and the degree to which he was trusted by the program's clinical staff. The interesting comparisons involved the ways in which psychopathic and nonpsychopathic patients differed. Psychopathic offenders showed much poorer adjustment, assessed in terms of problem behaviors, both in their first year and in their last year. However, when variables that reflect the degree of trust by clinical staff were considered, psychopathic and nonpsychopathic offenders showed no differences. It is interesting that the first set of variables, reflecting patient's behavior rather than staff trust, were consistently related to outcome.

Overall, then, the results showed no effect of the therapeutic community in reducing recidivism. However, the most important finding of this study was the differential effect of the program. Psychopathic offenders who participated in the therapeutic community exhibited higher rates of violent recidivism than did the psychopathic offenders who did not participate. The opposite result was obtained for nonpsychopathic offenders, and it should be noted that the nonpsychopathic groups comprised both psychotic and nonpsychotic individuals. Although there were more psychotic men among the treated offenders, and psychotic offenders showed lower rates of reoffense overall, those differences alone cannot explain the interaction of treatment and psychopathy. The interaction is especially surprising because the program was explicitly designed to effect positive changes in the psychopathic personality and was based on a solid theoretical background provided by the literature that existed at the time the program was designed, and it provided extensive opportunities for patients to gain insight into their own behavior and to learn to be caring and empathic. That is, it was exactly the program that most clinicians would have recommended to produce improvement in psychopathic offenders.

The results of this study gave strong support to the importance of the concept of psychopathy and to the PCL–R as a way to measure psychopathy. The PCL–R score was strongly related to recidivism (more strongly than a DSM–III diagnosis), but most important, it was a powerful predictor of response to treatment. Offenders who scored more than 25 on the PCL–R (i.e., those most likely to be psychopaths) showed a negative effect of treatment, whereas those who scored lower benefited from the therapeutic community program. To our knowledge, this is the most powerful predictor of response to treatment yet reported in the area of criminal behavior and recidivism. These results also lend support to the method used in arriving at a PCL–R score using very complete case files.

Given the pervasive pessimism about whether psychopathic individuals can change in any significant way, the finding that participation changed the rate of violent recidivism (albeit for the worse) is remarkable. The finding belies conventional wisdom about the immutability of psychopathic behavior and shows that an inappropriate institutional environment can actually increase criminal behavior. The results strongly suggest that the kind of therapeutic community described in this article is the wrong program for serious psychopathic offenders. It must be noted, however, that these psychopaths were an especially serious group of offenders; almost all (85%) had a history of violent crimes. It is unclear whether such a program would have the same results with a group of less violent, less criminal psychopaths. These results are consistent with those of another study on the effect of therapeutic community treatment on the recidivism of psychopathic offenders (Craft, Stephenson, & Granger, 1964). Although the two studies used very different operational definitions of psychopathy, the combined results suggest that a therapeutic community is not the treatment of choice for psychopathic offenders, particularly those with extensive criminal histories. A similar conclusion was also reached in a meta-analysis of treatments for psychopaths (Garrido, Esteban, & Molero, 1995).

It is important to note, too, that our results showed a positive effect (compared with prison) of the therapeutic community program in reducing recidivism for nonpsychopathic offenders. These results lend support to those clinicians who use therapeutic community treatment and suggest that, compared with prison, a therapeutic community may be a clinically sound institutional environment for psychotic and nonpsychotic offenders as long as they are not psychopaths. However, a meta-analysis of offender treatments suggests that more behaviorally oriented and structured interventions are indicated for the majority of offenders (Andrews, Zinger, et al., 1990). In addition, a more recent evaluation of a therapeutic community program for mentally disordered offenders suggested that it was not effective (McMurran, Egan, & Ahmady, 1998), although the outcomes for psychopathic and nonpsychopathic participants were not evaluated separately.

Why did the therapeutic community program we evaluated have different effects on psychopathic and nonpsychopathic offenders? The ways in which they performed in the program provide possible clues. Hare (1986) discussed the results of a lie detection study that suggested that psychopathic individuals are especially interested in social cues to learn how to "read" people. Compared with prison, where it has been reported that offenders learn surprisingly little (Zamble & Porporino, 1988), we hypothesize that both psychopathic and nonpsychopathic individuals in the therapeutic community learned how to perceive the feelings of others, take the perspective of others, use emotional language, act in a socially skilled manner, and delay gratification. However, such experiences represent a double-edged sword. To persons with generally prosocial, anticriminal values (i.e., nonpsychopathic individuals), such new abilities would be associated with successful marital, family, social, and vocational adjustment. However, to psychopathic offenders with antisocial, procriminal values, such new abilities could facilitate the manipulation and exploitation of others and could be associated with novel ways to commit violent crime. As well, we speculate that the program increased the self-esteem of the participants, which in turn increased the risk of aggression (Baumeister, Campbell, Krueger, & Vohs, 2003), especially among psychopaths.

We speculate, then, that patients learned a great deal from the intensive program but that the psychopathic offenders put their new skills to quite unintended uses. What could the clinical staff have done to prevent this? An obvious suggestion comes from the finding that psychopathic offenders were much more likely to be coded as having antisocial values compared with nonpsychopathic offenders and that this was also related to violent outcome (G. T. Harris et al., 1991b). According to modern behavioral formulations of differential association theory (Andrews, 1980), criminals behave as they do because they associate with other criminals and are thus exposed to criminal rather than anticriminal models. It has been suggested (Elliot, Huizinga, & Ageton, 1985) that therapeutic community programs fail because they place offenders in highly intensive interaction with one another and inadvertently place the most antisocial individuals in leadership roles. Such programs thereby foster rather than inhibit criminal identification and subsequent recidivism. Although there are no outcome data with adult psychopathic offenders, one could predict on the basis of differential association theory that programs that involve highly structured interaction with prosocial models who demonstrate anticriminal attitudes and ways of thinking would be a more promising treatment approach. Such programs have been described by Andrews, Kiessling, Robinson, and Mickus (1986); Serin and Kuriychuk (1994); and Wormith (1984). Similarly, Wong and Hare (in press) have developed program guidelines for the institutional treatment of psychopaths that incorporate the methods currently thought to hold most promise for the treatment of psychopaths.

A FOLLOW-UP OF INSANITY ACQUITTEES AND A COMPARISON SAMPLE OF CORRECTIONAL INMATES

The defense plea of insanity is based on the idea that the criminal behavior of insanity acquittees is caused by a mental disorder, whereas the same behavior from an offender found guilty is because of criminogenic factors. If it is true that the causal factors differ in the offenses of insanity acquittees and convicted offenders, then it follows that factors that predict recidivism in the two groups ought to be different. For example, whereas such factors as age and criminal history have consistently been found to be important for predicting recidivism among convicted persons (Monahan, 1981; Nuffield, 1982; Wormith & Goldstone, 1984), such psychiatric factors as diagnosis, psychiatric history, and symptom severity ought to be important in predicting recidivism among insanity acquittees.

In the study presented in this section, Rice, Harris, Lang, and Bell (1990) examined the long-term recidivism rates of a large group of insanity acquittees and compared them with those of a group of convicted men. The offenders were an exhaustive sample ($n = 280$) of all insanity acquittees present in the maximum-security institution for at least 1 day over a 7-year period (January 1, 1975 to December 31, 1981). A matched comparison group was formed by culling the records of patients admitted to the same institution during the same period for brief pretrial psychiatric assessments. A comparison offender was acceptable only if he met all of the following criteria:

- his original most serious criminal charge for the index offense was the same as that of the treated offender,
- his criminal offense history on the Akman–Normandeau Scale (Akman & Normandeau, 1967) was within 20% of that for the not guilty by reason of insanity (NGRI) offender for violent and nonviolent offenses separately,
- he was the same age within 1 year,
- his index offense and that of the insanity acquittee occurred within 12 months of each other, and
- he never returned to the institution for treatment.

The numbers of patients admitted to the institution for pretrial remand remained high throughout the 7-year study period, and matches were obtained for 86% of the insanity acquittees ($n = 238$). Comparisons showed that the insanity acquittees who were successfully matched did not differ from those who were not matched on any other study variables. Of the 516 insanity acquittees and comparison offenders, almost all (253 and 210, respectively) were at risk to reoffend or had reoffended at the time of the final follow-up (April 1, 1988).

The matching procedure produced two very comparable groups that were alike not only on the matching variables but on most other study variables as well. Of the 49 study variables, the two groups differed significantly on only six. The insanity acquittees had more psychiatric admissions and greater assertion deficits than the non-NGRI offenders. In addition, the insanity acquittees were less likely to have had alcohol involved in the index offense and less likely to have had a parent with an alcohol problem. Finally, the insanity acquittees were more likely to meet the DSM–III criteria for psychosis (schizophrenia, major affective disorder, or organic psychosis, 57%

vs. 13%) and less likely to meet the criteria for any personality disorder (22% vs. 41%) than the non-NGRI offenders.

During the average 78.2-month (SD = 50.2) follow-up period, 253 insanity acquittees and 210 comparison offenders had an opportunity to reoffend (or reoffended even though they had not technically been at risk). Overall, the insanity acquittees yielded a lower rate of violent recidivism (20% vs. 29%), and the effect was even larger when only matched offenders (n = 214) were included (19% vs. 29%).

The relationships between study variables and outcome for the insanity acquittees were almost identical to those for comparison offenders, even though the comparison offenders had a higher rate of recidivism. To examine the degree to which outcome was related to the same factors in both groups, a relatively strong statistical test was used: Multiple discriminant analyses were used to determine the linear combination of variables that best predicted outcome for each group. That same equation was then used to predict outcome for the other group. The equations constructed to predict violent recidivism for one sample worked quite well for the other. Although shrinkage in accounted-for variance occurred in both tests, the amount of shrinkage is approximately what would be expected if true cross-validations had been performed on a random split from a single population (Kerlinger & Pedhazur, 1973).

Overall, the predictors of violent recidivism in this study were consistent with those that have been found to predict reoffense in other studies of criminal recidivism: arrest at an early age, criminal history, alcohol abuse, aggression, impulsivity, school maladjustment, separation from parents, parental crime, employment, marital status, a diagnosis of personality disorder, and score on the Level of Supervision Inventory (LSI), an objective risk assessment tool for the prediction of criminal recidivism (Motiuk, Bonta, & Andrews, 1986; now available as the LSI–R, Andrews & Bonta, 2003a). In addition, the pattern of results revealed remarkable similarity between the two groups in the ways recidivism was related to each study variable. These findings are important because they lend strong support to the argument that the same variables that predict criminal recidivism among offenders in general also predict criminal recidivism among mentally disordered offenders. These findings are similar to those of other investigators (Bonta, Law, & Hanson, 1998; Hodgins, 1987; Morrow & Peterson, 1966; Pasewark, Bieber, Bosten, Kiser, & Steadman, 1982; D. Shore, Filson, & Johnson, 1988; D. Shore et al., 1989).

Because the antisocial behavior of mentally disordered offenders is related to the same factors that cause crime in non–mentally disordered offenders, basing the release of insanity acquittees solely on psychopathological symptoms and recovery would be a serious mistake. Our results suggest that treatment programs for insanity acquittees must include programs designed to attend to their "criminogenic needs" (Andrews, Bonta, & Hoge,

1990). Although it has been argued by some (Craig, 1982; Taylor, 1985) that clinicians treating psychotic offenders should attend to the psychotic symptoms and that the violent behavior will then disappear, our results suggest that clinicians who treat psychotic offenders should address the antisocial behavior directly in treatment. Problems such as substance abuse, antisocial attitudes and values, and criminal associates have been shown to be relevant treatment targets for correctional populations, and programs designed to address these problems have produced promising results (Andrews, Bonta, & Hoge, 1990). The data from the study described in this section suggest that similar attention to these sorts of problems holds promise for reducing criminal recidivism rates among insanity acquittees.

A COMPARISON OF CRIMINAL RECIDIVISM AMONG SCHIZOPHRENIC AND NONSCHIZOPHRENIC OFFENDERS

In another study, Rice and Harris (1992) examined the subset of 145 men in the study described in the preceding section who met the *DSM–III* criteria for schizophrenia. A matched comparison group was formed by culling the records of patients admitted to the same institution during the same period for brief pretrial psychiatric assessments. A matched comparison offender was acceptable only if he did not meet *DSM–III* criteria for schizophrenia and met all the following criteria:

- his original most serious criminal charge for the index offense was the same as that of the schizophrenic offender,
- his criminal offense history on the Akman–Normandeau Scale (Akman & Normandeau, 1967) was equivalent (within 20%) to that of the offender with schizophrenia,
- he was the same age within 1 year,
- his index offense and that of the schizophrenic offender occurred within 12 months of each other, and
- he never returned to the institution for treatment.

Matches were obtained for almost all of those with schizophrenia (*N* = 124), and preliminary comparisons showed that those with schizophrenia who were matched did not differ from those who were not. Unmatched offenders with schizophrenia were eliminated from the study. Also eliminated were any matched pairs in which either member was not at risk to recidivate (i.e., he was not released to the street or was not living in an open psychiatric facility) by the last follow-up. Fifteen offenders with schizophrenia and 13 comparison offenders were dropped at this point, resulting in 96 matched pairs. The matched groups were compared on all variables. On the matching variables (criminal history, age, index offense), the two groups were identical, and they were similar on most other variables as well.

Offenders with schizophrenia exhibited a lower rate of criminal recidivism (35%) than the comparison offenders (53%). For violent reoffense, the difference (16% for the schizophrenic offenders vs. 24% for the comparisons) was not statistically significant. However, inspection of the offenses in the two groups suggested that those of the schizophrenic offenders were less serious. Of the 15 violent reoffenses among those with schizophrenia, 10 were for assault (or its equivalent), 3 for assault causing bodily harm, and 2 for weapons charges or threatening. Among the 23 violent reoffenses by the nonschizophrenic offenders, there was 1 murder, 1 attempted murder, 1 wounding, 6 assaults causing bodily harm, 4 sexual assaults, 6 common assaults, and 4 in the robbery, threatening, and weapons offenses category.

The relationship between hospital adjustment variables and violent recidivism indicated that behavior in the institution was related to outcome. Among offenders with schizophrenia, clinicians and review boards tended to keep those who subsequently committed a new violent offense in custody longer than those who did not reoffend. It is interesting that many of the schizophrenic reoffenders (44%) committed their reoffense while they were patients in an open psychiatric hospital.

To examine further the relationship between severity of psychopathology and recidivism, we derived a measure of the severity of psychopathology at the time of the offense from among the variables we had coded. Offenders received a point for each of the following: emotional problems, severe emotional problems, receiving psychiatric treatment, delusional motive for the index offense, elevations on Scales 6 or 8 of the Minnesota Multiphasic Personality Inventory (MMPI; Hathaway & McKinley, 1967), and being seen by admitting clinicians as lacking insight. Not surprisingly, the groups differed greatly on this composite variable, but it was unrelated to recidivism for all offenders combined and for the offenders with schizophrenia separately (in fact, there was a nonsignificant trend in favor of lower recidivism for greater symptom severity).

Next, the recidivism of offenders with paranoid schizophrenia was compared with that of the others. There was no relationship between paranoid or nonparanoid schizophrenia and recidivism (17% vs. 15% for violent recidivism). Offenders with schizophrenia who were rated as having committed their index offenses in response to a delusion were compared with those with other motives. Again, there was no statistically significant relationship with outcome and a trend in the opposite direction (11% vs. 22% for violent recidivism).

In summary, schizophrenic offenders were less likely to commit any offense on release than their nonschizophrenic counterparts. The two groups were carefully matched on those characteristics most consistently found to be related to criminal recidivism. Among the group with schizophrenia, those who were more seriously disturbed at the time of the index offense were no more likely to commit another offense on release than those who were less disturbed. Although the violent recidivism rates between offenders with and without schizophrenia were not significantly different, an examination of the types of offenses committed by both groups suggested that the schizophrenic offenders were less dangerous on release.

As has been found in many other studies of mentally disordered offenders (Bonta et al., 1998), the best predictors of violent recidivism among schizophrenic offenders were the same as those found for non–mentally disordered offenders and included variables having to do with previous offense history, marital status, alcohol abuse, and past aggressive behavior. It is noteworthy that two instruments that were developed using offender or inmate populations predicted recidivism among schizophrenic offenders. Both the LSI and the PCL–R significantly predicted violent recidivism among the schizophrenic offenders in this study. Recently, other investigators have also reported that PCL–R scores predicted violent recidivism among criminal offenders with schizophrenia (Tengström, Grann, Långström, & Kullgren, 2000).

Similar to the results of several other studies (Lovell, Gagliardi, & Peterson, 2002; Rice, Quinsey, & Houghton, 1990, described earlier in this chapter; D. Shore et al., 1989), history of seclusions and other variables related to the commission of antisocial behavior within the institution were related to subsequent recidivism. Number of months spent in maximum security was also related to subsequent reoffense. This finding suggested that clinicians' judgments about who should and should not be released were better than chance (see also Quinsey & Maguire, 1986, discussed in chap. 4). Nevertheless, as we shall see in later chapters, clinicians' unstructured judgments are not nearly as good as those of an actuarial prediction instrument that includes clinical as well as nonclinical variables.

Why did schizophrenic offenders have a lower rate of recidivism than those without the disorder? The two groups differed on variables relating to alcohol problems. The nonschizophrenic offenders had had more alcohol problems both as teenagers and as adults, were more likely to have had an alcoholic parent, and were more likely to have been under the influence of alcohol at the time of the offense. Alcohol problems and substance abuse more generally have been found in a number of other studies to be related to criminality and especially to violence (Bonta et al., 1998; Hodgins & Janson, 2002; Monahan, 1981; Monahan et al., 2001; Ross & Lightfoot, 1985). Thus, greater alcohol problems in the nonschizophrenic offenders may have made them a higher risk group. In support of this hypothesis, we found that when alcohol abuse was statistically controlled, the two groups no longer exhibited statistically significant differences in recidivism.

Another possibility is that the treatment received by the schizophrenic offenders actually reduced their likelihood of recidivism. This argument is implausible, however, because the longer they stayed in a secure hospital, the more likely they were to recidivate. A more plausible explanation has to do with care following release from a secure hospital; almost all of the schizophrenic offenders remained under some form of clinical supervision and continuing care for an extended period after release. Whenever there were serious concerns, these individuals could be returned to the hospital. The nonschizophrenic offenders, by contrast, remained under supervision (at halfway houses or on parole or probation) for only short periods following release and were thereafter unsupervised. This difference in supervision and treatment may account for the different outcomes in the two groups.

Other researchers (Hodgins & Janson, 2002; Link, Andrews, & Cullen, 1992; Monahan, 1992; Swanson & Holzer, 1991; Tiihonen, Isohanni, Räsänen, Koiranen, & Moring, 1997; C. Wallace, Mullen, & Burgess, 2004; Wessely & Taylor, 1991) have investigated the relationship between severe mental disorder and the commission of illegal and violent acts, and they have concluded that there is a positive relationship. Yet our results suggest that the schizophrenic offenders were no more likely (and may even have been less likely) to commit a violent offense than nonschizophrenic offenders. How are the two sets of findings to be reconciled? We believe there are two possible explanations. The first, and to us most likely, explanation has to do with the composition of the seriously mentally ill and comparison groups. Studies that have found higher rates among mentally ill participants have not selected mentally disordered offenders as the mentally ill population and have used the general population as their comparison group. However, we (and others who have found similar findings) have compared offenders experiencing major mental disorders, or schizophrenia specifically, with other offenders.

The comparison offenders were more likely than the seriously mentally ill offenders to have a diagnosis of antisocial or some other personality disorder. As already mentioned, they were also more likely to have an alcohol problem than the schizophrenic offenders. However, in the studies that have compared persons with severe mental illness with the general population, the comparison population had fewer alcohol problems (Monahan et al., 2001) and likely had fewer persons with a personality disorder than the mentally ill group. Thus, the difference between the findings of the two types of study may be accounted for by the way the two groups were formed (see also Hodgins, 2000, for a similar discussion).

Alternatively, the answer may have to do with the recency of the psychotic symptoms. In the Link et al. (1992) study, for example, the violent and illegal behavior of mental patients and ex-patients was compared with that of never-hospitalized community control participants. It was found that current psychotic symptoms (presence of delusions or other false beliefs) were related to relatively recent occurrences of violent behavior among all groups and that when current symptoms were controlled, mental patient or nonpatient status was no longer significantly related to violence. In this study, our measure of psychotic symptoms was based on symptoms present at the time of the index offense and not those present on discharge or follow-up (see also Quinsey, Pruesse, & Fernley, 1975a). In fact, it is usually the case in Ontario, at least for released insanity acquittees, to receive follow-up psychiatric care on release, which includes remaining on antipsychotic medication. Thus, we believe it is likely that most of the schizophrenic offenders in this study would have had relatively low scores on measures of current psychotic symptoms on follow-up.

However, there are other recent data that cause us to doubt that current psychotic symptoms (and especially symptoms of schizophrenia) are positively related to violence (e.g., Grann & Fazel, 2005). In the MacArthur risk assessment study, psychotic symptoms and threat-control override symptoms specifically (see Link et al., 1992; Link & Stueve, 1994) were negatively related to violent behavior 20 weeks later (Monahan et al., 2001). Moreover, among the diagnostic categories, patients with schizophrenia were least likely to be violent on follow-up. Also, in two separate studies of dynamic predictors of violent recidivism among mentally disordered offenders, psychotic symptoms measured 1 month prior to a violent act were unrelated to violent recidivism, whereas measures of antisociality measured 1 month prior were positively related (Quinsey, Coleman, Jones, & Altrows, 1997; Quinsey, Jones, Book, & Barr, in press; see discussion in chap. 10). Finally, in a prospective study of criminal and violent criminal behavior among persons with major mental disorder, it was found that the criminal and violent behavior often appeared in early adolescence, well before the mental disorder became observable (Hodgins & Janson, 2002).

An additional intriguing result was that parental psychiatric history was very strongly related to recidivism among schizophrenic offenders. Only 13 of the offenders with schizophrenia were recorded as having parents with psychiatric problems, but 10 of those 13 recidivated. Examination of these 10 offenders' records showed that 4 had mothers who also had schizophrenia. Overall, the unstable rearing environment associated with parental psychiatric disturbance may be especially important in the subsequent adjustment of schizophrenic individuals. These findings are consistent with those of other studies in which offspring (especially the sons) of schizophrenic mothers were found to be at high risk for the subsequent development of early antisocial behavior, psychopathy, antisocial personality disorder, and schizophrenia (T. D. Cannon, Mednick, & Parnas, 1990; Mednick et al., 1978; Olin, John, & Mednick, 1995). The findings are also consistent, however, with a genetic transmission model. One possible mechanism for a genetic transmission model could have to do with assortative mating: That is, the schizophrenic mothers in the Mednick et al. (1978; see also Monahan & Arnold, 1996) study may have tended to mate with criminal men.

These results also have implications for the assessment and treatment of offenders with schizophrenia. They support the importance of a careful criminal history in the assessment of risk in mentally disordered persons. In our experience, many clinicians overlook gathering objective (i.e., not just self-report) data about past criminal behavior among mentally disordered offenders and concentrate instead on the history of the mental disorder. Our results strongly support the importance of attending to criminogenic needs (Andrews, Bonta, & Hoge, 1990) in addition to treatment needs having to do with the mental disorder itself. To reduce criminal behavior on release, one must treat those factors that are related to the commission of criminal behavior. Some of these problems have been included in or recommended for comprehensive treatment programs for chronically mentally ill persons (Farkas & Anthony, 1989; Liberman, 1988). For example, Liberman included life skills training and employment skills training, both of which address criminogenic needs. However, other criminogenic needs (e.g., alcohol problems, criminal attitudes) are often overlooked in the treatment of offenders with schizophrenia.

PSYCHIATRIC COMORBIDITY AND THE PREDICTION OF VIOLENCE

Concern has been raised about the rates of violence among persons who exhibit more than one disorder. For example, it has been suggested that individuals with both schizophrenia and substance abuse problems are more at risk for the commission of violent offenses than are persons with either alone, and there are now considerable data in support of this contention (Lindqvist & Allebeck, 1989; Swanson, Borum, Swartz, & Monahan, 1996; Swanson, Holzer, Ganju, & Jono, 1990). Swanson et al. (1990; see also Swanson & Holzer, 1991) reported that substance abuse and major mental disorder (which included schizophrenia as well as affective disorders) each added to the likelihood of violence. There are also data showing that persons with schizophrenia, compared with non–mentally disordered individuals, are more likely to abuse alcohol and other substances (Lindqvist & Allebeck, 1989; Monahan et al., 2001; Regier et al., 1990); the same is true of psychopaths (Smith & Newman, 1990).

Whatever the relationship between mental disorder or psychotic symptoms and violence in the general population, it cannot be assumed that the same relationships exist among offenders who already have a history of violence. Mental health professionals are under the most public scrutiny when called on to make assessments of dangerousness in cases where an individual has already committed a serious antisocial act. Furthermore, the more serious the prior act, the greater the public concern about future dangerousness. Does the combination of psychopathy and alcohol abuse make such a person more likely to commit a violent act? What about an individual who has schizophrenia, is psychopathic, and also has an alcohol abuse problem?

We examined the relationships among schizophrenia, psychopathy, alcohol abuse, and violent recidivism among a group of serious male offenders

(Rice & Harris, 1995a). The participants ($N = 685$) from two follow-up studies described earlier in this chapter (Rice et al., 1992; Rice, Harris, Lang, & Bell, 1990) were combined to address these empirical questions. Of the 618 at risk, 191 (31%) reoffended violently. Of the total sample, 347 (51%) were coded as having had an alcohol problem, 161 (24%) were schizophrenic, and 144 (22%) were psychopathic. Table 5.1 shows the conjoint frequencies of all study variables. Although schizophrenia and psychopathy were coded independently, the conjoint frequency of the two diagnoses was lower than expected; only 13 offenders met the criteria for both diagnoses. Psychopathic (compared with nonpsychopathic) offenders were more likely (57% vs. 41%) and schizophrenic (compared with nonschizophrenic) offenders much less likely (28% vs. 50%) to have had an alcohol problem. The intercorrelations of the four main study variables are shown in Table 5.2.

As Table 5.2 shows, schizophrenia was inversely related to violent recidivism; 16% of schizophrenic offenders reoffended, compared with 35% of the other offenders. Psychopathy and an alcohol abuse problem were positively related to violent recidivism. These significant main effects were qualified by two interactions: psychopathy by alcohol and schizophrenia by psychopathy. Alcohol abuse was related to violent recidivism only among nonpsychopathic offenders (30% vs. 20%, compared with 55% vs. 52%). Similarly, the difference in recidivism between psychopathic and nonpsychopathic offenders was much larger among offenders who did not have schizophrenia (57% vs. 27%, compared with 23% vs. 15%).

As a further check on these conclusions, a series of log-linear analyses (Norusis, 1992) were performed. These analyses indicated that a logit model including only the three main effects yielded a satisfactory fit to the results. According to the criteria proposed by Knoke and Burke (1980), no interactions needed to be included in the model. A logit model including the three main effects plus the interactions of psychopathy by alcohol abuse and of psychopathy by schizophrenia, however, also gave a very good fit to the data.

Finally, and consistent with the results described earlier in this chapter, offenders who had delusional motives for their index offense were less likely to commit another violent act than nondelusional offenders ($r = -.20$, $p < .001$). Even among the schizophrenic offenders, those who had committed their index offense in response to delusions were less likely (though not significantly so) than others to commit another violent act. Furthermore, even among delusional offenders, there were significant correlations between violent recidivism and each of PCL–R score ($r = .33$, $p < .001$) and alcohol abuse ($r = .19$, $p < .05$).

Among our sample of serious offenders, then, psychopathy proved to be more highly related to likelihood of violent recidivism than did alcohol abuse or schizophrenia. In fact, in this sample, schizophrenia was related negatively to violent recidivism. Lidz, Mulvey, and Gardner (1993) reported a similar finding among psychiatric patients, as did Monahan et al. (2001). Similarly,

TABLE 5.1
Numbers of Individuals in Each Category (N = 587)

| | Psychopaths | | | | Nonpsychopaths | | | |
| | Schizophrenia | | No schizophrenia | | Schizophrenia | | No schizophrenia | |
Category	Alcohol problem	No alcohol problem	Alcohol problem	No alcohol problem	Alcohol problem	No alcohol problem	Alcohol problem	No alcohol problem
Recidivists	2	1	39	28	8	11	49	42
Nonrecidivists	5	5	28	22	24	83	108	132

Note. Table excludes subjects (n = 31) for whom any of the categorizations above were coded as unknown.

TABLE 5.2
Intercorrelations (Pearson *r*s) of Study Variables

Variable	1	2	3	4
1. Psychopathy	—	−.172	.156	.268
2. Schizophrenia		—	−.237	−.179
3. Alcohol abuse			—	.101*
4. Violent recidivism				—

Note. All *p*s < .001, except for asterisked value (*p* < .01).

Bonta et al. (1998) found psychosis to be negatively related to violent recidivism among mentally disordered offenders (also see Grann & Fazel, 2005).

Although alcohol abuse was positively related to violent recidivism in this study, its relationship was much weaker than that of psychopathy. In fact, among the psychopathic offenders, the presence of alcohol abuse made no additional contribution to the already high likelihood of violent recidivism. At the same time, similar to other findings (e.g., Smith & Newman, 1990), psychopathic offenders were more likely to abuse alcohol than were nonpsychopathic offenders. Although alcohol may have had disinhibiting effects on nonpsychopathic offenders and thereby increased their likelihood of committing a violent act, it may not have had such effects on psychopathic offenders, whose behavioral controls were already chronically minimal. Our results suggest that even though alcohol abuse is likely to be a common problem of incarcerated psychopathic offenders, treatment for alcohol abuse may not reduce their likelihood of violent recidivism.

Another interesting result of this research was the finding that men diagnosed as having schizophrenia were less likely than other men in our study also to be psychopathic. Why was the comorbidity of schizophrenia and psychopathy so low? We examined the correlations between the diagnosis of schizophrenia and the individual items on the PCL–R and found that the items least likely to be endorsed for the schizophrenic offenders compared with other offenders were "juvenile delinquency," "early behavior problems," "glibness—superficial charm," and "conning—manipulative" (*r*s ranging from −.27 to −.15, all *p*s < .001). By contrast, there were no items that were significantly positively correlated with a diagnosis of schizophrenia. Speculations about the neurophysiological roots of violent behavior (Barratt, 1993; Eichelman, 1992) suggest that different neurotransmitter systems underlie different diagnoses. Whereas deficits in the serotonin system have been hypothesized to underlie the violent behavior of persons with antisocial personality disorder (e.g., G. L. Brown, Goodwin, Ballenger, Goyer, & Major; 1979; Elbogen & Huss, 2000; Virkkunen, 1991), different neurotransmitter imbalances may underlie violence associated with schizophrenia. Research on the effects of clozapine and risperidone on schizophrenia suggests that they may owe their therapeutic effects in reducing schizophrenic symptoms to antagonism of both dopamine and serotonin systems (Elbogen & Huss,

2000; Ereshefsky & Lacombe, 1993), leading to speculation that hyperactivity in both systems may be responsible for schizophrenia in the first place. Thus, one might speculate that serotonin (or at least 5-HT$_2$ serotonin receptor) hyperactivity underlies schizophrenia, whereas serotonin deficit underlies psychopathy, and thus individuals who qualify for both diagnoses should be especially rare. However, a subsequent study has found a positive relationship between psychopathy and schizophrenia (Rasmussen & Levander, 1996), so further interpretations should await replication.

We found that alcohol abuse was less common among men with schizophrenia than among the other men in our study. This finding is contrary to those of others who have used community comparison samples (Monahan et al., 2001; Regier et al., 1990). We believe that these discrepancies can be explained by the fact that our sample was (because of past history of violence) at high risk for future violence compared with a sample from the general population and that among high-risk samples, many nonschizophrenic offenders are likely to be personality disordered. In fact, 28% of the schizophrenic offenders in our study had an alcohol abuse problem, a figure similar to the 34% obtained in the Epidemiological Catchment Area (ECA; Regier et al., 1990) study. By contrast, the prevalence of alcohol abuse among the nonschizophrenic offenders was 50%, close to the 56% rate of alcohol disorders found among prisoners in the ECA study, and far higher than the 13.5% prevalence in the general population.

We also found that men with both schizophrenia and alcohol abuse were at much greater risk for violent recidivism than men with schizophrenia but no alcohol abuse. In our study, 26% of schizophrenic offenders with both disorders reoffended violently, compared with only 7% of schizophrenic offenders without an alcohol disorder. These results are similar to those of other studies in which alcohol-abusing persons with schizophrenia or other major mental disorder were much more likely than nonabusing persons with schizophrenia or other major mental disorder to commit acts of violence (Lindqvist & Allebeck, 1989; Monahan et al., 2001; Swanson et al., 1990; C. Wallace et al., 2004). These results point to the importance of addressing alcohol abuse in treatments to reduce the violent behavior of schizophrenic and other psychotic offenders.

In summary, among persons at high risk for future violence, psychopathic offenders are at especially high risk. Alcohol abusers are at higher risk than nonabusers. Contrary to findings for the population at large, persons diagnosed as having schizophrenia posed the least risk. We found that the comorbidity rate of schizophrenia and psychopathy was very low, although others have not found this to be the case. We also found that the comorbidity of schizophrenia and alcohol abuse was lower than it was among nonschizophrenic offenders. By contrast, the comorbidity of psychopathy and alcohol abuse was extremely high. Finally, among psychopathic offenders only, alcohol abuse conferred no additional risk of violence.

CONCLUSION

In this chapter, we have summarized several follow-up studies of mentally disordered offenders and compared their outcomes with those of men more similar to the general prison population. Although each study focused on somewhat different questions and different subpopulations of mentally disordered offenders, the results revealed a remarkable degree of consistency. The base rates of violent recidivism obtained in these studies ranged from 16% for the schizophrenic offenders in the follow-up of schizophrenic and nonschizophrenic offenders to 77% for the treated psychopathic offenders in the evaluation of the therapeutic community program. These base rates are, on average, considerably higher than those obtained in the studies described in the first part of this book. This is so, in part, because the follow-up periods for the studies reported in this chapter are longer than the follow-up periods reported in the earlier studies. It also appears that the greater the proportion of psychopathic offenders in the follow-up study, and the lower the proportion of schizophrenic offenders, the greater the rate of violent recidivism.

Consistent with the results of a meta-analysis (Bonta et al., 1998), the variables that were the best predictors of violent recidivism in the studies reported in this chapter are the same variables that have been shown to be related to the prediction of violent recidivism among other groups of offenders: criminal history, antisocial personality or psychopathy, early antisocial behavior, and alcohol abuse. Similar to some other recent findings among psychiatric and correctional populations, the presence of schizophrenia and psychotic symptoms exhibited around the time of the index offense or admission to hospital were negatively related to risk. Psychosis, psychotic symptoms, and exacerbation of those symptoms have little value as indicators of the risk of violence in offender populations. The level of predictive accuracy in these studies was consistently higher than those obtained in the studies published before 1990; the multiple correlations in most surpassed the .40 "sound barrier" previously thought to be the maximal achievable by some investigators (e.g., Menzies, Webster, & Sepejak, 1985). The accuracy of the predictions and the consistency of the predictor variables led us to develop an actuarial instrument for the prediction of violence, which we describe further in chapter 8.

6

FIRE SETTERS

Arson is a major problem worldwide. Per capita, Canada and the United States have among the most severe arson problems (Geller, 1992a). Arson has very low arrest and conviction rates compared with other crimes (Boudreau, Kwan, Faragher, & Denault, 1977), with only about 3% of all set fires leading to conviction (Geller, 1992a). Arson for profit, including insurance fraud, welfare fraud, bankruptcy scams, and other fraudulent activities, accounts for half of the fire-related property damage in the United States (Geller, 1992a). The majority of these arson offenses, as well as of fires set to conceal other crimes, are the work of professional criminals who rarely come to the attention of mental health professionals. However, a significant number of arsonists set fires for reasons that have little or nothing to do with monetary gain, and it is those persons, often called *mentally disordered fire setters*, that are the focus of this chapter. We begin by providing a historical overview of the literature on pathological fire setting and then review the empirical studies on the subject, with particular emphasis on studies done at Oak Ridge and studies pertaining to prediction of recidivism among fire setters.

HISTORICAL OVERVIEW

Pathological fire setting has intrigued those interested in mental disorder at least since the beginning of the 19th century (Geller, 1992b). Esquirol

115

(1845/1965) used the terms *incendiary monomania* and *pyromania* for a disorder characterized by fire-setting impulses that occurred without any necessary absence of reasoning abilities. Early German writers considered pathological fire setting to be especially common among pubescent girls (Geller, 1992b). In the latter half of the 19th century in the United States, there was considerable debate about the status of pyromania as a specific mental disorder (Geller, Erlen, & Pinkus, 1986). Some authorities agreed with the prevailing European view that pyromania was a specific disorder, whereas others argued that it was nothing more than a psychiatric label used to excuse what were more appropriately considered simply criminal actions.

Throughout much of the past hundred years, the literature on fire setting has been dominated by psychodynamic clinicians who believed in the existence of pyromania as a specific disorder. For example, Stekel (1924) believed that pyromania had a sexual root and used as evidence the claims of previous studies that awakening and ungratified sexuality impelled individuals to turn to fire setting. He also stated, "It is a fact that many pyromaniacs are suffering from urinary incontinence" (pp. 130, 131). Freud's (1932) formulation of the psychodynamics of fire setting centered on sexual deviations that he felt had their roots in a fixation or regression to the phallic–urethral stage of libidinal development.

Simmel (1949) described one case in considerable detail. He described the incendiary acts of the arsonist as "an unconscious attempt to find a substitute gratification for his reawakened and repressed infantile masturbating impulse. Due to the blockage of genital libido, this impulse had regressed to the level of infantile urethral autoeroticism" (p. 94). London and Caprio (1950) associated enuresis and pyromania, and they presented a case history that suggested that sadistic and homosexual tendencies were also linked with fire setting.

Scott (1978) described "fire bugs" as "unable to obtain sexual gratification in the usual way" (p. 261) and fire fetishists as those who derive pleasure "from seeing images of flames while masturbating and later from experimenting with harmless blazes. However, the impulse grows and there is a desire for larger and larger conflagrations" (p. 260). Mavromatis and Lion (1977) reviewed the literature on pyromania and concluded that observations supported the psychodynamic interpretation of fire setting as a sexual symbol and that masturbation, sexual dysfunction, and enuresis were all linked with fire setting. Macdonald (1977) stated that "the majority of pyromaniacs, both male and female, describe sexual excitement while watching the blaze, and some masturbate at the scene" (p. 191) and that "possession of obscene literature or female underclothing is another clinical indication of an association between sexual psychopathology and arson" (p. 192). He also stated that "the sadism of some fire setters is quite remarkable" (p. 192) and that "the clinical triad of fire setting, cruelty to animals, and enuresis has been noted by many clinicians" (p. 192).

The psychodynamic approach was based primarily on the accumulation of case histories. There were, however, serious problems with this approach. First, there was a tendency to report only about individuals who bore a high resemblance to those already reported in the literature. Case histories not consistent with the accepted pattern may not have been noticed, reported, or published. A second problem was that therapists writing about their own patients often also cited similar patients previously described by earlier writers. The same patient was often cited by several authors, so that a small number of patients had a disproportionate effect on the development of theories. The large number of articles in the literature that reported only case studies led to an unjustified belief that much was known about arson and arsonists. In addition, several modern reviews relied heavily on previously published case studies (Blumberg, 1981; Macdonald, 1977; Mavromatis & Lion, 1977; Prins, 1980), contributing further to the belief that much was known.

The case history literature about fire setting has been used by arson investigators in their attempts to apprehend fire setters. For example, one investigator, Barracato (1979), stated, "Pyromaniacs exhibit severe deviations from normal behavior. They set fires for no apparent rational reasons, although studies indicate that they achieve sexual gratification through the act of setting fires" (p. 3). He continued, "Most pyromaniacs have a history of bed-wetting (enuresis) problems" (p. 4) and a "childhood history of extreme cruelty to animals" (p. 5). Partly on the basis of his reading of the psychiatric literature, he advised fire investigators to escort and observe arson suspects while in the bathroom, because "urination is a psychological form of sexual gratification for the pyromaniac, and it's impossible for him to function in front of other people" (p. 4).

Although debate about the utility of the term *pyromania* persists (e.g., Geller et al., 1986; R. Robbins & Robbins, 1967), the concept continues to have an impact on modern psychiatric thinking about fire setters. Pyromania has been listed as a specific disorder in every version of the *Diagnostic and Statistical Manual of Mental Disorders* (DSM) except the second edition (American Psychiatric Association, 1968). The most recent edition, the *DSM–IV* (American Psychiatric Association, 1994), lists pyromania as a separate diagnostic entity under "Disorders of impulse control not elsewhere classified." Diagnostic criteria include a recurrent inability to resist impulses to set fires; an increasing sense of tension before setting the fire; an experience of intense pleasure, gratification, or release at the time of committing the act; an interest in fire-related paraphernalia; and a lack of such motivation as monetary gain, sociopolitical ideology, concealment of criminal activity, expression of anger or revenge, or improvement in one's living standard. A final criterion is that the fire setting is not better accounted for by manic disorder, antisocial personality disorder, or conduct disorder. According to the *DSM–IV*, individuals with the disorder are regular "watchers" at fires and frequently set off false fire alarms. The course of the disorder, predisposing factors, prevalence, and familial pattern are said to be unknown.

CHARACTERISTICS OF FIRE SETTERS

The first and still the largest empirical study of fire setters was that of N. D. C. Lewis and Yarnell (1951). They studied the characteristics of more than 1,500 arsonists, 1,145 of whom were men. Many of their findings were clearly at odds with the prevailing psychodynamic accounts. Male arsonists outnumbered female arsonists six to one, even though more liberal criteria for inclusion were applied to women. In their classification of motives, the researchers found evidence of sexual motives for only 40 of 1,145 men. They classified approximately half of their sample as pyromaniacs. Even though they reported their results objectively in terms of numbers and proportions, the authors were psychodynamically trained and seemed to disbelieve their own data. Thus, although sexual motivation involved only 3.5% of the arsonists, one of the eight chapters on the typology of adult male arsonists was devoted to those who were sexually motivated. Similarly, although they apparently did not discover urinary problems among the men in their sample, the researchers appeared to accept the psychoanalytic view that urinary factors were involved in fire setting. Thus, even though their data did not support many of the psychodynamic explanations of fire setting, their study did little to alter many of the commonly held views.

The N. D. C. Lewis and Yarnell (1951) study had serious limitations. First, the sample was neither random nor complete. Arsonists were selected by choosing complete cases from the files of the National Board of Underwriters and by adding cases brought to the attention of the investigators by fire investigators, fire marshals, and staff of psychiatric institutions. Furthermore, they had no non–fire setters to use for comparison. They also reported no reliability data and few methodological details about how they assigned individuals to categories. The sheer size of their sample, however, makes it possible to overlook many of the methodological shortcomings. Furthermore, many of their findings were replicated in later studies.

The characteristics of adult fire setters have been the focus of several other empirical studies since the N. D. C. Lewis and Yarnell (1951) study, and the results have consistently called into question some of the psychodynamic interpretations. In addition to the Oak Ridge study described later in this chapter, four studies have used control samples to compare with arsonists (Bradford, 1982; Hill et al., 1982; Hurley & Monahan, 1969; McKerracher & Dacre, 1966). The number of fire setters in each study was quite small, ranging from 30 (McKerracher & Dacre, 1966) to 50 (Hurley & Monahan, 1969). Although the findings of these studies were not entirely consistent, none provided support for the psychodynamic ideas of sexual motivation or enuretic problems among fire setters. McKerracher and Dacre (1966) studied 30 male arsonists admitted to a British special-security hospital and compared them with 147 patients admitted for other reasons.

Hurley and Monahan (1969) studied 50 male arsonists in a British psychiatric prison and compared them with 100 randomly selected other prisoners. Bradford (1982) studied 26 men and eight women charged with arson and sent for pretrial psychiatric assessments; the comparison group comprised 50 individuals charged with other offenses. Hill et al. (1982) studied 38 men charged with arson and sent to a psychiatric institution for psychiatric assessment and compared them with 30 male property offenders and 24 violent male offenders. In the only study that examined the issue, Bradford found no differences in self-reported enuretic problems between arsonists and control participants. Hurley and Monahan, Bradford, and Hill et al. all looked at the incidence of sexual motivation for fire setting and found that from 0% (Bradford, 1982) to 8% (Hill et al., 1982) of the fires were set for purposes of sexual gratification. The studies were equivocal in their support for the concept of pyromania. Bradford reported that only one participant in his study met the *DSM–III* criteria for pyromania (which were essentially the same as the *DSM–IV* criteria outlined in the Historical Overview section). However, 20% of the arsonists in the Hurley and Monahan study and 42% of the arsonists in the Hill et al. study were reported to have had no obvious motive.

Other studies of adult fire setters have not included a non–fire setting comparison group. In general, the results of these studies have confirmed the findings of the controlled studies (see Geller, 1992b, for a review). Sexual motivation was rare or nonexistent, and pyromania (using *DSM–III* or *DSM–III–R* criteria) was exceedingly rare. Among adult psychiatric inpatients, it has been noted that although pyromania is very rare (Geller et al., 1986), fire-setting behavior is not (Geller, 1987; Geller, Fisher, & Moynihan, 1992). Another common finding in all of the empirical studies of fire setting, controlled and uncontrolled, has been the high percentage of fires in which revenge has been identified as a motive. The targets of arson included employers, spouses, landlords, parents, relatives, and friends of the arsonist.

We have examined the characteristics of fire setters at Oak Ridge in several studies. In one study (Rice & Harris, 1991), we compared 243 adult male arsonists with 100 men admitted to Oak Ridge for other reasons. The arsonists were significantly younger (with a mean age of 29 years compared with 32 years for the comparison men), less intelligent (with a mean IQ of 93 compared with 99 for the comparison men; see also Barron, Hassiotis, & Banes, 2004; Lindsay & Macloed, 2001; Simpson & Hogg, 2001), less physically attractive (as rated from facial photographs on the patients' clinical records), and more socially isolated (less likely to be married and with solitary rather than social hobbies and interests). They were also less likely to have exhibited physically aggressive behavior and less likely to have had previous charges brought for violent behavior. Not surprisingly, they had more documented instances of fire setting in their histories, and their families were more likely to report that they had been interested in fire as children. Furthermore, they had more fire-related acts (e.g., setting false fire alarms and making bomb threats) than other patients, and their family members were more likely to have a history of fire setting. There were no significant differences between the two groups in diagnosis, occupational or educational history, socioeconomic status, or substance abuse history. The frequency of the "childhood triad" of fire setting, bed-wetting, and cruelty to animals was very low in both groups and was not more frequent among the fire setters.

We used discriminant analyses to determine how well a combination of variables could discriminate the two groups. We found that by using a combination of variables, the two groups could be differentiated with a high degree of accuracy ($R = .66$), confirming that mentally disordered fire setters present a clinical picture quite different from that of other mentally disordered offenders. In general, the fire setters exhibited social isolation and passivity, whereas the other mentally disordered offenders exhibited overt aggression and a generally criminal lifestyle.

We also examined the incidence of pyromania and sexual motivation in this study. We found only 1 individual (out of the 243 fire setters) who met the diagnostic criteria for pyromania (using DSM–III–R criteria, which were almost identical to the DSM–IV criteria outlined in the Historical Overview section). When we examined the primary motivation for the fire setting, we found that anger and revenge together were the most common. A sexual motive for fire setting could be ascertained from the clinical and offense information on file for only 6 of the 243 fire setters and was recorded as the primary motive for only 4.

In another study, we examined the sexual arousal patterns of fire setters and nonoffenders to fire-related stimuli, nonfire consenting sex stimuli, and nonsexual non-fire-related stimuli (Quinsey, Chaplin, & Upfold, 1989). When the responses of the two groups were examined using deviance indexes similar to those developed for rapists and child molesters (G. T. Harris, Rice, Quinsey, Chaplin, & Earls, 1992), we found that arsonists as a group showed relatively greater arousal to the fire-related stimuli (reported in Rice & Harris, 1991). The fire-related stimuli included two stories (of approximately 200 words each) illustrating each of the following motivations for fire setting: insurance fraud, revenge, heroism, control and secretiveness, unspecified excitement, and sexual excitement. The greatest difference between the arousal to stimuli in the nonfire consenting sex category of stories and each of the fire-related categories of stories was calculated for each individual. The fire-related stories most responsible for the group differences between the arsonists and control participants were the unspecified excitement and sexual excitement stories.

These findings are intriguing and provide a degree of empirical support for some of the psychodynamic interpretations of fire setting. The findings offer support for the idea that sexual arousal might play some role in fire setting, even though the offender would be very unlikely to qualify for a diagnosis of pyromania and even though the sexual motivation might be difficult to ascertain. Our results support the further use of behavioral treatments designed to alter sexual arousal patterns of those arsonists who show sexual arousal to the fire themes (see also Lande, 1980). Another intriguing result of our comparison of fire setters and non–fire setters was the finding of significantly more homosexual men (8.5%) among the fire setters than among the non–fire setters (2%), again providing empirical support for findings reported in the early case study literature.

SOCIAL COMPETENCE OF FIRE SETTERS

In another study conducted at Oak Ridge (G. T. Harris & Rice, 1984), we compared the social competence of 13 fire setters and 13 other offenders matched for age and IQ. On the basis of the common finding of revenge as a motive for fire setting, we hypothesized that arsonists were unassertive individuals who set fires because they were unable to express anger toward their victims in more acceptable ways. Participants engaged in two behavioral assessments of social skill and assertion and completed questionnaire measures of assertion and self-esteem. In addition, ward staff completed questionnaires about each patient. The behavioral measures consisted of role-play situations that required the patient to stand up for his rights to achieve a fair outcome. The other actor in the role-plays took the role of the patient's spouse, landlord, employer, family member, hospital staff, or fellow patient.

In general, our results supported the hypothesis that arsonists were less assertive than other hospitalized offenders. Arsonists described themselves as having less control over their own lives and behaved less assertively on behavioral tests. Shyness associated with fire setting has also been recently reported by others (Chen, Arria, & Anthony, 2003). It is interesting, however, that the social skill and assertion differences among our participants were not apparent to staff during the day-to-day hospital routine. Ward staff did not rate the groups differently in social interaction or social withdrawal. As suggested elsewhere (Quinsey, Maguire, & Varney, 1983; Rice & Josefowitz, 1983), assertive behavior by patients is not generally rated positively by staff.

The results of our studies showing that fire setters exhibited significant deficits in assertiveness and the commonly reported finding that revenge is a common motive for fire setting led us to believe that social skills in general and assertion deficits in particular represented important treatment targets for many mentally disordered fire setters. Thus, in two other studies we developed and evaluated a behavioral assertion training program for arsonists hospitalized at Oak Ridge. In the first study (Rice & Chaplin, 1979), 10 fire setters received eight sessions of assertion training and, as a placebo treatment, eight sessions of nondirective group psychotherapy. Half received the assertion training first, and half received the placebo treatment first. Blind ratings demonstrated increased social skills in role-play assessments after the assertion training, but not after the placebo treatment.

More recently, we conducted another study in which 22 fire setters received assertion training and 14 patients received life skills training (G. T. Harris & Rice, 1992). We collected a variety of pretreatment and posttreatment measures of therapeutic effectiveness: role-play measures, self-report questionnaires, and staff ratings of patient behaviors. The results showed that compared with life skills training, the assertion training improved patients' ability to perform assertively. In contrast, the control treatment produced significantly greater improvements on a paper-and-pencil assessment of life skills. It is also noteworthy that, compared with the control treatment, assertion training was associated with increases in staff ratings of belligerence and noncompliance. Thus, another important aspect of assertion training programs that take place inside institutions involves encouraging ward staff to observe and reward appropriate assertive behavior.

FIRE SETTER SUBTYPES

In another of the Oak Ridge studies of fire setters (G. T. Harris & Rice, 1996b), we used the 243 fire setters from a study described earlier in this chapter (Rice & Harris, 1991) to develop a typology of mentally disordered fire setters. Using cluster analyses, we found four subtypes that were internally homogeneous and clearly distinct from one another. The largest group (33%), which we labeled *psychotics*, comprised men whose motives for fire setting were primarily delusional. They had set few fires in their lives and had little history of criminal or aggressive behavior, but they did not appear to be unassertive, either. They were most likely to be diagnosed with schizophrenia and least likely to have an alcohol problem. They were less likely than members of other clusters to have used accelerants in their fires. The likelihood that they committed further violent, nonviolent, and fire-setting offenses on release was about average for the group as a whole.

The second largest group (28%), which we called *unassertives*, were men who had the best histories prior to the fire that had brought them to our institution and the lowest rates of all kinds of recidivism. They had little history of aggression as children or adults, and had little criminal activity in their backgrounds. They also had the best family backgrounds, were more intelligent, and had better employment histories compared with the other clusters. They were the least assertive (they resembled the individuals high in overcontrolled hostility described in chap. 4), and they were the most likely of all the clusters to have set their fires because of anger or revenge. More recent studies have identified anger and revenge, especially in the context of general interpersonal shyness, as important precursors to fire-setting behavior (Chen et al., 2003; Fritzon, 2001; Kocsis & Cooksey, 2002).

The *multifire setters* accounted for 23% of the total. These individuals had the worst childhood histories, characterized by unstable homes, poor school adjustment, and high amounts of aggression. Although they had little criminal history, they had set many fires as children and adults. They were also the least intelligent and had the poorest academic achievement. They were the most likely to have had psychiatric help and to have been institutionalized as children, and they were the most likely to have had parents with psychiatric problems. They had spent the longest time in psychiatric institutions, although they were the least likely to have been diagnosed with schizophrenia. They were the least likely ever to have married and were very unassertive. They were the most likely to have set fires in institutions and to have confessed to setting the fire when confronted. They were younger than fire setters in the other groups and were the most likely to have set their fires during the day. They were the most likely of all the fire setters to commit another offense of some kind, and their rates of recidivism were high for every type of crime. The cluster analyses suggested that this group was the least homogeneous of the four clusters and that in a five-cluster solution, this cluster was subdivided into two or more homogeneous clusters in which members of one group were motivated primarily by anger and revenge and had extremely high rates of fire-setting recidivism and members of a second, smaller group were motivated by excitement or attention seeking.

Finally, a cluster we labeled *criminals* constituted the smallest subtype (16%). These individuals had extensive criminal histories and poor childhood backgrounds marked by unaccepting, abusive parents, and they were the most likely to have histories of aggression as adults. They were the most likely to have been diagnosed with a personality disorder, the least likely to have known the victim of the fire, the most likely to have set the fire at night, and the least likely to have confessed or reported the fire at the time by activating an alarm. This was the most assertive group, and it was the group most likely to commit new fire and violent offenses on release.

Although we attempted to develop a typology of fires using the same methods used to develop the typology of fire setters, the results were disappointing. Using only information that investigators are likely to have available before they have a suspect in mind, the results yielded a large group of relatively nonserious fires and a small cluster of serious fires. However, few characteristics of perpetrators were related to these clusters. Thus, our study yielded little information that would be likely to assist fire investigators.

Perhaps the most important implications of this study were those pertaining to treatment. For the fire setters in the psychotic cluster, treatments designed to reduce their psychotic symptoms may have the greatest chance of reducing the likelihood of future fire setting, because their motives were frequently delusional.

We observed that two of the clusters of fire setters (the unassertives and the multifire setters), together accounting for over half of the sample, were extremely unassertive compared with both the general population and other psychiatric populations. Furthermore, in both these clusters of offenders, motives of anger and revenge were very common. For these offenders, then, assertion training holds considerable promise as a treatment to reduce the likelihood of future fire setting.

Surprisingly, the group most likely to commit further acts of fire setting were the "criminals," the same group most likely to commit other criminal and violent offenses. Members of this group, far from being unassertive, were considerably overassertive on our measures. For these offenders, who were also most likely to be diagnosed with a personality disorder, treatments designed to increase assertion are definitely not indicated, although cognitive–behavioral anger management techniques designed to reduce aggression may be helpful.

In summary, the results of this study revealed four subtypes of fire setters with different background characteristics, different fire-setting characteristics, and different likelihoods for future fire setting and violent and nonviolent recidivism. Examination of the four subtypes yielded information that may be useful in assessing risk among mentally disordered fire setters and in designing effective treatment programs.

ASSESSING RISK AMONG FIRE SETTERS

Fire setters are among the most difficult persons to release from secure settings because of the perceived risk that they will set further fires and endanger the lives of others. The psychiatric literature about fire setters has contributed to the belief that fire setters are a dangerous group with poor prognoses (e.g., N. Lewis, 1965; Mavromatis & Lion, 1977; Schmideberg, 1953). For example, it has been asserted that arsonists are likely to set new fires while in confinement or after release and that they should therefore be incarcerated with no chance to escape (Macdonald, 1977). The few available data on recidivism among arsonists provide little support for the contention that arsonists are likely to set further fires on release. Soothill and Pope (1973) examined the subsequent fire-setting offenses of 67 men and women who went to court in England and Wales on charges of arson in 1951. In a 20-year follow-up, only three individuals were convicted of another arson offense, although many were subsequently convicted of other, most often property, offenses. In another study (Sapsford, Banks, & Smith, 1978), 147 men who had served time in prison for arson in Britain and then been released were followed for up to 5 years in the community. Although half of those followed for 5 years committed another offense of some kind, only 5% were convicted of arson. It is interesting that the best single predictor of future convictions was past convictions, and the best predictor of future convictions for arson was past convictions for arson. Stewart and Culver (1982) followed up on 32 children who had set fires and had been admitted to a children's psychiatric ward. After a 1- to 5-year follow-up, seven children, all boys, were still setting fires. Recidivists came from less stable homes and engaged in more antisocial behaviors of other types in addition to fire setting. O'Sullivan and Kelleher (1987) studied 54 fire setters in hospital or prison and found a higher arson recidivism rate than other investigators, with 35% setting another fire as long as 10 years after the initial episode.

Geller, Fisher, and Bertsch (1992) conducted a 7-year follow-up of 50 psychiatric patients who had previous histories of fire setting or fire-related behaviors and 50 matched patients who did not. Patients with previous histories of fire setting or fire-related behavior were more likely to set a fire in the follow-up period.[1] Geller (1992a) reviewed the literature on fire setting and emphasized the need for the development of risk prediction tools for fire setters.

Researchers have debated whether arson should be considered a violent crime or a property crime and whether arsonists are more like property offenders or violent offenders. Hill et al. (1982) compared arsonists with property and violent offenders on a number of clinical measures. All had been sent to a psychiatric hospital for assessment prior to trial. Although arsonists were somewhat similar to both groups, they were more similar to the property offenders than to the violent offenders in terms of personality, diagnosis, history of criminal and violent behavior, family background, and substance abuse. Jackson, Hope, and Glass (1987) found that arsonists resembled violent offenders on demographic variables, but they had shown less interpersonal aggression and were less assertive. A number of studies have shown that arsonists sent for forensic assessment are biochemically similar to violent offenders in that both groups show lower cerebrospinal fluid levels of the serotonin metabolite 5-hydroxyindoleacetic acid than nonoffenders (Linnoila, DeJong, & Virkkunen, 1989; Virkkunen, DeJong, Bartko, Goodwin, & Linnoila, 1989; Virkkunen, Nuutila, Goodwin, & Linnoila, 1987). Sapsford et al. (1978) studied the similarity between arsonists and other offenders by examining the subsequent arson, violent, sex, and property offenses of their sample of arsonists. Although their data are somewhat difficult to interpret, they found that the arsonists were about as likely to commit a violent as a nonviolent offense on release, that arson and sex offenses were both about equally likely, and that the rates for both were much lower than those for violent and property offenses (which presumably ex-

---

[1]Geller et al. (1992) did not report this result, but we calculated $\chi^2(1, N = 100) = 5.83$ ($p < .05$) using the data they presented.

cluded sex and arson offenses). Thus, the evidence has been inconclusive about the relationship between arson and other violent and nonviolent criminal offenses.

OAK RIDGE STUDY OF RISK ASSESSMENT AMONG FIRE SETTERS

True follow-up studies of fire setters appear to be quite rare, and almost none identify predictors of recidivism (Brett, 2004). We undertook a study of the prediction of recidivism among fire setters (Rice & Harris, 1996). The fire setters in this study were the same 243 adult male arsonists used in previously described studies (G. T. Harris & Rice, 1996b; Rice & Harris, 1991). All of the study variables, except those pertaining to outcome, were retrospectively coded entirely from patients' clinical files. The variables were organized into several categories: offender characteristics, childhood and social history, and offense variables. In addition to variables similar to those used in our prediction studies for other offenders (e.g., previous criminal charges, previous psychiatric hospitalizations, alcohol problem at the time of offense, ratings of interpersonal aggression, socioeconomic status, IQ, psychiatric history, marital status), several were motivated by an examination of the literature about fire setting. For example, childhood history of bed-wetting, fire setting, and cruelty to animals were coded; so too were homosexuality, history of fire setting, shyness, and so on. Regarding the most serious fire leading to admission, several details were coded, including location, method of setting the fire, and up to three motives. All of the fire setters were coded on all variables, and the mean proportion of missing observations was .025.

Similar to the methods used in our other prediction studies, outcome was coded from data provided by the Canadian Police Information Centre, and institutional records were searched for individuals who were returned for behavior that, in the opinion of the research assistants, would otherwise have resulted in criminal charges. We used several different definitions of recidivism. *Fire-setting recidivism* was any charge (or conduct warranting a criminal charge) for fire setting, including arson, setting fire to a substance, or mischief, where documentation indicated that fire setting was involved. Charges of mischief associated with false alarms or bomb threats were not included in this category. *Violent recidivism* included any charge (or conduct warranting a criminal charge) for any offense against another person (e.g., homicide, assault, sexual assault, and armed robbery) and excluded fire setting. *Nonviolent recidivism* was any criminal charge (or conduct warranting a charge) for criminal behavior not subsumed by the two other definitions. Time until reoffense was calculated by determining the time between the date the individual first had an opportunity to reoffend (being released to the street, a halfway house, or an open psychiatric ward) and the date he actually reoffended, with time incarcerated for other offenses subtracted. Any individual could qualify for each of the three types of recidivism, and two qualified for all three.

Results

Of the 243 fire setters, 208 had an opportunity to reoffend by the date of last coding. On average, the 208 at-risk fire setters had 93.6 months (*SD* = 87.8 months) of opportunity to reoffend. Of these, 33 (16%) set another fire, 118 (57%) committed a nonviolent offense, and 64 (31%) committed a violent offense (of which 20, or 10%, committed sex offenses). In all, 137 (66%) exhibited some form of recidivism. For fire-related reoffenses, the mean time until reoffense was 36.2 months (*SD* = 64.4 months). For those who reoffended violently, the mean time until reoffense was 54.9 months (*SD* = 50.0 months); for nonviolent reoffense, the mean was 83.3 months (*SD* = 64.4 months).

Survival curves were also computed for each type of recidivism separately. Figure 6.1 depicts Kaplan–Maier survival curves for the 208 fire setters for the three types of criminal recidivism separately. The survival curves illustrate the relatively low rate of fire-setting recidivism, with virtually no further drop in survival beyond 10 years. However, the rates of subsequent violent and antisocial conduct were high, and survival continued to drop beyond 10 years. The rate and time course of violent recidivism was somewhat lower than that exhibited by all men released from the study institution (unselected by offense type) over the same period (G. T. Harris, Rice, & Quinsey, 1993). However, the rate of nonviolent recidivism was remarkably steady and linear throughout the 20-year follow-up period and suggests that virtually no individuals with that duration of opportunity would remain free of antisocial behavior.

When we examined the relationship between each background variable and each of the three discrete definitions of recidivism, we found that few variables were common to the prediction of the three types of recidivism. Only childhood fire setting and never having been married were significantly related to all three types of recidivism. Although adult aggression and violent offense history were significantly related to both fire-setting and violent recidivism, they were positively related to future violence but negatively related to future fire setting. In addition to childhood fire setting and never having been married, number of fires set was similarly and significantly related to both future fire-setting and nonviolent recidivism. Age at first fire setting and having another criminal charge concurrent to fire setting were significantly related to both, but in opposite directions; having set many fires and having no concurrent criminal charges were positively related to future fire setting but negatively related to future nonviolent recidivism (see Rice & Harris, 1996).

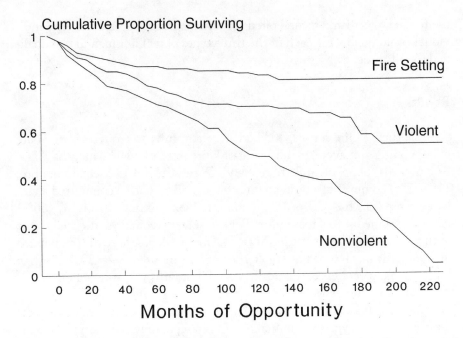

Cumulative Proportion Surviving

Fire Setting

Violent

Nonviolent

Months of Opportunity

Figure 6.1. Kaplan–Maier survival curves for three types of recidivism: Cumulative proportion surviving as a function of years of opportunity.

Three separate multiple regression equations were derived: one for each of fire setting, violent, and nonviolent recidivism. Separate stepwise multiple discriminant analyses ($\alpha = .05$ for both entry and removal of potential predictor variables) were conducted for each set of study variables (childhood and adult history and offender and offense characteristics) considering only those with significant univariate correlations. The variables selected by the stepwise analysis from each set were included in a final stepwise analysis (Rice & Harris, 1996). Scores on the three equations were significantly intercorrelated but not identical: fire setting and violence, $r(208) = .16$, $p < .05$; fire setting and nonviolence, $r(208) = .58$, $p < .0001$; and violent and nonviolent recidivism, $r(208) = .32$, $p < .001$. Because the regression weights computed in such an analysis would be subject to considerable shrinkage, and because such weights are difficult to apply to new cases, we used the method described by Nuffield (1982) to compute weights for a final instrument to predict fire-setting recidivism, which is described in chapter 8.

What Variables Predict Fire Setting?

The results of this study provide a starting point for the development of risk prediction tools for fire setters. The variables that predicted future fire setting in this study are consistent with the small existing literature on recidivism among arsonists. Future fire-setting rates among arsonists in our study were in the midrange of the rates reported in earlier studies (16% in an average follow-up of 7.8 years). The variables that made the largest contribution to the prediction of future fire setting had to do with a history of fire setting: age at first fire setting (the younger, the more likely to engage in future fire setting) and past history of fire setting (the more fires set in the past, the more likely to engage in future fire setting). Furthermore, other variables that predicted future fire setting are consistent with what is known about how arsonists differ from other mentally disordered offenders (Rice & Harris, 1991). Specifically, those who set future fires were less intelligent and less likely to have histories of aggression as adults than those who did not.

The variables that predicted further fire setting tended to be very different from those that predicted violent recidivism and somewhat different from those that predicted nonviolent recidivism. A multiple discriminant function predicting fire setting shared little common variance with a discriminant function for violent recidivism (3%) but considerable variance with that predicting nonviolent recidivism (34%). These results supported the idea that fire setting is an act different from both violent and nonviolent crime but especially from violent crime.

Although we were unable to gather detailed information about the recidivism offenses of the individuals in this study, we did have detailed information about the offense that brought them to our institution. In general, the fire-setting behavior of these men was quite minor in the sense that very few (9%) had caused nonfatal human injuries and extremely few (5%) had caused death. On follow-up, we were able to ascertain that none of the future fire setting involved death, and it is likely that only a small proportion involved human injury. Thus, we believe that the especially poor prognosis often assigned to mentally disordered fire setters is undeserved. However, the risk of violent reoffending among these men was substantial (31% over an average of 7.8 years). This rate was identical to the 31% violent recidivism rate obtained in an average 6.8-year follow-up of a mixed group of mentally disordered offenders (only 3% of whom had an index offense of fire setting) from the same institution (G. T. Harris, Rice, & Quinsey, 1993). Thus, we also believe that assessing fire setters' risk of future violent behavior is at least as important, if not more important, than assessing their risk for future fire setting.

7

SEX OFFENDERS

Of all the types of offenders discussed in this book, the literature on sex offenders is by far the largest. The size of this literature is a result of contemporary popular and ideological concerns and the location of sexual offending at the intersection of a number of very different academic subfields, including sexology, evolutionary psychology, criminology, forensic psychiatry and psychology, law, and so on. Simply the conjunction of sexual, aggressive, and legal elements found in sexual offending results in a very large and disparate literature. This chapter does not include a review of this voluminous literature,[1] nor does it include discussion of theories about the etiology of sexual aggression, which we have discussed elsewhere (Lalumière, Harris, Quinsey, & Rice, 2005; Quinsey, 2003).

This chapter focuses primarily on identified sex offenders, men who have been incarcerated or hospitalized because of illegal sexual behaviors involving bodily contact with a victim. Most of these men committed rape or child molestation. This chapter describes our efforts to identify characteristics of sex offenders that differentiate them from nonoffenders and from

---

[1]The interested reader is referred to reviews provided by Langevin (1983); Pallone (1990); Quinsey (1977a, 1984, 1986); Quinsey and Lalumière (1995a, 2001); and Ressler, Burgess, and Douglas (1988) and to edited books (Feierman, 1990; Greer & Stuart, 1983; Krivacska & Money, 1994; Marshall, Laws, & Barbaree, 1990; Prentky & Quinsey, 1988; Roberts, Doren, & Thornton, 2002).

men who have committed nonsexual offenses, as well as characteristics that predict future sexual recidivism. Among incarcerated sex offenders, the largest group comprises rapists (i.e., men who have assaulted adult women), and a smaller percentage are child molesters (Porporino & Motiuk, 1991). A sizeable proportion of incarcerated sex offenders (Porporino & Motiuk reported 28%) offended against both adults and children.

Under the sexual psychopath laws enacted between 1937 and the early 1970s, the overwhelming majority of the offenders who qualified were men who had offended against children exclusively or against both children and adults, because the diagnosis that most often qualified for the designation was a sexual deviation or paraphilia (almost always pedophilia or sexual sadism) in any edition of the Diagnostic and Statistical Manual of Mental Disorders (DSM; American Psychiatric Association, 1952, 1968, 1980, 1987, 1994). Because most rapists did not qualify for such a diagnosis, they were much less often included under the old sexual psychopath laws. However, under the sexually violent predator laws, personality disorders (which are much more common among rapists than among pedophiles) are explicitly recognized as sufficient diagnostically to qualify for designation as a "predator." Thus, under the sexually violent predator commitment laws, rapists are much more likely to be committed than under the older laws. Data from California and Washington State suggest that at least one third of the sexually violent predators are men who have convictions for offending exclusively against adults (J. Marques & L. Berliner, personal communication, August 15, 1997).

One of the earliest, most robust, and most important findings in the literature on sex offenders was that the frequency of offending and the likelihood of recidivism are strongly related to the type of victim and the relationship between offender and victim (Fitch, 1962; Frisbie, 1969; Frisbie & Dondis, 1965; Mohr, Turner, & Jerry, 1964). Among child molesters, heterosexual father–daughter incest offenders (who have no other victims) exhibit the lowest recidivism rates, heterosexual extrafamilial child molesters an intermediate recidivism rate, and homosexual child molesters the highest recidivism rate. The probability of recidivism is positively related to the number of past sex offenses and the frequency of the behaviors. The nature of past sex offenses is related to future sex offenses in that there is a tendency for offenders to recommit the same type of offenses rather than to randomly switch among them (Hanson, Scott, & Steffy, 1995; also see Quinsey, 1984, 1986, and Quinsey, Lalumière, Rice, & Harris, 1995, for reviews of this material).

Given these findings, the known groups or specificity design research strategy can seek variables that discriminate not only between sex offenders and non–sex offenders but also among offenders according to their history of sex offending. Although the discriminant validity of a variable does not prove its causal status, it is a reasonable first step in identifying potential causal variables (see also Garber & Hollon, 1991). More important in the present context, the discriminant validity of a variable is likely to be related to its predictive power, in the sense that poor discriminators of known groups are unlikely to be good predictors of future outcome. A great deal of our research on sex offenders has focused on variations in sexual preferences.

SEX OFFENDERS AND SEXUAL DEVIANCE

Phallometric Studies of Sexual Deviance Among Child Molesters

Phallometry involves the measurement of male sexual arousal by monitoring changes in penis size while stimuli are presented in a controlled fashion. In most studies, variations in the characteristics of the stimuli are used to test theories about how the sexual interests of sexual aggressors differ from those of nonoffenders and offenders who are not sexually aggressive. Phallometric studies most often come closest to true experimental research designs. We have addressed the scientific value of phallometry in detail elsewhere (G. T. Harris et al., 1992; G. T. Harris & Rice, 1996a; Lalumière & Harris, 1998). In this section, we summarize those discussions by saying that, under limited circumstances, phallometric tests can be valid and reliable scientific procedures. However, phallometric testing could not be used to determine whether a particular offender was guilty of an offense in the first place.

In pioneering research, Freund (1965) was the first to demonstrate that many child molesters preferred children to adults as sexual partners as indexed by their penile tumescence responses to photographs of persons who varied in age and sex. Quinsey, Steinman, Bergersen, and Holmes (1975) replicated Freund's basic observation by showing that phallometric assessment differentiated extrafamilial child molesters from both nonoffenders and offenders who had not committed sexual offenses. However, verbal rankings of preferences for similar stimuli did not differentiate the groups (see also G. T. Harris, Rice, Quinsey, & Chaplin, 1996). Among the child molesters, there was a close correspondence between magnitude of response to particular slide categories defined by age and gender and history of victim choice. This research showed that relative sexual age preference was important in sexual offending against children, as would be expected from its persistence and victim specificity, and that phallometric assessment was a better measure of this preference than self-report.

Quinsey and Chaplin (1988b) reported that aural stimuli also worked very well in phallometric assessment of age and gender preferences. Penile tumescence changes were monitored in response to audiotaped descriptions involving consenting sex with an adult partner, sex with a child (at three levels of force and violence), nonsexual violence with a child victim, and neutral interactions with a child. Extrafamilial child molesters preferred stories depicting sex with children to sex with adults, showed sexual interest in children of both sexes, and did not respond to depictions of nonsexual violence. Compared with other child molesters, those who had physically injured their victims responded relatively more to children than adults and more to coercive sex with children. Men in a comparison group recruited from both the institution and the local community showed little arousal to any of the child stimuli. Furthermore, Chaplin, Rice, and Harris (1995) found that child molesters were better discriminated from other men with stimuli that emphasized victim trauma than with stimuli that did not and that sexually deviant responding was negatively correlated with questionnaire measures of empathy.

Quinsey, Chaplin, and Carrigan (1979) compared the sexual age preferences of incestuous and matched nonincestuous child molesters. Child molesters with daughter or stepdaughter victims showed more appropriate age preferences (i.e., preferred older stimulus persons) than child molesters with unrelated victims. Child molesters with other female relatives as victims exhibited a nonsignificant trend toward more appropriate age preferences than their control participants. These data suggest that inappropriate sexual preferences are more common among extrafamilial than among incestuous child molesters. The relative proportion of child molesters who have deviant sexual age preferences among extrafamilial versus incestuous offenders remains unclear, however. Others have found these two groups of child molesters to be indistinguishable with phallometric assessment, with both groups showing more inappropriate age preferences than nonoffending heterosexual men (Barsetti, Earls, Lalumière, & Bélanger, 1998; Studer, Aylwin, Clelland, Reddon, & Frenzel, 2002). The results of other studies (e.g., Seto, Lalumière, & Kuban, 1997) have suggested that the number of victims is more important than whether the offender molested a child within the family.

Rice and Harris (2002a) compared 82 men who sexually molested prepubescent girls in their own families with 102 who had offended only against girls outside their families. Men who offended only against their daughters (especially when they were their own genetic daughters) exhibited much less serious criminal and antisocial histories and less deviant sexual interests than men who offended both against their own daughters and nonfamilial victims. These mixed offenders were at least as antisocial and sexually deviant as the exclusively extrafamilial child molesters. Although clearly more sexually deviant than non–sex offenders, the exclusively father–daughter child molesters exhibited lower rates of violent and sexual recidivism. The prediction of recidivism by static risk factors was the same in all groups, and the lower rates of recidivism in the incest offenders could be attributed entirely to their lower scores on empirically established static predictors of recidivism (Rice & Harris, 2002a).

Phallometric Studies of Sexual Deviance Among Rapists

Quinsey, Chaplin, and Varney (1981) compared rapists, non–sex offender patients, and nonpatient control participants using aural descriptions of consenting sex, rape, nonsexual violence, and neutral heterosocial interactions with a female adult (read in a male voice in the first person). Half of the nonpatient control participants were given a "permissive set" by informing them that sexual responses to unusual stimuli were common and thus not to be surprised if they found themselves sexually aroused by things they had never thought of before. The remainder were given the ambiguous instructions to listen to the audiotapes and imagine that they were the person "saying it." Rapists were differentiated from the other men on the basis of their relatively greater responses to rape stimuli in comparison to their responses to consenting sex. The permissive instructions increased responding to all of the nonneutral categories but did not affect relative arousal to the consenting sex and rape stimuli. Although few rapists showed large responses to nonsexual violence, the amount of sexual arousal to that category in relation to the consenting sex category was weakly but positively correlated with whether the offender had ever injured a victim in a sexual assault (Quinsey & Chaplin, 1982).

Quinsey and Chaplin (1984) attempted to determine which aspects of the rape stimuli were responsible for differentiating rapists from nonrapists. The following stimulus categories were used: active consent, in which the female sexual partner initiated and controlled sexual activity; passive consent, in which the male partner was active and the female partner passive; and four categories of rape stimuli. These vignettes varied in the initial response of the victim (either assertive refusal or pleading) and in her ultimate response (either pain and suffering or sexual arousal). The rapists' phallometric responses did not discriminate among these stimulus categories, whereas the nonrapists responded most to the consenting sex stimuli and least to the rape stimuli in which the woman's ultimate response was suffering.

In a further attempt to identify the critical aspects of the nonsexual violence stimuli, Quinsey, Chaplin, and Upfold (1984) compared 20 rapists with 10 non–sex offender forensic patients and 10 men recruited from the local community. All of the men reported that they considered themselves to be heterosexual. The story categories involving female partners or victims were as follows: neutral heterosocial, consenting sex, rape, nonsexual violence, consenting bondage and spanking, masochistic bondage and spanking, and nonconsenting bondage and spanking. The categories involving male partners or victims were neutral, consenting sex, rape, and nonsexual violence. Rapists showed more sexual arousal to rape descriptions and less to consenting sex stories than the control participants. It was predicted that violence per se was not sexually arousing and thus that rapists should respond to violence against a female victim but not a male victim. This prediction was confirmed; rapists were sexually aroused by stories involving nonsexual violence with female but not male victims. Surprisingly, rapists and control participants did not differ in their responsiveness to the spanking and bondage stories. It appeared that the amount of violence in the rape descriptions was critical in differentiating rapists from non–sex offenders.

Rice, Chaplin, Harris, and Coutts (1994) further studied the effects of the salience of victims' suffering. The stimulus categories all involved interactions between a man and a woman: rape with victim enjoyment, rape with victim suffering, nonsexual assault, consenting sexual activity, and neutral heterosocial interactions. In each category, stories were told either from the woman's or the man's viewpoint. Participants showed greater sexual arousal to consenting sex stories when described from a female perspective. However, for the rape stories, the maximal differentiation between rapists and nonrapists was obtained when the stories included victim suffering and were told from the female perspective. Rapists scored lower than nonrapists on self-report measures of empathy, and these measures were negatively correlated with relative indexes of sexual arousal to rape and nonsexual violence.

Lalumière and Quinsey (1993, 1994) conducted a meta-analysis to examine how well identified rapists could be discriminated from non–sex offenders using phallometric assessments, what variables might moderate this discrimination, and whether rapists respond more to descriptions of rape than to consenting sex. Eleven primary and five secondary phallometric studies involving 415 rapists and 192 non–sex offenders were examined. By conventional standards (e.g., Cohen, 1992), the average size of the difference was large. Stimuli sets that contained more graphic rape descriptions produced better discrimination between rapists and non–sex offenders and showed greater sensitivity (i.e., were more likely to correctly identify the rapists in the sample). Using these stimulus sets, the probability that a randomly chosen rapist had a higher rape index than a randomly chosen non–sex offender varied between .74 and .82. Rapists responded more to rape than to consenting sex stimuli (i.e., showed an absolute preference for rape stimuli) in 9 of the 16 data sets and in all 8 of those using the more effective stimulus sets. A meta-analysis by other investigators (Hall, Shondrick, & Hirschman, 1993) also reported significant differences in the phallometric responses of rapists and other men.

An update of these meta-analyses with new data clearly established that incarcerated rapists are sexually different from other men (Lalumière, Quinsey, Harris, Rice, & Trautrimas, 2003). The differences between self-reported rapists and other men do not appear to be as large but are also commonly reported. To the extent that phallometric stimuli emphasize brutality and victim suffering, these differences in sexual responding are consistently observed. What remains unclear is the meaning of the differences in sexuality between rapists and other men. We will return to the explanation of these differences later in this chapter.

Several conclusions can be drawn already. First, there are large differences in the responses of officially identified rapists and non–sex offenders in phallometric tests. Rapists and non–sex offenders groups can be classified on the basis of phallometric tests with few false positive errors if conservative criteria are adopted. Second, unequivocal support was given to an explanation of rape on the basis of a sexual preference hypothesis: Rapists, as a group, responded more to rape than to consenting sex in comparison to non–sex offenders, and non–sex offenders preferred consenting sex to rape. A stronger sexual preference hypothesis, that rapists respond more to rape than to consenting sex whereas nonrapists show the opposite preference, was also supported, but only with the use of graphic and brutal rape stimuli. Third, stimulus sets that included graphic and brutal rape stimuli and multiple rape exemplars discriminated rapists from non–sex offenders more effectively than stimulus sets that included less graphic and brutal stimuli or only one or few exemplars.

It was of interest that the study by Rice et al. (1994) was identified as a statistical outlier in this meta-analysis. This study produced an unusually high effect size as a result of low variance in each group. The low variance probably was caused by the study's use of 16 rape stories. The only other study that used such a high number of exemplars (Quinsey & Chaplin, 1984) also obtained a very large effect size. The best discrimination between rapists and non–sex offenders was obtained in Rice et al. (1994) when the rape story was told from the woman's point of view and when the woman experienced pain. It is therefore likely that the large effect size reflects the power of phallometric assessment when the quality and the quantity of stimuli are optimal. Procedures that maximize discriminant validity are those likely to maximize predictive accuracy.

Phallometry and Faking

The very high discriminant validity (i.e., the close correspondence between phallometric responses and sexual history) demonstrated for phallometric assessment when participants are tested for the first time means that very few of them fake their responses on initial testing. However, the discriminant and predictive validity of phallometric assessment can be compromised to the extent that participants can intentionally influence their responses. Almost always this dissimulation involves either not responding to any of the stimuli and so trying to produce an uninterpretable profile or feigning sexual preference for appropriate sexual stimuli. Such feigning can involve responding to nonpreferred sexual stimuli or not responding to preferred sexual stimuli. Because sex offenders are highly motivated to appear to have normal sexual preferences, the ability to fake means that deviant phallometric profiles are more readily interpreted than nondeviant phallometric profiles. Thus, the effect of faking is to reduce the sensitivity (ability to detect true deviance) of the test. In the case of child molesters, Freund and Blanchard (1989) calculated that their phallometric test of sexual age preferences had 55% sensitivity among child molesters who denied a sexual interest in children.

Quinsey and Bergersen (1976) administered phallometric sexual age preference assessments involving slide stimuli on four occasions to five non–sex offenders. The first and fourth of these assessments involved normal or neutral instructions, and in the second and third sessions participants were asked to try to appear as if they preferred male children on one session and female children on the other. Participants were told that they would earn extra money for the faking sessions to the extent that they could fake interest in children and lack of interest in women. Two of the five participants significantly altered their responses in accord with instructions; two others altered their responses to a degree, but the changes did not reach statistical significance. Participants were as successful in reducing their responses to preferred stimuli as they were in augmenting responses to nonpreferred stimuli.

A similar procedure was used by Quinsey and Carrigan (1978) to examine whether an audiotape of a sexual fantasy appropriate to the type of person depicted in the slide affected instructional control of penile responses. In this study, one of the two faking sessions involved the audiotape, and the other did not. Participants were instructed to fake preference for little girls. The audiotaped fantasies had no effect on participants' ability to fake: Seven of the 9 participants successfully altered their responses in both conditions.

Quinsey and Chaplin (1988a) evaluated a more sophisticated procedure designed to prevent faking. The aural stimuli designed for assessing rapists' sexual preferences (Quinsey et al., 1981) were presented four times to each of 16 nonoffender volunteers. Half of them were given normal instructions on the first and fourth session. On the second and third sessions they were asked to appear to prefer nonsexual violence and rape to consenting sexual activity. On the third session, participants were required to engage in a concurrent semantic tracking task in which they pressed one button when sexual activities were being described, a second button when violent activities were being described, and both when sexually violent activities occurred. This task was developed to ensure that they attended to the relevant aspects of the stimuli presented. For the other half of the participants, the sequence of sessions was as follows: normal instructions, normal instructions with the semantic tracking task, faking, and faking with the semantic tracking task. Participants were given the strong expectation that they could fake preferences in the phallometric assessment and were coached as to how they might accomplish this, although they were free to use any techniques they could imagine.

The first and fourth normal instruction sessions for the first eight participants did not differ; neither did the normal instruction session with and without the semantic task for the second eight participants. Fifteen of the 16 successfully (and significantly) faked a preference for nonsexual violence and rape in the faking session without the semantic task, but only two were successful when the semantic task was used. Two others modified their responses, but not to a statistically significant degree.

The semantic tracking task appears to be a useful technique to investigate in phallometric assessments of rapists. On the basis of these results, one would expect that more rapists would appear to have inappropriate sexual preferences when tested with the semantic task than without. G. T. Harris, Rice, Chaplin, and Quinsey (1999) tested this prediction by assessing the sexual preferences of 38 rapists with and without the semantic tracking task. Four categories of audiotaped vignettes describing neutral interactions, consenting sex, rape, and nonsexual violence were used as stimuli. In the semantic tracking task, participants were instructed to press one button when violent events were described in the vignette and another when sexual activities were described. Phallometric assessment with the semantic task better discriminated between rapists and non–sex offender participants (from the earlier study) than the same assessment when the task was not used, because the rapists responded relatively less to the consenting sex stimuli with the semantic task than without it. The results suggest that the semantic task may improve discriminant validity, particularly among sex offenders who have had previous experience with phallometric assessment. In a study of homosexual pedophiles who were either test experienced or not, Proulx, Côté, and Achille (1993) confirmed that among pedophiles who had prior phallometric assessments, the addition of the semantic tracking task increased the correspondence between phallometric data and sex offense history.

Phallometric Scoring

Many factors other than faking can affect the discriminant validity of phallometric assessment (Quinsey & Laws, 1990). One of the more important of these is the method of scoring the penile response. In all of the discriminant validity studies described in this section, standard z scores have proved to be superior to raw scores. Earls, Quinsey, and Castonguay (1987) found that z scores were superior to both percentage of full erection and raw scores in differentiating child molesters from non–sex offenders. Relative preference for sexual stimuli thus appears to lead to better differentiation of sexual offenders from non–sex offenders.

In a more ambitious methodological study, G. T. Harris, Rice, Quinsey, Chaplin, and Earls (1992) reanalyzed data from some of the studies reported in this section, plus some new data, to examine factors that might be related to discriminant validity. They concluded that discriminant validity could be enhanced in the following ways:

- by using scoring methods that compensate for individual differences in responsivity, such as z scores or percentage of full erection;
- by using deviance indexes, preferably difference scores, in which the mean response to the highest deviant category is compared with the mean response to the highest nondeviant category;

- by including stimuli that describe elements of violence and coercion; and
- in the assessment of child molesters with visual stimuli, by including adolescent stimuli provided that only early pubescent stimuli are included.

Discriminant validity was found to be unimpaired by including participants whose level of response was very low. Use of these guidelines in scoring phallometric data would be expected to enhance their predictive accuracy.

IS THERE A SEX OFFENDER PSYCHOLOGY?

Hanson, Cox, and Woszczyna (1991) provided an extensive and useful review of psychometric measures designed specifically for sex offenders. Most of these measures are intended to measure attitudes toward women, sexual offending, and so on. Most commonly, investigators have attempted to discriminate sex offenders from others with personality measures or measures of general psychopathology. These efforts have met with limited success (Levin & Stava, 1987; Quinsey, 1984, 1986). For example, Quinsey, Arnold, and Pruesse (1980) compared the Minnesota Multiphasic Personality Inventory (MMPI; Hathaway & McKinley, 1967) profiles of rapists, extrafamilial child molesters, and a variety of other categories of offenders in Oak Ridge. Although all groups showed significant psychopathology, they scored almost identically to each other.

The perceptions that child molesters have of themselves and others were investigated using the semantic differential and repertory grid in a specificity design (Horley & Quinsey, 1994, 1995). No differences were found on the grid between non–sex offender inmates, community controls, and child molester inmates. On the semantic differential, however, child molesters described themselves as relatively submissive and sexually unattractive, and they described women as oppressive and unattractive. It is interesting that no between-group differences were found for descriptions of children.

There are many other individual differences among men in their sexuality and sexual aggression in particular. Sexual aggressors have been reported to endorse "rape myths," traditional (as opposed to enlightened) sex roles, interpersonal violence, hostility toward women, adversarial sexual beliefs, sensation seeking, and generally right-wing sociopolitical ideas (Burt, 1980; Feild, 1978; Malamuth, 1996; Malamuth, Heavy, & Linz, 1993; Quinsey, 1984, 1986; W. D. Walker, Rowe, & Quinsey, 1993). In addition, sexual aggression has been shown to be related to general antisociality (e.g., juvenile delinquency, generally violent conduct) and, as discussed later in this chapter, to psychopathy and sexual deviance. As mentioned in the preceding section, such differences are candidates in causal theories about sexual aggression. Which are the causal and explanatory relationships here, and which are not? For example, attitudes hostile toward women might cause men to engage in sexual aggression, or they might be the result of sexual aggression—rationalizations adduced to justify behaviors actually caused by other things.

Stermac and Quinsey (1986) compared the social skillfulness of rapists, non–sex offenders from the same institution, and men of low socioeconomic status from the community. Ratings of social skillfulness were made by the men themselves and by raters who were blind to group membership. The latter were based on videotapes of a 5-minute conversation held individually with a male and a female confederate and on responses to audiotaped conversations between a man and either a male or a female confederate. Rapists were rated as equally skilled with male and female confederates in the 5-minute conversation. They were rated as less skilled in responding to the audiotaped vignettes involving female confederates versus male confederates but as skilled as the men in the other two groups. Rapists were as skilled as other men in identifying the nature of the confederate's response in the audiotaped vignettes.

Across groups, all of the men rated themselves as less socially skilled and as more anxious than did the external raters. Female raters rated the rapists as significantly less physically attractive than the community men, but there was no difference between the two institutional groups. Rapists were less assertive in both general assertion and heterosexual situations as measured by the Callner–Ross Assertiveness Scale (Callner & Ross, 1976).

This study did not find a skill deficit unique to rapists. Rapists were less skilled than the men recruited from the community but not different from other hospitalized individuals. Rapists were neither differentially unskilled with women in comparison to other men nor differentially inaccurate in their perceptions of social situations. These findings do not necessarily imply that social skill deficits are inappropriate targets for intervention in individual cases, but they do indicate that social skill deficits, at least when used as a single predictor, are not likely to be effective predictors of recidivism.

PREDICTORS OF RECIDIVISM AMONG SEX OFFENDERS

At first glance, it might seem that the most relevant research outcome for sex offenders is a repetition of the offense for which the offender was originally convicted—most probably another sex offense. However, *sexual recidivism* has variously been defined as any new arrest, charge, conviction, or (less often) hospital readmission for a sexual offense. Often official criminal records constitute the only available information. Although all official records are an underestimate of the actual rates of reoffending, there is extra cause for concern in the case of sexual offenses because of the tendency for the sexual component of the offense to be eliminated from the arrest, charge, or conviction offense (e.g., sexual assault becomes simply "assault") because of lack of sufficiently hard evidence of the sexual component, through a plea bargaining agreement, or because the offense involved was a homicide and whether or not there was a sexual component was viewed as secondary.

Another outcome measure used for predicting recidivism among sex offenders (Rice & Harris, 1997a) has been any charge, conviction, or readmission to hospital for any violent offense (defined as offenses ranging from assault or armed robbery to murder and including all hands-on sexual offenses). Although overinclusive, violent recidivism is likely to capture significantly more sexual reoffenses than the more commonly used sexual recidivism definition. In fact, when we have had the resources to check into more detailed information concerning recidivism offenses, we have found that many offenses that appear to be nonsexual violent offenses actually have a sexual component or sexual motivation.

Results of a new study (Rice, Harris, Lang, & Cormier, 2005a) suggest that for sex offenders, using violent recidivism as defined in the preceding paragraph is at least as accurate a measure of offenses that are truly sexually violent as is sexual recidivism that can be ascertained as clearly sexual from police rap sheets alone. That is, although it is an overestimate of the number of sexually motivated violent offenses that are detected by police and result in charges for some kind of criminal offense, it is at least as accurate as using only those charges or convictions recorded as sexual on the criminal rap sheet (which are, of course, underestimates of the true number of sexually motivated criminal offenses). Moreover, using only sexual charges or convictions recorded on the criminal rap sheet is biased inasmuch as it misses the most serious offenses (sexual murders), whereas using violent offenses does not.

Furthermore, many sex offenders, especially rapists, do not confine their recidivism offenses to clearly sexual crimes. We have found, for example, that whereas child molesters who reoffend are much more likely to be convicted of a new sex offense than another violent offense, rapists are just about as likely to be convicted of an apparently nonsexual violent offense as a sexual one. (However, both groups are also at risk for nonviolent, nonsexual offenses.) It appears that much of the problem may lie in the weakness of the criterion measure—sexual recidivism as determined from crude official records of arrests, charges, or reconvictions. When the definition of sexual recidivism includes all acts of violence, whether recorded as sexual or not, much better accuracy—indeed, accuracy that can be characterized as good—can be attained.

Most members of the public at large are concerned not just about sexual offenses but about violent offenses in general (Wolfgang, Figlio, Tracy, & Singer, 1985). The risk of an entirely non–sexually motivated murder certainly is at least as much of concern as a physically noninjurious sexual molestation, although fear of both underlies much of the current conservative tendency in criminal justice policy. We conclude, therefore, that the outcome of greatest relevance for the appraisal of risk among sex offenders is violent recidivism. Even if one is interested only in new sexually violent offenses, it may be argued that violent recidivism is a more valid outcome measure for evaluating prediction accuracy than sexual recidivism as usually defined.

Reviews of the prediction of recidivism among sex offenders before 1990 were pessimistic about the relative lack of progress in the area to that date. In many follow-up studies (e.g., Frisbie & Dondis, 1965; Gibbens, Soothill, & Way, 1981; Radzinowicz, 1957; Soothill, Jack, & Gibbens, 1976), the differences in the proportions of recidivists over studies were dramatic, and Quinsey (1984) concluded that "by selectively contemplating the various studies one can conclude anything one wants" (p. 101), a point also made several years before about sex offender treatment in general (Furby, Weinrott, & Blackshaw, 1989). Nevertheless, the studies clearly demonstrated that some groups of offenders were at significant risk of committing new acts of sexual violence on release. Frisbie and Dondis followed 70 men who had committed sexual acts accompanied by threats or force on women 18 years old or older and found that 36% of the men committed a new sexual offense within 5 years of their release from Atascadero, where they had been judged on admission as sexually dangerous. This was a high rate of recidivism, considering that one of the most commonly used arguments to explain the difficulty in predicting violence was that the base rate of violence was low.

In a 1986 review of the literature on child molesters, Quinsey found three variables that were consistent predictors of sexual recidivism. Recidivism was found to increase with number of previous sexual offenses, the selection of male victims (either exclusively or in addition to female victims), and the selection of unrelated victims. Perhaps the best of the early follow-up studies of child molesters was that of Frisbie and Dondis (1965), who studied 1,035 heterosexual, 428 homosexual, and 49 bisexual child molesters, all of whom were designated as *sexual psychopaths* treated in Atascadero and discharged to the court as improved. In addition to the three predictors mentioned previously, this study also showed that recidivists were younger and more frequently diagnosed as sociopaths. Furby et al. (1989) reviewed the literature on sex offender recidivism in general and concluded that by examining qualitative patterns across studies, it was possible to observe the following trends: recidivism (not necessarily sexual) increased with follow-up time, there was no evidence that clinical treatment reduced risk for any type of offender, and there was no indication that recidivism rates varied by subtype of offender.

Throughout the 1990s, several studies of the prediction of recidivism among sex offenders found more consistent patterns than had been observed earlier. Rice, Harris, and Quinsey (1990) examined the sexual and violent recidivism of a group of 54 rapists assessed in a forensic hospital and released (usually after serving time in prison). The follow-up period averaged 46 months. The predictors included those found to be related to violent reoffending among offenders in general (psychopathy, past criminal history, age, and marital status), those known from the previous research literature to be important for the prediction of sexual offenses (especially those having to do with past sexual offending), and those known to discriminate rapists from nonoffenders (phallometric deviance scores). Given the relatively short follow-up period, the violent recidivism rate of 43% was high (28% were convicted of a new sexual offense). As a group, then, these men constituted a high-risk sample for future violence. For the prediction of new sexual offense convictions specifically, the best predictors included previous convictions for violent offenses, previous sexual offenses, and phallometric deviance. It is interesting that predictions of later violent or sexual offenses could be made just as well from only two variables (phallometric deviance and psychopathy) as from a larger set of predictors. The data from this study supported an account of rape as an act of sexual violence differentially committed by men who exhibit a criminal lifestyle and an exploitive approach to others.

In a further study (Rice, Quinsey, & Harris, 1991), we examined the recidivism of 136 extrafamilial child molesters assessed in Oak Ridge and released (again, mostly from prison) over an average of 6.3 years of opportunity to reoffend. The violent recidivism rate for this group was 43% (31% were convicted of a new sexual offense). Psychopathy scores were not obtained in this study, and the focus of prediction was only on subsequent sexual convictions. We found that sexual recidivism was moderately well predicted by using a multivariate equation including whether the offender had ever been married, previous admissions to correctional institutions, previous property convictions, previous sexual convictions, a diagnosis of personality disorder, and a phallometric deviance index reflecting a sexual preference for children rather than adults. Unfortunately, there was no evidence that a behaviorally oriented treatment reduced the likelihood of recidivism.

Hanson and Bussière (1998) examined the predictors of sexual recidivism in a meta-analysis of studies available by the end of 1995 that examined the predictors of sexual recidivism among sex offenders. They found 87 articles based on 61 data sets, and half of the reports had been produced since 1989. The median sample size was 198, and the median follow-up period was 4 years. In total, 28,972 sexual offenders were included. Their results were largely in agreement with those just discussed in showing the importance of deviant sexual preferences and past criminal history. The strongest predictor of sexual recidivism in their meta-analysis was deviant sexual preferences measured phallometrically. Other important predictors included prior sexual offenses and early onset of sexual offending. Two other important predictors were ones commonly found to be important predictors of general recidivism among offenders: age (negatively related) and never having been married. Of less importance but still significantly related to sexual recidivism were having a male victim and having a victim who was a stranger. Because so many offenders were included in this meta-analysis, it was also possible to identify some factors that were not related to sexual recidivism. Having a history of being sexually abused as a child, substance abuse, and general psychological problems (including anxiety, low self-esteem, and depression) were unrelated to sexual recidivism. Treatment did not appear to reduce sexual recidivism. Hanson and Morton-Bourgon (2004) recently redid the meta-analysis using studies up to 2003 and obtained very similar results.

Although having deviant sexual preferences was related to sexual recidivism in the entire sample of sex offenders (comprising both rapists and child molesters), the strongest results were obtained for child molesters separately. Hanson and Bussière (see also Hanson & Morton-Bourgon, 2004) found no significant relationship between phallometric preferences for rape and sexual recidivism. However, as discussed earlier, research using stimulus sets that included more brutal and graphic stimuli found relative arousal to sexual or nonsexual violence to be a good predictor of sexual recidivism among rapists (Rice, Harris, & Quinsey, 1990).

Since the Hanson and Bussière (1998) meta-analysis, there was an interesting proliferation of follow-up studies of released sex offenders. We are aware of approximately 25 methodologically sound studies from six countries using both adult and juvenile sex offenders that have replicated already established predictors of recidivism among sex offenders:

- sexual deviance (English, Retzlaff, & Kleinsasser, 2002; Firestone et al., 2000; Gretton, McBride, Hare, O'Shaughnessy, & Kumka, 2001; G. T. Harris et al., 2003; Hildebrand, de Ruiter, & de Vogel, 2004; Kenny, Keogh, & Seidler, 2001; Langstroem, 2002; Langstroem & Grann, 2000; Proulx et al., 1997; Rabinowitz, Sharon, Firestone, Bradford, & Greenberg, 2002; Rice & Harris, 2002a; Roberts, Doren, & Thornton, 2002; Serin, Mailloux, & Malcolm, 2001; Seto, Harris, Rice, & Barbaree, 2004);
- young age (Firestone et al., 2000; Hanson, 2002; G. T. Harris et al., 2003; Hildebrand et al., 2004; Proulx et al., 1997);
- criminal and sex offense history (Craissati, Falla, McClurg, & Beech, 2002; English et al., 2002; Hagan, Gust-Brey, Cho, & Dow, 2001; G. T. Harris et al., 2003; Hildebrand et al., 2004; Langstroem & Grann, 2000; Proulx et al., 1997; Rabinowitz et al., 2002; Seto et al., 2004; Worling, 2001);
- juvenile antisociality (English et al., 2002; G. T. Harris et al., 2003; Kenny et al., 2001; Langstroem, 2002; Langstroem & Grann, 2000);
- psychopathy or personality disorder (Barbaree, Seto, Langton, & Peacock, 2001; Firestone et al., 2000; G. T. Harris et al.,

2003; Hildebrand et al., 2004; Langstroem & Grann, 2000; Rabinowitz et al., 2002; Serin et al., 2001);

- alcohol abuse (Firestone et al., 2000; G. T. Harris et al., 2003);
- extrafamilial victims (Greenberg, Bradford, Firestone, & Curry, 2000; Hanson, 2002; Rice & Harris, 2002a); and
- reports of having suffered abuse or lived apart from parents as a child (Craissati et al., 2002; Firestone et al., 2000; Hanson, 2002; G. T. Harris et al., 2003; Kenny et al., 2001; Worling, 2001).

This literature is remarkable for its consistency—these predictive effects seem highly robust and reliable—and for its lack of novelty—few new empirical predictors have been discovered in over a decade.

One exception is the finding of a multiplicative interaction between psychopathy and sexual deviance in violent or sexual recidivism that we first reported (Rice & Harris, 1997a). There have now been several replications of this relationship (Gretton et al., 2001; G. T. Harris et al., 2003; Hildebrand et al., 2004; Serin et al., 2001; Seto, 2005). In general, sex offenders who are both psychopathic and sexually deviant are especially likely to reoffend and to do so quickly; the risks conferred by the combination are greater than would be conferred by the additive combination of their independent effects alone. These results are consistent with the view that there are two separate components to risk of sexual recidivism among sex offenders—deviant sexuality and antisociality (Roberts, Doren, & Thornton, 2002). Another innovation is a new measure of sexual deviance that can be used when phallometry is unavailable (Seto, Harris, Rice, & Barbaree, 2004).

Partly because of the U.S. federal law obliging states to enact sexually violent predator statutes, there has been a burst of interest in the prediction of recidivism among sex offenders. Given this context, the burgeoning literature contains an odd contradiction, however. A search of the psychological literature (using as search terms *sex* offen* (risk or recid* or pred*)*) found 120 publications in the 5 years preceding November 2003. Other than our own research, only 14 (12%) of these presented any empirical data on risk factors or predictors of recidivism among sex offenders (mostly from Canada and Scandinavia), and another 21 (18%) presented non-follow-up data on the characteristics of sex offenders. The large majority (81, or 70%), including almost all the publications by U.S. writers, were nonempirical commentaries—advice about how to conduct sex offender risk assessment, perspectives on the legality or morality of formal risk assessment, or discourse on the authors' affection for or dislike of the current empirical literature. Perhaps the words of Mark Twain—"Many people talk about the weather but very few do anything about it"—apply to risk assessment, too. If there were a law to prevent hurricanes, one might expect an ensuing debate about whether and by what means hurricanes could be predicted and the futility of hurricane predictors that fail to aid hurricane prevention. The same kind of debate is needed to inform the prediction of sexual offenses.

Some of these nonempirical commentaries have argued that efforts to identify high-risk sex offenders (also called *sexually violent predators*) are pointless because the base rate of recidivism is so low that the most efficient "prediction" is to detain no one (e.g., Campbell, 2003; Wollert, 2001). The available evidence undermines these arguments (even granting the premise of sexually violent predator legislation that nonsexual violence is not worth preventing) in at least five ways. First, as discussed in the section on Predictors of Recidivism Among Sex Offenders, each sexually violent offense recorded on police rap sheets underrepresents by approximately 25% to 33% the actual number of sexually violent offenses detected by the police (because the sexual element of many offenses is lost; Rice et al., 2005b). Second, most follow-up studies of sex offenders are fairly short. Studies with long follow-up periods reveal higher base rates of recidivism (Hanson et al., 1995; Hanson, Steffy, & Gaulthier, 1993; Langevin et al., 2004; Prentky, Lee, Knight, & Cerce, 1997). Third, it can be concluded that the base rate of sexually violent recidivism among sex offenders referred for sexually violent predator determination, even on the basis of unaided clinical judgment (Milloy, 2003; Quinsey, 1980), is higher than that among adjudicated sex offenders in general. Fourth, it is quite clear that criminal charges and especially convictions underestimate actual criminal behavior (Langevin et al., 2004; Prentky et al., 1997). Finally, the assumption of these critiques is that the cost associated with a false positive (detaining a sex offender who will not commit another sex offense) is equivalent to the cost of failing to prevent sexually violent reoffenses. As discussed elsewhere (Rice & Harris, 1995b), this assumption is debatable and, if false, means that there are many circumstances in which efficient prediction of recidivism among sex offenders is clearly attainable.

Thus, recent years have seen a small proliferation of schemes or systems aimed at combining empirical predictors of recidivism among sex offenders to yield numerical estimates of risk of violent or sexual recidivism. Much more fully described in chapter 8, our own work in this area resulted in the Sex Offender Risk Appraisal Guide (SORAG). The 14-item SORAG is an actuarial system for the prediction of violent recidivism that, when used as specified, has consistently produced large predictive effects (Barbaree et al., 2001; Bartosh, Garby, Lewis, & Gray, 2003; Dempster, Hart, & Boer, 2002; G. T. Harris & Rice, 2003; G. T. Harris et al., 2003). Other actuarial systems have also been developed to assess the risk of violent recidivism that is known to be sexually motivated. Specifically, a four-item tool called the Rapid Risk Assessment for Sexual Offense Recidivism (RRASOR; Hanson, 1997) was expanded and improved to yield the Static–99 (Hanson & Thornton, 2000). Both have been found to significantly predict violent or sexual recidivism among sex offenders (e.g., Barbaree et al., 2001; Ducro, Claix, & Pham, 2002; Hanson & Morton-Bourgon, 2004; G. T. Harris et al., 2003; Nunes, Firestone, Bradford, Greenberg, & Broom, 2002). Nonactuarial "structured professional discretion" schemes (which do not provide probabilities or numerical estimates of risk) have also been promulgated, but these have not generally fared well in validation testing (Barbaree et al., 2001; Ducro et al., 2002; Sjoestedt & Langstroem, 2002; but see de Vogel et al., 2004) and have performed more poorly than actuarial assessments (Dempster, Hart, & Boer, 2002; Hanson & Morton-Bourgon, 2004).

TREATMENT AND RECIDIVISM AMONG SEX OFFENDERS

The phallometric data that have predicted sexual recidivism in the studies described previously in this chapter, as well as in our other research (Malcolm, Andrews, & Quinsey, 1993), were gathered at first assessment. Posttreatment phallometric data have not predicted sexual recidivism (despite positive results reported in an initial investigation by Quinsey, Chaplin, & Carrigan, 1980). This observation raises the issue of whether the dynamic predictor of most applied interest, the provision of treatment intended to lower the likelihood of recidivism, predicts outcome. Unfortunately, the results obtained to date in our research have been negative. Neither a behavioral laboratory program designed to aid offenders in gaining control over their inappropriate sexual interest nor the provision of social skills training and sex education[2] were found to affect the sexual recidivism of 136 child molesters released from a maximum-security psychiatric institution (Rice, Harris, & Quinsey, 1991; Rice, Quinsey, & Harris, 1991).

Similar negative effects were found in a larger study of a cognitive–behavioral sex offender treatment program in a federal correctional institution (Quinsey, Khanna, & Malcolm, 1998). The sample included 488 rapists and child molesters who were referred to a sex offender treatment program and who were followed for an average of 44 months of opportunity to reoffend: 213 completed the program, 185 were assessed as not requiring it, 54 refused to be assessed, 27 were judged to be unsuitable, and 9 were judged as requiring treatment but did not receive it. More than half of the total sample was charged and 28% reconvicted of a new violent or sexual offense. After statistically controlling for the static variables that predicted reoffending, the treatment program was associated with increased sexual recidivism and had no effect on the composite dependent variable, charges for violent or sex offenses. Among treated offenders, clinical assessment of improvement was not significantly associated with recidivism.

These negative treatment findings are in accord with the results of a meta-analysis of recent treatment studies. Hall (1995) found no treatment effect for behaviorally oriented interventions (e.g., Hanson et al., 1993; Rice, Quinsey, & Harris, 1991), whereas hormonal (e.g., Fedoroff, Wisner-Carlson,

---

[2]A detailed program description can be found in Quinsey, Chaplin, Maguire, and Upfold (1987).

Dean, & Berlin, 1992) and cognitive–behavioral approaches (e.g., Hildebran & Pithers, 1992; Marshall & Barbaree, 1988) produced medium effect sizes. Unfortunately, the contrast between behavioral and hormonal treatment was confounded with the use of different kinds of control groups. None of the behavioral treatment program evaluations compared treated offenders with treatment refusers or dropouts, whereas all of the evaluations of hormonal treatments (that reported positive effects) and some of the cognitive–behavioral programs did. Although the overall meta-analysis yielded a small effect size for treatment, the effect size closely approximates 0 for studies that used a matching or randomization design (Rice & Harris, 1997a; Rice, Harris, & Quinsey, 2001).

There has been some recent convergence on the question of whether there has been scientifically adequate demonstration of the ability of treatment to cause reductions in recidivism among sex offenders. A comprehensive meta-analysis of psychological treatment supported by the Association for the Treatment of Sexual Abusers (Hanson et al., 2002) concluded that the most methodologically sound evaluations showed no salutary effect of treatment on recidivism. Such studies were few in number, however, and the authors also examined the results from weaker designs. A subset of such weaker studies ($k = 11$) was identified in which treatment was associated with lower recidivism. In almost all of these 11 studies, however, the apparent effect of treatment could be attributed to the use of noncomparable groups. That is, men who received treatment were compared with sex offenders at least some of whom were not offered it. Such groups can be assumed to include a significant proportion who would have refused or quit treatment had it been offered to them and, therefore, are not appropriate comparison or control groups for the evaluation of offender treatment (Rice & Harris, 2003a, 2003b). Although this subset of studies yielded results consistent with treatment being effective, neither the authors of the meta-analysis nor we regard the evidence as meeting the usual standards for scientific adequacy (Hanson et al., 2002; Rice & Harris, 2003a, 2003b). A rigorous randomized controlled evaluation of the most comprehensive cognitive–behavioral program for sex offenders yet mounted yielded no evidence of a positive effect (Marques, Wiederanders, Day, Nelson, & Ommeren, 2005).

There is almost no empirical literature available on the ability of either supervision or community notification (either as added components of treatment or separately) to reduce the recidivism of sex offenders (Lieb, 2004). A 1995 study in Washington State compared recidivism rates of sex offenders subject to notification with matched sex offenders not subject to notification. The two groups had similar rearrest rates, but the notification offenders were rearrested significantly faster, and the majority of the new sex offenses occurred in the same jurisdiction as the notifications (Schram & Milloy, 1995). Although there has been much concern about vigilantism against the offender and his family, the data to date suggest that such occurrences are rare and that physical injury is extremely rare. Matson and Lieb (1996) reported that harassment of offenders occurred with 3.5% of 942 notification offenders and that the most serious incidents were two cases of physical assault and one case of a residence being burned.

The literature on the effects of supervision among criminals in general suggests that although intensive supervision programs run the risk of "widening the net" by including low-risk offenders, supervision that is limited to offenders of moderate to high risk and that includes rehabilitation components can reduce the risk of recidivism (Gendreau, Cullen, & Bonta, 1994). Such supervision might include the use of technology, such as cellular electronic monitoring and drug testing. However, no data are available on the effectiveness of such measures for sex offenders or sexually violent predators specifically. Because pathological lying and use of deceit are among the distinguishing characteristics of antisocial personality disorder and psychopathy, great care obviously must be taken by those charged with supervision to ensure that conditions of supervision are being followed.

Overall, it seems clear that the field of sex offender treatment is changing without progressing. New therapies are adopted (e.g., building intimacy and self-esteem; Marshall et al., 2003), and others are recommended for abandonment (e.g., relapse prevention; Marshall et al., 2003). Yet these changes appear more as a series of strategic retreats (or forays into unknown territory, perhaps) than as advances based on a scientifically sound evaluation of past efforts (one of the current authors praised this latter approach to applied research at a recent conference, and an eminent authority labeled him a "plodder"). The unfortunate result of the current unsystematic approach to clinical practice is that the changes are not occasioned by advances in knowledge about treatment specifically and are not consilient (i.e., consistent with more established theory) with advances in evolutionary psychology and biology or the psychology of antisocial behavior more generally. Practice and science gradually but inexorably diverge, to the dismay of everyone. Because practitioners' implicit rules permitting change are different from those of scientists, the dismay cannot halt this divergence.

CONCLUSION

In summary, measures of antisociality, most notably the Revised Psychopathy Checklist (Hare, 1991); aspects of criminal history, such as the number of previous sex offenses and the age, gender, and relationship of previous victims; and phallometrically measured sexual deviance are reliably and strongly related to sexual and violent reoffending among rapists and child molesters. Offenders who are both psychopathic and sexually deviant are the most likely to recidivate. Thus, two classes of variables predict sexual reoffending: measures of antisociality (which also predict violent reoffending among both sex offenders and non–sex offenders) and sexual deviance (which predicts primarily sexual reoffending). We return to the prediction of sex offending in the next chapter.

The most important practical need for future research is the identification of interventions, including methods of supervision, that can reliably and appreciably reduce the likelihood of sex offender recidivism. The development of effective interventions may depend on the formulation of new theories of etiology and maintenance, as well as greater emphasis on earlier intervention (see also Borduin, Henggeler, Blaske, & Stein, 1990; Borduin et al., 1995).

III

DEVELOPMENT OF VIOLENCE PREDICTION INSTRUMENTS

8

ACTUARIAL PREDICTION
OF VIOLENCE

In this chapter, we present our work on the development of actuarial instruments for the prediction of violent recidivism. First, we describe our general approach, highlighting decisions we made in the construction phase and how those decisions affect the applicability of the instruments. Second, we present specific results for the Violence Risk Appraisal Guide (VRAG). Third, we describe some of our work aimed at developing special instruments for the prediction of violent recidivism in three selected subpopulations: fire setters, sex offenders, and men who are assaultive in institutions. Fourth, we describe all the research on the replications of our actuarial instruments for the appraisal of violence risk. Finally, we conclude with comments on application and improvement of actuarial assessment.

CONSTRUCTION

We used data from follow-up studies described in chapters 5 and 7. The following sections describe several features of that research that are especially relevant to constructing an actuarial instrument.

Dependent and Independent Variables

The construction of an actuarial tool most obviously requires an outcome variable to be predicted and a set of "predictor" variables at least potentially related to that outcome. Our choice of the outcome variable was straightforward—any new criminal charge for a violent offense. Of all possible outcomes, that was the one most consistent with the intent of the important legislation (e.g., the Dangerous Offender provisions and sentencing guidelines of the *Criminal Code of Canada*, the provisions pertaining to civil commitment of the Mental Health Act of Ontario) in our own jurisdictions. It has been asserted (e.g., Litwack, 2001) that other outcomes (severity of bodily injury caused by violent crime, the total number of violent crimes, or just violent crimes that occur immediately after release) are more important and predicted much differently than our dichotomous outcome. As described later in this chapter, our research shows this assertion to be incorrect; all of these outcomes are predicted by the same characteristics.

Deciding how to measure this dichotomous outcome was not straightforward; we had to decide what criminal charges constituted violence. Here we tried to be conservative. Thus, we included the obvious: homicide, attempted homicide, kidnapping, forcible confinement, wounding, assault causing bodily harm, and rape. We also included armed robbery but not "simple" robbery. In our jurisdiction, a charge of assault can be laid even without physical contact between perpetrator and victim (as can attempted murder). In fact, however, criminal charges for "noncontact" assault are extremely rare, so we counted assault as a violent offense. Moreover, some sexual assaults, particularly those toward children, are often called "nonviolent child molestation," presumably because the perpetrator relies on trust or guile rather than force and because no great physical harm comes to the victim. Perhaps reflecting our own values and those we ascribed to most citizens, we decided to count all sexual assaults involving physical contact as violent. We did not count as violent noncontact sexual offenses such as exhibitionism and voyeurism, and, where possible, we consulted victims' statements and investigating officers' reports when the nature of the charges was unclear.

We operationalized *violent recidivism* as criminal charges rather than convictions. At first glance it seems that our choice runs an inherent methodological risk in that not everyone who is charged is guilty. Certainly, using either charges or convictions would be an imperfect measure of actual violent conduct. In addition to wrongful arrest and conviction, not every violent crime is reported to the authorities, not all police investigations result in the identification of a perpetrator, not all identified perpetrators are apprehended and charged, and some guilty perpetrators are not convicted. Our research indicates, however, that the use of charges entails less measurement error than the use of convictions. This is, in a real sense, a design feature of modern criminal justice systems. The maxim that it is better for

10 guilty men to go free than to convict one innocent man means maximum accuracy of the outcome is of less concern than is avoiding a false positive error. A researcher can, and probably should, adopt a different priority—the most accurate available outcome variable. Although criminal charges is a better outcome measure than criminal convictions, we have found that the latter are predicted by the same predictors as the former, only a little less accurately.

Because most of the offenders we studied were institutionalized, it was important that we not miss subsequent violent behavior in other institutions for which the offender would have been charged had it occurred in the community. Consequently, we examined records of subsequent institutionalizations (both correctional and psychiatric) and recorded those violent acts that, in the judgment of research assistants, would have resulted in criminal charges had the incident occurred outside an institution. It was also important that we not count as nonviolent those offenders who had no opportunity to be violent because they were held in secure custody or had died. Consequently, official records were examined to eliminate those possibilities. Finally, for the purposes of constructing the VRAG, all violent recidivism data were reduced to a single dichotomous variable, so that what was predicted was at least one instance of violent recidivism.

On average, offenders had 81.5 ($SD = 60.6$) months of opportunity to recidivate. Time was computed for each offender from his first opportunity until the study end date (April 1988) or until his first violent offense (whichever occurred first). Time spent institutionalized for nonviolent offenses (or other reasons) was subtracted.

The independent or predictor variables numbered about 50 and reflected all those for which there was any existing empirical support in the prediction of either violence or criminal behavior generally. Because many of the offenders were mental patients, we also included variables related to rehospitalization in psychiatric populations. Finally, we included variables without much empirical support but to which clinicians attached importance (e.g., expressions of remorse, whether clinicians reported that the offender had "insight") or about which we were curious (e.g., rated physical attractiveness, height, weight, and birth order). In the end, the list of variables reflected the following categories:

- sociodemographic information (e.g., socioeconomic status, age, marital status, educational attainment, employment history),
- childhood problems (e.g., *Diagnostic and Statistical Manual of Mental Disorders* [third edition; *DSM–III*; American Psychiatric Association, 1980] List B antisocial personality disorder items, whether the offender's biological family remained intact until he was 16, criminal history of parents and siblings, ratings of elementary school maladjustment and childhood aggression),

- adult adjustment (e.g., psychiatric history, criminal record, living situation, alcohol use, social supports, ratings of adult aggressiveness),
- characteristics of the index offense (e.g., offender's relationship to the victim, injury to the victim, weapon used, sex of victim, motive for the offense), and
- psychological assessment variables obtained or obtainable during the early part of his first postindex offense admission (e.g., IQ, results on the Minnesota Multiphasic Personality Inventory [MMPI; Hathaway & McKinley, 1967], Level of Supervision Inventory [LSI; Motiuk, Bonta, & Andrews, 1986] items, DSM–III diagnosis coded from the clinical record, and Revised Psychopathy Checklist score [PCL–R; Hare, 1991] also coded from the clinical record).

Given our earlier comments about the weaknesses of the use of variables of convenience (mostly those routinely found in institutional files), readers may wonder about the variables used in the construction of the VRAG. Certainly, some of our predictor variables (e.g., age, marital status, educational attainment) were conveniently available from the records, but we included them because of their well-established empirical relationship with violent criminality. Many variables were certainly inconvenient and to our knowledge had never before been studied when coded from institutional records. Even though the clinical records maintained in our institution were unusually detailed and complete, the coding of many variables demanded careful application of other coding systems. For example, the use of the PCL–R manual, originally designed for semistructured interviews, with clinical records required many carefully drawn inferences. Similarly, we applied guidelines from the manual for the LSI, DSM–III diagnostic criteria, and a complex system for coding socioeconomic status (Blishen & McRoberts, 1976). As such, then, many of the variables we used as predictors were definitely not those routinely available from ordinary institutional records, but rather reflected the existing state of the science on the prediction of violence. Of course, we learned that independent variables do not predict violent recidivism just because they are difficult to code—for example, the complex and labor-intensive socioeconomic variable never performed better than a simple, convenient classification of occupation scored in minutes from admission forms.

Finally, we addressed the issue of the reliability with which variables were measured. As noted in the original reports, all variables entertained for inclusion in our actuarial instrument, as well as the outcome measures, met high standards for reliability (for continuous variables a Pearson correlation of at least .80, and for categorical variables a kappa of at least .70). Reviewers have commented that these reliability statistics reflect interrater agreement in the coding of documents; the reliability of the information within the files is unknown. Although true, this criticism is not an especially telling one; the clinical files were compiled long before the offenders had the opportunity to reoffend, and there is no conceivable way that the clinical material was biased by the much-later-occurring outcome. The demonstrated relationships between the earlier clinical observations and later outcomes establish the validity of the material. Once validity is established, the question of reliability is much less important.

Samples

We decided early that our goal was an actuarial instrument that predicted violent recidivism for serious offenders in general. We addressed the question of special instruments for special populations as a subsidiary question. It was clear that what was needed was one tool that would work for all offenders for whom the courts, clinicians, and parole officials were required to make predictive decisions. As such, offenders who had committed only minor offenses and citizens who had committed no offenses were not the population of interest. Those persons for whom decisions must usually be made are those who have already committed at least one serious antisocial act. Toward that end, therefore, we sought an otherwise heterogeneous sample of offenders who met this criterion. The offenders chosen were those from the two large studies of Oak Ridge patients described in chapter 5 (Rice, Harris, Lang, & Bell, 1990; Rice, Harris, & Cormier, 1992). This resulted in a sample of 685 men, of whom 618 had an opportunity to recidivate. There were few differences between these 618 offenders and the 67 men who did not get an opportunity to reoffend. The offenders with opportunity had less serious prior offenses (even though this variable was inversely related to the probability of violent recidivism), were less likely to have a female victim in a prior offense, and were more likely to have married. That there were so few differences and so few men without opportunity to recidivate gave little reason to expect either that offenders with opportunity were less dangerous than the other men or that they were not representative of their cohort. Not surprisingly, however, the released group included no mass murderers (men who had killed more than three people), although there were a few in the unreleased group. The groups were different, therefore, in this one possibly important way. We discuss this point more fully in chapter 9.

By definition, this sample had been mental patients at least once. Although this may appear to be a serious threat to the generalizability of our results, we believe the threat is not as great as might be supposed for the following reasons:

- The clinical and criminal histories of sex offenders in our samples did not differ systematically from those in a correctional institution (G. T. Harris, Rice, Quinsey, Chaplin, & Earls, 1992). Similarly, offenders in the maximum-security prison samples did not differ from offenders reported in the samples used to construct and validate the VRAG (T. Glover & Bernfeld, 1997; Loza & Dhaliwal, 1997).

- Although a significant minority of the offenders in our samples qualified for diagnoses of psychosis, many offenders in prison also qualify for the same diagnoses (Coté & Hodgins, 1990, 1992; Hodgins & Coté, 1990). The incidence of psychosis was higher in our samples, but, as noted in chapter 5, there is now evidence that among offender populations, the presence of psychosis does not increase the likelihood of violent recidivism (see also Bonta, Law, & Hanson, 1998).

- The Bonta et al. meta-analysis showed further that the predictors of violence among mentally disordered offenders were the same as those among offenders in general. Indeed, psychiatric variables and symptoms do not predict violence even in nonforensic mental patients; even in such populations, the predictors of violence are the same as those in offenders (Monahan et al., 2001).

- In predicting recidivism, the results for individual variables, especially those used in the actuarial instrument, have all been reported by at least one other independent investigator.

We took steps, described in the next section, to ensure that the actuarial instrument would work as well with mentally disordered offenders as with offenders free of serious mental disorder.

Analytic Strategy

Our goal was to construct an actuarial instrument to predict which offenders would commit at least one further act of violence given the opportunity. *Opportunity* was defined as having been released to the community, a minimum-security psychiatric hospital, or a halfway house. A few offenders committed violent acts even though they did not technically have the opportunity to do so (e.g., by escaping from a medium-security psychiatric facility and attacking a member of the public). Three offenders who committed such offenses were included as violent recidivists.

The first step in analysis was to examine, one at a time, the relationships between the study variables and dichotomous violent recidivism. Variables without a significant bivariate relationship were not considered in the construction of the actuarial instrument. A few variables were highly correlated with others (e.g., prior criminal charges and prior convictions for violent offenses); from such pairs, the variable with lower correlation with violent recidivism was dropped. The second step was to use least squares stepwise multiple regression to select variables that added independently to the prediction of violent recidivism. We tackled this task in a staged manner. Separate regression analyses were run for variables in sets corresponding to each of childhood history (e.g., *DSM–III* conduct disorder items, elementary school maladjustment rating), adult adjustment (e.g., criminal history, employment, marital status), index offense characteristics (e.g., sex of victims, victim injuries, alcohol involvement), and assessment results (e.g., IQ, LSI score, PCL–R score). In addition, we subdivided the offenders in several ways (e.g., randomly, treated vs. assessed only) and ran the setwise stepwise regression analyses on each subgroup separately. Only variables selected in a majority of subgroups were eligible for a final stepwise regression analysis that considered all variables that had survived thus far. Only variables selected by this final regression analysis were chosen for the actuarial instrument that we eventually called the Violence Risk Appraisal Guide.

As mentioned, this approach used ordinary least squares linear regression to select predictor variables and a single dichotomous dependent variable. Much sophistication is available in multivariate statistical modeling. Maximum likelihood methods of estimation make fewer parametric assumptions about the data. Other methods to discover predictive relationships also exist, such as neural networks and entropy minimax (Christensen, 1986). Event history analyses make use of not just the dichotomous outcome event, but also the length of time until the event occurred. There also is no necessary requirement that only linear relationships between independent and dependent variables would exist; nonlinear models and interactions among variables might also increase predictive accuracy.

However, several investigators have shown that for the kinds of data we were concerned with, these statistical "improvements" make very little difference. For example, it has been well demonstrated that unitary weights or even randomly chosen weights do almost as well (on cross-validation) as optimal regression weights (Grove & Meehl, 1996). Similarly, when we used unitary weights for the actuarial instrument, its performance was close to that of the VRAG described later in this chapter (G. T. Harris, Rice, & Quinsey, 1993). We also used Cox proportional hazards event history analyses to select predictor variables in a subsequent study (Rice & Harris, 1997a) and found very few differences in the final list of predictor variables (compared with the list chosen by linear regression). This is not to say that improvements in predictive accuracy are impossible using more sophisticated models, such as models including interactions and nonlinear effects. However, given the amount of measurement error that must exist in such follow-up studies and the level of accuracy already achieved when all items are reliably scored as specified, it seemed to us that the room for improvement must be small (although given the importance of the issues involved, small improvements can still be worthwhile). We return to the question of improving the actuarial instrument at the end of this chapter.

EXHIBIT 8.1
Violence Risk Appraisal Guide (VRAG) Variables and Pearson Correlations With Violent Recidivism

Item	Variable	r
12	Revised Psychopathy Checklist score	0.34
2	Elementary school maladjustment score	0.31
10	Meets *DSM–III* criteria for any personality disorder	0.26
7	Age at index offense	−0.26
1	Separation from either biological parent by age 16 (except for death of parent)	0.25
6	Failure on prior conditional release	0.24
5	Criminal history score for nonviolent offenses (using the Cormier–Lang system; see Appendix E, Table E.2)	0.20
4	Never married	0.18
11	Meets *DSM–III* criteria for schizophrenia	−0.17
8	Victim injury	−0.16
3	Alcohol problems score	0.13
9	Female victim	−0.11

Note. See Appendix A for the complete Violence Risk Appraisal Guide.

We used variable weights for the 12 predictor variables selected for the actuarial instrument. The 12 variables used in the actuarial instrument and their bivariate correlations with violent recidivism are shown in Exhibit 8.1. We wanted a weighting system that nonstatisticians would find easy to use and that would not require much computation on the part of users. We adopted a system described by Nuffield (1982) that calculates the weight on the basis of how different the individual is from the base rate. To calculate the weight for a predictor variable, a score of 1 is assigned (plus or minus, as appropriate) for each difference of 5 percentage points from the mean overall violent recidivism rate (in this case, 31%). For example, in the original construction study (G. T. Harris, Rice, & Quinsey, 1993), offenders who had married had a violent recidivism rate of 21%—two full 5% increments below the base rate (31%). Those who had not married had a violent recidivism rate of 38%—one 5% increment above the 31% base rate. Thus, in scoring the actuarial instrument, an offender who has married gets a score of –2, whereas an offender who has not married gets a score of +1. In this way, a score for an individual is derived by adding up weights variable by variable. We originally recommended that a 0 be scored for a missing variable—the estimate was then the base rate. Although we liked this continual reference to the base rate in determining weights and in scoring, the procedure of adding 0 for missing items meant that missing items had the effect of pushing the final score toward the overall mean (overestimating the "true" score for low-risk offenders and underestimating the "true" score for high-risk offenders). We have since developed a method for prorating missing items to minimize the effect of missing data. This method is presented in Exhibit 8.2.

VIOLENCE RISK APPRAISAL GUIDE (VRAG)

The performance of the VRAG is illustrated in Figure 8.1, which shows the rate of violent recidivism for the offenders used in the original construction. To illustrate the relationship, the offenders were divided into nine groups on the basis of their scores on the VRAG. Scores on the VRAG ranged from –26 to +36 (totals as high as +38 are possible), and the nine groups were formed by dividing the range of scores (63 points) into nine equal-sized categories (of 7 points each). Although the categories were composed of equal-sized steps on the VRAG, they did not contain equal numbers of offenders. The distribution of offenders' scores was much more normal shaped (also shown in Figure 3.1). As described in chapter 3, a preferable way to describe the accuracy of predictions is the relative operating characteristic (ROC), shown in Figure 8.2. The proportional area under the ROC was .76 (95% confidence interval = ± .03). As mentioned in chapter 3, the common language effect size (CLES) was also .76, meaning that if an offender were drawn randomly from each of the recidivist and nonrecidivist groups, there was a probability of .76 that the recidivist had the higher score on the VRAG. We also calculated another, more traditional measure of effect size, Cohen's d (Cohen, 1969), which is numerically and conceptually similar to the d' statistic from signal detection theory. For the data in Figures 8.1 and 8.2, $d = 1.06$. Cohen's rule of thumb defines a $d \geq .80$ as large.

Although the purpose of the VRAG was to predict which offenders would commit at least one violent reoffense, application of the instrument would have been difficult if certain conditions had obtained. Most important, it could have been that offenders who received high scores were more likely to commit a violent offense but were relatively unlikely to commit the most serious violent offenses. After all, the seriousness of prior offenses was inversely related to risk. To evaluate this possibility, we examined not only each offender's first violent offense (after release) but all violent reoffenses recorded for him. Using normative data (e.g., Wolfgang, Figlio, Tracy, & Singer, 1985), we computed a score reflecting the seriousness of each offender's total violent outcome (Rice & Harris, 1995b). This score was positively related to VRAG score ($r = .18$, $p < .01$). Similarly, we calculated the correlation between VRAG score and the length of opportunity available to the recidivist until the reoffense occurred ($r = -.13$, $p < .05$). Thus, VRAG score was positively related to the probability of at least one violent reoffense, to the severity of the reoffenses that occurred, and to the speed with which violent reoffenses occurred (see also G. T. Harris, Rice, & Cormier, 2002; G. T. Harris et al., 2003, where larger predictive effects were reported for seriousness and imminence). The VRAG performed exactly as one would have wished.

EXHIBIT 8.2
Substituting and Prorating Items on the VRAG and SORAG

In the first edition of this book, we recommended assigning a 0 for items that could not be scored because of lack of information. We made that recommendation because it was the most conservative strategy, and given the relatively small amount of data available on replications of the instruments, it seemed the most scientifically defensible thing to do. Also, in the first edition of the book we stated that as long as the Revised Psychopathy Checklist (PCL–R; Hare, 1991) or Childhood and Adolescent Taxon Scale (CATS; see Exhibit 8.4) was available, it was acceptable to score an offender on the VRAG with as many as four other items missing. After many more studies establishing the validity of the instruments and after seeing the effects of missing items on the overall predictive accuracy, we have now revised our recommendations about what to do when not all items of the VRAG or SORAG can be scored according to the scoring criteria as outlined in Appendixes A and B, respectively. We now recommend that an offender's score be considered valid on either the VRAG or the SORAG as long as not more than four items are missing or approximated.

SUBSTITUTING ITEMS

If an item cannot be scored because of missing information, it can occasionally be substituted by using another highly correlated alternative variable. In every case where a substitution is made, the Actuarial Risk Appraisal Report should state the substitution that was made. Acceptable substitutions are as follows:
- For the PCL–R: The CATS as described in Exhibit 8.4 or the PCL–SV (Hare, 1998) score prorated to a score out of 40. As described in Appendix D, it is acceptable to use the Psychopathy Checklist—Youth Version (PCL–YV; Forth, Kosson, & Hare, 2004) in place of the PCL–R for an offender who was under age 18 at the time of the index offense; this does not count as a substitution.
- For *DSM–III* diagnosis of schizophrenia: The *DSM–IV* or other *DSM* revision for diagnosis of schizophrenia.
- For *DSM–III* diagnosis of personality disorder: The *DSM–IV* or other *DSM* revision for diagnosis of personality disorder.
- For phallometric test results (on the SORAG):
  - Evidence from the clinical record sufficient to justify a diagnosis (on any version of the *DSM*) of pedophilia or sadism would score +1. Evidence that the offender does not qualify for such a diagnosis would be scored –1.
  - A score of 4 or 5 on the Screening Scale for Pedophilia Interests (SSPI; Seto, Harris, Rice, & Barbaree, 2004; Seto & Lalumière, 2001) can be used to score +1. A score of 1 or 2 should be scored –1. A score of 3 should be scored 0.

If one or more of these substitutions is available, they may be used in place of the item as defined in the scoring instructions in Appendix A for the VRAG and Appendix B for the SORAG.

PRORATING SCORES

An offender's prorated score for as many as four missing items is calculated as follows:
- Add up the score, counting only those items that were scored according to the scoring criteria as outlined in Appendix A for the VRAG and Appendix B for the SORAG (i.e., not counting items scored by using substitutions listed earlier in this chapter).
- If the score is positive, determine the highest possible positive score an offender could have obtained on those items. Then determine the proportion of possible positive points the offender obtained on those items. Next, determine the highest

possible number of positive points an offender could have obtained on the missing items. Multiply that number by the proportion of possible positive points obtained on the items actually scored. Then add the resulting number to the previously obtained total score to obtain a prorated score. If any items were substituted, that number now needs to be added to obtain a final total score.

- If the score obtained by adding the scores for those items scored according to the criteria as outlined in the Appendixes is negative, follow the same procedure as previously mentioned, but add a negative number to the previously obtained negative number.

For example, suppose an offender is scored on the VRAG. Items 10 (meets *DSM–III* criteria for any personality disorder) and 11 (meets *DSM–III* criteria for schizophrenia) are scored as –2 and –3 as substitutions obtained by using *DSM–IV* diagnoses. Items 9 and 12 are unavailable. The offender obtains a score of –2 on the first 8 items of the VRAG scored according to the scoring criteria outlined in Appendix A. The total possible negative score for these items is –14. Thus, the offender obtained 2/14, or .14, of the available negative points for the 8 items that could be scored according to the scoring criteria outlined in Appendix A. The available negative points for the missing items (9 and 12) is 6. Multiplying .14 times 6 gives .86. Thus, the offender's total score including prorating is –2 (score on the 8 items scored by the scoring criteria in Appendix A) plus –.86 (the addition for prorating) plus –5 (for the substituted items), or –7.86. This number can then be rounded to the nearest integer: –8.

In another example, suppose an offender is scored on the SORAG. Item 13 (phallometric test results) is substituted by using a *DSM–IV* diagnosis of pedophilia, for which the offender scores +1. Items 2 and 14 cannot be scored. The offender obtains a score of +10 on items 1, 3, 4, 5, 6, 7, 8, 9, 10, 11, and 12, all scored according to the scoring criteria outlined in Appendix B. The available positive points for these items is 33. Thus, the offender obtained 10/33, or .30 of the available positive points for the 11 items that could be scored according to the scoring criteria outlined in Appendix B. The available positive points for the missing items is 5 + 12 = 17. Multiplying .30 times 17 gives 5.2. Thus, the offender's total score including prorating is +10 (score on the 11 items that could be scored by the scoring criteria in Appendix B) plus 5.2 (the addition for prorating) plus 1 (for the substituted item), or 16.2. This number can then be rounded to the nearest integer: 16.

Psychometrics

Not surprisingly, the mean VRAG score was close to 0 (.91), with a standard deviation of 12.9. To estimate the interrater reliability of the VRAG, we used the independent coding by two trained raters for each of the 12 VRAG variables using 20 randomly selected offenders (G. T. Harris, Rice, & Quinsey, 1993). The 20 pairs of scores yielded a correlation coefficient of .90. We also calculated the standard error of measurement, which was 4.1, roughly half the size of one VRAG category. The 95% confidence intervals for each category showed that confidence tended to decrease slightly as scores increased (G. T. Harris, Rice, & Quinsey, 1993). Nevertheless, overlap among categories and confidence intervals was not great; risk levels were quite distinct from each other. Reliability was sufficiently high that we were confident that an individual's actual risk did not differ by much more than one category from his obtained score.

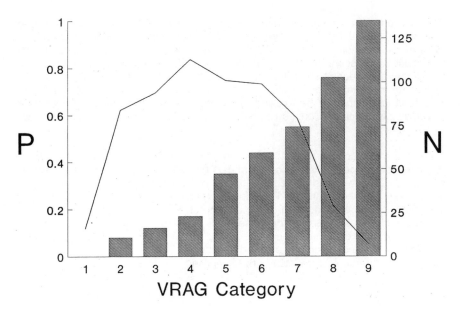

Figure 8.1. Probability of violent recidivism as a function of the score on the Violence Risk Appraisal Guide (VRAG).

Extension, Validation, and Replication

In this section, we present some of our own work extending and validating the VRAG. This and other research by the authors, as well as by other investigators, is summarized later in this chapter. We have demonstrated in new samples that the properties of the VRAG are consistent: Its mean and variance are similar to those reported in the construction sample, and the VRAG can be scored with very high interrater reliability ($r > .95$; G. T. Harris et al., 2002, 2003). We demonstrated that the accuracy of the VRAG, assessed using ROC statistics, did not depend on the base rate of violence (Rice & Harris, 1995b). We shortened the follow-up period by provisionally declaring any offender who recidivated after a shorter period of opportunity not to have reoffended. This yielded a mean follow-up of 3.5 years and a base rate of violent recidivism of 15%. We lowered the base rate by redefining violent recidivism to include only more serious violent offenses, resulting in a base rate of 29%.

We extended the length of the follow-up by adding sex offenders from another study (Quinsey, Rice, & Harris, 1995) and by collecting recidivism data again, resulting in a new study end date (January 1993). This yielded a mean follow-up of 10 years and a base rate of violent recidivism of 43%. We also raised the base rate by applying the VRAG only to a high-risk subpopulation—sex offenders—resulting in a base rate of 58%. In all of these cases, the performance of the VRAG in predicting violent recidivism was very similar. ROC areas ranged from .73 to .77.

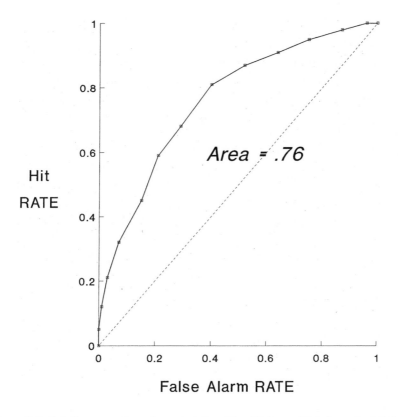

Hit RATE

False Alarm RATE

Area = .76

Figure 8.2. Relative operating characteristic of the Violence Risk Appraisal Guide.

Samples used in these investigations included the offenders who had been used in the construction of the VRAG. A true cross-validation would have entailed constructing the VRAG on a random sample from a larger group and then testing it on the offenders not selected for construction. We had used a similar approach to the selection of variables but had used the whole construction sample to derive weights. The fact that the choice of variable weights seems to make very little difference to predictive accuracy (Grove & Meehl, 1996) means that this approach nearly guaranteed successful cross-validation. Our first opportunity to replicate the VRAG on a different sample from the same population came from a study of sex offenders not used in construction of the VRAG (Rice & Harris, 1997a). The accuracy of the VRAG in predicting violent recidivism in this sample of 159 sex offenders was at least as good as that described previously—the ROC area was .77.

We have conducted other replications of the VRAG in new offender samples. In one (G. T. Harris et al., 2003), we examined the recidivism of 396 sex offenders referred from four different research sites (Oak Ridge, the local community served by our institution, and two federal penitentiaries, one a few hundred and the other a few thousand kilometers away). The predictive accuracy of the VRAG matched or exceeded that of other actuarial assessments designed specifically for sex offenders (the Rapid Risk Assessment for Sexual Offense Recidivism [RRASOR; Hanson, 1997] and Static–99 [Hanson & Thornton, 2000]) over a mean follow-up of approximately 5 years. The accuracy of VRAG predictions of violent recidivism corresponded to an ROC area of .73, with higher accuracy with rapists, invariant follow-up duration, reliable item scoring, and no missing items. When all of these conditions were met, VRAG scores yielded an ROC area of .84. VRAG scores also significantly predicted the speed of violent recidivism ($r = .33$), the severity of recidivistic offenses ($r = .21$), and the seriousness of injuries caused ($r = .35$). Scores on the RRASOR and Static–99 were unrelated to these latter two outcomes. We compared the obtained rates of violent recidivism with the norms provided in Appendix A and found no overall significant difference.

In the second replication, we conducted a prospective evaluation of the VRAG in a cohort of 347 male forensic patients where we scored the VRAG before patients were released (G. T. Harris et al., 2002). The accuracy of VRAG scores in predicting violent recidivism corresponded to an ROC area of .80 over a fixed 5-year follow-up. Again, there was no statistically significant difference between the obtained rates of violent recidivism and the VRAG norms (provided in Appendix A). VRAG scores were significantly more accurate in predicting recidivism than were averaged clinical judgments also gathered before release. The superiority of the VRAG was maintained over short follow-up periods (as brief as 6 months) and for very serious violent recidivism (homicide alone). Very few aspects of patients' prerelease clinical conditions (including clinical opinion) improved the accuracy obtained with the VRAG score. Even though they were unrelated to violent recidivism, VRAG scores outperformed clinical judgments among a small sample of released female patients.

An estimate of the effect size for the relationship between VRAG score and violent reoffending was computed from a study of eloping and reoffending among mentally disordered offenders (Quinsey, Coleman, Jones, & Altrows, 1997). The VRAG score difference between 19 offenders who committed an additional extremely serious offense and 50 comparison offenders was equivalent to about .7 of a standard deviation. Offenders were matched on age, diagnosis, and security level (all VRAG variables or likely to be related to VRAG variables and collectively responsible for roughly an additional .3 of a standard deviation). The total of roughly 1 standard deviation is the effect size we reported in the construction of the VRAG.

In another study, we applied the VRAG to nonforensic male and female psychiatric patients from the Monahan et al. (2001) MacArthur Risk Assessment Study (G. T. Harris, Rice, & Camilleri, 2004). A modified 10-item version of the VRAG exhibited a large effect (ROC area = .72) in predicting postdischarge serious violence reported by the patients and collaterals over both a 20-week and a 50-week follow-up. Accuracy was unrelated to patient sex, and VRAG scores significantly predicted the frequency and severity of postdischarge violence. As will be discussed later in this chapter, there have been a few other studies in which complete VRAG scores alone were compared either with clinical adjustments to actuarial VRAG scores (Hilton & Simmons, 2001) or with structured professional discretion schemes (e.g., Barbaree, Seto, Langton, & Peacock, 2001; Dempster, Hart, & Boer, 2002; Ducro, Claix, & Pham, 2002; Grann & Wedin, 2002; Polvi, 2001). In each case, VRAG scores yielded superior accuracy (all ROC areas $\geq$ .70) in the prediction of violent postrelease recidivism. A summary of all known evaluations of the VRAG follows later in this chapter, but the research described in this section settled for us in the affirmative the question of whether there is sufficient scientific evidence that the VRAG is a valid instrument for the assessment of violent recidivism.

APPLICATION OF THE VRAG

The research summarized in the preceding section gives us considerable confidence that the VRAG is ready for application to new cases. Most clinical statements about dangerousness, even if they were based on an accurate process, lack value because of the use of such vague terms as *moderate dangerousness* plus additional vagueness about exactly what is being predicted over what time period. As elucidated by others (Monahan & Steadman, 1996), many decisions are involved when making an actuarially based statement about an individual. The following factors are important: a statement about a specific numerical probability value (or range of values), the duration of time covered by the prediction, the operational definition of the outcome being predicted, and normative information about how this individual's risk score compares with others. In addition, we wanted to inform those using VRAG scores about how the individual scored on each VRAG variable as well as other variables known to be related to violent recidivism but not included in the VRAG. It seemed advisable further that a brief summary of the research on the construction of the VRAG be included. Finally, we wanted the VRAG scores to be presented in a format that was familiar to users (clinicians and criminal justice officials) and that used an absolute minimum of numerical characters.

An example of an Actuarial Risk Appraisal report is presented in Appendix J. Note that even such numbers as 82% are written out in words ("eighty-two percent"). To produce such a report, one needs an actuarial table (essentially Figure 8.1 in tabular form; also shown in Appendix A) and a tabulated frequency distribution for VRAG scores (Appendix C). Finally, we note that although forensic clinicians are generally unaccustomed to this form of risk assessment report and might even initially prefer something different (K. Heilbrun, O'Neill, Strohman, Bowman, & Phillipson, 2000), they can, without much training, get used to it and make proficient decisions using it (Hilton, Harris, Rawson, & Beach, 2005). We contend that the form of risk assessment report shown in Appendix J approaches "best practice" given current knowledge (Monahan & Steadman, 1996).

More recommendations about the appropriate use of actuarial predictions may be found in the last chapter, but we note here that the report in Appendix J does not address the ultimate question: Should the individual be released, receive an indeterminate sentence, be held in maximum security, receive intensive community supervision, or enter treatment? In our opinion, these decisions are not directly addressable with a risk appraisal. They can only be addressed with knowledge of the resources available (e.g., beds in secure custody, supervision resources, places in treatment) plus information about where the individual in question stands (in terms of risk) compared with other candidates for the same decisions (incarceration, supervision, or treatment). There is reason to believe that apportioning available resources (treatment, supervision, and custody) in relation to risk would increase public safety without changing expenditures on those resources. Actuarial methods could also be used to make less conservative decisions than those that tend to result from the exercise of clinical judgment. In this case, the same level of public safety could be achieved with less institutionalization, for example.

This view—that the VRAG score alone cannot render a final disposition without knowledge of available resources and where other offenders stand—has been criticized as an unhelpful intellectual exercise (e.g., "I know what to do with a hundred patients; I just don't know what to do with one!"). This struck us as odd (the usual complaint is that the VRAG does too much) and unfair. It seemed tantamount to criticizing Alfred Binet for measuring IQ because he failed to guarantee that schools achieved all their educational goals. Nevertheless, spurred by this critique, we began a new project to automate forensic disposition decisions in the same way that the VRAG automates risk assessments. We developed a formulaic process that outputs a disposition decision for each individual forensic patient given several inputs (e.g., recent misconducts of various kinds, lifetime violent offenses, resources available, and of course, VRAG score). Evaluation could involve comparing the violent recidivism of patients released by this formulaic system with that of the patients released by the existing tribunal system.

The issue of the appropriate index of predictive accuracy must be revisited. The accuracy of an actuarial instrument (or any decision-making system) needs to be considered in combination with the base rate of the outcome to be predicted. If the true base rate of violent recidivism in the population of interest were very low, say under 10% (and the costs of the two types of errors were equal), we have shown that it would not be worthwhile to use an actuarial tool, even with an instrument as accurate as the VRAG

(Rice & Harris, 1995b; see also Janus & Meehl, 1997). Instead, at a given accuracy and when the base rate is low enough, the optimal decision is to release everyone.

An important qualification to this statement (not considered by Janus & Meehl, 1997) concerns the relative costs of two types of errors: false positives (detaining a nondangerous person) and false negatives (releasing a dangerous one). The statement at the end of the previous paragraph (that the appropriate decision is to release everyone) presupposes that the costs of these two types of errors are equivalent. However, as discussed in chapter 3, how these costs are perceived undoubtedly depends on who is asked. Incarcerated offenders are likely to judge this differently than the victims of violent crime and their families. If the costs of false negatives were (or were perceived to be) much greater than the costs of false positives, there are populations (e.g., sexually deviant psychopathic sex offenders) where the base rate is so high that the optimal decision would be to detain everyone. Of course, the determination of relative costs is a (usually implicit) political question. Thus, our automated formula for disposition decisions uses available resources as a proxy for this value judgment about relative costs. That is, we assume that a government that funds few beds in secure custody has implicitly decided that the relative cost of false negatives is low, and a decision to fund many secure beds is a value decision to prefer false positives over false negatives. The Actuarial Risk Appraisal Report in Appendix J does not address ultimate questions, but on the basis of such assumptions, ultimate decisions may be automated in the same way that the VRAG automates risk assessment.

SPECIAL POPULATIONS

The samples used to develop the VRAG were deliberately selected to be as heterogeneous as possible (given that all offenders had already committed at least one serious criminal offense). Most experts on violent behavior would say, however, that violence has many idiosyncratic underlying causes. That is, the violence perpetrated by a predatory child molester has a different cause than the violence perpetrated by a persistently violent wife batterer. This kind of thinking has led us to ask whether special actuarial instruments for special subpopulations would perform better than the VRAG applied to the same population. This led, for example, to the development and cross-validation of a special actuarial instrument for the prediction of domestic violence (Hilton et al., 2004; see also Hilton & Harris, 2005), which estimates the probability that a man who has assaulted his female domestic partner will do so again. This actuarial tool, the Ontario Domestic Assault Risk Assessment (ODARA), which uses only information available to investigating police officers, has exhibited a large predictive effect for this particular outcome and predicts the frequency, severity, and latency of domestic assault recidivism (Hilton et al., 2004). In the following sections we consider three other special populations: fire setters, sex offenders, and men who are assaultive in institutions.

Fire Setters

Arson was not considered a violent offense in the research used to develop the VRAG. Nevertheless, as described in chapter 6, we have had a long-standing interest in fire setting as a special form of antisocial behavior. As described in that chapter, a follow-up study of fire setters identified quite different predictors of fire-related recidivism and violent recidivism (Rice & Harris, 1996). Only two variables (marital status and history of fire setting) predicted both. Some (e.g., childhood aggression, criminal history, whether the index offense victim was a stranger) predicted violent but not fire-setting recidivism. Some (e.g., low educational achievement, low IQ, having acted alone in committing the index offense, not having a concurrent criminal charge in the index offense) predicted fire setting but not violent recidivism. Indeed, two had opposite relationships with the two outcomes: Adult aggression and having a prior violent offense were positively related to violent recidivism but inversely related to fire-setting recidivism. On the basis of these results, we concluded that the VRAG was the optimal instrument for the prediction of violent recidivism even in this population. However, the prediction of fire-setting recidivism specifically would require a special instrument. Mainly out of theoretical interest, we followed the method described earlier in this chapter to construct an actuarial instrument to predict, among men who had already committed a fire-setting offense, which would commit further fire setting given the opportunity to do so.

The variables in the fire-setting prediction instrument (in decreasing order of the strength of their relationship) were age at the time of the first fire-setting behavior, the total number of fire-setting offenses, whether there was a childhood fire-setting problem, IQ, whether there were other criminal charges concurrent with the index fire, whether the offender had acted alone in setting the index fire, and the offender's aggression score. This last variable was particularly interesting because its relationship with fire-related recidivism was negative; more aggressive offenders were more likely to exhibit violent recidivism, but they were less likely to set future fires. The performance of the instrument is illustrated in Figure 8.3. Although the base rate of fire-setting recidivism was low (16%), the performance of the actuarial instrument in predicting that outcome matched that of the VRAG in predicting violent recidivism. The ROC area was .76, and d was 1.1.

This follow-up study did not examine the PCL–R, and in the absence of further validation, we are not ready to recommend clinical application. Nevertheless, this study leads to several conclusions about predicting recidivism in special populations. First, it provided some evidence that actuarial

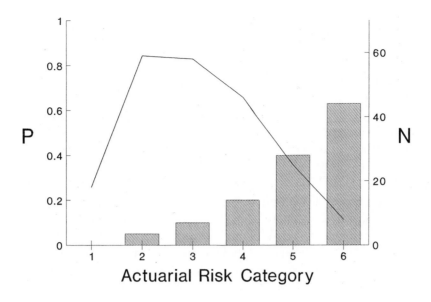

Figure 8.3. Probability of fire-setting recidivism as a function of the actuarial risk score.

instruments should be specialized according to the outcome to be predicted, perhaps more than it must be specialized according to the particular population to which they are applied. We do not know how well the VRAG would perform in populations we have never studied (e.g., adolescent offenders released under the age of 18). So far, however, the accuracy (in ROC terms) of the VRAG is quite robust. Second, we take these results to lend considerable support to our general method for the construction of actuarial instruments on the basis of detailed and corroborated official records, systematic coding of behavioral variables, selection of predictor variables using setwise multivariate analyses, and the Nuffield (1982) system to determine variable weights.

Third, although not a theory itself, an actuarial instrument lends itself to theoretical interpretations. In the case of fire setting, our results lent support to our general theory that fire setting is often an act of anger committed by an extremely unassertive individual. Fire setting is one of the few ways for a perpetrator to harm someone without having to be aggressive or assertive in a face-to-face confrontation, especially if the perpetrator is intellectually limited. The similarities, and especially the differences, in the optimal actuarial instruments for the prediction of violence and fire setting were quite consistent with this account (Rice & Harris, 1991, 1996).

Sex Offenders

We have done more work on the prediction of recidivism among sex offenders (child molesters and rapists) than among fire setters, and determining the definition of the outcome variable has been more complicated. It is clear that among sex offenders, many instances of sexual offending, even when they result in criminal charges, do not end up being registered as sex-related crimes. Sex offenders, when apprehended, often are charged with homicide, attempted murder, kidnapping, forcible confinement, assault, and even burglary. Police and prosecutors sometimes prefer laying charges for nonsexual violent offenses to avoid having to prove sexual motive and to spare witnesses from testifying to humiliating sexual activities. Sex offenders often agree to plead guilty to a criminal offense (sometimes even a more serious offense) without a sexual connotation to avoid being officially labeled as a sex offender. Often ambiguity can be resolved by examining police, witness, and victim statements, but there are probably also times when no one other than the offender knows that the offense was sexually motivated. Thus, unlike fire setting and violent offending, the outcomes of violent and sexual recidivism are much less distinct. It is probable that more measurement error is associated with sex offending than with violent offending generally. Consequently, in our research on the recidivism of sex offenders, we have used two primary definitions of recidivism: *Sexual recidivism* has been defined as any charge or conviction for an offense against another person that clearly involved sexual contact, and *violent recidivism* has been defined as any offense that involved violence, and as such, violent recidivism includes all sexual recidivism.

As discussed in chapter 7, we think there is good reason to appraise, for sex offenders, the risk of violence in general whether officially recorded as sexually motivated or not. It is hard for us to believe that the public would regard a nonsexual homicide or life-threatening assault as less worthy of protection and prevention than the most common forms of sexual assault. Of course, in a few jurisdictions the law requires an assessment of the likelihood of a sexually violent act (a violent *and* sexual assault), sometimes against a stranger. Even if sexual violence were the only form of violence one were concerned about, there is some evidence (Corbett, Patel, Erikson, & Friendship, 2003; Rice, Harris, Lang, & Cormier, 2005a) that, among sex offenders, violent recidivism (as usually measured) may be as good an index of that outcome as is sexual recidivism (as usually measured). Thus, even where commitment as a sexually violent person is the issue, violent recidivism might be just as appropriate an outcome for research and actuarial prediction.

Among sex offenders, there are some variables that predict violent (including all hands-on sexual) recidivism (e.g., psychopathy, criminal history, marital status), some that predict violence but not sexual recidivism (e.g., not having a female victim in the index offense), and some that predict sexual recidivism but not violence in general (prior sexual offenses). Indeed, among sex offenders, victim injury has been positively related to the probability of violent (including sexual) recidivism, whereas it is inversely related to the same outcome among offenders in general. It appears, then, that there may

EXHIBIT 8.3
Sex Offender Risk Appraisal Guide (SORAG) Variables

Item	Measure	
14	Revised Psychopathy Checklist score	.26
2	Elementary school maladjustment score	.18
1	Separation from either biological parent by age 16 (except for death of parent)	.19
5	Criminal history score for nonviolent offenses (using the Cormier–Lang system; see Appendix E, Table E.2)	.10
6	Criminal history score for violent offenses (using the Cormier–Lang system; see Appendix E, Table E.1)	.05
7	Number of convictions for previous sex offenses	.17
8	History of sex offenses against male children or adults	.13
4	Never married	.18
10	Age at index offense	−.18
9	Failure on prior conditional release	.13
13	Phallometrically determined sexual deviance	.14
11	Meets *DSM–III* criteria for any personality disorder	.25
12	Meets *DSM–III* criteria for schizophrenia	−.10
3	Alcohol problems score	.07

Note. See Appendix B for the complete Sex Offender Risk Appraisal Guide.

be a need for a special instrument for sex offenders. We have attempted to construct such a special sex offender instrument. The variables used in the Sex Offender Risk Appraisal Guide (SORAG) are shown in Exhibit 8.3, and the scoring details are shown in Appendix B. The variables were chosen using setwise multivariate methods in construction using sex offenders from four studies (Quinsey, Rice, & Harris, 1995; Rice & Harris, 1997a; Rice, Harris, & Quinsey, 1990; Rice, Quinsey, & Harris, 1991) with the goal to predict at least one reconviction for a violent or sexual offense. The SORAG's interrater reliability was equivalent (i.e., approximately .90) to that of the VRAG, and SORAG scores in the construction sample ranged from –17 to +42, with a mean of 8.90 (*SD* = 11.33, *SEM* = 3.58). Not surprisingly, given how it was constructed, the SORAG's accuracy in predicting sexual recidivism (recorded in police records) was lower than for the prediction of violent (including sexual) recidivism (ROC area in construction = .75). The best ROC area reported for its prediction of sexual recidivism was .77 (Dempster et al., 2002), but this was in the context of an ROC area of .88 for violent recidivism in the same study. It seems that the SORAG's predictive effect size is .05 to .15 lower (in terms of ROC area) for violent recidivism easily established to be sexually motivated than for violent recidivism overall.

There was a relatively narrow range of risk in the studies of sex offenders mentioned previously. That is, compared with our studies on violent recidivism in general, we had fewer low-risk offenders in our sex offender samples. Had we included more low-risk offenders, the predictive accuracy scores might have been higher. Implicit support for this supposition comes from an impressive meta-analysis of sex offender recidivism, using almost

30,000 offenders (Hanson & Bussière, 1998), that included a much higher proportion of low-risk offenders as indicated by the overall base rate. Hanson (1997) estimated the accuracy with which sexual recidivism could have been predicted by pooling variable intercorrelations. This estimate, using a very simple and short list of predictor variables, yielded an ROC area of .70 for sexual reconviction. In comparatively high-risk samples, the SORAG appears to outperform the RRASOR for both outcomes (G. T. Harris et al., 2003), whereas the RRASOR is a better predictor of sexual recidivism (as usually measured) in lower risk samples (Barbaree et al., 2001).

However, in thinking about whether our results agree in general with the whole field, we note the comment of Hunter and Schmidt (1990) that much study-to-study variation in the reported interrelationships among variables is probably illusory. They maintained that most apparent variations in estimates of population parameters are due to sampling error and that, until that parsimonious explanation is ruled out, investigators need not attempt to "explain" study-to-study variability by invoking putative moderators.

In the case of sex offenders, the empirical foundation provided by Hanson and Bussière's (1998) meta-analysis led us to use and recommend the SORAG for the prediction of violent and sexual recidivism among sex offenders. In our opinion, the construction method of the SORAG (incorporating several common variables) ensures that, at the very least, it equals the accuracy obtained with the VRAG and sometimes does better. There have been several tests of the SORAG that confirm these observations. Furthermore, one of these tests (G. T. Harris et al., 2003) indicated that rates of violent recidivism observed in a new replication sample of sex offenders did not significantly differ from those given as norms in Appendix B. That study also showed that (unlike actuarial tools specifically designed for violent recidivism registered as sexually motivated) the SORAG predicted the speed, severity, and frequency of recidivism.

Hanson and Bussière (1998; and subsequently Hanson & Morton-Bourgon, 2004) demonstrated the value in coding documentary variables, selecting on the basis of known outcomes (as opposed to clinical wisdom), and using multivariate combination to predict a dichotomous outcome. They reported that phallometrically determined sexual deviance was a strong predictor of sexual recidivism, supporting the centrality of sexual deviance in any explanation of sexual aggression; that measures of antisocial personality or psychopathy were also strong predictors of sexual recidivism, again lending support to the theoretical centrality of psychopathy as an explanatory construct; and that measures of psychological distress or psychopathology (exclusive of psychopathy) contribute little to the prediction of sexual aggression. These findings have implications for the treatment of sex offenders; they indicate a reduced likelihood that therapy aimed at psychological distress effectively alters the probability of recidivism. They also found no evidence that the provision of treatment (of any type) caused reductions in recidivism.

Another limitation on the ability of our actuarial instrument to predict sexual recidivism might have to do with our exclusive use of additive linear relationships in the construction of the SORAG. That is, as described in chapter 7, we have identified a multiplicative interaction between sexual deviance and psychopathy in predicting sexual recidivism: Sexually deviant psychopathic individuals were especially likely to exhibit sexual recidivism, whereas nonpsychopathic individuals and sexually nondeviant psychopathic individuals all exhibited much lower rates of sexual recidivism. We are pursuing improvements, described in the next section, to our actuarial instruments in current research aimed at improving test accuracy or efficiency or both.

Recently, many North American jurisdictions have passed laws providing for the indeterminate incarceration of "sexual predators." Generally, offenders designated as sexual predators have victimized strangers and have committed very frequent or very serious offenses. Elsewhere, we have provided extensive discussions of the issues involved in this type of legislation (Lieb, Quinsey, & Berliner, 1998; Rice & Harris, 1997b, 2002b); here, we outline the implications of our research for social policy in this area. Actuarial assessments of risk can be used to identify the most dangerous sex offenders. Criteria can be set in such a manner that very few false positives occur. It must be recognized, however, that actuarial instruments (or any other method) cannot identify all dangerous sex offenders without a high false positive rate.

Variations in specific legal criteria have an important effect on the precision with which actuarial instruments can accomplish the purpose of sexual predator laws. Laws concerned solely with sexual recidivism, as opposed to both violent and sexual reoffending, inevitably miss identifying more truly dangerous sex offenders as sexual predators than if they were concerned with both types of crime. This is because the likelihood of a new sexual offense is necessarily lower than the likelihood of a new sexual or violent offense. This is more true of rapists, who are at substantial risk to commit both sexual crimes and nonsexual violent crimes, than it is for child molesters, who show less criminal versatility. Our preliminary data suggest that the actual number of sexually motivated hands-on offenses that have been investigated by police and are recorded on the criminal record as a charge or conviction for some criminal offense is about one and a half times the number of offenses recorded on the criminal record as specifically sexual (Rice, Harris, Lang, & Cormier, 2005a). Finally, we believe there is more measurement error in identifying sexual crimes than in identifying sexual or violent crimes, because it is often difficult to determine whether a particular violent crime has a sexual component.

Sexual predator hearings can be applied at the time of the trial for the index offense. So far, there is no evidence that long-term predictive accuracy is increased by using information gathered after the beginning of the index offense sentence, as long as a thorough assessment has been conducted at sentencing, because current actuarial instruments use entirely or primarily static predictors. New information about offenses that occurred before the index offense is an exception to this recommendation and often leads to a changed level of actuarially determined risk. Occasionally, behavior during an inmate's sentence raises concerns about community safety. Typically, such behaviors include assaults, threats toward specific individuals, or more general threats, but they might also include postindex sex offenses. These concerns are probably best dealt with through less cumbersome and draconian methods than sexual predator statutes.

Institutional Violence

Elsewhere we have described our work on violence that occurs within institutions (Rice, Harris, Varney, & Quinsey, 1989). Most important for present purposes is our research on the characteristics of violent persons in institutions (G. T. Harris & Varney, 1986; Quinsey & Varney, 1977). That work identified several similarities between variables associated with committing assaults within the institution and those associated with engaging in violent recidivism on release. In both domains, only a small minority of individuals are responsible for the majority of the violence. In addition, youthfulness, poor social adjustment, a history of violent and antisocial behavior, not having committed a very serious index offense, not being an insanity acquittee, not having been married, and having poorer academic and vocational achievement were all associated with violent behavior in both domains. Similarly, having committed assaults inside the institution has been shown to predict violent recidivism (Rice et al., 1992; Rice, Quinsey, & Houghton, 1990), although not as strongly as many clinicians believe (Rice, Harris, & Quinsey, 1996).

More generally, we have reported a positive correlation between problems, symptoms, and deficits related to aggression, rule breaking, and noncompliance, on the one hand, and scores on the VRAG, on the other. Kroner and Mills (1997) reported that VRAG scores significantly predicted assaults and other disciplinary infractions in a maximum-security prison. As discussed later in this chapter, there have been several further demonstrations that VRAG scores predict violence that is entirely institutional or that includes violence that occurs in an institution (Doyle, Dolan, & McGovern, 2002; G. T. Harris et al., 2002; McBride, 1999; Nadeau, Nadeau, Smiley, & McHattie, 1999; Nicholls, Vincent, Whittemore, & Ogloff, 1999; Quinsey, Book, & Skilling, 2004). Thus, it is highly likely that the relationships between personal characteristics and subsequent violence captured by the VRAG are the same whether the violence occurs inside or outside an institution.

That said, however, interesting questions arise. Data about institutional violence reviewed in our earlier book (Rice et al., 1989) seem equivocal on some variables. For example, although violent crime in the community is very disproportionately committed by men, some studies suggest that among institutionalized persons, women are as violent as or more violent than men (e.g., Lam, McNiel, & Binder, 2000). Some studies suggest that institutional violence is disproportionately committed by psychotic patients (McNiel, Eisner, & Binder, 2000), whereas other studies suggest that personality (or character) disorder predicts violence by psychiatric patients (G. T. Harris & Varney, 1986; Monahan et al., 2001; Quinsey, Coleman, et al., 1997). In contrast to most of the empirical literature on the prediction of violence, one actuarial instrument for the prediction of inpatient violence (McNiel & Binder, 1994) assigns positive values for having been married. The answer to these apparent paradoxes probably lies in differential selection (Quinsey, 2000). For example, because women are incarcerated at much lower rates than men, those who do end up in institutions represent a much more highly selected population in several ways, most probably including predisposition to aggression.

Similarly, in some of our studies on institutional assaulters, the ways psychotic and nonpsychotic individuals were selected for admission undoubtedly varied, so that among psychotic patients, a history of violence within institutions was effectively a criterion for admission (G. T. Harris, 1989; Quinsey, 1981). At the time these studies of assaults were done at our institution, it is likely that psychotic and nonpsychotic patients received different types of staff supervision, so that psychotic patients had much less opportunity to commit undetected assaults. Finally, although rare (Rice & Harris, 1995a), some individuals are both psychotic (or mentally retarded) and personality disordered or psychopathic, and it might be that such rare individuals are especially likely to make up the small group of inmates who commit the vast majority of institutional assaults (see also Toch, 1982). Regardless of the direction of the association in any particular study, it appears that all researchers would agree that irrespective of diagnosis and symptoms, the personal characteristics most informative about subsequent institutional violence are history of antisocial behavior, substance abuse, treatment noncompliance, and especially interpersonal violence (R. L. Binder, 1999; McNiel, Gregory, Lam, Binder, & Sullivan, 2003; Monahan et al., 2001).

Why not use institutional behavior (e.g., misconduct, assaults, program attendance) to predict violent recidivism, instead of requiring the collection of preincarceration biographical material? So far, the empirical relationships between institutional behavior and recidivism, although reliable, are small. In addition, some of our research has shown that a significant subgroup of offenders represent a very high risk of violent recidivism but are very well behaved within the institution, at least as far as the impressions of clinicians are concerned (Rice et al., 1992, 1996). Thus, as a predictor of violent recidivism, institutional violence is likely to be specific but not sensitive; violent inmates are likely to be violent recidivists, but a good institutional record is not an indicator of low risk.

REDUNDANCY AND ROBUSTNESS OF THE VRAG

When applying the VRAG to individual cases, one wonders how well it performs for subsets of violent offenders. For example, how well it predicts the violent recidivism of men who were very young at the time of their index offenses is a common concern. Before tackling this general question, an important point should be addressed: To the extent that VRAG variables are used to define a subset, the expected effect size for the VRAG's predictions within that subset is lowered. To take the most obvious example, what is the accuracy of the VRAG among violent offenders who score less than 10 on the PCL–R? In this subgroup, the PCL–R cannot contribute to the VRAG (there would be no variability in VRAG scores for the PCL–R item), so that one should expect a smaller effect size. How much smaller would depend on the effect size for the VRAG variable or variables used to create a subgroup and on the intercorrelations (or redundancy) among the variables defining the subgroup and the rest of the variables.

In Table 8.1, we define several subgroups using VRAG variables and list the accuracy, expressed as ROC area, in predicting violent recidivism in the mean 10-year follow-up for the sample. The mean area for all subgroups was .73—significantly smaller than the original effect size of .75, but minimally so. Thus, the redundancy among the VRAG variables means that only small reductions in effect size occur even when three VRAG variables are used to create a subgroup (as in the last row of the table). Of course, it is also possible to define subgroups using non-VRAG variables. Here one might expect some decline in accuracy if the defining variables were highly correlated with VRAG items (e.g., whether the offender had been arrested under age 16), but one might not expect much change in VRAG accuracy within other subgroups (those based on socioeconomic status or physical attractiveness, for example). The only exception to that expectation was IQ; among those 128 offenders whose IQ was less than 85, the area for VRAG accuracy was .79 and the base rate of violent recidivism was .45. However, a separate study of closely supervised clients reported a similarly high base rate of violence but somewhat lower accuracy for a modified version of the VRAG (Quinsey, Book, & Skilling, 2004). Otherwise, it was not possible to identify a subgroup based on any variables where the VRAG's performance changed more than would be expected based on how the subgroup was defined in the first place.

TABLE 8.1
Accuracy of the VRAG With Offender Subpopulations

Subpopulation's characteristics at the time of the index offense	n	Area	Observed base rate[a]	Predicted base rate[b]
All offenders	799	.75	.43	.43
Murderers	277	.76	.30	.31
Psychotic offenders	222	.71	.26	.24
Teenagers	177	.70	.55	.58
Criminal history score using the Cormier–Lang system for all offenses = 0	265	.70	.26	.24
Criminal history score using the Cormier–Lang system for all offenses ≥ 10	195	.74	.50	.58
Insanity acquittees or received psychiatric treatment	432	.76	.40	.48
Convicted and never received psychiatric treatment	367	.73	.46	.48
Psychopath (≥ 25 on the PCL–R)	147	.73	.66	.64
Not a psychopath (< 10 on the PCL–R)	247	.72	.25	.24
Nonpsychopathic murderers who had been married	51	.72	.08	.10

Note. PCL–R = Revised Psychopathy Checklist (Hare, 1991).
[a]Observed base rate for subset. [b]Predicted base rate based on VRAG scores.

This matter of the redundancy inherent among the VRAG items leads to a more interesting question: What new variables would improve its accuracy? Of course, many more than the final dozen items had been considered for inclusion in the VRAG (see G. T. Harris, Rice, & Quinsey, 1993). Many bore a significant relationship with violent recidivism (e.g., prior psychiatric admissions, educational attainment, ever fired), and some of these were counterintuitive (e.g., severe emotional problems before the index offense were inversely related to violent recidivism). However, none of these were selected by the multivariate analyses because they did not significantly increase predictive accuracy beyond that achieved by the variables already included. Thus, in further testing, such variables as having procriminal attitudes and having a history of institutional escapes, although significantly correlated with violent recidivism, did not significantly add to the predictive accuracy, because such variables were also correlated with VRAG variables (criminal history and PCL–R score).

We were much more hopeful that new variables not considered for inclusion in the VRAG could improve predictive accuracy. Thus, in the study that extended the follow-up of the original VRAG construction sample (Rice & Harris, 1995b), we also coded some new variables (conduct disorder, learning disorder, pregnancy and birth difficulties, health problems in infancy, parental conflict, and childhood abuse). All of these were significantly correlated with violent recidivism, but to our surprise, none improved the accuracy already achieved by the VRAG. When we examined the relationships between each new variable and the VRAG, we could see why we could not seem to improve it: Conduct disorder, for example, was very highly correlated with PCL–R and *DSM–III* personality disorder. Similarly, being the victim of childhood psychological or physical abuse and neglect or witnessing familial abuse was positively correlated with violent recidivism but also highly correlated with PCL–R score, so that the abuse variables added nothing to the predictive accuracy of the VRAG.

It is interesting that the PCL–R items significantly correlated with these abuse variables were conning/manipulative, shallow affect, lack of realistic goals, glibness, and failure to accept responsibility for one's actions. Sexual abuse was correlated only with pathological lying. These results raised intriguing questions about which things caused what, but also meant that we were unable to find any static, historical variables that improved the accuracy of the VRAG. Indeed, we have also sought variables pertaining to patients' prerelease clinical presentation that would improve on VRAG score in predicting postrelease violent recidivism. Given the number of variables tested, we have been able to identify none that would not be expected on the basis of measurement error alone (G. T. Harris et al., 2002). Again, it is clear that for long-term (more than a year) assessment of risk, the personal characteristics that best predict violence are already captured by the VRAG.

In addition to their statistical implications about the VRAG, these results caused us to reconsider our advice (Webster, Harris, Rice, Cormier, & Quinsey, 1994) about the moderation of VRAG scores based on clinical judgment. If individual clinical adjustment of VRAG scores were to result in more accurate predictions, the clinician would need to sense which personal characteristics were actually related to subsequent violence (and the direction of that relationship), intuit which characteristics were not statistically redundant with existing actuarial predictors, and be able to measure them reliably. Needless to say, the literature on clinical judgment implies an extremely low likelihood that all these conditions can ever be met and, therefore, an extremely high probability that clinically adjusted VRAG predictions would be less accurate than unadjusted scores (Grove & Meehl, 1996).

As a final comment about redundancy, we are sometimes asked how much the VRAG adds to the predictive accuracy achieved by the PCL–R alone. In our largest follow-up sample (Rice & Harris, 1995b), the correlation between violent recidivism and PCL–R score alone was .33, and the addition of all the other 11 VRAG variables boosted the correlation to .45. It might seem that the gain from 11 variables was small (although the corresponding ROC area increase from .65 to .75 is a little more impressive). The converse situation puts things in perspective, however: The other 11 VRAG variables produced a correlation of .42 with violent recidivism, and the addition of PCL–R score boosted the correlation to .45. Obviously, this does not mean the PCL–R is unhelpful in predicting violent recidivism (any more than it means that the other 11 VRAG variables make a small contribution).

It means that the VRAG benefits from considerable redundancy among its predictor variables, and this redundancy is responsible for the robustness of its predictive accuracy in all the subgroups shown in Table 8.1.

Finally, are these studies on the prediction of recidivism really about prediction? If we merely examined the characteristics noted about some violent offenders after their violent offenses, we would have done a postdiction study. In most cases, however, the studies used a cohort of offenders who had been released long before we began to collect data. The information recorded in their clinical files, which we used to measure all predictor variables, was obtained long before the offender was released. In the study on the development of the VRAG (G. T. Harris, Rice, & Quinsey, 1993), for example, the offenders were institutionalized for an average of over 5 years after the compilation of the clinical material (used for coding all independent variables) before they even had the opportunity to recidivate. In addition, our coding of outcome variables was done by a different team of research assistants than the team who coded independent variables. Those who coded outcome were blind to scores on the independent variables, and those who coded the independent variables were blind to outcome. In every important sense, therefore, the follow-up studies used to construct and validate our actuarial instruments were truly predictive. Some additional questions and answers pertaining to technical issues involved in the development of the VRAG appear in Appendix D.

AN ANALYSIS OF REPLICATIONS OF THE VRAG AND SORAG

In this section we review recent follow-up research that has assessed the predictive accuracy of the VRAG and SORAG using a variety of new samples. The samples have been taken from forensic psychiatric, general psychiatric, convicted offender, and developmentally handicapped populations. Some of the studies have studied unselected groups of offenders, and some have focused on sex offenders. The outcomes examined have been violent (including sexual) recidivism, sexual recidivism alone, general recidivism, and institutional misbehaviors. A number of the studies include comparisons between the risk appraisal guides and other instruments. Lastly, we review recent research on dynamic risk and its implications for managing long-term risk. Overall, at the time of this writing (March 2005) we are aware of more than 35 replications or extensions of the VRAG and SORAG. Notwithstanding some problems in the implementation of the actuarial instruments, the median ROC area for the prediction of violent recidivism is .72.

Follow-Up Studies

The original VRAG construction sample consisted of men who were referred to a maximum-security psychiatric institution and later released from that institution as forensic psychiatric patients or from correctional institutions as former prison inmates. Studies of released forensic psychiatric patients and convicted offenders are replications, whereas studies of at-risk individuals from other populations are extensions. Even in replication studies, however, the samples sometimes differ in important ways from the original: Samples may be selected on various criteria (e.g., diagnosis or particular legal status) and may differ from the original sample in level of risk (the proportion of released individuals who commit a new offense) or in the nature of the outcome data that are collected (e.g., institutional charges as opposed to recidivism).

Before reviewing the follow-up literature, it may be useful to consider what effects variations in sample composition would be expected to produce. As we demonstrated earlier in this chapter by looking at accuracy statistics for subgroups of the original construction sample (e.g., murderers, schizophrenics), predictive accuracy, as measured by the ROC statistic, is often as high in subgroups as it is in the sample as a whole. There is a limit, however, imposed by the way the grouping is accomplished. To the degree that a subgroup is selected on VRAG variables or proxies thereof, the variance of the VRAG diminishes and predictive accuracy is expected to decline.

Variations in sample base rate will also have particular effects. Low base rate samples are, of course, expected to have low average VRAG scores. Some measures of predictive accuracy, notably those provided by an ROC analysis and the common language effect size, are unaffected by the base rate of the sample, although samples with very small absolute numbers of reoffenders will produce more variable study-to-study outcomes simply because of the law of small numbers. Other statistics pertaining to predictive accuracy, including relative improvement over chance, percent correct, and false positive rate, will be affected by the base rate because they express to varying degrees the consequences of adopting a particular decision rule in combination with a particular base rate. Other commonly used statistics, such as correlation coefficients, are measures of association that do not reflect accuracy directly because they are not tied to a particular selection ratio; they are, however, affected by the base rate.

Problems in scoring the VRAG such as missing data, errors in coding, and item misspecification (e.g., scoring an item in the wrong direction) lower measured predictive accuracy. The same applies for errors and omissions in recording the outcome data. Good scientific hygiene requires investigators to establish and report interrater agreement on the VRAG, even though most of the items (except the PCL–R) require little inference, to determine the degree to which predictive accuracy is attenuated by less-than-perfect interrater reliability (G. T. Harris & Rice, 2003).

The follow-up studies reviewed in this section have been divided into replications (follow-ups of unselected offenders drawn from forensic psychiatric and correctional populations and follow-ups of sex offenders) and extensions to special populations (wife assaulters, developmentally handicapped individuals, and general psychiatric patients). The narrative review that follows discusses only studies that have appeared since 1998. Details of all studies of which we are aware can be found at http://www.mhcp-research.com/ragreps.htm.

Forensic Psychiatric Patients

Pham (2002) compared the VRAG, PCL–R, and HCR–20 (Webster, Eaves, Douglas, & Wintrup, 1995) in a follow-up of 58 men released from a high-security prison or forensic psychiatric institution in Belgium. The ROC areas for all three instruments were very high (.85, .85, and .80, respectively).

Three studies have compared psychiatric symptoms or clinical judgment with the VRAG in the prediction of violent recidivism. As mentioned earlier in this chapter, G. T. Harris et al. (2002) followed 347 mentally disordered male offenders whose data were not used in the construction of the VRAG. Over the average follow-up time of 7 years (SD = 5.5 years), the VRAG (in which two items were approximated) significantly predicted violent recidivism with an ROC area of .76, the same as that reported for the construction sample. Psychotic symptoms and other indicators of psychological distress assessed while still hospitalized were unrelated to violent outcome. The only in-hospital behaviors that were significantly related to violent recidivism were selfishness, rule breaking, dishonesty, aggressive conduct, and antisocial attitudes.

Polvi (2001) found that the VRAG was more accurate than the HCR–20, the PCL–SV (Hare, 1998), and clinical judgment in a follow-up of 215 Ontario mentally disordered offenders examined before trial. Hilton and Simmons (2001) examined decisions made by clinicians and an autonomous review tribunal for maximum-security forensic patients. Detained and released patients did not differ in their VRAG scores. The best predictor of tribunal release decisions was the senior clinician's testimony before the board, but there was no significant association between the actuarial risk score and clinicians' opinions. Actuarial risk score, however, was significantly associated with criminal recidivism (r = .42), whereas clinical opinion was not.

There are also several studies of forensic psychiatric patients that have used modified versions of the VRAG, often because of the unavailability of information in the files. Douglas, Hart, Dempster, and Lyon (1999) found an ROC area of .60 in a study of maximum-security psychiatric patients. The level of predictive accuracy was not significantly different from that obtained with the PCL–R alone, presumably because approximations were used for most of the VRAG items. Grann, Belfrage, and Tengstroem (2000) similarly omitted or approximated a number of VRAG items in a follow-up of Swedish forensic patients using conviction data as the outcome. Despite a definition of violent reoffending different from that usually used (e.g., trespassing and arson were counted as violent, but attempted homicide was not), an ROC area of .68 was obtained. A similar level of accuracy was obtained for the historical items of the HCR–20. In a similar study, Tengstroem (2001) tested a variant of the VRAG (in which two items were not used, three items were estimated or modified, one item was apparently reverse scored, and one new item was apparently added) in a follow-up of Swedish male insanity acquittees. This study also found an ROC area of .68, similar to that obtained with the historical HCR–20 items.

In summary, the predictive accuracy of the VRAG in ROC terms has been found to range from .60 to .85 in the prediction of a variety of antisocial outcomes among forensic psychiatric patients. The VRAG performed as well as or better than a variety of other instruments and consistently better than clinical judgment. The VRAG appears to be somewhat robust in the face of missing data, misscored items, and variations in outcome criteria, although its predictive accuracy is reduced under these circumstances.

Convicted Offenders

Loza, Villeneuve, and Loza-Fanous (2002) reported a follow-up of 124 released federally sentenced Canadian male offenders (see also Loza & Loza-Fanous, 2001). Offenders were followed until they met any of the outcome criteria (any parole violation, any new charge, any new conviction, any return to custody, a violent offense, and any failure, including negative reports from parole supervisors). The base rates of general and violent recidivism were 43% and 13%, respectively. The VRAG correlated significantly ($r = .29$) with general recidivism but not significantly with violent recidivism. In addition, the VRAG was reported to overpredict violent recidivism. The performance of the VRAG in this study is difficult to interpret for a variety of reasons. First, because no interrater reliability data were reported and predictive accuracy was low, the extent to which this is a study of a particular rater or the characteristics of the VRAG cannot be ascertained. Second, the overprediction of violent recidivism was caused by the authors' use of 7-year actuarial tables in a follow-up with a maximum opportunity to reoffend of 2 years. Third, the procedure of dropping offenders from the study when they reached any of the follow-up criteria (some of which were very minor) means that violent offenses committed by an offender after he had reached lesser criteria were missed.

Kroner and Loza (2001) compared the predictive accuracy of the Self-Appraisal Questionnaire (Loza, Dhaliwal, Kroner, & Loza-Fanous, 2000) with the PCL–R, the General Statistical Information on Recidivism (SIR) Scale (Nuffield, 1982), and the VRAG in a sample of 78 federally sentenced male non–sex offenders. Predictive accuracy over a 20-month follow-up was over .70 for all measures in the prediction of general recidivism, but the ROC area for violent reoffending for the VRAG was .64.

Kroner and Mills (2001) compared the predictive accuracy of the PCL–R, the Level of Service Inventory—Revised (LSI–R; Andrews & Bonta, 2003a), the HCR–20, the VRAG, and a self-report measure, the Lifestyle Criminality Screening Form (Walters, White, & Denney, 1991) among federally sentenced Canadian male offenders. Official institutional charges were collected for 8 months following assessment for 97 offenders, and data on violent convictions (violence was defined to include robbery) were collected for an average of 760 days after release for 87 offenders. Thirty-six percent of the offenders were convicted of a major institutional misconduct. Thirteen percent of the sample committed a new violent offense in the follow-up period. The ROC areas for the institutional and violent recidivism outcomes were as follows: PCL–R, .58 and .56; LSI–R, .61 and .67; HCR–20, .57 and .62; VRAG, .63 and .60; and Lifestyle Criminality Screening Form, .53 and .62. There were no statistical differences in predictive accuracy among the instruments, but for reasons that are unclear, none of the instruments performed very well. Similarly, Mills, Jones, and Kroner (in press) studied 209 penitentiary inmates over a 3-year follow-up. How the VRAG was scored, the number of missing items, and reliability were not reported. VRAG scores significantly predicted violent recidivism with an ROC area of .67, and there was no significant difference between the observed rates for VRAG categories and VRAG norms (see Appendix A), goodness-of-fit chi-square ($df = 7$) = 11.08, ns.

Two studies of high-risk prison inmates have been reported. In the first of these, Nugent (2001) compared federal offenders who had been detained until the end of their sentences because they were judged to be at imminent risk of causing serious harm to others with nondetained high-risk offenders. Over a 2.4-year follow-up, 30% of the 123 released offenders were charged with a new violent or sexual offense. The common language effect size (equivalent to ROC area) in predicting charges for violent or sexual reoffending with the VRAG while controlling for time at risk was .68. In descending order of accuracy, the instruments used were the SIR Scale, the VRAG, the LSI, and the HCR–20; there were no significant differences among the instruments.

In the second study of high-risk prison inmates, A. J. J. Glover, Nicholson, Hemmati, Bernfeld, and Quinsey (2002) compared the accuracy of 10 risk measures in predicting violent recidivism among 106 federally sentenced male offenders who had been referred for assessments by parole officers concerned about the offenders' risk levels. Their concern turned out to be justified; 32% became violent recidivists in less than 2 years of opportunity to reoffend. Common language effect sizes in discriminating violent recidivists from other offenders were .73 for the SIR Scale and .72 for the VRAG. Effect sizes ranging from .58 to .68 were obtained for *DSM–IV* conduct disorder scored as a scale, the Violent Statistical Information on Recidivism—Revised (Nuffield, 1982), the Psychological Referral Screening Form (Serin,

EXHIBIT 8.4
Childhood and Adolescent Taxon Scale: Replacing the PCL–R

A. SCORING THE CHILDHOOD AND ADOLESCENT TAXON SCALE (CATS)

Assign one point for each of the following:
1. Elementary school maladjustment (at least a minor discipline or attendance problem)
2. Teenage alcohol problem
3. Childhood aggression problem (at least occasional minor physical assaults before age 15)
4. Childhood behavior problem before age 15
   Three or more of the *DSM–III* antisocial personality disorder criteria from List B (American Psychiatric Association, 1980, p. 320)
6. Ever suspended or expelled from school
7. Arrested under the age of 16
8. Parental alcoholism
9. Lived with both biological parents to age 16 (except for death of parent)—assign 1 point for *no.*

B. ASSIGNING PREDICTIVE WEIGHTS

Use the following weights instead of the weights for the PCL–R in computing VRAG scores (probability estimates for VRAG scores are the same as in the original instrument):
- CATS scores of 0 or 1: –3
- CATS scores of 2 or 3: 0
- CATS score of 4: +2
- CATS scores of 5 or more: +3

1991), the PCL–R total score and Factor 2, and the Childhood and Adolescent Taxon Scale (see Exhibit 8.4). Effect sizes of .58 and .51 were obtained with the *DSM–IV* antisocial personality disorder scored as a scale and PCL–R Factor 1, respectively.

Sex Offenders

We could find 10 studies of sex offenders in which the VRAG or SORAG, or both, were tested. Follow-up studies with samples of more than 200 offenders are commented on in this section.

As part of a study of dynamic prediction, Hanson and Harris (2000) compared the ability of a number of predictors to discriminate 208 sexual recidivists from 201 nonrecidivist sex offenders released from federal penitentiaries. The groups were matched on offense history, victim type, and jurisdiction. The three best discriminators among the static predictors were VRAG score ($r = .32$), IQ ($r = -.24$), and sexual deviance ($r = .24$). *Sexual deviance* was a composite of any juvenile sexual offense, any paraphilias, any stranger victims, and versatile (across gender and age) victim choice. Other significant discriminators included the SIR Scale and PCL–R scores. RRASOR score was not a significant predictor because the offenders were matched on several of its items.

Barbaree et al. (2001) followed 215 released federally sentenced sex offenders for 4.5 years. Twenty-four percent of the offenders committed a serious reoffense, and 9% committed a new sexual offense. The investigators concluded,

> Although they were not designed to predict general recidivism, the highest ROC area was obtained by the VRAG, followed closely by the SORAG and then the Static–99. Serious recidivism was also predicted by the VRAG, SORAG, RRASOR, and Static–99; the SORAG had the highest ROC area for this outcome (which it was designed to predict). The VRAG, SORAG, RRASOR, and Static–99 significantly predicted sexual recidivism; the RRASOR had the highest predictive accuracy for this outcome (which it was designed to predict). (pp. 507–508)

A similar follow-up study of 258 sex offenders was conducted by Nunes, Firestone, Bradford, Greenberg, and Broom (2002) comparing modified versions of the SORAG and the Static–99. Accuracy was somewhat lower for the SORAG than found by Barbaree et al., and no difference was found between the SORAG and the Static–99 in the prediction of violent or sexual recidivism.

As mentioned earlier in this chapter, G. T. Harris et al. (2003) compared the predictive accuracy of the VRAG, SORAG, RRASOR, and Static–99 in four samples of men who had sexually assaulted children or adult women (N = 396). The four samples comprised federally sentenced sex offenders from Ontario and from British Columbia, sex offenders assessed in a maximum-security psychiatric institution, and sex offenders under community correctional supervision. The average follow-up period was 5 years. Although all four instruments were successful in predicting violent (including sexual) recidivism, as well as recidivism known to be sexually motivated, ROC areas were consistently higher for the VRAG and the SORAG than for the RRASOR and the Static–99. For violent recidivism, the ROC areas were .73, .72, .56, and .63 for the four instruments, respectively. For sexual recidivism, the corresponding areas were .65, .66, .59, and .62. Predictive accuracy tended to be higher for child molesters than for rapists, especially for the Static–99 and the RRASOR.

Importantly, and in agreement with, past research (Gretton, McBride, Hare, O'Shaughnessy, & Kumka, 2001; Rice & Harris, 1997a), survival analyses revealed offenders who were high in both psychopathy and sexual deviance to be a uniquely high-risk group. The four instruments performed better when there were fewer missing items and when follow-up time was fixed, with an ROC area up to .84 for predicting violent or sexual recidivism (as usually measured) with the VRAG, for example, under such favorable conditions. That very high ROC areas were obtained under optimal conditions implies that the principal limitation on the accuracy of long-term prediction is error in the measurement of outcome (for a detailed discussion, see G. T. Harris & Rice, 2003).

Hanson and Morton-Bourgon (2004) conducted a recent meta-analysis of 94 follow-up studies of sex offenders, some of which included actuarial predictors. Although they are based on a relatively small number of studies, the results generally confirm the conclusions of our narrative review (which are based on substantially more studies) that the VRAG and the SORAG are superior to the Static–99 and the RRASOR in predicting violent and sexual recidivism of reoffenders (the outcome that the VRAG and the SORAG were designed to predict), and the reverse is true, although not to the same extent, for the forms of sexual recidivism that can easily be ascertained from police records alone (the outcome that the Static–99 and the RRASOR were designed to predict).

Special Populations

Incest Offenders

Rice and Harris (2002a) compared 82 men who had sexually offended against a daughter or stepdaughter with 102 men who sexually offended against only extrafamilial female victims. Men who offended against their daughters had less deviant sexual age preferences and were less likely to commit new violent and sexual offenses. However, the father–daughter offenders exhibited an average absolute phallometric preference for prepubertal children. Follow-up data were available for 114 offenders. Predictive accuracy was very good (e.g., the ROC for sexual recidivism was .81 for both the VRAG and the SORAG). The VRAG and the SORAG were as accurate for intrafamilial child molesters as for the other sex offenders, suggesting that the relatively low recidivism rate of incest offenders is a result of their low scores on the predictors included in the actuarial scales, not to any unique characteristics associated with incestuous offending.

Wife Assaulters

The VRAG has been shown to predict both violent recidivism generally and spousal battery specifically among male spousal batterers. Hilton, Harris, and Rice (2001) examined psychopathy, VRAG scores, and motives thought to be related to wife assault in predicting violent recidivism during an 83-month follow-up period among 80 men with a history of serious wife assault. Violent recidivism was lower among wife assaulters (24%) than among a larger sample of generally violent offenders (44%). Score on the PCL–R was a good predictor of subsequent violence ($r = .35$), and score on the VRAG was significantly better ($r = .42$), with an ROC area of .75. In a Swedish study, Grann and Wedin (2002) focused specifically on reconviction for spousal assault in a follow-up of 88 male spousal batterers who had had a court-ordered forensic assessment. During the 7-year follow-up, 28% were reconvicted of spousal assault. The SARA guide (Kropp, Hart, Webster, & Eaves, 1995) yielded a nonsignificant ROC area of .59 and the VRAG yielded an ROC area of .75 in a 1-year follow-up.

General Psychiatric Patients

G. T. Harris et al. (2004) examined the application of the VRAG to the prediction of self- or collateral-reported seriously violent acts of voluntary and civilly committed U.S. psychiatric patients of both sexes in a short (20-week) follow-up. The data for this study came from the MacArthur Violence Risk Assessment Study (Monahan et al., 2001). Modifications were made in the items of the VRAG to reflect the availability of information in the MacArthur Study and the nonforensic nature of the sample. In particular, items pertaining to the index offense were changed to the index admission. Two items, failure on a prior conditional release and most serious injury to a victim in the index offense, were dropped. The PCL–R was replaced with its 12-item screening version (Cooke, Michie, Hart, & Hare, 1999). Postdischarge outcome was assessed primarily by interviewing participants and collaterals using a modification of the Conflict Tactics Scale (Straus, 1979). The primary outcome measure in the modified VRAG analysis was the presence of at least one act of severe violence on the Conflict Tactics Scale. The overall ROC area for the sample was .72 (95% CI $\pm$ .04). The accuracy of the modified VRAG was unrelated to sex: ROC area = .71 (95% CI $\pm$ .06) for the 423 men and .73 (95% CI $\pm$ .06) for the 318 women, and the two sexes exhibited similar rates of violence, 27% and 23%, respectively.

Subsidiary analyses evaluated the association between modified VRAG score and continuous measures of the severity of violent outcome. Over the 20-week period, the modified VRAG significantly predicted the number of seriously violent incidents ($r = .33, p < .0001$), the total number of any violent incidents ($r = .34, p < .0001$), the most serious injury caused in a violent incident ($r = .25, p < .0001$), the total amount of injury caused in all violent incidents ($r = .24, p < .0001$), and the total Conflict Tactics Scale scores for all violent incidents ($r = .21, p < .0001$).

The results of this study provide the most compelling evidence of the robustness and generality of the VRAG to date. The VRAG worked at least as well for women as it did for men, predicted self- or collateral-reported violence in a very short follow-up period, and was successful among voluntary or civilly committed psychiatric patients released from U.S. psychiatric hospitals. As replications of the VRAG and SORAG accumulate, we post details of all studies at http://www.mhcp-research.com/ragreps.htm.

CONCLUSION

Why Is the VRAG Accurate?

A key reason behind the accuracy of the VRAG lies in the way independent variables were measured. Rather than depending on clinical impressions of abstract psychological concepts or on clinical interviews, the VRAG variables were measured with reference to detailed and complete psychosocial histories. As mentioned already, these histories more closely resemble biographies than autobiographies in their use of collateral sources and reliance on descriptions of actual behavior as opposed to self-report and hypothetical internal psychological states as explanations for behavior. As such, the accuracy of the VRAG further weakens any remaining support for the idea that clinical intuition (or indeed any variables relying on unstructured clinical judgment) is to be preferred for the accurate prediction of violent recidivism. In fact, the accuracy we have obtained for the VRAG, and especially the performance of file-based (as opposed to interview-based) PCL–R scores in prediction (higher than reported by most other users of the PCL–R), has led us to wonder about the use of the PCL–R for violence predictions. Given the defining properties of psychopathy (e.g., lying, conning, and glib speech), does the personal contact that occurs in an interview actually increase measurement error? Indeed, there is evidence that PCL–R scores based on documentary material might be better predictors of violent recidivism than PCL–R scores based on the more traditional file-plus-interview method (Walters, 2003; G. D. Walters, personal communication, October 29, 2003). A complete manual for the compilation of a psychosocial history (including information required for the scoring of the PCL–R according to its manual; Hare, 1991) to be used in risk appraisal is provided in Appendix F.

Second, as discussed in the section on Redundancy and Robustness of the VRAG, the VRAG contains considerable redundancy in its predictor variables.[1] Psychopathy is clearly an important source of violence, and the inclusion of a measure of psychopathy is one key to the VRAG's performance. Moreover, some other variables, in addition to making independent contributions, probably decrease the error associated with the measurement of psychopathy (*DSM–III* personality disorder, failure on conditional release, elementary school maladjustment, separation from parents, and perhaps the absence of *DSM–III*-defined schizophrenia). The VRAG variables, most of which have been reported to predict violence or crime by other investiga-

---

[1]We have also used a self-report version of this scale, the CATS–SR, to assess psychopathy in community samples (Belmore & Quinsey, 1994; Lalumière, Chalmers, Quinsey, & Seto, 1996; Lalumière & Quinsey, 1996; Seto, Khattar, Lalumière, & Quinsey, 1997; Seto, Lalumière, & Quinsey, 1995). Items are recoded to match the scoring of PCL–R items. Scores range from 0 to 16. Lalumière and Quinsey obtained significant correlations with Levenson's psychopathy scale (Levenson, Kiehl, & Fitzpatrick, 1995), sensation seeking, different measures of mating effort (i.e., promiscuity), and self-reported sexual aggression.

tors, undoubtedly provide independent predictive contributions and redundancy in measuring important factors in predicting violence. Just as in any other assessment, it is not the response to one stimulus (or to one item) that provides the most useful information, but rather the average response to a number of stimuli within a category (or to a number of items measuring the same thing). Including several items (compared with just one) per category invariably enhances reliability and hence validity. In predicting violent recidivism, the range and overlap in the VRAG variables are what guarantee both reliability and validity and also enhance the generalizability to new populations.

Improving the VRAG

As mentioned earlier, one could explore several avenues to improve the performance of the VRAG. An obvious first step is to explore ways to decrease measurement error for the independent and dependent variables already considered. That is, it is very unlikely that all the VRAG variables have been optimally measured. Perhaps a more detailed coding of childhood maladjustment (e.g., by coding *DSM–IV* conduct disorder items individually) would improve accuracy. This would of course result in larger effect sizes and, depending on how large, tend to decrease the apparent payoff available for pursuing other avenues. We have presented evidence that when the VRAG and SORAG are scored with high interrater reliability and without dropping or altering any items (and when there is no variance in the duration of the follow-up period), ROC areas approach .90 (G. T. Harris & Rice, 2003).

More substantive improvements in performance might be achieved by considering more than just linear predictive relationships. For example, we have already reported interactions between some other variables and PCL–R score: sexual deviance, age, and alcohol abuse. In the case of the latter two, the effects of the independent variables on violent recidivism were confined to nonpsychopaths. Psychopaths remained at much higher risk regardless of age or alcohol abuse history. In addition, in principle, nothing prevents predictive interactions from involving time at risk, such that, for example, the predictive strength of a variable would be much greater early in the follow-up period. Predictive interactions need not involve only two independent variables. It is clear that ordinary least squares regression and ROC analysis of dichotomous outcomes might not be up to this task; maximum likelihood event history analyses were designed for these purposes (Allison, 1984) but do not readily lend themselves to translation into ROC-type statistics.

This implies that the final number of VRAG variables need not necessarily be 12. It is entirely possible that 10 variables would perform just as well, and these are empirical questions that we are tackling in our current research. It also is possible that research might discover new variables to replace existing VRAG variables that would also improve accuracy. Perhaps other ways of assessing psychopathy (e.g., using childhood variables or psychoneurological variables) would more accurately identify members of the psychopathy class. We have already begun to examine this possibility.

On the basis of our taxometric work on the construct of psychopathy (described in chap. 11), we hypothesized that, at least for the purposes of predicting violent recidivism, psychopathic individuals could be identified more easily. That is, the use of the PCL–R requires scoring 20 separate items pertaining to an offender's whole life, but our analyses (G. T. Harris, Rice, & Quinsey, 1994) suggested that fewer variables reflecting antisocial and aggressive childhood conduct could discriminate the two classes (psychopaths and nonpsychopaths) just as efficiently. Consequently, we constructed, ex post facto, an eight-item scale to reflect these variables (the Childhood and Adolescent Taxon Scale, or CATS[2]; see Exhibit 8.4) and subjected the scale to the Nuffield system for determining item weights shown in Exhibit 8.4. Replacing the PCL–R in the VRAG with the CATS resulted in nearly identical performance ($d = 1.04$, ROC area = .75). There have been other replications of the predictive accuracy of the VRAG in which the PCL–R score was replaced by the CATS (Bartosh, Garby, Lewis, & Gray, 2003; Quinsey, Book, & Skilling, 2004).

The practical and theoretical significance of this result (if borne out in further research) is profound. First, from a practical point of view, actuarial appraisal of the risk of violent recidivism may be accomplished without reference to a restricted psychological test that, in some jurisdictions, requires a licensed professional for its administration. We would argue that a more appropriate approach to qualifying risk appraisers lies in the evaluation of the reliability and validity of predictions, irrespective of general professional certification.

Second, from a theoretical perspective, we would argue that a measure of psychopathy might be necessary for the prediction of violent recidivism but that the PCL–R might not be. That is, although the two PCL–R factors are highly correlated (with an r of approximately .50; see Harpur, Hakstian, & Hare, 1988), it has become clear that the second factor, reflecting a life history of exploitative, irresponsible, and antisocial conduct, is more responsible for the ability of the PCL–R to predict violence. The results suggesting that it may be possible to replace the entire PCL–R by variables pertaining only to antisocial childhood behavior imply that PCL–R Factor 1 items reflecting apparently adult personality (e.g., glibness, grandiosity, lying, conning, remorselessness, shallowness, callousness) do little or nothing to reduce uncertainty about the likelihood of violent recidivism. This is not to say that these characteristics are not associated with psychopathy, nor is it to say that these traits are not inherent to the phenomenon and even essential to its assessment for some purpose (e.g., suitability for treatment). It is also possible that our

---

[2]Preliminary data are very encouraging. For example, Quinsey, Skilling, and Rougier-Chapman (1997) found that VRAG scores calculated with the PCL–R correlated .975 with VRAG scores calculated with the CATS in a sample of 54 mentally disordered offenders.

record-based measurement was not the ideal way to measure these interpersonal behaviors (see Skilling, Harris, Rice, & Quinsey, 2002). This body of research does clearly imply that, irrespective of affective states and internal phenomena, the most informative variables about the risk of violence are those that pertain to overt aggression and antisociality, especially as a child.

Our current research is taking several paths to improving our actuarial instruments for predicting recidivism: seeking simpler and more accurate measures of independent variables (as in replacing PCL–R score with an improved version of the CATS), seeking new predictor variables based on theories about the etiologies of psychopathy and sexual deviance, incorporating interaction terms (as in using the interaction of psychopathy and sexual deviance in the prediction of sexual recidivism and the interactions between psychopathy and each of age and alcohol abuse history in the prediction of violent recidivism), and determining whether independent variables in interaction with opportunity time enhance prediction (necessitating the development of statistics analogous to ROCs based on event history analyses). We have previously recommended assigning the base rate value of 0 for missing VRAG variables, but we now recommend prorating (see Exhibit 8.2) because of its greater accuracy. We are also considering more sophisticated ways to measure outcome, including time at risk before recidivism, severity, and number of new violent offenses. The improved version of the VRAG is likely to comprise roughly the same number of variables and to use static historical variables but also to be easier to score.

All of these intriguing possibilities are part of our current and future investigations. There is a limit, however, to how much improvement in accuracy is possible. Given the unavoidable error in the measurement of violent crime, it is likely that there is a predictive "sound barrier," even though it is surely higher than the .40 correlation postulated by Menzies, Webster, and Sepejak (1985). The accuracy of the results of some diagnostic tests (concurrent rather than predictive validity) and of the prediction of certain weather phenomena (where there is essentially 0 outcome measurement error) of over .90 (in ROC terms) probably cannot be accomplished in the prediction of violent recidivism. Nevertheless, effect sizes already reported for the first-generation VRAG rival those reported in many fields (e.g., weather forecasting of violent storms; Swets, 1988).

Which Actuarial Instrument Should One Choose?

Webster et al. (1995) produced a professional discretion scheme to assist clinicians in making risk appraisals. The historical portion of the checklist was partly derived from the VRAG variables (e.g., psychopathy, substance abuse, personality disorder, supervision failure, early maladjustment) but also contained as risk factors items whose relationship to violent recidivism is actually negative or 0 in forensic and clinical populations (e.g., major mental illness, active symptoms of major mental illness; Bonta et al., 1998; Grann & Fazel, 2005; Monahan et al., 2001). The checklist was not actuarial—neither a follow-up study nor empirically measured relationships with outcome were used to construct it (although the selection of items was informed by the empirical literature available at the time). Its promulgation was accompanied by no data indicating reliability or validity, it does not render estimated likelihoods for any outcome, and there are no norms. The manual gives instructions about item coding but instructs clinicians not to compute a total score. Instead, one is to make a three-way classification (high, moderate, low) without necessarily resorting to the total; no guidelines or criteria for this judgment are provided. Citing no empirical evidence, it is asserted that the unguided summary clinical judgment (the professional discretion aspect) improves on totalling individual items (the structured aspect).

Thinking about developing other prediction devices raises an interesting hypothetical question: If several instruments were available, which would be the most important criteria in choosing one: the use of actuarial methods in construction, evidence of reliability, instrument validation, the size of the construction and validation samples, the number of independent validation studies, the availability of explicit scoring instructions and norms, the extent of the similarity between the construction and validation populations and the individuals to be evaluated, or the sheer size of the instruments' predictive effects? Of course, these considerations could be further complicated if different instruments varied in their administration costs and if instruments yielded ROCs that were lopsided in different ways so that some were generally more sensitive than specific and vice versa. The answer would also depend on the relative costs of the two types of decision errors. Of course, these questions become interesting only when different instruments produce very different estimates of the probability of violent recidivism for the same individuals. It is clear that if the candidate instruments used pretty much the same variables (and this seems inevitable for the foreseeable future, at least), their norms would be unable to give vastly differing estimates, and selection would therefore be rather straightforward.

In the end, these are fundamentally empirical matters that await the development of enough different actuarial instruments to make the questions more than moot. There have been some preliminary efforts and discussions of the issues (e.g., Bonta et al., 1998; Furr, 1993; Gardner, Lidz, Mulvey, & Shaw, 1996), but at this point the VRAG is the most widely validated actuarial assessment designed for the prediction of violence in general. A final matter concerns the combination of actuarial instruments: Can accuracy be improved further by using several actuarial assessment systems? So far, the answer to this last question is negative. No combination rule for a set of actuarial tools has yet demonstrated accuracy greater than that achieved by the most accurate tool in the set (Seto, 2005).

9

CRITICISMS OF
ACTUARIAL RISK ASSESSMENT

It says that 50% of individuals in this category reoffended violently. But I need to know which half this guy is in!

—Harried Forensic Clinician

In issuing a second edition of this book, we again call on clinicians to do risk appraisal in a new way—a way different from that in which most of us were trained. What we are advising is not the addition of actuarial methods to existing practice, but rather the replacement of existing practice with actuarial methods. This is a different view than we expressed a decade ago, when we advised the practice of adjusting actuarial estimates of risk by up to 10% when there were compelling circumstances to do so (Webster, Harris, Rice, Cormier, & Quinsey, 1994). In the preceding chapters, we explained why we no longer think this is justifiable: Actuarial methods are too good and clinical judgment is too poor to risk contaminating the former with the latter. Such advice leads to the empirically unjustified overuse of clinical overrides.

Hilton and Simmons (2001) showed that when clinicians anchor their estimates of risk with actuarial scores and then adjust their estimates with clinical opinion if required, decisions ended up being unrelated to actuarial scores. Similarly, when judges were given discretion to adjust empirically based federal sentencing guidelines, their judgments were unrelated to outcome and significantly worse than predictions based solely on empirically based guidelines (Krauss, 2004). As observed in other domains (Meehl, 1973), clinical overrides were overused. The compelling circumstances that tempt one to adjust an actuarial score should instead be considered separately in adjusting supervision and providing interventions to reduce risk.

Our advice to replace long-standing clinical practice with new methods has encountered resistance and skepticism. This is understandable and appropriate. The history of psychiatry, for example, is replete with uncritically accepted "treatments" that were actually useless or even harmful (Valenstein, 1986). However, medicine seems to have unnecessarily resisted beneficial improvements. When is there sufficient evidence of the right kind to warrant a change in practice? We argue that there is enough evidence of the right kind to warrant the replacement of clinical prediction of violence by actuarial instruments. That this conclusion is important and justified has been reached by others:

> All policymakers should know that a practitioner who claims not to need any statistical or experimental studies but relies solely on clinical experience as adequate justification, by that very claim is shown to be a nonscientifically minded person whose professional judgments are not to be trusted. . . . To say that the clinical–statistical issue is of little importance is preposterous. (Grove & Meehl, 1996, pp. 319–320)

Since the publication of the first edition of this book, we have heard fewer outright rejections[1] of actuarial methods and more assertions that actuarial results must be blended with clinical intuition. The blending takes different forms—adjusting actuarial scores with clinical opinion, overriding actuarial scores when clinical judgment says it is warranted, or structured professional discretion. This last approach generally comprises a list of risk factors gleaned from the literature or clinical experience with instructions to consider any factors that outweigh others on the list. Users then render a final judgment whether the person is at high, medium, or low risk (see Exhibit 9.1). No criteria for these judgments are given, no norms are provided, and no data on reliability or validity accompany the system. Assertions that the incorporation of clinical opinion improves predictive accuracy are, however, made, accompanied by some of the arguments against using actuarial methods alone. It is instructive, therefore, to examine these arguments in light of our research (also see G. T. Harris, 2003; Quinsey, Rice, & Harris, 2003). Anyone who advocates or uses actuarial risk appraisal probably encounters these arguments, and each has been presented as a serious basis for the rejection or blending of actuarial methods (the incredulous reader is re-

---

[1] It is interesting but not surprising that some objections are similar to objections to evolutionary theory. For example, arguments from personal incredulity used against evolution are similar to the fallacy of personal validation used to dismiss actuarial prediction. Dennett (1995) has written a sprightly defense of "Darwin's dangerous idea."

EXHIBIT 9.1
The Parable of the Lawn Mowers: Or, Why Structured Professional Judgment in Risk Appraisal Is an Idea Whose Time Has Gone

So I go to Canadian Tire and pick up a lawn mower for a couple of hundred bucks. Its operation is simple enough that, following the application of a little authoritarian persuasion, I can sit on my deck sipping mint juleps and increasing the likelihood of my developing a malignant melanoma while supervising my kids cutting the lawn.

One day a guy comes to my door with a very fancy-looking lawn mower. Now this lawn mower comes with a tweed or pinstripe dust cover and has a unique feature—the machine that drives the blades is mounted on springs! This feature means that the operator must apply exactly the right amount of downward pressure to cut all the grass at the same height. Difficult? You bet. Yet the operator has trained for 8 years (actually, mostly in the ethics and philosophy of lawn management) and is now a bored-certified and registered grass height consultant who can commit the controlled act of mowing as long as he uses tasteful fonts in his advertising. In addition, the operator has mowed courthouse and prison lawns all over North America and knows what he's doing.

So I ask him, "How high will you cut my grass?" He says, "How high would you like it? Very high, moderately high, or low?" "Well," I say, "How high is moderately high?" "Well, you know," he replies, ". . . moderate." "How many inches is moderate?" I say, betraying my age. He smiles secretively. "That all depends on how hard I'm pushing."

"So how consistent will 'moderate' be across my lawn? Right now, I cut it all at exactly 2 inches." "We've looked into this in great detail," he says. "Our spring-loaded model in the hands of a bored-certified operator is almost as consistent as the completely mechanical ones. And you know what?" he confides. "The newer models have shorter and stiffer springs that make them just as good as the mechanical models in some studies."

As prestigious and dynamic as this guy is, I can't afford to pay him to cut my lawn—he's just too expensive. However, for only 10 times the cost of my old lawn mower, he'll run a training workshop for me in the use of the spring-loaded machine in the privacy of my own backyard. I think there's a living to be made here, and I'm thinking about taking advantage of it. As for capital investment, all I have to do is add four springs to my old lawn mower.

Note. A French version of this parable, entitled "Il faut que je meau de lawne avec les petites spirales de fer" is permanently unavailable from the authors.

ferred to Price, 1997, and Litwack, 2001). Answers to less common and more technical questions are provided in Appendix D. The following sections state each argument in the first paragraph and then provide our response.

TWENTY ARGUMENTS AGAINST ACTUARIAL RISK APPRAISAL

Argument 1

This call for actuarial methods to replace existing practice is too radical. Other experts in the field are more conciliatory, advising a significant role for clinical intuition in finalizing an individual assessment. Imagine a discharge interview with a client with the lowest possible score on the Violence Risk Appraisal Guide (VRAG) who soberly says he is going home to stab his wife to death with a carving knife. Obviously, it's a big mistake not to override the VRAG here, and you wouldn't adhere to your own actuarial-only position. Actuarial instruments lead to ignoring unusual, individual characteristics related to recidivism. Your position abrogates professional responsibility. Professional standards require clinicians to exercise their judgment; they must not default to a mechanical process. The only reasonable, responsible, and ethical course is a compromise between strict actuarial assessment and unfettered professional discretion.

With respect to the issue of this type of compromise, Kendall (1949, quoted in Meehl, 1973) observed,

> A friend of mine once remarked to me that if some people asserted that the earth rotated from East to West and others that it rotated from West to East, there would always be a few well meaning citizens to suggest that perhaps there was something to be said for both sides and that maybe it did a little of one and a little of the other; or that the truth probably lay between the extremes and perhaps it did not rotate at all. (p. 229)

It is tough to get data on imaginary events, but as a matter of policy[2] (as opposed to risk assessment) it is wise to require the renunciation of violence from anyone considered for a less restrictive disposition. It is also reasonable to detain a threatening individual because credible threats are presumptively but sensibly considered a dynamic (i.e., short-term) risk factor. That is, we recommend that the estimate of long-term risk be unaltered and, when the threats stop, that the actuarially determined estimate of long-term risk have the same meaning and be treated the same way as if the threats had never occurred.

Such hypothetical instances, however, are so rare as to have never occurred in the careers of the most experienced forensic clinicians. Meehl (1973) best summarized the idea of overriding actuarial assessment with clinical judgments:

> [A] decision *policy* of this kind is almost certain to have a cost that exceeds its benefits. The research evidence strongly suggests that a policy of making such departures, except very sparingly, will result in the misclassifying of other cases that would have been correctly classified had such nonactuarial departures been forbidden; it also suggests that more of this second kind of misclassification will occur than will be compensated for by the improvement in the first kind. . . . That there are occasions when you should use your head instead of the formula is perfectly clear. But which occasions they are is most emphatically *not* clear. What *is* clear on the available empirical data is that these occasions are much rarer than most clinicians suppose. (pp. 234–235)

---

[2] Is this not clinical override? No. A strict policy requiring the renunciation of violence alters no long- (or short-) term appraisal of risk and permits no discretion in application.

Hilton and Simmons (2001) showed that clinicians and forensic decision makers advised to apply clinical overrides sparingly in using an actuarial instrument departed so often from the actuarial device that clinical advice and dispositions bore no relationship to actuarial scores (and produced demonstrably inferior decisions as a consequence).

In making this call to replace existing practice with actuarial methods, we refer to the means whereby assessments of violence risk are derived—the selection of relevant personal characteristics and other factors and their weighting and combination into a final assessment. In our view, no evidence supports (and much evidence contradicts) the application of informal or unaided judgments by clinicians in adjusting or overriding the actuarial score.

Quite clearly, considerable expertise and experience are required to evaluate important predictors of violent recidivism. It takes know-how to properly read a police rap sheet in order, for example, to correctly infer the number and type of offenses, whether any constituted a failure on conditional release, and the verdict and criminal sanction for each. More obviously, the assessment of psychopathy with the Revised Psychopathy Checklist (PCL–R; Hare, 1991) demands clinical skill. Training and practice with the PCL–R manual are obviously necessary to achieve acceptable interrater reliability. We also note that psychological assessment (and science, in general) advances primarily through formalization and "algorithmization." In any field, opportunities for the application of intuition inevitably decrease as knowledge about measurement improves. If it is true that some professional standards require the application of discretion of some unspecified character in appraising violence risk, we argue that the professional standards should be changed to proscribe the use of demonstrably suboptimal methods.

Argument 2

> This research was conducted in Penetanguishene (Ontario, or Canada, or North America) in a mental hospital (or prison, or maximum-security facility) on insane (or psychopathic, or deranged, or sadistic, or dangerous) offenders (or patients). It does not apply to the population with which I have to deal; at least, we do not know that it applies. Thus, I must use some form of clinical judgment.

There is no evidence that clinical judgment can counteract the problems of generalization across populations for actuarial measures (or anything else). The evidence is very strong that the VRAG and the Sex Offender Risk Appraisal Guide (SORAG) would work as well (as we reported for its construction) with those offenders who have committed relatively serious offenses (mostly offenses against persons) because of the way we used cross-validation in its construction. For example, we checked to ensure that it worked as well with those Oak Ridge patients who were only remanded for assessment and who were later convicted as with those who remained for psychiatric treatment. Thus, our group comprised men convicted and imprisoned for serious offenses as well as forensic patients. This group fairly represents serious offenders in North American and Western European correctional systems. In addition, as described in chapter 5, all of the variables in the actuarial instrument have been reported to predict violent or criminal recidivism by other investigators in other settings with other populations. We know of no evidence that serious violent crime is predicted by different variables in different ethnic groups. It is highly unlikely that the VRAG would not be correlated with recidivism in new samples.

In this connection, it is of interest that the base rate of the construction sample for violent and sexual recidivism is virtually identical to that found for a large sample of Canadian federal correctional inmates (Nuffield, 1982). Moreover, as discussed at length in chapter 8, we have demonstrated replications of our instrument (e.g., G. T. Harris, Rice, & Cormier, 2002; G. T. Harris et al., 2003; Rice & Harris, 1997a, 2002a; and a re-analysis of the data provided by Quinsey, Coleman, Jones, & Altrows, 1997), and further replications have been reported by independent investigators in several samples (e.g., Barbaree, Seto, Langton, & Peacock, 2001; Bartosh, Garby, Lewis, & Gray, 2003; Bélanger & Earls, 1996; Doyle, Dolan, & McGovern, 2002; Polvi, 2001; see www.mhcp-research.com/ragreps.htm for the most current research) from at least five different countries. When compared with any other violence prediction methods, we know of no demonstration that anything performed significantly better than the VRAG and the SORAG, and many findings that the VRAG and the SORAG performed better than other methods have been reported (see chap. 8). We have also demonstrated large predictive effects for the VRAG's performance in a mixed-sex sample of nonforensic psychiatric patients where the outcome was self-reported aggression over a 5-month follow-up (G. T. Harris, Rice, & Camilleri, 2004). These findings afford added confidence in the generalizability of the VRAG.

Altogether, this constitutes considerably greater support than that available for unaided clinical judgment, irrespective of the population. However, an actuarial instrument cannot be applied directly to a new population in a way that yields the same probability estimates as derived in populations in which it has been tested. For example, if police apprehension rates were greatly lower in a different jurisdiction, the probability estimates (based on the likelihood of a new criminal charge) would also be expected to be lower. It might be possible to provide guidelines to correct actuarial risk estimates for such factors as police arrest practices and differences in official definitions of criminal violence, but data from different jurisdictions would be required, and thus such corrected rates would themselves be actuarial estimates. We see no reason to suppose that difficulties in applying an actuarial assessment to new populations are remedied by the unguided application of clinical intuition (but see Monahan et al., 2001).

Even when the base rate for the offender population at hand cannot be known, the rank ordering of offenders according to risk would be the same as in the original population even if the absolute probability estimates were not. Moreover, as described elsewhere in this book, when an appropriate index (relative operating characteristic, or ROC) is used, the instrument's accuracy is the same, even though the base rate of violent recidivism is different. Also, as discussed in chapter 8, where the violent recidivism rates from different studies have been compared over similar follow-up times with those of the construction sample, observed rates for each category have not deviated significantly from the norms.

Argument 3

> This approach predicts only trivial violence. The research (on which the actuarial instrument is based) included violence in subsequent hospitalizations in the definition of violent recidivism. Violence in hospitals is partly produced by inappropriate staff behaviors. Predicting such staff conduct is impossible and unimportant. Many of the other violent offenses predicted by the actuarial instrument in the research were also unimportant—bar fights, for example. There is no point in engaging all that effort to predict and control such trivial violence.

In our research, *violent recidivism* was defined as any criminal charge for an offense against persons or any parole revocation or return to Oak Ridge for actions that would otherwise have resulted in a criminal charge for an offense against persons. Thus, violent recidivism included charges of murder, manslaughter, sexual assault, wounding, assault causing bodily harm, simple assault, kidnapping, armed robbery (but not simple robbery), pointing a firearm (but not simply uttering threats), and acts that could have resulted in such charges. The criteria for violent recidivism were the same whether the offense occurred inside or outside a hospital. The behaviors we defined as violent in our research are those regarded as violent by Canadian courts and citizens.

Very few "bar fights" are represented in the violent recidivism in our studies. Our research shows that the actuarial instrument predicted serious violence (e.g., more severe than a simple assault) just as well as violence in general (also see the discussion of the prediction of serious violence in Appendix D). In addition, as described in chapter 8, scores on the instrument were correlated with both the severity and the speed of violent recidivism in several studies (G. T. Harris et al., 2002, 2003, 2004). Even when the definition of violent recidivism was restricted to very serious violence or even just murder, the VRAG significantly predicted the outcome whereas clinical judgment did not. Despite suggestions to the contrary, there is evidence that structured professional discretion offers nothing to the specific prediction of severe and imminent violence alone (Douglas & Ogloff, 2003). Not all violent recidivism is detected by the criminal justice system, but it is very likely that our actuarial instruments identify as high risk those offenders who cause the most frequent and severe violence after release. The VRAG was designed to predict which offenders would commit at least one violent offense within a specified opportunity. In most cases, that also is the concern of decision makers.

The triviality of a violent act depends on one's point of view. A victim of assault undoubtedly regards it as more serious than does the perpetrator. The ultimate seriousness of crime is a value judgment and not a scientific issue, although scientists have studied opinions about crime severity in which perceptions depend on the physical harm done (Wolfgang, Figlio, Tracy, & Singer, 1985) and on how closely related the person doing the judging is to the victim (Quinsey, Lalumière, Querée, & McNaughton, 1999). It is also clear that some violent offenses everyone would regard as very serious cause no physical harm (e.g., many sexual assaults against children, kidnapping at knifepoint, attempted murder in which the assailant's gunshots miss their target). It is clear too that opinions change; many men who have assaulted their spouses presently serve sentences for behavior that 20 years ago would not have resulted even in criminal charges. It is difficult for a researcher to anticipate what will be regarded as serious violence in the future. Nevertheless, if a violent crime merits police investigation, prosecution, and conviction (as were almost all violent reoffenses in our research), surely it merits attempts to predict and prevent it.

In the G. T. Harris, Rice, and Quinsey (1993) study, there were 23 offenders (of the 191 violent recidivists) whose recidivism resulted in no criminal charges and only a return to Oak Ridge. For these offenders, in-hospital violence was the only basis on which they were classified as recidivists. Removing them from the study actually increased the accuracy of the VRAG from an effect size (Cohen's d) of 1.0 to 1.2. Similarly, leaving them in the study and reclassifying them as nonrecidivists (as one might do if such violence were so trivial as to be unworthy of prevention) produced the same increase in effect size. Most people would say that institutional staff and inmates are no less deserving of protection than other citizens. Moreover, ordinary citizens are sometimes the victims of violence by institutionalized individuals when an escape occurs.

Argument 4

A fair test of the actuarial–clinical competition has not been made. Research studies force clinical judgment into a domain where it is never exercised in ordinary practice. When clinicians assess risk using unaided judgment, they are actually rendering an opinion only about very serious violence over the very short term and not the trivial violence over long periods predicted by actuarial tools. Clinicians actually estimate the severity of violence should an incident occur and not whether a violent incident is likely. Clinicians almost always act as part of a multidisciplinary team in which members decline to give an opinion if they lack the requisite confidence.

In a "fair" comparison in which all these questionable assertions were granted, actuarial assessment was significantly better than unaided clinical judgment rendered under optimal conditions (G. T. Harris et al., 2002). That is, even for very short follow-up periods and for very serious violence, actuarial assessment outperformed the aggregate clinical judgments of multidisciplinary teams.

Argument 5

> This actuarial system is not accurate enough (has too many false positives, or has too low a correlation, or accounts for too small a proportion of the variance in the outcome) to be used to make such important decisions.

Many of the responses to this argument rest on the idea that the actuarial method under consideration actually is correlated with subsequent violent criminal behavior. In a sense, this entire book is about how we satisfied ourselves that this relationship actually existed. Unless a prediction device is perfectly accurate, however, it remains a somewhat open question as to how accurate is "accurate enough." Again, this book is about the fact that many investigators have not used appropriate indexes of accuracy and have been misled by the index they used. We have repeatedly demonstrated that the effect size we and others have obtained for our actuarial instruments under a variety of circumstances is large and certainly large enough to be useful under a wide range of base rates. As shown elsewhere, accuracy is lowered by poor implementation (inconsistent definition of outcome; unreliable scoring; changing, adding, or deleting items) and increased by reducing variance in the follow-up duration (G. T. Harris & Rice, 2003).

More important however, is that demonstrably less accurate methods of risk appraisal are widely used instead. Arguments about whether a proposed system is sufficiently accurate collapse when it is clear that clinicians, courts, and parole officials all use less accurate methods, and (almost) no one seriously proposes the elimination of all discretion from all disposition decisions for all serious offenders in all situations. Our point here is that when decisions about risk are made, some system is always in use. When none is specified, it can be assumed that informal, intuitive, unaided (clinical) judgment is being used. Under such circumstances, obviously, the only ethical course of action is to use the most accurate system available, even if it is imperfect.

Argument 6

More accurate systems to predict violent recidivism have already been developed. Using serotonin (or evoked potentials, or PET scans, or soft neurological signs, or insecure attachment) is the way to tell who's going to be violent. This actuarial method does not incorporate situational variables.

Other researchers have reported that several systems, such as the Level of Service Inventory (Andrews & Bonta, 2003a) and the General Statistical Information on Recidivism (SIR) Scale (Bonta, Harman, Hann, & Cormier, 1996), succeed quite well in predicting general criminal recidivism. However, the VRAG has shown more success than other actuarial instruments in the prediction of violence. Other variables not yet included in our research have been reported to predict violence. To date, however, no single variable or combination has been reported to exceed the level of accuracy (in construction and cross-validation) that we have attained. An important strength of the VRAG is that it uses several overlapping predictor variables independently; error in measuring one is compensated for by others.

Eventually, research is likely to result in improvements in our actuarial methods or in their replacement by better tools. Such improvements might include physiological measures (e.g., serotonin levels) or situational variables (e.g., postdischarge social supports). The research to allow such improvements has not yet been done, however. It is completely unknown whether these new variables would improve on predictions made by the VRAG. Whatever new results the future yields, the most accurate predictions will be made by actuarial instruments. Realistically, clinical judgment will not supersede statistical methods. Whether aided or "structured" clinical judgment (e.g., using checklists) improves on unstructured clinical judgment is unknown. The incremental value of structured professional discretion to actuarial, mechanical, or formulaic methods has not been demonstrated and is hard to study because structured discretion schemes cannot be accompanied by norms that can be evaluated.

Argument 7

Each human being is unique and cannot be reduced to a number. It is morally wrong to do so. It is illegal or unethical to use group data to make statements about individuals. It is inappropriate to use nomothetic knowledge or methods when ideographic knowledge and methods are called for.

How unique people are is largely an empirical question. Undoubtedly, humans exhibit great similarity in many aspects of their nature. In fact, one of the authors of this book believes that people are unique only in scientifically uninteresting ways. Although people also show many individual differences, research clearly shows that some personal characteristics are consistently and strongly associated with future violent behavior.

People routinely use information about groups to make individual decisions. Examples abound. The insurance industry is based on the idea that the risks for identifiable groups can be assessed and premiums determined accordingly. When buying a car, wise consumers ask about the repair record for cars of the same model. If a physician tells a person he or she has a serious disease, the person will want to know the prognosis—that is, what proportion of the group of people with the same disease recover from it. When a physician states, "You have an 80% chance of survival," it actually means, "Of all the people like you who get this disease, 80% survive." People want to know these statistics so that they can make wise decisions about what to do.

It is, in our opinion, quite appropriate, ethical, and legal to use group data in this way. In principle, the use of an actuarial instrument to assess risk of violent recidivism is based on exactly the same reasoning. Trying to treat an offender as though he were unique in any true sense (i.e., a member of no group whatsoever) would mean ignoring all relevant research.

For example, consider a man whose childhood was marked by family instability, poor school adjustment, and juvenile delinquency. Assume also that as an adult he never married and has a history of many property crimes, alcohol abuse, failure while on parole, and sexual assaults. Assume further that the offenses that brought him to the institution at the age of 20 were coercive sexual assaults against young boys; that, on examination, he exhibited deviant sexual interests according to phallometric testing; that his detailed psychosocial history showed that he met the *DSM–III* criteria for a personality disorder; and that he had a very high score on the PCL–R. Our research (and that of other investigators) shows that no matter what unique psychological qualities such a man might possess, he represents an extremely high risk of violent recidivism.

We used the phrase "unique *psychological* qualities" in the preceding sentence. Are there physical qualities that reduce the risk of violent recidivism? What if the offender had become blind? Although it makes some intuitive sense that blindness would lessen risk, there is little evidence about such "broken leg countervailings," as Grove and Meehl (1996, p. 307) called them.[3] In practice, we have found that some quite disabling conditions did not prevent violent recidivism. As an anecdotal example, a released Oak Ridge patient who scored in the highest VRAG category committed murder on his first day at risk, even though he was over 50 and had become legally blind.

[3]Grove and Meehl (1996) discussed the hypothetical man who rode his bicycle daily so that his behavior could be predicted with great accuracy except on the day he broke his leg. On that day, special unique knowledge about the broken leg was required to predict accurately. Grove and Meehl refuted claims (e.g., Monahan et al., 2001) that overriding actuarial scores must be permitted because clinicians do well in predicting violence in such special and unique situations, which can never be captured by actuarial methods.

Argument 8

> Heisenberg's Uncertainty Principle proved that the prediction of any-thing is impossible. Chaos theory reveals the impossibility of predicting complex phenomena, and what could be more complex than human behavior? In the very limited technical sense that actuarial assessments work, they have little or no practical value. Actuarial assessment has little or no use to most clinicians whose task is to manage violent offend-ers under supervision in the community. Thus, useful prediction is im-possible, and what is possible is irrelevant. This whole prediction of vio-lence idea ought to be abandoned in favor of the narrative management of violence.

Even if the "management of hazards" were the only worthwhile activ-ity, such an enterprise would also be impossible in a truly unpredictable uni-verse. Poor Heisenberg; no other discovery in physics has been so misunder-stood. It is clear that, compared with the behavior of organisms on Earth, different types of scientific statements are required for the "behavior" of very, very small things like quarks and for very, very big things like quasars. Heisenberg's principle was a statistical statement about the momentum and position of electrons, and not about phenomena at the level of human con-duct and criminal violence. In no sense did Heisenberg (nor does chaos theory) deny the existence of regularities in nature. Actuarial assessment is merely the most accurate available exploitation of some well-established regulari-ties in nature. No scientific finding, principle, or theory precludes this ex-ploitation.

Although chaos theory can be applied to phenomena of any size and does limit the predictability of many, the degree to which a given phenom-enon is chaotic must be demonstrated rather than assumed. As discussed in chapter 8, reliable scoring of the complete VRAG over invariant follow-up periods yields predictive effect sizes approaching .90 (expressed as ROC ar-eas, or approximately .70 expressed as point-biserial correlation coefficients with a 50% base rate). Given the inevitable error inherent in measuring violent recidivism, there is limited variance left to be accounted for by cha-otic processes. Casti (1990) provided an illuminating and accessible account of the actual and potential success of efforts in prediction across different areas of science.

Long-term risk (based on the actuarial selection and combination of static historical variables) is relevant to many aspects of the criminal justice system and the clinical practice of professionals who work there—bail, in-carceration, sentence, preventive detention, and parole, for example. At this point, however, little is known about what changes in which fluctuating per-sonal or situational characteristics actually predict subsequent violent crimi-nal behavior among adults in the community (see also Quinsey, Coleman, et al., 1997) after static measures have been incorporated. Even less is known about what interventions bring about changes in such characteristics that are then reflected in parallel changes in violent behavior. There is evidence that, in standard clinical practice, clinicians cannot make the accurate conditional probability estimates required by the idea that clinicians' primary role in preventing violence is about the judicious management of fluctuating hazards (Skeem, Mulvey, & Lidz, 2000). The idea of managing risk via the modulation of clinical interventions is appealing, but the empirical foundation for such an endeavor is unfortunately very scant as yet.

Lack of an empirical foundation notwithstanding, community management of offenders still requires periodic monitoring and adjustment of services and supervision conditions in response to fluctuations in measures thought to be related to the probability that an offense is imminent. This effort cannot be approached without a way to determine which offenders will be candidates for how much supervision. Determining which offenders are candidates clearly depends on long-term, actuarial risk, because it would be impossible to make such decisions on the basis of fluctuating characteristics.

Adjusting the intensity or components of supervision must partly depend on actuarially assessed risk also. Adjustments in supervision would have to depend on fluctuations in circumstances, but the best policy would permit this to occur within limits set by long-term, actuarial assessment. Thus, offenders at the high end of an actuarial risk scale (the specific level to be determined by the resources available) would have to demonstrate longer periods of greater stability and compliance before supervision conditions would be eased compared with offenders from the low end of the scale. "Tolerance" for noncompliance and supervision failure would (at least partly) be inversely associated with risk as assessed actuarially. Finally, actuarially assessed risk would, we propose, set limits on supervision relaxation—actuarially high-risk offenders, no matter how compliant, would, for example, never receive unannounced supervision visits less often than monthly. Forensic clinicians' management of the violence risk posed by offenders should heavily depend on actuarially assessed risk (G. T. Harris & Rice, 2003; but see K. L. Heilbrun, 1997).

Argument 9

Actuarial instruments are about selective incapacitation. We know that selective incapacitation cannot work on logical grounds—the only offenders who can accumulate a criminal history suggestive of high risk are so old that they have already "burned out." Meanwhile, essentially all serious violence is committed by youthful offenders who cannot yet have accumulated an antisocial history that would produce a high actuarial score, and they could not be considered for incapacitation.

Some violent acts are committed by persons, young or old, who have no previous history of violent or antisocial conduct. By definition, attempts to predict and prevent violent recidivism cannot affect the rates of violence committed by novices. The empirical relationship between youthfulness and violent crime is not that large, however. Although generally criminal conduct is very disproportionately exhibited by men between the ages of 15 and 25, violent crime does not show nearly so large a peak.

Considerable evidence demonstrates that a disproportionately large amount of violence is committed by a small group of persistently violent individuals whose history of aggression extends back through childhood (e.g., Loeber & Stouthamer-Loeber, 1998). A very large proportion of such individuals have, in fact, come to official attention before. It is quite possible for an individual to receive a high actuarial risk score even though he is young and does not already have an extensive documented history of violent crime. The opportunity to prevent violent crime exists when many offenders (youthful or not) come to official attention after having committed at least one serious crime and when scores on a prediction tool are, in fact, related to subsequent violence (regardless of whether the offenders who exhibit violent recidivism are young). That is the existing state of affairs.

Argument 10

> Violent crime is the product of social forces outside individuals' control. Poverty, unemployment, and discrimination cause violence. Predicting crime with personal characteristics cannot work. The use of most actuarial variables is immoral: Psychopathy is caused by ineffective or abusive parents, or it is genetic. Alcoholism is genetic, or it is caused by stress. No one chooses to be abandoned by his parents as a child. Not marrying might be an appropriate thing for a troubled person to do. No one has any control over his own age. Yet all these things are held against a person when an actuarial risk appraisal is completed. Holding someone responsible and blaming him for things over which he has no control is obviously immoral. Using actuarial instruments to prolong incarceration is punishing a person for something that has not even happened. Actuarial instruments, risk appraisal, and incapacitation promote imprisonment and institutionalization. Actuarial assessments are used to justify capital punishment. All of these constitute abusive, repressive, and cruel social control. Doing and using science to support an authoritarian Establishment is evil.

The role of discrimination, poverty, and unemployment in causing violence is unclear, but the available research indicates that these problems are unlikely to be the direct causes of much serious violent crime (Andrews & Bonta, 2003b). In any case, an actuarial instrument is not necessarily about the cause of violence. It is about reducing the uncertainty about who (among those who have already committed serious offenses) will commit new violence. It is possible that (but in practice irrelevant whether) poverty, discrimination, unemployment, and other social ills are among the causes of the relationships between actuarial scores and violent recidivism. A great strength of actuarial methods is that relationships can be used without knowing why they exist.

In our opinion, it is moral, and indeed desirable, for authorities to use information about those individuals who have already done harm to prevent further harm. The prevention of further victimization is, in our view, a moral good, and it is appropriate and desirable that science be used to aid in this enterprise. There is no moral necessity that the information used to prevent that further harm refer only to things the violent individual has had under his control (whatever *control* means in this context). Of course, even though it can rarely be verified, offenders often claim that the forces that drove them to violence were beyond their control—negligent parents, authoritarian school systems, past head injuries. Once an offender has committed a serious crime, society has a moral right (and obligation, we would argue) to prevent violence to future victims by using the most accurate methods available.

There is no logical or clinical necessity that living in an institution or under official supervision in the community be cruel, inhumane, or abusive. It is clearly possible to operate institutions and supervisory systems, even very secure ones, that are fair and humane (even though offenders might prefer to live elsewhere). Experience with actuarial systems, in general, shows that such systems result in decisions that are, on average, less restrictive. Actuarial systems (compared with clinical judgment) result in lower average estimates of dangerousness because the base rate is necessarily reflected, whereas clinicians tend to overestimate base rates (Quinsey, 1981). Many would argue that one does an offender no favors by inappropriately providing him an opportunity to commit further violence.

None of the present authors supports capital punishment. Although VRAG scores have been shown to predict institutional misconduct and aggression, it is not presently possible to provide actuarial estimates for the serious institutional violence that would occur if an offender spent the rest of his life in a maximum-security prison instead of being executed (the criterion for execution in some jurisdictions). That said, if (and it is a very big *if*) the state is to execute some convicted offenders and not others, some means will be found to select those to be killed. We strongly disagree with capital punishment, but would using actuarial assessment not at least ensure that such decisions were explicitly based on risk rather than, for example, ethnicity, social class, or IQ?

Argument 11

This research is fine for researchers, but I don't understand statistics and am uncomfortable using something I don't understand. I am unqualified to use actuarial methods, so I stick with what I do understand—my clinical judgment.

This objection presupposes that one understands the operation of one's own decision making. In fact, there is abundant evidence that people do not actually know how they make their own decisions—much of our own individual psychology is not open to introspection. For that reason alone, clinical judgment is even less justified than actuarial methods because no one knows how one's own clinical judgment works. Many studies have shown that clinicians are unable to produce predictions that are consistent with their own decision-making processes (see chap. 4). The comfort afforded by clinical judgment in its various forms is based largely on illusion.

One does not have to defend the statistics and research to use them. A health care professional can use the results of a computed tomography (CT) scan without fully understanding all of the complex technology. The scan is useful because it works: Research and experience have shown that structures apparent on CT scans are actually found when patients are examined surgically or on postmortem. By the same token, actuarial risk appraisals work—patients identified as high risk actually exhibit rates of violent recidivism much greater than those exhibited by patients identified as low risk.

Argument 12

> This system is based solely on a person's history and on only a very few aspects of his history, at that. Yes, I consider the actuarial score, but it is just one piece of information that I include in my more comprehensive assessment. I have to get to know him to incorporate all aspects of his clinical condition into my appraisal.

There is good evidence that clinicians' appraisals of patients' current clinical conditions are, at best, weakly related to recidivism. With regard to static, historical variables, more is not necessarily better. Our research shows that adding more historical predictors from the long list we have studied (even if they are actually related to recidivism) did not improve predictions because of the overlap among the predictors. Trying mentally to incorporate too many historical factors worsens decisions because of increased error and the likelihood that important predictors are overlooked. In a comparison, the VRAG outperformed clinical judgment rendered under the latter's optimal conditions. As mentioned in the response to Argument 11, many studies have shown that clinicians are unable to produce predictions consistent with their own decision-making processes, resulting in decisions that are even less accurate than clinicians could make if they were consistent. After extensive testing, it is clear that getting to know individuals, as in typical interviews, does not improve the prediction of behavior in any domain (e.g., violent recidivism, academic attainment, job performance) beyond what is possible without a personal interview by the decision maker. For example, a meta-analysis of the ability of the PCL–R to predict criminal recidivism showed that scoring on the basis of documentary material alone was at least as accurate as the more traditional scoring also using a clinical interview (Walters, 2003; G. D. Walters, personal communication, October 29, 2003).

Argument 13

> This actuarial instrument is great, and I incorporate it into my clinical judgment. I cannot use it for all patients, but I certainly apply it to the ones I know are high risk. On the basis of clinical experience, the instrument does not work nearly as well with psychotic individuals. Moreover, I have tried it on two serial murderers, and they did not get very high scores, so it obviously does not work in all cases.

The data do not support the tempering, modification, or adjusting of actuarial estimates with clinical opinion. To the extent that unaided clinical opinions are blended with actuarial estimates, the result is very, very likely to be less accurate than actuarial estimates alone. The VRAG might not yield a high score for a person who has already demonstrated that he is very dangerous by committing horrific crimes. That, however, is not the purpose of the VRAG. It is designed to predict violent recidivism, not postdict offenses. It is unknown how well the VRAG (or anything else) would predict the recidivism of mass or serial murderers or the assassins of American presidents. Such individuals are naturally rare, and even rarer are decisions to release them—in other words, the predictors of violent recidivism for such individuals are unknown.

How can it be decided a priori which offenders are high risk? If it is to be done using clinical judgment, this statement really constitutes an unfounded rejection of actuarial methods. So too does the statement that in someone's clinical experience the actuarial methods perform poorly (or well, for that matter). The only appropriate test of the validity of any method (actuarial or clinical) is a systematic empirical evaluation (for which two cases would obviously be insufficient). Clinical impressions of the accuracy of a prediction scheme are no more valid than clinical impressions of dangerousness.

Argument 14

> This patient says there are mistakes in his Actuarial Risk Appraisal Report. He says he had no behavior problems in school. He says he did not have a drinking problem. He says the score on the Psychopathy Checklist is wrong. He says he was innocent of those things for which he was arrested when he was younger. How am I going to prove any of this one way or the other? A clinical appraisal is preferable because it would not depend on "facts" to be argued about—it is based on impressions.

Without question, the quality of any decision can be only as good as the information on which it is based. Whether they use our actuarial risk appraisal system or not, clinicians, parole officials, and review boards make poor decisions with many errors when they rely on inaccurate, irrelevant, or vague information about offenders. The only way to improve decision making is with the right kind of accurate information about offenders. Because offenders' memories may err and because they have reason to minimize the seriousness of their past antisocial behavior, it is essential to gather independent information from families, schools, other institutions, and the police. Generally, in our experience, a lot of information is available in institutional files if one looks for it carefully. However information is obtained, it is obviously very important to clearly identify its ultimate source in compiling a psychosocial history. If only some information is available, a VRAG can be completed as long as at least eight variables are recorded. Of course, case historians and VRAG scorers can make mistakes. If anyone brings our attention to a possible error, we investigate as much as possible and issue a corrected report. In so doing, it would be unwise to assume that an offender's report was accurate in the face of evidence to the contrary.

In using past criminal charges (rather than convictions) in the instrument, one need not presume guilt. It merely turned out in our research studies that prior criminal charges were more strongly related to subsequent violent recidivism than were criminal convictions. Consequently, the actuarial instrument uses charges. By the same token, the procedures used in our research studies are those with demonstrated predictive validity. Consequently, those methods are to be used in actuarial risk appraisal.

Argument 15

> Actuarial methods must require consent. What if a patient refuses? I do not have the patient's consent to contact his family (or school, or former therapists, or former employer, or friends, or juvenile authorities) to compile his history. Because I do not necessarily need information from other sources to use my clinical judgment, I appraise risk with that—then I obviously do not need consent.

There are many technicalities and intricacies of the law. Here is our understanding of legalities in most jurisdictions: For individuals under the control of the criminal justice system—prisoners, probationers, parolees—no legal or ethical impediments prevent legally constituted authorities from gathering information relevant to risk. For hospital patients, the patient's permission is not required to *gather* information, although it often is required to *release* personal records. Thus, some institutions and agencies may require patients' permission before information is released. Other kinds of records (e.g., criminal records, some records from correctional institutions) are not protected, and in many cases no permission is required.

Legally, a clinician does not require a patient's permission to gather information from a patient's family. In many cases, of course, a clinician could not reveal private information without the patient's permission. Technically, a clinician could not even reveal that the patient was in hospital without permission. However, the disposition of a forensic patient is generally a matter of public record. In addition, some forensic patients are not mentally competent to make decisions, and family members are responsible for substitute decision making. Thus, if an informant knows, by whatever means, where the patient is, nothing need be revealed by gathering information. Finally, many patients would grant permission to other agencies for the release of information if asked. Most patients are likely to perceive that the collection of such information is in their best interest because clinicians, tribunals, and judges are likely to (and should) be very cautious in the face of inadequate data.

In our opinion, actuarial risk appraisals of the sort we describe in this book are based on the reorganization of existing documentary information. As such, they contain no material that is not (or should not be) already contained in the patient's institutional record. Thus, in our view, producing a risk appraisal based on material in the patient's record discloses no private information to the patient's hospital and its staff, and anyone who would have legal access to the record would also have legal access to VRAG reports. In contrast, the structured professional discretion schemes that we are aware of require an interview, making them problematic for use with nonconsenting or incapable individuals.

Argument 16

> For an expert opinion (including an expert opinion about violence risk) to be admissible, it must be based on a generally accepted scientific theory. Because you plainly admit that actuarial assessments are not a theory of violence, they are, by definition, inadmissible and irrelevant to forensic clinical practice.

What generally accepted scientific theory underlies expert testimony about matching latent fingerprints to those of a suspect, or a bullet from a victim to a confiscated firearm? There are two main senses of the term *theory*. The first, informal sense is that of an educated hunch or hypothesis—the notion that human fingerprints or bullet markings from a gun barrel might be unique. Extensive testing reveals that such hypotheses are, from a practical point of view, correct. A similar hypothesis is that certain aspects of past behavior predict subsequent violent behavior and that carefully measuring and selecting the former on the basis of incremental efficiency would usefully reduce uncertainty about the latter.

The second, formal sense of *Theory* is an elaborated and organized set of scientific principles that explain a set of phenomena. As such, a theory is anything but an educated hunch or hypothesis; it is as close to a law as one gets in science. It is correct to say that an actuarial assessment device itself is not a theory in either sense but is based on theory in both senses. As we illustrate in chapter 11, our actuarial assessments inform explanations of criminal and violent behavior and, we hope, are consilient with much generally accepted scientific theory about behavior and aggression. On the basis of these definitions of theory, the same kind of scientific theory underlies both ballistics evidence and the VRAG to assess violence risk.

What generally accepted scientific theory underlies "expert" testimony on the basis of unaided clinical judgment (or, for that matter, structured professional discretion or the clinical adjustment of an actuarial score)? Because it could be argued that there are no generally accepted scientific theories of criminal violence specifically, we suppose that the application of a strict version of such a premise could render all assessments (actuarial and clinical) inadmissible. Of course, this would mean that clinical judgment, by a judge, for example, instead of a clinician, would be the only permissible basis for decisions about violence risk—on the basis of all the evidence, a suboptimal and unacceptable result. The author of the opinion requiring that expert evidence be based on generally accepted scientific theory was probably not well informed about the definitions of *theory* and role of theory in developing forensic techniques. It is more appropriate to require that expert opinion be based on empirical evidence and generally accepted scientific methods.

Argument 17

> Risk is inherently contextual, because hazards arise in particular circumstances. Actuarial instruments based on static (and distal) factors can never, by definition, take into account dynamic fluctuations in contextual or proximal factors.

The role of dynamic variables in the assessment of violence risk has become seriously confused. We address this issue in chapter 2 and again at length in chapter 10. The argument here is trivially true but profoundly misleading in this context. Estimating the likelihood of the occurrence of at least one event of a particular kind over a long time (say, 6 months or more) into the future means estimating over changing and unspecifiable contexts. That is, given enough time, most things that can happen, do happen. Even more important, this remark ignores one of the principal theoretical interpretations of behavior genetics—people do much to make their own circumstances by actively choosing congenial environments (which then affect their own behavior).

Thus, the assertion that actuarial instruments based on static (and distal) factors can never take into account fluctuations in contextual or proximal factors is correct but misleading. All characteristics assessed before the follow-up period begins are static predictors in a data analytical sense, even though they may be changeable later. Estimates of long-term probabilities must ignore rapidly fluctuating factors, even if these are causes of the behavior of interest, precisely because these factors vary over the follow-up interval. Being frequently drunk prior to admission or being diagnosed as an alcoholic may function as a static predictor that can be used for long-term estimates of risk, but the fact that an offender might be drunk on a particular occasion during the follow-up interval of necessity makes a poor and even nonsensical long-term predictor. Changes in dynamic factors during the follow-up period can be used for short-term prediction (essentially to look at imminence) but do not compete with static predictors for variance in long-term prediction. As discussed in chapter 8, given the error inherent in measuring violent recidivism, there is little variance left once there is an optimally selected and scored actuarial assessment. Thus, there is only a modest amount of room for undiscovered (changeable) prerelease factors to improve the prediction of violence.

Argument 18

> Almost all my clients get actuarial scores indicating some non-zero likelihood of violent recidivism, and many probabilities seem high. However, most citizens would demand, as a criterion for parole or discharge, an estimated lifetime probability of violent recidivism close to the base rate for the general population. People do not realize that such a release criterion is impossible. If I conduct actuarial appraisals, I then have documents about the people I evaluate showing that virtually all of them (even the ones I say are low risk) are of a higher risk than the public would accept. When the inevitable violent reoffense occurs, my client's Actuarial Risk Appraisal Report will be used to hang me in the liability suit brought by the victims. Would it not be safer for me to avoid or destroy Actuarial Risk Appraisal Reports and use clinical judgment instead? That way, I could say that all my estimates of the risk of violent recidivism were less than 5%, say—who could prove they weren't?

In most North American jurisdictions, the law explicitly requires review boards and forensic clinicians to attend to the issue of public safety in making decisions. A clinician's best protection against liability is documentary evidence that the issue of public safety was explicitly addressed and that the clinician followed a systematic and clinically sensible approach to deal with identified risk factors. In our view, the approach described in this book provides excellent grounds for defense against any charges of negligence or liability should an "error" occur. From a legal standpoint, *negligence* means failure to meet professional standards, not simply making a factual error of judgment. It is very unlikely that the courts would regard deliberate ignorance of relevant information as an adequate defense against such charges, and deliberate ignorance could constitute negligence in and of itself.

Argument 19

> Before I can accept this (admit it into evidence), I need proof that others (judges, clinicians) have accepted it. Until then, I will rely on clinical judgment.

Other expert witnesses and legal scholars have accepted the VRAG and the use of actuarial instruments in general. According to Monahan (1995), "for use with male patients with histories of serious violence, the [VRAG] is so far superior to anything previously available that not to seriously consider its use . . . would be a difficult choice to justify" (p. 447). Grove and Meehl (1996) discussed the superiority of actuarial over clinical prediction in a large number of situations, including release on parole, and in psychiatric decision making: "To use the less efficient of two prediction procedures in dealing with such matters is not only unscientific and irrational, it is unethical" (p. 320). Grisso and Appelbaum (1993) argued in favor of the ethical propriety of risk assessments by focusing "on that type that was most easily defended: testimony based on actuarial indicators offering probability estimates of future violence for persons manifesting various measurable characteristics" (p. 483). The actuarial–clinical judgment debate has been called a "dead horse" (Monahan et al., 2001). The VRAG is widely used, and a VRAG score has been admitted as evidence in many legal proceedings.

Argument 20

> This actuarial approach both lowers my status and makes my job more difficult. Before, I could conduct interesting interviews with patients, make a few notes, and comfortably write a report on the basis of my wisdom and experience. Now you want me to engage in the tedious and time-consuming process of gathering detailed biographical information from reluctant family members, rule-bound bureaucrats, and overworked public servants, none of whom appreciate the importance of my work. Then the credit for producing the prediction goes to an actuarial table. Don't disparage my clinical acumen, and at least grant me the right to adjust and modify the actuarial score when I need to.

One might have some sympathy for this position. That sympathy is not relevant, however, to the decision about how risk ought to be appraised. In another domain, performing surgery might confer greater status, income, and personal satisfaction to practitioners than recommending physiotherapy, prescribing medication, or changing patients' diets. That fact could not (and should not) make it morally acceptable for a surgeon to operate in the knowledge that the surgery leads to poorer patient outcomes. The modern concept of "profession" obliges professionals to place the welfare of clients and the public ahead of their self-interest. We acknowledge this is not always easy to do.

PRESENTING EVIDENCE ABOUT ACTUARIAL RISK APPRAISAL

Over the past several years, members of our research team have had many opportunities to present evidence about actuarial risk appraisal in court and before boards of review. This experience of testifying can be a daunting one. Although scientists are accustomed to a certain amount of debate and controversy, most would shy away from the nakedly adversarial forum represented by the criminal trial process. As noted in the introduction to this chapter, skepticism is warranted whenever someone presents findings that purport to demand a change in clinical practice. Most of the arguments and responses we have addressed in this chapter are based on a sincere desire to learn more and not make mistakes. Among the 20 arguments, one can find, of course, some honest misconceptions and some unabashed self-interest. Nevertheless, in academic discourse, the implicit ground rules allow time for reflection with the stated goal of approaching the truth. Not so in adversarial proceedings, however. There, the clear desire of some lawyers is to obfuscate and confuse; shake witnesses' confidence; make them angry; get them to misspeak; or make them seem foolish, arrogant, or naive to the court.[4] These tactics include the following:

- raising one or more of the 20 objections in this chapter or having the objections raised by a rebuttal witness. Sometimes this is attempted by packing objections into the premise of a question—for example, "Because the VRAG has only static variables and does not take account of the more important dynamic aspects of risk (e.g., personality, attitudes, and support systems), how can you use my client's VRAG score to say anything about his risk of violence when he gets to another institution?"
- quibbling about each actuarial variable and bringing up small (atypical) examples of behavior inconsistent with the variable. For example, one might mention the times the offender did not fail on conditional release, argue that his teenage drinking was not so abnormal, or claim that a previous relationship was equivalent to a marriage.
- exhibiting exasperation ("You dance around every one of my questions!") or mock confusion, as if the witness were being evasive or deceitful.

---

[4]Offenders' lawyers do not, however, debate the value of low VRAG scores.

Most of these tactics are self-defeating, generally causing the court or tribunal to listen to the witness describe in great detail the many instances of mean, selfish, and antisocial conduct recorded for the accused. In the case of real or feigned hostility and rudeness, most trial lawyers realize that judges and jurors regard such behavior as more damaging to the lawyer's case than to the witness. Opposing lawyers commonly use "experts" with contradictory opinions. In our experience, opposing experts often counter the Actuarial Risk Appraisal Report using versions of the 20 arguments in this chapter. The most popular arguments used are based on the idea that our research was not conducted on the same population, at the same ages, with the same diagnoses, from the same kind of institution, with the same treatment experiences, from the same era in time, or in the same jurisdiction to which the individual in question belongs. The expert then usually uses a method with even less empirical support—clinical judgment (regardless of the population, institution, diagnosis, era, or jurisdiction at hand). Moreover, no method could satisfy all of the conditions implied in the objection, which is akin to rejecting an actuarial method for predicting tornadoes next summer because it was developed on last summer's tornadoes (after all, it could be that the two populations of tornadoes differ in some way), then using a Ouija board instead.

There are instances of a clinician giving opposite testimony (as to the appropriateness of actuarial methods, for example) depending on who retained him. We have seen an opposing expert assert that an interview is required to complete the PCL–R, when we knew he was aware that the PCL–R manual stated the opposite. We are confident that the legal concept of an expert does not include deliberate mendacity and the outright selling of opinions. Perhaps these witnesses rationalized their actions with the idea that justice or truth emerges when two adversaries tackle each other in the legal crucible. This seems highly debatable to us and raises the possibility that the comparative accuracy (i.e., validity) of different approaches to the criminal trial process could be evaluated empirically. In the end, legal systems are not organized according to scientific understandings of human conduct or data about the accuracy of verdicts. Rather, the law is explicitly based on common sense, with all its inherent strengths and weaknesses.[5]

Useful advice about preparation, attire, and demeanor is available for those testifying as expert witnesses. The advice is commonsensical and reminds one of the counsel one might give a doctoral candidate preparing for an oral dissertation defense. Courtroom strategy is beyond our scope, but "expertise" warrants further discussion.

---

[5]Some scholars have compared the accuracy and perceived fairness of various models of the trial process, concluding that adversarial proceedings are at least as accurate as, for example, inquisitorial methods common in Europe. Notwithstanding this, the accuracy of various approaches and procedural details remains an empirical question, because the design of existing criminal justice systems has not been informed by data about accuracy.

Society in general and professionals often seem confused about what constitutes expertise in the legal sense. An informal understanding of the matter suggests that if one can get paid for doing something for a long time, one must have a lot of specialized knowledge. However, everyone has known people who practiced their professions for a lifetime apparently without knowing very much about them. The following is an example of a legal opinion about true expertise.

> To warrant the use of expert testimony, then, two elements are required. First, the topic of the testimony must be so uniquely related to some science, profession, business, or occupation as to be beyond the understanding of the typical layperson; and, second, the witness must have such knowledge or experience in that field as to make it seem that the opinion will likely assist the trier in the search for truth. (McCormick, 1954)

Depending on how it was determined, in practice, that something was "beyond the understanding of the typical layperson" and how it could be determined that the requisite skill, knowledge, or experience was present, this hurdle seems a low one indeed. Ironically, there is evidence that triers (i.e., judges) want testimony from mental health professionals for just those legal questions about which mental health professionals are least expert (Melton, Petrila, Poythress, & Slobogin, 1987). Some commentators have concluded,

> First, professionals have considerably less to contribute than is commonly supposed; second, for legal purposes, laypersons are quite competent to make judgements concerning mental disorder; third, all mental health law cases involve primarily moral and social issues and decisions, not scientific ones; fourth, overreliance on experts promotes the mistaken and responsibility-abdicating view that these hard moral questions (i.e., whether and in what way to treat mentally ill persons differently) are scientific ones; and fifth, professionals should recognize this difference and refrain from drawing social and moral conclusions about which they are not expert. (Morse, 1978, cited in Melton, Petrila, Poythress, & Slobogin, 1987, p. 15)

It is likely, however, that clinicians will continue to be qualified as experts, especially to give testimony about clinical appraisals of dangerousness. This desire on the part of the courts means that, in any forum, both sides could have as many witnesses as desired, each testifying as "experts" to exactly opposite things: psychopathic or not psychopathic, dangerous or not dangerous, treatable or not treatable, suitable for community placement or not, insane or sane, and so forth. This has prompted what can only be called a massive assault on the legal idea of clinical expertise (Ziskin & Faust, 1988). Rather than the traditional legal view of expertise established by experience and credentials, Ziskin and Faust argued that the sine qua non of expertise (in the legal sense) ought to be evidence of accuracy. In addition, it can be argued (Quinsey & Ambtman, 1979) that, by definition, true experts base their decisions on specialized methods, so that they would not always arrive at the same decisions as laypeople and agree among themselves (the amount of disagreement places an absolute upper bound on accuracy). On the basis of these criteria, Ziskin and Faust reviewed the overwhelming body of evidence demonstrating that, in their proposed legal sense, clinical expertise (based on unstructured opinion) simply does not exist. Nowhere is this assertion more true than in the clinical prediction of violent behavior.

Ziskin and Faust (1988) are so strong in their assault that they call into question some aspects of psychology for which there is impressive evidence of validity. For example, they concluded that the scientific evidence underlying IQ testing is weak. The one place where they accord scientific status, however, is actuarial prediction (see also Grove & Meehl, 1996). They asserted that actuarial methods are the only scientifically (and, by their criteria, legally) valid means to make predictions about human conduct. Thus, testimony by an expert (properly prepared and knowledgeable about the methods) using a purely actuarial approach would meet the Ziskin and Faust standard for true expertise.

Some authorities attempted to refute Ziskin and Faust (1988), arguing that their characterization of the law was inaccurate. Hoge and Grisso (1992) asserted that U.S. federal law established a lower hurdle for expertise. That is, U.S. courts did not demand that experts be accurate; only that they use the procedures and methods accepted within their own fields of knowledge. Hoge and Grisso provided examples of inaccurate (even absurd) "expert" testimony that was nevertheless ruled admissible. These examples, however, buttress the idea that accuracy ought to be among the requisite standards for admissibility, even if it has not been required in all jurisdictions. Indeed, a subsequent decision (*Daubert v. Merrell Dow Pharmaceuticals, Inc.*, 1993) seemed to tip the balance in favor of accuracy as the legal criterion for expertise.

The lower standard discussed by Hoge and Grisso (1992) raised fundamental epistemological questions. For example, without evidence for the accuracy of assertions in a particular field, could it be argued that the field comprised "knowledge"? If astrologers or psychics used methods established in those fields, should their "expert" testimony be ruled admissible? The Hilton and Simmons (2001) study showed that clinicians used override so much that their opinions were related neither to actuarial assessment nor recidivism. In addition, Quinsey and Ambtman (1979) described a study in which forensic psychiatrists and laypersons were given information about offenders' current offenses, history, and clinical assessments then asked to make predictions about future violence (see chap. 4). Contrary to psychiatrists' assertions about their use of specialized clinical data, both groups used the same information (current offense and past behavior). Neither group made use of clinical assessment data, and the ratings of (and level of agreement among) clinicians were no different from those of the laypeople.

Accuracy aside, it cannot be argued (à la Hoge & Grisso, 1992) that when making unaided judgments about dangerousness, forensic clinicians use procedures and methods accepted within their own fields, unless it is also argued that their field of knowledge is that naturally also used by untrained persons. In the assessment of dangerousness, at least, unaided clinical judgment is an odd form of expertise indeed—that possessed by everyone. The only defensible conclusion is that expert opinion about the likelihood of violent recidivism can presently be rendered only by actuarial systems.

IV

ALTERING THE RISK
OF VIOLENCE AND
CONCLUSIONS

10

TREATMENT AND MANAGEMENT

Andrews, Zinger, and their colleagues (1990) asserted that criminal recidivism is most effectively reduced by well-structured treatment programs focused on the criminogenic needs of relatively high-risk offenders that are delivered in a manner that matches the learning styles of the offenders to be treated. *Criminogenic needs* are those modifiable characteristics of offenders that are related to their propensity to reoffend. These are the principles of need, risk, and responsivity. The meta-analyses referred to in chapter 4 by Andrews, Zinger, et al. (1990) and Lipsey (1992) strongly support Andrews, Zinger, et al.'s conceptualization.

Regrettably, the treatment outcome literature on the recidivism of sexual, chronic, and psychopathic offenders is difficult to square with the moderate effect sizes identified in the meta-analyses. This apparent contradiction is probably because the large majority of studies in the meta-analyses involved juvenile or young adult offenders.

Moffitt (1993) usefully distinguished between adolescent-limited and lifelong-persistent offenders. If one examines the number of male offenders convicted each year as a function of their age, the curve looks like a testosterone output curve, rising steeply with puberty and declining gracefully after young adulthood. Female offenders show the same shaped conviction curve at an extremely reduced level.[1] The large majority of offenders, therefore, are of the adolescent-limited variety: They start offending in their teenage years and desist before their mid-20s. This pattern of offending represents part of what Wilson and Daly (1985, 1993) termed the *young male syndrome* of risk taking and violence. From a theoretical perspective, such activity appears to represent intermale competition for status. In contrast, lifelong-persistent offenders start offending prior to adolescence and continue to commit offenses throughout their lives. These persistent offenders therefore form a greater proportion of older offenders as opposed to younger offenders (G. T. Harris & Hilton, 2001) and a greater proportion of chronic offenders than offenders with a more limited offense history.

Our interpretation of the treatment literature is that the best of the current treatment technologies induce adolescent-limited offenders to desist earlier than they otherwise would have. However, none of these appropriate interventions, such as cognitive–behavioral programs, directed toward the criminogenic needs of high-risk offenders or any other approach has been shown to reduce the recidivism rates of serious adult offenders. New treatment technologies are needed for repetitive adult offenders. Until this development work has been completed, however, we must rely on the best of what is available. To the extent that treatment is ineffective, supervision must be emphasized. The remainder of this chapter outlines our view of the current state of the arts of intervention and supervision.

PLANNING INSTITUTIONAL TREATMENT PROGRAMS

Although treatment programs designed to lower risk are focused on the specific criminogenic needs of individual offenders, they are delivered to individuals in an organizational context. Moreover, high-risk individuals may suffer from a variety of social or mental health problems that determine the kind of interventions that may be appropriate. Some of these problems, although not relevant to risk per se, affect the responsiveness of offenders to interventions designed to lower it; many are serious enough to justify treatment as mental health issues.

Treatment programs thus need to be structured to take into account individual differences among offenders that affect the type of service most likely to be effective. The type of service is determined by the types of clinical needs or problems an offender has. It is clear that particular problems are likely to be correlated with one another, so that if an offender has a particu-

---

[1]Androgens secreted by the adrenal glands begin to rise in both sexes at age 10, before the physical changes of puberty (McClintock & Herdt, 1996); testosterone is positively associated with aggression and negatively associated with prosocial behaviors in both men and women (J. A. Harris, Rushton, Hampson, & Jackson, 1996).

lar problem, he is more or less likely to have particular kinds of other problems. Thus, from a clinical perspective, one can define offender types by the pattern of clinically relevant problems that they exhibit.

In a series of studies using a 66-item clinician-rated checklist called the Problem Identification Checklist (Quinsey, Cyr, & Lavallee, 1988; Rice & Harris, 1988; Rice, Harris, Quinsey, & Cyr, 1990), we determined the different interpersonal, psychiatric, and criminal problems in cross-sectional populations of mentally disordered offenders[2] in Oak Ridge and at the Philippe Pinel maximum-security psychiatric institution in Montreal. We accomplished this by surveying staff who were most familiar with the offenders. The individual problems were factor analyzed to yield Clinical Problem Scales. The Problem Identification Checklist data have been shown to be related to mentally disordered offenders' ratings of their own problems, to their demographic and clinical characteristics, and to both static and dynamic risk of reoffending.

Cluster analyses were conducted using scores on each of the factor analytically derived Clinical Problem Scales and a measure of level of intellectual functioning. Cluster analyses were used to identify relatively homogeneous subgroups of mentally disordered offenders, all of which shared similar patterns of scores on the various Clinical Problem Scales. These data were then used to assign individuals to particular programs and living units within Oak Ridge (Rice, Harris, Quinsey, & Cyr, 1990).

Building on these initial studies, Rice, Harris, and Quinsey (1996) conducted a survey of mentally disordered offenders in Ontario during June 1990, known as the Ontario Survey of Mentally Disordered Offenders. The survey included all 467 individuals occupying beds in one of the province's seven secure hospital units and all insanity acquittees living on open wards of psychiatric hospitals or in the community. Individuals held on warrants of remand and those who had been found unfit to stand trial since January 1990 were excluded. File data indicated that the survey population resembled other mentally disordered offenders described in the literature: Most had committed a serious offense against other individuals (47% had committed a homicide). Most were men (88%), had a hospital diagnosis of schizophrenia (63%), had psychiatric medication prescribed (81%), and had prior correctional (53%) and psychiatric (75%) admissions. They tended to have had chronically poor social adjustment, together with antisocial conduct. Since their index offense, they had spent, on average, slightly less than 5 years in secure settings and were living in one of four levels of security (community, minimum, medium, and maximum) at the time of the study. In general, offenders

---

[2]We use the phrase *mentally disordered offenders* here in a very general way: All the offenders were or had been admitted to psychiatric institutions, almost all had committed at least one serious violent act, and many qualified for a diagnosis of schizophrenia or affective psychosis.

held at higher levels of security had more serious antisocial histories and poorer community adjustment than those held at lower levels of security.

Using the Violence Risk Appraisal Guide (VRAG), each individual was assigned to one of nine risk levels where the predicted rate of *violent recidivism*, defined as a charge for a violent offense or return to a maximum-security hospital for a violent offense, within 7 years at risk ranged from 0% for those in the lowest of the nine risk categories to 100% for those in the highest. Their current level of placement showed very little relationship to actuarial risk, even though the disposition of each was entirely at the discretion of clinicians and review boards. In other words, and as expected from the literature on the clinical appraisal of dangerousness, high-risk offenders were nearly as likely as low-risk offenders to be found in each setting.

The survey also gathered data on the clinicians' perceptions of the offenders' clinical problems. Clinicians who knew them well rated them from 0 (no problem) to 5 (severe problem) using the Problem Identification Survey. Clinical Problem Scales were again developed using factor analysis. The resulting eight Clinical Problem Scales were labeled Life Skills Deficits, Aggression, Health Problems, Management Problems, Family Problems, Social Withdrawal, Active Psychotic Symptoms, and Depression.

According to clinicians' ratings, the offenders exhibited great variability in the number of clinical problems they had. Twelve percent of them had no problems of even moderate severity, but one individual had 51 problems endorsed. Hospital diagnosis or historical variables alone did not adequately represent the heterogeneity of individual clinical presentations. Among the problem scales, Aggression, Management Problems, and Life Skills Deficits were related to actuarial risk scores, suggesting that treatments that target these problems would be most promising in reducing risk of violent recidivism.

Indicative of the treatment problems posed by many offenders was that the most commonly endorsed single item was *denies all problems*. Ironically, this item was highly correlated with the total number of problems and with such other management problems as lack of consideration for others and refusing therapy. In other words, offenders who were perceived by clinicians as denying problems were also likely to have been perceived as having problems characterized by aggression and antisocial behavior and as not being amenable to treatment. *Denies all problems* was also positively related to actuarial risk.

Clinicians were asked to respond to three security-related questions for each patient regarding which of seven types of institutional security (ranging from completely open access to the community to maximum perimeter security with maximal internal monitoring and security precautions) would be most appropriate, the degree of direct access the individual should have to the community (ranging from total freedom to absolutely none), and what conditions they would apply to any community access (10 possibilities were provided, such as take prescribed medication, avoid alcohol, or wear an electronic monitor). In addition, clinicians could write in any other recommended conditions.

On average, clinicians agreed with one another more frequently when clients had either very high or very low security assignments (or risk levels); clinicians were less likely to be in agreement when offenders were at the intermediate security or actuarial risk levels. These analyses also showed that clinicians' perceptions of risk were more strongly related to the number of obvious psychiatric problems (of any kind) than to actuarially determined risk. A significant minority of clients were seen as unsuitable for community access under any circumstances.

Patient Clusters

Scores on the Clinical Problem Scales and on the VRAG were used in cluster analyses to assign each offender to one of eight homogeneous groups for the purpose of examining treatment and security needs. The largest cluster comprised 30% of the population. Members of this "low risk, low need" cluster were very low in actuarially estimated risk and exhibited almost no clinical problems. Although it seemed as though these individuals could be managed well in the community, only 41% of them were actually in the community at the time of the study.

The second largest group, comprising 17% of the population, were of low actuarially determined risk and exhibited a moderate number of clinical problems that are typical of chronic psychiatric patients (as measured on the Social Withdrawal, Life Skills Deficits, Depression, Family Problems, and Active Psychotic Symptoms scales). The treatments indicated for this "typical psychiatric" group (as described later in this chapter) include primarily skills training for life skills and social skill deficits, cognitive–behavioral (and sometimes pharmacological) treatment for depression, family therapy, and behavioral and pharmacological treatment for active psychotic symptoms. The literature on psychosocial rehabilitation suggests that these treatments can be most effectively delivered while the client lives in the community, and their low actuarial risk scores suggested that placement in the community would have posed little risk.

The third largest group, 16% of the population, were offenders whom clinicians rated as having almost no clinical problems, yet who were high on actuarial risk—"model but dangerous patients." An estimated 44% of this group would have committed a violent offense within 7 years of opportunity. Although they required high levels of supervision as determined by their actuarial risk score, nearly half were in the community or in open settings at the time of the survey.

The fourth cluster, comprising 11% of the population, also had high actuarial risk scores (44% would be expected to reoffend violently within 7 years at risk) and also exhibited moderate clinical problems, especially problems of management and aggression. There is little question that these of-fenders required both the internal and perimeter security available in a maxi-mum-security facility. The treatments recommended for these "dangerous problem" patients included primarily behavioral, cognitive–behavioral, and skills training programs.

The fifth cluster was of relatively low actuarial risk (an estimated 12% would reoffend within 7 years of risk) but had significant clinical problems indicating a need for treatment, as measured by the Aggression, Manage-ment Problems, and Active Psychotic Symptoms scales. For these "problem" patients (6% of the total population), movement to less secure units and eventually to the community would be expected to pose little risk to the community.

The members of the sixth cluster (9% of the population) were of low to moderate risk (it was estimated that 17% would reoffend violently within 7 years at risk) and also exhibited very significant clinical problems in the areas measured by the Life Skills Deficits, Active Psychotic Symptoms, and Social Withdrawal scales. They also exhibited problems measured by the Family Problems and Depression scales, as well as moderate difficulties as measured by the Aggression and Management scales. These "social isolates" would have been best suited to a setting with at least moderate internal and perimeter security. The treatments recommended as highest priority for these patients were those that address management problems and aggression, be-cause these were the problems that required that they be held in a unit of moderate internal security. Once problems in these areas were addressed in treatment, it is possible that many could be moved to minimum-security units for treatment of their other clinical problems, from which they could eventually be released to the community. Because of their moderate risk to the community, however, they would require relatively intensive supervi-sion, whether inside or outside an institution.

The smallest offender cluster (4% of the population) was very problem-atic, obtaining the worst ratings on most measures, and we labeled them "dangerous troublemakers." These were the offenders of very high actuarial risk (an estimated 55% would commit a violent offense within 7 years at risk). These offenders also exhibited significant problems as measured by the Management Problems and Aggression scales. Maximum perimeter and in-ternal security over a lengthy period was indicated.

A cluster comprising 7% of the population were of moderate actuarial risk (an estimated 35% of these patients would reoffend within 7 years at risk) and exhibited significant problems in every area. These "high need" forensic patients obviously required maximum internal security and at least moderate perimeter security. It was recommended that treatment while in maximum security should focus primarily on aggression and management problems and that once these were under control, these patients could be transferred to a unit with less internal security for further treatment.

In summary, the factor and cluster analyses indicated that the heterogeneity in the clinical problems exhibited by the offenders studied in the survey could be considerably reduced to several clinical problem scales or domains. These domains are consistent with the ways in which clinicians, correctional officials, and indeed laypersons think about the problems that people experience. Furthermore, the heterogeneity in individual problem "profiles" could also be considerably simplified by classifying offenders into relatively homogeneous subgroups. Some subgroups resembled the patients one might expect in psychiatric facilities. Other subgroups resembled the inmates one might expect in correctional facilities. Still others seemed to have the characteristics of both. The largest subgroup seemed to have no significant criminogenic or mental health needs. The point of all this is not to argue that these subtypes (or especially that their relative sizes) would be found in all populations. That is, it is to be expected that some groups would be smaller (and other groups larger) if the offenders had been the inmates of a maximum-security prison. On the basis of this survey and our previous research, we do think that the clinical problems and the way they grouped together are stable aspects of offender populations, that clinically homogeneous subgroups also exist in all populations, and that many subgroups would match those found in the present study. Thus, we conclude that planning treatment for violent offenders need not be as difficult a task as might be suggested by the wide array of problems exhibited by offenders. The commonalities in problem and offender "types" are captured, however, not by diagnosis or history, but by broadly conceived individual symptoms, skill deficits, and problematic behaviors. Finally, we note that although the Problem Identification Checklist used in this survey did a good job of characterizing the patterns of clinical problems experienced by the large group of offenders, planning treatment for individuals requires the use of standardized, psychometrically sound measurement.

Clinical Judgment

The information obtained in the Ontario Survey permitted an evaluation of clinicians' judgments and recommendations. This assessment pertains to the correspondence among clinicians' ratings of offenders' problems; their treatment, disposition, and supervision recommendations; and offenders' documented histories. With regard to disposition and supervision, there was good agreement among clinicians on the recommended level of security. Recommendations about level of security, security precautions, and degree of community access were all significantly related to actuarial risk and to other historical variables known to predict antisocial behavior. Thus, on average, there was evidence that clinicians' recommendations were reliable and had some validity. However, there was evidence that the recommendations could have been improved. For example, there was a halo effect inasmuch as scores in all problem areas were positively related to the recommended level of security and negatively related to the degree of community access and intensity of supervision. In other words, on average, offenders with large numbers of problems were more likely to be rated as requiring greater security and less community access by clinicians. Because scores in many problem areas (as measured by the Active Psychotic Symptoms, Family Problems, and Social Withdrawal scales) were, in fact, unrelated to actuarially determined risk, the halo effect led to less than optimal decisions about placement. This phenomenon of halo-influenced recommendations was most apparent with the third cluster, the model but dangerous offenders (those with high actuarial risk but very few clinical problems). The data suggested that because they exhibited few clinical problems, they were inappropriately judged to be safe to release to open settings or the community.

Implications for a System to Manage Mentally Disordered Offenders

The clinical problems most frequently endorsed were *denies all problems*, anger, and impulsivity, all three of which were on the Management Problem scale. That *denies all problems* was the most frequently reported problem makes an important statement about these offenders and sets them apart from most other psychiatric patients. The fact that they do not believe themselves to have clinical needs makes them an especially difficult group to treat. Anger has been noted as a very common problem among forensic and nonforensic populations (e.g., G. T. Harris, Hilton, & Rice, 1993; Novaco, 2003; Quinsey & Cyr, 1986). Impulsivity has been less commonly noted as a problem among nonforensic patients.

It is also of interest that although the majority of offenders had several problems of at least moderate magnitude, a sizeable minority (12%) were rated by clinicians as having no clinical problems. Two clusters were rated as having virtually no clinical treatment needs: the low risk, low needs first cluster had very low actuarial risk scores, and the model but dangerous patients in the third cluster had high actuarial risk scores. It would seem obvious that the individuals in the first group should mostly be found in the community; however, as previously noted, only 41% of that first cluster were actually living in the community. In general, most offenders were not living in settings that seemed to match the level of risk and problem areas of their cluster membership. Thus, only 35% of the typical psychiatric patients in the second cluster were living in the community or on nonforensic units; 77% of the social isolates in the sixth cluster were held in maximum or medium security; 50% of the dangerous individuals in the fourth cluster were in settings with less than medium security; and 69% of the rather nondangerous problem patients of cluster 5 were in maximum or medium security. However, 75% of the dangerous troublemakers and 84% of the high-need patients in the eighth cluster were in maximum- or medium-security facilities.

From a forensic policy viewpoint, the fourth cluster, a group of 77 model but dangerous patients, was very problematic. The considerable risk posed to the community by this subgroup suggested that many require long-term placement in a setting with careful and close supervision and high perimeter security to protect the public. Their lack of manifest clinical problems, however, indicated that as far as current clinical technology is concerned, they would require little treatment. These results suggest that because these patients presented no difficulty in management, clinicians regarded them as good candidates for transfer to low-security facilities and to the community. In fact, examination of the actual location of these high-risk offenders revealed that 43% of them lived in the community or on open psychiatric wards, and 54% were rated by clinicians as appropriate for such settings.

It is possible that model but dangerous offenders had real clinical needs that were missed in this staff survey but would be discovered through specialized assessments. According to file information, for example, alcohol had been involved in the index offenses of many of these patients (as well as those of many other patients in the study). Because alcohol was not usually available to offenders who lived inside an institution, it may not be surprising that it was not commonly endorsed as a clinical problem. Even if clinical needs could have been found, however, many of these offenders had very serious criminal histories that, in combination with their high-risk scores, would have warranted very cautious approaches to reductions in supervision following any therapeutic improvement.

In this survey, as in most jurisdictions, a range of internal and external security was available for the mentally disordered offenders. Internally, available facilities were currently maximum, double-locked medium, single-locked medium, and minimum (open) security. The internal security in each of the institutions was roughly matched to that of the perimeter security. Thus, in the maximum-security institution, internal security was also relatively tight; all patients had individual rooms (cells), all patients were locked in their rooms at night, staff–patient ratios were high, internal movement was closely monitored, furniture was carefully selected for safety, any instruments (including cutlery) were carefully counted, and rooms were periodically searched for contraband. In the medium-security units, patients generally did not have individual rooms, security checks were not so tight, and staffing ratios were not so high. Internal security precautions were even fewer in the single-locked and open facilities.

The survey data suggested that the internal security required to safely treat and manage mentally disordered offenders may have borne little relation to the degree of perimeter security required to protect the public. For example, the high-need individuals in the last cluster presented only moderate risk to the community, but their high scores on the Management Problems, Aggression, and Active Psychotic Symptoms scales suggested that they would require maximal internal security to be safely managed. By contrast, at least some of the model but dangerous offenders in the third cluster required high levels of perimeter security to protect the public yet required much less in the way of internal security (other than that necessary to ensure that the perimeter remained secure).

Recommended Treatments for Problems Common Among Forensic Patients

The Ontario Survey of Mentally Disordered Offenders indicated the need to consider clinical problems that are empirically related to the risk of future violent behavior as treatment targets. The following overview of recommended treatments relies on our previous reviews of the literature on recommended treatments for offenders and mentally disordered offenders (G. T. Harris & Rice, 1997; G. T. Harris, Rice, Quinsey, & Durdle, 1995; Rice & Harris, 1997b; Rice, Harris, Quinsey, & Cyr, 1990; Rice et al., 1996). Extensive references to the treatment literature can be found in these reviews.

Management Problems and Criminal Propensity

The largest group of problems among the offenders, and the single most important contributor to the cluster solution of patient subtypes, was the Management Problems scale. The problems were those that pertained to the management difficulties that individuals presented within the institution. Anger was also a problem on this scale, but because it was such a common problem, it is considered separately.

Those familiar with institutions can immediately recall individuals who present such problems, and they can recognize the disruption and stress created when these inmates regularly exhibit problem behaviors. Individuals who exhibit such behaviors are difficult to treat, and staff frustration with them often makes them candidates for "bus therapy" (Toch, 1982). Many of the problems of offenders in this category (e.g., lying, lack of consideration for others, impulsivity, superficiality, manipulation, denying all problems) are diagnostic of antisocial personality disorder and psychopathy. There was also a very close correspondence in the Ontario Survey data between Management Problems scores as rated by clinicians and background variables associated with psychopathy, criminal history, and the actuarially determined risk of future violent offending.

The problems associated with these disorders have been found to be extremely resistant to treatment. One of the first challenges for mental health professionals called on to provide treatment for persons who are serious management problems is to help them acknowledge that some problems might be addressed by programs. For some offenders who do not refuse treatment, problem solving combined with social skills training, moral reasoning (sometimes again combined with social skills training), and academic programs that focus on the humanities and social sciences (and that emphasize democratic teaching methods used by an instructor selected to be a good role model) are helpful (e.g., Duguid, 1983, 1985). Contingency management procedures to reduce conflict at work and attitudes toward work, as well as deliberately contrived opportunities for interactions with prosocial models who are interpersonally skilled and who have been trained in how to respond to antisocial comments and rationalizations for law violation, can also have positive effects on management problems (e.g., Daigle-Zinn & Andrews, 1980).

To date, data demonstrating that any of these interventions reduce criminal or violent recidivism among high-risk adult offenders are limited. However, some research indicates positive effects of training in moral reasoning, academic programs, and provision of prosocial models who model anticriminal values and attitudes for young offenders of moderate risk. In general, behavioral treatment programs aimed at teaching and strengthening skills and modeling prosocial attitudes have been shown to be more effective in reducing recidivism than relationship or insight-oriented therapies (for a review, see Andrews & Bonta, 2003b). Although interventions that reduce recidivism among psychopathic individuals have not yet been identified, the evidence presented in chapter 5 indicates that confrontational milieu-type treatments raised the recidivism rates of psychopathic mentally disordered offenders. Similarly, a structured, social learning, coping skills approach was found to be more effective than an interactional insight-oriented approach with sociopathic alcoholic individuals (Kadden, Cooney, Getter, & Litt, 1989).

Considerable evidence suggests that institutional violence is not just the product of individual pathology but rather a result of a variety of variables, including personal characteristics, staff behaviors, institutional routines, and other environmental factors (Rice et al., 1996; Rice, Harris, Varney, & Quinsey, 1989). These variables are discussed later in this chapter.

Aggression

Aggression (toward self and others), which includes problems of assaultiveness, property destruction, weapons possession, and suicide threats, were infrequent among the offenders surveyed, but such considerations are extremely important to placement decisions. Even the occasional occurrence of these behaviors within an institution is likely to mean that an individual is not considered for release or any intervention other than pharmacotherapy. Moreover, the possibility of these behaviors is a primary reason for the implementation of a wide variety of expensive and therapeutically unwieldy security precautions that must often be applied to all institutional inhabitants even though only a small minority is likely to require them. Thus, the reduction or elimination of problems of physical aggression inevitably has very high priority in secure treatment facilities.

Interventions frequently used to reduce assaultiveness include drugs, seclusion and mechanical restraint, behavioral treatment, and staff training. Drugs and restrictive or punitive management strategies alone are unlikely to be successful. Rather, careful and consistent behavioral consequation of problem conduct and the training and on-ward reinforcement of incompatible prosocial behaviors are required. Staff training in verbal calming and defusing skills combined with fair and reasonable management policies are probably essential (Rice et al., 1989). It is also necessary to ensure effective prosocial models in the institutional environment and to control patients' exposure to the media. Indeed, as will be discussed later in this chapter, the real challenge in reducing aggression in institutions appears to lie in achieving effective control of staff behaviors.

Anger

Anger was second only to *denies all problems* in frequency in the current population. Most treatments for the reduction of anger use social skills training techniques to teach effective, nonhostile verbal strategies for dealing with provocative situations. Many treatments also use cognitive components directed at clients' hostile outlook or at the emotional and attitudinal components of anger, and they may include a relaxation training component aimed at equipping individuals with a strategy to use when they determine that they are becoming unduly or inappropriately aroused. Because it is currently perhaps the most promising of potentially dynamic predictors, we note that a comprehensive approach to the assessment and treatment of anger may be found in the work of Novaco and colleagues (Novaco, 2003; Renwick, Black, Ramm, & Novaco, 1997). The anger literature also indicates that encouraging angry individuals to relieve anger through catharsis (e.g., boxing, using a punching bag) is contraindicated because it may lead to increased hostility and aggression.

Substance Abuse

Substance abuse problems were common in the histories of the offenders surveyed. Fifty-two percent of the population had documented evidence of a problem of alcohol abuse, and it was noted as a problem at the time of the offense for 39%. Alcohol abuse is associated with both parole failure and crimes against others. Substance abuse should be a treatment target whenever it figures as a causal factor in a clinical theory of an offender's offense history. Some evidence supports aversion therapy, behavioral training in self-control, relaxation, communication, assertion, social skills, and family therapy (especially perhaps for schizophrenic alcohol abusers). Cognitively based approaches, including relapse prevention and skills training, have gained support in other populations; however, more research is necessary before it can be claimed that such techniques are successful with offender populations. Consistent with a relapse prevention approach, programs for alcohol abuse should extend into the community. Whereas there is some debate in the alcoholism treatment literature about whether the goal of treatment should be moderation or abstinence, abstinence is the appropriate goal in a forensic population if alcohol use had been related to the commission of serious crimes.

Life Skills Deficits

There is a very large and sophisticated literature on educational and behavioral programs directed toward the normalization of intellectually handicapped patients that serve as a model for the effective psychosocial rehabilitation of mentally disordered offenders (whether or not they are intellectually handicapped). Contingency management approaches to basic literacy and mathematics skills as well as vocational skills have increased proficiencies among prison inmates, and there is evidence that token economy programs that emphasize vocational and educational training in prison settings reduce postrelease recidivism. Using the principles of contingency management, token economies involve the specification of desired, attainable behaviors and of reinforcers on which the desired behaviors are contingent.

Active Psychotic Symptoms

Serious mental disorder (i.e., psychosis) has not been found to be a risk factor for violent recidivism. Indeed, as reviewed extensively in chapter 5, our own follow-up studies and Bonta, Law, and Hanson's meta-analysis (1998) suggest that those with serious mental illness may be at lower risk of violent recidivism compared with other offenders. Although psychosis appears to be modestly related to violence in samples from the general population, there is scant evidence that such difficulties are associated with violence in any samples of offenders. Consequently, it cannot be expected that treatment targeting psychotic symptoms does much to reduce the risk of violent recidivism in any identified offender population. It is, however, likely that psychotic symptoms interfere with offenders' ability to benefit from other programs. Because of that and because such symptoms represent real human suffering, clinicians should address these symptoms.

There is little question that neuroleptic drugs have, for most patients, a powerful ameliorative effect on active psychotic symptoms; lithium appears to be the drug of choice for mania. There is also substantial evidence that nondrug psychosocial treatments can (independently or in combination with drugs) help ameliorate active psychotic symptoms; however, their effectiveness requires the institutional administration to engage in extensive planning and to exercise considerable control over the behavior of staff at all levels.

G. T. Harris (1989) investigated how changes in neuroleptic drug dose affected the performance of mentally disordered offenders participating in a maximum-security token economy program. Many participants showed improvements in program performance after relatively few changes to their medication. For a substantial number of participants, however, a much different pattern emerged. These individuals showed no improvements in performance despite numerous medication changes. This research addressed a problematic process familiar to mental health professionals: Frequently, a chronic patient exhibits an aberrant or symptomatic behavior, and concerned staff request that the attending physician "do something." Generally, the physician adjusts the medication. If the medication change is followed by deterioration, another change quickly follows; if improvement follows, the desired result is attributed to the medication change. The difficulty with the repetition of this process is that random or unexplained fluctuations in patients' behaviors result in unnecessary prescription changes and create an unwarranted confidence in simple pharmacological solutions for problems when, in fact, fluctuations in patients' conditions are totally unrelated to changes in medication.

Owing to interdisciplinary rivalries and shortages of appropriately trained clinicians, psychosocial treatments that are known to be effective are frequently not provided for mentally disordered offenders. The delivery of drugs alone rarely requires such a high degree of effective administration. An interesting social policy dilemma is whether to expend limited research resources to find yet newer drugs to treat psychotic symptoms or to find better ways to deliver the effective behavioral and psychosocial treatments we already have.

Social Withdrawal

In general, there is little evidence that targeting social withdrawal substantially alters the likelihood of violent recidivism. However, for the purposes of improving response to other programs and on humanitarian grounds, programs to reduce social withdrawal are often indicated. The treatment of choice for socially inadequate behavior among psychiatric patients is social skills training. *Social skills training* refers to a variety of techniques that have been used to change a person's social behavior in particular social situations. The training involves behavioral components (e.g., role-playing, modeling, feedback, and coaching), and anxiety reduction components are often included. The training has been found to be just as beneficial for very acute and low-functioning schizophrenic patients as it is for higher functioning individuals or patients with other diagnoses. The best treatment strategy for problems of social withdrawal includes a careful assessment of the problematic situations to be linked with specific treatment components, such as anxiety reduction, problem-solving skills, coping skills, and conversational skills. When these skills are being taught in an institutional rather than a community setting, one must take precautions to ensure that the ward environment does not punish the newly learned behaviors to promote generalization of treatment effects on the ward environment.

Family Problems

Family and marital problems were common among the offenders in our survey, and their victims frequently included family members. Because reductions in both criminal and psychiatric recidivism as the result of family therapy have been reported, it is worth attempting family therapy whenever offenders are returning to live with their families, although family dissolution might be more appropriate in cases of spouse battery or incest. Psychoeducational programs for patients' families have had positive effects on the community adjustment of schizophrenic patients (Hogarty et al., 1986).

Conclusions

The relationship between various clinical problems and the dangerousness of individuals is sometimes direct (e.g., assaultiveness), sometimes indirect (e.g., suspiciousness), and sometimes unknown (e.g., life skills deficits). What is evident from the foregoing discussion is that the relationship between response to any particular form of treatment and subsequent dangerousness is largely uncharted empirically. Like other clinicians, we regard the improvement of patients' conditions and behaviors as desirable in themselves. Moreover, the relationship between therapeutic interventions and subsequent behaviors cannot be established until the interventions are appropriate, implemented properly, and guided by plausible theory. Progress will not be made unless coherent treatment programs can be developed, delivered, and evaluated.

A repetition of the survey several years later (Rice, Harris, Cormier, et al., 2004) revealed that some of the anticipated problems were realized. That is, the size of the forensic population continued to increase, as did the base rate of violence among released forensic patients. As discussed in chapter 4, these trends were attributed to the failure of the forensic system to uniformly incorporate current findings about effective risk appraisal and management into regular practice (Rice, Harris, Cormier, et al., 2004). That is, by making release decisions dependent on characteristics unrelated to future violence (Hilton & Simmons, 2001), forensic decision makers achieved suboptimal results in the assessment and treatment of their clientele. This in turn meant that the numbers of forensic patients and the violent behavior of those released to the community were higher than necessary given current empirical findings (Rice, Harris, Cormier, et al., 2004).

Assuring Program Integrity

Proper implementation of treatment programs in secure institutions presents formidable difficulties. Program Development Evaluation (G. D. Gottfredson, 1984) emphasizes the accurate measurement of the internal integrity or quality control aspects of interventions. In any institution, it is important that clinical staff interact with patients in a manner that fosters the attainment of rehabilitative goals. Of general concern, therefore, is the extent to which staff behavior creates a therapeutic atmosphere as opposed to an antitherapeutic one. More specifically, it is essential to focus on whether and how well staff perform specific tasks related to particular treatment programs. An extensive literature demonstrates that the condition of psychiatric inpatients is often worsened during hospitalization through the process of institutionalization. Institutionalization has often been associated with punitive staff attitudes toward clients, discouragement of initiative, and lack of meaningful tasks or direction for frontline workers.

It is not difficult to understand why staff behavior is quite resistant to change in typical institutions. Most institutions are strongly hierarchical, and frontline staff have little say in management decisions. Programs are often so poorly specified that no one is sure what is supposed to be done. Frontline staff are not rewarded for therapeutic interactions with institutional residents, and supervisory staff often do not model such behaviors. Moreover, program managers, who might be expected to implement interventions known to affect staff performance, almost never have line authority over frontline staff. Managers frequently use ineffective methods in attempting to improve staff behaviors; memos and in-service training programs alone are insufficient to develop or maintain appropriate staff behaviors. Administrators inadvertently signal that treatment is unimportant (e.g., by basing staff assignments and promotions on criteria unrelated to program performance). Security issues in secure psychiatric settings further exacerbate efforts to change the interactions of frontline workers with patients.

Whereas the technology of implementing rehabilitation programs is not well developed, improvement is possible in at least some situations. In an environment where program managers have relatively complete control over staff hiring and duties, nonprofessional staff can maintain a therapeutic atmosphere and can systematically interact with chronic and assaultive mental patients in therapeutic interactions, as documented by Paul and Lentz (1977). Frontline staff are enabled to perform and maintain therapeutic behaviors under the following conditions:

- they receive detailed written description of the desired behaviors;
- their supervisors offer frequent approval of enactments of the behaviors and a description of precisely what was being approved;
- they receive continuous posted feedback describing progress on staff target behaviors;
- they are given rewards for superior performance; and
- they have input into decision making.

Prerequisites for these interventions are a well-managed institution with a detailed overall program plan and individualized treatment objectives.

Institutional managers frequently do not know how staff behave, whether change is occurring on the front line, or what important clinical events transpire. Institutional records of assaults, seclusions, and most other events are notoriously unreliable. For this reason, specifically developed information systems are required to measure important clinical events and staff behaviors.

Assaults and Other Incidents

Because assaults on other inmates or on staff are relatively commonplace (assaultiveness was rated for 22% of the offenders in our Ontario Survey), assault frequency is one area that can be singled out for precise and continuous measurement to obtain information about the integrity of interventions. Institutional assaultiveness does not emanate solely from psychopathology but relates in an intimate way to institutional social systems, of which frontline staff are an integral part. Because variations in staff behaviors affect assault frequency, assaults are an important, if indirect, indicator of staff clinical skills. Moreover, assaults are clinically significant in their own right and can be measured in an accurate manner by carefully defining assaults and having investigators interview patient and staff witnesses within a day or two of each incident. As might be inferred from the discussion in chapter 4, informal impressions, even by victims, of the levels of interpersonal violence are surprisingly inaccurate (e.g., Hilton, Harris, & Rice, 1998, 2003b). Changes in staff behaviors can reduce institutional violence (Rice et al., 1989).

Staff–Patient Interactions

The daily interactions between staff and participants are of most direct concern in any rehabilitative program. To obtain accurate, quantitative measurements of these interactions, they must be observed as they occur. Such information not only allows rigorous prospective evaluation of institutional changes, but also can provide a stimulus for improvement and tangible evidence of progress if they are continuously communicated to staff and supervisors. Such direct observation measures as the Staff–Resident Interaction Chronograph (Paul & Lentz, 1977) permit the monitoring of treatment integrity and yield data that are directly comparable across and among institutions.

Institutional Atmosphere

Although the Staff–Resident Interaction Chronograph is the most important measure of staff performance, measures of ward atmosphere can play a valuable supplementary role. Because data can be gathered from both staff and clients, it is possible to examine the extent to which these perceptions agree. Ward atmosphere measures also are important because they provide an index of consumer satisfaction.

Clinical Notes

Another area in which management can obtain reliable information about the quality of ward-based interventions involves the measurement of the quality of clinical records and notes. Notes reflect the training, ability, and motivation of the staff who make them and can be used in studies of staff performance. Because entries in an individual patient's or inmate's file are designed to satisfy legal requirements and to convey information for use in assessment, it is of crucial importance that the information in these records provide an accurate description of those aspects relevant to clinical decision making. A clinical file should identify the behaviors that are to be changed before the client can be safely discharged or transferred, provide an accurate description of the individual's condition and behaviors that appear relevant to his ability to behave responsibly in a less secure setting, and describe the treatments provided and the outcome of these treatments.

Deficiencies in typical clinical records of progress are commonly observed. One of these involves the frequent noncomparability of observations recorded at different times. To detect clinical change, at least two comparable observations of behavior must be obtained. For instance, one could not infer that someone had improved on the basis of observations made in two very different situations, because the time the observation was made is confounded with the observational context. A more insidious kind of noncomparability results from the different interpretations of descriptive phrases used by different observers. The imprecision of commonly used negative descriptors (e.g., surly, hostile, threatening, confused) results in very poor agreement among staff members. Moreover, recorded observations typically vary in a nonrandom manner. An examination of clinical files shows that the frequency of notes increases as the inmate or patient disturbs others, thereby presenting a gloomy caricature of behavior; comparable observations made at random or regular intervals are required to provide an unbiased assessment of performance. A possible, albeit radical, solution might be to discontinue informal anecdotal clinical notes and to replace them with standardized rating scales of behaviors and counts of specific types of significant incidents.

Institutional Violence Revisited

Aggression within institutions warrants further discussion in light of the foregoing discussion on treatment integrity, because it is of great concern to those involved with secure facilities. Research and the development of theory on institutional assaultiveness (G. T. Harris & Rice, 1992) indicates that three classes of variables influence the frequency of institutional violence and, consequently, the effectiveness of interventions; they pertain to assaulters, victims of assault, and violence-promoting environments.

Most studies of institutional assaultiveness have been conducted in psychiatric institutions where the medical model predominates. It is perhaps not surprising, therefore, that most researchers begin with the assumption that the problem lies within the assaulter, and so they examine the pathology of the assaulter. Because the majority of assaults are committed by a small proportion of individuals, and because the best predictor of future institutional aggression is past institutional aggression, developing programs for those persons who have exhibited institutional violence makes good sense. As previously noted, seclusion, drugs, and restraint have been most commonly used with assaultive institutional inhabitants. The most important observation to make about these "solutions" is that although they are ubiquitous, there is almost no evidence that they reduce violence. What can be concluded is that the use of such strategies varies greatly over institutions with similar populations. Moreover, their use is related to such institutional characteristics as the amount of structured activities for clients, management style, and staff morale.

Considerable evidence (e.g., Paul & Lentz, 1977) demonstrates that behavior therapy techniques are effective in teaching assaultive individuals alternative behaviors. Difficulties with the implementation of social skills training, such as anger management and assertiveness training, however, are frequently experienced because of the tendency of institutional staff to discourage socially skillful client behaviors. Social norms for inhabitants of most institutions require them to be quiet and compliant. Thus, prosocial behaviors learned and rewarded in treatment are consequated quite differently (punished) by staff and peers. Behavioral interventions for assaultiveness at the individual level alone may not render any service to assaulters at all.

There is abundant and persuasive evidence that interventions aimed at altering the social environment in the form of token economies can have profoundly positive effects on a wide variety of behaviors, including institutional assaultiveness. Maintaining the integrity of token economies has been difficult for a variety of reasons. Bureaucratic practice is often incompatible with effective behavioral programming. It is difficult to retrain custodially oriented staff, who traditionally reward both appropriate and inappropriate behavior inconsistently, to use behavioral techniques that require the careful application of contingencies. In addition, frontline staff invariably seek to punish assaultiveness but frequently do not reinforce incompatible, appropriate responses. In token economies, frontline staff tend to lobby for more and larger penalties for misbehaviors and simultaneously to give fewer and fewer rewards for appropriate behaviors.

A second method by which attempts have been made to alter the institutional environment has been to reduce the effects of aggressive models. For example, an effort to manipulate the amount of television violence viewed by Oak Ridge patients was unsuccessful because, despite administrative approval, staff did not comply with the prescribed television regimen. Compliance fell as the rate of violence in the television diet fell; during the nonviolent regimen, staff ignored the prescription and watched what they liked (which often included violent programs). Ironically, staff were in agreement with researchers that televised violence probably increases aggressive behavior (G. T. Harris & Rice, 1992).

Probably the most radical way to reduce assaultiveness comes from studying the staff victims of assault. Victims of assault and their attackers frequently have sharply different perceptions concerning their interactions. Thus, it would seem that assaults can be decreased by changing the interpersonal behavior of peer and staff victims of assaults. Attempts at changing assaulter–victim relations by improving the social skills of unpopular patients and teaching a variety of prevention skills to staff are expensive in terms of staff time but have been given high priority at Oak Ridge relative to other training. Institutional management has frequently hired staff who had no training and experience in mental health, so it is not entirely surprising that a training course in managing aggression might be regarded as desirable but not essential.

One wonders about the actual contingencies that apply to staff behaviors, especially those consistent with reductions in assaults by inmates or patients. For instance, the impact of decisions affecting labor–management relations, such as compensating staff for working in a dangerous environment, renders the issue of incentive to reduce institutional violence questionable.

The primary reason that most behavioral interventions in institutions are difficult to maintain is that they exist in an environment that is not behavioral. That is, the contingencies that apply to the behavior of staff, administrators, and government bureaucrats often do not promote the long-term maintenance of offender behavior change. Managers rarely use behavioral principles in attempting to alter staff behaviors. Staff learn that promotions are not contingent on commitment to treatment and that their performance is more likely to be judged on such criteria as having a neat work area, "meeting well with others," or having all their paperwork done.

Effective behavioral change in both patients and staff can be maintained when consistent, appropriate contingencies for behaviors are provided (Paul & Lentz, 1977). Unless program managers and their supervisors have some knowledge about offender treatment in general and behavior modification in particular and about violence and behaviorally sound ways to reduce violence, they are unlikely to recognize, let alone reward, desirable behaviors in their subordinates. Staff trainees must be carefully selected for the necessary intellectual, social, and technical skills, as well as self-confidence and enthusiasm. Within secure treatment facilities, the optimal staff for behavioral programs, including those to reduce levels of violence, might be behavioral technicians rather than nurses. Although changing the qualifications of staff requires interventions at high levels in the system and can take considerable time, it is another way to increase the likelihood that behavioral interventions are adopted and maintained.

Despite the declarations of politicians, bureaucrats, administrators, and clinicians to the contrary, an examination of the existing contingencies reveals that reductions in institutional violence (or any other improvements in patients' adaptive behaviors) are not always the primary concern of service organizations. When such laudable ideals are the genuine goals of the organization's leaders, they are often ineffective because their efforts do not embody what is already known about human behavior change. The behavior of violent offenders, institutional staff, program managers, and bureaucrats does not change (and stay changed) simply because such changes are virtuous, moral, desirable, or dictated from above. Changes occur when the contingencies applied to the behavior support and continue to support that behavior change.

A Final Note on the Institutional Environment

The operation of secure facilities for the treatment of dangerous or aggressive clients requires a complex set of policies and procedures to promote prosocial, cooperative behavior; to provide appropriate and humane consequences for assaultive, dangerous conduct; to guide the day-to-day conduct of staff and ensure therapeutic interactions with clients to encourage them to participate in therapeutic activities; to provide criteria for the access clients have to their peers, potential weapons, and the community; and finally to guide decisions about and recommendations for discharge. Institutional token economy programs provide an effective system of policies and procedures to guide client and staff behavior. Token economies have no serious rivals as institutionwide systems to guide administrative and clinical decision making. There is good evidence that a more typical, unstructured milieu actually does harm to its inhabitants by inadvertently promoting aggressive, psychotic, and dependent behaviors.

An interesting dilemma emerges for those who consider using token economies. Some patients in our jurisdiction have made a legal challenge to the use of token economy programs, arguing that they should be able to avoid program consequences because the program is a form of treatment and they are constitutionally protected from receiving unwanted therapy. This argument, if accepted, would place clinicians in the position of having to arrange an institutional environment in which client behaviors have either no consequences or only unplanned consequences. The clinical and administrative dangers inherent in such an environment are obvious.

It is our view that the clinical leaders of an institution are obliged to use the systematic application of consequences to influence the behavior of the institution's inhabitants, including encouraging participation in treatment.

Modern scientific understandings of human behavior share the conception that behavior is strongly influenced by its consequences. This influence occurs whether or not anyone plans the consequences or whether influence is intended. Thus, behavior and attitudes are controlled in every environment. The only choice that can be made is whether the clinical leaders explicitly decide which behaviors are to be promoted and which are to be discouraged, or whether they leave this to chance. There cannot be a completely neutral (in the sense of having no effect) alternative to a carefully planned, systematic, and humane institutional program. There can be unplanned or unknown consequences of behavior, but this is not "no treatment" in the same sense that there are nontreatment alternatives to drugs, electroconvulsive therapy, or individual counseling.

Treatment and Supervision in the Community

Almost all of the treatments suggested for use with offenders and mentally disordered offenders could be provided in the community. In fact, some of the treatments (e.g., social skills training, life skills training, relapse prevention programs) actually might be more successful in a community setting. With the exception of high scorers on the Management Problems, Aggression, and Active Psychotic Symptoms scales, who may require a degree of control over the environment only possible within an institution (although rarely found there), it is difficult to argue that institutionalization is necessary, or even desirable, for treatment. Rather, in most cases the only reason for institutionalization is to protect the public.

Did our survey data suggest anything about how many offenders really needed to be in institutions? Those in the dangerous but model offender cluster were at high risk of violent recidivism but had few clinical needs. If these patients were kept in custody, they would need a high degree of perimeter security while at the same time needing little internal security and little in the way of treatment, at least as currently conceived. The task of clinicians would be to house them safely and humanely and to provide as many educational, vocational, and recreational activities as possible. It is very costly to keep these offenders institutionalized.

It would be possible for some of the survey offenders to live under supervision in the community. The key to providing adequate supervision would lie in having a well-specified theory, developed while the offender was institutionalized, about his risk factors and likely antecedents of reoffense. Close monitoring of such dynamic predictors as alcohol consumption, medication compliance, or attendance at work or school (for about half of the population for whom spare time or problems at work were criminogenic factors) would be tailored to that client's risk factors. By using the VRAG to retain the highest risk cases and tailoring treatment and supervision to the criminogenic risk factors of each offender, the number of persons held in secure institutions could be reduced (at a substantial financial savings) without increasing the risk to society.

Alternatively, the same strategy could be used to reduce the instances of violent recidivism without changing the number of individuals held in secure units. For the highest risk offenders (the exact criterion of high risk would be a political, not a clinical, decision), permanent institutionalization should be implemented. For low-risk individuals, treatment for criminogenic needs could be provided under modest supervision in the community. For higher risk clients, treatment for criminogenic factors could occur within the institution, or at least begin in the institution, and continue under aggressive community supervision. Noncriminogenic factors for these persons could be treated entirely in the community.

As we demonstrate in the next section and as the literature suggests, postrelease factors are closely related to recidivism. It is strongly recommended, therefore, that the purpose of intervention be reconceptualized from attempting to produce a cure with an intervention given in an institutional environment to enhancing long-term adjustment through continuing intervention extending into the community. Furthermore, because it is likely that the effects of institutional interventions seldom generalize across settings and because of the previously discussed punitive atmosphere of institutional environments, interventions should occur in the settings in which the behaviors occur.

PROCESS OF RECIDIVISM AND RELAPSE PREVENTION

Zamble and Quinsey (1997) studied men who had committed one of three kinds of offense while under supervision and had been returned to a federal prison. The offense types were assault (n = 102), robbery (n = 100), and property (n = 109). Offenders were interviewed very shortly after their readmission to prison. The interview focused on the recidivists' patterns of socialization, moods, and cognitions prior to their reoffense. They were also administered a large number of other instruments, including the Level of Supervision Inventory (LSI; Andrews, Kiessling, & Kominos, 1983), the Beck Depression Inventory (A. T. Beck, 1967), the State Anxiety Scale (Spielberger, Gorsuch, & Lushene, 1970), the Multimodal Anger Inventory (Siegel, 1986), the Alcohol Dependence Scale (Skinner & Horn, 1984), and the Drug Abuse Screening Test (Skinner, 1982). Offenders' coping skills were assessed by having them propose solutions to five common problem scenarios comprising the Coping Vignettes Scale (Zamble & Porporino, 1988).

The recidivists' coping skills were very poor, poorer than a comparison sample of 39 nonrecidivists and much poorer than those found in nonoffender samples. Not surprisingly, therefore, living outside of prison had been difficult for most of them. They were subject to the variety of problems faced by most people, plus those associated with their recent release from prison, such as serious difficulties in finding legal employment. Moreover, the inadequate coping skills of the recidivists appeared to create even more difficulties, such as frequent interpersonal conflicts. As a result of their problems, their predominant moods were dysphoric, with depression, anxiety, frustration, and anger very common.

For many recidivists, there appeared to have been a downward trend in their moods and the tenor of their thoughts about their lives. There was also evidence of emotional change, with a shift toward anger for some (especially assaulters). These changes were particularly visible for those who had been released less than a month before their new offense, because the measurements in the study captured the entire period of their release. These data, although obtained retrospectively, support the belief that there are identifiable precursors to reoffending. Once initiated, however, the time course for the commission of these offenses was extremely brief. Premeditation often involved only minutes.

Recidivists frequently articulated a linkage between negative emotional states and the problems they experienced. When asked what had set off their (mostly negative) feelings in the preoffense period, recidivists differed significantly from nonrecidivists in the choices of interpersonal problems, lack of money, and substance (especially alcohol) abuse. The largest difference was in the interpersonal problems category, cited by 37% of recidivists and only 6% of nonrecidivists.

When static variables such as age and criminal history were covaried, patterns of socialization or drug and alcohol use still differentiated reliably between the recidivists and nonrecidivists. Reoffenders still perceived more (and more serious) problems in interpersonal relationships and in substance abuse. The differences in emotional responses and coping adequacy and the changes over time in mood and cognitions remained significant. Each measure of emotional states indicated that the substantial incidence of emotional problems reported by recidivists in the preoffense period is not characteristic of all ex-offenders.

The "coping–criminality" hypothesis supported by this research appears to support some form of relapse prevention approach to the reduction of recidivism. However, although dysphoria appears to be a dynamic antecedent of reoffending, the reason for this link is not immediately obvious (some ideas are offered in the next section and are based on documentary evidence obtained before the reoffending). A theoretical explanation for this link may be provided by Leith and Baumeister's (1996) studies on emotion and decision making that demonstrate that negative emotions, such as depression and anger, increase risk acceptance in suboptimal ways when combined with high arousal. The mechanism producing self-defeating behavior appears to involve a decline in self-regulation as opposed to changes in perceived utilities:

When people become upset, they take risks that seem ill-advised, at least in light of rational analysis. Furthermore, it appears that being upset causes people to abandon that very light of rational analysis in making such decisions. Undoubtedly the capacity for such rational analysis is one of the greatest treasures of human nature, and it is sad to realize how easily emotional distress can induce people to spurn that treasure–often with costly and tragic results. The combination of high arousal and unpleasantness appears to be crucial: Neither feeling bad nor feeling aroused was alone sufficient to elicit such irrational, self-defeating patterns of choice. These aroused, bad moods cut short rational consideration of options, promote risky choices, and hence leave people at the mercy of long odds. When they are upset, they seem not to recognize that they are stacking the deck against themselves. (Leith & Baumeister, 1996, p. 1265)

Treatment of high-risk offenders is ultimately aimed at preventing repetition of the inappropriate, dangerous, or criminal behaviors that led to their commitment. The treatments described in this chapter can be placed in the context of relapse prevention, or relapse prevention can be offered as a treatment module separate from other intervention targets because it is thought that the conditions underlying the maintenance of treatment-induced behavioral change are different than those involved in its initiation. Recidivism may result from a failure to maintain treatment effects (Laws, 1989).

Annis and Davis (1989) suggested that relapse is a failure to maintain behavior change rather than a failure to initiate it. Their model of relapse suggests that in a high-risk situation, individuals begin a cognitive appraisal that leads to a judgment of their ability to cope with the situation. For many, this cognitive appraisal is automatic or has never been consciously scrutinized. Thus, they may not be aware of the choices, decisions, and expectations that precede and accompany their inappropriate behaviors. The behaviors or high-risk situations just seem to happen on their own. This interpretation is supported by interview data from recidivists (Zamble & Quinsey, 1997).

Maintenance of treatment-induced behavioral change is conceptualized in a relapse prevention model as dependent on three things: (a) self-efficacy, the confidence in one's ability to cope with a situation in which the risk of relapsing is high; (b) coping skills, the possession of the requisite skills to cope with various risk situations; and (c) motivation, the desire or the incentive not to relapse. Relapse prevention thus attempts to increase offenders' self-efficacy, coping skills, and motivation. Coping skills are often also covered in stand-alone modules, such as those dealing with anger management and substance abuse. Through cognitive (providing insight into the how and why of their behavior) and behavioral (providing actual experiences of mastery and success) means, a relapse prevention approach teaches offenders new ways of coping that may allow them to break the cycle before they relapse completely: "Relapse prevention relies heavily on the client's ability to learn and to initiate appropriate coping behaviors at the earliest possible point in the relapse process" (Laws, 1989, p. 139). By understanding their behavior and what led up to it, offenders can learn to plan and rehearse alternative, prosocial behaviors. Appropriate contingencies must be in place for the maintenance of these behaviors.

DYNAMIC RISK

The idea that there is a process of recidivism implies that there are dynamic risk factors that are able to change and that, when changed, alter the risk of recidivism. A distinction must be made between those dynamic risk factors that are fixed before a follow-up period begins (e.g., change occasioned by an in-prison treatment program) and those that change during a period of opportunity to reoffend (e.g., changes in mood or degree of compliance). Because the former are fixed at a point in time, they function as static predictors for the purposes of prediction. Variables that are dynamic during the follow-up period must be measured periodically. Changes in these variables can be used to predict variations in risk over short time intervals.

Retrospective Study of Dynamic Risk

Although the historical items that predict violent and sexual recidivism cannot change, certain characteristics of offenders do change over time, and changes in these characteristics are related to violent and sexual recidivism. In the first of a series of three studies of dynamic predictors that vary during the follow-up period, Quinsey, Coleman, Jones, and Altrows (1997) compared 60 mentally disordered male offenders who had eloped from a hospital or reoffended while under supervision with 51 male offenders who had done neither. Offenders were matched on diagnosis, age, and level of supervision. In addition to the VRAG and other static measures, potentially dynamic variables were coded from clinical file information recorded either in the 1-month or 6-month period before the elopement or reoffense or control date (i.e., a date chosen for the comparison offenders to match that of the recidivists) for all offenders, as well as from a control period of equal length a year earlier for the elopers and offenders. It was thus ensured that the predictors were completely independent of static risk by either using a within-patient comparison or, less satisfactorily, by covarying VRAG scores in between-patient comparisons. The 1-month predictors were four subscales, Dynamic Antisociality, Psychiatric Symptoms, Poor Compliance, and Medication Noncompliance, collectively termed the Proximal Risk Factor Scale. The 6-month predictors were five subscales of the Problem Identification Checklist (modified from the staff rating version of G. T. Harris & Rice, 1990; Rice & Harris, 1988; Rice et al., 1996; Rice, Harris, Quinsey, & Cyr,

1990; see Appendix L): Psychotic Behaviors, Skill Deficits, Inappropriate and Procriminal Social Behaviors, Mood Problems, and Social Withdrawal.

Seven dynamic variables statistically differentiated elopers and reoffenders from other patients after controlling for actuarial risk level and also differentiated the period preceding eloping or reoffending from an earlier period among elopers and reoffenders. These predictors were thus extremely robust in surviving both the within-patient and between-patient comparisons. They involved primarily two kinds of items: those pertaining to noncompliance and procriminal sentiment and those pertaining to dysphoric mood or psychiatric symptoms. The 1-month predictors produced generally larger effect sizes, probably because of their closer temporal relationship with eloping or reoffending.

Only the items reflecting antisocial traits were related to violent reoffending. These violent reoffenses were quite serious: Of 19 violent reoffenders, 3 committed murder, 5 attempted murder, 1 wounding, 2 assault causing bodily harm, 3 common assault, 4 rape, and 1 indecent assault. The best predictor of violent reoffending was a factor in the 1-month data labeled Dynamic Antisociality. Dynamic Antisociality includes items reflecting procriminal sentiments. A factor in the 6-month data, the Inappropriate and Procriminal Social Behaviors scale of the Problem Behavior Checklist was correlated with Dynamic Antisociality and was a somewhat weaker predictor of violent reoffending. Both of these dynamic factors contain items that are similar to static items of the PCL–R.

The static nature of the PCL–R and the continuously varying dynamic nature of Dynamic Antisociality are not contradictory. The scoring of the PCL–R uses a lifetime perspective approach in which the items that are not simply historical are scored using the person's entire previous history, whereas Dynamic Antisociality items are scored using data from only a 1-month period.

A further factor in the 1-month data labeled Psychiatric Symptoms contained items reflecting both positive and negative schizophrenic symptoms. Psychiatric Symptoms was not significantly correlated with violent reoffending and was inconsistently correlated with nonviolent reoffending but was strongly related to eloping. The finding that Psychiatric Symptoms did not predict violent reoffending is not inconsistent with the finding that a diagnosis of schizophrenia is associated with reduced risk of violent reoffending (Gardner, Lidz, Mulvey, & Shaw, 1996; G. T. Harris, Rice, & Cormier, 2002; G. T. Harris, Rice, & Quinsey, 1993; Monahan et al., 2001; Villeneuve & Quinsey, 1995) because a diagnosis of schizophrenia is a static variable. In this study, schizophrenic symptoms were treated as a dynamic variable. The question being addressed was in essence a conditional one: Given a schizophrenic patient, does the exacerbation of symptoms relate to eloping or reoffending? The answer to this question was positive with respect to elopement and negative with respect to violent reoffending. This study suggests that early intervention in response to psychotic symptoms and to noncompliance with medication may reduce the likelihood of elopement, but it is unlikely to much affect violent reoffending.

The finding that worsening psychiatric symptoms predicted elopement but not violent reoffending is consistent with the static differences between elopers who were more frequently psychotic and the violent reoffenders who were more frequently personality disordered. There is thus an interaction between static patient characteristics and the prognostic significance of changes in particular behaviors. Psychotic offenders are, in comparison to personality-disordered offenders, more likely to elope (and not reoffend) and to do so when their symptoms worsen. However, increases in Dynamic Antisociality predicted both elopement and violent reoffending. It is thus a poor prognostic sign for simple elopement and for violent reoffending among both psychotic and personality-disordered patients.

This first study of dynamic predictors was encouraging but limited in several ways. The most important limitation was the retrospective nature of the design. The coders could not be kept completely blind with respect to when incidents occurred. We attempted to address this issue of potential retrospective bias by having a second coder rate a subset of the files when completely blind to the outcomes; the second coder achieved excellent agreement with the first coding. Nevertheless, a prospective demonstration was required. A second limitation was that specially trained and highly qualified coders had to laboriously extract the information from the files. Although clinicians clearly record information in files that can be coded as successful dynamic predictors, can they, if untrained, explicitly make ratings of the variables that we originally identified in their written records?

Before turning to this question, we might wonder whether the dynamic risk indicators identified among forensic psychiatric patients are unique to that population or, like static predictors, are similar across offender populations. An answer is provided by Hanson and Harris (2000), who conducted a study of 208 recidivist and 201 nonrecidivist sex offenders released from Canadian federal corrections. Offenders were matched on sex offense history, victim type, and jurisdiction. Data were obtained from offenders' institutional files and interview and file information from community supervision officers. The community data pertained to a period beginning a month before the interview for the nonrecidivists and a month before the sexual reoffense for the recidivists (Time 1) and a month period 6 months earlier (Time 2). The three best static predictors of sexual recidivism were the VRAG ($r = .32$), sexual deviance ($r = .24$), and IQ ($r = -.24$). The best three predictors from the officer interview classified as stable dynamic factors were *sees self as no risk* ($r = .47$), *poor social influence* ($r = .39$), and *sexual entitlement* ($r = .37$). Lastly, the three best acute dynamic factors identified from the officer interview were *access to victims* ($r = .28$), *noncooperation with supervision* ($r = .25$), and *anger* ($r = .19$). Only two significant differences between Time 1 and Time 2 data were found: Officers noted an increase in anger for the recidivists, and the recidivists were more likely to have begun taking antiandrogen therapy. Because the interview data could be contaminated by retrospective bias, data from the Time 2 officer notes were examined separately. Only a Sexual Preoccupation scale predicted recidivism after static predictors were controlled. Hanson and Harris concluded,

> This study attempted to control for retrospective recall biases by examining the case notes completed by the officers before they knew of the recidivism event. This strategy was only partially successful due to the limited information available in the case notes. Nevertheless, the major dynamic risk factors reported in the interview were also present in the contemporaneous case notes. The officers recorded concerns about sexual preoccupation/compulsivity, poor self-management strategies (sees self as no risk), increased victim access, and increased anger in the 4 to 6 weeks before recidivating. (p. 30)

Field Study of High-Risk Men With Intellectual Disabilities

Two field trials to address the limitations of our retrospective study of dynamic risk factors have been conducted. The first (Quinsey, 2004; Quinsey, Book, & Skilling, 2004) followed the transfer or release of 58 men with intellectual disabilities and histories of serious antisocial behaviors who were residing in institutions about to be closed. The histories of the antisocial behaviors in which clients had engaged varied widely in seriousness and chronicity. About 70% of the clients had documented incidents or charges for sex offenses of various kinds; almost all of these were hands-on offenses. It was common for clients to have committed sexual offenses against children in the community and to offend against adult peers in the institution. Clients were sometimes charged for their misbehaviors, particularly if they occurred in a community setting, but often these charges were dropped on their institutionalization or transfer to a more secure institution. More than half of the clients presented chronic management problems involving sexual or physical aggressiveness, or both, within the institution.

The 58 clients who had been transferred to community settings were followed for 16 months. Staff reported more than 500 incidents during the follow-up period. Most of these were minor, and two clients contributed more than half of them; 39 of the 58 clients had at least one incident. In terms of the most serious incident per client, there were seven AWOL incidents, one incident of fire setting, four incidents involving hands-on sexual misbehaviors, and 27 violent incidents involving physical contact between the client and another person. All the violent or sexual incidents involved staff or other clients, and none involved community members. Only two of the victims of

violent incidents required medical attention, although minor physical injuries involving scratches, bite marks, and bruising were common. Many of the
incidents required staff to intervene physically to restrain the client. The
most serious violent incident occurred during an outing in which a client
pursued and repeatedly punched his lone female escort.

The VRAG was scored using the CATS to replace the PCL–R because
the former is much simpler to score than the latter, particularly for individuals with intellectual disabilities. There were, however, some missing data in
the files that pertained to the CATS item of the VRAG. VRAG scores were
not prorated. The correlation between the number of missing items and the
VRAG score was –.22, indicating that on average, missing data resulted in
an underestimation of static risk. The interrater agreement on the VRAG
was good; the average interrater correlation based on five cases and four independent raters was .89.

Trained raters completed the Problem Identification Checklist (see
Appendix L) and a shortened version of the Proximal Risk Factor Scale (see
Appendix M) from institutional files. These predictors were treated analytically as static variables because they were scored before the follow-up period
began (and thus could not change).

A number of the predictors were significantly related to whether clients were involved in an incident of any type. In descending order of magnitude of effect, the significant predictors were Mood Problems, Inappropriate
and Procriminal Social Behaviors, Dynamic Antisociality, and a single item,
denies all problems.

The VRAG exhibited the highest correlation with whether clients committed a new violent or sexual misbehavior ($r = .32$). Predictive accuracy, as
defined by the area under the relative operating characteristic curve, was .69
($SE = .07$, $p = .02$). The mean VRAG scores for the 21 clients who had
committed a new violent offense and the 37 who had not were 11.38 ($SD =
6.26$) and 6.89 ($SD = 6.70$), respectively. The only other variable that sig-
nificantly predicted violent and sexual incidents was the Inappropriate and
and Procriminal Social Behaviors score (from the Problem Identification
Checklist), although a stepwise multiple regression analysis selected only the
VRAG as a predictor of violent and sexual incidents, $t(58) = 2.19$, $p = .032$.
The VRAG showed low positive correlations with predictors reflecting antisocial conduct and attitudes. Ratings of Mood Problems, Inappropriate and
Procriminal Social Behaviors, Dynamic Antisociality, and *denies all problems*
showed substantial intercorrelations.

A number of variables predicted incidents of any kind (in addition to
violent and sexual incidents, primarily elopement, threats, and property destruction). Ratings of Mood Problems were the most successful of these, although ratings of antisocial tendencies were also significant. Most of these
other variables were correlated with each other, suggesting that they measured the same or related underlying dimensions.

The correlations among the measures were in the direction and of the magnitude expected. The VRAG was not expected to correlate highly with measures that potentially change over time, because for an individual client, the VRAG is fixed at the time of the index offense or admission to the current facility. This expectation remains even if the measures that change over time are treated as static predictors because they were measured only once. Thus, the VRAG should correlate positively with the Dynamic Antisociality scale and the Inappropriate Social and Procriminal Social Behaviors scale from the Problem Behavior Checklist and negatively with the Psychotic Behavior scale of the Problem Behavior Checklist. The expected pattern of correlations was obtained.

The level of predictive accuracy obtained with the VRAG was moderate but a little lower than that achieved in previous studies. Nevertheless, given the circumstances of this follow-up study, the performance of the VRAG was very good. The VRAG significantly predicted new violent or sexual misbehaviors in supervised settings (not primarily charges in the community, as in most previous research) in a relatively small sample consisting exclusively of men with intellectual disabilities, with some amount of missing data, over a relatively short time period, and while substituting the CATS for the PCL–R. More important, men identified as higher risk on the basis of the VRAG were afforded a great deal more supervision than those assessed as lower risk. The VRAG, for example, correlated .29 (44, $p < .014$, one-tailed) with whether a professional had been consulted about the treatment or management of a client in the receiving facility.

In summary, the VRAG was the best static predictor of those examined of new violent or sexual misbehaviors among men with intellectual disabilities and histories of antisocial behavior. Rates of such incidents were high. The VRAG results confirm the enduring nature of the risk for reoffending, suggesting that programs for high-risk clients must be available for the indefinite future.

Following client transfer to the community settings, staff assisting the clients in their new placements provided monthly ratings of client behaviors in addition to the incident report forms. Our analyses were designed to address three key questions:

1. Are the rating scales internally consistent when used in a field trial with untrained raters?
2. Do clients who become involved in incidents have higher risk scores on average than those who do not?
3. Do ratings of risk rise before clients become involved in incidents?

All of the 58 clients reported on were included, save one for whom we received incident data but no staff ratings because he was transferred to his family home. Each month staff filled out shortened versions of the Problem

Identification Checklist (26 items plus a single item scale—the Therapeutic Alliance Scale; Beauford, McNiel, & Binder, 1997, shown in Appendix N) and the Proximal Risk Factor Scale (18 items plus the Therapeutic Alliance Scale), as well as an incident report form. At most sites these first two scales were filled out independently, the former by the frontline worker most closely involved with the client and the latter by a nonfrontline worker associated with the case.

Between-client analyses were conducted on the average ratings obtained over all months and, for those clients who had incidents, up to 6 months preceding the first incident (hereafter, *previous months*), as well as the month preceding the first incident (hereafter, the *prior month*). The between-client analyses were repeated covarying the VRAG. Within-client analyses for those clients who had incidents were conducted on the previous months, the prior month, and the month containing the incident (the *index month*).

Considering ratings of clients in the preceding or prior months, Medication Compliance/Dysphoria, Poor Compliance, Dynamic Antisociality, and Inappropriate and Procriminal Social Behaviors significantly discriminated clients who subsequently had incidents from those who did not. All but Inappropriate and Procriminal Social Behaviors were significant predictors when the VRAG was statistically controlled. Four subscales failed to differentiate the groups: Psychiatric Symptoms, Psychotic Behaviors, Mood Problems, and Social Withdrawal.

The same variables were the best discriminators of clients who subsequently had violent or sexual incidents from those who had none. Medication Compliance/Dysphoria, Poor Compliance, Dynamic Antisociality, and Inappropriate and Procriminal Social Behaviors were significant predictors whether rated in the previous months or prior month. However, when the VRAG was statistically controlled, Inappropriate and Procriminal Social Behaviors was not a significant predictor, and none of the variables were significant when taken from just the prior month.

Within-client analyses using only clients who had incidents of any kind or violent or sexual incidents were conducted to examine the relation of changes in ratings to antisocial incidents. Because these analyses focused on changes within clients, no variables were covaried. The index month could have been contaminated by retrospective bias because the ratings may have been completed *after* the incident was recorded for that month. Because of this, the cleanest comparison for showing that ratings of risk increase in the period before an incident is prior month versus previous months, although for this comparison to be relevant, one must assume that the dynamic risk variables change very slowly.

Considering the outcome of incidents of any kind, trend tests over previous months, prior month, and index month were significant for six of the nine dynamic predictors (Psychotic Symptoms, Poor Compliance, and Medication Compliance/Dysphoria did not achieve significance). Turning to pairwise comparisons among the three time periods, there were some significant differences among months leading up to an incident of any type for all four Problem Identification Checklist subscales. Inappropriate and Procriminal Social Behaviors was the best predictor of subsequent incidents of any kind. For violent or sexual incidents, only trend tests for Psychotic Behaviors and Inappropriate and Procriminal Social Behaviors achieved significance. However, none of the predictors were significant with the cleanest but very conservative test of previous months versus prior months for either incidents of any kind or violent or sexual incidents.

In summary, the data from the field trial were surprisingly orderly. The subscales of the rating instruments had very good internal reliability or consistency. Staff showed moderate agreement among themselves about client ratings. There were very large differences in the ratings taken from months before the first incident occurred between clients who had incidents and those who did not, even when the best measure of static risk, the VRAG, was statistically controlled. Clients' risk scores appeared to increase before events occurred, although these differences were not significant in the cleanest comparison of prior versus previous months. The scales that were most closely related to incidents were those that have been found to predict eloping, aggression, and criminal conduct in our previous research (Quinsey, Coleman, et al., 1997).

Monthly staff ratings of client characteristics from months in which clients exhibited no antisocial behaviors differentiated clients who subsequently had antisocial incidents from those who did not, suggesting that these changes may be useful for establishing treatment targets and titrating supervision. There was also evidence from within-client analyses that changes in staff ratings foreshadowed new antisocial behaviors, but these results await confirmation.

Future risk management strategies for intellectually handicapped offenders may benefit from static and dynamic risk appraisal. An appropriate model for the provision of services for this population appears to be assertive community treatment (e.g., Burns & Santos, 1995; Lafave, de Souza, & Gerber, 1996). The need for long-term support of the type involved in assertive community treatment is, of course, not restricted to clients who are at risk to reoffend, but also applies to persons with intellectual disabilities who have behavioral or psychiatric problems (A. H. Reid & Ballinger, 1995) and chronic mental patients. We have described specific treatment methods for clusters of forensic clients who present different patterns of risk and need in detail earlier in this chapter and in a model of service delivery for intellectually handicapped men with histories of sexual offending (Griffiths, Quinsey, & Hingsburger, 1989). Interventions for intellectually disabled clients that have the potential to reduce long-term risk have been reviewed in books edited by Cipani (1989) and Lindsay, Taylor, and Sturmey (2004). In addition to interventions designed to reduce the dangerousness of high-risk clients, however, two further elements of programming require careful attention: supervision and crisis intervention.

The degree of risk that an agency is able to assume depends on the amount and quality of supervision available in the community and the characteristics of the environment, such as access to young or vulnerable persons, in which the client is placed. Supervision for very high risk clients requires that a particular person be responsible for authorizing a particular level of supervision for an individual client and for coordinating its implementation. It is also necessary that that person have the legal authority to compel compliance (Wiederanders, 1992; Wiederanders, Bromley, & Choate, 1997).

One of the components of assertive community treatment is 24-hour availability of staff. In the "Rochester Model," Davidson et al. (1995) documented the importance of the availability of a crisis team in the management of persons with intellectual disabilities together with behavioral and psychiatric problems. The crisis team's resources included inpatient beds where clients could be stabilized before re-entering the community. This is a particularly important capability in the management of high-risk clients.

A reasonably accurate estimate of long-term risk is required to determine the appropriate level of supervision required for individual clients. The VRAG appears capable of providing such an estimate. Ongoing management of risk and changes in level of supervision, however, require monitoring of changes in dynamic risk so as to proactively adjust supervision. The dynamic variables rated in the field trial appear promising for this task because they differentiated clients who subsequently exhibited antisocial behaviors from those who did not, although they did not significantly differentiate clients who had exclusively violent or sexual incidents from those who did not. Further research is required to demonstrate that temporal changes in dynamic variables within individual clients are related to the imminence of their antisocial behaviors. To accomplish this, it may be necessary to obtain staff ratings more frequently than once a month. Our previous research (Quinsey, Coleman, et al., 1997) documented dynamic risk factors by comparing measures documented during the month leading up to an incident of antisocial behavior in comparison to measures taken in a month period a year earlier. Even ratings made weekly would be more likely to reflect changes in client characteristics that are temporally more closely linked to the occurrence of antisocial events.

Preliminary results from a small sample of intellectually handicapped offenders in a security hospital setting (Lindsay et al., manuscript submitted) indicate that daily ratings of proximal risk factors, such as mood, compliance, self-regulation, and aberrant thoughts yielded substantial effect sizes in the prediction of incidents such as institutional violence, drug offenses, and absconding. Assessments were recorded on the day of the incident, the day before the incident, and a control day at least 7 days before or after an incident. These results suggest that better temporal resolution of changes in dynamic risk may result in better prediction.

Field Study of Forensic Psychiatric Patients

Quinsey, Jones, Book, and Barr (in press) conducted a field investigation of staff ratings of dynamic predictors on a large multisite sample of forensic psychiatric patients who had been found unfit for trial or not criminally responsible by reason of mental disorder. The study used a method similar to that used with the developmentally handicapped sample described earlier in this chapter and the same measures (shortened versions of the Problem Identification Checklist and the Proximal Risk Factor Scale to which the Therapeutic Alliance Scale had been added). The study was designed to answer three questions:

1. whether postrelease dynamic predictors were related to violent offenses and antisocial behaviors of any kind under field conditions in which regular staff completed the ratings and received little or no training in doing so,
2. which of these predictors were best suited to this purpose, and
3. the degree to which the dynamic predictors operated in the same manner among offenders who varied in their levels of static risk.

There were 467 male patients and 64 female patients in the study (information on the sex of 34 individuals was missing). The majority were diagnosed with a psychotic disorder (primarily schizophrenia), and most had been charged with a violent offense. The 565 patients were followed for an average of 33 (SD = 14.67) months and a maximum of 54 months. Nearly half of them lived in the community at some point. There were 265 incidents over the follow-up period involving 144 patients. Eighty-six of these were violent incidents (excluding threats, attempted assaults, and property destruction), 52 involved escape or escape attempts, 37 were nonviolent offenses, and 6 were hands-on sexual offenses (hereafter classified as violent). The remaining incidents were not clearly specified but were not violent. There were 144 patients who could be included in within-patient analyses of incidents of any kind because they had at least two incident-free months preceding an incident and 42 patients who had at least two incident-free months preceding a violent incident.

Patients who had an incident of any type scored in significantly higher VRAG ranges or categories (actual VRAG scores were not available) than patients who had none. Patients who had incidents received higher ratings on most subscales of the instruments than patients who had none, as expected. In these analyses, ratings were averaged over all months that did not contain an incident (index months were excluded to eliminate retrospective bias). Similarly, patients with incidents had more variable ratings on most subscales than those with none, providing a necessary condition for them to function as dynamic predictors. Over all patients, there was a nonsignificant trend for the probability of a violent incident to increase with higher VRAG categories. However, most of the subscales of the instruments scored during the follow-up period reliably distinguished between patients with and without violent incidents. Finally, patients with violent incidents had more variable ratings over months on most subscales than those without.

Within-patient analyses of variance for those patients who had incidents were conducted on the average of up to 6 months preceding the month before the index month, the month immediately preceding the index month (the prior month), and the index month (the month containing the incident). Of course, the comparison between the previous months and the prior month is the most important, because it could not be contaminated by retrospective bias. For the key comparison between the prior month and the average of previous months, Dynamic Antisociality, Poor Compliance, and the Therapeutic Alliance item (all rated by the nursing staff) were found to increase significantly prior to an incident. However, only Inappropriate and Procriminal Social Behaviors and Therapeutic Alliance (rated by the nonnursing staff) changed significantly before a violent incident.

Using only patients who had incidents of the relevant type, each item was run through a dependent-samples t test comparing the prior month to the 6 months previous to that. Any items that showed an increase in magnitude and a p of less than .25 were retained for the Dynamic Risk Appraisal Scale. Analyses were conducted separately for any incident and violent incidents. For General Risk the analysis resulted in a 23-item subscale and for Violence Risk, a 10-item subscale. The items are shown in Appendix N. Alpha coefficients were .93 and .79 for the General Risk and Violent Risk subscales, respectively. The mean rating for general risk was 16.89 (SD = 13.93) out of a possible 92 and for Violent Risk 5.57 (SD = 5.03) out of a possible 40. Both subscales (averaged over nonincident months for each patient) correlated significantly with static risk as measured by the VRAG categories.

The total scores for each of the new subscales were calculated for each individual and were analyzed using repeated-measures ANOVAs. As would be expected because of the way in which the items were chosen, General Risk ratings rose in a linear fashion leading up to incidents of any type and Violent Risk scores rose linearly leading up to violent incidents.

To determine whether changes in the Dynamic Risk Appraisal Scale ratings were related to changes in the probability of an incident over time using data from all patients (not just those who had incidents), we conducted trajectory analyses using all patients. Nagin and his colleagues (B. L. Jones, Nagin, & Roeder, 1998; Nagin, 1999) developed a procedure that combines growth curve modeling (i.e., tracking change over time) with the ability to look for distinct clusters or groups within the growth curves and to assess what characteristics define these distinct groups. That is, this procedure can be used when the population does not comprise a continuous distribution, as is assumed in other growth curve modeling techniques, but is rather a mixture of different groups defined by different probability distributions. Trajectory analysis was developed to analyze repeated-measures data (developmental trajectories) by fitting a latent mixture model, involving semiparametric or discrete distributions, to longitudinal data.

This method applies to this data set because the dependent variable was discrete (incident vs. no incident) and was measured multiple times for each participant. It is important that the procedure allows for time-dependent covariates to be entered into the model. The General Risk rating and whether the individual lived in the community were entered as time-dependent covariates in the model predicting an incident of any type. The Violence Risk rating and community variable were used as time-dependent covariates in the model predicting only violent incidents. For these analyses, an additional 30 patients who were not included in the rest of the study because they had less than 6 months of follow-up data were included, making the total sample size for the trajectory analysis 595 patients. Once again, ratings for the index month were not included in these analyses. In these analyses, a patient could have multiple incidents (but only one in a particular month).

The best model for general risk identified a high- and a low-incident group. Two regression equations, one for each group, predicting the probability of an incident in any given month resulted from the analysis. As previously mentioned, the variables included as predictors were the General Risk score for each month and whether the individual was living in the community that month. The predictors acted slightly differently for the two groups. For the low general risk group, increases in General Risk over months and moving into the community significantly increased the odds of having an incident. However, for the high general risk group, only increases in the General Risk score over months predicted incidents.

The best model for Violence Risk involved only one group, because the predictors acted similarly across patients. Increases in Violence Risk score over the prior months resulted in an increased probability of having a violent incident, but moving into the community was not related to the probability of a violent incident.

Because the items for the Dynamic Risk Appraisal Scale were identified on the basis of their relation to outcome, cross-validation is essential. Fortunately, the data from the field study of high-risk men with intellectual disabilities described earlier provide an opportunity for cross-validation because the same items were used in both field studies, even though the samples were quite different. The General Risk subscale differentiated clients who had at least one incident from those who had none using the average of nonindex months ($p < .009$, one-tailed), and the Violence Risk subscale differentiated clients who had at least one violent incident from those who had none using the average of nonindex months ($p < .022$, one-tailed). With respect to detecting changing risk, the General Risk subscale increased between previous and prior months for any incident ($p = .052$, one-tailed). The Violence Risk subscale showed an increase between previous and prior months for violent incidents ($p < .006$).

How should the Dynamic Risk Appraisal Scales be interpreted? A unit change in dynamic risk score reflects a change in the probability of an incident occurring in the near future. However, the overall probability of an event occurring is very different for individuals who have high as opposed to low average scores. The probability of at least one event of any type occurring each month for the approximately 10% of high-risk patients was .08, whereas the probability of an event occurring each month was .004 for the remainder. Therefore, even though the change in probability of a subsequent incident with a unit change in General Risk Scale score from one month to the next is lower for the high-risk patients (.03) than the change for low-risk patients (.06), the absolute probability of high-risk patients' involvement in an incident is higher. The base rate situation for violent incidents was more extreme. The probability of a violent incident over the 54 months was .002. Each 1-point increase or decrease in the Violence Risk score from one month to the next corresponded to a .15 increase or decrease in the probability of a violent incident in the next month.

These statistics show that clinicians must take into account both the absolute probability of an incident for a given patient (the base rate) and the amount of change in the risk score that has occurred. The base rate would be determined, as in the analyses for this study, by the patient's average risk score or, alternatively, his or her actuarially determined level of static risk. An even simpler method for clients who have been observed for a time might be to assign all individuals to the higher risk category on the basis of their having already had at least one incident, because having had an incident was also a good predictor of group membership.

Although we have used probabilities to illustrate how changes in the Dynamic Risk Appraisal Scale could be interpreted, it is important to understand that the scale is not an actuarial instrument. At its present state of development, it could be used informally by visually examining the direction and magnitude of changes over time for individual patients to make short-term decisions in which a high rate of false positive errors are acceptable and the nature of the decisions are constrained by actuarial estimates of long-term risk. Although there are few data that speak directly to the issue, we expect that more frequently made observations would be associated with more accurate prediction and that reliability would be enhanced by combining the independent ratings of different clinicians. What seems certain on the basis of the research to date is that there are observable patient characteristics that change prior to the commission of incidents of any kind and violent incidents.

Comment

The dynamic items reflecting antisocial traits potentially represent targets for both supervision and treatment. Although their informal use in supervision is comparatively straightforward, their use as treatment targets is not. With respect to procriminal sentiments, as reflected in some of the items of the Dynamic Risk Appraisal Scale, a number of cognitive–behavioral interventions have shown some success. Andrews and Bonta (2003b) and Andrews (1980) reviewed interventions designed to ameliorate procriminal attitudes. The appropriateness of many of the other dynamic factors as treatment targets, however, is problematic. Although all of these characteristics change over time, it is unclear at present how to make some of the nonattitudinal ones change. For example, how is it possible to increase an offender's empathy? More important, it is unclear whether the changes that are observed reflect real changes in the offender's underlying characteristics or whether these changes simply become more or less apparent with variations in the offender's degree of compliance. Do observed changes in empathy reflect the degree to which an offender really cares about others, or simply the amount of effort he expends in attempting to demonstrate that he does, or in attempting to conceal that he does not? Considerably more work is required before an intervention is developed that can reduce the violence risk of psychopathic individuals. In the long run, the most effective means of improving community safety are likely to involve preventative efforts rather than remediation (see Yoshikawa, 1994). A preventative approach probably depends on understanding the etiology of the condition, a goal toward which progress has been accelerating in recent years.

CONCLUSION

Because the VRAG and SORAG yield estimates of long-term risk established at the beginning of a follow-up period (i.e., the probability of an offender being identified as committing at least one violent or sexual crime following release), investigators have studied how changes in predictors that vary during the time in which an offender has an opportunity to reoffend are related to reoffending. Because these predictors fluctuate during the follow-up period, they are in principle unsuited for estimating long-term risk—just as static predictors are unsuited to examining fluctuations in risk over time. Static predictors are suitable for making dispositional decisions that affect long-term security issues, whereas dynamic predictors are suitable for making short-term risk management decisions. The studies that we have reviewed demonstrate that changes in a substantial number of predictors measured over several months of opportunity are related to reoffending, although further research and development will be required to make dynamic risk scales useful in an actuarial sense.

11

CONCLUSIONS

In broad terms, risk management consists of treatment, the application of some intervention designed to reduce an offender's risk of violent reoffending, and supervision—anything that reduces the opportunity to reoffend. To the extent that treatment reduces a person's risk, less supervision is necessary. To the extent that treatment fails in its purpose, intervention must rely on the elimination of opportunities for reoffending. The key to determining the extent to which an offender requires treatment or supervision is an accurate appraisal of his dangerousness. We have argued for an actuarial approach to this task on the grounds that it is accurate enough to be practically useful and that, on empirical and ethical grounds, there are no serious alternatives.

Actuarial systems using static or historical predictors work in part because current treatment technology is not very effective in reducing the likelihood of violent recidivism among serious adult offenders. An effective intervention would be an important predictor (i.e., offenders who had received the treatment would be unlikely to reoffend regardless of their static risk score), and the accuracy of predictions made on the basis of pretreatment variables would be lowered. Ironically, therefore, a by-product of successful treatment program development would be the degradation of the predictive accuracy of static prediction instruments. An exception to this outcome would occur if a treatment were to reduce recidivism equally across all risk levels (and only treated offenders were considered). In this scenario, the treatment of an individual offender would lead to a lowered actuarially determined probability of recidivism, but the rank ordering of risk for offenders who had received treatment would be the same as if none of them had.

The provision of treatment is one of a class of dynamic predictors for which the value is fixed at a point in time. From an analytic viewpoint, these predictors become static or historical at the time they occur and can, in principle, be used to predict recidivism over a subsequent period of any desired length. In contrast, continuously fluctuating dynamic predictors cannot sensibly be used to make predictions over lengthy time intervals. Thus, such fluctuating predictors are not in competition for outcome variance with either static or temporally fixed dynamic predictors; rather, they track temporal variations in the likelihood of reoffending.

We have seen that the issues of prediction, risk management, supervision, and treatment are interwoven. They are related to each other not only conceptually and methodologically, but also in their dependence on the approach society takes to them. In chapter 1, we outlined some of the legal and historical contexts within which the management of offenders occurs. The process appears to be one of change without much progress. This vacillating approach is reflected in the peculiar inertia of practices within the forensic health and correctional services, the endless swinging of the pendulum between extremely harsh and somewhat less harsh sentencing, the upholding or abolishment of the death penalty, the definition of greater or fewer numbers of offenders as mentally ill, the alternation between treatment for offenders or just deserts, variations on the intervention of the month (wilderness programs, boot camps, community notification, diversion, empathy enhancement therapy, intimacy enhancement, incapacitation, and so forth), determinate versus indeterminate sentences, community versus institutional dispositions, and so on, ad nauseum.

None of the foregoing is meant to gainsay the real advances that have been made in the conceptualization of interventions for offenders or the meta-analytic evidence for treatment efficacy outlined in chapter 3. For mentally ill persons, the continuing improvements in pharmacological agents for schizophrenia and affective disorders and the empirical support for what has come to be called *psychosocial rehabilitation* provide concrete evidence of true progress. Unfortunately, these latter interventions are not as widely and systematically applied as they should be.

Because VRAG predictors cannot change, what is their relevance to intervention? Their primary relevance is in identifying offenders whose risk level is high enough to warrant intervention. Aside from the small proportion of offenders who, because of the severity of their offending and their high actuarial risk scores, are proper candidates for incapacitation, actuarial measures of risk are best suited for ensuring that more intense treatments and more rigorous supervisory techniques are used with the offenders who need them the most, those at high risk. The difficulty at present is that the characteristics of offenders that make them high risk are also those that are related to poor response to intervention. Moreover, no treatments have yet been identified that reduce the recidivism of psychopathic offenders. If ever a problem cried out for a solution, it is this one.

ACTUARIAL PREDICTION AND THEORY

An actuarial instrument for predicting violent recidivism is not a theory of violent crime. That is, the VRAG does not imply an explanation of violent crime in which past antisocial acts are causes of future ones. The instrument merely implies that uncertainty about future violence can be reduced by knowledge about an offender's personal characteristics and past antisocial conduct. The instrument does not necessarily imply that youthfulness, personality disorder, and being unmarried are causes of violence (although it might be tempting to think so). Fortunately, empirical relationships can be used without knowing why they exist. The history of technology is full of examples of people using phenomena without understanding them. People used aspirin, compasses, sailing ships, fermentation, distillation, and the selective breeding of domesticated plants and animals (to name but a few examples) long before they could accurately explain why such things worked. An actuarial instrument is merely another example of the use of a phenomenon even though its usefulness has not been fully explained.

Science, however, aspires to more than useful predictions. The goal of science is explanation, and a useful technology cries out for scientists to provide valid causal explanations (Quinsey, 1995). Thus, scientists spent great effort trying to understand and explain magnetism, aerodynamics, and genetics as soon as compasses, sails, and animal husbandry were known to work. Why and how does the Violence Risk Appraisal Guide work? An obvious and compelling component to an explanation lies with the phenomenon of life-course-persistent antisociality and psychopathy in particular. A very clear theoretical implication of the success of the VRAG is that psychopaths are responsible for a lot of violence. In the section that follows, we describe some of our research on the characteristics of psychopathy as a clinical and natural entity. After that, we briefly describe how our research on psychopaths and the prediction of violence leads to a theoretical reinterpretation of psychopathy.

Psychopaths: A Separate Class of Violent Offenders?

Many beds in forensic psychiatric and correctional facilities are occupied by people labeled *psychopaths* (Wong, 1988). Psychopaths commit a disproportionately large number of crimes and violent crimes (e.g., Hare & McPherson, 1984; G. T. Harris, Rice, & Cormier, 1991b). Evidence suggests that psychopathic characteristics emerge early in life and persist well into middle age (G. T. Harris et al., 1991b; G. T. Harris, Skilling, & Rice, 2001). Cleckley (1941) provided the first systematic clinical account of psychopathy and identified its salient clinical features. Hare (1985, 1991) used Cleckley's conceptualization of psychopathy and developed and validated a checklist containing items that reflected 22 (20 in the revised version) characteristics of psychopaths. Hare and his colleagues (1990) provided evidence that Revised Psychopathy Checklist (PCL–R; Hare, 1991) scores are composed of two correlated factors: The first is thought to reflect interpersonal and affective personality traits (e.g., callousness, manipulation, shallow affect) and the second to reflect a chronically unstable and antisocial lifestyle (e.g., juvenile delinquency, poor behavioral controls). This two-factor conceptualization appears to be undergoing some theoretically motivated revision toward four (or even more) conceptually distinct components (Hare, 2003), but the two-factor view continues to dominate the field.

Although Cleckley (1941, and subsequent editions) and Hare (1996, 2003) adopted the view that psychopaths are different from nonpsychopaths in fundamental ways, neither has argued that psychopathy should be construed as a discrete class, or *taxon*, rather than as a continuous dimension. Hare (1991), however, conceived of scores on the checklist as representing the extent to which an individual matches the "prototypical" psychopath, with a maximal score being closest to the prototype.

Meehl and Golden (1982) defined a *taxon* in psychopathology as an "entity, type, syndrome, species, disease, or more generally, a nonarbitrary class" (p. 127). The goal of taxometric analysis is to identify classes of individuals that are "really in nature" and exist independently of clinicians' awareness of them. Some generally accepted taxa are sex and species. Within psychopathology, there is evidence for both a "schizotypy" taxon underlying schizophrenia (Golden & Meehl, 1979) and a dementia taxon (Golden, 1982). Our purpose in the study described here was to examine whether psychopathy is better conceptualized as reflecting an underlying taxon or a dimension.

Past research has provided little or no scientific evidence on the discreteness of psychopathy. Although PCL–R scores are continuous, a measurement device that yields such scores can be used to detect a discrete entity. More to the point, where there is imperfect identification of key characteristics combined with measurement error, a taxon can yield continuous scores on a measurement tool or on a set of variables designed to indicate its defining properties (Meehl & Golden, 1982).

The simplest procedure to detect a taxon is to examine the distribution of scores on an indicator believed to discriminate between members of the taxon and its complement. A sharply bimodal distribution is strong evidence for a taxon. Even if there is a taxon, however, the observed distribution is much more likely to be a flattened normal distribution. One can test for the existence of two overlapping normal distributions—one for taxon members and one for nonmembers (Golden & Meehl, 1979). Estimates of the means, variances, and base rates of the latent distributions (Harding, 1949; Hasselblad, 1966) are compared with observed values with goodness-of-fit tests.

The logic behind more sophisticated taxometric techniques is similar. To detect a taxon, it is assumed that within the taxon and within its complement, the indicators of the taxon are uncorrelated with each other. Only when one mixes individuals from both taxometric classes do the various indicators covary.

The *maxcov–hitmax* method (Meehl & Golden, 1982) requires a subset of dichotomous items that actually measure the phenomenon of interest, correlate highly with the total score on the instrument, and do not have similar manifest content. If one has eight such items, one then removes two of them and constructs a subscale using the sum of the remaining items. Then a sample of individuals is divided into subsamples, one for each possible score on this 0–6 scale. If a taxon exists, then the covariance between the two set-aside items plotted as a function of the sum of the remaining six should be peaked, with maximal values where individuals in both classes are mixed together, and near-0 values at the extremes where the subsamples should comprise individuals from only one class. Meehl (1996) has reported strong evidence of the validity of this method from computer simulations.

Two related methods involve a set of iterative procedures, called *consistency tests*, to select from a large number of possible dichotomous indicators a subset that is optimal in its ability to discriminate between the taxon and its complement. Using the final set of indicators, estimates of the true base rate of the taxon and the valid and false positive rates for each indicator are derived. Finally, these parameters are used to calculate a Bayesian probability estimate that any particular individual is a taxon member given his or her specific set of indicator scores. If the set of indicators allows for effective classification of individuals into classes, the Bayesian probabilities should be either very high ($p > .90$) or very low ($p < .10$). In addition, individuals classified as members of the taxon by one of these methods should also have a high likelihood of being classified as a member of the taxon by other methods, and the base rate estimates should be similar to one another.

The fourth method (parabolic function) requires another dichotomous variable (in this research, criminal recidivism) also likely to discriminate fairly well between the taxon and its complement. Except for the endpoints on a continuous variable assumed to indicate the taxon, every possible integer value of the variable is entertained as the best score for discriminating between the taxon and the complement. Then, the mean rate on the other, dichotomous indicator for individuals above and below this cut score is calculated, as are the sum of the squares of the deviations about this mean. If a taxon exists, then the sum of these two sums of squared deviations should be a parabolic function of the continuous variable with a minimum approximately at that cut score that optimally discriminates between the taxon and its complement. Meehl (1996) provided strong evidence based on computer simulations for the validity of a conceptually identical procedure called the MAMBAC ("mean above minus mean below a cut score").

G. T. Harris, Rice, and Quinsey (1994) used the methods described earlier in this chapter to evaluate the hypothesis that a taxon underlies psychopathy, with the PCL–R providing the main operational definition of psychopathy. We also sought evidence of the taxon in the two PCL–R factors separately as well as in some measures not from the PCL–R. Finally, we examined the ability of each of the taxometric methods to reject the taxon hypothesis for adult criminal history, which we hypothesized to be continuous. The offenders were 653 men from two follow-up studies of mentally disordered offenders described in chapter 5 and previously reported in the literature (Rice, Harris, & Cormier, 1992; Rice, Harris, Lang, & Bell, 1990).

We found that the evidence supported the validity of the PCL–R (especially Factor 2 items) and other variables having to do with childhood history as indicators of a taxon underlying psychopathy. Curve-fitting procedures suggested that the hypothesis of two underlying normal distributions was not unreasonable. Subsequent analyses using taxometric methods to decompose the overall distribution yielded two distributions that were clearly distinct. Two normal distributions whose parameters were estimated from the scores of the individuals assigned to each group provided an adequate fit, and the obtained parameters were very similar to those obtained using the entire sample. Further evidence for the idea that psychopaths and nonpsychopaths come from two different populations comes from K. Rasmussen and S. Levander (personal communication, January 7, 1997), who reported a bimodal distribution of PCL–R scores among patients in a secure psychiatric hospital in Norway.

The maxcov–hitmax method yielded a highly peaked covariance curve for the eight best PCL–R items, for items exclusively from Factor 2, and for non-PCL–R variables reflecting antisocial childhood behavior. The two iterative methods using items from the PCL–R each provided further evidence of a taxon, the categorization of offenders into the taxon and complement showed very high agreement, and both methods also classified almost all offenders as members either of the taxon or the complement with high probability. Finally, the parabolic function method yielded a near-parabolic function using both criminal recidivism and the PCL–R as indicators of the taxon.

Evidence for the taxon was strengthened by the finding that variables reflecting participants' history of adult criminality alone did not yield evidence of a taxon on most of the same tests. The only exception was that adult criminality variables yielded a bimodal distribution on the iterative tests (although not as sharply bimodal as the hypothesized taxon indicators), suggesting that the iterative methods may be weaker tests than other methods. Evidence for the existence of a taxon was further strengthened by the finding that the four taxometric methods agreed on the proportion of offenders who were taxon members. That is, these methods would place the proportion at .46 for the two iterative approaches and at .44 for the maxcov–hitmax and parabolic methods. The taxometric methods are designed to detect discontinuity in the patterns of item-by-item covariation and are, consequently, not necessarily the best methods for individual diagnosis. Nevertheless, all methods showed good agreement (65% to 92%, correlations ranged from .30 to .83) on which offenders were likely to be taxon members.

Where it could be estimated, a PCL–R cutoff of approximately 19 would optimally distinguish the two groups (i.e., maximize hit rate and minimize both false positives and incorrect rejections). In the evaluation of the therapeutic community study described in chapter 5 (G. T. Harris, Rice, & Cormier, 1991a), a cutoff of 25 on the PCL–R optimized the prediction of criminal and violent recidivism; this cutoff of 25 would have identified 24% of this sample. The results of this study suggest that there were substantially more taxon members in the sample. However, our results suggested that our use of 25 as a cutoff score on the PCL–R probably yielded a nearly "pure" subsample. Thus, the choice of "best" cutoff depends on the purpose of identification. It is interesting that about 10% of the entire sample were identified as taxon members by all methods (including the non-PCL–R childhood variables). The records of these "prototypical psychopaths" showed some of them to be responsible for particularly heinous reoffenses.

More evidence for the taxon came from Factor 2 than Factor 1. It is possible that more evidence of a taxon from Factor 1 would have been found if interviews had been used to complete the PCL–R rather than using file information alone. Nevertheless, these data provide evidence that a taxon does not underlie adult criminality per se. As has been asserted elsewhere (G. T. Harris et al., 1991a, discussed in chap. 5; Hart, Kropp, & Hare, 1988), psychopathy, as operationalized by the PCL–R, captures much more than a history of or propensity for crime. Perhaps more than the interpersonal and affective characteristics reflected by PCL–R Factor 1 (e.g., callousness, lack of remorse, shallow affect), chronic antisocial behavior beginning in childhood may be the most central feature of psychopathy. The very high correlation between the PCL–R and the criteria for both the *DSM–III* and *DSM–IV* (American Psychiatric Association, 1980 and 1994, respectively) diagnosis of antisocial personality disorder (when the criteria are scored in the same manner as the PCL–R items and summed to yield a total continuous score) strongly supports this notion (Skilling, Harris, Rice, & Quinsey, 2002). As expected from this result, the antisocial personality disorder criteria exhibit evidence of the same underlying taxon and also identify the same offenders as psychopathy taxon members as do the PCL–R and Childhood/Adolescent Psychopathy Scale (Skilling et al., 2002). Again, the best evidence for this discrete class came from antisocial and aggressive behavior from childhood on. Evidence consistent with a discrete class underlying antisocial personality has been reported elsewhere (Ayers, 2000; also see Haslam, 2003), but there has also been a failure to find the same result using a self-report assessment of psychopathy (Marcus, John, & Edens, 2004).

The finding that childhood behavior problems were good taxon indicators means that it may be possible to identify psychopaths early in life. Forth, Hart, and Hare (1990; see also Forth, Kosson, & Hare, 2004) found that the distribution and psychometric properties of a modification of the PCL–R in a sample of male offenders averaging 16 years of age were similar to those of adult offenders. Could it be detected even earlier? In a review of the literature on the prediction of delinquency, Loeber (1990) concluded that the greatest continuity in antisocial offending is found among the children who exhibit antisocial behavior earliest. The best predictors of juvenile delinquency identified in his review are similar to the childhood taxon indicators in these analyses. In descending order of accuracy, Loeber's predictors of delinquency among boys (together with our closest childhood indicator of a taxon variable in parentheses) are the following: drug use (teen alcohol abuse score, parental alcoholism), stealing (arrested under age 16), aggression (childhood aggression), general problem behaviors (childhood behavior problems), truancy (suspended or expelled, elementary school maladjustment), educational achievement, and lying (conduct disorder). Furthermore, Tremblay et al. (1992) found school disruptiveness (a taxon indicator) and not school achievement (the predictor in Loeber's review) to predict later delinquency. There is increasing support for the idea that children who exhibit both early hyperactivity–impulsivity–attention problems and conduct disorder may be fledgling psychopaths (Lynam, 1996).

Skilling, Quinsey, and Craig (2001) addressed this issue by conducting taxometric analyses on a community sample of 1,111 boys who were nearly 12 years old on average. Taxometric analyses were applied to several self-report measures of antisocial behavior. These measures were similar in content to the *DSM–IV* conduct disorder criteria, the Psychopathy Checklist—Youth Version (PCL–YV; Forth et al., 2004), and the Childhood and Adolescent Taxon Scale (CATS; see Exhibit 8.4). Taxometric analyses yielded evidence of a discrete entity underlying scores on the three different measures of antisocial behavior. A distinct class of boys (9% of the total) who report already engaging in serious antisocial behavior can be identified in childhood.

A further possible implication of the taxon is that criminal behavior is related to different factors in psychopaths and nonpsychopaths. The mixture of both in studies of offender treatment and prediction of recidivism may mask relationships that are important in only one subgroup. For example, as described in chapter 5, we have found that both age and alcohol abuse history were strongly related to recidivism among nonpsychopathic offenders but unrelated among psychopathic offenders (G. T. Harris et al., 1991a).

Psychopathy as a Life History Strategy

Thus, we have found evidence for the existence of a psychopathy taxon in both young men and adult male offenders. Although not all taxa are genetically caused (Meehl, 1992), many are (e.g., gender and species). Behavior genetic analyses are required to determine the degree to which psychopathy taxon membership may be genetically based (Mednick, Gabrielli, & Hutchings, 1983; Zuckerman, 1989), perhaps involving a combination of genetic factors and early experiences (e.g., Caspi et al., 2002). Blum and Noble (1997) and Bock and Goode (1996) discussed work on genetics and antisocial behavior, and Quinsey, Skilling, Lalumière, and Craig (2004) provided an extensive discussion of this research in relation to psychopathy as a life history strategy. Barr and Quinsey (2004) reviewed the implications of a life history view of psychopathy for interventions designed to reduce criminal behavior.

Our research on the prediction of violence implies more about what psychopaths are like and, perhaps, why they are that way. With respect to predicting violence, it is quite clear that the most useful psychopathic characteristics are those that appear very early (conduct disorder, elementary school maladjustment) as opposed to those most apparent in adulthood (glibness, proneness to boredom). Indeed, it is the childhood and adolescent indicators of psychopathy (as opposed to those putatively associated with adult personality) that allow one to say with confidence that psychopathic offenders form a distinct subgroup of serious offenders (G. T. Harris, Rice, & Quinsey, 1994). This is not to say, of course, that adult psychopaths are not discriminably different from other adults, especially on these perceived personality traits, but rather that these traits, at least as currently measured, are not as diagnostic as childhood and adolescent conduct.[1]

The demonstration that the accuracy of the VRAG is very nearly the same when historical predictors taken from childhood and adolescence (CATS) are used in place of the PCL–R is not surprising for two reasons. First, the univariate correlation of the CATS with violent or sexual recidivism is almost identical to that of the PCL–R, and second, the CATS identifies essentially the same individuals as being in the psychopathy taxon as (primarily Factor 2) PCL–R items in taxometric analyses (G. T. Harris, Rice,

[1]It has been reported (Cooke & Michie, 1997) that the PCL–R items associated with Factor 1 are better because they afford better discrimination, but it is unclear how this squares with the finding that Factor 2 items are better indicators of the underlying taxon and are more highly predictive of all socially relevant criminal justice outcomes.

& Quinsey, 1994). The predictive ability of items taken only from childhood and adolescence is a striking illustration of the static nature of the VRAG.

These observations lead to more basic questions about how best to conceive of psychopathy. Is it a disorder of personality? Wakefield (1992a, 1992b) has usefully conceptualized a disorder as a harmful dysfunction. Thus, the concept of a disorder is at the interface of the given natural world and the constructed social world. In this view, a person is considered to have a disorder when a failure of the person's internal mechanisms to perform their natural function impinges harmfully on the person's well-being as defined by social values and meanings.

In Wakefield's (1992a) view,

> a condition is a mental disorder, therefore, if and only if:
> (a) the condition causes some harm or deprivation of benefit to the person as judged by the standards of the person's culture (the value criterion), and
> (b) the condition results from the inability of some mental mechanism to perform its natural function, wherein a natural function is an effect that is part of the evolutionary explanation of the existence and structure of the mental mechanism (the explanatory criterion). (p. 385)

In the present context, the value criterion might usefully be expanded to include harm or deprivation of benefit to others. The idea that psychopathy is a disorder or defect is a powerful one. It explains the findings showing that psychopaths react to punishment in an apparently inefficient way. The disorder idea explains why psychopaths do not seem to benefit from experience, especially therapy, in the way that nonpsychopaths do. The defect idea seems to explain why psychopaths are not affected by emotionally laden material the way other people are. Moreover, the disorder idea fits comfortably with neuropsychological findings implying that the brains of psychopaths are different and seem to operate with less serotonin than the brains of other people. Of course, all of this kind of thinking leads to research aimed at "personality tests," diagnostic questions, and therapy, all using theories and modes of explanation common to psychopathology.

All the same findings can, however, lead in quite a different direction. Perhaps rather than conceiving of psychopathy as a disorder, it is better conceived of as a life history strategy (G. T. Harris, Rice, & Cormier, 2002; G. T. Harris, Skilling, & Rice, 2001, in press; Mealey, 1995; Quinsey & Lalumière, 1995b; Rice, 1997). This strategy may have conferred reproductive advantages in the ancestral environment, especially under conditions in which psychopaths were infrequent and mobile. Perhaps aggression and belligerence were the earliest (ontologically as well as phylogenetically) features of this adaptation, with deceitfulness and dishonesty relatively later and "optional" additions. Perhaps acting quickly in the presence of potential rewards, being resistant to punishment and social influence, and being relatively unaffected by emotionally distressing stimuli are advantages in such a "warrior-hawk" strategy. A compelling example of how a warrior-hawk strategy might confer advantages is given by the fearless and fierce "berserkers" in Viking society. Berserkers were sought-after allies and bodyguards. If a berserker chanced to kill one of one's relatives, however, it was more prudent to accept a monetary payment than to seek revenge (Dunbar, Clark, & Hurst, 1995).

If psychopathy is a life history strategy, then the behaviors most closely associated with it should be coherent and plausibly related to reproductive success in ancestral environments. We propose that psychopathy can be considered to be a life history strategy consisting of short-term mating tactics, an aggressive and risky (warrior-hawk) approach to achieving social dominance, and frequent use of nonreciprocating and duplicitous (cheating) tactics in social exchange. As well, the sexual behavior of psychopaths seems to be uniquely characterized less by high adult mating effort (which is also common in other life strategies) and more by coercive and precocious sexuality (G. T. Harris, Hilton, Rice, Lalumière, & Quinsey, 2005).

There clearly must be proximal causes of such a life history strategy, and individuals in the psychopathy taxon must have detectable differences in the nervous system. Such a view, we think, explains the unusual differential effects of treatment observed in our earlier studies (G. T. Harris, Rice, & Cormier, 1994; Rice et al., 1992). It may explain why PCL–R scores based on corroborated file reviews show such high validity, because historical behavioral factors are the most important and not as vulnerable to the dissimulation that might occur in an interview. It explains why the eight-item CATS can replace the entire PCL–R in the prediction of violent recidivism with little decrement in predictive accuracy. It explains why PCL–R Factor 2 predicts violent recidivism better than the personality-based Factor 1.[2] It may explain why psychopaths show fewer signs of developmental perturbations than violent offenders with such mental disorders as schizophrenia, bipolar disorder, and developmental delay (Lalumière, Harris, & Rice, 2001). Indeed, the path to criminal violence associated with various neurodevelopmental perturbations appears to be quite independent of psychopathy (G. T. Harris, Rice, & Lalumière, 2001).

Much more research is required before we can begin to understand whether psychopathy is better conceived as a lifelong strategy than as a disorder and, if so, whether the adoption of that strategy is facultative (i.e., dependent on environmental conditions) or obligate (independent of environmental conditions). Whether conceptualized as pathology, a facultative

---

[2]It is almost inevitable that both PCL–R factors (PCL–R items load on two correlated factors with three items left over) predict violent recidivism, although not necessarily equally, because the two factors correlate with each other at between .50 and .70. The individual PCL–R items are correlated at most about .60 or .70 with the total score.

strategy (most likely dependent on the environment in the first few years of life, including perhaps the intrauterine environment), or an obligate strategy, however, the finding that a discrete entity underlies the early expression of extremely persistent antisocial traits suggests that psychopathy might profitably be considered to be a behavioral phenotype (O'Brien & Yule, 1995). A *behavioral phenotype* is a characteristic pattern of motor, cognitive, linguistic, and social features associated with a biological condition that is not necessarily pathological in itself.

Flint (1995) discussed strategies for elucidating the paths leading from genotype to phenotype in those cases where it is likely that a behavioral phenotype is causally associated with genetic variation. In his view, a promising alternative to linkage analysis of DNA polymorphisms is the molecular dissection of a behavioral phenotype. This approach does not rely on normal allelic variation but rather attempts to determine how the aberration determines the phenotype. It is always an empirical question whether a complex behavioral phenotype is caused by many genes, the interactions among a very few genes, or (as appears likely in the case of extremely aggressive behavior found among developmentally delayed male individuals of a Dutch extended family) a single gene (Brunner, Nelen, Breakefield, Ropers, & van Oost, 1993; Brunner, van Zandvoort, et al., 1993). Of course, as pointed out by others (e.g., Mealey, 1995), it may be that in particular individuals the behavioral phenotype is a phenotypic copy of a behavioral disorder without being a genetic copy—there may be more than one path to the same cluster of traits.

Our point here is not so much to make a case for psychopathy as an adaptation as opposed to a disorder, but rather to illustrate how the results showing the predictive validity of an actuarial instrument call on us to explain them, constrain such an explanation, and lead to new and interesting research questions.

EPILOGUE

We began this book by describing some of the history of the management of offenders and psychiatric patients presumed to be dangerous. We provided a general historical context followed by a context that specifically pertained to Oak Ridge, the maximum-security forensic setting where our program of research originated. Perhaps the best way to conclude this book is to examine some of the ways our own ideas have changed since we began, both as a result of our own findings and as a result of findings and conceptual advances that have occurred in science more generally. The dangers of hindsight bias must be braved if we are to make sense of our own scientific and professional careers and to explain why we now think as we do.

THE HUMBLING POWER OF ALGORITHMS

We very quickly became disenchanted with intuitive approaches to prediction and treatment. Contrary to our initial expectations, there appeared to be nothing useful in the realm of practice (as opposed to metapractice, like program evaluation) that an individual professional could do that could not be formalized in some sort of simple algorithm.

THE TENACITY OF CIRCUMSTANCES

We learned gradually about the limits of reform. Even if a practice could be improved through a combination of research and advocacy, it would not necessarily stay improved. We discovered that the behavioral contingencies associated with working in an institutional bureaucracy exerted inertial drag to the extent of obliterating the effects of individual differences among administrative and frontline staff that we knew were very real. These observations are as true of risk assessment practices as of any other clinical issues with which we have been involved. The effort required to change a clinical practice is much greater than that involved in doing the research that justifies changing the practice in the first place.

QUANTITATIVE LENSES

All of us were originally trained primarily in analysis of variance techniques. We learned about the liberating power of other statistical and psychometric methods as they became essential to the problems we were investigating. New mathematical tools have allowed us to consider and answer questions that we could not have addressed with our graduate statistical training.

THE UNITY OF SCIENCE

We suppose that we were naive about what had relevance to the problems we were considering. Originally, we were primarily consumers of the behavior therapy and behavior modification literatures on treatment and the special hospital literature on forensic issues. If an investigator was not reporting behavioral frequencies in real time or physiological measures, we were generally dismissive. For these reasons and because of an unfounded belief in the uniqueness of our population, we tended to discount such things as the importance of psychopathy, the literatures on predicting suicide and on psychotherapy outcome, and much of the correctional treatment literature. This parochialism had to be overcome before we could benefit from the lessons and insights that had been hard won in other areas of inquiry.

WHAT IS POSSIBLE?

Our most important cognitive shift occurred very gradually. It is certain that in the 1970s, the focus of our research was entirely on more or less obvious and immediate clinical and management problems. Our hope was that our applied work would result in a more humane institution with more interesting and more effective programs. We conceived of our task as primarily one of applying what was already known to local institutional issues, and we expected that incremental improvements would follow. Even with respect to these practical issues, our expectations were very limited. We were, for example, profoundly and wrongly pessimistic about improving the accuracy with which we could predict future violent behavior.

It never occurred to us then that solutions to the etiological problems associated with violent offending might actually be found, not in the distant future, but within our own lifetimes. We now think of theories of violent offending not as things that one gathers data about but as things that can be put to definitive test. Although there are a number of exciting recent empirical findings, it is not just these findings themselves that inspire such optimism, but also the incredibly rapid pace of advances in neuroscience and behavior genetics that, together with the conceptual advances in evolutionary psychology, promise a full scientific understanding of the problems with which we have grappled in this book. We like to think that, in a tiny way, we are part of this grand enterprise.

PROGRESS

Finally, significant progress in the scientific knowledge of antisocial behavior and the technology of prediction has occurred since the first edition of this book. The quality of the research continues to improve and the rate of publication to grow. We believe that this scientific progress is the direct result of increasing rigor in the research methods used and of the increasing awareness of scientific work in other fields. These developments have markedly increased the number of well-replicated findings, permitting the execution of ever more sophisticated meta-analyses. Learning how best to apply this expanding body of scientific knowledge to the improvement of clinical practice and interventions designed to promote public safety is a more important problem now than ever.

APPENDIX A

Violence Risk Appraisal Guide (VRAG)

SCORING THE VRAG

1. Lived with both biological parents to age 16 (except for death of parent)
   Score *no* if offender did not live continuously with both biological parents until age 16, except if one or both parents died. In the case of parent death, score as for *yes*.
   Yes = –2, No = +3

2. Elementary school maladjustment
   (up to and including Grade 8)
   No problems   = –1
   Slight or moderate discipline or attendance problems   = +2
   Severe (i.e., frequent or serious) behavior or
   attendance problems (e.g., truancy or disruptive
   behavior that persisted over several years or resulted
   in expulsion)   = +5

3. History of alcohol problems
   Allot one point for each of the following: alcohol abuse in biological parent, teenage alcohol problem, adult alcohol problem, alcohol involved in a prior offense, alcohol involved in the index offense.
   0 points = –1, 1 or 2 points = 0, 3 points =
   +1, 4 or 5 points = +2

Note. Variables are listed in the order in which they are addressed in the final report. *DSM–III* = *Diagnostic and Statistical Manual of Mental Disorders* (3rd ed.; American Psychiatric Association, 1980).

4. Marital status (at time of index offense)
Ever married (or lived common law in the same home for at least 6 months) = −2
Never married = +1

5. Criminal history score for convictions and charges for nonviolent offenses prior to the index offense (from the Cormier–Lang system shown in Table A.1)
Score of 0 = −2
Score of 1 or 2 = 0
Score of 3 or above = +3

6. Failure on prior conditional release (includes parole violation or revocation, breach of or failure to comply with recognizance or probation, bail violation, and any new charges, including the index offense, while on a conditional release)
No = 0, Yes = +3

7. Age at index offense (at most recent birthday)
≥39 = −5
34–38 = −2
28–33 = −1
27 = 0
≤26 = +2

8. Victim injury (index offense only; most serious injury is scored)
Death = −2
Hospitalized = 0
Treated and released = +1
None or slight (includes no victim) = +2

9. Any female victim (for index offense)
Yes = −1, No (includes no victim) = +1

10. Meets *DSM–III* criteria for any personality disorder
No = −2, Yes = +3

11. Meets *DSM–III* criteria for schizophrenia
Yes = −3, No = +1

12. Hare Psychopathy Checklist—Revised score (PCL–R; Hare, 1991)
≤4 = −5
5–9 = −3
10–14 = −1
15–24 = 0
25–34 = +4
≥35 = +12

TABLE A.1
Cormier–Lang Criminal History Scores for Nonviolent Offenses

Offense	Score
Robbery (bank, store)	7
Robbery (purse snatching)	3
Arson and fire setting (church, house, barn)	5
Arson and fire setting (garbage can)	1
Threatening with a weapon, dangerous use of or pointing firearm	3
Threatening (uttering threats)	2
Theft over[a] (includes car theft and possession of stolen property over[a])	5
Mischief to public or private property over[a]	5
Break and enter and commit indictable offense (burglary)	2
Theft under[b] (includes possession of stolen property under[b])	1
Mischief to public or private property under[b]	1
Break and enter (includes break and enter with intent to commit an offense)	1
Fraud (extortion, embezzlement)	5
Fraud (forged check, impersonation)	1
Possession of a prohibited or restricted weapon	1
Procuring a person for or living on the avails of prostitution	1
Trafficking in narcotics	1
Dangerous driving, impaired driving (driving while intoxicated)	1
Obstructing a peace officer (including resisting arrest)	1
Causing a disturbance	1
Wearing a disguise with the intent to commit an offense	1
Indecent exposure	2

Note. [a]Roughly equivalent to grand larceny based on the value of the stolen property—as of 2003, over $5,000.00.
[b]Roughly equivalent to larceny based on the value of the stolen property—as of 2003, under $5,000.

Score and then total all charges and convictions for all counts for nonviolent criminal offenses, including juvenile record. Do *not* count both a charge and a conviction if they are known to pertain to the same incident. In a case where sufficient information is known and there is a discrepancy between the charge and conviction, use the more serious of the two, which almost exclusively will be the charge. For example, an incident involving the destruction of a house by fire may result in a charge of arson that is later reduced to mischief for conviction; score this incident as arson only. There may, however, be more than one charge pertaining to the same incident (e.g., charged originally for arson and theft for first stealing a television from the house and then setting fire to the house, but convicted of mischief, with the first two charges withdrawn). This incident would be scored for both arson and theft, but not for mischief. When a particular criminal code is different from the *Criminal Code of Canada*, some amount of judgment will be required to approximate offenses in other jurisdictions. For example, larceny does not appear in the Canadian code but is usually equivalent to theft. See the Notes and Instructions in Appendix E to the full Cormier–Lang system for additional scoring details.

TABLE A.2

Probability of Violent Recidivism at Two Different Mean Lengths of Opportunity as a Function of Nine Equal-Sized Violence Risk Appraisal Guide (VRAG) Categories

VRAG category	VRAG score	Probability of recidivism	
		7 years	10 years
1	≤ −22	0.00	0.08
2	−21 to −15	0.08	0.10
3	−14 to −8	0.12	0.24
4	−7 to −1	0.17	0.31
5	0 to +6	0.35	0.48
6	+7 to +13	0.44	0.58
7	+14 to +20	0.55	0.64
8	+21 to +27	0.76	0.82
9	≥ +28	1.00	1.00

Note. Seven-year base rate of violent recidivism was 31%. Ten-year base rate of violent recidivism was 43%.

APPENDIX B

Sex Offender Risk Appraisal Guide (SORAG)

SCORING THE SORAG

1. Lived with both biological parents to age 16 (except for death of parent)
   Score *no* if offender did not live continuously with both biological parents until age 16, except if one or both parents died. In case of parent death, score as for *yes*.
   Yes = –2, No = +3

2. Elementary school maladjustment
   (up to and including Grade 8)
   No problems = –1
   Slight or moderate discipline or attendance problems = +2
   Severe (i.e., frequent or serious) behavior or attendance problems (e.g., truancy or disruptive behavior that persisted over several years or resulted in expulsion) = +5

3. History of alcohol problems
   Allot one point for each of the following: alcohol abuse in biological parent, teenage alcohol problem, adult alcohol problem, alcohol involved in a prior offense, alcohol involved in the index offense.
   0 points = –1, 1 or 2 points = 0, 3 points = +1,
   4 or 5 points = +2

Note. Variables are listed in the order in which they are addressed in the final report. *DSM–III* = *Diagnostic and Statistical Manual of Mental Disorders* (3rd ed.; American Psychiatric Association, 1980).

4. Marital status (at time of index offense)
   Ever married (or lived common law in the same home
   for at least 6 months)   = –2
   Never married   = +1

5. Criminal history score for convictions and charges for nonviolent offenses prior to the index offense (from the Cormier–
   Lang system shown in Table A.1)

   Score of 0 = –2
   Score of 1 or 2 = 0
   Score of 3 or above = +3

6. Criminal history score for convictions and charges for violent
   offenses prior to the index offense (from the Cormier–Lang
   system shown in Table B.1)

   Score of 0 = –1
   Score of 2 = 0
   Score of 3 or above = +6

7. Number of convictions for previous sexual offenses (pertains
   to convictions for sexual offenses that occurred prior to the
   index offense)
   Count any offenses known to be sexual, including, for example,
   indecent exposure.

   0 = –1
   1 or 2 = +1
   $\geq$3 = +5

8. History of sex offenses against girls under age 14 *only* (includes
   index offense; if offender was less than 5 years older than victim, always score +4)
   Yes = 0, No = +4

9. Failure on prior conditional release (includes parole violation
   or revocation; breach of or failure to comply with recognizance or probation; bail violation; and any new charges, including the index offense, while on a conditional release)
   No = 0, Yes = +3

10. Age at index offense (at most recent birthday)

    $\geq$39 = –5
    34–38 = –2
    28–33 = –1
    27 = 0
    $\leq$26 = +2

11. Meets *DSM–III* criteria for any personality disorder
    No = –2, Yes = +3

12. Meets *DSM–III* criteria for schizophrenia
    Yes = –3, No = +1

13. Phallometric test results
    All indicate nondeviant sexual preferences   = –1
    Any test indicates deviant sexual preferences   = +1

14. Hare Psychopathy Checklist—Revised score (PCL–R; Hare, 1991)
    ≤ 4 = –5
    5–9 = –3
    10–14 = –1
    15–24 = 0
    25–34 = +4
    ≥ 35 = +12

TABLE B.1
Cormier–Lang Criminal History Score for Violent Offenses

Offense	Score
Homicide (murder, manslaughter, criminal negligence causing death)	28
Attempted murder, causing bodily harm with intent to wound	7
Kidnapping, abduction, and forcible confinement	6
Aggravated assault, choking, administering a noxious substance	6
Assault causing bodily harm	5
Assault with a weapon	3
Assault, assaulting a peace officer	2
Aggravated sexual assault, sexual assault causing bodily harm	15
Sexual assault with a weapon	12
Sexual assault, gross indecency (vaginal or anal penetration, victim forced to fellate offender)	10
Sexual assault (attempted rape, indecent assault)	6
Gross indecency (offender fellates or performs cunnilingus on victim)	6
Sexual assault (sexual interference, invitation to sexual touching)	2
Armed robbery (bank, store)	8
Robbery with violence	5
Armed robbery (not a bank or store)	4

Score and then total all charges and convictions for all counts for violent criminal offenses, including juvenile record. Do *not* count both a charge and a conviction if they are known to pertain to the same incident. In a case where sufficient information is known and there is a discrepancy between the charge and conviction, use the more serious of the two, which almost exclusively will be the charge. For example, an incident involving the sexual assault of a woman may result in a charge of sexual assault that is later reduced to assault for conviction; score this incident as sexual assault only.

There may, however, be more than one charge pertaining to the same incident (e.g., charged originally with sexual assault and armed robbery for taking her purse and having a weapon as well as for sexually assaulting her, but convicted for assault only, with the first two charges withdrawn). This incident would be scored for both sexual assault and armed robbery, but not for assault. With the exception of attempted murder, charges of "attempted" offenses, such as attempted armed robbery, are scored the same as the offense itself. Documents with details of offenses can (and should whenever possible) be used for scoring. In general, for example, armed robbery and robbery with violence are scored as violent offenses, but robbery is considered to be nonviolent. However, if investigating officers' reports indicated that a robbery charge was associated with violent conduct (e.g., a victim was injured), record the offense as violent. See the Notes and Instructions in Appendix E to the full Cormier–Lang system for additional scoring details.

TABLE B.2
Probability of Violent Recidivism at Two Different Mean Lengths of
Opportunity as a Function of Nine Equal-Sized Sex Offender Risk
Appraisal Guide (SORAG) Categories

SORAG category	7 years		10 years	
	SORAG score	Probability	SORAG score	Probability
1	≤ -10	0.07	≤ -11	0.09
2	−9 to −4	0.15	−10 to −5	0.12
3	−3 to +2	0.23	−4 to +1	0.39
4	+3 to +8	0.39	+2 to +7	0.59
5	+9 to +14	0.45	+8 to +13	0.59
6	+15 to +19	0.58	+14 to +19	0.76
7	+20 to +24	0.58	+20 to +25	0.80
8	+25 to +30	0.75	+26 to +31	0.89
9	$\geq +31$	1.00	$\geq +32$	1.00

Note. Seven-year base rate of violent recidivism was 42%. Ten-year base rate of violent recidivism was 58%.

APPENDIX C

Normative Data on the Distribution of Violence Risk Appraisal Guide (VRAG) and Sex Offender Risk Appraisal Guide (SORAG) Scores

VRAG				SORAG					
Score	Percentile	Score	Percentile	Score	Percentile	Score	Percentile	Score	Percentile
≤−24	<1	1	54	≤−17	<1	1	27	15	71
−23	1	2	56	−16	1	2	30	16	73
−22	2	3	59	−12	2	3	39	17	76
−20	3	4	62	−11	4	4	40	18	79
−19	5	5	63	−10	5	5	41	19	81
−18	7	6	66	−9	6	6	44	20	84
−17	9	7	67	−7	8	7	47	21	86
−16	11	8	69	−6	10	8	50	22	88
−15	13	9	72	−5	13	9	55	23	90
−14	16	10	74	−4	15	10	57	24	91
−13	18	11	76	−3	16	11	60	25	92
−12	20	12	79	−2	18	12	64	26	93
−11	22	13	81	−1	21	13	65	27	94
−10	25	14	83	0	24	14	67	28	96
−9	28	15	85					30	98
−8	30	16	87					34	99
−7	32	17	89					≥40	>99
−6	35	18	90						
−5	38	19	92						
−4	40	20	93						
−3	42	21	94						
−2	45	22	95						
−1	47	23	96						
0	50	25	97						
		26	98						
		28	99						
		≥32	>99						

291

APPENDIX D

Technical Questions About the Violence Risk Appraisal Guide (VRAG) and the Sex Offender Risk Appraisal Guide (SORAG)

Since we first developed the VRAG and the SORAG, we have received many questions from people using them. Many questions pertain to technical matters, such as how we defined certain things, who exactly our research participants were, and so forth. In the hopes that answers to these technical matters will aid those who use the VRAG or the SORAG, we provide the most accurate answers we can to some of those questions here. This appendix gives particular attention to the more common questions we have received. Questions that have been addressed by subsequent research that is summarized in chapter 8 are not dealt with here.

We have grouped the questions into those concerning the applicability of the risk appraisal guides to various populations, those concerning general methodological or substantive questions, issues of ethics and bias, and issues concerning the scoring of the risk appraisal guide items. The section on questions concerning scoring treats the VRAG items in the order in which they appear in the scoring key. The SORAG items that are unique to it follow.

GENERALITY OR APPLICABILITY OF THE VRAG AND THE SORAG

We have received a great many questions about whether the VRAG or the SORAG applies to specific kinds of offenders.

1. *Can the VRAG and SORAG be used with juveniles? Were all the offenders in the construction sample adults at the time of their index offenses?*

A significant minority (17%) of the VRAG construction sample were under age 18 at the time of their index offense. The predictors of recidivism among juveniles were the same as those among adults, but overall the juveniles exhibited higher rates of recidivism than did the adults. Predictive accuracy was about the same for these young offenders as it was for those who were adults at the time of their offense (and the same was true of the 3% of the sample who were under 16 years old). Note, however, that the juveniles in the construction sample were adults (i.e., over 18 years old) when they had an opportunity to reoffend. In our view, therefore, it is appropriate to use the VRAG for individuals whose index offense occurred when they were juveniles if their opportunity to reoffend begins after they turn 18 years old.

2. *How do I score psychopathy for offenders under age 18?*

At the time we conducted the research that led to the construction of the VRAG and the SORAG, the Psychopathy Checklist—Youth Version (PCL–YV; Forth, Kosson, & Hare, 2004) was just being developed. We used a modified version of the PCL–R (Hare, 1991) for offenders who were under age 18 at the time of their index offense (as described in Forth, Hart, & Hare, 1990). Now that it is available, we recommend using the PCL:YV.

3. *Does the VRAG work with persons who are intellectually handicapped?*

Yes, the effect size for those in the construction sample with IQs below 85 (n = 122, r = .45) is identical to that for those with IQs above 85 (n = 596, r = .45). The VRAG also predicts violent incidents in group homes among intellectually handicapped men (Quinsey, Book, & Skilling, 2004). It has not been tested, to our knowledge, on individuals with IQs below the mildly mentally retarded range. Substituting the CATS for the PCL–R in the VRAG makes the VRAG easier to score with intellectually handicapped individuals. However, the full PCL–R should be used where possible.

4. *What do the minus signs mean beside the VRAG items pertaining to age, severity of the index offense, diagnosis of schizophrenia, and female victim?*

These items have negative weights on the VRAG because increasing age (at index offense), greater offense severity, presence of schizophrenia, and having a female victim are associated with violent recidivism rates that are lower than the overall average for the construction sample. A negative weighting of a predictor item in the VRAG is not an indication that the test is inapplicable for individuals identified by that item. With regard to age, however, we note that we have few empirical data on offenders assessed in their 60s or older.

A related question about age pertains to whether VRAG (and other actuarial assessment) scores should be "discounted" for older offenders being considered for release. Analyses of our data indicate that offenders released at older ages are less likely to recidivate violently. However, this effect is significantly subsumed by the age at index offense and, even more so, by age at first criminal offense (G. T. Harris & Rice, 2005a). There is presently no sound research basis to discount VRAG scores based on the age offenders are when considered for release.

5. *Was the VRAG construction sample of uncharacteristically high risk?*

No, the violent recidivism rates we have reported are the same as those reported by Nuffield (1982) in a study of a representative sample of Canadian federal inmates.

6. *Can the VRAG be used for female offenders?*

We have tested the ability of the VRAG to predict violent recidivism among women in two studies. In the first study (G. T. Harris, Rice, & Cormier, 2002), all forensic patients in the province of Ontario were followed up for approximately 7 years of opportunity to reoffend. Of the 406 patients who had an opportunity to reoffend, 59 were women. The violent recidivism rate for women was low (14%, $n = 8$), and the VRAG did not predict violent recidivism for the women in this study. In the second study (G. T. Harris, Rice, & Camilleri, 2004), the VRAG (modified to suit the predictor variables available in the archived data set) predicted violence in both 20-week and 1-year follow-ups of 403 women in the MacArthur Violence Risk Assessment Study (Monahan et al., 2001). The VRAG worked at least as well for women as it did for men. Violence in this study was primarily self-reported violence, and the base rate of violence for women was substantial (23% in 20 weeks). More generally, the predictors of crime and violence among women are the same as those among men, but the base rate of criminal violence in most female populations is much, much lower than the base rate among male populations. Note that the primary measure of violence in the MacArthur Violence Risk Assessment Study (Monahan et al., 2001; Robbins, Monahan, & Silver, 2003) was self-reported violence rather than criminal violence.

7. *Shouldn't the VRAG or the SORAG be used only for offenders that the examiner knows to be of at least moderately high risk?*

No, this practice unjustifiably assumes examiner omniscience. If this omniscience existed, it would obviate the use of actuarial instruments. The same objection applies to the practice of using the VRAG or the SORAG only for offenders that the examiner "knows" to be of low risk.

These comments are not meant to preclude the development of a triage system in which VRAG assessments would be reserved only for offenders who were identified as moderate risk or higher on the basis of a briefer, less expensive actuarial screening instrument of known validity. Unfortunately, no such instrument yet exists.

8. *Did all the index and recidivism offenses occur in Ontario, Canada?*

No. Although exact numbers are not available for the construction sample, we know that a small minority occurred outside Ontario and that a few occurred outside Canada. The applicability of the VRAG and the SORAG in jurisdictions other than those already studied is an empirical question. It is possible that the absolute likelihoods of recidivism vary over jurisdictions. It is, however, highly unlikely that the relative risk ranking of individuals would vary over geographic locations because of the universal nature of the correlates of crime. The VRAG and the SORAG have performed well in different locations in recent research. (See http://www.mhcp-research.com/ragreps.htm for an up-to-date list of replications.)

9. *What is the base rate for insanity acquittees?*

The 10-year base rate of violent recidivism for 799 men in our follow-up studies was 43% and for a subsample of 476 insanity acquittees, 34%.

GENERAL QUESTIONS

1. *I am assessing an offender who has been living in the community without incident for more than 10 years, after having served a 10-year sentence. Surely, his estimated probability of recidivism is lower now than that indicated by a VRAG score obtained upon his initial incarceration over 20 years ago. Should I adjust this probability, and if so, how and by how much?*

There are two parts to this question. The first pertains to whether the probability of violent recidivism should be adjusted according to the length of the period between the index offense and the time of release. This period of incarceration does not include an opportunity to reoffend and should not be used to adjust the probability. The offenders in the original construction sample all had varying periods of institutionalization before the follow-up period began.

The second part of the question concerns adjusting the probability of violent recidivism based on the length of offense-free time during which an offender has had an opportunity to reoffend. Analyses of our data indicate lower (than VRAG norms would suggest) recidivism rates as offense-free time at risk increases (G. T. Harris & Rice, 2005). The data suggest lowering estimated risk by approximately 1 percentile for each offense-free year in the community. However, this correction does not apply to the three highest VRAG categories. We also do not know how many offenders who appear to be offense free after decades have actually been lost to follow-up (by, unbeknownst to us, dying, changing their names, or moving far away). We recommend in such rare cases that one state the probability and qualify it with the observation that the research suggests it is actually likely to be lower because of the length of the offense-free period of opportunity.

2. *I am working with a paroled offender who has full community access. This offender has a high VRAG score but low scores on all dynamic risk indicators. How should I adjust his estimated likelihood of reoffending?*

The actuarially determined probability provided by the VRAG is not altered by changes in dynamic risk factors, because it is an estimate of the probability of at least one violent offense over a 7- or 10-year period during which dynamic indicators are expected to fluctuate. Dynamic risk indicators should be used to manage an offender's risk over short time periods.

3. *Doesn't the fact that the VRAG or SORAG scores of some well-known serial sexual murderers are not in the highest category show that the instruments are totally useless or at least useless for serial sexual murderers?*

It is possible that the VRAG and the SORAG underestimate the dangerousness of multiple murderers, but it is difficult to know, because most jurisdictions have some variant of the "too many bodies rule" that prevents these offenders from getting a new opportunity to reoffend. However, we have looked at our data for the 39 sexual murderers (but not serial murderers) who were released and followed for a 10-year period. On the basis of this small sample, the base rate for violent (including sexual) reoffending was .46, the correlation between the VRAG score and violent recidivism was .27, and Cohen's *d* was .58.

4. *If it is known that a sex offender is sexually deviant, why would one bother to score the SORAG?*

   It should be scored, because the SORAG is a more accurate predictor of recidivism than a phallometric score alone.

5. *What was the outcome variable in the VRAG research?*

   It was a charge or conviction for a violent offense or a return to either prison (as a parole violator) or maximum-security psychiatric hospital for a violent offense for which the offender could have been charged.

6. *Can the CATS be substituted for the PCL–R in the SORAG as well as the VRAG?*

   Yes. However, because the range of possible scores on the VRAG and the SORAG for the CATS is only –3 to +3, compared with –5 to +12 for the PCL–R, the risk assessment report should state that the CATS was used to substitute for the PCL–R.

7. *What are the correlations among the PCL–R, the CATS, and violent recidivism?*

   For 799 men in our follow-up studies, the correlations are as follows: The CATS correlates .56 with the PCL–R (.35 with Factor 1 and .61 with Factor 2). Violent recidivism correlated .32 with the CATS and .36 with the PCL–R.

8. *Is it the case that the VRAG works best in the prediction of fairly minor offenses?*

   Its ability to predict violent recidivism is unaffected by the adoption of even very extreme definitions (e.g., murder committed within 6 months at risk; G. T. Harris et al., 2002). See more comments on this issue in the answer to questions 4 and 5 in the Ethics and Bias section.

9. *The VRAG and the SORAG are more accurate in predicting violent than specifically sexual recidivism; should one not use another method for sex offenders?*

   First, the question assumes that sexual recidivism is the only relevant outcome for sex offenders. We argue that from a policy perspective, the prediction of violent (including sexual) recidivism is an appropriate goal for sex offenders. As explained in chapter 8, we believe that sexual recidivism (as measured so far) entails considerably more measurement error than other measures of recidivism. Nevertheless, it is true that some U.S. sexual predator statutes specify that the legally relevant outcome is specifically sexual recidivism. In these jurisdictions, one must estimate the likelihood that an offender meets the legally mandated criterion. In most cases, that means that one must assess the likelihood that an offender will commit a violent sexual offense at some time during the rest of his life. At the present time, there are no such norms available for any actuarial instrument. Moreover, because many sexual offenses end up in charges or convictions for nonsexual offenses, it is undoubtedly the case that norms based on charges or convictions for offenses that are known to be sexual because of the name of the charge or conviction underestimate the number of truly sexual offenses (Rice, Harris, Lang, & Cormier, 2005a). For this reason, we have not published norms for predicting specifically sexual recidivism, but they are available for other actuarial instruments such as the RRASOR (Hanson, 1997) and the Static–99 (Hanson & Thornton, 2000).

10. *What is the correlation between latency to reoffend and VRAG score among sex offenders?*

The correlation between VRAG score and latency to a sexual or violent reoffense among 343 sex offenders was $-.34$, $p < .0001$.

ETHICS AND BIAS

1. *Did you have ethics approval to conduct the research leading to the VRAG?*

Yes. The research was approved by our institution's Research and Ethics Committee.

2. *Doesn't the VRAG unfairly penalize members of minorities because it holds them responsible for their histories? For example, Aboriginals and Blacks are more likely than others to have criminal histories, and in the VRAG aspects of criminal history translate into higher risk scores.*

First, Whites formed the overwhelming majority of the VRAG construction sample. Second, a VRAG score is not moral judgment or a finding of criminal responsibility. In general, the correlates of crime are the same across ethnic and racial groups. In the general population, these groups differ in their base rate of criminal offending, such that the base rates for violence are higher. However, it is not as clear that the base rates for the recidivism of identified offenders vary as much as the base rates for criminality in the general population. Lastly, lowering the level of risk based on allowances for ethnic differences could inadvertently lead to a lack of sufficient supervision and, quite possibly, a new offense (and possibly one in which a member of the same ethnic minority is the victim).

3. *Isn't it illegal or at least immoral to use static predictors?*

No, it is not illegal to use static predictors. Neither is it, in our view, immoral, if the goal is to achieve a proper balance between public safety and the civil liberties of offenders. It is important to remember that one of the difficulties with the use of clinical judgment or informal criteria to inform dispositional decisions is its association with inappropriate conservatism.

4. *Does the SORAG count trivial offending in its measurement of criminal history or outcome? For example, did exhibitionism or other noncontact sex offenses count in the computation of sex offense history or the definition of violent recidivism?*

No. We excluded such offenses from the definitions of sexual or violent history and sexual and violent recidivism. Note, however, that there are two items (7 and 8) on the SORAG that do include noncontact offenses that are known to be sexual. Note also that among sex offenders, the SORAG and the VRAG correlate with both severity of offense and victim injury in the recidivism offense ($rs = .35, p < .001$).

5. *Does the VRAG predict very serious reoffending?*

Yes. Of 617 men in the original construction sample who had an opportunity to reoffend (G. T. Harris, Rice, & Quinsey, 1993), 101 scored 15 or more on the VRAG. Of these 101, 67 (66%) met our criteria for violent recidivism over a 7-year follow-up. These 67 men were convicted of a total of 46 serious offenses as follows:

- Homicide–3
- Attempted murder–2
- Wounding–1
- Assault causing bodily harm–18
- Hands-on sex offenses–11
- Kidnapping–1
- Weapons–6
- Armed robbery–4

In addition, 10 men were convicted of common assault and an additional 11 men had been charged but not (or not yet) convicted for a violent offense. Many of the charges were later cleared by conviction for something on the first section of the list. The violent recidivism charge rate for this same group of 101 after an average 10-year follow-up was 73%.

Seventy-eight offenders scored +17 or more on the VRAG in this sample. Of these, 59 (76%) violently recidivated within an average of 10 years. Twenty had been charged but not convicted before the end of the first follow-up period of 7 years (Rice & Harris, 1995b) or were convicted of "only" a common assault. Thus, this group's conviction rate for serious violent crime was 50% over 7 years.

Twenty offenders scored +25 or more on the VRAG in this sample. Of these, all violently recidivated, but 5 were not convicted before the end of the 7-year follow-up or committed "only" a common assault. The 7-year conviction rate for serious violent crime was 75%.

In a subsequent study (Quinsey, Coleman, Jones, & Altrows, 1997), the VRAG differentiated 19 recidivists in the Ontario forensic system (they committed 3 murders, 5 attempted murders, 1 wounding, 2 assaults causing bodily harm, 3 common assaults, 4 rapes, and 1 indecent assault) from 92 nonrecidivist forensic patients.

SCORING ISSUES

General Questions

1. *What is the "index" offense?*
   The index offense is the offense that led to the current assessment or institutionalization, whether violent or not.
2. *Can one replace missing VRAG or SORAG variables with other similar variables that are known to be risk indicators? For example, can one replace elementary school maladjustment with early psychiatric history or a PCL–R score with a clinical ascertainment of psychopathy?*
   In general, no. Such substitutions turn an actuarial method into a clinical impression. However, in Exhibit 8.2 we present a short list of acceptable substitutions.
3. *Can one replace the PCL–R with the PCL–SV in scoring the VRAG?*
   See Exhibit 8.2.

VRAG Item 1: Lived With Both Biological Parents to Age 16 (Except for Death of Parent)

1. *How is Item 1 scored? What if the offender was adopted, sent to live with relatives in another country for political reasons, lived in a*

boarding school, or spent 2 months at a summer camp before age 16? What if the offender was adopted because one or both parents died?

In the original research used to construct the VRAG, this item was scored as follows: Did the offender live with *both* biological parents until the age of 16? The question was answered *yes* unless there was a traumatic event that separated the child from at least one of his parents for longer than 1 month. The most common traumatic events were parental marital breakup or paternal absence. Other examples of traumatic events were having a parent die, being in an incubator for several months because of prematurity, or being sent to juvenile corrections (training school). Of these, having a parent die turned out *not* to increase risk. All other traumatic separations that were longer than 1 month increased risk.

Certain nontraumatic separations (i.e., those that were intended to be positive experiences for the child and were not due to child misbehavior or to shirking of parental duty) were not counted. Thus, for example, being sent to summer camp for 2 months, when it was intended as a positive experience and when there was no indication that it was because the offender was difficult to manage or because of marital problems, was not counted as separation. Although it was very rare in our study population, the question has often arisen (especially in queries from other countries) whether being sent to boarding school should be counted as separation. Using the same logic applied to summer camp, we recommend that being sent to boarding school, when intended as a positive experience for a child and not as a way to correct behavior problems, *not* count as separation.

If an offender's parents died and the child was then adopted, this was scored as –2. If the rater believes there is not sufficient information to score this item confidently, we recommend omitting the item and prorating.

VRAG Item 2: Elementary School Maladjustment

1. *What are the criteria for having an elementary school problem?*

   First, *elementary school* means kindergarten through grade 8 (on average, until a child turns 14 years old). Any mention of behavior problems qualifies as slight maladjustment. Mention of any behavior problems that resulted in suspension or that occurred in more than 1 year of elementary school qualifies as at least moderate maladjustment. Minor acts of aggression against other pupils count as moderate maladjustment. Examples of slight or moderate problems are being suspended for smoking on school property, being told to report to the principal's office for refusing to cooperate with assignments or for interfering with other students' class participation or for "talking back" to a teacher, having parents notified because of incidents of pushing students down in the schoolyard, and being suspended for truancy.

Behavior problems that resulted in expulsion or that were persistent throughout elementary school qualify as severe maladjustment. Any act of actual or attempted aggression against a teacher counts as severe. A score of severe is also given for a serious act of aggression against another pupil (e.g., being suspended for beating up another pupil).

Use the information at hand to make an "at least" decision. That is, if you are certain that there were at least slight problems, give a score of +2.

In countries where there is no equivalent of eighth grade, use the time at school until the offender turns 14 years old for scoring.

2. *What if the offender did not complete elementary school until the age of 18 or later?*

Count the time until the offender completed the eighth grade or equivalent if the offender actually attended an elementary school. However, if the offender completed an eighth-grade equivalency without attending a school, count only the years the offender was actually enrolled in an elementary school (or until the offender turned 14 years old).

3. *What if the offender was in a special school (e.g., an institution for intellectually handicapped individuals) or a reform school?*

If the offender was in a special or reform school, score the item for the period up to the time the offender turned 14 years old.

4. *What if there is no documentation apart from the offender self-report?*

If the offender self-reports behavior problems at school, count them. However, if the offender reports no problems, and that is the only information available, omit the item and score by prorating.

VRAG Item 3: History of Alcohol Problems

1. *What are the criteria for deciding if there was alcohol involvement in an offense? How "involved" does alcohol have to be in an of-*

fense to be scored in the affirmative? If the offender had one beer before he forged a check, would that count? Is it simply a case of the offender having alcohol in his system when the offense was committed, or is the item meant to get at something more pathological in terms of alcohol being a significant factor in the crime?

The criterion is a determination that alcohol of any amount was consumed just prior to or during the offense.

VRAG Item 4: Marital Status

1. *Do same-sex marriages count?*

   No, only marriages or common-law relationships with opposite-sex partners.

VRAG Item 5: Criminal History Score for Nonviolent Offenses

1. *Do you count charges and convictions?*

   Yes. Refer to the more detailed explanation of the Cormier–Lang system in the notes to Table A.1 of Appendix A and in Appendix E.

2. *What about "carrying a concealed weapon"?*

   Score as +1, the same as possession of a weapon.

3. *What about "hit and run"?*

   Without further information, score it as a nonviolent offense (it could be that the offender hit a parked car as opposed to a person). The same applies for failure to remain at the scene of an accident, dangerous operation of a motor vehicle, or careless driving.

4. *What about "criminal trespass"?*

   Score as +1.

5. *What about "prowl by night" or "possession of house-breaking tools"?*

   Score each as +1.

6. *What about "taking an auto without consent"?*

   Score as theft of auto, +5.

7. *How does one score failure to return leased property?*

   Score it as theft. Without further details (e.g., whether it is a rented movie or a Porsche), assign it a +1. When there is uncertainty, we use the strategy of scoring an item according to the least score the offender could get for that item.

VRAG Item 6: Failure on Prior Conditional Release

1. *What does failure on prior conditional release include?*

Failure on conditional release includes failure on bail, promise to appear, probation, or parole. Supervision by mental health authorities subsequent to release from the hospital does not count. Of course, if the offender was on a conditional release at the time of the index offense, this item is scored as *yes*.

VRAG Item 7: Age at Index Offense

1. *What age is used if the index offense involves a series of crimes?*
   Use the age at the time of the first offense for which the offender is currently being assessed.

VRAG Item 8: Victim Injury

1. *If the index offense involves a series of crimes, how does one determine injury?*
   For this item, count the injury to the most seriously injured victim among the victims of the offenses for which the offender is currently being assessed.

VRAG Item 9: Any Female Victim

1. *How is this item scored when there are a series of crimes that constitute the index offenses, some of which involve female victims and some of which do not?*
   Score this as −1 if there is any female victim for any of the index offenses.
2. *What if the index offense was armed robbery of a bank, but it is not specified whether the tellers were men or women?*
   Omit the item and prorate.
3. *Is there a female victim for offenses that do not involve personal contact, such as forging a woman's checks or breaking into a woman's home?*
   No.

VRAG Item 10: Meets DSM–III Criteria for Any Personality Disorder

1. *Shouldn't clinicians be using current (DSM–IV) criteria for personality disorder (and, for Item 11, schizophrenia) when scoring the VRAG and the SORAG?*
   No, because the instrument was developed using DSM–III criteria. If only DSM–IV (or some other version of DSM) is available, use that diagnosis, but qualify in the risk assessment report that that item was approximated.

2. *When is the diagnosis supposed to be made? Is it "currently meets" or is it "ever met" the diagnostic criteria?*
   Factors are coded as they were at the time of the index offense. Therefore, the individual must have met the criteria at the time of the index offense. However, because of the temporal stability and historical nature of the criteria for the diagnosis, both past functioning and present functioning are relevant.

VRAG Item 11: Meets DSM–III Criteria for Schizophrenia

1. *Does schizoaffective disorder count as schizophrenia in this item?*
   No. In the construction sample, of all the diagnoses recorded, only schizophrenia and personality disorder were related to violent recidivism.

VRAG Item 12: Hare Psychopathy Checklist—Revised Score

1. *Doesn't the PCL–R require an interview?*
   No. According to the PCL–R manual, an interview is not required as long as sufficient documentary information is available. The norms in the PCL–R manual include scores obtained solely from file review. The PCL–R was scored from institutional files in the follow-up studies that were used to construct and cross-validate the VRAG and SORAG (e.g., G. T. Harris, Rice, & Quinsey, 1993; G. T. Harris et al., 2003; Rice & Harris, 1997a).

SORAG Item 6: Criminal History Score for Violent Offenses

1. *What if an offender reports sex offenses for which he was never charged?*
   Count only charges and convictions for this item.

SORAG Item 7: Number of Convictions for Previous Sexual Offenses

1. *Should I count offenses against boys that resulted in a breach of a term of probation or found to be a parole violation when no new conviction was involved?*
   No, count only convictions for this item. Information on offenses for which an offender was not convicted can, however, be used in SORAG Item 8 (and, of course, SORAG Item 9).

SORAG Item 8: History of Sex Offenses Against Girls Under Age 14 Only

If an offender has ever committed a sex offense (whether involving physical contact or not) against a person 14 years of age or over or, if under age 14, within 5 years of his own age when the offense occurred, he gets "high-risk" points (+4). Or if a sex offender has ever sexually offended against a boy or a man of any age, he gets high-risk points. If his only sex offenses have been against girls under age 14 and more than 5 years younger than himself, he gets a score of 0.

1. *I am assessing an offender whose index offense involves a female child. Should I count offenses against boys that were used to revoke a term of probation or found to be a parole violation, even if no new conviction was involved?*

    Yes, that information is used to score this item. Include any offense for which you have sufficient documentation that the offense was of a sexual nature and occurred against either a male or female adult, or against a male child. Violating parole or breaching probation as a result is sufficient evidence to satisfy the criteria. Be sure that clear and acceptable evidence is used to score this item. When the evidence only "suggests" offending against one of the other categories, leave the item out and state why. This item must be scored in the affirmative for offending against female children only when there is absolutely no doubt that the offense pattern is exclusive.

SORAG Item 13: Phallometric Test Results

1. *Can you score the SORAG without the phallometric item?*

    Yes. Use the substitute in Exhibit 8.2, or prorate the item.

APPENDIX E

Cormier–Lang System for Quantifying Criminal History

NOTES AND INSTRUCTIONS

This system is an adaptation of an earlier one by Akman and Normandeau (1967). It can be used to quantify an offender's history of criminal offenses, a current or index offense, or a particular subgroup of offenses (e.g., violent offenses or property offenses). Add up each count of an offense to determine the seriousness within that type. For example, if there are two counts of break and enter ($2 \times 1 = 2$) and three counts of theft under ($3 \times 1 = 3$), then the resulting score would be 5. Scores can be cumulative or separated into desired categories (e.g., separated into violent and nonviolent or sexual and nonsexual). In cases where the exact offense type is unknown, use an "at least" method to score. For example, if an offense is known to be assault but there are no details as to whether it was assault causing bodily harm or aggravated assault, score the offense in the lowest category, as 2. Charges of attempted offense, such as attempted armed robbery, are scored the same as if the offense had been completed, with the exception of attempted murder, which has a separate assigned value.

This system can be used when only official police information is available (e.g., records from the Royal Canadian Mounted Police Fingerprint Service), but when possible, documents such as police reports from investigating officers and witnesses should also be used to clarify details. In general, for example, armed robbery and robbery with violence are scored as violent offenses, but robbery is considered to be nonviolent. However, if investigating officers' reports indicate that a robbery charge was associated with violent conduct (e.g., a victim was injured), the offense would be recorded as violent. As another example, a charge for pointing a firearm or possession of a restricted weapon would be recorded as nonviolent without additional information. However, if police reports from witnesses indicated that the charges were associated with violent conduct (e.g., attempting to fire a weapon at someone), the offense would be recorded as violent. Similarly, a conviction for a fire setting offense may be recorded as mischief (with a score of 1), but if details of the offense clearly indicate that the offense was actually setting fire to a home and causing substantial damage, then the score would be 5 for the most serious of the arson offenses.

For scoring Item 5 of the VRAG and Items 5 and 6 of the SORAG, all charges and convictions (including juvenile record) prior to the index offense are scored separately for nonviolent and violent criminal history. In scoring the VRAG and the SORAG, offenses listed in Group 1 are generally considered to be violent, and offenses listed in Group 2 are nonviolent, but exceptions are possible. Some criminal offenses do not appear here, for a variety of reasons. First, some offenses (e.g., sedition, bestiality, bribery, counterfeiting, or hijacking) are so rare that we did not derive a score for them. In the case of such rare offenses, the listed offense closest to the rare one should be used: kidnapping for hijacking or fraud for counterfeiting, for example. Second, some offenses (prostitution, possession of narcotics, public intoxication and drinking under age, bookmaking, and other so-called victimless crimes) were too minor to include. Third, parole and mandatory supervision violations; breach of probation, recognizance, or bail; failure to appear; and escapes and unlawfully at large were addressed separately in other areas of the original research and are therefore not included here unless these crimes resulted in additional offenses (e.g., a murder by a prison escapee), which then would be scored.

This system (and the earlier one by Akman & Normandeau, 1967) is based on the *Criminal Code of Canada,* which itself is based on British Common Law, as are criminal statutes throughout the English-speaking world. Thus, the *Criminal Code of Canada* is very similar to the statutes in individual states in the United States. To the extent that a particular state code is different, some amount of judgment is required to approximate as closely as possible the names of offenses in other jurisdictions. For example, an offense commonly listed in U.S. state codes is battery, which usually involves some physical injury. It would therefore be comparable to the assault causing bodily harm listed in this scoring method. Similarly, larceny does not appear in the Canadian code but is usually equivalent to theft.

In addition, the *Criminal Code of Canada* entails two classes for some offenses (e.g., theft, mischief, possession of stolen property) against property (offenses resulting in a loss over a particular monetary value versus those involving a loss under that value). This is similar to the grand larceny versus larceny distinction in some other jurisdictions. The scoring system presented here reflects that distinction by assigning larger values to offenses exceeding that criterion (over) compared with those that do not (under). Because of inflation, the critical value has changed from time to time (from $50 to $200 to $1,000; it is currently $5,000). Scoring is done according to whether the offense exceeded the cutoff value at the time.

TABLE E.1

Cormier–Lang Criminal History Score for Violent Offenses (Group 1)

Offense	Score
Homicide (murder, manslaughter, criminal negligence causing death)	28
Attempted murder, causing bodily harm with intent to wound	7
Kidnapping, abduction, and forcible confinement	6
Aggravated assault, choking, administering a noxious substance	6
Assault causing bodily harm	5
Assault with a weapon	3
Assault, assaulting a peace officer	2
Aggravated sexual assault, sexual assault causing bodily harm	15
Sexual assault with a weapon	12
Sexual assault, gross indecency (vaginal or anal penetration, victim forced to fellate offender)	10
Sexual assault (attempted rape, indecent assault)	6
Gross indecency (offender fellates or performs cunnilingus on victim)	6
Sexual assault (sexual interference, invitation to sexual touching)	2
Armed robbery (bank, store)	8
Robbery with violence	5
Armed robbery (not a bank or store)	4

TABLE E.2
Cormier–Lang Criminal History Scores for Nonviolent Offenses (Group 2)

Offense	Score
Robbery (bank, store)	7
Robbery (purse snatching)	3
Arson and fire setting (church, house, barn)	5
Arson and fire setting (garbage can)	1
Threatening with a weapon, dangerous use of or pointing firearm	3
Threatening (uttering threats)	2
Theft over[a] (includes car theft and possession of stolen property over[a])	5
Mischief to public or private property over[a]	5
Break and enter and commit indictable offense (burglary)	2
Theft under[b] (includes possession of stolen property under[b])	1
Mischief to public or private property under[b]	1
Break and enter (includes break and enter with intent to commit an offense)	1
Fraud (extortion, embezzlement)	5
Fraud (forged check, impersonation)	1
Possession of a prohibited or restricted weapon	1
Procuring a person for or living on the avails of prostitution	1
Trafficking in narcotics	1
Dangerous driving, impaired driving (driving while intoxicated)	1
Obstructing a peace officer (including resisting arrest)	1
Causing a disturbance	1
Wearing a disguise with the intent to commit an offense	1
Indecent exposure	2

Note. [a]Roughly equivalent to grand larceny based on the value of the stolen property—as of 2003, over $5,000.00.
[b]Roughly equivalent to larceny based on the value of the stolen property—as of 2003, under $5,000.

APPENDIX F

Guidelines for the Compilation of a
Psychosocial History Suitable for Risk Appraisal

These guidelines were written to aid in the information-gathering process for the assessment of criminal offender and forensic psychiatric populations. The questions included in these guidelines are intended to yield sufficient information to allow scoring of the Violence Risk Appraisal Guide (VRAG), the Sex Offender Risk Appraisal Guide (SORAG), and the Hare Psychopathy Checklist—Revised (PCL–R; Hare, 1991).

These guidelines are based on many years of experience in collecting research data based on psychosocial case history information on offender and forensic psychiatric populations. Because many case historians have never been trained in using structured information-gathering procedures, their reports are often inadequate for the task of scoring formal assessment instruments. For maximal usefulness, the information gathered should be presented in such a way as to aid the reader in making decisions about diagnosis, security issues, risk factors, and community adjustment and to provide guidance in initiating further specific assessments of treatment needs.

GENERAL GUIDELINES

The goal of this assessment format is to present accurate and pertinent information about an offender. The following key issues should guide the psychosocial history assessment:

1. Information should be gathered from as many sources as possible. The issue of confidentiality governing information col-

lection from these sources must be addressed in accordance with legal guidelines of the jurisdiction. Case historians should request records from schools, centralized databases of arrests and convictions (in Canada, Royal Canadian Mounted Police Fingerprint Services), police, social agencies, hospitals, and corrections to provide the information necessary to complete all areas of the assessment. The historian should also request information from family members in a personal interview or, if this is not possible, by telephone. Gathering information from all of these sources alleviates the need to depend on offenders as the sole source of information; they often prove to be poor historians. We recommend that case historians review the information from other sources before interviewing offenders to ensure that specific areas of questioning are dealt with completely in an informed manner.

2. Case historians must attribute statements to their sources so that readers of the psychosocial history report can determine the validity of the information. For example, if the offender says during the interview that he never had any problems as a child, the information should be presented as being reported by the offender. Too often, misinformation in written reports is assumed to be fact because the historian did not clearly indicate that the statement was made by a particular person only. The historian should check other sources to validate the information.

3. We have not explicitly defined some of the terms used in these guidelines because we assume that case historians have a working knowledge of these terms. The historian must be able to define and interpret terms for an offender and family members who are uncertain of their meanings in a manner that accommodates their level of comprehension. If the historian is uncertain about the definition of any term in these guidelines, he or she should seek clarification before beginning to compile a history.

4. When reporting on behaviors, it is advisable to give age of onset, frequency, and severity of the action. This information assists readers in evaluating the seriousness of that particular behavior. With regard to age, the historian should always specify age at last birthday for consistency.

5. These guidelines are designed to aid clinicians from all disciplines in acquiring psychosocial history information for any number of purposes, but especially to allow the scoring of the VRAG and the SORAG. Not everyone using the report will be familiar with the names of other clinicians or the relevance

of certain placements, so when referring to a particular staff member the historian should identify him or her by discipline or position held. Likewise, in referring to a particular ward or unit or to other agencies and facilities, the historian should identify it by type and security level.

6. The first page should be set up to provide quick access to key identifiers such as the offender's full name, age, reason for admission, and parole eligibility date (for correctional inmates). Case historians should date the report and identify themselves, including their title and unit or department.

7. Dividing the assessment into categories with headings serves two purposes: It unifies all the information pertaining to that category, and it allows readers to easily find a particular area of interest.

8. Style is important. Case historians should avoid a bullet list format, because this format does not make clear the connections between points, making it more difficult for the reader to get the full meaning. Slang words are not advisable in a formal report, unless the historian is specifically quoting the offender or a significant informant. The historian must be objective, because the purpose of the assessment is to present the information as clearly and factually as possible for a reader to make accurate decisions.

9. Finally, the case historian should sign the report at the end, with his or her name and title typed below. It is also advisable, and often an accepted standard, to identify the top of each page with the offender's name and case number or date of birth for administrative reasons. In addition, each page should be numbered (e.g., 1 of 10).

PSYCHOSOCIAL ASSESSMENT REPORT

The following format guides the psychosocial assessment and can be used to structure the report. The item number from the VRAG, the SORAG, or the PCL–R is noted in parentheses following each item; it is particularly important that the case historian gather enough information on these questions to meet the criteria for the information collection methods or instructions for these systems.

Name: First, middle, and last names of the offender, as well as aliases

Institution: Institution name

Case number: Institutional case number

Centralized police database number:	In Canada, the Royal Canadian Police Fingerprint Services
Date of report:	Report date
Date of admission:	Admission date to the current facility
Legal documentation:	Formal convictions and sentencing, with dates and parole eligibility dates
Date of birth:	Month, day, year (indicate current age)
Birthplace:	City or town and province or state
Marital status:	Single, married (includes common-law relationships), divorced, widowed

Note the time frame (e.g., at time of report, at time of admission, or at time of current offense)

Legal next of kin:	Name and relationship to offender
Address:	Most recent residence of next of kin
Religion:	Information about religious affiliation
Occupation:	Description of most recent job prior to admission
Information sources:	May include offender, relatives, Royal Canadian Mounted Police Fingerprint Services (or other centralized police database), police reports, jail summaries, court transcripts, correctional or psychiatric institutional records, parole and probation reports, school records, community agency records, and psychiatric reports
Case historian:	Name, job title, and unit or department of author of the psychosocial history report

Circumstances Leading to Admission

The report briefly describes the legal circumstances that led to the current admission, including, for example, the formal charge, conviction, and disposition and the dates of each. It is advisable in most cases to list charges, because frequently they are notably different from convictions. For example, a charge of sexual assault may be reduced to assault causing bodily harm for a conviction, and unless the charge is clearly stated, readers will remain uninformed of the sexual component to the offense. This section should state which court the offender was convicted in and the facility he was transferred from and by whom. The details of the offense are addressed in the following section. (PCL–R 11, 18, 19, 20)

Current Offense Information

This section discusses the current offense or offenses for which the offender was admitted to the facility. The section should start with a description of the immediate circumstances preceding the offense and should include accurate dates, locations (e.g., in the case of sexual assault, where the offender encountered the victim and where the assault took place), and the approximate time of day. The case historian should record the offender's age at the time of this offense; the victim's age, gender, and relationship to the offender (e.g., stranger, casual acquaintance, friend, relative); and a narrative description of the offense. For confidentiality reasons, victims' names should be substituted with initials. The narrative description should be complete and should include whether a weapon was present, type of weapon, how it was used, and the amount of victim injury and cause, for a personal offense, or value of property or extent of damage, for a property offense. If an accomplice was involved, information about that person should be noted (i.e., age, relationship, criminality, and amount of involvement in the current offense). If possible, the report should state how the offender was arrested. When more than one offense is involved, each should be treated as a separate incident, and the historian should give an accurate description of each in chronological order. (VRAG 3, 7, 9; SORAG 3, 8, 10; PCL–R 5, 6, 8, 10, 11, 14, 18, 19)

Family History

The family history section describes each member of the offender's immediate family, beginning with parents and followed by siblings in order of birth. If he was separated from either of his biological parents before the age of 16 because of such circumstances as divorce, death, or incarceration, the report should include the same information about the replacement caregiver if a significant amount of involvement occurred; when only temporary or short involvement occurred, it is considered sufficient only to identify the individual or agency. In either case, the report should briefly give the details of the situation that led to the replacement caregiver's involvement with the offender.

If other family members beyond the immediate family have experienced significant psychiatric, medical, or criminal problems, a brief description should also be included in this section (applicable persons include those who are biologically related or who have had a significant amount of contact with the offender). The report should specify the relationship of each family member to the offender.

For the offender's father and mother, the report should give full name, current age, occupational summary, and history of criminal charges and convictions, drug and alcohol use, psychiatric problems, and mental health contacts such as hospitalized psychiatric admissions or counseling. This description should include information about significant medical history, psychiatric diagnosis, epilepsy, retardation, and suicide and attempted suicide. The report should provide a brief description of each parent's current functioning, with emphasis on his or her present relationship with the offender. (VRAG 1, 3; SORAG 1, 3; PCL–R 7)

For siblings, the report should record the same information as for parents, in order of birth, beginning with the eldest and stating the offender's birth order.

Childhood

The section on the offender's childhood includes background, relationship with his family, and social adjustment up to about 18 years of age. When noting aspects of abnormal behavior, the age of onset, frequency, and seriousness are as important as the characteristics of the behavior. Questions concerning childhood drug and alcohol use, criminality, sexuality, and schooling can be detailed specifically in other sections. The following interview questions can help the case historian gather sufficient information:

1. Until what age did the offender live with both biological parents? If the offender did not live with both parents until adulthood, the report should specify the offender's age at separation and the reasons for the separation (e.g., parental death, divorce, institutionalization). The report should also describe any substitute caregivers (e.g., relative, adoptive parents, foster parents, admission to juvenile corrections) and the duration of the caregiving relationship. (VRAG 1, SORAG 1)
2. Describe the offender's home life as a child (e.g., frequent moves, financial stability, close-knit family relations).
3. What were the offender's parents like as individuals and in their marital relationship (e.g., hard workers, socially isolated, alcoholic, abusive, happy, compatible)?
4. Describe the offender's relationship with his parents (e.g., frequent arguments, harsh punishments, emotionally positive interaction, supportive relationship).
   (PCL–R 4, 5, 6, 7, 8, 12, 16)
5. Describe the offender's relationship with his brothers and sisters (e.g., distant, close, physically aggressive, protective).
   (PCL–R 4, 5, 6, 7, 8, 11, 12, 16)
6. How was the offender disciplined or punished (e.g., slapped, denied privileges, beaten), how often, and for what reasons?
   (PCL–R 4, 5, 10, 12, 16)
7. Did the offender run away from home for more than a day? At what age? How often, and why? (PCL–R 3, 12)
8. Did the offender ever have any sleep disorders (e.g., somnambulism, night terrors)?
9. Was the offender involved in physical fights? At what age, and how often? (PCL–R 3, 10, 12, 14)

10. Did the offender ever threaten someone, control someone by threats, or force someone to do something he or she did not want to do? (PCL–R 5, 11, 12)
11. Did the offender ever pick out another child seen as weaker or controllable and torment that child for a period of time? Describe. (PCL–R 3, 5, 8, 12)
12. Was the offender ever picked on or tormented by someone for a period of time?
13. Was the offender ever involved in thefts, vandalism, fire setting, or hurting animals? (PCL–R 3, 8, 12, 15, 18)
14. Was the offender ever involved with police, social services, or young offender (juvenile) courts (e.g., had formal charges laid, been assessed by child protection agency)? (PCL–R 11, 12, 18, 19, 20)
15. Was the offender ever involved in criminal acts not resulting in charges? (PCL–R 5, 6, 11, 12, 14, 15)
16. What was the nature of the offender's relationships with his peers (e.g., mutually rewarding interactions, acquaintances only, preferred to be a loner, used others for own gain)? Did he have any close friends? Describe. (PCL–R 2, 5, 7, 8, 11, 12, 16)

Education

Information in this section should describe the offender's behavior and adjustment in the educational system, academic ability, and achievements.

1. What was the highest grade the offender completed?
2. Did the offender ever fail a grade? Which one, and why? (PCL–R 3, 12, 13, 14, 15)
3. What were the offender's grades like in elementary school and in high school (e.g., generally poor, above average, good only during a particular period of schooling)?
4. Was the offender ever diagnosed with any learning or reading disability (e.g., dyslexia; inability to read, or dysphasia; loss of ability to understand or use language as a result of brain damage)? How was the diagnosis made?
5. In what areas did the offender perform well (e.g., mathematics, writing, sports, mechanics)?
6. In what areas did the offender perform poorly?
7. Did the offender leave high school before graduation? What was the reason for quitting school? (PCL–R 3, 10, 13, 15, 16)

8. Was the offender ever truant? How often, and at what age? (VRAG 2; SORAG 2; PCL–R 3, 12, 14, 15)

9. What were the offender's relationships with teachers like in both elementary and high school?
(VRAG 2; SORAG 2; PCL–R 2, 4, 5, 10, 12, 13, 15, 16)

10. What were the offender's relationships with other students like? (VRAG 2; SORAG 2; PCL–R 2, 4, 5, 7, 10, 12)

11. How would the offender's elementary school and high school teachers describe him?
(VRAG 2; SORAG 2; PCL–R 1, 2, 3, 4, 5, 7, 12, 13, 14, 15, 16)

12. Was the offender ever in trouble with teachers, principals, and other students? For what, when, and how often?
(VRAG 2; SORAG 2; PCL–R 3, 4, 5, 6, 10, 12, 14, 15, 16)

13. Was the offender ever suspended, expelled, or asked to transfer? Why? At what grade?
(VRAG 2; SORAG 2; PCL–R 12, 15, 18)

14. Did the offender attend any college or university, receive any technical training, or obtain a high school equivalency diploma? Describe the offender's educational experiences after leaving high school, and include education obtained while institutionalized. (PCL–R 13)

15. Did the offender ever find school boring or uninteresting? (PCL–R 2, 3)

16. What did the offender like and dislike about school? (PCL–R 2, 3)

Occupational

The occupational section should describe the offender's degree of functioning within occupational settings, as well as type and length of employment.

1. Occupation or usual type of employment.

2. Position held, length of stay, and reason for leaving for at least the most recent five jobs. (PCL–R 2, 3, 5, 9, 13, 14, 15)

3. Number of jobs held as an adult since leaving formal education. (PCL–R 3, 9, 14, 15)

4. How often was the offender late or absent from work? Why? (PCL–R 3, 5, 14, 15)

5. Was the offender ever fired? Why, and from how many jobs? (PCL–R 2, 3, 9, 10, 15)

6. What were the offender's relationships with his bosses like? (PCL–R 2, 5, 10, 15)

7. What were the offender's relationships with other employees like? (PCL–R 2, 5, 7, 10, 15)

8. Describe the offender's job performance.
   (PCL–R 2, 14, 15, 16)
9. Did the offender ever find jobs too difficult, boring, or too low paying? Explain. (PCL–R 2, 3, 14, 15)
10. How often was the offender unemployed as an adult, and for how long? (PCL–R 9, 14, 15)
11. Did the offender ever collect welfare, unemployment, or disability payments? Why, and for how long? (PCL–R 5, 9, 13, 15)
12. Did the offender ever sell drugs, and was he ever involved in prostitution or pimping, fraud, thefts, or fencing to make money? (PCL–R 5, 9, 11, 14, 20)
13. What type of work has the offender planned for after release? (PCL–R 2, 9, 13, 15, 16)
14. Did the offender engage in any military service? If so, describe his involvement, including when, how long, type of classification, and type of discharge. (Any psychiatric and criminal activities and dispositions that occurred during this time should be recorded in the appropriate categories. PCL–R 2, 3, 13, 14, 15, 20)

Medical

The medical section provides a short, general description of the offender's overall health throughout his lifetime. It should specify any physical disabilities, major illnesses, surgeries, and physical trauma (e.g., a difficult birth, a head injury as a result of a car accident), in both childhood and adulthood.

1. Describe the offender's overall general health.
2. Has the offender had any serious illnesses (e.g., hepatitis, cancer)?
3. Has the offender had any admissions to a general hospital for medical reasons (e.g., respiratory infection) or major surgery (e.g., appendectomy)?
4. Describe any medical problems or physical disabilities (e.g., diabetes, arthritis, blindness). (PCL–R 2, 5)
5. Describe the types of medication the offender receives at present for any of the aforementioned physical problems. (PCL–R 3, 5)
6. Did the offender experience any problems or side effects with medications now or in the past?
7. Has the offender ever experienced problems with compliance with prescribed medications? (PCL–R 3, 5, 15)
8. Has the offender ever been knocked unconscious or received a head injury (e.g., severe beating, car accident)? (PCL–R 2, 3, 5, 14, 15)

9. Has the offender ever had a CAT scan or an EEG? Why, when, and what were the results, if known?
10. Indicate the offender's handedness (i.e., right-handed, left-handed, ambidextrous).
11. Did the offender's biological mother experience miscarriages or spontaneous abortions prior to the offender's birth?
12. Did the offender's mother experience any of the following pregnancy difficulties?
    a. maternal malnutrition
    b. toxemia (presence of toxic substance in the blood)
    c. high fever
    d. serious accident, physical abuse, or injury
    e. prescribed medication use
    f. alcohol or drug abuse (VRAG 3, SORAG 3)
    g. mental illness
13. Did the offender or his mother experience any of the following perinatal problems?
    a. prolonged labor or delivery
    b. umbilical or placental abnormality
    c. asphyxia (inability to breathe)
    d. anoxia (permanent damage caused by lack of oxygen to tissues)
    e. use of forceps or other instruments
    f. low birth weight
    g. cesarian section
    h. abnormal fetal posture
    i. fetal distress
    j. prematurity
    k. Rh problems
    l. infections
14. Did the offender experience any of the following childhood illnesses and physical problems before age 15?
    a. infections or diseases (e.g., measles, chicken pox, asthma, tuberculosis, high fever, severe allergies)
    b. disabilities (e.g., hearing problems, serious headaches, blurred vision, stuttering, major coordination problems)
    c. injuries (e.g., head injury resulting in loss of consciousness, dizziness, or dazedness)
    d. other (e.g., colic, malnutrition, fainting, dizziness)

Psychiatric

The psychiatric section discusses the offender's formal contacts with professionals in mental health care and reports psychiatric problems that have interfered with his life functioning in accordance with formal diagnostic criteria. (VRAG 10, 11; SORAG 11, 12)

1. Psychiatric admissions, including admissions to psychiatric wards of general hospitals. The report should describe each admission in chronological order and should specify when, where, and why the offender was admitted; the type of ward and level of security; and one of the following types of legal documentation (or a similar documentation):
   a. Informal, voluntary
   b. Involuntary; certified as a danger to self or others
   c. Remand; referred by a court for assessment
   d. Not criminally responsible (or not guilty by reason of insanity) for an offense
   e. Unfit to stand trial for an offense

2. Was the offender ever assessed or treated by a psychiatrist, psychologist, or other mental health worker? When, and for what reason (for each contact)? (PCL–R 3, 5, 10, 12, 18)

3. Was the contact a single-visit assessment (e.g., school referral for assessment of behavior problems) or a series of ongoing psychotherapy sessions for each separate contact (e.g., weekly group therapy at an outpatient clinic)? (PCL–R 3, 5, 10, 12)

4. Was the offender ever diagnosed as hyperactive or as having an attention deficit disorder (ADD) as a child? (PCL–R 3, 10, 12, 14)

5. Has the offender ever experienced emotional problems (e.g., depression, anxiety), psychosis, or delusions? (PCL–R 7, 10)

6. Has the offender ever experienced significant periods of withdrawal or seclusiveness?

7. Has the offender ever received medication for psychiatric problems?

8. Has the offender ever experienced any side effects or problems in relation to these prescribed medications?

9. Has the offender ever had problems complying with prescribed psychiatric medication? (PCL–R 5, 15)

10. Has the offender ever received an assessment of sexual preferences (i.e., phallometric testing) in the past or following the current offense, if sexual? (SORAG 13)

11. Has the offender ever been prescribed an antiandrogen (sex drive–reducing medication)? Describe when, why, and the medication's effectiveness and side effects, if any.

12. Has the offender ever attempted suicide? Why? When? (PCL–R 5, 14, 15)

13. Was the offender under psychiatric supervision at the time of the current offense? (PCL–R 19)
14. Has the offender ever escaped or attempted to escape from a secure psychiatric ward? (PCL–R 5, 14, 15)
15. Has the offender ever been absent without permission from a psychiatric ward or failed to return when required to? (PCL–R 5, 14, 15)
16. Has the offender ever been readmitted to a psychiatric facility because of community problems or charges laid while on a supervised leave from a psychiatric facility to the community? (PCL–R 14, 15, 18, 19, 20)

Substance Use

The substance use section describes the frequency and severity of the offender's alcohol and drug use (including inhalants like glue and gas) over his lifetime, as well as his intake at the time of the current offense. It is important to explore the level of social interference as well as the pathological indicators of alcohol abuse (VRAG 3, SORAG 3), drug abuse, or any other substance abuse. (PCL–R 3, 9, 12, 14, 15, 16, 18, 19, 20)

1. Does the offender have a history of alcohol use?
2. At what age did the offender first start to drink alcohol? What were the circumstances? (PCL–R 3, 12)
3. What were the offender's usual drinking situations as a teenager? as an adult? How often has the offender used alcohol, and how much has he used? (PCL–R 3, 9, 15)
4. Has the offender ever exhibited any of the following pathological indicators of alcohol abuse? (PCL–R 3, 14, 15)
   a. inability to reduce the amount of intake
   b. repeated efforts to abstain
   c. continuation of drinking despite serious physical problems caused by alcohol
   d. blackouts (i.e., amnesia regarding events that occurred while intoxicated)
   e. binges (i.e., remaining intoxicated for at least 2 days)
   f. tolerance (i.e., need for markedly increased amounts of alcohol)
   g. withdrawal (i.e., development of physical symptoms, such as fever, diarrhea, insomnia, or shakes, after cessation of drinking)
5. Does the offender have a history of illegal drug use? (PCL–R 3, 18, 20)
6. At what age did the offender first start to take illegal drugs? (PCL–R 3, 12)

7. What types of illegal drugs has the offender used, and how often? (PCL–R 3, 9, 14, 15, 18, 20)
8. Does the offender have a history of abuse of prescribed medications, such as tranquilizers? (PCL–R 5, 15)
9. Has the offender ever exhibited any of the following pathological indicators of drug abuse? (PCL–R 3, 14, 15)
   a. Inability to reduce the amount of intake or to stop
   b. Continuation of drug taking despite serious physical problems caused by drugs
   c. Prolonged heavy use of the substance
   d. Tolerance (i.e., need for markedly increased amount of the substance)
   e. Withdrawal (i.e., development of physical symptoms, such as fever, diarrhea, insomnia, or shakes, after cessation of drug use)
10. Has the offender's alcohol or drug use ever caused problems with his spouse or partner, family, friends, or work? Describe. (PCL–R 3, 9, 10, 11, 12, 14, 15, 16, 17)
11. Has the offender ever been absent or fired from work because of alcohol or drug use? (PCL–R 3, 14, 15)
12. Has the offender ever been violent while using alcohol or drugs? (PCL–R 10, 12, 15, 16)
13. Has the offender ever exhibited marked behavior change while using alcohol or drugs? Describe. (PCL–R 3, 11, 12, 14, 15, 16)
14. Has the offender ever been charged with an offense related to alcohol or drug use, such as impaired driving, possession, trafficking, or "double-doctoring" narcotics (i.e., illegally obtaining the same medication from more than one doctor)? (PCL–R 5, 9, 14, 15, 18, 19, 20)
15. Was alcohol or drug use involved in any prior offenses? Describe. (PCL–R 3, 5, 10, 14, 15, 16)
16. Was alcohol or drug use involved in the current offense? Describe. (PCL–R 3, 5, 10, 14, 15, 16)
17. Does the offender have a history of tobacco use? Currently or in the past? How often, and how much? (PCL–R 3)

Criminal History

The criminal history section relies heavily on information from other sources, including incident and arrest reports from police, correctional services, a centralized police database (in Canada, the Royal Canadian Mounted Police Fingerprint Services), child protection agencies (in Canada, the Children's Aid Society), family members, and the offender's report. The charges, dates, and disposition of each offense should be recorded for juvenile and adult criminal offenses. A *disposition* is the final result of formal charges; it could be a conviction with possible incarceration, a withdrawal, or a dismissal; a suspended sentence, community time, or probation are other forms of sentencing. The report should clearly note both the charges and the conviction that resulted; they may be somewhat different (e.g., because of plea bargaining). Previous charges and convictions should also be provided as evidence of the frequency, severity, and versatility of prior criminal involvement. Whenever possible, the report should describe the circumstances of previous offenses that are similar to the current offense.

1. History of criminal offenses. (PCL–R 10, 11, 12, 18, 19, 20)
2. Age at first criminal activity. (PCL–R 3, 12, 18)
3. Charges and convictions, including dates and dispositions. (VRAG 5; SORAG 5, 6, 7; PCL–R 12, 18, 19, 20)
4. Does the offender have a history of juvenile correctional involvement (including training school)? At what age? Was it the result of formal charges or of behavior and discipline problems at home or school? Describe behavior while in a juvenile facility. (PCL–R 12, 18)
5. Has the offender ever been detained in jail or in remanded custody? (PCL–R 19)
6. Age at first incarceration. (PCL–R 12, 18, 20)
7. What other institutions has the offender been incarcerated in, including type of facility and level of security? Did he experience any institutional charges or misconducts? (PCL–R 10, 12, 14)
8. Has the offender ever escaped or attempted to escape from custody in a jail or correctional institution or while being escorted by police or correctional officers or been absent while on leave? (PCL–R 14, 15, 19, 20)
9. Has the offender ever violated a community supervision order such as parole, mandatory supervision, or probation or while released on bail or recognizance order? (PCL–R 19)
10. Has the offender committed any criminal offense (including the current offense) while on community supervisions? (VRAG 6; SORAG 9; PCL–R 15, 18, 19)
11. Has the offender ever experienced violation or revocation of parole or failed to comply with probation or recognizance order? Describe. (VRAG 6; SORAG 9; PCL–R 19)
12. Has the offender ever committed an offense for which he was never formally charged? Describe. (PCL–R 5, 6, 8, 10, 11, 12, 14, 15)

13. What is the offender's attitude toward the police and criminal system? What is his attitude about his responsibility for his criminal violations? Does he rationalize his offenses or appear supportive of a criminal lifestyle or critical of the judicial system? (PCL–R 1, 2, 5, 6, 9, 13, 15, 16)

Adult Relationships and Sexual History

This section should indicate the extent of the offender's social functioning as an adult. Occupational, substance use, criminal, and psychiatric variables have already been dealt with in previous sections; this section, therefore, should focus on the quality of sexual, familial, and general interpersonal relationships. The offender's general level of functioning is described in terms of his interests, religious practices, leisure activities, and responsibilities.

1. Age at onset of puberty (e.g., appearance of pubic hair, voice change).
2. Age at first sexual experience involving another person. (PCL–R 11, 12, 14)
3. Was the offender's first sexual experience consensual? Give age, gender, and relationship of first sexual partner. (PCL–R 5, 8, 11, 12, 14)
4. Has the offender ever been married or in a common-law relationship with a woman (for male offenders only; VRAG 4, SORAG 4) or a man? How many relationships has he been involved in, when, and for how long? (PCL–R 3, 14, 17)
5. Describe the offender's intimate relationships (i.e., quarrelling, threatening, assaultiveness, supportiveness, good and bad qualities) and describe why they ended. (PCL–R 3, 7, 8, 9, 10, 11, 14, 15, 16)
6. Has the offender been involved in sexual relationships with women or men other than marriage or common-law relationships? How many, and how long did they last? Describe. (PCL–R 3, 5, 7, 8, 11, 14)
7. What was the offender's current marital or relationship status and level of satisfaction at the time of the current offense? Describe. (PCL–R 7, 9, 11)
8. What was the offender's living situation at time of current offense (e.g., with wife, parents, siblings, male lover, alone, transient)? (PCL–R 3, 5, 7, 9)
9. How does the offender describe his sexual and romantic interests and behaviors? (PCL–R 1, 2, 3, 7, 11, 14, 15, 17)
10. How desirable does the offender perceive himself as a mate (e.g., attractiveness, physical fitness, earning potential, financial resources, level of caring)? (PCL–R 2, 7, 11, 13, 15, 16)

11. Does the offender have a history of sexual problems or concerns that have interfered with his life (e.g., premature ejaculation, impotence, fetishes)? (PCL–R 11)
12. Has the offender ever been forced to have sex or do a sex act he was not willing to do? Describe.
13. Has the offender ever forced someone else to have sex or perform a sex act he or she was not willing to do? Describe. (PCL–R 5, 6, 8, 11)
14. Does the offender have any children? If so, how many, and what are their ages (distinguish between biological and stepchildren brought to a union)? (PCL–R 9, 14, 15)
15. What type of relationship has the offender had with all of his children? (PCL–R 7, 15)
16. What type of contact does the offender have with other family members (e.g., parents, siblings)?
(PCL–R 5, 7, 8, 9, 15, 16)
17. Does the offender have any close nonsexual relationships? Describe. (PCL–R 3, 7, 8, 9, 14)
18. Does the offender have a history of financial problems (e.g., inability to provide for self or others, incurred debts, credit misuse)? (PCL–R 5, 9, 13, 14, 15, 16)
19. Does the offender participate in any sports, leisure, recreational, or religious activities and interests? (PCL–R 3)
20. Does the offender have any language, religious, or cultural customs that might affect assessment, treatment planning, incarceration, and placement?
21. Has the offender ever travelled around without any plans or goals? At what age, how often, and for how long?
(PCL–R 3, 9, 13, 14, 15)
22. How well does the offender generally get along with others? Has he ever been verbally and physically assaultive? What kinds of assaults (e.g., threats, arguments, minor assaults, serious injury to someone), how often, and why?
(PCL–R 2, 5, 7, 8, 9, 10, 14, 15, 16)
23. What is the offender's usual lifestyle when in the community (e.g., social isolate, transient, "party animal," criminal associations, good worker, family man)?
(PCL–R 2, 3, 7, 9, 11, 13, 14, 15, 16)
24. What is the offender's attitude toward convention and social norms (e.g., is he supportive of or does he reject or deny the validity or worth associated with family, work, or society as a whole)? (PCL–R 2, 5, 6, 8, 9, 13, 15)
25. What is the offender's description of himself in general? (PCL–R 1 to 20)

Interviewer's Impressions

Whenever possible, the case historian should interview the offender as part of the psychosocial assessment. It is just as important to record how the offender presents himself during the interview as it is to summarize the content provided by other sources. This interview assists a reader in assessing the offender's personality, motivation level, interpersonal skills, and treatment needs. The role of the historian is to objectively present how the offender appears during the interview for the reader to evaluate. The historian can offer an opinion about his behavior in this section but should avoid being judgmental.

Generally, the case historian should describe how polite and cooperative the offender appeared to be in the interview. Some specific things to describe are eye contact, posture and movements, facial expressions of emotions, and voice expression (e.g., volume and tone).

1. Did the offender answer interview questions appropriately, or did he attempt to control the conversation, overelaborate on his answers, or give evasive or indirect answers? (PCL–R 1, 2, 5, 7)
2. Did the offender tend to provide overly short answers or refuse to answer? (PCL–R 1, 2, 5)
3. Was the offender's affect appropriate to the situation? (PCL–R 7)
4. How did the offender express how he felt about the crime, incarceration, and his future? (PCL–R 1, 2, 5, 6, 7, 8, 13, 16)
5. Did the offender's statements about himself concur with his actions? (PCL–R 2, 5, 6, 7, 16)
6. How concerned did the offender seem about the consequences of his actions for his life? (PCL–R 6, 7, 8, 13, 16)
7. What was the offender's attitude about receiving treatment? (PCL–R 6, 13, 16)
8. What did the offender say about the victims of his crimes? (PCL–R 6, 7, 8, 11, 15, 16)
9. Did the offender appear superficial and overly charming? Explain. (PCL–R 1, 2, 5)
10. Was the offender easily irritated, impatient, or verbally abusive? (PCL–R 1, 2, 5, 10)
11. Could the historian confirm from other sources that information the offender gave is true or false? (PCL–R 4, 5)

APPENDIX G

Sample Psychosocial History Suitable for Use in Scoring the Violence Risk Appraisal Guide (VRAG) and the Sex Offender Risk Appraisal Guide (SORAG)

Name: David Robert Moore (fictitious)

Institution: Regional Reception Centre, Millhall Penitentiary

Case number: 000001

Date of report: May 1, 2000

Date of admission: April 17, 2000

Legal documentation: Found guilty for sexual assault with a weapon and sentenced to 5 years on March 21, 2000

Parole eligibility date: November 21, 2001

Warrant expiry date: March 21, 2005

Date of birth: September 10, 1967 (32)

Birthplace: Burketon, Ontario, Canada

Marital status: Single

Legal next of kin: Martha Louise Moore (mother; 200 Park Road, Apt. 217, Burketon, Ontario)

Religion: Roman Catholic (nonpracticing)

Occupation: Construction worker

Information sources: Offender, Ontario Provincial Police (OPP) report, mother, brother, Royal Canadian Mounted Police (RCMP) Fingerprint Service, Gatby Provincial Correctional Institution, Burketon High School, Children's Aid Society

Case historian: Minny Quester, Case Historian, Admission Unit, Regional Reception Centre, Millhall Penitentiary

CIRCUMSTANCES LEADING TO ADMISSION

Mr. David Moore, a 32-year-old, single, Caucasian man was admitted to the Regional Reception Centre at the Millhall Penitentiary on April 17, 2000. He had been charged and subsequently found guilty of sexual assault with a weapon. He was sentenced on March 21, 2000, in the Burketon provincial court and received a sentence of 5 years. A further charge of forcible confinement incurred at the same time was withdrawn. He had been detained at the Burketon North Detention Centre since his arrest and was brought to this facility by the Ontario Provincial Police from the Burketon Detachment.

Current Offense Information

The police report indicated that on October 11, 1999, the victim, Ms. Donna W, age 26, had been drinking beer with two girlfriends in the bar at the Georgian Hotel in Burketon, Ontario, from approximately 9:00 p.m. until midnight, at which time the bar closed. Witnesses stated that she drank only two beers during the evening.

Mr. Moore had joined the three women at 11:00 p.m., being invited by one of the victim's girlfriends, who knew him as a coworker. He apparently consumed two beers while with the three women. As they were all leaving the hotel at midnight, Mr. Moore offered the victim, Ms. W, a ride home, claiming he was driving in the same direction anyway. The victim stated that instead of following her directions to her mother's home, where she lived, Mr. Moore turned off on a road in the opposite direction and drove out of Burketon to a secluded park near the Burke River. During the drive, Mr. Moore had locked the car doors and repeatedly told the victim, "Just relax. I knew all night you really wanted me to screw you." The victim was crying throughout the trip, and several times she pleaded with Mr. Moore to take her home and promised not to tell anyone. According to her statement, he apparently laughed each time, until finally he withdrew a knife from his coat pocket and said, "See this? This is going to make sure you fuck me."

When they arrived at the park, Mr. Moore forced Ms. W into the back seat of the car and forced her to remove all of her clothes while he removed his clothes also. Mr. Moore then demanded that she fondle his penis while he fondled her breasts and genitals. He then lay on top of the victim, forced his penis into her vagina, and intercourse took place for about 10 minutes. During that time, according to the victim, he kept saying how good it was and how much he knew she was enjoying the sex. Throughout the offense, Ms. W claimed, the knife was always present. She also stated that during the time they were in the back seat of the car, Mr. Moore continued to hold the knife near her face, but she claimed that she did not offer resistance at any time because she was too frightened. She further stated that he did not physically injure her during the assault.

After he ejaculated, Mr. Moore allowed the victim to dress, and she pleaded with him to let her go and not to hurt her, but he ignored her pleas. After approximately 20 minutes, he drove back to Burketon. Once there, he dropped her off near the Burketon bus station, but before driving away, he threatened to cut up her face if she told anyone. Ms. W contacted the Burketon detachment of the OPP from the bus station and was taken to the Burketon General Hospital by police for an examination by the Sexual Assault Clinic. Mr. Moore, who was identified by the victim, was arrested at his place of employment on the following morning of October 12, 1999, and he was formally charged the same day with sexual assault with a weapon and forcible confinement. A bail hearing was arranged for Mr. Moore for October 13, 1999, at which time he was not successful in being released on bail. He was subsequently remanded to the Burketon Jail until his trial date.

Family History

Father

Joseph Robert Moore, age 60, has been self-employed for many years as an electrician. He was divorced from Mr. Moore's mother in 1977 when Mr. Moore was 10 years old. He has had two convictions for common assault, one in 1972 and the other in 1977, for which he was given a suspended sentence with probation each time. Both were the result of charges laid by Mr. Moore's mother. The family reported that the father has been a heavy drinker since the age of 21 and that this was the cause of his recently diagnosed cirrhosis of the liver. The Children's Aid Society reported that the father physically abused all members of his family until the time of the divorce. Since the divorce, he has seen Mr. Moore about twice a year on holidays.

Mother

Martha Louise Moore, age 58, currently works as a sales clerk in a shoe store in Burketon. After divorcing Joseph Moore, she began living common law with Dale Brown in 1979 when Mr. Moore was 12 years old. She has always been in good physical health but has had one admission to the psychiatric ward of the Burketon General Hospital in 1978 for depression when Mr. Moore was 11 years old. She claims that her relationship with Mr. Moore is currently poor and that they have frequent arguments.

Stepfather

Dale Benjamin Brown died of a heart attack in 1989 at the age of 53 when Mr. Moore was 22. He had been employed as a machinist in a factory until his death. For many years prior to his death, he had had frequent leaves of absence because of ill health. Mr. Moore reported that he was never very close to his stepfather but that he thought that Mr. Brown and his mother had a good relationship.

Brother

John Michael Moore, age 35, is employed as a bricklayer and lives in Riverton, Ontario. He is 3 years older than Mr. Moore. The mother reported that he abuses alcohol and that this was the cause of the breakdown of his marriage after 2 years. At that time, he attempted suicide by drug overdose and is currently involved in drug and alcohol rehabilitation. His relationship with Mr. Moore has mainly involved going drinking together.

Inmate

David Robert Moore, currently age 32, is the younger of two boys.

Childhood

Until age 10, when Mr. Moore's parents divorced, the family moved frequently while the father attempted to establish his electrical business. The mother reported that the father frequently physically assaulted her and the children when drinking. She reported that the father, who was responsible for disciplining the children, beat the two boys with a belt for almost any type of misbehavior. Mr. Moore reported that he and his brother ran away from home overnight on at least three occasions beginning when he was 9 years old. When Mr. Moore was 12 years old, he and another youth stole Mr. Moore's stepfather's car. Only the other youth involved, age 15, was charged with taking auto without consent.

The Children's Aid Society reported that the family was referred to them by Family Court when Mr. Moore was 10 years old, originally because of the assault charges laid against the father. They reported that Mr. Moore had been involved in several thefts at neighborhood stores beginning when he was 10 years old. The Children's Aid Society also provided information about his once having set fire to garbage at his school when he was 11 years old. Mr. Moore claimed he liked to fight and is proud of beating up an older boy, at the age of 12, who apparently called Mr. Moore a "goofball." He was never formally charged for any of these incidents. During his teenage years, his mother claimed that he was argumentative and rarely at home and that he spent a great deal of his time at a pool hall with two other boys. Mr. Moore claimed that these two acquaintances were "drinking buddies" and were just kids to get into trouble with. He said that he had not seen them or any other childhood friends since leaving school.

Schooling

Mr. Moore began school at the age of 5 and left school at the age of 16, having completed Grade 9. He blamed the family's frequent moves for his inability to do well at school, including failing Grade 8. However, school records indicated that in elementary school he was frequently disciplined for disruptive behavior in his classes and for fighting with other students. He did well in sports and the technical shops but never achieved good grades in other courses. He was suspended from school at age 11 for setting a fire and at age 13 for fighting. During Grade 9, he was frequently truant, and the school suggested that he consider quitting, which he did during Grade 10. Before he left high school he was given IQ testing, which placed him in the average range of intelligence. When he was 29 years old, he attempted and failed to finish high school equivalency diploma while incarcerated at Gatby Correctional Institute. He claimed that the teacher was not good enough for the task and that she did not really know how to teach properly. Overall, Mr. Moore stated that he felt that school was boring and a waste of time and that it did not teach him anything important.

Occupational

Mr. Moore has held only short laboring jobs on construction sites and in factories. His last employment, and his longest, was for the 5 months prior to his arrest for the current offense. He claimed the arrest "screwed up" his life and that he felt that the construction company would have made him foreman by now. He stated that before this job, he worked for three summers on construction sites doing general labor work just long enough to collect unemployment insurance three times. Before that, he was employed twice in factory work for 3 months each time. Mr. Moore claimed that he worked well with his coworkers, but on two jobs he felt that the foremen did not know what they were doing. This led to occasional arguments with them about his performance. His mother stated that he was fired from both his factory jobs for consuming alcohol on the job. His mother also stated that she has supported him financially several times between jobs and incarcerations. Mr. Moore felt that after his release, he would do construction work again. He hoped to depend on his brother, who had found him several jobs in the past.

Medical

Mr. Moore's mother stated that she had had no pregnancy difficulties, that his birth weight was average, and that the delivery, although long, had no complications. She also stated that she did not smoke or drink during the pregnancy, which was unplanned but not unwanted. Prior to this pregnancy, she did not have any miscarriages or spontaneous abortions. Mrs. Moore was 26 years old when he was born.

Mr. Moore claimed to have had good health all his life and has had only one admission to a general hospital, in 1985 at the age of 18, for an appendectomy. In 1990, when Mr. Moore was 23, he was involved in a physical fight that resulted in his left hand being broken. The injury, although not serious, causes occasional pain in his hand for which he takes prescribed painkillers. His mother reported that when Mr. Moore was 8, his father threw him against a wall, causing a laceration to the head that required five stitches to close. She also stated that Mr. Moore had the usual childhood diseases, such as measles at age 5 and chicken pox at age 8. Mr. Moore stated that he is right-handed.

Psychiatric

School records indicate that Mr. Moore was assessed twice by a school psychologist at the age of 11 in 1978 for behavior problems in the class. The psychologist recommended that a behavior management program be instituted by his teachers, but no further involvement occurred. When Mr. Moore was 29 years old, he was admitted to Lowen Psychiatric Hospital from February 12 to April 6, 1996. His status was that of a court-remanded assessment patient in connection with a charge of sexual assault resulting from an incident that occurred in January 1996. According to an assessment report by Dr. Barry Brown, the forensic unit psychiatrist at that hospital, Mr. Moore claimed that he was innocent, stating that the sex was consensual. He then stated that he did not know what was going on because he was very drunk at the time and just "did it because she wanted it so badly." He was discharged to court with a diagnosis of personality disorder, antisocial type.

In our interview, Mr. Moore claimed to have had no problems with depression or anxiety, stating that when he feels restless, he goes drinking and cruising in his car. In response to questions about psychotic symptoms, Mr. Moore stated that he has never had any hallucinations or delusions. Both he and his mother claimed that as an adult, Mr. Moore has had no other involvement with any mental health worker apart from his remanded psychiatric assessment prior to his last conviction. Subsequent to his admission to this institution, Mr. Moore was offered participation in a phallometric assessment of his sexual preferences. Results of this assessment by Dr. S. Tester, which can be found in the report dated April 21, 2000, in Mr. Moore's Mental Health Services clinical file, indicated that Mr. Moore exhibited a preference for rape scenarios over consensual sexual activity.

Substance Use

Mr. Moore claimed that he started to consume alcohol at the age of 12, when he and his brother would steal liquor that belonged to their stepfather. He continued to drink beer through his teenage years, claiming that there was nothing else to do for fun in Burketon. At the age of 16, he was fined $50 for drinking under age.

Mr. Moore stated that since age 18, he liked to get drunk every weekend at a local bar with his "buddies." He had been involved in several physical fights while drinking, including the incident in which his hand was broken. He had experienced blackouts from drinking to excess on several occasions, stating that he would wake up not knowing how he had got to where he found himself or what had happened while he was drinking. He also claimed that from age 18, he had occasionally used illegal drugs, mostly at parties. He said that on these occasions, he had used "uppers," snorted cocaine, and smoked marijuana. He stated that he had on occasion used his prescribed painkillers for hangovers, taking several at a time so he could go to work. Mr. Moore blamed alcohol for this conviction and his previous sexual assault conviction, stating, "Things just get out of hand when I get drunk."

Mr. Moore stated that he had smoked a pack of cigarettes per day since the age of 16. He claimed that he smoked to alleviate boredom and had no plans to discontinue.

Criminal History

As stated in the Childhood section, Mr. Moore was involved in thefts beginning at the age of 10 but was not charged for these, including the car theft when he was 12. His first conviction occurred in October 1983 at age 16 for drinking under age, and he was fined $50.

As an adult, he was convicted and fined $200 in 1988 when he was 21 for a possession of marijuana charge. In 1991, at age 24, he was charged with assault with a weapon, but this was reduced to assault causing bodily harm for conviction. For this offense, he was sentenced to 3 months in the Braydon Correctional Institute. By the age of 25, he had received two convictions for theft under $1,000, one in August 1991 and the other in October 1992, and he served 2 months for each in the Burketon Jail.

Mr. Moore's previous conviction for sexual assault was the result of an offense that occurred on January 28, 1996, late in the evening. At that time, the victim, Ms. Susan M, a 26-year-old woman who was a stranger to the offender, accepted a ride from him while hitchhiking near Kittell, Ontario. He drove the victim to a construction company garage, where he forced her to remove her clothes and perform oral sex on him. At one point, the victim attempted to escape, whereupon Mr. Moore became enraged, according to the victim, and slapped her repeatedly, causing extensive bruising and swelling to her face. He then returned the victim to the highway where he had initially met her and drove off. Mr. Moore was arrested and charged on January 30, 1996, and was remanded for a psychiatric evaluation prior to conviction. He was convicted in the provincial court in Kittell on April 27, 1996, for sexual assault, and he received a sentence on May 13, 1996, of 2 years less a day to be served at the Gatby Provincial Correctional Institution and probation for 2 years to follow. He served 17 months for this conviction before his release on parole in October 1997. He was on parole until May 1998, at which time he began the probationary period of his sentence, which would have expired in May 2000. Mr. Moore was still on this probation when the current offense of sexual assault occurred.

Adult Relationships and Sexual History

Mr. Moore recalled that he experienced the onset of puberty at age 13 and began to masturbate at that time. At that age, he also had his first sexual experience with a girl. According to Mr. Moore, he and several friends were drinking beer at a party when he attempted intercourse with a 14-year-old girl but was unable to penetrate her vagina. He claimed that she had also been drinking at the party and consented to having sex with him. He stated that he has had sexual intercourse fairly frequently since age 16. He stated that he has never had any problems getting girlfriends but claimed he gets bored with them easily and ends relationships quickly. His longest relationship occurred when he was 24 years old and lasted for 6 months with a woman who was 18 years old at the time. His mother reported that he had been physically abusive to some of his girlfriends and that he had stated they had been "fooling around" with other men. He admitted to a preference for picking up women at bars for sex because he did not care to get involved with "all the demands women make" in relationships. Up to the time of the current offense, he had never been married or involved in a common-law relationship. He reported never having any homosexual involvement, although he was approached by several inmates while in the Gatby Correctional Institute. That institution reported that on one of those occasions, he severely kicked and punched the inmate involved. He claimed never to have forced someone to have sex but laughed and stated, "They are usually too drunk to put up a fight."

When not incarcerated, Mr. Moore had lived mostly with his mother. She provided for him financially whenever he was not working. For a short period when he was 22 years old, he lived with his brother while working for him, but this arrangement ended after 3 months because of frequent arguments. Mr. Moore was again living with his mother at the time of the current offense. He stated that he liked this arrangement because, aside from the occasional argument with him, she cooked and cleaned up after him, and he did not have to pay her anything.

His mother also reported that about a year ago she bought a car for him with the agreement that he would pay her monthly. Apparently, he had yet to pay her any money toward the car. Both his mother and his brother stated that he had no close friends, just drinking partners. Mr. Moore described himself as "a pretty good guy, but don't make me angry." He stated that partying with people was okay for a few laughs but that he was really a loner who did not need or depend on anybody. Besides partying, he stated that his only interests are watching hockey on television and playing pool.

Interviewer's Impressions

I spoke with David Moore on two occasions for 2 hours each time. Throughout most of the interview, he was polite and answered questions with full answers. Several times, though, such as when I asked specific questions about his criminal activities, he would fail to answer as if he did not hear me. Instead, he would start talking about hockey or divert the conversation to construction, attempting to impress me by telling me that he knew so much about building luxury homes that he could have been an "architecturer." When I asked that we restrict our focus to the assessment questions, he stated rather indignantly and in a loud voice, "Hey, I know you people want me to talk. I was just trying to open up to you." Occasionally, he also would not look at me directly when I asked questions related to the sexual offenses and shifted in his chair frequently. He asked twice how long this would take because he did not want to miss a soccer game in the yard.

He often seemed irritated about his family and blamed his father and mother for his unhappy childhood and his drinking. Mr. Moore justified his past thefts and drug conviction on the basis of "just being a kid." He claimed that the two victims of the sexual assault offenses knew the risks when they put themselves in those situations, as all women do. When discussing these incidents, he would occasionally snicker. He stated that because he did not really hurt them, he felt that he should not have been given such "fucking long sentences." At another point in our conversation, he claimed that the offenses happened because he was too drunk and stoned on drugs. Then he suddenly stated, "Who knows. Maybe I was sexually molested as a child or something and I just don't remember and that made me do it." He did not elaborate any further.

I requested to speak to him on a third occasion with the view of discussing some information from other sources. To this he replied that he had already talked enough and that any more would be a waste of his time. He stated that he had no problems and was not interested in a treatment plan because he felt confident that he would make an early parole and it would just be wasting everybody's time for him to start "one of those stupid groups." He finished by emphatically remarking that he was definitely appealing this conviction because he had "one of the best lawyers you can get" and he could prove that the police were "just out to get me." The lawyer was apparently going to "show the judge you can't mess up my life."

Minny Quester, Case Historian
Admission Unit, Regional Reception Centre
Millhall Penitentiary

APPENDIX H

Scoring the Violence Risk Appraisal Guide (VRAG) From a Psychosocial History

The numbered items are the items on the VRAG, and the lettered items are other related factors. The other related factors are not used in scoring the VRAG but can be presented in the final Violence Risk Appraisal Guide Report (see Appendix J). Space is provided on the worksheet below each item for the clinician to write in details regarding the offender (the complete Psychosocial History for this offender is provided in Appendix G); these details are in italics on this sample worksheet. This is a suggested format for a worksheet for use in calculating scores and compiling notes in completing a VRAG report based on Appendix G to prepare the formal report shown in Appendix J. As such, this document would not normally form part of the offender's official record.

Name:	*David Robert Moore (fictitious)*
Case number:	*000001*
Date of birth:	*September 10, 1967*
Index offense:	*Sexual assault with a weapon*
Date of offense:	*October 11, 1999*
Date and type of disposition:	*March 21, 2000; received sentence of 5 years*
Parole eligibility date:	*November 21, 2001*
Warrant expiry date:	*March 21, 2005*
Date of admission:	*April 17, 2000*
Referral source:	*Dr. Diane Agnosis, Director of Mental Health Services (MHS), Millhall Penitentiary, Correctional Services Canada*
Information source:	*MHS clinical file compiled at Millhall Penitentiary*

CHILDHOOD HISTORY

1. Lived with both biological parents to age 16 (except for death of parent)

   Score *no* if offender did not live continuously with both biological parents until age 16, except if one or both parents died. In the case of parent death, score as for *yes*.

   Yes = –2
   No = +3 √

   Parents divorced when he was 10 years old.

   Score: +3 (high)

2. Elementary school maladjustment (up to and including Grade 8)

No problems	= –1
Slight or moderate discipline or attendance problems	= +2

   Severe (i.e., frequent or serious) behavior or attendance problems (e.g., truancy or disruptive behavior that persisted over several years or resulted in expulsion)   = +5 √

   Frequently disciplined for disruptive behavior in class and for fighting; assessed twice at age 11 for school problems; suspended at age 11 for fire setting; suspended at age 13 for fighting.

   Score: +5 (high)

A. Suspended or expelled from school (elementary or secondary)

   No = Low   Yes = High √

   See Factor 2.

B. Highest grade (prior to index offense)

   ≥ Grade 9 = Low √   < Grade 9 = High

   Left school while in Grade 10.

C. Arrested before age 16

   No = Low √   Yes = High

   First arrested at age 16 for drinking under age, in October 1983.

D. Childhood behavior problem before age 15

   Allot one point for each of the following: repeated truancy __√__, delinquency __√__, repeated sex ____, runaway overnight (≥ 2) __√__, repeated lying __√__, fights __√__, repeated substance abuse __√__, grades < IQ ____, vandalism __√__, school suspension ____, violations of rules __√__, thefts (at home or at school) __√__ : Total = 9 points

   < 3 = Low   ≥ 3 = High √

   Car theft, age 12; thefts from stores, age 10; alcohol use, age 12; running away, age 9; assaultive, age 12; truancy, Grade 9; school behavior problems, see Factor 2.

ADULT ADJUSTMENT

3. History of alcohol problems
   Allot one point for each of the following: parental alcohol
   abuse __√__ , teenage alcohol problem __√__ , adult alcohol problem __√__ , alcohol involved in prior offense __√__ , alcohol involved in index offense __√__): Total = 5 points
   0 points = –1
   1 or 2 points = 0
   3 points = +1
   4 or 5 points = +2 √
   Parental alcohol abuse: Father was alcoholic, had charges laid, was
   assaultive, experienced marital problems, was diagnosed with cir-
   rhosis—1 point.
   Teenage alcohol problem: Started drinking at age 12, drank through
   teens, was charged at age 16 for drinking under age—1 point.
   Adult alcohol problem: Experienced binges, fights, blackouts, job
   loss—1 point.
   Prior offense: Was charged with drinking under age; received past
   conviction for sexual assault involving alcohol—1 point.
   Index offense: Drank two beers prior to offense; stated that alcohol
   was a factor in index offense—1 point.
                                                    Score: +2 (high)
4. Marital status (at the time of the index offense)
   Ever married (or lived common law in the same home for at
   least 6 months)   = –2
   Never married   = +1 √
   Always single; never married or involved in a common-law rela-
   tionship.
                                                    Score: +1 (high)
5. Criminal history score for convictions and charges for non-
   violent offenses prior to the index offense (from the Cormier–
   Lang system shown in Table A.1)
   Score of 0   = –2
   Score of 1 or 2   = 0 √
   Score of 3 or above   = +3
   Theft under in 1991 = 1 point; theft under in 1992 = 1 point:
   Total = 2 points.
                                                         Score: 0
6. Failure on prior conditional release (includes parole violation
   or revocation, breach of or failure to comply with recogni-
   zance or probation, bail violation, and any new charges, in-
   cluding the index offense, while on a conditional release)

No   = 0
Yes   = +3 √

Previously convicted May 1996; paroled October 1997 to May 1998; probation started May 1998; expiry date would have been May 2000; index occurred October 1999.

Score: +3 (high)

E. Significant period of employment (at least 6 months)
  ≥ 6 months = Low   < 6 months = High √
  Short labor jobs only; longest just prior to index lasted 5 months.

F. Living situation at time of index offense
  With someone (includes group home and
  institutions)   = Low √
  Alone (own accommodation or transient)   = High
  Lived with his mother since last released from corrections.

G. Admission to corrections
  No = Low   Yes = High √
  1991: 3 months; again in 1991: 2 months; 1992: 2 months; 1996: 2 years minus 1 day.

H. History of convictions or charges for violent offenses prior to index offense
  No = Low   Yes = High √
  1991 conviction for assault causing bodily harm; 1996 conviction for sexual assault.

I. Escape or attempted escape from secure custody
  No = Low √   Yes = High
  No history reported.

OFFENSE CHARACTERISTICS

7. Age at index offense (at most recent birthday)
  ≥ 39 = –5
  34–38 = –2
  28–33 = –1 √
  27   = 0
  ≤ 26 = +2
  Index offense date October 11, 1999; birth date September 10, 1967: (1999 – 1967 = 32).

  Score: –1 (low)

8. Victim injury (index offense only; most serious injury is scored)
  Death   = –2
  Hospitalized   = 0
  Treated and released   = +1
  None or slight (includes no victim)   = +2 √

Sexually assaulted the victim; weapon was present, but no injury occurred.

Score: +2 (high)

9. Any female victim (for index offense)
   Yes = –1 √   No (includes no victim) = +1
   Victim was a 26-year-old woman.

Score: –1 (low)

J. Relationship of victim to offender
   Previously known   = Low
   Stranger (includes peace officer or psychiatric hospital
   staff)   = High √
   Victim met offender in a bar for the first time the evening of the index offense.

ASSESSMENT INFORMATION

10. Meets *DSM–III* criteria for any personality disorder
    No = –2   Yes = +3 √
    Met antisocial personality disorder criteria from diagnostic manual; diagnosis by Dr. Brown, 1996.

Score: +3 (high)

11. Meets *DSM–III* criteria for schizophrenia
    Yes = –3   No = +1 √
    See Factor 10; no report of psychosis or hallucinations.

Score: +1 (high)

12. Hare Psychopathy Checklist—Revised score (PCL–R; Hare, 1991)
    ≤ 4 = –5
    5–9   = –3
    10–14 = –1
    15–24 = 0
    25–34 = +4 √
    ≥ 35 = +12
    Results of a PCL–R assessment by Dr. Agnosis from an MHS assessment report dated May 1, 2000, on file indicated a score of 33. (To score this item, the PCL–R assessment must have been completed by a clinician trained to use the PCL–R.)

Score: +4 (high)

K. Results of IQ testing
   ≥ 90 = Low √   < 90 = High
   Results from only testing done prior to leaving high school indicated an average IQ.

L. Attitudes supportive of crime

No = Low   Yes = High √
*Criminal history from early age, denial of responsibility, criticism
of judicial system, callous attitude toward victims and crimes.*

M. Attitudes unfavorable toward convention
No = Low   Yes = High √
*Poor work history, substance abuse, little responsibility for self,
little attachment to others, criminal attitudes.*

Total score: +22
Risk category: 8 (see Table H.1)
Percentile: Only 4% score higher (see Appendix C)
Probability of recidivism: 82% (see Table H.1)
Date assessed: May 15, 2000

TABLE H.1
Probability of Violent Recidivism as a Function of Risk Score

Category	Risk score range	Probability of violent recidivism within 10 years at risk
1	≤ −22	.08
2	−21 to −15	.10
3	−14 to −8	.24
4	−7 to −1	.31
5	0 to 6	.48
6	+7 to +13	.58
7	+14 to + 20	.64
8√	+21 to + 27	.82√
9	≥ +28	1.00 (100%)

APPENDIX I

Scoring the Sex Offender Risk Appraisal Guide (SORAG) From a Psychosocial History

The numbered items are the items on the SORAG, and the lettered items are other related factors. The other related factors are not used in scoring the SORAG but can be presented in the final Sex Offender Risk Appraisal Guide Report (see Appendix J). Space is provided on the worksheet below each factor for the clinician to write in details regarding the offender (the complete Psychosocial History for this offender is provided in Appendix G); these details are in italics on this sample worksheet. This is a suggested format for a worksheet for use in calculating scores and compiling notes in completing a SORAG report based on Appendix G to prepare the formal report shown in Appendix J. As such, this document would not normally form part of the offender's official record.

Name:	*David Robert Moore (fictitious)*
Case number:	*000001*
Date of birth:	*September 10, 1967*
Index offense:	*Sexual assault with a weapon*
Date of offense:	*October 11, 1999*
Date and type of disposition:	*March 21, 2000; received sentence of 5 years*
Parole eligibility date:	*November 21, 2001*
Warrant expiry date:	*March 21, 2005*
Date of admission:	*April 17, 2000*
Referral source:	*Diane Agnosis, Director of Mental Health Services (MHS), Millhall Penitentiary, Correctional Services Canada*
Information source:	*MHS clinical file compiled at Millhall Penitentiary*

347

CHILDHOOD HISTORY

1. Lived with both biological parents to age 16 (except for death of parent)
    Score *no* if offender did not live continuously with both biological parents until age 16, except if one or both parents died. In the case of parent death, score as for *yes*.
    Yes = –2
    No = +3 √
    Parents divorced when he was 10 years old.

    Score: +3 (high)

2. Elementary school maladjustment (up to and including Grade 8)
    No problems   = –1
    Slight or moderate discipline or attendance problems = +2
    Severe (i.e., frequent or serious) behavior or attendance problems (e.g., truancy or disruptive behavior that persisted over several years or resulted in expulsion)   = +5 √
    Frequently disciplined for disruptive behavior in class and for fighting; assessed twice at age 11 for school problems; suspended at age 11 for fire setting; suspended at age 13 for fighting.

    Score: +5 (high)

A. Suspended or expelled from school (elementary or secondary)
    No = Low   Yes = High √
    See Factor 2.

B. Highest grade (prior to index offense)
    ≥ Grade 9 = Low √   < Grade 9 = High
    Left school while in Grade 10.

C. Arrested before age 16
    No = Low √   Yes = High
    First arrested at age 16 for drinking under age, in October 1983.

D. Childhood behavior problem before age 15
    Allot one point for each of the following:
    repeated truancy __√__ , delinquency __√__ , repeated sex ___ , runaway overnight (≥ 2) __√__ , repeated lying ___ , fights __√__ , repeated substance abuse __√__ , grades < IQ ___ , vandalism __√__ , school suspension __√__ , violations of rules __√__ , thefts (at home or at school) __√__ : Total = 9 points
    < 3 = Low   ≥ 3 = High √
    Car theft, age 12; thefts from stores, age 10; alcohol use, age 12; running away, age 9; assaultive, age 12; truancy, Grade 9; school behavior problems, see Factor 2.

3. History of alcohol problems
    Allot one point for each of the following: parental alcohol abuse _√_ , teenage alcohol problem _√_ , adult alcohol problem _√_ , alcohol involved in prior offense _√_ , alcohol involved in index offense _√_): Total = 5 points
    0 points = −1
    1 or 2 points = 0
    3 points = +1
    4 or 5 points = +2 √

    Parental alcohol abuse: Father was alcoholic, had charges laid, was assaultive, experienced marital problems, was diagnosed with cirrhosis—1 point.
    Teenage alcohol problem: Started drinking at age 12, drank through teens, was charged at age 16 for drinking under age—1 point.
    Adult alcohol problem: Experienced binges, fights, blackouts, job loss—1 point.
    Prior offense: Was charged with drinking under age; received past conviction for sexual assault involving alcohol—1 point.
    Index offense: Drank two beers prior to offense; stated that alcohol was a factor in index offense—1 point.

    Score: +2 (high)

4. Marital status
    Ever married (or lived common law in the same home
    for at least 6 months)   = −2
    Never married   = +1 √
    Always single; never married or involved in a common-law relationship.

    Score: +1 (high)

5. Criminal history score for convictions and charges for nonviolent offenses prior to the index offense (from the Cormier–Lang system shown in Table A.1)
    Score of 0   = −2
    Score of 1 or 2   = 0 √
    Score of 3 or above   = +3
    Theft under in 1991 = 1 point; theft under in 1992 = 1 point. Total = 2 points.

    Score: 0

6. Criminal history score for convictions and charges for violent offenses prior to the index offense (from the Cormier–Lang system shown in Table B.1)
    Score of 0   = −1
    Score of 2   = 0

Score of 3 or above   = +6 √
Assault causing bodily harm in 1991 = 5 points; sexual assault in 1996 = 6 points. Total = 11 points.

Score: +6 (high)

7. Number of convictions for previous sexual offenses (pertains to convictions for sexual offenses that occurred prior to the index offense)
   Count any offenses known to be sexual, including, for example, indecent exposure.
   0   = –1
   1 or 2 = +1 √
   ≥ 3   = +5
   One conviction for a previous sexual offense in 1996.

Score: +1 (high)

8. History of sex offenses against girls under age 14 *only* (includes index offense; if offender was less than 5 years older than victim, always score +4)
   Yes = 0   No = +4 √
   Sexual assault on 26-year-old woman in 1996; index sexual assault on 26-year-old woman.

Score: +4 (high)

9. Failure on prior conditional release (includes parole violation or revocation, breach of or failure to comply with recognizance or probation, bail violation, and any new charges, including the index offense, while on a conditional release)
   No = 0   Yes = +3 √
   Previously convicted May 1996; paroled October 1997 to May 1998; probation started May 1998; expiry date would have been May 2000; index occurred October 1999.

Score: +3 (high)

E. Significant period of employment (at least 6 months)
   ≥ 6 months = Low   < 6 months = High √
   Short labor jobs only; longest just prior to index lasted 5 months.

F. Living situation at time of index offense
   With someone (includes group home and
   institutions)   = Low √
   Alone (own accommodation or transient)   = High
   Lived with his mother since last released from corrections.

G. Admission to corrections
   No = Low   Yes = High √
   1991: 3 months; again in 1991: 2 months; 1992: 2 months; 1996: 2 years minus 1 day.

H. Escape or attempted escape from secure custody

No = Low √   Yes = High
No history reported.

OFFENSE CHARACTERISTICS

10. Age at index offense (at most recent birthday)
    ≥ 39 = –5
    34–38 = –2
    28–33 = –1 √
    27   = 0
    ≤ 26 = +2
    Index offense date October 11, 1999; birth date September 10,
    1967: (1999–1967 = 32).

    Score: –1 (low)

I.   Relationship of victim to offender
    Previously known   = Low
    Stranger (includes peace officer or hospital staff)   = High √
    Victim met offender in a bar for the first time the evening of the
    index offense.

ASSESSMENT INFORMATION

11. Meets *DSM–III* criteria for any personality disorder
    No = –2   Yes = +3 √
    Met antisocial personality disorder criteria from diagnostic manual;
    diagnosis by Dr. Brown, 1996.

    Score: +3 (high)

12. Meets *DSM–III* criteria for schizophrenia
    Yes = –3   No = +1 √
    See Factor 10; no report of psychosis or hallucinations.

    Score: +1 (high)

13. Phallometric test results
    All tests indicate nondeviant sexual preferences   = –1
    Any test indicates deviant sexual preferences   = +1 √
    Results of tests conducted by Dr. S. Tester from an MHS assess-
    ment report dated April 21, 2000, on file indicated that he exhib-
    ited a higher magnitude of response to rape over consensual sexual
    activity.

    Score: +1 (high)

14. Revised Psychopathy Checklist score (PCL–R; Hare, 1991)
    ≤ 4 = –5
    5–9   = –3
    10–14 = –1

15–24 = 0
25–34 = +4 √
≥ 35 = +12

Results of a PCL–R assessment by Dr. Agnosis from an MHS assessment report dated May 1, 2000, on file indicated a score of 33. (To score this item, the PCL–R assessment must have been completed by a clinician trained to use the PCL–R.)

Score: +4 (high)

J. Results of IQ testing
≥ 90 = Low √   < 90 = High
Results from only testing done prior to leaving high school indicated an average IQ.

K. Attitudes supportive of crime
No = Low   Yes = High √
Criminal history from early age, denial of responsibility, criticism of judicial system, callous attitude toward victims and crimes.

L. Attitudes unfavorable toward convention
No = Low   Yes = High √
Poor work history, substance abuse, little responsibility for self, little attachment to others, criminal attitudes.

Total score: +33
Risk category: 9 (see Table I.1)
Percentile: Only 1% score higher (see Appendix C)
Probability of recidivism: 100% (see Table I.1)
Date assessed: May 15, 2000

TABLE I.1
Probability of Violent Recidivism as a Function of Risk Score

Category	Risk score range	Probability of violent recidivism within 10 years at risk
1	≤ −11	.09
2	−10 to −5	.12
3	−4 to +1	.39
4	+2 to +7	.59
5	+8 to +13	.59
6	+14 to +19	.76
7	+20 to +25	.80
8	+26 to +31	.89
9 √	≥ +32	1.00 (100%) √

APPENDIX J

Actuarial Risk Appraisal Report for an Offender

The resulting final report would contain the indicators (or factors) and scoring details for either the Violence Risk Appraisal Guide (VRAG) or the Sex Offender Risk Appraisal Guide (SORAG). Because this example (on the basis of Appendixes G, H, and I) is intended for instructional purposes only, indicators and scoring for both instruments are outlined. Indicators that are exclusive to one or the other are noted as such in brackets. We recommend that offenders being assessed because of a sexually motivated offense be scored using the SORAG, which was normed for sex offenders.

Name: David Robert Moore (fictitious)
Case number: 000001
Date of birth: September 10, 1967
Index offense: Sexual assault with a weapon
Date of offense: October 11, 1999

Mr. Moore was referred for an assessment of risk of violent recidivism by Dr. Dianne Agnosis, director of Mental Health Services (MHS), Millhall Penitentiary, Correctional Services Canada. Mr. Moore was convicted for the offense stated above on March 21, 2000, and was admitted to the Millhall Penitentiary on April 17, 2000. The instrument used to assess Mr. Moore was the Sex Offender Risk Appraisal Guide (SORAG) [or the Violence Risk Appraisal Guide (VRAG)], and it was constructed using available information from Mr. Moore's institutional file compiled at the Millhall Penitentiary.

This report summarizes the statistically determined risk of violent recidivism for the offender named above. The appraisal concerns only those indicators up to and including the time immediately after the index offense indicated above. The indicators considered are all static characteristics inasmuch as they cannot change over time. Each of the indicators mentioned below was coded from the offender's available file information. For the purposes of risk appraisal, *violent recidivism* was defined as any criminal charge for a violent offense (or violating parole or hospitalization in a secure facility for a violent act that could otherwise have resulted in a criminal charge) occurring once the offender has access to the community after the index offense.

The risk appraisal instrument used was originally constructed using data from a study of more than 600 offenders, and data from this sample were supplemented by data from another study of approximately 200 sex offenders to allow for the inclusion of some variables specific to sex offenders. "Hands-on" sexual offenses were counted as violent offenses. The risk appraisal instrument is designed to assess the risk that the offender will commit a violent offense within 10 years of his release to the community, where the base rate of violent recidivism was 43% for the VRAG sample and 58% for the sex offenders in the SORAG samples.

The static indicators (or factors) and their relationship with violent recidivism are listed at the end of this report under the heading Predictors Used in the Risk Appraisal Instrument. The static indicators of violent recidivism (both high risk and low risk) used to determine this offender's level of risk are indicated throughout the report **in bold** for easier identification. The summary for each category also includes other indicators (not in bold) that were related to violent recidivism but that were also highly related to the indicators already used in the risk appraisal instrument and therefore did not add to the accuracy of predictions. A list of these other indicators is also on the final page of this report under the heading Predictors Not Used but Related to Recidivism.

The report is organized into four sections: childhood history, adult adjustment, offense characteristics, and assessment information. Within each section, indicators for which the offender's scores reflect low risk are discussed first, and indicators for which the offender's scores reflect high risk are discussed next. Indicators that reflected neither low risk nor high risk or that were unscorable because of lack of information are discussed last. Finally, where necessary, following the indicators is detailed information (*in italics*) about how the determination was made for this offender.

CHILDHOOD HISTORY

Indicators of *low risk* of violent recidivism are that Mr. Moore completed at least a Grade 9 education and was not arrested before the age of 16.

Mr. Moore left school while in grade 10, and his first arrest occurred in October 1983 when he was 16 years old.

Indicators of *high risk* of violent recidivism are that Mr. Moore **did not live continuously with both of his biological parents at least to the age of 16; he had an elementary school maladjustment problem (including attendance and discipline problems up to and including Grade 8);** he was suspended or expelled from school (includes elementary and secondary school); and he had a significant childhood behavior problem before the age of 15 (includes delinquency, running away overnight, thefts, vandalism, lying, inappropriate sexual activity, substance abuse, fighting, and school and home violations of rules).

Mr. Moore's parents divorced when he was 10 years old. According to elementary school records, Mr. Moore was frequently disciplined for disruptive behavior in classes and for fighting with other students. He was suspended at age 11 for setting a fire and again at the age of 13 for fighting. Mr. Moore's behavior problems included running away three times, thefts from neighborhood stores from the age of 10, abuse of alcohol from age 12, serious assault of an older youth also at the age of 12, and the above-mentioned school problems.

ADULT ADJUSTMENT

Indicators of *low risk* are that Mr. Moore did not have a history of escape or attempted escape from secure custody and that he was not living alone at the time of the index offense.

From the time of his release from corrections in October of 1997 until the time of his arrest for the index offense, Mr. Moore was living with his mother.

Indicators of *high risk* are that Mr. Moore had a **history of alcohol problems (includes parental alcohol abuse, teenage alcohol problem, adult alcohol problem, alcohol involvement in prior offense, and alcohol involvement in the index offense);** he did not have a history of significant employment while living in the community; **he had not been involved in a marital relationship (includes common-law relationships of more than 6 months);** he had previously been admitted to corrections; **he had a history of convictions or charges for violent offenses (includes hands-on sexual offenses and offenses as an adult or juvenile) [SORAG only]; he had previously been convicted for a sexual offense [SORAG only]; he had a history of sexual offenses that did not exclusively involve female children under the age of 14 (includes prior and index offenses) [SORAG only]; and he had failed while on a prior supervised release to the community (includes parole violations, charges while on parole or probation, and breach of probation, recognizance or bail).**

Mr. Moore's father had been an alcoholic for many years and had dysfunctional social behavior, several arrests, and serious physical problems associated with alcoholism. Mr. Moore himself started to abuse alcohol at the age of 12 and admitted to regular consumption through his teens. As an adult, he often drank to excess and was physically assaultive when drinking, and he had experienced blackouts. Mr. Moore was fired from two jobs because of alcohol consumption on the job, and he had a prior conviction for drinking under age. Mr. Moore's previous conviction for sexual assault and the current conviction of sexual assault with a weapon both involved alcohol consumption. Mr. Moore's longest employment prior to the index offense lasted only 5 months. Mr. Moore had been incarcerated for convictions that he received in 1991, 1992, and 1996. Mr. Moore's index offense was a sexual assault on an adult woman, as was his previous conviction for sexual assault in 1996. As well, Mr. Moore had been convicted for assault causing bodily harm in 1991. Mr. Moore was released from corrections in October 1997 having served 17 months of a 2-year sentence. He was on parole until May 1998 and then on a 2-year probation order. It was during this probationary period that he committed the index offense.

Mr. Moore's **history of convictions or charges for nonviolent offenses (includes theft, mischief, dangerous or impaired driving, drug trafficking, fraud, property damage, and threatening as an adult or juvenile)** was such that it did not factor either positively or negatively in his risk score. *Mr. Moore was convicted in 1991 and again in 1992 for theft under.*

OFFENSE CHARACTERISTICS

Indicators of *low risk* are that Mr. Moore's **age was greater than 27 years old at the time of the index offense and that the victim was a woman [VRAG only].**

As stated at the beginning of the report, the index offense occurred in October 1999; at that time, Mr. Moore was 32 years old. His victim was a 26-year-old woman.

Indicators of *high risk* are that Mr. Moore did not previously know the victim; **slight or no injury occurred to the victim [VRAG only];** and the offense was sexual. *The victim of the index sexual offense was previously unknown to Mr. Moore, and she did not experience injury.*

ASSESSMENT INFORMATION

An indicator of *low risk* is that Mr. Moore's IQ testing indicated at least average intellectual functioning.

Results of IQ testing completed while Mr. Moore was attending high school indicated an average IQ.

Indicators of *high risk* are that Mr. Moore **met the criteria for a DSM–III psychiatric diagnosis of personality disorder; he did not meet the criteria for a DSM–III diagnosis of schizophrenia; during his first post–index** offense phallometric assessment of his sexual preferences, he exhibited a deviant profile [SORAG only]; and his score on the Hare Revised Psychopathy Checklist—Revised (PCL–R) was greater than 24 out of a possible total score of 40. He was recorded as having attitudes supportive of crime (includes justifying or rationalizing violations, denying responsibility, and being critical of the judicial system); and he was recorded as having attitudes unfavorable toward convention (includes values about family, work, relationships, and society).

As stated in the Childhood History section, Mr. Moore had a significant onset of behavior problems prior to age 15. Mr. Moore had a history of criminal offenses dating back to his adolescence resulting in incarcerations, substance abuse since childhood, a poor employment record, violation of other (e.g., theft, assault), sexually inappropriate behavior, and aggressiveness. During a previous psychiatric admission to the Lowen Psychiatric Hospital in 1996, he received a diagnosis of antisocial personality disorder by Dr. Barry Brown. During his present incarceration, Mr. Moore was referred to Dr. S. Tester in MHS for a phallometric assessment of his sexual preferences. The results of the assessment (see MHS report on file dated April 21, 2000) indicated that Mr. Moore exhibited a higher magnitude of responses to the scenarios depicting rape than to those depicting consensual sexual activity.

The PCL–R assessment conducted by Dr. Agnosis (see MHS report on file dated May 1, 2000) resulted in a score of 33. The PCL–R is a 20-item rating scale developed for the assessment of psychopathy to classify or diagnose individuals for research and clinical purposes. Psychopathy has an early onset, is characteristic of the individual's long-term functioning, and results in social dysfunction or disability. Psychopathy is associated with unstable interpersonal relationships, poor occupational functioning, and increased risk of involvement in criminal activities. Each of the 20 items is rated on a 3-point scale: 0 if the item does not apply, 1 if the item applies to a certain extent, or 2 if it applies to the individual. Thus, this patient scored 33 out of a possible maximum of 40 points.

APPRAISAL

[If using the SORAG:] On the basis of his score on a sex offender risk appraisal instrument (the SORAG) constructed from the variables discussed above, Mr. Moore's category for risk of violent recidivism is the highest of nine categories. Among sex offenders in the studies described above, fewer than one percent obtained higher scores, and all, or one hundred percent, in Mr. Moore's category reoffended violently within an average of ten years after release.

[If using the VRAG:] On the basis of his score on a violent offender risk appraisal instrument (the VRAG) constructed from the variables used to predict violent recidivism for violent offenders discussed above, Mr. Moore's category for risk of violent recidivism is the eighth, or second highest, of nine categories. Among offenders in the studies described above, only four percent obtained *higher* scores, and *approximately eighty-two percent* in Mr. Moore's category reoffended violently within an average of ten years after release.

Report date: May 15, 2000
Dr. Anne Assess, PhD, CPsych
Mental Health Services
Millhall Penitentiary
Correctional Services Canada

PREDICTORS OF VIOLENT RECIDIVISM

The variables in the following lists are listed in descending order of the strength of relationship with violent recidivism, from greatest to least. All variables were coded entirely from clinical information available around the period of the first–index offense admission. The notation [-] indicates that the variable has a negative relationship with violent recidivism. Thus, in the research studies, offenders who met the *DSM–III* criteria for schizophrenia were less likely to recidivate violently than other offenders (many of whom met the criteria for personality disorder). Similarly, in the research studies, offenders (other than sex offenders) whose index offense involved maximal victim injury (i.e., victim death) were, on average, *less* likely to violently recidivate than offenders who caused no injury or only minor injury to their victims.

Variables listed under Predictors Not Used but Related to Recidivism are variables that were related to violent recidivism but that were also highly related to variables used in the risk appraisal instrument. Therefore, they did not add to the accuracy of predictions based on just those variables that were used. (Note that, independent of other predictors, sex offenders exhibited greater likelihood of violent recidivism, hence our recommendation that the SORAG be used for that population.)

Predictors Used in the Risk Appraisal Instrument

- Revised Psychopathy Checklist score
- Criminal history score for nonviolent offenses
- Elementary school maladjustment score
- Never married
- *DSM–III* criteria for personality disorder
- *DSM–III* criteria for schizophrenia[-]
- Age at index offense[-]
- Victim injury in index offense[-]
- Separation from biological parents before age 16
- Alcohol problems score

- Failure on prior conditional release
- Female victim in index offense[(-)]

Predictors Not Used but Related to Recidivism

- Age at first psychiatric admission[(-)]
- Arrested under age 16
- Number of admissions to correctional institutions
- Criminal history score for violent offenses
- Highest grade achieved[(-)]
- Age at first admission to corrections[(-)]
- History of escapes from institutions
- Attitude unfavorable toward convention at index offense
- Procriminal attitude at index offense
- Index victim a stranger
- Childhood behavior problems before age 15
- History of stable employment[(-)]
- Suspended or expelled from school
- Parental alcohol problem
- Parental crime involvement
- Higher family socioeconomic status[(-)]
- Patient lived alone at time of index offense[(-)]
- Higher intelligence as assessed after index offense[(-)]

Variables Used for Sex Offenders Only

- Number of convictions for previous sexual offenses
- Criminal history score for violent offenses
- Exclusively female victims under age 14[(-)]
- Deviant sexual preference during the first post–index offense assessment

APPENDIX K

Sample Psychosocial History and Scoring of the Violence Risk Appraisal Guide (VRAG) for a Psychiatric Offender

PSYCHOSOCIAL HISTORY

Name:	*Elvin Matthew Nelson (fictitious)*
Institution:	*North Haven Psychiatric Hospital*
Case number:	*11111*
Date of report:	*May 15, 2003*
Date of admission:	*April 15, 2003*
Legal documentation:	*Found not criminally responsible (NCR) for arson and criminal negligence causing death on March 30, 2003*
Date of birth:	*February 28, 1974*
Birthplace:	*Brownsville, Ontario*
Marital status:	*Single*
Legal next of kin:	*Frances Nelson (mother; R.R. #1, Appleby, Ontario)*
Religion:	*Agnostic*
Occupation:	*Student*
Information sources:	*Family members, Lakeview Psychiatric Hospital, Appleby Wellness Clinic, Crown Briefs, Rogers Polytechnical University, Lyons College, Lakeview Police Service (LPS), Dearing General Hospital, Appleby–Kerr District Hospital*
Case historian:	*Theresa Pines, Social Worker, Forensic Unit, North Haven Psychiatric Hospital*

Circumstances Leading to Admission

Mr. Elvin Nelson, a 29-year-old, single, White man was at Lakeview Psychiatric Hospital from January 31, 2003, until March 30, 2003, on a 60-day judicial order, having been charged with arson and criminal negligence causing death. Mr. Nelson was found fit to stand trial, and his discharge diagnosis was paranoid schizophrenia. Mr. Nelson was returned to court and found not criminally responsible for the above charges on March 30, 2003. He was subsequently admitted to this facility, the North Haven Psychiatric Hospital, on April 15, 2003.

Current Offense Information

Mr. Nelson was 28 years old at the time of the index offense and was attending Rogers Polytechnical University in Lakeview, Ontario. He was enrolled in the political science program on a full-time basis. On January 27, 2003, Mr. Nelson set fire to his apartment, killing a male resident in the same building.

The circumstances of the offense, as related in reports received from Lakeview Psychiatric Hospital, are as follows: At the time of the offense, the patient was in a state of active paranoid psychosis. He had become convinced that he was being watched and followed and that others were attempting to kill him. He believed that the Mafia was involved in his persecution. The onset of his delusional thinking appears to have been approximately 2 months prior to the offense. Mr. Nelson had been admitted briefly to Lakeview Psychiatric Hospital in early January 2003, 3 weeks prior to the offense, and was treated for a short period of time with antipsychotic medications. Mr. Nelson was discharged from the hospital with a condition that he take medication as prescribed.

Following his discharge from the hospital, Mr. Nelson attempted to return to his university studies and moved into a bachelor apartment in a building where other students also resided. However, Mr. Nelson stated that he kept to himself and had not met any of the residents there. His thinking remained delusional. He became increasingly apprehensive and fearful for his life. He had not been taking his medication following his release from the hospital, and it is strongly suspected that he had used illegal drugs at least once. On the day of the offense, Mr. Nelson recalled having felt extremely frightened. He thought that he was to be killed that morning and that his assailant resided in the next apartment and was waiting outside the door to his apartment. His plan was to set fire to his own apartment so as to create a diversion and escape his assailant. Mr. Nelson set his apartment on fire and then left his residence. He was arrested shortly thereafter by police, walking down the road. At the time of his arrest, he was said to have been covered in soot and to smell strongly of smoke. He was taken into custody and questioned by the police.

It is further reported by police that the student who resided in the next apartment, Mr. Michael G, who had been drinking heavily, was asleep when the fire started and was not awakened by the fire alarms. He died of smoke inhalation before being discovered by firefighters. There was also approximately $15,000 in damages to the apartment building.

Family

Father

Reg Nelson, age 59, resides in Appleby, Ontario. He has a degree in optometry and has been self-employed as an optometrist for the past 35 years. Mr. Nelson's father reported that he did not have a history of criminal charges or convictions or a family history of psychiatric problems. He also reported no major physical problems and had had no contacts of a personal nature with the mental health system. In terms of alcohol and drug use, Mr. Nelson and his father stated that Reg Nelson does consume alcohol but that it does not pose a problem. He apparently enjoys a drink or two in the evening before going to bed. He reported no involvement with illicit street drugs. Mr. Nelson described his relationship with his father as being good during the past several years. However, Mr. Nelson reported that they did not communicate well when he was between the ages of 15 and 19, because they "did not see eye to eye on matters."

Mother

Frances Nelson, age 53, has a degree in business administration and currently assists her husband with the day-to-day operation of his optometry practice. According to Mr. Nelson and his mother, she had never had any criminal charges or convictions, and although she personally had not had any psychiatric difficulties, there is a history in her family; it was reported in his clinical record compiled during a previous admission that Mrs. Nelson's cousin had been diagnosed as schizophrenic. Mrs. Nelson had no history of illegal drug use and considered herself an occasional drinker. Both she and her son reported that her consumption of alcohol usually occurs during social gatherings or on special occasions. Mrs. Nelson indicated that she had a good relationship with her son and that they had always gotten along well. She did note, however, that there had been a shift in the relationship since Mr. Nelson had been diagnosed as mentally ill in that he relied more on his father for advice. She viewed this as positive, because she believed that Mr. Nelson previously felt that his father was unapproachable.

Siblings

Mr. Nelson has two sisters; he is the middle child. Karen Nelson is the oldest and is 31 years old. She is single and resides in Kerr, Ontario. Although she has a 2-year college degree in travel and tourism, she has been employed as a waitress at Buffalo Pizza in Kerr for the past 13 years. Mr. Nelson and his parents reported that Karen will have an occasional social drink but does not use illegal drugs. She is a heavy smoker but has no major physical problems, and she has had no criminal or psychiatric difficulties. Mr. Nelson's other sister, Julia Miller, is 26 years old. She has been residing in Appleby since June 2000 and was recently married, in August 2001. Julia has a 3-year college degree in nursing. She is currently employed as a registered nurse at the Appleby Retirement Residence. Mr. Nelson reported that Julia drinks occasionally and had also been known to use marijuana from time to time when she was at social gatherings. He and his parents indicated that Julia is in good health, has had no major physical problems, and has had no encounters with the mental health, correctional, or judicial systems. In Mr. Nelson's opinion, he has a very good relationship with Julia and is closer to her than to his older sister. He reported that they maintain monthly contact.

Childhood

Mr. Nelson recalled a fairly stable childhood. He was born in Brownsville, Ontario, and lived there until the age of 5. His family then moved to Kerr, Ontario. He reported that he lived with his parents continuously during his childhood and adolescent years and that they were never separated. Mr. Nelson stated that his parents have a good marital relationship and have been married for 35 years. They talk openly, and he cannot recall any arguing between them when he was growing up. Mr. Nelson reported that he felt his father was a workaholic when he was a child, given that he was so busy looking after two optometry practices, one in Kerr and the other in Appleby. However, he said his father spent any spare time that he did have with the family.

Mr. Nelson also reported that his father was the disciplinarian, but he did not feel that the punishments were too severe. He recalled always receiving an explanation as to why he was being punished and reported that his punishments usually involved being scolded or denied privileges. Mr. Nelson reported that he had a good relationship with his parents during his childhood and early adolescent years but openly admitted that he became more rebellious starting at age 17.

With regard to his siblings, Mr. Nelson stated that he got along with both of his sisters but felt closer to Julia, the youngest. He felt that Karen was jealous of him because he was the only boy and seemed to be able to get away with more than she did. He recalled that Karen was always trying to be good to gain his parents' approval, whereas he never tried to be good because his parents' approval did not matter as much to him.

Mr. Nelson denied ever being in physical fights as a child, being threatening toward others, or forcing others to do things they did not want to do.

Neither he nor his parents recalled any instance of Mr. Nelson's being threatened. Mr. Nelson also reported that he had never harmed animals or engaged in vandalism. He did indicate that there was some early involvement with the police. At the age of 15, Mr. Nelson took his mother's car without permission and went "joy riding." He recalled that he was following his 16-year-old friend, who was driving his own parents' car. He attempted to pass his friend but cut in too quickly and hit the ditch, thus damaging the front end of his mother's car. Mr. Nelson stated that he was charged with taking auto without consent and driving under age and was placed on probation for 1 year. Also at the age of 15, he was caught shoplifting a tape from a music store. He recalled being taken to the police station but was not charged. He was given a warning and told to return the merchandise, and his parents were contacted to pick him up.

Both Mr. Nelson and his parents also reported that he began using marijuana at the age of 16. He recalled that at this same time, he grew a marijuana plant in his home but eventually had to get rid of it when his parents discovered what it was.

According to Mr. Nelson and his parents, he had a small circle of friends until high school. However, he reported that during his high school years, he became less involved with these friends and presently does not maintain contact with any of this group.

Schooling

Mr. Nelson attended Grades 1 to 8 at Little Creek Public School in Kerr, Ontario. The family then moved to Appleby, and he attended Upperhill Secondary School, where he completed Grade 13. He reported that he was always an average student, did not experience any learning difficulties, and never failed any grade. He indicated that there was a general decline in his grades starting in Grade 10, when he was 16, that was due to truancy and using cannabis. Mr. Nelson reported that he found high school boring and that he was "just putting in time." He admitted that he never really applied himself and occasionally did not do his assignments or study. According to school records, his teachers reported that starting in Grade 10, he had little social involvement with classmates and no involvement in extracurricular activities. Mr. Nelson also reported that there was one incident when he was approximately 17 years old when he arrived at school under the influence of drugs and was caught. As a result, he was suspended for 1 week. However, he indicated that beginning at that age, it was a fairly regular occurrence for him to smoke marijuana and then go to school.

Following high school, Mr. Nelson traveled for a period of 3 years before returning to Ontario for further education. From September 1996 to April 1998, he attended Lyons College in Kerr, Ontario, on a full-time basis, enrolled in the business administration program. According to Mr. Nelson, he completed the first year of the program but lost interest in the second year, failed some courses, and therefore did not receive his degree. In September 1999, he again attempted to complete the second year of this program; however, in January 2000 he withdrew because of psychiatric problems. In September 2002, Mr. Nelson enrolled in the political science program at Rogers Polytechnical University (RPU) in Lakeview, Ontario. Except for a short admission to Lakeview Psychiatric Hospital, he continued to attend the university but was on academic probation at the time of the index offense. Mr. Nelson's parents funded each of his educational attempts.

Occupational

Most of Mr. Nelson's jobs had been short term and, except for one, had always involved working as a sales clerk or laborer for lumber stores. He stated that during the period in which he traveled around British Columbia from 1993 to 1996, he worked on three occasions for approximately 2 months each time. He stated that all of these jobs involved sorting lumber. He also stated that he left each job to continue traveling. However, his mother reported that he was fired from two of these jobs for not showing up for his shifts. While still in British Columbia, he attempted employment on one further occasion; however, he was unable to continue this job after 1 month because he was hospitalized in the psychiatric ward of Dearing General Hospital in Port Bernard. Following this discharge, his parents arranged for him to return home to live with them and sent him money for the trip back to Ontario.

His next two employment periods, as a clerk, began in August 1998 for 2 months at Lumber World in Kerr and March 1999 for 4 months at another Lumber World in Appleby. He resigned from the second job because he had applied for and was accepted again into the second year of the business administration program at Lyons College.

As previously stated, he had to withdraw from the program, and it was not until April 2001 that he again attempted employment. This was working part time as a laborer at Frank's Home and Garden Centre, but he quit after 4 months. His last employment, which started in October 2001, was at a family friend's office supply store in Appleby and was arranged by his father. This job involved Mr. Nelson computerizing stock inventory. He quit after 4 months because of delusional beliefs that his coworkers were part of the Mafia and that they were watching and following him.

Mr. Nelson reported that during periods of employment, he usually got along well with his bosses until he became undependable and unreliable. He admitted that he was occasionally late or absent from work and that there were times when he had a feeling he was going to be fired so he quit first. Mr. Nelson reported that basically he was a good worker if he liked the job he was doing and that he would strive to do his best. However, he indicated that for the most part, he found his jobs boring and low paying.

Mr. Nelson stated that he had seldom collected welfare, but he did receive a few checks while living in British Columbia when he was between jobs. After withdrawing from college for the second time in January 2000, Mr. Nelson received a disability pension from the Ministry of Community and Social Services until March 2002 because of his mental illness.

Mr. Nelson admitted to selling drugs as a teenager but not in large quantities. He related that when he was 17 he would sell "pot or hash" from time to time but was never caught. He denied engaging in pimping, fencing, or any kind of fraud.

Mr. Nelson stated that he would like to be a political journalist, which would require that he obtain a degree in political science and a degree in journalism before he could enter the workforce. His long-term goal is to work for a newspaper as a reporter.

Medical

Mrs. Nelson reported that her pregnancy was normal and that her son was not premature. She indicated that the delivery was a breech birth and was physically difficult. Although she would not allow the physician to use forceps, there were no major complications. Mrs. Nelson was 24 years old when he was born.

Mr. Nelson described his overall general health as average. He denied ever experiencing any serious illness or being hospitalized for any medical reason or major surgery. He did not report any physical disabilities. However, Mrs. Nelson did report that from the ages of 3 to 7, Mr. Nelson was asthmatic and that, on a number of occasions, his asthmatic symptoms had to be treated with bronchial inhalation.

Mr. Nelson indicated that he is not currently on any medications for physical ailments. According to his recollection, he had never been knocked unconscious or received a head injury. His mother, however, did recall an incident when Mr. Nelson was 2 years old when he fell from a chair onto his head. She stated that he was examined by a doctor after this incident, who found no injuries.

Psychiatric

According to Mr. Nelson and his parents, Mr. Nelson was never diagnosed as hyperactive or having an attention disorder as a child. Mrs. Nelson did report that her son had a problem when he was 2 or 3 years old with frustration and anger. She reported that he would bang his head on the floor if he did not get his own way. Mr. Nelson was assessed by his family doctor at the time, who did not see the behavior as a problem. Mr. Nelson's parents did not recall any significant emotional problems that may have interfered with their son's life, nor did they recall him ever threatening or attempting to commit suicide.

Mr. Nelson's first involvement with the mental health field occurred in 1996. He was admitted to the psychiatric ward of the Dearing General Hospital in Port Bernard, British Columbia, as an involuntary patient. He was admitted after jumping in front of a bus in an attempt to injure himself so that he could escape from apparent persecutors. He was delusional at that time and felt that his life was in danger. Mr. Nelson was hospitalized from January 12, 1996, to February 28, 1996. His condition did improve, but a report from the Dearing General states that he lacked complete insight into his illness. The final diagnosis was of a psychotic disorder, unspecified.

As reported above, after discharge he returned home to live with his parents and registered as an outpatient at the Appleby Wellness Clinic under the care of Dr. Jennings. His parents encouraged him to pursue further education, and he started the business administration course in September 1996. Over the next 2 years, he continued as an outpatient with the clinic while attending school and commuting from his parents' home.

In the spring of 1998, he started to deteriorate, became withdrawn from his parents, and attended classes less until he officially left the course without completing the second year. He attempted to complete the second year again in September 1999; however, in January 2000 it became clear that he was unable to continue. It was reported by the Appleby Wellness Clinic that Mr. Nelson believed that other students were able to read his mind and were watching him through his computer. He continued his involvement with Dr. Jennings, who arranged a disability pension because of his mental illness. His diagnosis was changed to paranoid schizophrenia. He again attempted employment on two occasions but left the second employment when he started to experience delusional thinking about coworkers.

After he stopped communicating with his parents and refused to leave his room, his parents arranged to have him admitted as a voluntary patient on March 17, 2002, to the psychiatric unit of the Appleby–Kerr District Hospital. After being stabilized on medication, he was discharged on April 17, 2002, with a diagnosis of paranoid schizophrenia and was referred back to the clinic for a follow-up appointment. However, Mr. Nelson did not attend the clinic again, and his parents were unaware of this. On January 1, 2003, after repeated attempts to contact their son at the townhouse he shared with some other students, Mr. Nelson's parents drove to his apartment in Lakeview from their home. Upon finding him actively psychotic and delusional and believing that his coresidents were plotting to kill him, they took him to the Emergency Services at the Lakeview Psychiatric Hospital. He was admitted that evening as an involuntary patient and placed on lithium carbonate and desipramine. He remained there until January 6, 2003, which was 3 weeks prior to the index offense. On that date, his status was changed to voluntary, and he was discharged with arrangements to continue outpatient treatment. His final diagnosis was again paranoid schizophrenia.

Following the index offense, Mr. Nelson was admitted to the Forensic Unit at the Lakeview Psychiatric Hospital on January 28, 2003. He was admitted on a judicial order for an assessment of fitness to stand trial in relation to the index offenses of arson and criminal negligence causing death. It was reported by Dr. Fox that on admission,

> Mr. Nelson was clearly psychotic. . . . He was disheveled in appearance, guarded and suspicious in his attitude, and volunteering little information. . . . His thinking was dominated by paranoid delusions. He thought that he was the victim of a plot of persecution, and that he was to be killed.

The diagnosis at the time was paranoid schizophrenia, and psychological testing that was completed confirmed this. The testing further "suggested a high probability of aggressive acting out behavior when symptoms are not controlled by medication." The results of testing at that time also indicated an average IQ.

While in the hospital, Mr. Nelson made steady progress. He was treated with an antipsychotic medication, risperidone, 3 mg per day. He was found to be fit to stand trial, and a recommendation of a not criminally responsible (NCR) disposition was made to the court. He was returned to court on March 30, 2003, and was subsequently found NCR. Following this disposition, Mr. Nelson was admitted to the Forensic Unit at the North Haven Psychiatric Hospital, where he remains at the time of this report. Mr. Nelson's attending psychiatrist is Dr. Hines, and his medication since admission has been 1.5 mg b.i.d. of risperidone. He has remained stable during this period; however, he has had occasional periods of suspiciousness involving newly admitted patients to the unit.

With regard to Mr. Nelson's psychiatric hospitalizations, he reported that he has always been compliant with taking his medications. This is not disputed, but compliance is and has been an issue when he is in the community. Mr. Nelson's parents agreed that he required supervision in this regard and that he had to be continually reminded to take it at the designated times when he was in the community. They also stated that when not living with them, they believed that he stopped taking his medication, which in turn had led to deteriorated functioning.

According to Mr. Nelson, he had never escaped or attempted to escape or been absent without permission from any psychiatric facility. It was documented in records from the Appleby–Kerr District Hospital, however, that there had been several occasions when he had returned late from some passes, but that no significant problems were encountered. Mr. Nelson also reported that at the time of his offense, there was no psychiatric outpatient appointment booked. This is contrary to records from Lakeview Psychiatric Hospital, which indicated that "he was discharged with an arrangement for continuing outpatient treatment."

It should also be noted that during this hospitalization at the North Haven Psychiatric Hospital, he has also undergone psychological testing. The findings were consistent with the results already documented by Lakeview Psychiatric Hospital.

Substance Use

As stated in the Childhood section, Mr. Nelson reported that he consumed alcohol occasionally on weekends at parties starting at age 16 and that he would usually drink until intoxicated. He indicated that he had never suffered blackouts, amnesic periods, the shakes, or major withdrawal symptoms when he had been drinking. According to Mr. Nelson, he had abstained from the use of alcohol altogether since January 2002. His parents related, however, that in September 2002, at a party given by relatives to celebrate a wedding anniversary, their son consumed three beers.

He stated that at the age of 16, he started to use marijuana partly out of curiosity and partly out of boredom. Mr. Nelson reported that he also experimented with acid and had used it three times while he was a teenager. He indicated that his use of drugs was quite limited at first and was contingent on how available it was. He reported that his use gradually increased and peaked at the age of 17, when he was smoking marijuana at least once a day. According to Mr. Nelson, his use of street drugs began to taper off while he was traveling in British Columbia. He claimed that while there he was involved in a religious cult for a period of 6 months, during which time he experienced bad effects from marijuana. Rather than become "high," as was the norm, Mr. Nelson reported having "bad trips" in which he would become paranoid. He reported that consequently he reduced his intake to very infrequent use. Since 1999, he had been "almost drug free" and used marijuana only "every once in a blue moon." He did admit that he "might have" smoked marijuana two times while attending university in Lakeview. According to Mr. Nelson, his tolerance for street drugs had never changed, and he had never experienced any severe withdrawal symptoms.

He claimed that his use of drugs and alcohol had not caused any significant problems for him. He had never lost a job as a result, and although his parents never approved, there were no major confrontations. Mr. Nelson claimed that he had never been violent while using drugs or alcohol, nor was he under the influence of either substance at the time of the index offense.

Mr. Nelson stated that he had been a regular cigarette smoker since age 16 and had been smoking a pack every 2 days up to his first admission following the index offense.

Criminal History

As already indicated, the only history of a criminal offense occurred at the age of 15, when Mr. Nelson took his mother's car without permission and got into an accident. He was placed on probation for 1 year. According to Mr. Nelson, he had completed his probationary period without any compliance failures or further charges.

In regard to his attitudes about the police, Mr. Nelson felt that they have a job to do, but that the criminal system did not always work. He believed sex offenders "get off too easily." When speaking about his own criminal violations, Mr. Nelson would say only that it was proved that he was "not responsible."

Adult Relationships and Sexual History

Mr. Nelson believed that he experienced the onset of puberty at the age of 14 and stated that he had his first sexual experience at the age of 16 with a consenting 15-year-old girl. He is single, has never been married or involved in a common-law union, and has no children. His longest relationship was 6 months long and occurred in 1998 when he was living in Port Bernard, British Columbia. The woman was 3 years his senior, and he recalled that the relationship was not that good because they quarreled a great deal. Mr. Nelson claimed that when the relationship ended, he was involved with another woman for 2 to 3 months but became ill and returned to Ontario. According to Mr. Nelson, both of the relationships were mainly for sexual gratification. He reported that there was never any deep commitment to either woman, and he viewed his relationships as superficial in nature. At the time of the index offense, Mr. Nelson was not involved in any relationship.

Mr. Nelson reported that he felt comfortable with his sexuality and had not had any sexual problems that could have interfered with his life. He reported no homosexual experiences or ever being forced to have sex or to do a sex act against his will. He in turn claimed that he had never forced anyone against his or her will, nor had he had any sexual encounters with children. Mr. Nelson stated that he would still like to have a girlfriend so that he would have a companion and someone to talk to. He reported that although he finds it easier to "deal" with women, he had always found it difficult to trust people. He stated, however, that he did not see this as a major issue. Mr. Nelson reported that he had no close friends, claiming, "They have all moved away."

At the time of the index offense, Mr. Nelson was living alone in his own bachelor apartment. He had been sharing a townhouse with three other students but was moved to his own apartment by his parents because his roommates had complained about his behavior and following his first admission to Lakeview Psychiatric Hospital.

Mr. Nelson received a disability pension in 2001 and part of 2002 on account of his mental illness. Previous to that, he had difficulties providing for himself because he was unable to maintain employment for a prolonged period of time. He recalled no incurred debts but did remember an incident in 1993 when he bought a leather jacket on credit and had no way of paying for it. He reported that his parents paid for it instead.

Mr. Nelson claimed that he enjoyed playing hockey as a child but now prefers to watch it on television. He also indicated an interest in writing in a private journal. According to Mr. Nelson, when he left home at the age of 19 and traveled across Canada, it was without any real plans or goals. Although he indicated an interest in furthering his education in the past as a result of his parents' urging and offering to pay for it, he agreed to register for courses "just on a whim."

He reported that he felt that he generally gets along well with others. He stated that he is not an outgoing person and is generally withdrawn. He described himself as being an introvert when in the community and basically keeping to himself. He stated that he made no effort to socialize and that this was by choice, because he was not interested in making friends. According to Mr. Nelson, he basically agreed with social norms, stating that he saw family as important and believed in the work ethic.

Writer's Impressions

The information for this history was gathered during several sessions with Mr. Nelson. Throughout the sessions, he was polite and answered questions with full answers. He often would avoid eye contact, sat slouched in his chair, was disheveled in appearance, lacked emotion in his responses, and displayed a flat affect. Mr. Nelson was evasive in talking about his offense other than to say that he was not responsible for what he had done and that this had been proved in a court of law. He also believed that he was being treated unfairly by being held in a secure psychiatric facility and that he should be living in the community.

The information Mr. Nelson provided remained fairly consistent over the sessions, and it was verifiable through his parents and the other sources used.

Theresa Pines
Social Worker, Forensic Unit
North Haven Psychiatric Hospital

SCORING THE VIOLENCE RISK APPRAISAL GUIDE

The numbered items are the items on the VRAG, and the lettered items are other related factors. The other related factors are not used in scoring the VRAG but can be presented in the final report. Details regarding this offender are in italics.

Name:	*Elvin Nelson*
Case number:	*11111*
Date of birth:	*February 24, 1974*
Index offense:	*Arson and criminal negligence causing death*
Date of offense:	*January 27, 2003*
Date and type of disposition:	*March 30, 2003; found NCR*
Date of admission:	*April 15, 2003*
Referral source:	*Dr. Hines, Psychiatrist, Forensic Unit, North Haven Psychiatric Hospital*
Information source:	*Clinical file compiled at North Haven Psychiatric Hospital*

Childhood History

1. Lived with both biological parents to age 16 (except for death of parent)
   Score *no* if offender did not live continuously with both biological parents until age 16, except if one or both parents died. In the case of parent death, score as for *yes*.
   Yes = –2 √
   No = +3
   Lived with both parents until age 19, when he left to travel around British Columbia.

   Score: –2 (low)

2. Elementary school maladjustment (up to and including Grade 8)
   No problems   = –1√
   Slight or moderate discipline or attendance problems = +2
   Severe (i.e., frequent or serious) behavior or attendance problems (e.g., truancy or disruptive behavior that persisted over several years or resulted in expulsion)   = +5
   No behavior problems until high school.

   Score: –1 (low)

A. Suspended or expelled from school (elementary or secondary)
   No = Low   Yes = High √
   Suspended once in high school for being under the influence of drugs at school.

B. Highest grade (prior to index offense)
   ≥ Grade 9 = Low √   < Grade 9 = High

Completed grade 13 and 1 year of a college business course.

C. Arrested before age 16

No = Low   Yes = High √

First arrested at age 15 for stealing his mother's car.

D. Childhood behavior problem before age 15

Allot one point for each of the following:

repeated truancy ___, delinquency ___, repeated sex ___, runaway overnight (≥ 2) ___, repeated lying ___, fights ___, repeated substance abuse___, grades < IQ ___, vandalism ___, school suspension ___, violations of rules ___, thefts (at home or at school) ___: Total = 0

< 3 = Low √ ≥ 3 = High

No major problems in the home or at school prior to age 15; theft of music tape and mother's car occurred at age 15.

Adult Adjustment

3. History of alcohol problems

Allot one point for each of the following: parental alcohol abuse ___, teenage alcohol problem _√_, adult alcohol problem ___, alcohol involved in prior offense ___, alcohol involved in index offense ___

0 points   = –1

1 or 2 points   = 0 √

3 points   = +1

4 or 5 points   = +2

Parents: No problems for either parent.

Teenager: Started drinking at age 16, usually drank to intoxication.

Adult: No problems.

Prior offenses: No involvement.

Index offense: No involvement.

Score: 0

4. Marital status (at the time of the index offense)

Ever married (or lived common law in the same home

for at least 6 months)   = –2

Never married   = +1 √

Always single; never married or involved in a common-law relationship.

Score: +1 (high)

5. Criminal history score for convictions and charges for non-violent offenses prior to the index offense (from the Cormier–Lang system shown in Table A.1)

Score of 0   = –2
Score of 1 or 2   = 0
Score of 3 or above   = +3 √
Convicted for taking auto without consent (theft over) at age 15: Total = 5 points.

Score: +3 (high)

6. Failure on prior conditional release (includes parole violation or revocation, breach of or failure to comply with recognizance or probation, bail violation, and any new charges, including the index offense, while on a conditional release)
   No = 0 √   Yes = +3
   One year of probation for conviction for theft of auto was completed with no failures.

Score: 0

E. Significant period of employment (at least 6 months)
   ≥ 6 months = Low   < 6 months = High √
   Short labor jobs only; longest was for 4 months.

F. Living situation at time of index offense
   With someone (includes group home and
   institutions)   = Low
   Alone (own accommodation or transient)   = High√
   Lived alone in a bachelor apartment after last discharge from hospital.

G. Admission to corrections
   No = Low √   Yes = High
   Never incarcerated.

H. History of convictions or charges for violent offenses prior to index offense
   No = Low √   Yes = High
   No history reported.

I. Escape or attempted escape from secure custody
   No = Low √   Yes = High
   No history reported.

Offense Characteristics

7. Age at index offense (at most recent birthday)
   ≥ 39   = –5
   34–38 = –2
   28–33 = –1 √
   27   = 0
   ≤ 26   = +2
   Index offense date January 27, 2003; birth date February 28, 1974: (2002 – 1974 = 28).

Score: −1 (low)

8. Victim injury (index offense only; most serious injury is scored)

Death	= −2 √
Hospitalized	= 0
Treated and released	= +1
None or slight (includes no victim)	= +2

   Delusional; set fire to his apartment, causing death of neighbor.

Score: −2 (low)

9. Any female victim (for index offense)

   Yes = −1   No (includes no victim) = +1 √

   Victim was a man residing in neighboring apartment.

Score: +1 (high)

J. Relationship of victim to offender

Previously known	= Low
Stranger (includes peace officer or hospital staff)	= High√

   Victim was neighbor unknown to him.

Assessment Information

10. Meets *DSM–III* criteria for any personality disorder

    No = −2 √   Yes = +3

    See Factor 11.

Score: −2 (low)

11. Meets *DSM–III* criteria for schizophrenia

    Yes = −3 √   No = +1

    Paranoid delusions, withdrawn, seclusive, flat affect, deteriorated functioning, and psychiatric admission for testing and diagnosis.

Score: −3 (low)

12. Hare Psychopathy Checklist—Revised score (PCL–R; Hare, 1991)

≤ 4	= −5
5–9	= −3
10–14	= −1 √
15–24	= 0
25–34	= +4
≥ 35	= +12

    Score was 11 from PCL-R assessment report. (To score this item, the PCL–R assessment must have been completed by a clinician trained to use the PCL–R.)

Score: −1 (low)

K. Results of IQ testing

   ≥ 90 = Low √   < 90 = High

   Results from testing done at Lakeview Psychiatric Hospital indicated an average IQ.

L. Attitudes supportive of crime
No = Low   Yes = High?
Unclear how much of attitudes and lifestyle are results of schizo-phrenia.

M. Attitudes unfavorable toward convention
No = Low   Yes = High?
Unclear how much of attitudes and lifestyle are results of schizo-phrenia.

Total score: −7
Risk category: 4 (see Table H.1)
Percentile: 30% score lower (see Appendix C)
Probability of recidivism: 31% (see Table H.1)
Date assessed: June 1, 2003

APPENDIX L

Problem Identification Checklist
(File Version)

On the following pages is a checklist of problems that the patient may or may not have presented in the past 6 months. (This checklist is a shortened form of the original checklist developed for a psychiatric patient population that can be applied to the offender population.) To complete this checklist, rate the severity of each problem behavior using the following 5-point scale: 1 = no problem, 3 = moderate problem, and 5 = severe problem. Code *not applicable* or *unknown* as 0. If the file information does not indicate whether a patient has exhibited a particular problem, try to obtain the information from a staff member who knows the patient. If the information is still unavailable, rate the problem as unknown (0).

Sometimes a patient previously had a problem but because of treatment or for some other reason no longer has it. To avoid ambiguity about such changes, confine your observations to the past 6 months to standardize the observation period. In other words, if the patient has exhibited the problem at any time in the past 6 months, he has the problem. For problems that cannot apply (e.g., problems in supportive housing for a patient who lives alone or in an institution), rate as unknown (0). Rate problems for all patients in the same way.

A. PSYCHOTIC BEHAVIORS

1. *Unusual thought content:* Thoughts that seem unusual, bizarre, or strange. Fixation on topics of no consequence. Putting together of ideas that obviously do not go together (does not include silliness or feeble attempts at humor).

379

2. *Hallucinatory behavior:* Perceptions without normal external stimulus correspondence; evidence is usually in the form of the individual holding conversations with persons who are not present, rearing back from a nonexistent threat, or giving explicit descriptions of perceptions that are obviously wrong.

3. *Conceptual disorganization:* Thoughts that seem confused, disconnected, or disrupted. Inability to maintain a train of thought (does not include silliness or feeble attempts at humor).

4. *Psychotic actions:* For example, stereotypes, bizarre mannerisms, facial grimaces, obviously inappropriate laughter, talking, singing, or perseverative movements. Does not include tics, spastic movements from a physical illness or disability, or movements that may be due to medications.

5. *Inappropriate suspicion:* Suspicion that is definitely inappropriate (e.g., belief that food is poisoned, aliens are reading his thoughts, or "everyone is out to get me"). Does not include suspicions that may be appropriate; in some cases, because of the nature of the patient's offense, personality, or some physical abnormality, other patients may indeed "pick on" him.

6. *Grandiosity:* Exaggerated self-opinion, arrogance, conviction of unusual power, continual bragging, claims to be able to do something that he could not possibly do. Includes claims the patient makes about his past and present that are not true and projections he makes about his future that are not probable.

B. INAPPROPRIATE AND PROCRIMINAL SOCIAL BEHAVIORS

1. *Impulsivity:* Failure to consider consequences of actions for self or others; failure to plan ahead.

2. *Insulting, teasing, and obnoxious verbal behavior:* Behaviors that are beyond good-natured play and not just isolated incidents.

3. *Lack of consideration for others:* Callousness, little empathy, or anything that shows an attitude of thinking only about his own concerns and never about the thoughts or feelings of or consequences for other patients or staff.

4. *Unconventional attitudes:* Attitudes that are nonsupportive of, reject, or deny the validity or worth of conventional (anticriminal) persons, activities, or settings such as those associated with work, school, or family. Includes obvious contempt for or a general cynical attitude about conventional persons, activities, or settings.

5. *Criminal attitudes:* In general, identification with criminals— for example, approval of criminals, disapproval of police, or

cheering for the "bad guy" when watching television.

6. *Shallow affect, superficiality:* General "so what?" attitude. Lack of response to normally emotional circumstances.

7. *Tension:* Physical and motor manifestations of nervousness and overactivation, including tics, grinding teeth, pacing, and chewing fingernails.

8. *Medication noncompliance:* Lack of compliance with medication regimens. Includes all types of medication and both not taking medication and overreliance on medication (e.g., requesting nonprescription medication for an extended period of time). Evidence may be sought through drug testing, especially if the patient has access to or is living in the community.

9. *Poor housekeeping or cooking:* Messy sleeping area. Messes in kitchen or common areas. Failure to pick up after self.

10. *Poor self-care and personal hygiene:* Failure to wash at all or frequently enough. Clothing that is dirty or in poor condition. Dirty appearance or smell.

11. *Substance abuse:* Alcohol or drug abuse. Any use of alcohol, for patients who are not permitted to drink, or of (nonprescription) drugs. For patients who are permitted to drink, drunkenness or interference of alcohol use with their lives.

12. *Physical self-abuse:* Deliberate self-injury—for example, burning self with cigarette, cutting or bruising self. Includes "jailhouse tattoos."

13. *Suggestible and easily led:* Frequent incidents of being duped by other patients or going along with what other patients tell him without question.

14. *Problems with money management:* Frequent incidents of running out of money. Frequent episodes of borrowing money from or lending money to other patients. Selling of possessions to pay debts.

15. *Sexual misbehaviors:* Inappropriate touching, exposure, talk, dress (e.g., underwear with the crotch removed).

16. *Fire starting:* Fire-related action and talk, even on a seemingly minor scale (e.g., burnt matches in sleeping area).

17. *Criminal associates:* Association with other patients who are frequently in trouble or who are suspected of criminal activity. If the patient is living in the community, even suspected association with criminals, such as being seen at bars or other spots frequented by criminals.

18. *Inappropriate dependence:* Clinging, monopolization of the time of staff or other patients. Need to be told what to do even for very simple things.

C. MOOD PROBLEMS

1. *Excitement:* Heightened emotional tone, agitation, increased activity.
2. *Anxiety:* Expressions of excessive fear and worry, even for minor problems.
3. *Mania:* Hyperactivity; being worked up for no obvious reason. Does not include that caused by the effects of medication.
4. *Anger:* Inappropriate displays of temper (if the anger expressed is minor, an isolated instance can be ignored).
5. *Blunted affect:* Reduced emotional tone, flatness. Does not include that caused by medication.
6. *Depression:* Real sadness. Lack of pleasure from ordinarily pleasurable acts that permeates most of day-to-day behavior.
7. *Guilt feelings:* Excessive self-blame, shame, or remorse for past behavior or for events that were beyond his control.

D. SOCIAL WITHDRAWAL

1. *Poor use of leisure time:* Complaints of boredom. Excessive TV watching, listening to music, or just laying about.
2. *Unpopular:* Few friends. Left out of group activities (includes treatment by staff).
3. *Social withdrawal:* Deliberate avoidance of contact with others. Does not include others' avoidance of him.
4. *Inactivity:* Lack of engagement in physical exercise. Tendency to spend a great deal of time sleeping or lying about.
5. *Excessive shyness:* Social anxiety, lack of ability to start a conversation. Discomfort in most social situations.
6. *Refusal to participate in nonmedical therapy:* Includes psychological, social work, and vocational therapy.
7. *Preoccupation with staying in the institution:* Actual preference shown for being hospitalized. Apprehensiveness about future release or access to the community.

APPENDIX M

Proximal Risk Factor Scale

The following is a list of problems that the offender may or may not have presented in the *past month*. Rate the severity of each of the client's problems. If the problem does not apply to this client (i.e., medication non-compliance for a client who is not prescribed any medications), or if insufficient information is available to make a judgment, record "N/A". If the client has clearly not had the particular problem at any time during the past month, record "0". If the problem has existed at any in the past month, rate its severity from 1 to 4, where "2" corresponds to a "moderate problem" and "4" corresponds to a "severe problem."

DYNAMIC ANTISOCIALITY

1. *Complains about staff*: Makes any complaints against staff, justified or not.
2. *Shows no remorse*: Does not feel responsible for index offense. Is not sorry for what he has done to others.
3. *Takes no responsibility for behavior*: Tries to blame others or circumstances for his acts or problems. Sees himself, inappropriately, as a victim.
4. *Ignores or passes over previous violent acts*: Is uncaring about violent acts he has perpetrated. Dismisses his violent acts as unimportant.
5. *Has antisocial attitudes and values.*
6. *Shows no empathy and concern for others.*
7. *Has unrealistic discharge plans*: Has unrealistic plans about being released and unrealistic plans about postrelease activities.
8. *Has psychiatric symptoms that are not in remission.*

9. *Voices threats of harm to a specific person or persons; shows a fixedness on specific types of victims:* For example, tends to be abusive toward female staff. Is obsessed with (evidenced by watching or talking about) children, women, or people who are like the victim of his index offense.
10. *Has same delusion as that involved in index offense.*

PSYCHIATRIC SYMPTOMS

11. *Has unusual thought content:* Has thoughts that seem unusual, bizarre, or strange. Fixates on topics of no consequence. Puts together ideas that obviously do not go together (does not include silliness or feeble attempts at humor).
12. *Exhibits hallucinatory behavior:* Perceives without normal external stimulus correspondence; evidence is usually in the form of the patient holding conversations with persons who are not present, rearing back from a nonexistent threat, or giving explicit descriptions of perceptions that are obviously wrong.

POOR COMPLIANCE

13. *Has escaped or attempted escape:* Has escaped or attempted to escape from supervised care.
14. *Exhibits few positive coping skills:* Deals inappropriately with anger (e.g., reacts aggressively rather than assertively). Does not deal with stressful or upsetting events in a constructive way (e.g., is aggressive or self-defeating).
15. *Has shown poor compliance with current supervision restrictions:* Is late returning from pass. Drifts away from group when out on group activity. Does not report when required. Does not deal with stressful or upsetting events in a constructive way (e.g., is aggressive or self-defeating).

POOR MEDICATION COMPLIANCE/DYSPHORIA

16. *Has shown poor compliance with psychiatric medication:* Does not take medication or misses medication (if living in the community, drug testing can be used as evidence).
17. *Exhibits anxiety, anger, or frustration.*

ADDED SINGLE ITEMS

18. *Denies all problems:* Just "goes through the motions" of treatment.
19. Therapeutic Alliance Scale (see description in Appendix N).

APPENDIX N

Dynamic Risk Appraisal Scale

INSTRUCTIONS

For each item below, rate the severity level of the client's behavior. This scale yields two scale scores—one for predicting any incident, and one for predicting violent incidents. There are two columns on the right, one for each scale score. Simply transfer the score for each item to the appropriate column or columns on the right. If the item does not count toward the total for a particular scale score, that cell is shaded. If both cells are blank, transfer that score to both cells.

For each item, choose the *one* number that best describes the client's presentation *over the past month,* and record it in the appropriate scoring column. If the problem does not apply to this client (e.g., medication noncompliance for a client who is not prescribed any medications) or if insufficient information is available to make a judgment, record N/A in the appropriate scoring column. If you are able to assert that the client has *not* had the particular problem at *any time* during the past month, record 0 for No Problem in the appropriate scoring column. If the problem has existed *at any time in the past month,* record 1, 2, 3, or 4 in the appropriate scoring column. The Therapeutic Alliance items are coded somewhat differently; however, the scoring is the same. Select the number that best describes the client's behavior *over the past month,* and place that number in the appropriate answer column or columns.

ITEM DESCRIPTIONS: FRONTLINE STAFF

- *Ignores or passes over previous violent acts:* Is uncaring about violent acts he has perpetrated. Dismisses his violent acts as unimportant.

Behavior	No problem		Moderate problem		Severe problem	N/A or unknown	Score for predicting any incident	Score for predicting a violent incident
			Frontline staff					
1. Ignores or passes over previous violent acts	0	1	2	3	4	N/A		
2. Takes no responsibility for behavior	0	1	2	3	4	N/A		
3. Exhibits anxiety, anger, or frustration	0	1	2	3	4	N/A		
4. Shows no remorse	0	1	2	3	4	N/A		
5. Has unrealistic discharge plans	0	1	2	3	4	N/A		
6. Has escaped or attempted escape	0	1	2	3	4	N/A		
7. Has unusual thought content	0	1	2	3	4	N/A		
8. Complains about staff	0	1	2	3	4	N/A		
9. Shows no empathy and concern for others	0	1	2	3	4	N/A		
10. Has antisocial attitudes and values	0	1	2	3	4	N/A		
11. Has shown poor compliance with current supervision restrictions	0	1	2	3	4	N/A		
12. Exhibits few positive coping skills	0	1	2	3	4	N/A		
13. Has shown poor compliance with psychiatric medication	0	1	2	3	4	N/A		
14. Has psychiatric symptoms that are not in remission	0	1	2	3	4	N/A		
15. Therapeutic Alliance item	0	1	2	3	4	N/A		
16. Denies all problems	0	1	2	3	4	N/A		

Clinical staff

	0	1	2	3	4	N/A
17. Exhibits psychotic actions	0	1	2	3	4	N/A
18. Displays inactivity	0	1	2	3	4	N/A
19. Refuses to participate in nonmedical therapy	0	1	2	3	4	N/A
20. Exhibits social withdrawal	0	1	2	3	4	N/A
21. Exhibits shallow affect, superficiality	0	1	2	3	4	N/A
22. Lacks consideration for others	0	1	2	3	4	N/A
23. Exhibits mania	0	1	2	3	4	N/A
24. Exhibits anger	0	1	2	3	4	N/A
25. Exhibits inappropriate suspicion	0	1	2	3	4	N/A
26. Holds unconventional attitudes	0	1	2	3	4	N/A
27. Shows conceptual disorganization	0	1	2	3	4	N/A
28. Has shown medication noncompliance	0	1	2	3	4	N/A
29. Therapeutic Alliance item	0	1	2	3	4	N/A
Totals						

- *Takes no responsibility for behavior:* Tries to blame others or circumstances for his acts or problems. Sees himself, inappropriately, as a victim.
- *Exhibits anxiety, anger, or frustration.*
- *Shows no remorse:* Does not feel responsible for index offense. Is not sorry for what he has done to others.
- *Has unrealistic discharge plans:* Has unrealistic plans about being released and unrealistic plans about postrelease activities.
- *Has escaped or attempted escape:* Has escaped or attempted to escape from supervised care.
- *Has unusual thought content:* Has thoughts that seem unusual, bizarre, or strange. Fixates on topics of no consequence. Puts together ideas that obviously do not go together (does not include silliness or feeble attempts at humor).
- *Complains about staff:* Makes any complaints against staff, justified or not.
- *Shows no empathy and concern for others.*
- *Has antisocial attitudes and values.*
- *Has shown poor compliance with current supervision restrictions:* Is late returning from pass. Drifts away from group when out on group activity. Does not report when required. Does not deal with stressful or upsetting events in a constructive way (e.g., is aggressive or self-defeating).
- *Exhibits few positive coping skills:* Deals inappropriately with anger (e.g., reacts aggressively rather than assertively). Does not deal with stressful or upsetting events in a constructive way (e.g., is aggressive or self-defeating).
- *Has shown poor compliance with psychiatric medication:* Does not take medication or misses medication (if living in the community, drug testing can be used as evidence).
- *Has psychiatric symptoms that are not in remission.*
- *Denies all problems:* Just "goes through the motions" of treatment programs.

ITEM DESCRIPTIONS: CLINICAL STAFF

- *Exhibits psychotic actions:* For example, exhibits stereotypes, bizarre mannerisms, facial grimaces, obviously inappropriate laughter, talking, or singing, or perseverative movements. Does not include tics, spastic movements from a physical illness or disability, or movements that may be due to medications.
- *Displays inactivity:* Gets no physical exercise. Spends a great deal of time sleeping or lying about.

- *Refuses to take part in nonmedical therapy:* Includes psychological, social work, and vocational therapy.
- *Exhibits social withdrawal:* Deliberately avoids contact with others. Does not include others' avoidance of him.
- *Exhibits shallow affect, superficiality:* Has a general "so what?" attitude. Does not respond to normally emotional circumstances.
- *Lacks consideration for others:* Is callous, has little empathy, shows an attitude of thinking only about his own concerns and never about the thoughts or feelings of or consequences for other patients or staff.
- *Exhibits mania:* Is hyperactive; gets worked up for no obvious reason. Does not include that caused by the effects of medication.
- *Exhibits anger:* Has inappropriate displays of temper (if the anger expressed is minor, an isolated instance can be ignored).
- *Exhibits inappropriate suspicion:* Suspicions are definitely inappropriate (e.g., belief that food is poisoned, aliens are reading his thoughts, or "everyone is out to get me"). Does not include suspicions that may be appropriate; in some cases, because of the nature of the patient's offense, personality, or some physical abnormality, other patients may indeed "pick on" him.
- *Holds unconventional attitudes:* Has attitudes that are nonsupportive of, reject, or deny the validity or worth of conventional (anticriminal) persons, activities, or settings such as those associated with work, school, or family. Includes obvious contempt for or a general cynical attitude about conventional persons, activities, or settings.
- *Shows conceptual disorganization:* Has thoughts that seem confused, disconnected, or disrupted. Is unable to maintain a train of thought (does not include silliness or feeble attempts at humor).
- *Has shown medication noncompliance:* Does not comply with medication regimens. Includes all types of medication and both not taking medication and overreliance on medication (e.g., requesting nonprescription medication for an extended period of time). Evidence may be sought through drug testing, especially if the client is living in the community.

THERAPEUTIC ALLIANCE ITEM

The Therapeutic Alliance item is coded as follows:
- 1 = Client is enthusiastically involved in treatment activities, recognizes and explores problem areas, seeks out staff assistance, and makes realistic plans for the future.

- 2 = Client is passively receptive to treatment efforts, attends programs as scheduled, and participates when engaged directly; future plans are vague and poorly formulated.
- 3 = Client is variable in treatment and irregular attendance at programs, is a reluctant participant, and is difficult to engage in dialogue on problem areas.
- 4 = Client declines most treatments offered, sees no need for further hospitalization, and is passively waiting for discharge.
- 5 = Client actively refuses most treatments, sees no purpose to the hospital stay, denies all problems, and constantly demands discharge.

APPENDIX O

Cross-Sectional Oak Ridge Statistics
Over 35 Years

Variable	January 1961	January 1976	February 1995
N	262	287	137
Age (years)			
M	32.8[a]	27.9	37.6
SD	Unavailable	10.1	8.6
Referred from (%)			
Court	33	41	53
Psychiatric hospital	45	22	42
Corrections	20	31	4
Primary diagnosis (%)			
Psychosis	69	47	69
Personality disorder	6	42	25
Mental retardation	21	11	4
Admission offense[b] (%)			
Against persons	58	57	82
Property or economic	28	10	4
Other or none	13	33	13
% Never married (or equivalent)	78	76	72
Less than grade 8 education (%)	62	66	22
Insanity acquittal or unfit (%)	39	42	67
Cumulative length of admission (months)	Unavailable	27.5	43.9
M			
SD		35.2	58.4

Note. [a]Median. [b]Most serious criminal charge leading to admission.

REFERENCES

Adams, K. (1983). Former mental patients in a prison and parole system: A study of socially disruptive behavior. *Criminal Justice and Behavior, 10,* 358–384.

Akman, D. D., & Normandeau, A. (1967). The measurement of crime and delinquency in Canada: A replication study. *British Journal of Criminology, 7,* 129–149.

Alexander, J. F., & Parsons, B. V. (1973). Short-term behavioral intervention with delinquent families: Impact on family process and recidivism. *Journal of Abnormal Psychology, 81,* 219–225.

Allison, P. D. (1984). *Event history analysis.* Newbury Park, CA: Sage.

Allyon, T., & Azrin, N. (1968). *The token economy: A motivational system for therapy and rehabilitation.* New York: Appleton-Century-Crofts.

American Psychiatric Association. (1952). *Diagnostic and statistical manual of mental disorders.* Washington, DC: Author.

American Psychiatric Association. (1968). *Diagnostic and statistical manual of mental disorders* (2nd ed.). Washington, DC: Author.

American Psychiatric Association. (1980). *Diagnostic and statistical manual of mental disorders* (3rd ed.). Washington, DC: Author.

American Psychiatric Association. (1987). *Diagnostic and statistical manual of mental disorders* (3rd ed., rev.). Washington, DC: Author.

American Psychiatric Association. (1994). *Diagnostic and statistical manual of mental disorders* (4th ed.). Washington, DC: Author.

American Psychological Association. (1982). *Report of the Task Force on the Evaluation of Education, Training, and Service in Psychology.* Washington, DC: Author.

Andrews, D. A. (1980). Some experimental investigations of the principles of differential association through deliberate manipulations of the structure of service systems. *American Sociological Review, 45,* 448–462.

Andrews, D. A., & Bonta, J. (2003a). *Level of Service Inventory–Revised (LSI–R).* Toronto, Ontario, Canada: Multi-Health Systems.

Andrews, D. A., & Bonta, J. (2003b). *The psychology of criminal conduct* (3rd ed.). Cincinnati, OH: Anderson.

Andrews, D. A., Bonta, J., & Hoge, R. D. (1990). Classification for effective rehabilitation: Rediscovering psychology. *Criminal Justice and Behavior, 17,* 19.

Andrews, D. A., & Friesen, W. (1987). Assessments of anticriminal plans and the prediction of criminal futures: A research note. *Criminal Justice and Behavior, 14,* 33–37.

Andrews, D. A., Kiessling, J. J., & Kominos, S. (1983). *The Level of Supervision Inventory (LSI–6): Interview and scoring guide.* Toronto, Ontario, Canada: Ontario Ministry of Correctional Services.

Andrews, D. A., Kiessling, J. J., Robinson, D., & Mickus, S. (1986). The risk principle of case classification: An outcome evaluation with young adult probationers. *Consulting Journal of Criminology, 28,* 377–384.

Andrews, D. A., Zinger, I., Hoge, R. D., Bonta, J., Gendreau, P., & Cullen, F. T. (1990). Does correctional treatment work? A clinically relevant and psychologically informed meta-analysis. *Criminology, 28,* 369–404.

Annis, H. M., & Davis, C. S. (1989). Relapse prevention. In R. K. Hester & W. R. Miller (Eds.), *Handbook of alcoholism treatment approaches* (pp. 170–182). New York: Pergamon Press.

Appelbaum, P. S. (1989). Titicut follies: Patients' rights and institutional reform. *Hospital and Community Psychiatry, 40,* 679–680.

Ashford, J. B., & LeCroy, C. W. (1988). Predicting recidivism: An evaluation of the Wisconsin juvenile probation and aftercare risk instrument. *Criminal Justice and Behavior, 15,* 141–151.

Ashton, R. H. (1986). Combining the judgments of experts: How many and which ones? *Organizational Behavior and Human Decision Processes, 38,* 405–414.

Ayers, W. A. (2000). Taxometric analysis of borderline and antisocial personality disorders in a drug and alcohol dependent population. *Dissertation Abstracts International, 61*(3), 1684B.

Backer, T. E., Liberman, R. P., & Kuchnel, T. G. (1986). Dissemination and adoption of innovative psychosocial interventions. *Journal of Consulting and Clinical Psychology, 54,* 111–118.

Barbaree, H. E., Seto, M. C., Langton, C. M., & Peacock, E. J. (2001). Evaluating the predictive accuracy of six risk assessment instruments for adult sex offenders. *Criminal Justice and Behavior, 28,* 490–521.

Barker, E. T. (1980). The Penetanguishene program: A personal review. In H. Toch (Ed.), *Therapeutic communities in corrections* (pp. 73–81). New York: Praeger.

Barker, E. T., & Buck, M. H. (1977). L.S.D. in a coercive milieu therapy program. *Canadian Psychiatric Association Journal, 22,* 311–314.

Barker, E. T., & Mason, M. H. (1968). The insane criminal as therapist. *Canadian Journal of Corrections, 10,* 553–561.

Barker, E. T., Mason, M. H., & Wilson, J. (1969). Defence-disrupting therapy. *Canadian Psychiatric Association Journal, 14,* 355–359.

Barker, E. T., & McLaughlin, A. J. (1977). The total encounter capsule. *Canadian Psychiatric Association Journal, 22,* 355–360.

Barr, K. N., & Quinsey, V. L. (2004). Is psychopathy a pathology or a life strategy? Implications for social policy. In C. Crawford & C. Salmon (Eds.), *Evolutionary psychology, public policy, and personal decisions* (pp. 293–317). Hillsdale, NJ: Erlbaum.

Barracato, J. S. (1979). *Fire—Is it arson?* (Available from the Aetna Casualty and Surety Company, 151 Farmington Avenue, Hartford, CT 06156)

Barratt, E. S. (1993). The use of anticonvulsants in aggression and violence. *Psychopharmacology Bulletin, 29,* 75–81.

Barron, P., Hassiotis, A., & Banes, J. (2004). Offenders with intellectual disability: A prospective comparative study. *Journal of Intellectual Disability Research, 48*, 69–76.

Barsetti, I., Earls, C. M., Lalumière, M. L., & Bélanger, N. (1998). The differentiation of intrafamilial and extrafamilial heterosexual child molesters. *Journal of Interpersonal Violence, 13*, 275–286.

Barton, C., Alexander, J. F., Waldron, H., Turner, C. W., & Warburton, J. (1985). Generalizing treatment effects of functional family therapy: Three replications. *American Journal of Family Therapy, 13*, 16–26.

Barton, R. R., & Turnbull, B. W. (1979). Evaluation of recidivism data: Use of failure rate regression models. *Evaluation Quarterly, 3*, 629–641.

Bartosh, D. L., Garby, T., Lewis, D., & Gray, S. (2003). Differences in the predictive validity of actuarial risk assessments in relation to sex offender type. *International Journal of Offender Therapy and Comparative Criminology, 4*, 422–438.

Baumeister, R. F., Campbell, J. D., Krueger, J. I., & Vohs, K. D. (2003). Does high self-esteem cause better performance, interpersonal success, happiness, or healthier lifestyles? *Psychological Science in the Public Interest, 4*, 1–39.

Beauford, J. E., McNiel, D. E., & Binder, R. L. (1997). Utility of the initial therapeutic alliance in evaluating psychiatric patients' risk of violence. *American Journal of Psychiatry, 154*, 1272–1276.

Beck, A. J., & Shipley, B. E. (1987). *Recidivism of young parolees* (Bureau of Justice Statistics Special Report). Washington, DC: Department of Justice, Bureau of Justice Statistics.

Beck, A. T. (1967). *Depression: Clinical, experimental, and theoretical aspects.* New York: Harper & Row.

Beck, N. C., Menditto, A. A., Baldwin, L., Angelone, E., & Maddox, M. (1991). Reduced frequency of aggressive behavior in forensic patients in a social learning program. *Hospital and Community Psychiatry, 42*, 750–752.

Bélanger, N., & Earls, C. M. (1996). Sex offender recidivism prediction. *Forum on Corrections Research, 8*, 22–24.

Bellack, A. S. (1986). Schizophrenia: Behavior therapy's forgotten child. *Behavior Therapy, 17*, 199–214.

Belmore, M. F., & Quinsey, V. L. (1994). Correlates of psychopathy in a non-institutional sample. *Journal of Interpersonal Violence, 9*, 339–349.

Berman, J. S., & Norton, N. C. (1985). Does professional training make a therapist more effective? *Psychological Bulletin, 98*, 401–407.

Bieber, S., Pasewark, R., Bosten, K., & Steadman, H. J. (1988). Predicting criminal recidivism of insanity acquittees. *International Journal of Law and Psychiatry, 11*, 105–112.

Binder, J. L. (1993). Is it time to improve psychotherapy training? *Clinical Psychology Review, 13*, 301–318.

Binder, R. L. (1999). Are the mentally ill dangerous? *Journal of the American Academy of Psychiatry & the Law, 27*, 189–201.

Blishen, B. R., & McRoberts, H. A. (1976). A revised socioeconomic index for occupations in Canada. *Canadian Review of Sociology and Anthropology, 13*, 71–79.

Blum, K., & Noble, E. P. (Eds.). (1997). *Handbook of psychiatric genetics.* New York: CRC Press.

Blumberg, N. H. (1981). Arson update: A review of the literature on fire setting. *Bulletin of the American Academy of Psychiatry and the Law, 9*, 255–265.

Bock, G. R., & Goode, J. A. (Eds.). (1996). *Genetics of criminal and antisocial behaviour.* New York: Wiley.

Bogenberger, R. P., Pasewark, R. A., Gudeman, H., & Bieber, S. L. (1987). Follow-up of insanity acquittees in Hawaii. *International Journal of Law and Psychiatry, 10*, 283–296.

Bonta, J., Harman, W. G., Hann, R. G., & Cormier, R. B. (1996). The prediction of recidivism among federally sentenced offenders: A re-validation of the SIR scale. *Canadian Journal of Criminology, 38*, 61–79.

Bonta, J., Law, M., & Hanson, R. K. (1998). The prediction of criminal and violent recidivism among mentally disordered offenders: A meta-analysis. *Psychological Bulletin, 123*, 123–142.

Bonta, J., & Motiuk, L. L. (1985). Utilization of an interview-based classification instrument: A study of correctional halfway houses. *Criminal Justice and Behavior, 12*, 333–352.

Bonta, J., & Motiuk, L. L. (1987). The diversion of incarcerated offenders to correctional halfway houses. *Journal of Research in Crime and Delinquency, 24*, 302–323.

Bonta, J., & Motiuk, L. L. (1990). Classification to halfway houses: A quasi-experimental evaluation. *Criminology, 28*, 497–506.

Boothroyd, R. A., Poythress, N. G., McGaha, A., & Petrila, J. (2003). The Broward mental health court: Process, outcomes, and service utilization. *International Journal of Law and Psychiatry, 26*, 55–71.

Borduin, C. M., Henggeler, S. W., Blaske, D. M., & Stein, R. J. (1990). Multisystemic treatment of adolescent sexual offenders. *International Journal of Offender Therapy and Comparative Criminology, 34*, 105–113.

Borduin, C. M., Mann, B. J., Cone, L. T., Henggeler, S. W., Fucci, B., Blaske, D. M., et al. (1995). Multisystemic treatment of serious juvenile offenders: Long-term prevention of criminality and violence. *Journal of Consulting and Clinical Psychology, 63*, 569–578.

Boudreau, J. F., Kwan, Q. Y., Faragher, W. E., & Denault, G. C. (1977). *Arson and arson investigation: Survey and assessment.* Washington, DC: U.S. Government Printing Office.

Bowden, P. (1981). What happens to patients released from the special hospitals? *British Journal of Psychiatry, 138*, 340–345.

Bradford, J. M. (1982). Arson: A clinical study. *Canadian Journal of Psychiatry, 27*, 188–192.

Braff, J., Arvanties, T., & Steadman, H. J. (1983). Detention patterns of successful and unsuccessful insanity defendants. *Criminology, 21*, 439–449.

Brett, A. (2004). Kindling theory in arson: How dangerous are firesetters? *Australian and New Zealand Journal of Psychiatry, 38*, 419–425.

Brown, G. L., Goodwin, F. K., Ballenger, J. C., Goyer, P. F., & Major, L. F. (1979). Aggression in humans correlates with cerebrospinal fluid amine metabolites. *Psychiatry Research, 1*, 131–139.

Brown, R. C., D'Agostino, C. A., & Craddick, R. A. (1978). Prediction of parole outcome based on discriminant function. *Corrective and Social Psychiatry and Journal of Behavior Technology, Methods and Therapy, 24*, 93–101.

Brunner, H. G., Nelen, M., Breakefield, X. O., Ropers, H. H., & van Oost, B. A. (1993). Abnormal behavior associated with a point mutation in the structural gene for monoamine oxidase A. *Science, 262*, 578–580.

Brunner, H. G., van Zandvoort, P., Abeling, N. G. G. M., van Gennip, A. H., Wolters, E. C., Kuiper, M. A., et al. (1993). X-linked borderline mental retardation with prominent behavioral disturbance: Phenotype, genetic localization, and evidence for disturbed monoamine metabolism. *American Journal of Human Genetics, 52*, 1032–1039.

Burgess, E. M. (1925). *The working of the indeterminate sentence law and the parole system in Illinois*. Springfield: Illinois Parole Board.

Burns, B. J., & Santos, A. B. (1995). Assertive community treatment: An update of randomized trials. *Psychiatric Services, 46*, 669–675.

Burt, M. R. (1980). Cultural myths and supports for rape. *Journal of Personality and Social Psychology, 38*, 217–230.

Butler, B., Long, A., & Rowsell, P. (1977). *Evaluative study of the social therapy unit Oak Ridge division: Report to the Ombudsman of Ontario*. Unpublished report. Office of the Ombudsman, Toronto, Ontario, Canada.

Callahan, L. A., Steadman, H. J., McGreevy, M. A., & Robbins, P. C. (1991). The volume and characteristics of insanity defense pleas: An eight-state study. *Bulletin of the American Academy of Psychiatry and Law, 19*, 331–338.

Callner, D. A., & Ross, S. M. (1976). The reliability and validity of three measures of assertion in a drug addict population. *Behavior Therapy, 7*, 659–667.

Campbell, T. W. (2003). Sex offenders and actuarial risk assessments: Ethical considerations. *Behavioral Sciences and the Law, 21*, 269–279.

Cannon, C. K., & Quinsey, V. L. (1995). The likelihood of violent behaviour: Predictions, postdictions, and hindsight bias. *Canadian Journal of Behavioural Science, 27*, 92–106.

Cannon, T. D., Mednick, S. A., & Parnas, J. (1990). Antecedents of predominantly negative and predominantly positive-symptom schizophrenia in a high risk population. *Archives of General Psychiatry, 47*, 622–632.

Carlson, K. A. (1973). Some characteristics of recidivists in an Ontario institution for adult male first-incarcerates. *Canadian Journal of Criminology and Corrections, 15*, 397–411.

Caspi, A., McClay, J., Moffitt, T. E., Mill, J., Martin, J., Craig, I. W., et al. (2002). Role of genotype in the cycle of violence in maltreated children. *Science, 297*, 851–854.

Casti, J. L. (1990). *Paradigms lost: Tackling the unanswered mysteries of modern science.* New York: Avon Books.

Chaplin, T. C., Rice, M. E., & Harris, G. T. (1995). Salient victim suffering and the sexual responses of child molesters. *Journal of Consulting and Clinical Psychology, 163*, 249–255.

Chapman, L., & Chapman, J. (1967). Genesis of popular but erroneous psychodiagnostic observations. *Journal of Abnormal Psychology, 72*, 193–204.

Chen, Y., Arria, A. M., & Anthony, J. C. (2003). Firesetting in adolescence and being aggressive, shy, and rejected by peers: New epidemiologic evidence from a national sample survey. *Journal of the American Academy of Psychiatry and the Law, 31*, 44–52.

Christensen, R. (1986). Entropy minimax multivariate statistical modeling: II. Applications. *International Journal of General Systems, 12*, 227–305.

Christiansen, L. B. (1988). *Experimental methodology.* Boston: Allyn & Bacon.

Christie, R. (1882). *Fifteenth annual report by the inspector of prisons and public charities upon the common gaols, prisons, and reformatories of the province of Ontario.* Toronto, Ontario, Canada: Legislative Assembly of the Province of Ontario.

Cipani, E. (Ed.). (1989). *The treatment of severe behavior disorders: Behavior analysis approaches.* Washington, DC: American Association on Mental Retardation.

Cleckley, H. (1941). *The mask of sanity.* St. Louis, MO: Mosby.

Cleckley, H. (1982). *The mask of sanity* (4th ed.). St. Louis, MO: Mosby.

Cocozza, J. J., Melick, M. E., & Steadman, H. J. (1978). Trends in violent crime among ex-mental patients. *Criminology, 16*, 317–334.

Cohen, J. (1969). *Statistical power analysis for the behavioral sciences.* New York: Academic Press.

Cohen, J. (1992). A power primer. *Psychological Bulletin, 112*, 155–159.

Community Protection Act, WA, Part X. RCW 71.09.020. Civil commitment. 1001–1013 (1990).

Cooke, D. J., & Michie, C. (1997). An item response theory analysis of the Hare Psychopathy Checklist–Revised. *Psychological Assessment, 9*, 3–14.

Cooke, D. J., Michie, C., Hart, S. D., & Hare, R. D. (1999). Evaluating the screening version of the Hare Psychopathy Checklist–Revised (PCL:SV): An item response theory analysis. *Psychological Assessment: A Journal of Consulting and Clinical Psychology, 11*, 1–11.

Copas, J. B., O'Brien, M., Roberts, J., & Whiteley, J. S. (1984). Treatment outcome in personality disorder: The effect of social psychological and behavioural variables. *Personality and Individual Differences, 5*, 565–573.

Corbett, C., Patel, V., Erikson, M., & Friendship, C. (2003). The violent reconvictions of sexual offenders. *Journal of Sexual Aggression, 9*, 31–39.

Corsini, R. (1958). Psychodrama with a psychopath. *Group Psychotherapy, 11*, 33–39.

Cosden, M., Ellens, J. K., Schnell, J. L., Yamini-Diouf, Y., & Wolfe, M. M. (2003). Evaluation of a mental health treatment court with assertive community treatment. *Behavioral Sciences and the Law, 21*, 415–427.

Costa, P. T., & McCrae, R. R. (1992). Development and validation. In *Revised NEO Personality Inventory (NEO PI–R) and NEO Five-Factor Inventory (NEOFFI) professional manual* (pp. 39–74). Odessa, FL: Psychological Assessment Resources.

Coté, G., & Hodgins, S. (1990). Co-occurring mental disorders among criminal offenders. *Bulletin of the American Academy of Psychiatry and the Law, 18*, 271–281.

Coté, G., & Hodgins, S. (1992). The prevalence of major mental disorders among homicide offenders. *International Journal of Law and Psychiatry, 15*, 89–99.

Craft, M. J., Stephenson, G., & Granger, C. (1964). A controlled trial of authoritarian and self-governing regimes with adolescent psychopaths. *American Journal of Orthopsychiatry, 34*, 543–554.

Craig, T. J. (1982). An epidemiological study of problems associated with violence among psychiatric inpatients. *American Journal of Psychiatry, 139*, 1262–1266.

Craissati, J., Falla, S., McClurg, G., & Beech, A. (2002). Risk, reconviction rates and pro-offending attitudes for child molesters in a complete geographical area of London. *Journal of Sexual Aggression, 8*, 22–38.

Cullen, E. (1993). The Grendon reconviction study, Part 1. *Prison Service Journal, 90*, 35–37.

Daigle-Zinn, W. J., & Andrews, D. A. (1980). Interpersonal skill training for young adult prisoners. *Canadian Journal of Criminology, 22*, 320–327.

Daly, M., & Wilson, M. (1988). Evolutionary social psychology and family homicide. *Science, 242*, 519–524.

Daubert v. Merrell Dow Pharmaceuticals, Inc., 509 U.S. 579 (1993).

Davidson, P. W., Cain, N. N., Sloan-Reeves, J. E., Giesow, V. E., Quijano, L. E., Van Heyningen, J., & Shoham, I. (1995). Crisis intervention for community-based individuals with developmental disabilities and behavioral and psychiatric disorders. *Mental Retardation, 33*, 21–30.

Dawes, R. M. (1994). *House of cards: Psychology and psychotherapy built on myth.* New York: Free Press.

Dawes, R. M., Faust, D., & Meehl, P. E. (1989). Clinical versus actuarial judgment. *Science, 243*, 1668–1674.

Deitch, D. A., Carleton, S., Koutsenok, I. B., & Marsolais, K. (2002). Therapeutic community treatment in prisons. In C. G. Leukefeld & F. Tims (Eds.), *Treatment of drug offenders: Policies and issues* (pp. 127–137). New York: Springer Publishing.

DeLeon, G. (1985). The therapeutic community: Status and evolution. *International Journal of the Addictions, 20*, 823–844.

Dempster, R. J., Hart, S. D., & Boer, D. P. (2002). *Prediction of sexually violent recidivism: A comparison of risk assessment instruments.* Unpublished manuscript.

Dennett, D. C. (1995). *Darwin's dangerous idea: Evolution and the meanings of life.* New York: Simon & Schuster.

Department of the Solicitor General of Canada. (2002). Recidivism and age: Follow-up data from 4,673 sexual offenders. *Journal of Interpersonal Violence, 17,* 1046–1062.

Dolan, B. (1998). Therapeutic community treatment for severe personality disorders. In T. Millon, E. Simonsen, M. Birket-Smith, & R. D. Davis (Eds.), *Psychopathy: Antisocial, criminal, and violent behavior* (pp. 407–430). New York: Guilford Press.

Douglas, K. S., Hart, S. D., Dempster, R. J., & Lyon, D. R. (1999, July). *Violence Risk Appraisal Guide (VRAG): Attempt at validation in a maximum-security forensic psychiatric sample.* Paper presented at the joint meeting of the American Psychology–Law Society and the European Association of Psychology and Law, Dublin, Ireland.

Douglas, K. S., & Ogloff, J. R. (2003). Multiple facets of risk for violence: The impact of judgmental specificity on structured decisions about violence risk. *International Journal of Forensic Mental Health, 2,* 19–34.

Downey, J. P. (1915). The separate care of the criminal insane. *Bulletin of the Ontario Hospitals for the Insane, 8,* 51–57.

Doyle, M., Dolan, M., & McGovern, J. (2002). The validity of North American risk assessment tools in predicting in-patient violent behaviour in England. *Legal & Criminological Psychology, 7,* 141–152.

Ducharme, J. M., & Feldman, M. A. (1992). Comparison of staff training strategies to promote generalized teaching skills. *Journal of Applied Behavior Analysis, 25,* 165–179.

Ducro, C., Claix, A., & Pham, T. H. (2002, September). *Assessment of the Static–99 in a Belgian sex offenders forensic population.* Paper presented at the European Conference on Psychology and Law, Leuven, Belgium.

Duguid, S. (1983). Origin and development of university education at Matsqui Institution. *Canadian Journal of Criminology, 25,* 295–308.

Duguid, S. (1985). What works in prison education? *Adult Education, 4,* 325–334.

Dunbar, R. I. M., Clark, A., & Hurst, N. L. (1995). Conflict and cooperation among the Vikings: Contingent behavioral decisions. *Ethology and Sociobiology, 16,* 233–246.

Durlak, J. A. (1979). Comparative effectiveness of paraprofessional and professional helpers. *Psychological Bulletin, 86,* 80–92.

Dvoskin, J. A., & Heilbrun, K. L. (2001). Risk assessment and release decision-making: Toward resolving the great debate. *Journal of the American Academy of Psychiatry and the Law, 29,* 6–10.

Dwyer, E. (1988). The history of the asylum in Great Britain and the United States. *Law and Mental Health: International Perspectives, 4,* 110–160.

Earls, C. M., Quinsey, V. L., & Castonguay, L. G. (1987). A comparison of three methods of scoring penile circumference changes. *Archives of Sexual Behavior, 16,* 493–500.

Eichelman, B. (1992). Aggressive behavior: From laboratory to clinic. *Archives of General Psychiatry, 49,* 488–489.

Einhorn, H. J. (1974). Expert judgment: Some necessary conditions and an example. *Journal of Applied Psychology, 59,* 562–571.

Einhorn, H. J., & Hogarth, R. M. (1978). Confidence in judgment: Persistence of the illusion of validity. *Psychological Review, 85,* 395–416.

Elbogen, E. B., & Huss, M. T. (2000). The role of serotonin in violence and schizophrenia: Implications for risk assessment. *Journal of Psychiatry and Law, 28,* 19–48.

Elbogen, E. B., Tomkins, A. J., Pothuloori, A. P., & Scalora, M. J. (2003). Documentation of violence risk information in psychiatric hospital patient charts: An empirical examination. *Journal of the American Academy of Psychiatry and the Law, 31,* 58–64.

Elliot, D. S., Huizinga, D., & Ageton, S. (1985). *Explaining delinquency and drug use.* Beverly Hills, CA: Sage.

English, K., Retzlaff, P., & Kleinsasser, D. (2002). The Colorado sex offender risk scale. *Journal of Child Sexual Abuse, 11,* 77–96.

Ereshefsky, L., & Lacombe, S. (1993). Pharmacological profile of risperidone. *Canadian Journal of Psychiatry, 38,* 80–88.

Esquirol, J. E. D. (1965). *Mental maladies: A treatise on insanity.* New York: Hafner. (Original English edition published 1845)

Estes, W. K. (1976). The cognitive side of probability learning. *Psychological Review, 83,* 37–64.

Fairweather, G. W., Saunders, D. H., Maynard, H., Cressler, D. L., & Black, D. S. (1969). *Community life for the mentally ill.* Chicago: Aldine.

Farkas, M. D., & Anthony, W. A. (1989). *Psychiatric rehabilitation programs: Putting theory into practice.* Baltimore: Johns Hopkins University Press.

Farrington, D. P. (2000). Adolescent violence: Findings and implications from the Cambridge Study. In G. Boswell (Ed.), *Violent children and adolescents: Asking the question why* (pp. 19–35). London: Whurr.

Fazel, S., & Danesh, J. (2002). Serious mental disorder in 23,000 prisoners: A systematic review of 62 surveys. *Lancet, 359,* 545–550.

Fedoroff, J. P., Wisner-Carlson, R., Dean, S., & Berlin, F. S. (1992). Medroxyprogesterone acetate in the treatment of paraphilic sexual disorders. *Journal of Offender Rehabilitation, 18,* 109–123.

Feierman, J. R. (1990). *Pedophilia: Biosocial dimensions.* New York: Springer-Verlag.

Feild, H. S. (1978). Attitudes toward rape: A comparative analysis of police, rapists, crisis counselors, and citizens. *Journal of Personality and Social Psychology, 36,* 156–179.

Firestone, P., Bradford, J. M., McCoy, M., Greenberg, D. M., Curry, S., & Larose, M. R. (2000). Prediction of recidivism in extrafamilial child molesters based on court-related assessments. *Sexual Abuse: Journal of Research & Treatment, 12,* 203–221.

Fisher, W. H., Dickey, B., Normand, S. L., Packer, I. K., Grudzinskas, A. J., & Azeni, H. (2002). Use of a state inpatient forensic system under managed mental health care. *Psychiatric Services, 53*, 447–451.

Fitch, J. H. (1962). Men convicted of sexual offences against children: A descriptive follow-up study. *British Journal of Criminology, 3*, 18–37.

Flint, J. (1995). Pathways from genotype to phenotype. In G. O'Brien & W. Yule (Eds.), *Behavioural phenotypes* (pp. 75–89). London: MacKeith Press.

Forer, B. R. (1949). The fallacy of personal validation: A classroom demonstration of gullibility. *Journal of Abnormal and Social Psychology, 44*, 118–123.

Forth, A. E., Hart, S. D., & Hare, R. D. (1990). Assessment of psychopathy in male young offenders. *Psychological Assessment: A Journal of Consulting and Clinical Psychology, 2*, 1–3.

Forth, A. E., Kosson, D. S., & Hare, R. D. (2004). *Hare Psychopathy Checklist: Youth version*. Toronto, Ontario, Canada: Multi-Health Systems.

Fowler, F. G., & Fowler, H. W. (1970). *The pocket Oxford dictionary of current English* (5th ed.). Oxford, England: Oxford University Press.

Freud, S. (1932). The acquisition of power over fire. *International Journal of Psycho-analysis, 13*, 405–410.

Freund, K. (1965). Diagnosing heterosexual pedophilia by means of a test for sexual interest. *Behavior Research and Therapy, 3*, 229–234.

Freund, K., & Blanchard, R. (1989). Phallometric diagnosis of pedophilia. *Journal of Consulting and Clinical Psychology, 57*, 100–105.

Friedman, M. L. (1986). *The case of Valentine Shortis: A true story of crime and politics in Canada*. Toronto, Ontario, Canada: University of Toronto Press.

Frisbie, L. V. (1969). *Another look at sex offenders in California* (California Mental Health Research Monograph No. 12). Sacramento: State of California Department of Mental Hygiene.

Frisbie, L. V., & Dondis, E. H. (1965). *Recidivism among treated sex offenders* (California Mental Health Research Monograph No. 5). Sacramento: State of California Department of Mental Hygiene.

Fritzon, K. (2001). An examination of the relationship between distance travelled and motivational aspects of firesetting behavior. *Journal of Environmental Psychology, 21*, 45–60.

Furby, L., Weinrott, M. R., & Blackshaw, L. (1989). Sex offender recidivism: A review. *Psychological Bulletin, 105*, 3–30.

Furr, K. D. (1993). Prediction of sexual or violent recidivism among sexual offenders: A comparison of prediction instruments. *Annals of Sex Research, 6*, 271–286.

Gabor, T. (1986). *The prediction of criminal behavior: Statistical approaches*. Toronto, Ontario, Canada: University of Toronto Press.

Gale, T. M., Hawley, C. J., & Sivakumaran, T. (2003). Do mental health professionals really understand probability? Implications for risk assessment and evidence-based practice. *Journal of Mental Health, 12*, 417–430.

Garb, H. N., & Boyle, P. A. (2003). Understanding why some clinicians use pseudoscientific methods: Findings from research on clinical judgment. In S. O. Lillienfeld, S. J. Lynn, & J. M. Lohr (Eds.), *Science and pseudoscience in clinical psychology* (pp. 17–38). New York: Guilford Press.

Garber, J., & Hollon, S. D. (1991). What can specificity designs say about causality in psychopathology research? *Psychological Bulletin, 110,* 129–136.

Gardner, W., Lidz, C. W., Mulvey, E. P., & Shaw, E. C. (1996). Clinical versus actuarial predictions of violence in patients with mental illnesses. *Journal of Consulting and Clinical Psychology, 64,* 602–609.

Garrido, V., Esteban, C., & Molero, C. (1995). The effectiveness in the treatment of psychopathy: A meta-analysis. *Issues in Criminological & Legal Psychology, 24,* 57–59.

Gathercole, C. E., Craft, M. J., McDougall, J., Barnes, H. M., & Peck, D. F. (1968). A review of 100 discharges from a special hospital. *British Journal of Criminology, 8,* 419–424.

Geller, J. L. (1987). Fire setting in the adult psychiatric population. *Hospital and Community Psychiatry, 38,* 501–506.

Geller, J. L. (1992a). Arson in review: From profit to pathology. *Clinical Forensic Psychiatry, 15,* 623–645.

Geller, J. L. (1992b). Pathological fire setting in adults. *International Journal of Law and Psychiatry, 15,* 283–302.

Geller, J. L., Erlen, J., & Pinkus, R. L. (1986). A historical appraisal of America's experience with "pyromania": A diagnosis in search of a disorder. *International Journal of Law and Psychiatry, 9,* 201–229.

Geller, J. L., Fisher, W. H., & Bertsch, G. (1992). Who repeats? A follow-up study of state hospital patients' fire setting behavior. *Psychiatric Quarterly, 63,* 143–157.

Geller, J. L., Fisher, W. H., & Moynihan, K. (1992). Adult lifetime prevalence of fire setting behaviors in a state hospital population. *Psychiatric Quarterly, 63,* 129–142.

Gendreau, P., Cullen, F. T., & Bonta, J. (1994). Intensive rehabilitation supervision: The next generation in community corrections. *Federal Probation, 58,* 72–78.

Gendreau, P., Grant, B. A., & Leipciger, M. (1979). Self-esteem, incarceration and recidivism. *Criminal Justice and Behavior, 6,* 67–73.

Gendreau, P., Madden, P. G., & Leipciger, M. (1979). Norms and recidivism for first incarcerates: Implications for programming. *Canadian Journal of Criminology, 21,* 1–26.

Gendreau, P., Madden, P. G., & Leipciger, M. (1980). Predicting recidivism with social history information and a comparison of their predictive power with psychometric variables. *Canadian Journal of Criminology, 22,* 328–337.

Gibbens, T. C. N., Pond, D. A., & Stafford-Clark, D. (1959). A follow-up study of criminal psychopaths. *Journal of Mental Science, 105,* 108–115.

Gibbens, T. C. N., Soothill, K. L., & Way, C. K. (1981). Sex offences against young girls: A long-term record study. *Psychological Medicine, 11,* 351–357.

Giles, T. R. (1990). Bias against behavior therapy in outcome reviews: Who speaks for the patient? *Behavior Therapy, 13,* 86–90.

Glover, A. J. J., Nicholson, D. E., Hemmati, T., Bernfeld, G. A., & Quinsey, V. L. (2002). A comparison of predictors of general and violent recidivism among high risk federal offenders. *Criminal Justice and Behavior, 29,* 235–249.

Glover, T., & Bernfeld, G. (1997, February). *Concurrent validation of the VRAG— Clinical and actuarial measures.* Symposium presented at the annual convention of the Ontario Psychological Association, Toronto, Ontario, Canada.

Goldberg, L. R. (1968). Simple models or simple processes? *American Psychologist, 23,* 483–496.

Goldberg, L. R. (1970). Man versus model of man: A rationale plus some evidence for a method of improving on clinical inferences. *Psychological Bulletin, 73,* 422–432.

Golden, R. R. (1982). A taxometric model for the detection of a conjectured latent taxon. *Multivariate Behavioral Research, 17,* 389–416.

Golden, R. R., & Meehl, P. E. (1979). Detection of the schizoid taxon with MMPI indicators. *Journal of Abnormal Psychology, 88,* 217–233.

Gordon, D. A., & Arbuthnot, J. (1987). Individual, group and family interventions. In H. C. Quay (Ed.), *Handbook of juvenile delinquency* (pp. 290–324). New York: Wiley.

Gordon, R. M., & Verdun-Jones, S. N. (1986). Mental health law and law reform in the Commonwealth: The rise of the "New Legalism"? In D. N. Weisstub (Ed.), *Law and mental health: International perspectives* (pp. 1–82). New York: Pergamon Press.

Gottfredson, G. D. (1984). A theory-ridden approach to program evaluation: A method for stimulating researcher–implementer collaboration. *American Psychologist, 39,* 1101–1112.

Gottfredson, M. R., Mitchell-Herzfeld, S. D., & Flanagan, T. J. (1982). Another look at the effectiveness of parole supervision. *Journal of Research in Crime and Delinquency, 19,* 277–298.

Government of Canada. (1977, March). *Minutes of proceedings and evidence of the House of Commons subcommittee on the penitentiary system in Canada* (2nd session of the 30th parliament, Issue No. 36). Ottawa, Ontario, Canada: Author.

Grann, M., Belfrage, H., & Tengstrom, A. (2000). Actuarial assessment of risk for violence: Predictive validity of the VRAG and historical part of the HCR–20. *Criminal Justice and Behavior, 27,* 97–114.

Grann, M., & Fazel, S. (2005, March). *Is mental disorder a risk factor for violent recidivism in offenders?* Paper presented at the Annual Conference of the American Psychology Law Society, La Jolla, CA.

Grann, M., & Wedin, I. (2002). Risk factors for recidivism among spousal assault and spousal homicide offenders. *Psychology, Crime and Law, 8,* 5–23.

Green, B., & Baglioni, A. J. (1998). Length of stay, leave and re-offending by patients from a Queensland security patients hospital. *Australian & New Zealand Journal of Psychiatry, 32,* 839–847.

Greenberg, D., Bradford, J., Firestone, P., & Curry, S. (2000). Recidivism of child molesters: A study of victim relationship with the perpetrator. *Child Abuse & Neglect, 24,* 1485–1494.

Greenland, C. (1984). Dangerous sexual offender legislation in Canada, 1948–1977: An experiment that failed. *Canadian Journal of Criminology, 26,* 1–13.

Greer, J. G., & Stuart, I. R. (1983). *The sexual aggressor: Current perspectives on treatment.* Toronto, Ontario, Canada: Van Nostrand Reinhold.

Gretton, H. M., McBride, M., Hare, R. D., O'Shaughnessy, R., & Kumka, G. (2001). Psychopathy and recidivism in adolescent sex offenders. *Criminal Justice and Behavior, 28,* 427–449.

Griffiths, D., Quinsey, V. L., & Hingsburger, D. (1989). *Changing inappropriate sexual behaviors: A community based approach for persons with developmental disabilities.* Toronto, Ontario, Canada: Brookes.

Grisso, T., & Appelbaum, P. S. (1993). Structuring the debate about ethical predictions of future violence. *Law and Human Behavior, 17,* 482–485.

Grove, W. M., & Meehl, P. E. (1996). Comparative efficiency of informal (subjective, impressionistic) and formal (mechanical, algorithmic) prediction procedures: The clinical–statistical controversy. *Psychology, Public Policy, and Law, 2,* 293–323.

Gulevich, G. D., & Bourne, P. G. (1970). Mental illness and violence. In D. N. Daniels, M. F. Gilula, & F. M. Ochburg (Eds.), *Violence and the struggle for existence* (pp. 309–326). Boston: Little, Brown.

Gunn, J. (1977). Criminal behaviour and mental disorder. *British Journal of Psychiatry, 130,* 317–329.

Gunn, J., Robertson, G., & Dell, S. (1978). *Psychiatric aspects of imprisonment.* London: Academic Press.

Hagan, M. P., Gust-Brey, K. L., Cho, M. E., & Dow, E. (2001). Eight-year comparative analyses of adolescent rapists, adolescent child molesters, other adolescent delinquents, and the general population. *International Journal of Offender Therapy & Comparative Criminology, 45,* 314–324.

Hall, G. C. N. (1995). Sexual offender recidivism revisited: A meta-analysis of recent treatment studies. *Journal of Consulting and Clinical Psychology, 63,* 802–809.

Hall, G. C. N., Shondrick, D. D., & Hirschman, R. (1993). The role of sexual arousal in sexually aggressive behavior: A meta-analysis. *Journal of Consulting and Clinical Psychology, 61,* 1091–1095.

Hanson, R. K. (2002). Recidivism and age: Follow-up data from 4,673 sexual offenders. *Journal of Interpersonal Violence, 17,* 1046–1062.

Hanson, R. K. (1997). *The development of a brief actuarial risk scale for sexual offense recidivism* (User Report 97-04). Ottawa, Ontario: Department of the Solicitor General of Canada.

Hanson, R. K., & Bussière, M. T. (1998). Predicting relapse: A meta-analysis of sexual offender recidivism studies. *Journal of Consulting and Clinical Psychology, 66,* 348–362.

Hanson, R. K., Cox, B. J., & Woszczyna, C. (1991). *Sexuality, personality and attitude: Questionnaires for sexual offenders: A review.* Ottawa, Ontario: Corrections Branch, Ministry of the Solicitor General of Canada.

Hanson, R. K., Gordon, A., Harris, A. J. R., Marques, J. K., Murphy, W., Quinsey, V. L., et al. (2002). First report of the collaborative outcome data project on the effectiveness of psychological treatment for sex offenders. *Sexual Abuse: A Journal of Research and Treatment, 14,* 169–194.

Hanson, R. K., & Harris, A. J. R. (2000). Where should we intervene? Dynamic predictors of sexual offense recidivism. *Criminal Justice and Behavior, 27,* 6–35.

Hanson, R. K., & Morton-Bourgon, K. (2004). *Predictors of sexual recidivism: An updated meta-analysis* (User Report 2004-02). Ottawa, Ontario: Public Safety and Emergency Preparedness Canada.

Hanson, R. K., Scott, H., & Steffy, R. A. (1995). A comparison of child molesters and nonsexual criminals: Risk predictors and long-term recidivism. *Journal of Research in Crime and Delinquency, 32,* 325–337.

Hanson, R. K., Steffy, R. A., & Gauthier, R. (1993). Long-term recidivism of child molesters. *Journal of Consulting and Clinical Psychology, 61,* 646–652.

Hanson, R. K., & Thornton, D. (2000). Improving risk assessments for sex offenders: A comparison of three actuarial scales. *Law and Human Behavior, 24,* 119–129.

Harding, J. P. (1949). The use of probability paper for the graphical analysis of polymodal frequency distribution. *Journal of the Marine Biological Association, 28,* 141–153.

Hare, R. D. (1970). *Psychopathy: Theory and research.* New York: Wiley.

Hare, R. D. (1983). Diagnosis of antisocial personality disorder in two prison populations. *American Journal of Psychiatry, 7,* 887–889.

Hare, R. D. (1985). Comparison of procedures for the assessment of psychopathy. *Journal of Consulting and Clinical Psychology, 53,* 7–16.

Hare, R. D. (1986). Twenty years of experience with the Cleckley psychopath. In W. H. Reid, D. Door, J. J. Walker, & J. W. Bonner (Eds.), *Unmasking the psychopath* (pp. 3–27). New York: Norton.

Hare, R. D. (1991). *The Revised Psychopathy Checklist.* Toronto, Ontario, Canada: Multi-Health Systems.

Hare, R. D. (1996). Psychopathy: A clinical construct whose time has come. *Criminal Justice and Behavior, 23,* 25–54.

Hare, R. D. (1998). *Scoring guidelines for the Hare PCL:SV.* Toronto, Ontario, Canada: Multi-Health Systems.

Hare, R. D. (2003). *Hare PCL–R* (2nd ed.). New York: Multi-Health Systems.

Hare, R. D., Harpur, T. J., Hakstian, A. R., Forth, A. E., Hart, S. D., & Newman, J. P. (1990). The revised Psychopathy Checklist: Reliability and factor structure. *Psychological Assessment: A Journal of Consulting and Clinical Psychology, 2,* 338–341.

Hare, R. D., Hart, S. D., & Harpur, T. J. (1991). Psychopathy and the *DSM–IV* criteria for antisocial personality disorder. *Journal of Abnormal Psychology, 100,* 391–398.

Hare, R. D., & McPherson, L. M. (1984). Violent and aggressive behavior by criminal psychopaths. *International Journal of Law and Psychiatry, 7*, 35–50.

Harpur, T. J., Hakstian, A. R., & Hare, R. D. (1988). Factor structure of the psychopathy checklist. *Journal of Consulting and Clinical Psychology, 56*, 741–747.

Harris, B., & Harvey, J. (1981). Attribution theory: From phenomenal causality to the intuitive social scientist and beyond. In C. Antaki (Ed.), *The psychology of ordinary explanations of social behavior* (pp. 57–95). New York: Academic Press.

Harris, G. T. (1989). The relationship between neuroleptic drug dose and the performance of psychiatric patients in a maximum security token economy program. *Journal of Behavior Therapy and Experimental Psychiatry, 20*, 57–67.

Harris, G. T. (2003). Men in his category have a 50% likelihood, but which half is he in? *Sexual Abuse: A Journal of Research and Treatment, 15*, 389–393.

Harris, G. T., & Hilton, N. Z. (2001). On interpreting moderate effects in interpersonal violence. *Journal of Interpersonal Violence, 16*, 1094–1098.

Harris, G. T., Hilton, N. Z., & Rice, M. E. (1993). Patients admitted to psychiatric hospital: Presenting problems and resolution at discharge. *Canadian Journal of Behavioural Sciences, 25*, 267–285.

Harris, G. T., Hilton, N. Z., Rice, M. E., Lalumière, M. L., & Quinsey, V. L. (2005, March). *Psychopathic sexuality*. Paper presented at the Annual Conference of the American Psychology–Law Society, La Jolla, CA.

Harris, G. T., & Rice, M. E. (1984). Mentally disordered fire setters: Psychodynamic versus empirical approaches. *International Journal of Law and Psychiatry, 7*, 19–24.

Harris, G. T., & Rice, M. E. (1990). An empirical approach to classification and treatment planning for psychiatric inpatients. *Journal of Clinical Psychology, 46*, 3–14.

Harris, G. T., & Rice, M. E. (1992). Reducing violence in institutions: Maintaining behaviour change. In R. D. Peters, R. J. McMahon, & V. L. Quinsey (Eds.), *Aggression and violence throughout the life span* (pp. 261–282). Newbury Park, CA: Sage.

Harris, G. T., & Rice, M. E. (1996a). The science in phallometric measurement of male sexual interest. *Current Directions in Psychological Science, 5*, 156–160.

Harris, G. T., & Rice, M. E. (1996b). A typology of mentally disordered fire setters and the fires they set. *Journal of Interpersonal Violence, 11*, 351–363.

Harris, G. T., & Rice, M. E. (1997). Mentally disordered offenders: What research says about effective service. In C. D. Webster & M. A. Jackson (Eds.), *Impulsivity: Theory, assessment and treatment* (pp. 361–393). New York: Guilford Press.

Harris, G. T., & Rice, M. E. (2003). Actuarial assessment of risk among sex offenders. *Annals of the New York Academy of Sciences, 989*, 198–210.

Harris, G. T., & Rice, M. E. (2005). *Aging, passage of time, psychopathy, and risk of violent recidivism*. Manuscript in preparation.

Harris, G. T., & Rice, M. E. (2005). Treatment of psychopathy: A review of empirical findings. In C. Patrick (Ed.), *The handbook of psychopathy* (pp. 555–572). New York: Guilford Press.

Harris, G. T., Rice, M. E., & Camilleri, J. A. (2004). Applying a forensic actuarial assessment (the Violence Risk Appraisal Guide) to nonforensic patients. *Journal of Interpersonal Violence, 19,* 1063–1074.

Harris, G. T., Rice, M. E., Chaplin, T. C., & Quinsey, V. L. (1999). Dissimulation in phallometric testing of rapists' sexual preferences. *Archives of Sexual Behavior, 28,* 223–232.

Harris, G. T., Rice, M. E., & Cormier, C. A. (1991a). Length of detention in matched groups of insanity acquittees and convicted offenders. *International Journal of Law and Psychiatry, 14,* 223–236.

Harris, G. T., Rice, M. E., & Cormier, C. A. (1991b). Psychopathy and violent recidivism. *Law and Human Behavior, 15,* 625–637.

Harris, G. T., Rice, M. E., & Cormier, C. A. (1994). Psychopaths: Is a therapeutic community therapeutic? *Therapeutic Communities, 15,* 283–300.

Harris, G. T., Rice, M. E., & Cormier, C. A. (2002). Prospective replication of the Violence Risk Appraisal Guide in predicting violent recidivism among forensic patients. *Law and Human Behavior, 26,* 377–394.

Harris, G. T., Rice, M. E., & Lalumière, M. L. (2001). Criminal violence: The roles of psychopathy, neurodevelopmental insults, and antisocial parenting. *Criminal Justice and Behavior, 28,* 402–426.

Harris, G. T., Rice, M. E., & Quinsey, V. L. (1993). Violent recidivism of mentally disordered offenders: The development of a statistical prediction instrument. *Criminal Justice and Behavior, 20,* 315–335.

Harris, G. T., Rice, M. E., & Quinsey, V. L. (1994). Psychopathy as a taxon: Evidence that psychopaths are a discrete class. *Journal of Consulting and Clinical Psychology, 62,* 387–397.

Harris, G. T., Rice, M. E., Quinsey, V. L., & Chaplin, T. C. (1996). Viewing time as a measure of sexual interest among child molesters and normal heterosexual men. *Behaviour Research and Therapy, 34,* 389–394.

Harris, G. T., Rice, M. E., Quinsey, V. L., Chaplin, T. C., & Earls, C. M. (1992). Maximizing the discriminant validity of phallometric assessment data. *Psychological Assessment: A Journal of Consulting and Clinical Psychology, 4,* 502–511.

Harris, G. T., Rice, M. E., Quinsey, V. L., & Durdle, B. M. (1995). *The assessment and treatment of mentally disordered offenders in Ontario.* (Available from Mental Health Programs and Services Branch, Ontario Ministry of Health, 5th Floor, 5700 Yonge Street, Toronto, Ontario, Canada M2M 4K5)

Harris, G. T., Rice, M. E., Quinsey, V. L., Lalumière, M. L., Boer, D., & Lang, C. (2003). A multi-site comparison of actuarial risk instruments for sex offenders. *Psychological Assessment: A Journal of Consulting and Clinical Psychology, 15,* 413–425.

Harris, G. T., Skilling, T. A., & Rice, M. E. (2001). The construct of psychopathy. In M. Tonry (Ed.), *Crime and justice: An annual review of research* (pp. 197–264). Chicago: University of Chicago Press.

Harris, G. T., & Varney, G. W. (1986). A ten year study of assaults and assaulters on a maximum security psychiatric unit. *Journal of Interpersonal Violence, 1,* 173–191.

Harris, J. A., Rushton, J. P., Hampson, E., & Jackson, D. N. (1996). Salivary testosterone and self-report aggressive and pro-social personality characteristics in men and women. *Aggressive Behavior, 22*, 321–331.

Hart, S. D., Kropp, P. R., & Hare, R. D. (1988). Performance of male psychopaths following conditional release from prison. *Journal of Consulting and Clinical Psychology, 56*, 227–232.

Haslam, N. (2003). The dimensional view of personality disorders: A review of the taxometric evidence. *Clinical Psychology Review, 23*, 75–93.

Hasselblad, V. (1966). Estimation of parameters for a mixture of normal distributions. *Technometrics, 8*, 431–444.

Hathaway, S. R., & McKinley, J. C. (1967). *Minnesota Multiphasic Personality Inventory, revised manual.* New York: Psychological Corporation.

Hattie, J. A., Sharpley, C. F., & Rogers, H. J. (1984). Comparative effectiveness of professional and paraprofessional helpers. *Psychological Bulletin, 95*, 534–541.

Hawkins, S. A., & Hastie, R. (1990). Hindsight: Biased judgments of past events after the outcomes are known. *Psychological Bulletin, 107*, 311–327.

Hedlund, J. L., Sletten, I. W., Altman, H., & Evenson, R. C. (1973). Prediction of patients who are dangerous to others. *Journal of Consulting and Clinical Psychology, 29*, 443–447.

Heilbrun, A. B., Heilbrun, L. C., & Heilbrun, K. L. (1978). Impulsive and premeditated homicide: An analysis of subsequent parole risk of the murderer. *Journal of Criminal Law and Criminology, 69*, 108–114.

Heilbrun, K. L. (1997). Prediction versus management models relevant to risk assessment: The importance of legal decision-making context. *Law & Human Behavior, 21*, 347–359.

Heilbrun, K. L., O'Neill, M. L., Strohman, L. K., Bowman, Q., & Philipson, J. (2000). Expert approaches to communicating violence risk. *Law and Human Behavior, 24*, 137–148.

Henderson, M., & Hewstone, M. (1984). Prison inmates' explanations for interpersonal violence: Accounts and attributions. *Journal of Consulting and Clinical Psychology, 52*, 789–794.

Henggeler, S. W. (1989). *Delinquency in adolescence.* Newbury Park, CA: Sage.

Hiday, V. A. (1999). Mental illness and the criminal justice system. In A. V. Horwitz & T. L. Scheid (Eds.), *A handbook for the study of mental health* (pp. 508–525). Cambridge, England: Cambridge University Press.

Hildebran, D. D., & Pithers, W. D. (1992). Relapse prevention: Application and outcome. In W. O'Donohue & J. H. Geer (Eds.), *The sexual abuse of children: Clinical issues* (Vol. 2, pp. 365–393). Hillsdale, NJ: Erlbaum.

Hildebrand, M., de Ruiter, C., & de Vogel, V. (2004). Psychopathy and sexual deviance in treated rapists: Association with sexual and nonsexual recidivism. *Sexual Abuse, 16*, 1–24.

Hill, R. W., Langevin, R., Paitich, D., Handy, L., Russon, A., & Wilkinson, L. (1982). Is arson an aggressive act or a property offense? A controlled study of psychiatric referrals, assaultive offenders and property offenders. *Canadian Journal of Psychiatry, 27*, 648–654.

Hilton, N. Z., & Harris, G. T. (2005). Predicting wife assault: A critical review and implications for policy and practice. *Trauma, Violence, & Abuse, 6*, 3–23.

Hilton, N. Z., Harris, G. T., Rawson, K., & Beach, C. (2005). Communication of risk information to forensic decision-makers. *Criminal Justice and Behavior, 32*, 97–116.

Hilton, N. Z., Harris, G. T., & Rice, M. E. (1998). On the validity of self-reported rates of interpersonal violence. *Journal of Interpersonal Violence, 13*, 58–72.

Hilton, N. Z., Harris, G. T., & Rice, M. E. (2000). The functions of aggression by male teenagers. *Journal of Personality and Social Psychology, 79*, 988–994.

Hilton, N. Z., Harris, G. T., & Rice, M. E. (2001). Predicting violence by serious wife assaulters. *Journal of Interpersonal Violence, 16*, 408–423.

Hilton, N. Z., Harris, G. T., & Rice, M. E. (2003a). Adolescents' perceptions of the seriousness of sexual aggression: Influence of gender, traditional attitudes, and self-reported experience. *Sexual Abuse: A Journal of Research and Treatment, 15*, 201–214.

Hilton, N. Z., Harris, G. T., & Rice, M. E. (2003b). Correspondence between self-report measures of interpersonal aggression. *Journal of Interpersonal Violence, 18*, 223–229.

Hilton, N. Z., Harris, G. T., Rice, M. E., Lang, C., Cormier, C. A., & Lines, K. J. (2004). A brief actuarial assessment for the prediction of wife assault recidivism: The Ontario Domestic Assault Risk Assessment. *Psychological Assessment, 16*, 267–275.

Hilton, N. Z., & Simmons, J. L. (1999). Adverse effects of poor behavior management on an inpatient's difficult behaviors. *Psychiatric Services, 50*, 964–966.

Hilton, N. Z., & Simmons, J. L. (2001). Actuarial and clinical risk assessment in decisions to release mentally disordered offenders from maximum security. *Law and Human Behavior, 25*, 393–408.

Hodgins, S. (1983). A follow-up study of persons found incompetent to stand trial and/or not guilty by reason of insanity in Quebec. *International Journal of Law and Psychiatry, 6*, 399–411.

Hodgins, S. (1987). Men found unfit to stand trial and/or not guilty by reason of insanity: Recidivism. *Canadian Journal of Criminology, 29*, 51–70.

Hodgins, S. (2000). Building mental health professionals' decisional models into tests of predictive validity: The accuracy of contextualized predictions of violence. In L. R. Bergman & R. B. Cairns (Eds.), *Developmental science and the holistic approach* (pp. 317–337). Mahwah, NJ: Erlbaum.

Hodgins, S., & Coté, G. (1990). Prevalence of mental disorders among penitentiary inmates in Quebec. *Canada's Mental Health, 38*, 1–4.

Hodgins, S., & Janson, C. G. (2002). *Criminality and violence among the mentally disordered.* Cambridge, England: Cambridge University Press.

Hoffman, P. B. (1994). Twenty years of operational use of a risk prediction instrument: The United States Parole Commission's Salient Factor Score. *Journal of Criminal Justice, 22,* 477–494.

Hoffman, P. B., & Beck, J. L. (1985). Recidivism among released federal prisoners: Salient factor score and five-year follow-up. *Criminal Justice and Behavior, 12,* 501–507.

Hogarty, G. E., Anderson, C. M., Reiss, D. J., Kornblith, S. J., Greenwald, D. P., Javna, C. D., Madonia, M. J., et al. (1986). Family psychoeducation, social skills training, and maintenance chemotherapy in the aftercare treatment of schizophrenia: I. One-year effects of a controlled study on relapse and expressed emotion. *Archives of General Psychiatry, 43,* 633–642.

Hoge, S. K., & Grisso, T. (1992). Accuracy and expert testimony. *Bulletin of the American Academy of Psychiatry and the Law, 20,* 67–76.

Holland, T. R., Holt, N., & Brewer, D. L. (1978). Social roles and information utilization in parole decision-making. *Journal of Social Psychology, 106,* 111–120.

Holloway, E. L., & Neufeldt, S. A. (1995). Supervision: Its contributions to treatment efficacy. *Journal of Consulting and Clinical Psychology, 63,* 207–213.

Horley, J., & Quinsey, V. L. (1994). Assessing the cognitions of child molesters: Use of the semantic differential with incarcerated offenders. *Journal of Sex Research, 31,* 171–178.

Horley, J., & Quinsey, V. L. (1995). Child molesters' construal of themselves, other adults, and children. *Journal of Constructivist Psychology, 8,* 193–212.

Howard, A. (1987). Work samples and simulations in competency evaluation. In B. A. Edelstein & E. S. Berler (Eds.), *Evaluation and accountability in clinical training* (pp. 55–76). New York: Plenum Press.

Hunter, J. E., & Schmidt, F. L. (1990). *Methods of meta-analysis: Correcting error and bias in research findings.* Newbury Park, CA: Sage.

Hurley, W., & Monahan, T. (1969). Arson. *British Journal of Criminology, 9,* 4–21.

Huss, M. T., Odeh, M. S., & Zeiss, R. A. (2004, March 6). *The use of risk cues in clinical predictions of violence.* Paper presented at the Annual Conference of the American Psychology–Law Society, Scottsdale, AZ.

Jackson, H. F., Hope, S., & Glass, C. (1987). Why are arsonists not violent offenders? *Therapy and Comparative Criminology, 31,* 143–151.

Janus, E. S., & Meehl, P. E. (1997). Assessing the legal standard for predictions of dangerousness in sex offender commitment proceedings. *Psychology, Public Policy and Law, 3,* 33–64.

Jenkins, W. O., Burton, M. C., de Valera, E. K., DeVine, M. D., Witherspoon, A. D., & Muller, J. B. (1972). *The measurement and prediction of criminal behavior and recidivism: The Environmental Deprivation Scale (EDS) and the Maladaptive Behavior Record (MBR).* Elmore, AL: Rehabilitation Research Foundation.

Jones, A. (1978). Closing Penetanguishene Reformatory: An attempt to deinstitutionalize treatment of juvenile offenders in early twentieth century Ontario. *Ontario History, 70,* 227–244.

Jones, B. L., Nagin, D. S., & Roeder, K. (1998). *A SAS procedure based on mixture models for estimating developmental trajectories.* Pittsburgh, PA: Carnegie Mellon University.

Jones, M. (1956). The concept of a therapeutic community. *American Journal of Psychiatry, 38,* 647–650.

Jones, M. (1968). *Social psychiatry in practice.* Harmondsworth, England: Penguin.

Kadden, R. M., Cooney, N. L., Getter, H., & Litt, M. D. (1989). Matching alcoholics to coping skills or interactional therapies: Posttreatment outcomes. *Journal of Consulting and Clinical Psychology, 57,* 698–704.

Kahneman, D., & Tversky, A. (1973). On the psychology of prediction. *Psychological Review, 80,* 237–251.

Kanji, G. K. (1993). *100 statistical tests.* Thousand Oaks, CA: Sage.

Kazdin, A. E. (1987). Treatment of antisocial behavior in children: Current status and future directions. *Psychological Bulletin, 102,* 187–203.

Kelly, E. L., & Fiske, D. W. (1951). *The prediction of performance in clinical psychology.* Ann Arbor: University of Michigan Press.

Kenny, D. T., Keogh, T., & Seidler, K. (2001). Predictors of recidivism in Australian juvenile sex offenders: Implications for treatment. *Sexual Abuse: Journal of Research & Treatment, 13,* 131–148.

Kerlinger, F. N., & Pedhazur, E. J. (1973). *Multiple regression in behavioral research.* New York: Rinehart & Winston.

Klassen, D., & O'Connor, W. A. (1988). A prospective study of predictors of violence in adult male mental health admissions. *Law and Human Behavior, 12,* 143–158.

Klein, N. C., Alexander, J. F., & Parsons, B. V. (1977). Impact of family systems intervention on recidivism and sibling delinquency: A model of primary prevention and program evaluation. *Journal of Consulting and Clinical Psychology, 45,* 469–474.

Knoke, D., & Burke, P. J. (1980). *Log-linear models.* Newbury Park, CA: Sage.

Kocsis, R. N., & Cooksey, R. W. (2002). Criminal psychological profiling of serial arson crimes. *International Journal of Offender Therapy and Comparative Criminology, 46,* 631–656.

Konecni, V., & Ebbesen, E. B. (1984). The mythology of legal decision making. *International Journal of Law and Psychiatry, 7,* 5–18.

Kozol, H. L., Boucher, R. J., & Garofalo, R. F. (1972). The diagnosis and treatment of dangerousness. *Crime and Delinquency, 18,* 371–392.

Krauss, D. (2004, March). *Judges' ability to clinically adjust risk of recidivism under the Federal Sentencing Guidelines.* Paper presented at the Conference of the American Psychology–Law Society, Scottsdale, AZ.

Krivacska, J. J., & Money, J. (1994). *Handbook of forensic sexology: Biomedical and criminological perspectives.* New York: Prometheus Books.

Kroner, D. G., & Loza, W. (2001). Evidence for the efficacy of self-report in predicting violent and nonviolent criminal recidivism. *Journal of Interpersonal Violence, 16,* 168–177.

Kroner, D. G., & Mills, J. F. (1997, February). *The VRAG: Predicting institutional misconduct in violent offenders.* Paper presented at the Annual Convention of the Ontario Psychological Association, Toronto, Ontario, Canada.

Kroner, D. G., & Mills, J. F. (2001). The accuracy of five risk appraisal instruments in predicting institutional misconduct and new convictions. *Criminal Justice and Behavior, 28,* 471–489.

Kropp, R. P., Hart, S. D., Webster, C. D., & Eaves, D. (1995). *The Spousal Assault Risk Assessment Guide (SARA).* Vancouver: British Columbia Institute Against Family Violence.

Lafave, H. G., de Souza, H. R., & Gerber, G. J. (1996). Assertive community treatment of severe mental illness: A Canadian experience. *Psychiatric Services, 47,* 757–759.

Lalumière, M. L., Chalmers, L. J., Quinsey, V. L., & Seto, M. C. (1996). A test of the mate deprivation hypothesis of sexual coercion. *Ethology and Sociobiology, 17,* 299–318.

Lalumière, M. L., & Harris, G. T. (1998). Common questions regarding the use of phallometric testing with sexual offenders. *Sexual Abuse: A Journal of Research and Treatment, 10,* 227–237.

Lalumière, M. L., Harris, G. T., Quinsey, V. L., & Rice, M. E. (2005). *The causes of rape: Understanding male propensity for sexual aggression.* Washington, DC: American Psychological Association.

Lalumière, M. L., Harris, G. T., & Rice, M. E. (2001). Psychopathy and developmental instability. *Evolution and Human Behavior, 22,* 75–92.

Lalumière, M. L., & Quinsey, V. L. (1993). The sensitivity of phallometric measures with rapists. *Annals of Sex Research, 6,* 123–138.

Lalumière, M. L., & Quinsey, V. L. (1994). The discriminability of rapists from non-sex offenders using phallometric measures: A meta-analysis. *Criminal Justice and Behavior, 21,* 150–175.

Lalumière, M. L., & Quinsey, V. L. (1996). Sexual deviance, antisociality, mating effort, and the use of sexually coercive behaviors. *Personality and Individual Differences, 21,* 33–48.

Lalumière, M. L., & Quinsey, V. L., Harris, G. T., Rice, M. E., & Trautrimas, C. (2003). Are rapists differentially aroused by coercive sex in phallometric assessments? *Annals of the New York Academy of Sciences, 989,* 211–224.

Lam, J. N., McNiel, D. E., & Binder, R. L. (2000). The relationship between patients' gender and violence leading to staff injuries. *Psychiatric Services, 51,* 1167–1170.

Lande, S. D. (1980). A combination of orgasmic reconditioning and covert sensitization in the treatment of a fire fetish. *Journal of Behavior Therapy and Experimental Psychiatry, 11,* 291–296.

Langevin, R. (1983). *Sexual strands: Understanding and treating sexual anomalies in men.* Hillsdale, NJ: Erlbaum.

Langevin, R., Curnoe, S., Federoff, P., Bennett, R., Langevin, M., Peever, C., et al. (2004). Lifetime sex offender recidivism: A 25-year follow-up study. *Canadian Journal of Criminology, 46,* 531–552.

Langstroem, N. (2002). Long-term follow-up of criminal recidivism in young sex offenders: Temporal patterns and risk factors. *Psychology, Crime & Law, 8,* 41–58.

Langstroem, N., & Grann, M. (2000). Risk for criminal recidivism among young sex offenders. *Journal of Interpersonal Violence, 15,* 855–871.

Law Reform Commission of Canada. (1976). *A report to parliament on mental disorder in the criminal process.* Ottawa, Ontario: Information Canada.

Laws, D. R. (Ed.). (1989). *Relapse prevention with sex offenders.* New York: Guilford Press.

Leith, K. P., & Baumeister, R. F. (1996). Why do bad moods increase self-defeating behavior? Emotion, risk tasking, and self-regulation. *Journal of Personality & Social Psychology, 71,* 1250–1267.

Levin, S. M., & Stava, L. (1987). Personality characteristics of sex offenders: A review. *Archives of Sexual Behavior, 16,* 57–79.

Levenson, M. R., Kiehl, K. A., & Fitzpatrick, C. M. (1995). Assessing psychopathic attributes in a noninstitutionalized population. *Journal of Personality and Social Psychology, 68,* 151–158.

Lewis, N. (1965). Pathological fire setting and sexual motivation. In R. Slovenko (Ed.), *Sexual behavior and the law* (pp. 627–641). Springfield, IL: Charles C Thomas.

Lewis, N. D. C., & Yarnell, H. (1951). Pathological fire setting (pyromania). *Nervous and Mental Disease Monographs, 82.* New York: Coolidge Foundation.

Liberman, R. P. (Ed.). (1988). *Psychiatric rehabilitation of chronic mental patients.* Washington, DC: American Psychiatric Press.

Liberman, R. P., Mueser, K. T., & Wallace, C. J. (1986). Social skills training for schizophrenic individuals at risk for relapse. *American Journal of Psychiatry, 143,* 523–526.

Lidz, C. W., Mulvey, E. P., & Gardner, W. (1993). The accuracy of predictions of violence to others. *Journal of the American Medical Association, 269,* 1007–1011.

Lieb, R. (2004, October). *Community notification: A decade of lessons.* Plenary session at the annual conference of the Association for the Treatment of Sexual Abusers, Albuquerque, NM.

Lieb, R., Quinsey, V. L., & Berliner, L. (1998). Sexual predators and social policy. *Crime and Justice: A Review of Research, 23,* 43–114.

Lindqvist, P., & Allebeck, P. (1989). Schizophrenia and assaultive behaviour: The role of alcohol and drug abuse. *Acta Psychiatrica Scandinavica, 82,* 191–195.

Lindsay, W., & Macloed, F. (2001). A review of forensic learning-disability research. *British Journal of Forensic Practice, 3,* 4–10.

Lindsay, W. R., Murphy, L., Smith, G., Murphy, D., Edwards, Z., Grieve, A., et al. (2004). *The Dynamic Risk Assessment and Management System: An assessment of immediate risk of violence for individuals with offending and challenging behaviour.* Manuscript submitted for publication.

Lindsay, W., Taylor, J., & Sturmey, P. (Eds.). (2004). *Offenders with developmental disabilities.* New York: Wiley.

Link, B. G., Andrews, D. A., & Cullen, F. T. (1992). The violent and illegal behavior of mental patients reconsidered. *American Sociological Review, 57,* 275–292.

Link, B. G., & Stueve, A. (1994). Psychotic symptoms and the violent/illegal behavior of mental patients compared to community controls. In J. Monahan & H. J. Steadman (Eds.), *Violence and mental disorder: Developments in risk assessment* (pp. 137–159). Chicago: University of Chicago Press.

Linnoila, M., DeJong, J., & Virkkunen, M. (1989). Family history of alcoholism in violent offenders and impulsive fire setters. *Archives of General Psychiatry, 46,* 613–616.

Lipsey, M. W. (1992). Juvenile delinquency treatment: A meta-analytic inquiry into the variability of effects. In T. D. Cook (Ed.), *Meta-analysis for explanation: A casebook* (pp. 83–126). New York: Russell Sage.

Lipsey, M. W., & Wilson, D. B. (1993). The efficacy of psychological, educational, and behavioral treatment: Confirmation from meta-analysis. *American Psychologist, 48,* 1181–1209.

Lipton, D. S. (1998). Therapeutic community treatment programming in corrections. *Psychology, Crime & Law, 4,* 213–263.

Lipton, H. (1950). The psychopath. *Journal of Criminal Law, Criminology, and Police Science, 6,* 399–411.

Litwack, T. R. (2001). Actuarial versus clinical assessments of dangerousness. *Psychology, Public Policy, and Law, 7,* 409–443.

Loeber, R. (1990). Development and risk factors of juvenile antisocial behavior and delinquency. *Clinical Psychology Review, 10,* 1–41.

Loeber, R., & Stouthamer-Loeber, M. (1998). Development of juvenile aggression and violence: Some common misconceptions and controversies. *American Psychologist, 53,* 242–259.

London, L. S., & Caprio, F. S. (1950). *Sexual deviations.* Washington, DC: Linacre Press.

Lovell, D., Gagliardi, G. J., & Peterson, P. D. (2002). Recidivism and use of services among persons with mental illness after release from prison. *Psychiatric Services, 53,* 1290–1296.

Loza, W., & Dhaliwal, G. K. (1997). Psychometric evaluation of the Risk Appraisal Guide (RAG): A tool for assessing violent recidivism. *Journal of Interpersonal Violence, 12,* 779–793.

Loza, W., Dhaliwal, G., Kroner, D. G., & Loza-Fanous, A. (2000). Reliability, construct, and concurrent validities of the Self-Appraisal Questionnaire: A tool for assessing violent and nonviolent recidivism. *Criminal Justice & Behavior, 27,* 356–374.

Loza, W., & Loza-Fanous, A. (2001). The effectiveness of the Self-Appraisal Questionnaire in predicting offenders' postrelease outcome. *Criminal Justice and Behavior, 28,* 105–121.

Loza, W., Villeneuve, D. B., & Loza-Fanous, A. (2002). Predictive validity of the Violence Risk Appraisal Guide: A tool for assessing violent offenders' recidivism. *International Journal of Law and Psychiatry, 25,* 85–92.

Lynam, D. R. (1996). Early identification of chronic offenders: Who is the fledgling psychopath? *Psychological Bulletin, 120,* 209–234.

Lynch, D. O. (1937). Some observations on the criminally insane with special reference to those charged with murder. *Ontario Journal of Neuro-Psychiatry, 12,* 39–52.

Macdonald, J. M. (1977). *Bombers and fire setters.* Springfield, IL: Charles C Thomas.

Maden, A. (2003). Standardised risk assessment: Why all the fuss? *Psychiatric Bulletin, 27,* 201–204.

Maier, G. J. (1976). Therapy in prisons. In J. R. Lion & D. J. Madden (Eds.), *Rage, hate, assault and other forms of violence* (pp. 113–133). New York: Spectrum.

Malamuth, N. M. (1996). The confluence model of sexual aggression: Feminist and evolutionary perspectives. In D. M. Buss & N. M. Malamuth (Eds.), *Sex, power, conflict: Evolutionary and feminist perspectives* (pp. 269–295). New York: Oxford University Press.

Malamuth, N. M., Heavy, C. L., & Linz, D. (1993). Predicting men's antisocial behavior against women: The interaction model of sexual aggression. In G. C. N. Hall, R. Hirschman, J. R. Graham, & M. S. Zaragoza (Eds.), *Sexual aggression: Issues in etiology, assessment, and treatment* (pp. 63–97). Bristol, PA: Taylor & Francis.

Malcolm, P. B., Andrews, D. A., & Quinsey, V. L. (1993). Discriminant and predictive validity of phallometrically measured sexual age and gender preferences. *Journal of Interpersonal Violence, 8,* 486–501.

Maller, J. O. (1971). *The therapeutic community with chronic mental patients.* Basel, Switzerland: S. Karger.

Mamuza, J. (2000). *Do actuarial assessments fall victim to base rate neglect?* Unpublished doctoral dissertation, Queen's University at Kingston, Ontario, Canada.

Mandelzys, N. (1979). Correlates of offense severity and recidivism probability in a Canadian sample. *Journal of Clinical Psychology, 35,* 897–907.

Marcus, D. K., John, S. L., & Edens, J. (2004). A taxometric analysis of psychopathic personality. *Journal of Abnormal Psychology, 113,* 626–635.

Marques, J. K., Nelson, C., West, M. A., & Day, D. M. (1994). The relationship between treatment goals and recidivism among child molesters. *Behavior Research and Therapy, 32,* 577–588.

Marques, J. K., Wiederanders, M., Day, D. M., Nelson, C., & Ommeren, A. V. (2005). Effects of a relapse prevention program on sexual recidivism: Final results from California's Sex Offender Treatment and Evaluation Project (SOTEP). *Sexual Abuse: A Journal of Research and Treatment, 17,* 79–107.

Marshall, W. L., & Barbaree, H. E. (1988). The long-term evaluation of a behavioral treatment program for child molesters. *Behavior Research and Therapy, 26*, 499–511.

Marshall, W. L., Fernandez, Y. M., Serran, G. A., Mulloy, R., Thornton, D., Mann, R. E., et al. (2003). Process variables in the treatment of sexual offenders: A review of the relevant literature. *Aggression & Violent Behavior, 8*, 205–234.

Marshall, W. L., Laws, D. R., & Barbaree, H. E. (1990). *Handbook of sexual assault: Issues, theories, and treatment of the offender.* New York: Plenum Press.

Matson, S., & Lieb, R. (1996). *Community notification in Washington State: 1996 survey of law enforcement.* Olympia: Washington State Institute for Public Policy.

Mavromatis, M., & Lion, J. R. (1977). A primer on pyromania. *Diseases of the Nervous System, 38*, 954–955.

McBride, M. (1999, February). *Predicting violence among federal inmates: Corrections Research Forum, Toronto.* Unpublished doctoral dissertation, University of British Columbia, Canada.

McClintock, M. K., & Herdt, G. (1996). Rethinking puberty: The development of sexual attraction. *Current Directions in Psychological Science, 5*(6), 178–183.

McCord, J. (1978). A thirty-year follow-up of treatment effects. *American Psychologist, 33*, 284–289.

McCord, W. M. (1982). *The psychopath and milieu therapy.* New York: Academic Press.

McCormick, C. T. (1954). *Handbook of the law of evidence.* St. Paul, MN: West.

McGarry, A. L. (1970). Titicut follies revisited: A long range plan for the mentally disordered offender in Massachusetts. *Mental Hygiene, 54*, 20–27.

McGraw, K. O., & Wong, S. P. (1992). A common language effect size statistic. *Psychological Bulletin, 111*, 361–365.

McKerracher, B., & Dacre, A. (1966). A study of arsonists in a special security hospital. *British Journal of Psychiatry, 11*, 1151–1164.

McKnight, C. K., Mohr, J. W., & Swadron, B. B. (1962). The mentally ill offender in the Oak Ridge Hospital Unit. *Criminal Law Quarterly, 5*, 248–258.

McMurran, M., Egan, V., & Ahmady, S. (1998). A retrospective evaluation of a therapeutic community for mentally disordered offenders. *Journal of Forensic Psychiatry, 9*, 103–113.

McNiel, D. E., & Binder, R. L. (1994). Screening for risk of inpatient violence: Validation of an actuarial tool. *Law and Human Behavior, 18*, 579–586.

McNiel, D. E., Eisner, J. P., & Binder, R. L. (2000). The relationship between command hallucinations and violence. *Psychiatric Services, 51*, 1288–1292.

McNiel, D. E., Gregory, A. L., Lam, J. N., Binder, R. L., & Sullivan, G. R. (2003). Utility of decision support tools for assessing acute risk of violence. *Journal of Consulting and Clinical Psychology, 71*, 945–953.

Mealey, L. (1995). The sociobiology of sociopathy: An integrated evolutionary model. *Behavioral and Brain Sciences, 18*, 523–599.

Mednick, S. A., Gabrielli, W. F., & Hutchings, R. (1983). Genetic influences in criminal behavior: Evidence from an adoption cohort. In K. T. VanDusen & S. A. Mednick (Eds.), *Prospective studies of crime and delinquency* (pp. 39–71). Boston: Kluwer–Nijhoff.

Mednick, S. A., Schulsinger, F., Teasdale, T. W., Schulsinger, H., Venables, P., & Rock, D. (1978). Schizophrenia in high-risk children: Sex differences in predisposing factors. In G. Serban (Ed.), *Cognitive defects in the development of mental illness* (pp. 169–197). New York: Brunner/Mazel.

Meehl, P. E. (1954). *Clinical vs. statistical prediction.* Minneapolis: University of Minnesota Press.

Meehl, P. E. (1973). *Psychodiagnosis: Selected papers.* Oxford, England: University of Minnesota Press.

Meehl, P. E. (1992). Factors and taxa, traits and types, differences in degree and differences in kind. *Journal of Personality, 60,* 117–173.

Meehl, P. E. (1996). Bootstraps taxometrics: Solving the classification problem in psychopathology. *American Psychologist, 50,* 266–275.

Meehl, P. E., & Golden, R. R. (1982). Taxometric methods. In P. C. Kendall & J. N. Butcher (Eds.), *Handbook of research methods in clinical psychology* (pp. 127–181). New York: Wiley.

Megargee, E. I. (1970). The prediction of violence with psychological tests. In C. D. Spielberger (Ed.), *Current topics in clinical and community psychology* (Vol. 2, pp. 98–156). New York: Academic Press.

Megargee, E. I., Cook, P. E., & Mendelsohn, G. A. (1967). Development and evaluation of an MMPI scale of assaultiveness in overcontrolled individuals. *Journal of Abnormal Psychology, 72,* 519–528.

Melton, G. B., Petrila, J., Poythress, N. G., & Slobogin, C. (1987). *Psychological evaluations for the courts: A handbook for mental health professionals and lawyers.* New York: Guilford Press.

Melton, G. B., Petrila, J., Poythress, N. G., & Slobogin, C. (1997). *Psychological evaluations for the courts.* New York: Guilford Press.

Menditto, A. A. (2002). A social-learning approach to the rehabilitation of individuals with severe mental disorders who reside in forensic facilities. *Psychiatric Rehabilitation Skills, 6,* 73–93.

Menditto, A. A., Beck, N. C., Stuve, P., Fisher, J. A., Stacy, M., Logue, M. B., et al. (1996). Effectiveness of clozapine and a social learning program for severely disabled psychiatric inpatients. *Psychiatric Services, 47,* 46–51.

Menzies, R. J., Chunn, D. E., & Webster, C. D. (1992). Female follies: The forensic psychiatric assessment of women defendants. *International Journal of Law and Psychiatry, 15,* 179–193.

Menzies, R. J., & Webster, C. D. (1987). Where they go and what they do: The longitudinal careers of forensic patients in the medicolegal complex. *Canadian Journal of Criminology, 29,* 275–293.

Menzies, R. J., Webster, C. D., & Sepejak, D. S. (1985). Hitting the forensic sound barrier: Predictions of dangerousness in a pre-trial clinic. In C. D. Webster, M.

H. Ben-Aron, & S. J. Hucker (Eds.), *Dangerousness: Probability and prediction, psychiatric and public policy* (pp. 115–143). New York: Cambridge University Press.

Mewett, A. W. (1961). Habitual criminal legislation under the criminal code. *Canadian Bar Review, 39*, 43–58.

Michelson, L. (1987). Cognitive–behavioral strategies in the prevention and treatment of antisocial disorders in children and adolescents. In J. D. Burchard & S. N. Burchard (Eds.), *Prevention of delinquent behavior* (pp. 275–310). Newbury Park, CA: Sage.

Milan, M. A. (1987). Token economy programs in closed institutions. In E. K. Morris & C. J. Braukmann (Eds.), *Behavioral approaches to crime and delinquency: A handbook of application, research and concepts* (pp. 195–222). New York: Plenum Press.

Miller, G. E., & Prinz, R. J. (1990). Enhancement of social learning family interventions for childhood conduct disorder. *Psychological Bulletin, 108*, 291–307.

Milloy, C. (2003). *Six-year follow-up of released sex offenders recommended for commitment under Washington's sexually violent predator law, where no petition was filed* (Document Number 03-12-1101). Olympia, WA: Washington State Institute for Public Policy.

Mills, J. F., Jones, M. N., & Kroner, D. G. (in press). An examination of the generalizability of the LSI–R and VRAG probability bins. *Criminal Justice and Behavior*.

Moffitt, T. E. (1993). Adolescence-limited and life-course-persistent antisocial behavior: A developmental taxonomy. *Psychological Review, 100*, 674–701.

Mohr, J. W., Turner, R. E., & Jerry, M. B. (1964). *Pedophilia and exhibitionism.* Toronto, Ontario, Canada: University of Toronto Press.

Molof, M. J. (1965). *Prediction of future assaultive behavior among youthful offenders* (Research Report 41). Sacramento: California Department of Youth Authority.

Monahan, J. (1978). Prediction research and the emergency commitment of dangerous mentally ill persons: A reconsideration. *American Journal of Psychiatry, 135*, 198–201.

Monahan, J. (1981). *Predicting violent behavior: An assessment of clinical techniques.* Beverly Hills, CA: Sage.

Monahan, J. (1992). Mental disorder and violent behavior. *American Psychologist, 47*, 511–521.

Monahan, J. (1995). Review of the book *The violence prediction scheme. Criminal Justice and Behavior, 22*, 446–455.

Monahan, J., & Arnold, J. (1996). Violence by people with mental illness: A consensus statement by advocates and researchers. *Psychiatric Rehabilitation Journal, 19*, 67–70.

Monahan, J., & Davis, S. K. (1983). Mentally disordered sex offenders. In J. Monahan & H. J. Steadman (Eds.), *Mentally disordered offenders: Perspectives from law and social science* (pp. 191–204). New York: Plenum Press.

Monahan, J., Davis, S. K., Hartstone, E., & Steadman, H. J. (1983). Prisoners transferred to mental hospitals. In J. Monahan & H. J. Steadman (Eds.), *Mentally disordered offenders: Perspectives from law and social science* (pp. 233–244). New York: Plenum Press.

Monahan, J., Heilbrun, K., Silver, E., Nabors, E., Bone, J., & Slovic, P. (2002). Communicating violence risk: Frequency formats, vivid outcomes, and forensic settings. *International Journal of Forensic Mental Health, 1*, 121–126.

Monahan, J., & Silver, E. (2003). Judicial decision thresholds for violence risk management. *International Journal of Forensic Mental Health, 2*, 1–6

Monahan, J., & Steadman, H. J. (1983). *Mentally disordered offenders: Perspectives from law and social science.* New York: Plenum Press.

Monahan, J., & Steadman, H. J. (1996). Violent storms and violent people: How meteorology can inform risk communication in mental health law. *American Psychologist, 51*, 931–938.

Monahan, J., Steadman, H., Silver, E., Appelbaum, P. S., Clark Robbins, P., Mulvey, E. P., et al. (2001). *Rethinking risk assessment: The MacArthur study of mental disorder and violence.* New York: Oxford University Press.

Morrow, W. R., & Peterson, D. G. (1966). Follow-up of discharged psychiatric offenders (not guilty by reason of insanity and criminal sexual psychopaths). *Journal of Criminal Law, 57*, 31–34.

Morton, A. (2003). *Philosophy in practice: An introduction to the main questions.* London: Blackwell.

Mossman, D. (1994). Assessing predictions of violence: Being accurate about accuracy. *Journal of Consulting and Clinical Psychology, 62*, 783–792.

Motiuk, L. L., Bonta, J., & Andrews, D. A. (1986). Classification in correctional halfway houses: The relative and incremental predictive criterion validities of the Megargee MMPI and LSI systems. *Criminal Justice and Behavior, 13*, 33–46.

Motiuk, L. L., & Porporino, F. J. (1989). *Offender risk/needs assessment: A study of conditional releases.* Ottawa, Ontario: Solicitor General Canada.

Motiuk, L. L., & Porporino, F. J. (1991). *The prevalence, nature and severity of mental health problems among federal male inmates in Canadian penitentiaries* (Research Report No. R-24). Ottawa, Ontario: Correctional Service Canada.

Nadeau, J., Nadeau, B., Smiley, W. C., & McHattie, L. (1999, November). *The PCL–R and VRAG as predictors of institutional behaviour.* Paper presented at the conference on Risk Assessment and Risk Management: Implications for the Prevention of Violence, Vancouver, British Columbia, Canada.

Nagin, D. S. (1999). Analyzing developmental trajectories: A semiparametric, group-based approach. *Psychological Methods, 2*, 139–157.

Neale, J. M., & Oltmanns, T. F. (1980). *Schizophrenia.* New York: Wiley.

Nicholls, T. L., Vincent, G. M., Whittemore, K. E., & Ogloff, J. R. P. (1999, November). *Assessing risk of inpatient violence in a sample of forensic psychiatric patients: Comparing the PCL:SV, HCR–20, and VRAG.* Paper presented at the conference Risk Assessment and Risk Management: Implications for the Prevention of Violence, Vancouver, British Columbia, Canada.

Nielson, R. F. (2000). *Total encounters: The life and times of the Mental Health Centre Penetanguishene*. Hamilton, Ontario, Canada: McMaster University Press.

Nietzel, M. T., & Himelein, M. J. (1987). Probation and parole. In E. K. Morris & C. J. Braukmann (Eds.), *Behavioral approaches to crime and delinquency: Application, research, and theory* (pp. 109–133). New York: Plenum Press.

Norusis, J. J. (1992). *SPSS*. Chicago: SPSS, Inc.

Novaco, R. W. (2003). *The Novaco Anger Scale and Provocation Inventory*. Los Angeles: Western Psychological Services.

Nuffield, J. (1982). *Parole decision-making in Canada: Research towards decision guidelines*. Ottawa, Ontario: Supply and Services Canada.

Nugent, P. M. (2001). *The use of detention legislation: Factors affecting detention decisions and recidivism among high-risk federal offenders in Ontario* (Doctoral dissertation, Queen's University at Kingston, Ontario, Canada). *Dissertation Abstracts International, 61*(12), 6716B.

Nunes, K. L., Firestone, P., Bradford, J. M., Greenberg, D. M., & Broom, I. (2002). A comparison of modified versions of the Static–99 and Sex Offender Risk Appraisal Guide. *Sexual Abuse: A Journal of Research and Treatment, 14*, 253–269.

O'Brien, G., & Yule, W. (1995). Why behavioural phenotypes? In G. O'Brien & W. Yule (Eds.), *Behavioural phenotypes* (pp. 1–23). London: MacKeith Press.

Olin, S. S., John, R. S., Mednick, S. A. (1995). Assessing the predictive value of teacher reports in a high risk sample for schizophrenia: A ROC analysis. *Schizophrenia Research, 16*, 53–66.

O'Marra, A. J. C. (1993). Hadfield to Swain: The criminal code amendments dealing with the mentally disordered accused. *Criminal Law Quarterly, 36*, 49–107.

Osipow, S. H., & Reed, R. A. (1987). Training and evaluation in counselling psychology. In B. A. Edelstein & E. S. Berter (Eds.), *Evaluation and accountability in clinical training* (pp. 117–133). New York: Plenum Press.

O'Sullivan, G. H., & Kelleher, M. J. (1987). A study of fire setters in the southwest of Ireland. *British Journal of Psychiatry, 151*, 818–823.

Overall, J. E., & Gorham, D. R. (1962). The Brief Psychiatric Rating Scale. *Psychological Reports, 10*, 799–812.

Packer, I. (1985). Insanity acquittals in Michigan 1969–1988: The effects of legislative and judicial changes. *Journal of Psychiatry and Law, 13*, 419–434.

Pallone, N. J. (1990). *Rehabilitating criminal sexual psychopaths: Legislative mandates, clinical quandaries*. New Brunswick, NJ: Transaction.

Pantle, M. L., Pasewark, R. A., & Steadman, H. J. (1980). Comparing institutionalization periods and subsequent arrests of insanity acquittees and convicted felons. *Journal of Psychiatry and Law, 8*, 305–316.

Parloff, M. B. (1986). Placebo controls in psychotherapy research: A sine qua non or a placebo for research problems? *Journal of Consulting and Clinical Psychology, 54*, 79–87.

Pasewark, R. A., Bieber, S., Bosten, K. J., Kiser, M., & Steadman, H. J. (1982). Criminal recidivism among insanity acquittees. *International Journal of Law and Psychiatry, 5*, 365.

Patterson, G. R., & Fleischman, M. J. (1979). Maintenance of treatment effects: Some considerations concerning family systems and follow-up data. *Behavioral Therapy, 10,* 168–185.

Paul, G. L. (1986). *Assessment in residential treatment settings: Principles and methods to support cost-effective quality operations.* Champaign, IL: Research Press.

Paul, G. L., & Lentz, R. J. (1977). *Psychosocial treatment of chronic mental patients: Milieu versus social learning programs.* Cambridge, MA: Harvard University Press.

Penrose, L. (1939). Mental disease and crime: Outline of a comparative study of European statistics. *British Journal of Medical Psychology, 18,* 1–15.

Perlman, D. (1980). Attributions in the criminal justice process: Concepts and empirical illustrations. In P. D. Lipsitt & B. D. Sales (Eds.), *New directions in psycholegal research* (pp. 51–67). Toronto, Ontario, Canada: Van Nostrand Reinhold.

Petrunik, M. (1982). The politics of dangerousness. *International Journal of Law and Psychiatry, 5,* 225–253.

Pham, T. H. (2002, October). *Risk assessment and biological markers.* Paper presented at the Belgian Congress of Neuropsychology. Leuven, Belgium.

Phillips, H. K., Gray, N. S., MacCulloch, S. L., Taylor, J., Moore, S. C., Huckle, P., & MacCulloch, M. J. (2005). Risk assessment in offenders with mental disorders: Relative efficacy of personal demographic criminal history, and clinical variables. *Journal of Interpersonal Violence, 20,* 833–847.

Pithers, W. D., Martin, G. R., & Cumming, G. F. (1989). Vermont treatment program for sexual aggressors. In D. R. Laws (Ed.), *Relapse prevention with sex offenders* (pp. 292–310). New York: Guilford Press.

Polvi, N. H. (2001, February). *The relative efficacy of statistical versus clinical predictions of dangerousness* (Doctoral dissertation, Simon Fraser University). *Dissertation Abstracts International, 61*(7), 3856.

Porporino, F. J., & Motiuk, L. L. (1991). *Preliminary results of national sex offender census* (Research Report No. 29). Ottawa, Ontario: Correctional Service Canada.

Porporino, F. J., & Motiuk, L. L. (1995). The prison careers of mentally disordered offenders. *International Journal of Law and Psychiatry, 18,* 29–44.

Prentky, R. A., Lee, A. F. S., Knight, R. A., & Cerce, D. (1997). Recidivism rates among child molesters and rapists: A methodological analysis. *Law & Human Behavior, 21,* 635–659.

Prentky, R. A., & Quinsey, V. L. (1988). (Eds.). Human sexual aggression: Current perspectives [Special issue]. *Annals of the New York Academy of Sciences, 528.*

Price, R. (1997). The risks of risk prediction. *Journal of Forensic Psychiatry, 8,* 1–4.

Prins, H. (1980). *Offenders, deviants or patients?* London: Tavistock.

Proulx, J., Côté, G., & Achille, P. A. (1993). Prevention of voluntary control of penile response in homosexual pedophiles during phallometric testing. *Journal of Sex Research, 30,* 140–147.

Proulx, J., Pellerin, B., Paradis, Y., McKibben, A., Aubut, J., & Ouimet, M. (1997). Static and dynamic predictors of recidivism in sexual aggressors. *Sexual Abuse: A Journal of Research and Treatment, 9,* 7–27.

Pruesse, M. G., & Quinsey, V. L. (1977). The dangerousness of patients released from maximum security: A replication. *Journal of Psychiatry and Law, 5,* 293–299.

The Psychological Corporation. (1994). *Technical manual for the Miller Analogies Test: A guide to interpretation.* San Antonio, TX: Author.

Quen, J. M. (1981). Anglo-American concepts of criminal responsibility: A brief history. In S. J. Hucker, C. D. Webster, & M. H. Ben-Aron (Eds.), *Mental disorder and criminal responsibility* (pp. 1–10). Toronto, Ontario, Canada: Butterworth.

Quinsey, V. L. (1977a). The assessment and treatment of child molesters: A review. *Canadian Psychological Review, 18,* 204–220.

Quinsey, V. L. (1977b). Problems in the treatment of mentally disordered offenders. *Canada's Mental Health, 25,* 2–3.

Quinsey, V. L. (1979). Assessments of the dangerousness of mental patients held in maximum security. *International Journal of Law and Psychiatry, 2,* 389–406.

Quinsey, V. L. (1980). The base rate problem and the prediction of dangerousness: A reappraisal. *Journal of Psychiatry and Law, 8,* 329–340.

Quinsey, V. L. (1981). The long term management of the mentally disordered offender. In S. J. Hucker, C. D. Webster, & M. Ben-Aron (Eds.), *Mental disorder and criminal responsibility* (pp. 137–155). Toronto, Ontario, Canada: Butterworth.

Quinsey, V. L. (1982). The Ontario Reformatory at Penetanguishene: 1882. *Canada's Mental Health, 30,* 14–15.

Quinsey, V. L. (1984). Sexual aggression: Studies of offenders against women. In D. N. Weisstub (Ed.), *Law and mental health: International perspectives* (Vol. 1, pp. 84–121). New York: Pergamon Press.

Quinsey, V. L. (1986). Men who have sex with children. In D. N. Weisstub (Ed.), *Law and mental health: International perspectives* (Vol. 2, pp. 140–172). New York: Pergamon Press.

Quinsey, V. L. (1988). Assessments of the treatability of forensic patients. *Behavioral Sciences and the Law, 6,* 443–452.

Quinsey, V. L. (1995). The prediction and explanation of criminal violence. *International Journal of Law and Psychiatry, 18,* 117–127.

Quinsey, V. L. (1999). Comment on Fallon, P., et al. Report of the Committee of Inquiry Into the Personality Disorder Unit, Ashworth Special Hospital, Vol. 1. *The Journal of Forensic Psychiatry, 10,* 635–648.

Quinsey, V. L. (2000). Institutional violence among the mentally ill. In S. Hodgins (Ed.), *Violence among the mentally ill: Effective treatments and management strategies* (pp. 213–235). Dordrecht, The Netherlands: Kluwer.

Quinsey, V. L. (2003). Etiology of anomalous sexual preferences in men. *Annals of the New York Academy of Sciences, 989,* 105–117.

Quinsey, V. L. (2004). Risk assessment and management in community settings. In W. Lindsay, J. Taylor, & P. Sturmey (Eds.), *Offenders with developmental disabilities* (pp. 131–141). New York: Wiley.

Quinsey, V. L., & Ambtman, R. (1979). Variables affecting psychiatrists' and teachers' assessments of the dangerousness of mentally ill offenders. *Journal of Consulting and Clinical Psychology, 47,* 353–362.

Quinsey, V. L., Arnold, L. S., & Pruesse, M. G. (1980). MMPI profiles of men referred for pre-trial psychiatric assessment as a function of offense type. *Journal of Clinical Psychology, 36,* 410–417.

Quinsey, V. L., & Bergersen, S. G. (1976). Instructional control of penile circumference. *Behavior Therapy, 7,* 489–493.

Quinsey, V. L., Book, A. S., & Skilling, T. A. (2004). A follow-up of deinstitutionalized men with intellectual disabilities and histories of antisocial behaviour. *Journal of Applied Research in Intellectual Disabilities, 17,* 243–253.

Quinsey, V. L., & Carrigan, W. F. (1978). Penile responses to visual stimuli: Instructional control with and without auditory sexual fantasy correlates. *Criminal Justice and Behavior, 5,* 333–342.

Quinsey, V. L., & Chaplin, T. C. (1982). Penile responses to nonsexual violence among rapists. *Criminal Justice and Behavior, 9,* 372–384.

Quinsey, V. L., & Chaplin, T. C. (1984). Stimulus control of rapists' and non-sex offenders' sexual arousal. *Behavioral Assessment, 6,* 169–176.

Quinsey, V. L., & Chaplin, T. C. (1988a). Penile responses of child molesters and normals to descriptions of encounters with children involving sex and violence. *Journal of Interpersonal Violence, 3,* 259–274.

Quinsey, V. L., & Chaplin, T. C. (1988b). Preventing faking in phallometric assessments of sexual preference. *Annals of the New York Academy of Sciences, 528,* 49–58.

Quinsey, V. L., Chaplin, T. C., & Carrigan, W. F. (1979). Sexual preferences among incestuous and non-incestuous child molesters. *Behavior Therapy, 10,* 562–565.

Quinsey, V. L., Chaplin, T. C., & Carrigan, W. F. (1980). Biofeedback and signaled punishment in the modification of inappropriate sexual age preferences. *Behavior Therapy, 11,* 567–576.

Quinsey, V. L., Chaplin, T. C., Maguire, A. M., & Upfold, D. (1987). The behavioral treatment of rapists and child molesters. In E. K. Morris & C. J. Braukmann (Eds.), *Behavioral approaches to crime and delinquency: Application, research, and theory* (pp. 363–382). New York: Plenum Press.

Quinsey, V. L., Chaplin, T. C., & Upfold, D. (1984). Sexual arousal to nonsexual violence and sadomasochistic themes among rapists and non-sex offenders. *Journal of Consulting and Clinical Psychology, 52,* 651–657.

Quinsey, V. L., Chaplin, T. C., & Upfold, D. (1989). Arsonists and sexual arousal to fire setting: Correlation unsupported. *Journal of Behavior Therapy and Experimental Psychiatry, 20,* 203–209.

Quinsey, V. L., Chaplin, T. C., & Varney, G. W. (1981). A comparison of rapists' and non-sex offenders' sexual preferences for mutually consenting sex, rape, and physical abuse of women. *Behavioral Assessment, 3,* 127–135.

Quinsey, V. L., Coleman, G., Jones, B., & Altrows, I. (1997). Proximal antecedents of eloping and reoffending among mentally disordered offenders. *Journal of Interpersonal Violence, 12,* 794–813.

Quinsey, V. L., & Cyr, M. (1986). Perceived dangerousness and treatability of offenders: The effects of internal versus external attributions of crime causality. *Journal of Interpersonal Violence, 1,* 458–471.

Quinsey, V. L., Cyr, M., & Lavallee, Y. (1988). Treatment opportunities in a maximum security psychiatric hospital: A problem survey. *International Journal of Law and Psychiatry, 11,* 179–194.

Quinsey, V. L., Jones, G. B., Book, A. S., & Barr, K. N. (in press). The dynamic prediction of antisocial behavior among forensic psychiatric patients: A prospective field study. *Journal of Interpersonal Violence.*

Quinsey, V. L., Khanna, A., & Malcolm, P. B. (1998). A retrospective evaluation of the Regional Treatment Centre Sex Offender Treatment Program. *Journal of Interpersonal Violence, 13,* 621–644.

Quinsey, V. L., & Lalumière, M. L. (1995a). Evolutionary perspectives on sexual offending. *Sexual Abuse: A Journal of Research and Treatment, 7,* 301–315.

Quinsey, V. L., & Lalumière, M. L. (1995b). Psychopathy is a non-arbitrary class. *Behavioral and Brain Sciences, 18,* 571.

Quinsey, V. L., & Lalumière, M. L. (2001). *Assessment of sexual offenders against children* (2nd ed.). Thousand Oaks, CA: Sage.

Quinsey, V. L., Lalumière, M. L., Querée, M., & McNaughton, J. K. (1999). Perceived crime severity and biological kinship. *Human Nature, 10,* 399–414.

Quinsey, V. L., Lalumière, M. L., Rice, M. E., & Harris, G. T. (1995). Predicting sexual offenses. In J. C. Campbell (Ed.), *Assessing dangerousness: Violence by sexual offenders, batterers, and child abusers* (pp. 114–137). Thousand Oaks, CA: Sage.

Quinsey, V. L., & Laws, D. R. (1990). Validity of physiological measures of pedophilic sexual arousal in a sexual offender population: A critique of Hall, Proctor, and Nelson. *Journal of Consulting and Clinical Psychology, 58,* 886–888.

Quinsey, V. L., & Maguire, A. (1983). Offenders remanded for a psychiatric examination: Perceived treatability and disposition. *International Journal of Law and Psychiatry, 6,* 193–205.

Quinsey, V. L., & Maguire, A. (1986). Maximum security psychiatric patients: Actuarial and clinical prediction of dangerousness. *Journal of Interpersonal Violence, 1,* 143–171.

Quinsey, V. L., Maguire, A., & Varney, G. W. (1983). Assertion and over controlled hostility among mentally disordered murderers. *Journal of Consulting and Clinical Psychology, 51,* 550–556.

Quinsey, V. L., Pruesse, M. G., & Fernley, R. (1975a). A follow-up of patients found not guilty by reason of insanity or unfit for trial. *Canadian Psychiatric Association Journal, 20,* 461–467.

Quinsey, V. L., Pruesse, M. G., & Fernley, R. (1975b). Oak Ridge patients: Prerelease characteristics and postrelease adjustment. *Journal of Psychiatry and Law, 3,* 63–77.

Quinsey, V. L., Rice, M. E., & Harris, G. T. (1995). Actuarial prediction of sexual recidivism. *Journal of Interpersonal Violence, 10,* 85–105.

Quinsey, V. L., & Sarbit, B. (1975). Behavioral changes associated with the introduction of a token economy in a maximum security psychiatric institution. *Canadian Journal of Criminology and Corrections, 17,* 177–182.

Quinsey, V. L. , Skilling, T. A., Lalumière, M. L., & Craig, W. M. (2004). *Juvenile delinquency: Understanding individual differences.* Washington, DC: American Psychological Association.

Quinsey, V. L., Skilling, T. A., & Rougier-Chapman, C. (1997). *Inter-ministerial population review initiative: Final report.* Toronto, Ontario, Canada: Ministry of Community and Social Services.

Quinsey, V. L., Steinman, C. M., Bergersen, S. G., & Holmes, T. F. (1975). Penile circumference, skin conductance, and ranking responses of child molesters and "normals" to sexual and nonsexual visual stimuli. *Behavior Therapy, 6,* 213–219.

Quinsey, V. L., & Varney, G. W. (1977). Characteristics of assaults and assaulters in a maximum security psychiatric unit. *Crime and Justice, 5,* 212–220.

Quinsey, V. L., & Walker, W. D. (1992). Dealing with dangerousness: Community risk management strategies with violent offenders. In R. D. Peters, R. J. McMahon, & V. L. Quinsey (Eds.), *Aggression and violence throughout the lifespan* (pp. 244–260). Newbury Park, CA: Sage.

Quinsey, V. L., Warneford, A., Pruesse, M. G., & Link, N. (1975). Released Oak Ridge patients: A follow-up of review board discharges. *British Journal of Criminology, 15,* 264–270.

Rabinowitz, G., Sharon, R., Firestone, P., Bradford, J. M., & Greenberg, D. M. (2002). Prediction of recidivism in exhibitionists: Psychological, phallometric, and offense factors. *Sexual Abuse: Journal of Research & Treatment, 14,* 329–347.

Radzinowicz, L. (1957). *Sexual offences: A report of the Cambridge Department of Criminal Science.* Toronto, Ontario, Canada: Macmillan.

Rasmussen, K., & Levander, S. (1996). Symptoms and personality characteristics of patients in a maximum security psychiatric unit. *International Journal of Law and Psychiatry, 19,* 27–37.

Rawlings, B. (1999). Therapeutic communities in prisons: A research review. *Therapeutic Communities: International Journal for Therapeutic & Supportive Organizations, 20,* 177–193.

Regier, D. A., Farmer, M. E., Rae, D. S., Locke, B. Z., Keith, S. J., Judd, L. L., et al. (1990). Comorbidity of mental disorders with alcohol and other drug abuse. *Journal of the American Medical Association, 264,* 2511–2518.

Regina v. Swain, 63 C.C.C. (3d) 193, 5 C.R. (4th) 253, (1991) 1 S.C.R. 933.

Reid, A. H., & Ballinger, B. R. (1995). Behaviour symptoms among severely and profoundly mentally retarded patients: A 16–18 year follow-up study. *British Journal of Psychiatry, 167*, 452–455.

Reid, W. H. (1989). *The treatment of psychiatric disorders.* New York: Brunner/Mazel.

Renwick, S., Black, L., Ramm, M., & Novaco, R. W. (1997). Anger treatment with forensic hospital patients. *Legal and Criminological Psychology, 2*, 103–116.

Ressler, R. K., Burgess, A. W., & Douglas, J. E. (1988). *Sexual homicide: Patterns and motives.* Toronto, Ontario, Canada: Lexington.

Rhodes, W. (1986). A survival model with dependent competing events and right-hand censoring: Probation and parole as an illustration. *Journal of Quantitative Criminology, 2*, 113–137.

Rice, M. E. (1985). Violence in the maximum security hospital. In M. H. BenAron, S. J. Hucker, & C. D. Webster (Eds.), *Clinical criminology: The assessment and treatment of criminal behavior* (pp. 57–79). Toronto, Ontario, Canada: M&M Graphics.

Rice, M. E. (1986). Medium- and maximum-security units for psychiatric patients in Ontario. *Canada's Mental Health, 34*, 17–20.

Rice, M. E. (1997). Violent offender research and implications for the criminal justice system. *American Psychologist, 52*, 414–423.

Rice, M. E., & Chaplin, T. C. (1979). Social skills training for hospitalized male arsonists. *Journal of Behavior Therapy and Experimental Psychiatry, 10*, 105–108.

Rice, M. E., Chaplin, T. C., Harris, G. T., & Coutts, J. (1994). Empathy for the victim and sexual arousal among rapists and nonrapists. *Journal of Interpersonal Violence, 9*, 435–449.

Rice, M. E., & Harris, G. T. (1988). An empirical approach to the classification and treatment of maximum security psychiatric patients. *Behavioral Sciences and the Law, 6*, 497–514.

Rice, M. E., & Harris, G. T. (1990). The predictors of insanity acquittal. *International Journal of Law and Psychiatry, 13*, 217–224.

Rice, M. E., & Harris, G. T. (1991). Fire-setters admitted to a maximum security psychiatric institution: Characteristics of offenders and offenses. *Journal of Interpersonal Violence, 6*, 461–475.

Rice, M. E., & Harris, G. T. (1992). A comparison of criminal recidivism among schizophrenic and nonschizophrenic offenders. *International Journal of Law and Psychiatry, 15*, 397–408.

Rice, M. E., & Harris, G. T. (1993). Ontario's maximum security hospital at Penetanguishene: Past, present and future. *International Journal of Law and Psychiatry, 16*, 195–215.

Rice, M. E., & Harris, G. T. (1995a). Psychopathy, schizophrenia, alcohol abuse, and violent recidivism. *International Journal of Law and Psychiatry, 18*, 333–342.

Rice, M. E., & Harris, G. T. (1995b). Violent recidivism: Assessing predictive validity. *Journal of Consulting and Clinical Psychology, 63*, 737–748.

Rice, M. E., & Harris, G. T. (1996). Predicting the recidivism of mentally disordered fire setters. *Journal of Interpersonal Violence, 11,* 364–375.

Rice, M. E., & Harris, G. T. (1997a). Cross validation and extension of the Violence Risk Appraisal Guide for child molesters and rapists. *Law and Human Behavior, 21,* 231–241.

Rice, M. E., & Harris, G. T. (1997b). The treatment of mentally disordered offenders. *Psychology, Public Policy, and Law, 3,* 126–183.

Rice, M. E., & Harris, G. T. (2002a). Men who molest their sexually immature daughters: Is a special explanation required? *Journal of Abnormal Psychology, 111,* 329–339.

Rice, M. E., & Harris, G. T. (2002b). Sexual aggressors: Scientific status. In D. L. Faigman, D. H. Kaye, M. J. Saks, & J. Sanders (Ed.), *Modern scientific evidence: The law and science of expert testimony* (Vol. 1, 2nd ed., pp. 471–504). St. Paul, MN: West Publishing.

Rice, M. E., & Harris, G. T. (2003a). The size and sign of treatment effects in therapy for sex offenders. In R. A. Prentky, E. S. Janus, & M. C. Seto (Eds.), *Understanding and managing sexually coercive behavior* (*Annals of the New York Academy of Sciences,* Vol. 989, pp. 428–440). New York: New York Academy of Sciences.

Rice, M. E., & Harris, G. T. (2003b). What we know and don't know about treating adult sex offenders. In B. J. Winick & J. Q. La Fond (Eds.), *Protecting society from sexually dangerous offenders* (pp. 101–117). Washington, DC: American Psychological Association.

Rice, M. E., Harris, G. T., & Cormier, C. A. (1992). Evaluation of a maximum security therapeutic community for psychopaths and other mentally disordered offenders. *Law and Human Behavior, 16,* 399–412.

Rice, M. E., Harris, G. T., Cormier, C. A., Lang, C., Coleman, G., & Smith Krans, T. (2004). An evidence-based approach to planning services for forensic psychiatric patients. *Issues in forensic psychology, 5,* 13–49.

Rice, M. E., Harris, G. T., Lang, C., & Bell, V. (1990). Recidivism among male insanity acquittees. *Journal of Psychiatry and Law, 18,* 379–403.

Rice, M. E., Harris, G. T., Lang, C., & Cormier, C. A. (2004, March). *Developing actuarial tools to predict sexual recidivism: What is the best criminal record outcome measure?* Paper presented at the American Psychology–Law Society Conference, Phoenix, AZ.

Rice, M. E., Harris, G. T., Lang, C., & Cormier, C. A. (2005a). *Developing actuarial tools to predict sexual recidivism: What is the best criminal record outcome measure?* Paper submitted for publication.

Rice, M. E., Harris, G. T., Lang, C., & Cormier, C. A. (2005b). *Sexually violent offenses: How are they best measured from official records of charges and convictions?* Manuscript submitted for publication.

Rice, M. E., Harris, G. T., & Quinsey, V. L. (1990). A follow-up of rapists assessed in a maximum security psychiatric facility. *Journal of Interpersonal Violence, 5,* 435–448.

Rice, M. E., Harris, G. T., & Quinsey, V. L. (1991). Evaluation of an institution-based treatment program for child molesters. *Canadian Journal of Program Evaluation, 6,* 111–129.

Rice, M. E., Harris, G. T., & Quinsey, V. L. (1996). Treatment for forensic patients. In B. D. Sales & S. A. Shah (Eds.), *Mental health and law: Research, policy and services* (pp. 141–189). New York: Academic Press.

Rice, M. E., Harris, G. T., & Quinsey, V. L. (2001). Research on the treatment of adult sex offenders. In J. B. Ashford, B. D. Sales, & W. Reid (Eds.), *Treating adult and juvenile offenders with special needs* (pp. 291–312). Washington, DC: American Psychological Association.

Rice, M. E., Harris, G. T., Quinsey, V. L., & Cyr, M. (1990). Planning treatment programs in secure psychiatric facilities. In D. N. Weisstub (Ed.), *Law and mental health: International perspectives* (Vol. 5, pp. 162–230). New York: Pergamon Press.

Rice, M. E., Harris, G. T., Varney, G. W., & Quinsey, V. L. (1989). *Violence in institutions: Understanding, prevention, and control.* Toronto, Ontario, Canada: Hans Huber.

Rice, M. E., & Josefowitz, N. (1983). Assertion, popularity, and social behavior in maximum security psychiatric patients. *Corrective and Social Psychiatry and Journal of Behavior Technology Methods and Therapy, 29,* 97–104.

Rice, M. E., Quinsey, V. L., & Harris, G. T. (1991). Sexual recidivism among child molesters released from a maximum security psychiatric institution. *Journal of Consulting and Clinical Psychology, 59,* 381–386.

Rice, M. E., Quinsey, V. L., & Houghton, R. (1990). Predicting treatment outcome and recidivism among patients in a maximum security token economy. *Behavioral Sciences and the Law, 8,* 313–326.

Robbins, P. C., Monahan, J., & Silver, E. (2003). Mental disorder, violence, and gender. *Law and Human Behavior, 27,* 561–571.

Robbins, R., & Robbins, L. (1967). Arson. *New York State Journal of Medicine, 67,* 795–798.

Roberts, C. F., Doren, D. M., & Thornton, D. (2002). Dimensions associated with assessments of sex offender recidivism risk. *Criminal Justice and Behavior, 29,* 569–589.

Robins, L. N., Helzer, J. E., Croughan, J., & Ratcliff, K. S. (1981). National Institute of Mental Health Diagnostic Interview Schedule: Its history, characteristics, and validity. *Archives of General Psychiatry, 38,* 381–389.

Rodgers, T. (1947). Hypnotherapy and character neuroses. *Journal of Clinical Psychopathology, 8,* 519–524.

Rosenthal, R. (1991). Effect sizes: Pearson's correlation, its display via the BESD, and alternative indices. *American Psychologist, 46,* 1086–1087.

Rosow, H. M. (1955). Some observations on group therapy with prison inmates. *Archives of Criminal Psychodynamics, 1,* 866–897.

Ross, R. R., & Lightfoot, L. O. (1985). *Treatment of the alcohol-abusing offender.* Springfield, IL: Charles C Thomas.

Rothman, D. J. (1971). *The discovery of the asylum: Social order and disorder in the New Republic.* Toronto, Ontario, Canada: Little, Brown.

Rothman, D. J. (1980). *Conscience and convenience: The asylum and its alternatives in progressive America.* Toronto, Ontario, Canada: Little, Brown.

Salekin, R. T. (2002). Psychopathy and therapeutic pessimism: Clinical lore or clinical reality? *Clinical Psychology Review, 22,* 79–112.

Sapsford, R. M., Banks, C., & Smith, D. D. (1978). Arsonists in prison. *Medicine, Science and the Law, 18,* 247–254.

Saulnier, K., & Perlman, D. (1981a). The actor–observer bias is alive and well in prison: A sequel to Wells. *Personality and Social Psychology Bulletin, 7,* 559–564.

Saulnier, K., & Perlman, D. (1981b). Inmates' attributions: Their antecedents and effects on coping. *Criminal Justice and Behavior, 8,* 159–172.

Schmideberg, M. (1949). The analytic treatment of major criminals: Therapeutic results and technical problems. *International Journal of Psychoanalysis, 30,* 197.

Schmideberg, M. (1953). Pathological fire setting. *Journal of Criminal Law, Criminology and Police Science, 44,* 30–39.

Schram, D., & Milloy, C. (1995). *Community notification: A study of offender characteristics and recidivism.* Olympia: Washington State Institute for Public Policy.

Scott, D. (1978). The problems of malicious fire setting. *British Journal of Hospital Medicine, 19,* 259–263.

Sechrest, L., & Chatel, D. M. (1987). Evaluation and accountability in training for professional psychology: An overview. In B. A. Edelstein & E. S. Berler (Eds.), *Evaluation and accountability in clinical training* (pp. 1–37). New York: Plenum Press.

Serin, R. C. (1991). *Development and validation of a psychological referral screening tool.* Ottawa, Ontario, Canada: Research and Statistics Branch, Correctional Service of Canada.

Serin, R. C., & Kuriychuk, M. (1994). Social and cognitive processing deficits in violent offenders: Implications for treatment. *International Journal of Law and Psychiatry, 17,* 431–441.

Serin, R. C., Mailloux, D. L., & Malcolm, P. B. (2001). Psychopathy, deviant sexual arousal and recidivism among sexual offenders: A psycho-culturally determined group offense. *Journal of Interpersonal Violence, 16,* 234–246.

Serran, G., Fernandez, Y., Marshall, W. L., & Mann, R. E. (2003). Process issues in treatment: Application to sexual offender programs. *Professional Psychology: Research and Practice, 34,* 368–374.

Seto, M. C. (2005). Is more better? Combining actuarial risk scales to predict recidivism among adult sex offenders. *Psychological Assessment, 17,* 156–167.

Seto, M. C., Harris, G. T., & Rice, M. E. (2004). The criminogenic, clinical, and social problems of forensic and civil psychiatric patients. *Law and Human Behavior, 28,* 577–586.

Seto, M. C., Harris, G. T., Rice, M. E., & Barbaree, H. E. (2004). The Screening Scale for Pedophilic Interests and recidivism among adult sex offenders with child victims. *Archives of Sexual Behavior, 33*, 455–466.

Seto, M. C., Khattar, N. A., Lalumière, M. L., & Quinsey, V. L. (1997). Deception and sexual strategy in psychopathy. *Personality and Individual Differences, 22*, 301–307.

Seto, M. C., & Lalumière, M. L. (2001). A brief screening scale to identify pedophilic interests among child molesters. *Sexual Abuse: A Journal of Research and Treatment, 13*, 15–25.

Seto, M. C., Lalumière, M. L., & Kuban, M. (1997, April). *The sexual age preference of incestuous and non-incestuous child molesters.* Paper presented at the Forensic Psychiatry Program First Annual Research Day, Penetanguishene, Ontario, Canada.

Seto, M. C., Lalumière, M. L., & Quinsey, V. L. (1995). Sensation seeking and males' sexual strategy. *Personality and Individual Differences, 19*, 669–676.

Shah, S. A. (1986). Criminal responsibility. In W. J. Curran, A. L. McGarry, & S. A. Shah (Eds.), *Forensic psychiatry and psychology: Perspectives and standards for interdisciplinary practice* (pp. 167–208). Philadelphia: F. A. Davis.

Shoom, S. (1972). The Upper Canada Reformatory, Penetanguishene: The dawn of prison reform in Canada. *Canadian Journal of Criminology and Corrections, 14*, 220–267.

Shore, D., Filson, C. R., & Johnson, W. E. (1988). Violent crime arrests and paranoid schizophrenia: The White House case studies. *Schizophrenia Bulletin, 14*, 279.

Shore, D., Filson, R., Johnson, W. E., Rae, D. S., Muchrer, P., Kelley, D. J., et al. (1989). Murder and assault arrests of White House cases: Clinical and demographic correlates of violence subsequent to civil commitment. *American Journal of Psychiatry, 146*, 645–651.

Shore, M. F., & Massimo, J. L. (1979). Fifteen years after treatment: A follow-up study to comprehensive vocationally-oriented psychotherapy. *American Journal of Orthopsychiatry, 49*, 240–245.

Showstack, N. (1956). Treatment of prisoners at the California Medical Facility. *American Journal of Psychiatry, 112*, 821–824.

Siegel, J. M. (1986). The Multidimensional Anger Inventory. *Journal of Personality and Social Psychology, 51*, 191–200.

Simmel, E. (1949). Incendiarism. *Yearbook on Psychoanalysis, 5*, 90–101.

Simmons, H. G. (1990). *Unbalanced: Mental health policy in Ontario, 1930–1989.* Toronto, Ontario, Canada: Watt & Thompson.

Simpson, M. K., & Hogg, J. (2001). Patterns of offending among people with intellectual disability: A systematic review. Part I: Methodology and prevalence data. *Journal of Intellectual Disability Research, 45*, 384–396.

Sjoestedt, G., & Langstroem, N. (2002). Assessment of risk for criminal recidivism among rapists: A comparison of four different measures. *Psychology, Crime and Law, 8*, 25–40.

Skeem, J. L., Monahan, J., & Mulvey, E. P. (2002). Psychopathy, treatment involvement, and subsequent violence among civil psychiatric patients. *Law and Human Behavior, 26,* 577.

Skeem, J. L., Mulvey, E. P., & Lidz, C. W. (2000). Studying the etiology of crime and violence among persons with major mental disorders: Challenges in the definition and the measurement of interactions. *Law and Human Behavior, 24,* 607–628.

Skilling, T. A., Harris, G. T., Rice, M. E., & Quinsey, V. L. (2002). Identifying persistently antisocial offenders using the Hare Psychopathy Checklist and the DSM Antisocial Personality Disorder criteria. *Psychological Assessment, 14,* 27–38.

Skilling, T. A., Quinsey, V. L., & Craig, W. M. (2001). Evidence of a taxon underlying serious antisocial behavior in boys. *Criminal Justice and Behavior, 28,* 450–470.

Skinner, H. A. (1982). The Drug Abuse Screening Test (DAST–20). *Addictive Behaviors, 7,* 363–371.

Skinner, H. A., & Horn, J. I. (1984). *Alcohol Dependence Scale user's guide.* Toronto, Ontario, Canada: Addiction Research Foundation.

Slate, R. N. (2003). From the jailhouse to Capitol Hill: Impacting mental health court legislation and defining what constitutes a mental health court. *Crime and Delinquency, 49,* 6–29.

Slovic, P., Fischhoff, B., & Lichtenstein, S. (1982). Facts versus fears: Understanding perceived risk. In D. Kahneman, P. Slovic, & A. Tversky (Eds.), *Judgment under uncertainty: Heuristic and biases* (pp. 463–489). Cambridge, England: Cambridge University Press.

Slovic, P., & Monahan, J. (1995). Probability, danger, and coercion: A study of risk perception and decision making in mental health law. *Law and Human Behavior, 19,* 49–65.

Slovic, P., Monahan, J., & MacGregor, D. (2000). Violence risk assessment and risk communication: The effects of using actual cases, providing instruction, and employing probability versus frequency formats. *Law and Human Behavior, 24,* 271–296.

Smiley, A. (2001). Forensic mental health in the United States—an overview. In G. Landsberg & A. Smiley (Eds.), *Forensic mental health: Working with offenders with mental illness* (pp. 1–14). Kingston, NJ: Civic Research Institute.

Smith, S. S., & Newman, J. P. (1990). Alcohol and drug abuse-dependence disorders in psychopathic and nonpsychopathic criminal offenders. *Journal of Abnormal Psychology, 99,* 430–439.

Solicitor General of Canada. (2001). *High risk offenders: A handbook for criminal justice professionals.* Ottawa, Ontario: Public Safety and Emergency Preparedness, Canada.

Soothill, K. L., Jack, A., & Gibbens, T. C. N. (1976). Rape: A 22–year cohort study. *Medicine, Science, and the Law, 16,* 62–68.

Soothill, K. L., & Pope, P. J. (1973). Arson: A twenty-year cohort study. *Medicine, Science, and Law, 13,* 127–138.

Spielberger, C. D., Gorsuch, R. I., & Lushene, R. E. (1970). *Manual for the State–Trait Anxiety Inventory ("Self-Evaluation Questionnaire")*. Palo Alto, CA: Consulting Psychologists Press.

Spitzer, R. L., Endicott, J., & Robins, E. (1978). *Research diagnostic criteria (RDC) for a selected group of functional disorders.* New York: Biometrics Research.

Spruit, J. E. (1998). The penal conceptions of the emperor Marcus Aurelius in respect of lunatics: Reflections on D. 1, 18,14. *International Journal of Law and Psychiatry, 21,* 315–333.

Statistics Canada. (1975). *Homicide in Canada: A statistical synopsis.* Ottawa, Ontario: Information Canada.

Steadman, H. J., & Cocozza, J. J. (1974). *Careers of the criminally insane: Excessive social control of deviance.* Toronto, Ontario, Canada: Lexington Books.

Steadman, H. J., Fabisiak, S., Dvoskin, J. A., & Holohean, E. J. (1987). A survey of mental disability among state prison inmates. *Hospital and Community Psychiatry, 38,* 1086–1090.

Steadman, H. J., & Halfon, A. (1971). The Baxstrom patients: Backgrounds and outcomes. *Seminars in Psychiatry, 3,* 376–385.

Steadman, H. J., & Keveles, G. (1972). The community adjustment and criminal activity of the Baxstrom patients: 1966–1970. *American Journal of Psychiatry, 129,* 304–310.

Steadman, H. J., McGreevy, M. A., Morrissey, J. P., Callahan, L. A., Robbins, P. C., & Cirincione, C. (1993). *Before and after Hinckley: Evaluating insanity defense reform.* New York: Guilford Press.

Steadman, H. J., Monahan, J., Duffee, B., Hartstone, E., & Robbins, P. C. (1984). The impact of state mental hospital deinstitutionalization on United States prison populations, 1968–1978. *Journal of Criminal Law and Criminology, 75,* 474–490.

Steadman, H. J., Pasewark, R. A., Hawkins, M., Kiser, M., & Bieber, S. (1983). Hospitalization length of insanity acquittees. *Journal of Clinical Psychology, 39,* 611–614.

Stein, D. M., & Lambert, M. J. (1995). Graduate training in psychotherapy: Are therapy outcomes enhanced? *Journal of Consulting and Clinical Psychology, 63,* 182–196.

Stekel, W. (1924). *Peculiarities of behavior* (Vol. 2). New York: Liveright.

Stermac, L. E., & Quinsey, V. L. (1986). Social competence among rapists. *Behavioral Assessment, 8,* 171–185.

Stewart, M. A., & Culver, K. W. (1982). Children who set fires: The clinical picture and a follow-up. *British Journal of Psychiatry, 140,* 357–363.

Straus, M. A. (1979). Measuring intrafamily conflict and violence: The Conflict Tactics (CT) Scales. *Journal of Marriage and the Family, 41,* 75–88.

Strong, E. K. (1943). *Vocational interests of men and women.* Palo Alto, CA: Stanford University Press.

Studer, L. H., Aylwin, A. S., Clelland, S. R., Reddon, J. R., & Frenzel, R. R. (2002). Primary erotic preference in a group of child molesters. *International Journal of Law & Psychiatry, 25,* 173–180.

Studer, L. H., Clelland, S. R., Aylwin, A. S., Reddon, J. R., & Monro, A. (2000). Rethinking risk assessment for incest offenders. *International Journal of Law and Psychiatry, 23,* 15–22.

Sturgeon, V. H., & Taylor, J. (1980). Report of a five-year follow-up study of mentally disordered sex offenders released from Atascadero State Hospital. *Criminal Justice Journal, 4,* 31–63.

Swanson, J. W., Borum, R., Swartz, M. S., & Monahan, J. (1996). Psychotic symptoms and disorders and the risk of violent behaviour in the community. *Criminal Behaviour and Mental Health, 6,* 309–329.

Swanson, J. W., & Holzer, C. (1991). Violence and the ECA data. *Hospital and Community Psychiatry, 42,* 474–490.

Swanson, J. W., Holzer, C., Ganju, V., & Jono, R. (1990). Violence and psychiatric disorder in the community: Evidence from the Epidemiologic Catchment Area Surveys. *Hospital and Community Psychiatry, 41,* 761–770.

Swets, J. A. (1988). Measuring the accuracy of diagnostic systems. *Science, 240,* 1285–1293.

Swets, J. A. (1992). The science of choosing the right decision threshold in high-stakes diagnostics. *American Psychologist, 47,* 522–532.

Szmukler, G. (2003). Risk assessment: "Numbers" and "values." *Psychiatric Bulletin, 27,* 205–207.

Takagi, P. (1975). The Walnut Street jail: A penal reform to centralize the powers of the state. *Federal Probation, 34,* 18–26.

Talbott, J. A. (1978). *The death of the asylum: A critical study of state hospital management services and care.* New York: Grune & Stratton.

Taylor, P. J. (1985). Motives for offending among violent and psychotic men. *British Journal of Psychiatry, 147,* 491–498.

Tengstroem, A. (2001). Long-term predictive validity of historical factors in two risk assessment instruments in a group of violent offenders with schizophrenia. *Nordic Journal of Psychiatry, 55,* 243–249.

Tengstroem, A., Grann, M., Langstroem, N., & Kullgren, G. (2000). Psychopathy (PCL–R) as a predictor of violent recidivism among criminal offenders with schizophrenia. *Law and Human Behavior, 24,* 45–58.

Teplin, L. A. (1984). Criminalizing mental disorder: The comparative arrest rate of the mentally ill. *American Psychologist, 39,* 794–803.

Teplin, L. A. (1990a). Detecting disorder: The treatment of mental illness among jail detainees. *Journal of Clinical and Consulting Psychology, 58,* 233–236.

Teplin, L. A. (1990b). The prevalence of severe mental disorder among male urban jail detainees: Comparison with the epidemiologic catchment area. *American Journal of Public Health, 80,* 663–669.

Teplin, L. A. (1991). The criminalization hypothesis: Myth, misnomer, or management strategy. In S. A. Shah & B. D. Sales (Eds.), *Law and mental health: Major developments and research needs* (pp. 149–183). Rockville, MD: National Institute of Mental Health.

Thornberry, T. P., & Jacoby, J. E. (1979). *The criminally insane: A community follow-up of mentally ill offenders*. Chicago: Chicago University Press.

Thorne, F. C. (1959). The etiology of sociopathic reactions. *American Journal of Psychotherapy, 13*, 310–330.

Tiihonen, J., Isohanni, M., Räsänen, P., Koiranen, M., & Moring, J. (1997). Specific major mental disorders and criminality: A 26-year prospective study of the 1966 Northern Finland birth cohort. *American Journal of Psychiatry, 154*, 840–845.

Toch, H. (Ed.). (1980). *Therapeutic communities in corrections*. New York: Praeger.

Toch, H. (1982). The disturbed disruptive inmate: Where does the bus stop? *Journal of Psychiatry and Law, 10*, 327–349.

Tong, J. E., & MacKay, G. W. (1959). A statistical follow-up of mental defectives of dangerous or violent propensities. *British Journal of Delinquency, 9*, 276–284.

Tremblay, R. E., Masse, B., Perron, D., Leblanc, M., Schwartzman, A. E., & Ledingham, J. E. (1992). Early disruptive behavior, poor school achievement, delinquent behavior, and delinquent personality: Longitudinal analyses. *Journal of Consulting and Clinical Psychology, 60*, 64–72.

Trupin, E., & Richards, H. (2003). Seattle's mental health courts: Early indicators of effectiveness. *International Journal of Law and Psychiatry, 26*, 33–53.

Tucker, J. O. (1970). Dispensing with selection interview. *Australian Psychologist, 5*, 141–153.

U.S. Supreme Court. (1966). *Baxstrom v. Herold*. Reports 383:107.

Valenstein, E. S. (1986). *Great and desperate cures: The rise and decline of psychosurgery and other radical treatments for mental illness*. New York: Basic Books.

Villeneuve, D. B., & Quinsey, V. L. (1995). Predictors of general and violent recidivism among mentally disordered inmates. *Criminal Justice and Behavior, 22*, 397–410.

Virkkunen, M. (1991). Brain serotonin and violent behaviour. *Journal of Forensic Psychiatry, 3*, 171–173.

Virkkunen, M., DeJong, J., Bartko, J., Goodwin, F. K., & Linnoila, M. (1989). Relationship of psychobiological variables to recidivism in violent offenders and impulsive fire setters. *Archives of General Psychiatry, 46*, 600–603.

Virkkunen, M., Nuutila, A., Goodwin, F. K., & Linnoila, M. (1987). Cerebrospinal fluid monoamine metabolite levels in male arsonists. *Archives of General Psychiatry, 44*, 241–247.

de Vogel, V., de Ruiter, C., van Beek, D., & Mead, G. (2004). Predictive validity of the SVR-20 and Static-99 in a Dutch sample of treated sex offenders. *Law & Human Behavior, 28*, 235–251.

Vogt, W. P. (1993). *Dictionary of statistics and methodology*. Newbury Park, CA: Sage.

Wakefield, J. C. (1992a). The concept of mental disorder: On the boundary between biological facts and social values. *American Psychologist, 47*, 373–388.

Wakefield, J. C. (1992b). Disorder as harmful dysfunction: A conceptual critique of *DSM–III–R*'s definition of mental disorder. *Psychological Review, 99*, 232–247.

Walker, N. (1968). *Crime and insanity in England: Volume 1. The historical perspective.* Edinburgh, Scotland: Edinburgh University Press.

Walker, N., Hammond, W., & Steer, D. (1967). Repeated violence. *Criminal Law Review, 207*, 465–472.

Walker, N., & McCabe, S. (1973). *Crime and insanity in England: Vol. 2. New solutions and new problems.* Edinburgh, Scotland: Edinburgh University Press.

Walker, W. D., Rowe, R. C., & Quinsey, V. L. (1993). Authoritarianism and sexual aggression. *Journal of Personality and Social Psychology, 65*, 1036–1045.

Wallace, C., Mullen, P. E., & Burgess, P. (2004). Criminal offending in schizophrenia over a 25-year period marked by deinstitutionalization and increasing prevalence of comorbid substance use disorders. *American Journal of Psychiatry, 161*, 716–727.

Wallace, N. C. (1925). The criminally insane at Guelph. *Ontario Journal of Neuro-Psychiatry, 5*, 72–77.

Waller, I. (1974). *Men released from prison.* Toronto, Ontario, Canada: University of Toronto Press.

Walters, G. D. (2003). Predicting institutional adjustment and recidivism with the Psychopathy Checklist factor scores: A meta-analysis. *Law and Human Behavior, 27*, 541–558.

Walters, G. D., White, T. W., & Denney, D. (1991). The Lifestyle Criminality Screening Form: Preliminary data. *Criminal Justice and Behavior, 18*, 406–418.

Watson, A., Hanrahan, P., Luchins, D., & Lurigio, A. (2001). Mental health courts and the complex issue of mentally ill offenders. *Psychiatric Services, 52*, 477–481.

Watson, D., & Friend, R. (1969). Measurement of social-evaluative anxiety. *Journal of Consulting and Clinical Psychology, 33*, 448–457.

Webster, C. D., Eaves, D., Douglas, K. S., & Wintrup, A. (1995). *The HCR–20 scheme: The assessment of dangerousness and risk.* Vancouver, British Columbia, Canada: Simon Fraser University and British Columbia Forensic Psychiatric Services Commission.

Webster, C. D., Harris, G. T., Rice, M. E., Cormier, C. A., & Quinsey, V. L. (1994). *The violence prediction scheme: Assessing dangerousness in high risk men.* Toronto, Ontario, Canada: University of Toronto, Centre of Criminology.

Weisman, R. (1995). Reflections on the Oak Ridge experiment with mentally disordered offenders, 1965–1968. *International Journal of Law and Psychiatry, 18*, 265–290.

Weisz, J. R., Weiss, B., Han, S. S., Granger, D. A., & Morton, T. (1995). Effects of psychotherapy with children and adolescents revisited: A meta-analysis of treatment outcome studies. *Psychological Bulletin, 117*, 450–468.

Wenk, E. A., Robison, J. O., & Smith, G. W. (1972). Can violence be predicted? *Crime and Delinquency, 18,* 393–402.

Wessely, S., & Taylor, P. J. (1991). Madness and crime: Criminology versus psychiatry. *Criminal Behaviour and Mental Health, 1,* 193–228.

Whiteley, J. S. (1970). The response of psychopaths to a therapeutic community. *British Journal of Psychiatry, 116,* 517–529.

Wiederanders, M. (1992). Recidivism of disordered offenders who were conditionally vs. unconditionally released. *Behavioral Sciences and the Law, 10,* 141–148.

Wiederanders, M., Bromley, D. L., & Choate, P. A. (1997). Forensic conditional release programs and outcomes in three states. *International Journal of Law and Psychiatry, 20,* 249–257.

Wiggins, J. S. (1973). *Personality and prediction: Principles of personality assessment.* Don Mills, Ontario, Canada: Addison-Wesley.

Wilson, M., & Daly, M. (1985). Competitiveness, risk taking, and violence: The young male syndrome. *Ethology and Sociobiology, 6,* 59–73.

Wilson, M., & Daly, M. (1993). Lethal confrontational violence among young men. In N. J. Bell & R. W. Bell (Eds.), *Adolescent risk taking* (pp. 84–106). Newbury Park, CA: Sage.

Wiseman, F. (1967). *Titicut follies.* Cambridge, MA: Zipporah Films.

Wolfgang, M. E., Figlio, R. M., Tracy, P. E., & Singer, S. I. (1985). *The National Survey of Crime Severity.* Washington, DC: U.S. Department of Justice, Bureau of Justice Statistics.

Wollert, R. (2001). An analysis of the argument that clinicians under-predict sexual violence in civil commitment cases. *Behavioral Sciences and the Law, 19,* 171–184.

Wong, S. P. (1984). *The criminal and institutional behaviours of psychopaths.* Ottawa, Ontario, Canada: Ministry of the Solicitor General.

Wong, S. P. (1988). Is Hare's Psychopathy Checklist reliable without the interview? *Psychological Reports, 62,* 931–934.

Wong, S. P., & Hare, R. D. (in press). *Program for the treatment of psychopaths (PTP): Institutional treatment of violent psychopathic offenders.* Toronto, Ontario, Canada: Multi-Health Systems.

Woody, G. E., McLellan, A. T., Rubersky, L., & O'Brien, C. P. (1985). Sociopathy and psychotherapy outcome. *Archives of General Psychiatry, 42,* 1081–1086.

Worling, J. A. (2001). Personality-based typology of adolescent male sexual offenders: Differences in recidivism rates, victim-selection characteristics, and personal victimization histories. *Sexual Abuse: Journal of Research and Treatment, 13,* 149–166.

Wormith, J. S. (1984). Attitude and behavior change of a correctional clientele: A 3-year follow-up. *Criminology, 22,* 595–618.

Wormith, J. S., & Borzecki, M. (1985). *Mental disorder in the criminal justice system* (Programs Branch User Report 1985-14). Ottawa, Ontario: Ministry of the Solicitor General of Canada.

Wormith, J. S., & Goldstone, C. S. (1984). The clinical and statistical prediction of recidivism. *Criminal Justice and Behavior, 11,* 3–34.

Wormith, J. S., & Ruhl, M. (1986). Preventive detention in Canada. *Journal of Interpersonal Violence, 1,* 399–430.

Wright, C. (1991). Homicide in Canada 1990. *Juristat Service Bulletin, 11*(15), 1–15.

Yoshikawa, H. (1994). Prevention as cumulative protection: Effects of early family support and education on chronic delinquency and its risks. *Psychological Bulletin, 115,* 28–54.

Zamble, E., & Porporino, F. (1988). *Coping behavior and adaptation in prison inmates.* New York: Springer-Verlag.

Zamble, E., & Quinsey, V. L. (1997). *The process of recidivism.* Cambridge, England: Cambridge University Press.

Zarb, J. M. (1978). Correlates of recidivism and social adjustment among training-school delinquents. *Canadian Journal of Behavioural Science, 10,* 317–328.

Ziskin, I., & Faust, D. (1988). *Coping with psychiatric and psychological testimony* (Vols. 1–3). Marina del Rey, CA: Law and Psychology Press.

Zuckerman, M. (1989). Personality in the third dimension: A psychobiological approach. *Personality and Individual Differences, 10,* 391–418.

AUTHOR INDEX

SUBJECT INDEX

and serotonin deficits, 111
in sex offenders, 89
and sexual deviance, 146
APD. *See* Antisocial personality disorder
Arson, 115, 118, 119
Assaults
definition of, 92
measurement of institutional, 241
Assertion training, 66n, 121–122, 124
Assertiveness, 65–66, 141
Association for the Treatment of Sexual
Abusers, 149
Assortative mating, 107
Atascadero State Hospital, 85–86, 143
Atheoretical actuarial approach, 42
Attention-seeking motivation, 123
Attribution theory, 68
Auburn penitentiary system, 13
Aural stimuli, phallometric assessment and,
133–135, 138
Averaged judgments, 66–67

"Back-end" reforms, 25
Base rates, 46–47
Baumeister, R. F., 249
Baxstrom, Johnny K., 36
Baxstrom cohort, 36–37
Baxstrom v. Herold, 36
Bed-wetting. *See* Urinary incontinence
Behavioral assertion training program, 121–
122
Behavioral treatments
for arsonists, 121
effectiveness of, 78–79
for institutional violence, 243–245
at Oak Ridge, 30
for sex offenders, 148–149
Behavior family management, 80
"Being at risk to offend" (term), 95
Bias
in measurement of outcome, 35
sample, 46
Binet, Alfred, 170
Board of Review, 38
Bridgewater Institution, 38–39
Britain, 124–125
Brutality, 136
Bunyan, John, 16–17
Burden of proof, 25
Burgess method, 38, 41
"Bus therapy," 88, 234

California, 25, 132
California Youth Authority, 40
Cambridge–Somerville Youth Study, 78–79
Canada, 40, 41, 71, 95, 115
Canadian Charter of Rights and Freedoms,
22
Canadian Habitual Offender legislation, 27
Canadian jurisprudence, 22–23
Canadian Police Information Centre, 126
Canadian Supreme Court, 22
Case history literature, 117
The Case of Valentine Shortis (M. L. Fried-
man), 24
Case study method, 15, 16
CATS. *See* Childhood and Adolescent
Taxon Scale
CATS–SR, 192n
Chaos theory, 208
Chatel, D. M., 76
Child and adolescent psychotherapy, 78–79
Childhood and Adolescent Taxon Scale
(CATS), 187, 188, 193–194
Childhood fire setting, 123, 127
Childhood history
actuarial risk appraisal of, 354–355
psychosocial assessment of, 317–319,
334, 341–342, 347–348, 364–365
Childhood problems, 157, 273–374
"Childhood triad," 120
Child molesters
faking on phallometry studies of, 137–
138
as percentage of sex offenders, 132
prediction of future violence by, 63
recidivism among, 142–145
self-perceptions of, 140
sexual deviance among, 133–134
Circumstances leading to admission, 331–
332, 361
Civil liberties, 36
Civilly committed patients, 38
Clarke, C. K., 24
Cleckley, H., 270
CLES. *See* Common language effect size
Clinical judgment, 61–81
and actuarial models, 69–73
averaged, 66–67
evidence-based, 73–74
expectations about, 62–63
faulty, 197–198
and human judgment, 61–62

VRAG scoring for, 341–346
Nonviolent recidivism, 126
"Not criminally responsible on account of mental disorder (NCRMD), 22
"Not guilty by reason of insanity" (NGRI), 4
    convictions *vs.*, 23
    follow-up study of cases of, 101–102

Oak Ridge Division of the Mental Health Centre, 5, 29–31
    base rates as perceived by staff of, 46–47
    and clinical judgment, 63–65, 69, 70
    cross-sectional statistics over 35 years, 391
    fire setters at, 119, 121–122, 126–129
    follow-up studies at, 89–90
    as most secure psychiatric institution in Ontario, 28
    patient population characteristics at, 29
    problem identification in offenders at, 227
    reducing aggression models at, 244
    referrals to, 29
    "Robert Phillip" at, 6
    ROC technique used at, 59
    sex offender studies at, 140, 144
    Valentine Shortis at, 24
    structure/staffing of, 29
    studies of patient dangerousness in, 37, 38
    treatment programs at, 29–30
Obedience, 13
Occupational assessment, 320–321, 335, 366–367
ODARA (Ontario Domestic Assault Risk Assessment), 171
Offender management, 3–4, 12
Offender–victim relationship, 132
Offense information, 332–333, 362
    actuarial risk appraisal of, 356
    psychosocial assessment of, 316–317, 344–345, 351
O-H subscale. *See* Overcontrolled–Hostility subscale
Ontario
    mental hospitals in, 18–19
    mentally disordered offenders in, 27–28
    studies of patient dangerousness in, 37
Ontario Domestic Assault Risk Assessment (ODARA), 171

Ontario Reformatory at Penetanguishene, 13–14
Ontario Review Board, 22, 23, 90
Ontario Survey of Mentally Disordered Offenders, 227, 234
Opportunity(-ies)
    definition of, 160
    and human judgment, 62
    and recidivism, 51
Orderliness, 13
Overcontrolled hostility, 122
Overcontrolled–Hostility (O-H) subscale, 64–66

Parabolic function, 271–272
Paranoid schizophrenia, 103
Paraphilias, 89, 132
Paraprofessionals, 76–77
Parental psychiatric history, 107, 123
Parole system, 15
Passivity, 120, 121
Patient consent, 214–215
PCL–R. *See* Psychopathy Checklist—Revised
Pedophiles, 139
Peel, Robert, 21
Penetanguishene (Ontario), 5, 13–14
Pennsylvania penitentiary system, 13
Penrose's law, 4, 87
Percent correct, 53
Personal injury offenses, 26–27
Personality-disordered patients/inmates
    and clinical judgment, 67–68
    and fire setting, 123
    and insanity acquittees, 87
    recidivism rates of, 38
    sex offenders as, 132
Personality disorders, 40
Personal violence, 40
Phallometric deviance indexes, 45, 164, 176
Phallometric studies of sexual deviance, 133–140
    among child molesters, 133–134
    among rapists, 134–137
    and faking, 137–139
    scoring of, 139–140
Philippe Pinel maximum-security psychiatric institution, 227
Physical attractiveness, 119, 141
Planning, lack of, 19–20

ABOUT THE AUTHORS

Vernon L. Quinsey, PhD, is a professor of psychology, biology, and psychiatry at Queen's University in Kingston. He is a fellow of the Canadian Psychological Association and has served on the editorial boards of a variety of journals. He has chaired research review panels of the American National Institute of Mental Health and the Ontario Mental Health Foundation. He was awarded the Significant Achievement Award of the Association for the Treatment of Sexual Abusers and a Career Contribution Award from the Canadian Psychological Association. He has authored or coauthored more than 100 publications on forensic topics, including 8 books.

Grant T. Harris, PhD, is the director of research at the Mental Health Centre in Penetanguishene, Ontario, Canada. He is also an associate professor of psychology at Queen's University in Kingston and associate professor of psychiatry at the University of Toronto. He is a fellow of the Canadian Psychological Association and was awarded the Amethyst Award for outstanding achievement by an Ontario public servant. He has been awarded several research grants on the topics of actuarial violence risk assessment, sexual aggression, the nature of psychopathy, and the assessment and treatment of violent offenders. This research has resulted in more than 100 publications on forensic topics.

Marnie E. Rice, PhD, is the scientific director of the Centre for the Study of Aggression and Mental Disorder and is the former director of the Research Department of the Mental Health Centre in Penetanguishene, Ontario, Canada, where she continues her research part time. She is also a part-time professor of psychiatry and behavioral neurosciences at McMaster University, adjunct professor of psychiatry at the University of Toronto, and adjunct associate professor of psychology at Queen's University. She was the

461

1995 recipient of the American Psychological Association's award for Distinguished Contribution to Research in Public Policy and a 1997 recipient of the Amethyst Award for outstanding contribution by an Ontario public servant. Dr. Rice was recently elected a fellow of the Royal Society of Canada in recognition of her scholarly contribution.

Catherine A. Cormier, BA, is a psychometrist in the Research Department at the Mental Health Centre in Penetanguishene, Ontario, Canada. Her research and clinical work has mostly been in the assessment and treatment of violent offenders, particularly sex offenders and psychopaths. More recently, she and her colleagues have developed an actuarial prediction instrument for domestic assaulters in conjunction with the Ontario Provincial Police, provincial corrections, and emergency clinics. She is a member of the research team that has received several awards including the Amethyst Award for outstanding contribution to public service in the province of Ontario.